D0710283

CRITICAL SURVEY OF

Shakespeare's Sonnets

SHAKE-SPEARES

SONNETS.

Neuer before Imprinted.

AT LONDON
By G. Eld for T. T. and are
to be solde by William Aspley.
1609.

Title page of *Shake-Speare's Sonnets*, *Quarto 1* published by Thomas Thorpe, London, 1609

CRITICAL SURVEY OF

Shakespeare's Sonnets

SALEM PRESS
A Division of EBSCO Information Services
Ipswich, Massachusetts

GREY HOUSE PUBLISHING

Critical Survey of Shakespeare's Sonnets, 2014, published by Grey House Publishing, Inc., Amenia, NY, under exclusive license from EBSCO Information Services, Inc.

∞ The paper used in this book conforms to the American National Standard for Permanence of Paper for Printed Library Materials, Z39.48 1992 (R1997).

Publisher's Cataloging-In-Publication Data
(Prepared by The Donohue Group, Inc.)

Critical survey of Shakespeare's Sonnets / [edited by Salem Press]. --
  [First edition].

  pages : illustrations ; cm

  Includes bibliographical references and index.
  ISBN: 978-1-61925-499-2

  1. Shakespeare, William, 1564-1616--Criticism and interpretation. 2. Sonnets, English--History and criticism. I. Shakespeare, William, 1564-1616. Sonnets. Selections. II. Salem Press.

                                        PR2848.A2 S35 2014
                                        821/.3

Contents

CRITICAL READINGS 1: FORM & TECHNIQUE

CRITICAL READINGS 2: MAIN THEMES

RESOURCES

About This Volume

Although Shakespeare is considered a leading dramatist in the English language—perhaps in any language—his poetry, particularly his sonnets, has gotten just as much scrutiny in academia as his famous plays. What is it about those one-hundred-fifty-four sonnets from the collection originally published in 1609 that makes them emotionally demanding even to contemporary readers with so much literary criticism at their disposal? How can Shakespeare's sonnets still provide so much wisdom and remain so elusive at the same time? How many more generations of scholars, one wonders, will attempt to unravel their mysteries until we reach a point at which another book on the sonnets would indeed be unnecessary?

The amount of scholarship focused on Shakespeare's *Sonnets* is truly considerable, spanning centuries, and the number of scholars attempting to shed new light on the sonnets continues to grow well into the twenty-first. There is also renewed interested in the sonnets across high school programs and community colleges, brought on in recent years by the Common Core initiative, which encourages close readings of shorter literary texts, including poetry. So a volume that serves as a one-stop resource on Shakespeare's sonnets for students encountering the form for the first time as well as those studying it in more depth seems both timely and necessary in 2014. This book serves that dual purpose: to provide the context for the beginner as well as to broaden literary horizons with new critical analysis for more advanced students.

The volume is divided into six distinct sections: The Author and His Work, Historical and Literary Contexts, Close Readings of 25 Sonnets, Critical Readings 1 (Form and Technique), Critical Readings 2 (Main Themes), and Resources. Taken together, the essays in these sections provide a sweeping overview of the sonnets, the time in which they were written, key biographical details that may help explain some of the obvious and less obvious themes, the way in which they were written, the historical events that may have influenced Shakespeare's fascination with love, pain, and aging, among other topics, and the literary influences that may explain their peculiar form.

The Author and His Work eases the reader into William Shakespeare's life and his work both as a dramatist and poet. It then introduces Shakespeare as the author of the *Sonnets* and ends with an essay that focuses on the sonnets' lasting allure. Here Rafeeq McGiveron brings the reader into the twenty-first century and explains why our fascination with the sonnets continues and is likely to continue.

Historical and Literary Contexts consists of four essays that provide the context students need to fully grasp the time in which Shakespeare lived and created, including those years immediately preceding the original publication in 1609. Although not focused on Shakespeare exclusively, the opening essay, "English Poetry in the Sixteenth Century," provides an overview of a "consistently poetic" century in which poets "were constantly aware of themselves as poetic craftsmen." Indeed, the poetry of the latter part of the century—commonly referred to as the Elizabethan poetry—is said to have heavily influenced the Bard. The essay that follows almost stands in opposition and challenges us to question how much of this history is truly necessary when interpreting works of art. Just how much importance does historical context play when we are attempting to read a life, asks Andrew Hadfield in "Does Shakespeare's Life Matter?," concluding: "We cannot always know the lives of the poets and, even if we do, reading literary works in terms of what we know is problematic and fraught with difficulties...." In the end, however, Shakespeare's life does matter, but Hadfield warns the reader that it may not mean quite what we think, or perhaps not as much as we think because writers have always been able to manipulate the ways in which they were read, even in Elizabethan England.

"Sins of the Sonnets" is an overview of the various editions of the *Sonnets* that have been published over the years (and there have been countless versions in the last one hundred years alone; see Resources section for a full listing). It is an attempt to analyze how previous scholars have interpreted the sonnets. William Logan, who hardly needs an introduction in the world of literary criticism, leaves no stone unturned—even at the expense of appearing confrontational—and doesn't shy away from challenging even the most revered critics and their widely-accepted theories. Logan's essay provides the necessary literary context to help us understand how we've come to collectively perceive the sonnets, but it also serves as a reminder of just how controversial and inconclusive Shakespeare scholarship has been.

The last essay in this section plays on the title of Jan Kott's famous book, *Shakespeare Our Contemporary*. Here Robert C. Evans explores both the similarities and (especially) the differences between Shakespeare's sonnets and various more recent examples of the form. The essay focuses on "Shakespearean" sonnets by E. E. Cummings (the notorious experimental writer); on a work by the African American woman poet Gwendolyn Brooks; on a sonnet by Eavan Boland, one of Ireland's most important modern authors; and on a final Shakespearean sonnet by Carol Ann Duffy, the United Kingdom's current Poet Laureate. Together, these comparisons of Shakespeare's sonnets with those by more recent authors help the contemporary reader understand how the form of the sonnet has evolved since Elizabethan England and what it's morphed into in modern times.

Section 3 is a collection of twenty-five shorter essays that provide new critical analysis of some of the most famous and beloved sonnets. Three scholars, including Robert C. Evans, Ashleigh Imus, and T. Fleischmann, provide close readings of select sonnets while paying special attention to recurring themes and their key meanings, place each in the context of the original collection of the sonnets and, when appropriate, draw useful thematic comparisons to other works of literature, both classic and contemporary. The three scholars also point to various examples of how the themes explored by Shakespeare hundreds of years ago continue to be explored in the twenty-first century, with unexpected references to popular culture, including film franchises and music by teenage icons. Each essay provides a listing of keywords, an abstract, and a "for further reading" listing.

Sections 4 and 5 delve deeper by providing more advanced treatments of the recurring themes and the sonnets' delicate structure. This part of the book demands some preliminary knowledge and is recommended for the undergraduate student of literature looking to expand his or her basic understanding. The essays here discuss both the form and technique of the sonnets (Critical Readings 1) as well as persistent themes (Critical Readings 2), including, among others, love, passion, sexuality, aging, and death. The essays that appear in these two sections are reprinted from various journals and books published in the past fifteen years, and with permission from copyright holders. We are grateful to the various publishers and authors for giving us permission to make their works part of this new collection.

Finally, the last section of the book consists of various resources designed to enrich further research. These include a detailed chronology of Shakespeare's life, a listing of the various editions of the *Sonnets*, a fully annotated and up-to-date guide to free online resources that provide more information and analysis, another annotated guide to literary criticism, a general bibliography, and an index. The last section also reprints the entire collection of one-hundred-fifty-four sonnets as it was originally published.

Mirela Roncevic

CRITICAL SURVEY OF

Shakespeare's Sonnets

The Author & His Work

Biography of William Shakespeare

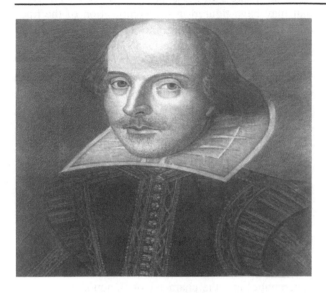

April 23, 1564 - April 23, 1616
(*Library of Congress*)

More has been written—with less certainty—about the life of William Shakespeare than about any other literary figure. Despite murmurings to the contrary, enough records and references exist to enable scholars to outline with confidence Shakespeare's life and career as poet, playwright, actor, and entrepreneur—but not to expose the inner workings of his genius. The register of Holy Trinity Church in Stratford-upon-Avon notes the christening of William Shakespeare on April 26, 1564. Shakespeare's birthday is traditionally celebrated on April 23, the feast day of Saint George, England's patron saint, and the day the dramatist died in 1616.

William was the son of John Shakespeare and Mary Arden. John worked with leather goods and traded in wool and farm produce. He rose to be the equivalent of mayor of Stratford but suffered reversals and stopped attending council meetings and church. William very likely attended Stratford's free grammar school, where he was drilled in Latin and introduced to Plautus and Terence, Ovid, Plutarch, and Seneca, among other classical sources he would later use.

At age eighteen William hastily married Anne Hathaway, who was eight years his senior and pregnant. Their daughter Susanna was born on May 26, 1583. On February 2, 1585, twins Hamnet and Judith Shakespeare—named after Stratford friends Hamnet and Judith Sadler—were baptized. The domestic life of the Shakespeare family in Stratford has given rise to much speculation, but we lack evidence to make meaningful observations. All we know is that sometime between 1585 and 1592 Shakespeare became involved in London's theater world.

In 1592 a bitter playwright, Robert Greene, published a deathbed confessional that includes an attack on other dramatists including Shakespeare, whom he calls "an upstart Crow, beautified with our feathers." Greene then parodies a line from *Henry VI, Part III* and continues, Shakespeare "supposes he is as well able to bombast out a blank verse as the best of you, and being an absolute *Johannes Factotum*, is in his own conceit the only Shake-scene in a country." The *Johannes Factotum* (jack-of-all-trades) reference suggests that Shakespeare was acting as well as writing by 1592. We do not know the circumstances of Shakespeare's shift from Stratford to London, but he kept a residence there as well as in Stratford for the next twenty years.

Within a few years Shakespeare was among the players in the Lord Chamberlain's company. During the period of 1592–94, when the theaters were closed because of the high number of plague deaths, Shakespeare wrote two long narrative poems, *Venus and Adonis* and *The Rape of Lucrece* (simply *Lucrece* on the title page), published with dedications to his patron, Henry Wriothesley, Earl of Southampton, and signed "William Shakespeare." These poems were much admired. When the theaters reopened, Shakespeare continued writing plays and acting. In 1598 Francis Meres writes, "the sweet, witty soul of Ovid lives in mellifluous and honey-tongued Shakespeare: witness his *Venus and Adonis*, his *Lucrece*, his sugared sonnets among his friends, etc." "His sugared sonnets" were not published until 1609, and then without permission. Meres goes on to list Shakespeare's plays: *Two Gentlemen of Verona*, *Comedy of Errors*, *Love's Labour's Lost*, *A Midsummer Night's Dream*, *Merchant of Venice*, *Richard II*, *Richard III*, *Henry IV*, *King John*, *Titus Andronicus*, and *Romeo and Juliet*, as well as *Love's Labours Won*—a lost play or alternative title. Meres concludes, "The Muses would speak with Shakespeare's fine-filed [polished] phrase if they would speak English."

During this period, Shakespeare and his fellow Lord Chamberlain's Men acted in England's first purpose-built theater, called simply the Theatre. The Theatre had been built in 1576 by James Burbage, father of two company members: the entrepreneurial Cuthbert and the chief tragedian Richard. James died in 1597, two months before the lease on the Theatre was to expire, and his heir Cuthbert was unable to negotiate an extension. On a freezing December night in 1598 the Burbages and a dozen other men made the bold move of dismantling the Theatre timber by timber and carrying the wood south across the Thames, where it was used to construct a new theater on the Bankside. To finance this enterprise the Burbages invited a handful of actors to contribute money and become shareholders. The new playhouse was called the Globe Theatre, and William Shakespeare held a ten percent share of the company and its new acting venue. The economic decision to cover the roof with thatch instead of tiles later proved to be unfortunate.

Records show that Shakespeare was taxed on a residence in London, and he also purchased land in and around Stratford. In 1596 the application for a coat of arms that Shakespeare had filed in his father's name was approved, and in the next year he moved his family to New Place, one of the largest houses in town. Now he could display his coat of arms on his door and call himself "gentleman." Yet amid these signs of success and prosperity, there was also personal loss. Shakespeare's son Hamnet died in August 1596, at the age of eleven.

During the last years of Queen Elizabeth I's life, Shakespeare was London's leading dramatist. Responding with patriotic pride to the defeat of the Spanish Armada in 1588, and then with concern over questions of succession to the throne, playwrights provided audiences with a variety of English history plays. Early in his career, Shakespeare wrote a group of four plays looking at the reign of Lancastrian King Henry VI and the transfer of power to the Yorkist monarchs culminating with the treacherous King Richard III and his defeat by Henry Tudor, the founder of the Tudor dynasty. Shakespeare then wrote another tetralogy providing the earlier history with vivid accounts of the Wars of the Roses: *Richard II*; *Henry IV, Part I* and *Part II*; and *Henry V*.

Although perhaps his greatest comic creation, Sir John Falstaff, took life in these history plays, Shakespeare also excelled in comedy, especially romantic and lyric plays suffused with illusion and witty battles between the sexes. To the plays listed by Meres we can add

The Taming of the Shrew, Much Ado About Nothing, As You Like It, and *Twelfth Night*.

Shakespeare's father John died in 1601, an event that may have figured in the composition of the tragedy *Hamlet* at around that time. In March 1603 Queen Elizabeth I died, ending Gloriana's forty-five-year reign as England's Protestant monarch. Almost immediately King James VI of Scotland, estranged son of Mary, Queen of Scots, but himself nominally a Protestant, journeyed to England, where he was crowned King James I. James spoke with a thick Scots accent, had a shuffling walk and awkward appearance, and disliked crowds. Although intelligent, James showed little interest in state affairs unless with handsome young courtiers. Although the king preferred hunting to theater, he authorized the Lord Chamberlain's Men to become the King's Men, and Shakespeare and his fellow shareholders were named Grooms of the Royal Chamber.

Shakespeare responded by writing *Macbeth*, which incorporated James's strong interest in witches and the supernatural and the character of Banquo, from whom James traced his own regal lineage. This was also the period of the composition of the other great tragedies *Othello, King Lear, Antony and Cleopatra*, and *Coriolanus*. Shakespeare's comedies became darker and more concerned with sexual intrigue, as in *Measure for Measure* and *Troilus and Cressida*.

Since 1576 a small indoor theater had operated on the grounds of a former Dominican monastery within the City of London. The black-robed monks gave the district and the theater its name: Blackfriars. James Burbage, the builder of the Theatre, was interested in this site for the Lord Chamberlain's Men, and in 1596 he bought more property and built a larger indoor Blackfriars Theatre. But residents of the area, including the company's patron, petitioned the Privy Council to forbid the Lord Chamberlain's Men to play there. The theater was instead leased to a children's company, the "aerie of children, little eyasses" of which Hamlet complains. Finally, in the summer of 1609, the King's Men were able to lease Blackfriars.

Blackfriars was totally enclosed and artificially lighted. With two galleries, it could hold around six hundred spectators, while the Globe held closer to three thousand. All the Blackfriars patrons were seated; there were no groundlings such as those who paid a penny each to stand in front of the Globe stage. Indeed, the lowest admission to Blackfriars was sixpence. Naturally, Blackfriars attracted a more affluent, aristocratic, and homogeneous audience than did the Globe, although Shakespeare's company performed plays in both venues.

The opening of Blackfriars, with its coterie audience, coincided with the growth of importance of the king's court and its attendant courtiers and ladies-in-waiting. James's queen consort, Anne of Denmark, was a lover of theater. She commissioned a series of extravagant entertainments—court masques—with allegorical stories written by Ben Jonson and other playwrights and with elaborate sets and costumes designed by Inigo Jones, whom she had met at the Danish court. Queen Anne and her circle performed these lavish spectacles. Public playwrights, Shakespeare included, began to add masquelike elements to their plays as well (such as Prospero's entertainment for Miranda and Ferdinand in *The Tempest*).

In the first decade of the seventeenth century, writers Francis Beaumont and John Fletcher introduced a new dramatic genre: tragicomedy. Tragicomedy is an amalgam rather than a mixture of comedy and tragedy. Characters undergo the suffering associated with tragedy, but forces in the universe keep humankind from making irreversible mistakes leading to tragic results. Thus everything is resolved at the end of such a play, and the focus is on forgiveness, reunion, regeneration, and renewal. Four of Shakespeare's last plays, *Pericles*, *Cymbeline*, *The Winter's Tale*, and *The Tempest* are written in this genre, and each contains music and dance associated with the spectacle of the court masque.

Although Shakespeare was influential in developing the tragicomedy or romance, he may not have felt comfortable in the genre, as he recycled several plots and devices from his earlier tragedies. It is almost irresistible to see Shakespeare himself in the figure of Prospero taking off his magical robe and burying his magic book to return to the everyday world of his home. Shakespeare's revels were, indeed, almost ended.

The last record we have of Shakespeare the actor is of his performance in Jonson's unsuccessful tragedy *Sejanus* in 1603. By 1610, he appears to have traveled more often to Stratford, where he continued to make investments in property and goods. Shakespeare probably gave up his London lodgings by 1612, although he continued to receive his share of money generated by the King's Men.

Despite his presumed retirement to Stratford, Shakespeare bought a house in the Blackfriars district of London, but there is no indication that he ever lived there. It was probably another sound investment. In 1612 he provided a deposition in a lawsuit between a master and a servant who married the master's daughter and now averred that his father-in-law had promised a dowry. Shakespeare had lived in the house where these events took place eight years earlier, but he was unable to remember the specifics. This deposition provides some details about his time in London. In 1613 Shakespeare probably attended the Globe Theatre for the opening of his final history play, *Henry VIII*, or *All Is True*, written with John Fletcher, but he was back in Stratford on June 29 when a cannon fired during a performance of that play accidently ignited the theater's thatched roof, and the Globe burned to the ground. (It was rebuilt the next year with a tile roof).

On March 25, 1616, Shakespeare was concerned enough about his health to call his lawyer to make final provisions in his last will and testament. He included bequests to his daughters, to his sister Joan and her children, to the poor of Stratford, and to various neighbors and fellow actors. Strangely, he added a provision leaving his "second best bed" to his wife, Anne. Anne would naturally inherit a third of his estate, but whether this last-minute addition was an insult or an inside joke eludes us. The signatures on the will are shaky; a month later, William Shakespeare died of unknown causes. It was April 23, 1616, his fifty-second birthday. As Ben Jonson declared, "He was not of an age but for all time."

Barry Gaines

For Further Study

Bate, Jonathan. *The Genius of Shakespeare*. New York: Oxford UP, 1998. One of our finest critics looks at the authorship question and the nature of Shakespeare's brilliance.

Chambers, E. K. *William Shakespeare: A Study of Facts and Problems*. 2 vols. Oxford: Clarendon Press, 1930. Older but highly respected compendium of information about Shakespeare.

Greenblatt, Stephen. *Will in the World: How Shakespeare Became Shakespeare*. New York: W. W. Norton, 2004. A bold new historical approach to Shakespeare's life and composition.

Schoenbaum, S. *Shakespeare's Lives*. 2d ed. Oxford: Clarendon Press, 1991. A scholarly and witty examination of Shakespeare biography.

_____. *William Shakespeare: A Documentary Life*. Oxford: Clarendon Press, 1975. The culmination of Schoenbaum's extensive study of Shakespeare biography.

_____. *William Shakespeare: Records and Images*. New York: Oxford UP, 1981. A vivid presentation of the surviving documents related to Shakespeare.

Shakespeare, William. *The Complete Works of Shakespeare.* Ed. David Bevington. 4th ed. New York: Longman, 1997. Perhaps the best single-volume collection of Shakespeare's works.

Shapiro, James. *Contested Will: Who Wrote Shakespeare?* New York: Simon & Schuster, 2010. Thoroughly reviews the candidates and arguments presented regarding the supposed writer of Shakespeare's plays, and refutes them with evidence that Shakespeare wrote the works.

_____. 1599: *A Year in the Life of William Shakespeare.* London: Faber & Faber, 2005. A delightful account of the pivotal year in Shakespeare's life.

Shakespeare the Poet

William Shakespeare is perhaps the world's greatest dramatist—certainly, at the very least, the greatest to write in English. Of his thirty-seven plays, written over a career in the theater that spanned, roughly, 1588 to 1613, the most important are *Romeo and Juliet* (pr. c. 1595–1596); *Henry IV, Parts I and II* (pr. c. 1597–1598; 1598); *Hamlet, Prince of Denmark* (pr. c. 1600–1601); *Othello, The Moor of Venice* (pr. 1604); *Measure for Measure* (pr. 1604); *King Lear* (pr. c. 1605–1606); *Macbeth* (pr. 1606); *Antony and Cleopatra* (pr. c. 1606-1607); *The Winter's Tale* (pr. c. 1610–1611); and *The Tempest* (pr. 1611).

Shakespeare also wrote some of the greatest love poems in English. His short erotic narratives, *Venus and Adonis* and *The Rape of Lucrece*, were typical examples of fashionable literary genres. Other minor poems include contributions to the miscellany *The Passionate Pilgrim* and *The Phoenix and the Turtle*, written for a collection of poems appended to *Love's Martyr* (1601), an allegorical treatment of love by Robert Chester. All these pale alongside the sonnets, which, in an age of outstanding love poetry, attain a depth, suggestiveness, and power rarely duplicated in the history of humankind's passionate struggle to match desire with words.

Shakespeare spent most of his adult life in the London theaters and quickly attained a reputation as a dramatist, actor, and poet. His company prospered under the reign of James I, and by the time of his retirement from playwriting about 1612, Shakespeare had acquired a respectable fortune. His career as a poet, distinct from his more public career as a dramatist, was probably confined to perhaps a decade, between 1591 and 1601, although the sonnets were later collected and published (perhaps without his permission) in 1609. Because of the absurd controversies that grew, mainly in the nineteenth century, about whether Shakespeare actually existed, it is worthwhile pointing out that there are many official records (christening record, marriage license, legal documents, correspondence, and so on) which may be consulted by the skeptical.

One of Shakespeare's great advantages as a writer was that, as a dramatist working in the public theater, he was afforded a degree of autonomy from the cultural dominance of the court, his age's most powerful institution. All over Europe, even if belatedly in England, the courts of the Renaissance nation-states conducted an intense campaign to use the arts to further their power. The theater, despite its partial dependency on court favor, achieved through its material products (the script and the performance) a relative autonomy in comparison with the central court arts of poetry, prose fiction, and the propagandistic masque. When Shakespeare briefly turned to Ovidian romance in the 1590s and, belatedly, probably also in the 1590s, to the fashion for sonnets, he moved closer to the cultural and literary dominance of the court's taste—to the fashionable modes of Ovid, Petrarch, and Neoplatonism—and to the need for patronage. Although the power of the sonnets goes far beyond their sociocultural roots, Shakespeare nevertheless adopts the culturally inferior role of the petitioner for favor, and there is an undercurrent of social and economic powerlessness in the sonnets, especially when a rival poet seems likely to supplant the poet.

In short, Shakespeare's nondramatic poems grow out of and articulate the strains of the 1590s, when, like many ambitious writers and intellectuals on the fringe of the court, Shakespeare clearly needed to find a language in which to speak—and that was, necessarily, given to him by the court. What he achieved within this shared framework, however, goes far beyond any other collection of poems in the age. Shakespeare's occasional poems are unquestionably minor, interesting primarily because he wrote them; his sonnets, on the other hand, constitute perhaps the language's greatest collection of lyrics. They are love lyrics, and clearly grow from the social, erotic, and literary contexts of his age. Part of their greatness, however, lies in their power to be read again and again in later ages, and to raise compellingly, even unanswerably, more than merely literary questions.

Venus and Adonis

In his first venture into public poetry, Shakespeare chose to work within the generic constraints of the fashionable Ovidian verse romance. Venus and Adonis appealed to the taste of young aristocrats such as the earl of Southampton to whom it was dedicated. It is a narrative poem in six-line stanzas, mixing classical mythology with surprisingly (and incongruously) detailed descriptions of country life, designed to illustrate the story of the seduction of the beautiful youth Adonis by the comically desperate aging goddess Venus. It is relatively static, with too much argument to make it inherently pleasurable reading. Its treatment of love relies on Neoplatonic and Ovidian commonplaces, and it verges (unlike Christopher Marlowe's *Hero and Leander*, 1598, to which Shakespeare's poem is a fair but decidedly inferior fellow) on moralizing allegory, with Venus as flesh, Adonis as spiritual longing. The poem's articulation of the nature of the love that separates them is abstract and often unintentionally comic—although Shakespeare's characterization of Venus as a garrulous plump matron brings something of his theatrical power to enliven the poem. The poem was certainly popular at the time, going through ten editions in as many years, possibly because its early readers thought it fashionably sensual.

The Rape of Lucrece

The Rape of Lucrece is the "graver labor" that Shakespeare promised to Southampton in the preface to *Venus and Adonis*. Again, he combines a current poetical fashion—the complaint—with a number of moral commonplaces, and writes a novelette in verse: a melodrama celebrating the prototype of matronly chastity, the Roman lady Lucrece, and her suicide after she was raped. The central moral issue—that of honor—at times almost becomes a serious treatment of the psychology of self-revulsion; but the decorative and moralistic conventions of the complaint certainly do not afford Shakespeare the scope of a stage play. There are some fine local atmospheric effects that, in their declamatory power, occasionally bring the directness and power of the stage into the verse.

The Phoenix and the Turtle

The Phoenix and the Turtle is an allegorical, highly technical celebration of an ideal love union: It consists of a funeral procession of mourners, a funeral anthem, and a final lament for the dead. It is strangely evocative, dignified, abstract, and solemn. Readers have fretted, without success, over the exact identifications of its characters. Its power lies in its mysterious, eerie evocation of the mystery of unity in love.

Sonnets

Probably more human ingenuity has been spent on Shakespeare's sonnets than on any other work of English literature. In *Shakespeare's Sonnets* (1978), Stephen Booth briefly summarizes the few facts that have led to a plethora of speculation on such matters as text,

authenticity, date, arrangement, and, especially, biographical implications. The sonnets were first published in 1609, although numbers 138 and 144 had appeared in *The Passionate Pilgrim* a decade before. Attempts to reorder the sonnets have been both varied and creative, but none represents the "correct" order. Such attempts simply fulfill an understandable anxiety on the part of some readers to see narrative continuity rather than variations and repetition in the sonnets. The "story behind" the sonnets has, as Booth puts it, "evoked some notoriously creative scholarship": speculation on the identity of the young man mentioned in many of the first 126 sonnets, of Mr. W. H., to whom the sequence is dedicated by the printer, of the "Dark Lady" of sonnets 127-152, and of the rival poet of some of the earlier sonnets—all these matters have filled many library shelves.

Such speculations—which reached their peak in critics and readers wedded to the sentimental Romantic insistence on an intimate tie between literary and historical "events"—are in one sense a tribute to the power of the sonnets. They are arguably the greatest collection of love poems in the language, and they provide a crucial test for the adequacy of both the love of poetry and the sense of the fascinating confusion that makes up human love. In a sense, the sonnets are as "dramatic" as any of Shakespeare's plays inasmuch as their art is that of meditations on love, beauty, time, betrayal, insecurity, and joy. Each sonnet is like a little script, with (often powerful) directions for reading and enactment, with textual meanings that are not given but made anew in every performance, by different readers within their individual and social lives. What Sonnet 87 terms "misprision" may stand as the necessary process by which each sonnet is produced by each reader.

It is conventional to divide the sonnets into two groups—1-126, purportedly addressed or related to a young man, and 127-152, to the "Dark Lady." Such a division is arbitrary at best—within each group there are detachable subgroups, and without the weight of the conventional arrangement, many sonnets would not seem to have a natural place in either group. Sonnets 1-17 (and perhaps 18) are ostensibly concerned with a plea for a young man to marry; but even in this group, which many readers have seen to be the most conventional and unified, there are disruptive suggestions that go far beyond the commonplace context.

What may strike contemporary readers, and not merely after an initial acquaintance with the sonnets, is the apparently unjustified level of idealization voiced by many of the sonnets—an adulatory treatment of noble love that, to a post-Freudian world, might seem archaic, no matter how comforting. The continual self-effacement of the anguished lover, the worship of the "God in love, to whom I am confined" (110), the poet's claim to immortalizing "his beautie . . . in these blacke lines" (63), are all idealizations born out of a world of serene affirmation. Some of the most celebrated sonnets, such as "Shall I compare thee to a summer's day" (18) or "Let me not to the marriage of true minds" (116), may even seem cloyingly affirmative, their texts seemingly replete, rejecting any subtextual challenges to their idealism.

In the two hundred years since Petrarch, the sonnet had developed into an instrument of logic and rhetoric. The Shakespearian sonnet, on the other hand, with its three quatrains and a concluding couplet, allows especially for the concentration on a single mood; it is held together less by the apparent logic of many of the sonnets (for example, the "when . . . then" pattern) than by the invitation to enter into the dramatization of a brooding, sensitive mind. The focus is on emotional richness, on evoking the immediacy of felt experience. Shakespeare uses many deliberately generalized epithets, indeterminate signifiers and floating referents that provoke meaning from their readers rather than providing it. Each line contains contradictions, echoes, and suggestions that require an extraordinary degree of emotional activity on the part of the reader. The couplets frequently offer a reader indeterminate statements, inevitably breaking down any attempt at a limited formalist reading. The greatest of the sonnets—60, 64, 129, as well as many others—have such an extraordinary combination of general, even abstract, words and unspecified emotional power that the reader may take it as the major rhetorical characteristic of the collection.

In particular lines, too, these poems achieve amazing power by their lack of logical specificity and emotional open-endedness. As Booth points out, many lines show "a constructive vagueness" by which a word or phrase is made to do multiple duty—by placing it "in a context to which it pertains but which it does not quite fit idiomatically" or by using phrases that are simultaneously illogical and amazingly charged with meaning. He instances "separable spite" in Sonnet 36 as a phrase rich with suggestion; another example is the way in which the bewilderingly ordinary yet suggestive epithets sit uneasily in the opening lines of Sonnet 64. Often a reader is swept on through the poem by a syntactical movement that is modified or contradicted by associations set up by words and phrases. There is usually a syntactical or logical framework in the sonnet, but so powerful are the contradictory, random, and disruptive effects occurring incidentally as the syntax unfolds that to reduce the sonnet to its seemingly replete logical framework is to miss the most amazing effects of these extraordinary poems.

Shakespeare is writing at the end of a very long tradition of using lyric poems to examine the nature of human love, and there is a weight of insight as well as of rhetorical power behind his collection. Nowhere in the Petrarchan tradition are the extremes of erotic revelation offered in such rawness and complexity. Northrop Frye once characterized the sonnets as a kind of "creative yoga," an imaginative discipline meant to articulate the feelings that swirl around sexuality. Most of the conventional topoi of traditional poetry are the starting points for the sonnets—the unity of lovers (36-40), the power of poetry to immortalize the beloved (18, 19, 55), contests between eye and heart, beauty and virtue (46, 141), and shadow and substance (53, 98, 101). As with Petrarch's Rerum vulgarium fragmenta (1470, also known as Canzoniere; Rhymes, 1976) or Sir Philip Sidney's Astrophel and Stella (1591), it would be possible to create a schematic account of commonplace Renaissance thinking about love from the sonnets. To do so, however, would be to nullify their extraordinary power of creation, the way they force ejaculations of recognition, horror, or joy from their readers.

After half a century of existentialism, readers in the late twentieth century understood that one of the most urgent subjects of the sonnets is not the commonplaces of Renaissance thinking about love, nor even the powerful concern with the power of art, but what Sonnet 16 calls people's "war upon this bloody tyrant Time." It is no accident that the "discovery" of the sonnets' concern with time and mutability dates from the 1930's, when the impact of Søren Kierkegaard, Friedrich Nietzsche, and the existentialists, including Martin Heidegger, was starting to be widely felt in England and the United States. The sonnets' invitation to see humans' temporality not merely as an abstract problem but as part of their inherent nature—what Heidegger terms humans' "thrownness," their sense of being thrown into the world—seems central to a perception of the sonnets' power. Unpredictability and change are at the heart of the sonnets—but it is a continually shifting heart, and one that conceives of human love as definable only in terms of such change and finitude. The sonnets avoid the transcendentalism of Geoffrey Chaucer beseeching his young lovers to turn from the world, or of Edmund Spenser rejecting change for the reassurance of God's eternity and his providential guidance of time to a foreknown, if mysterious, end. Shakespeare's sonnets rather overwhelm readers with questions and contradictions. In Sonnet 60, for example, time is not an impartial or abstract background. Even where it is glanced at as a pattern observable in nature or humanity, it is evoked as a disruptive, disturbing experience that cannot be dealt with as a philosophical problem. Some sonnets portray time as a sinister impersonal determinant; some thrust time at the reader as an equally unmanageable force of unforeseeable chances and changes, what Sonnet 115 calls humanity's "million'd accidents."

In Sonnet 15, it may be possible to enter into an understandable protest against time destroying its own creations (a commonplace enough Renaissance sentiment), and to accede to a sense of helplessness before a malignant force greater than the individual human being. When the sonnet tries, however, by virtue of its formally structured argument, to create a consciousness that seeks to understand and so to control this awareness, the reader encounters lines or individual words that may undermine even the temporary satisfaction of the aesthetic form. Such, for example is the force of the appalling awareness that "everything that grows/ Holds in perfection but a little moment." What is the application of "everything" or the emotional effect of the way the second line builds to a seemingly replete climax in "perfection" and then tumbles into oblivion in "but a little moment"? The sonnet does not and need not answer such questions. In a very real sense, it cannot answer them, for readers can only acknowledge time's power in their own contingent lives. What is shocking is not merely the commonplace that "never-resting time leads summer on/ To hideous winter, and confounds him there" (5) but that each reading fights against and so disrupts the logical and aesthetic coherence of the reader's own sense of change and betrayal.

To attempt criticism of the sonnets is, to an unusual extent, to be challenged to make oneself vulnerable, to undergo a kind of creative therapy, as one goes back and forth from such textual gaps and indeterminacies to the shifting, vulnerable self, making the reader aware of the inadequacy and betrayal of words, as well as of their amazing seductiveness. Consider, for example, Sonnet 138. When one falls in love with a much younger person, does one inevitably feel the insecurity of a generation gap? What is more important in such a reading of the sonnets is the insistence that age or youthfulness are not important in themselves: It is the insistence itself that is important, not the mere fact of age—just as it is the anxiety with which a man or woman watches the wrinkles beneath the eyes that is important, not the wrinkles themselves. The note of insistence, in other words, is not attached merely to the speaker's age: It stands for an invitation to participate in some wider psychological revelation, to confess the vulnerability that people encounter in themselves in any relationship that is real and growing, and therefore necessarily unpredictable and risky.

Without vulnerability and contingency, without the sense of being thrown into the world, there can be no growth. Hence the poet invites the reader to accept ruefully what the fact of his age evokes—an openness to ridicule or rejection. The sonnet's insistence on being open to the insecurity represented by the narrator's age points not merely to a contrast between the speaker and his two lovers but rather to a radical self-division. This is especially so in the Dark Lady sonnets, where there is a savage laceration of self, particularly in the fearful exhaustion of Sonnet 129, in which vulnerability is evoked as paralysis. At once logically relentless and emotionally centrifugal, Sonnet 129 generates fears or vulnerability and self-disgust. Nothing is specified: The strategies of the poem work to make the reader reveal or recognize his or her own compulsions and revulsions. The poem's physical, psychological, and cultural basis forces the reader to become aware of his or her awful drive to repress words because they are potentially so destructive.

Even in the seemingly most serene sonnets, there are inevitably dark shadows of insecurity and anxiety. In Sonnet 116, for example, the argument is that a love that alters with time and circumstance is not a true, but a self-regarding love.

The poem purports to define true love by negatives, but if those negatives are deliberately negated, the poem that emerges may be seen as the dark, repressed underside of the apparently unassailable affirmation of a mature, self-giving, other-directed love. If lovers admit impediments, and play with the idea that love is indeed love which "alters when it alteration finds," that it is an "ever-fixed mark" and, most especially, that love is indeed "time's fool," then the poem connects strikingly and powerfully with the strain of insecurity about the nature of change in human love that echoes throughout the whole collection. Such apparent affirmations may be acts of repression, an attempt to regiment the unrelenting unexpectedness and challenge of love. There are poems in the collection that, although less assertive, show a willingness to be vulnerable, to reevaluate constantly, to swear permanence within, not despite, transience—to be, in the words of Saint Paul, deceivers yet true. Elsewhere, part of the torture of the Dark Lady sonnets is that such a consolation does not emerge through the pain.

In short, what Sonnet 116 represses is the acknowledgment that the only fulfillment worth having is one that is struggled for and that is independent of law or compulsion. The kind of creative fragility that it tries to marginalize is that evoked in the conclusion to Sonnet 49 when the poet admits his vulnerability: "To leave poor me thou hast the strength of laws,/ Since, why to love, I can allege no cause." This is an affirmation of a different order—or rather an acknowledgment that love must not be defined by repression and exclusion. Lovers can affirm the authenticity of the erotic only by admitting the possibility that it is not absolute. Love has no absolute legal, moral, or causal claims; nor, in the final analysis, can love acknowledge the bonds of law, family, or state—or if finally they are acknowledged, it is because they grow from love itself. Love moves by its own internal dynamic; it is not motivated by a series of external compulsions. Ultimately it asks from the lover the nolo contendere of commitment: Do with me what you will. A real, that is to say, an altering, bending, never fixed and unpredictable love is always surrounded by, and at times seems to live by, battles, plots, subterfuges, quarrels, and irony. At the root is the acknowledgment that any affirmation is made because of, not despite, time and human mortality. As Sonnet 12 puts it, having surveyed the fearful unpredictability of all life, lovers must realize that it is even "thy beauty" that must be questioned. At times this thought "is as a death" (64), a "fearful meditation" (65)—that even the most precious of all human creations will age, wrinkle, fade, and die. Just how can one affirm in the face of that degree of reality?

Under the pressure of such questioning, the affirmation of Sonnet 116 can therefore be seen as a kind of bad faith, a false dread—false, because it freezes lovers in inactivity when they should, on the contrary, accept their finitude as possibility. Frozen in the fear of contingency, which Sonnet 116 so ruthlessly represses in its insistent negatives, readers may miss Shakespeare's essential insight that it is in fact the very fragility of beauty, love, poetry, fair youth, and dark lady alike that enhances their desirability. Paradoxically, it is precisely because they are indeed among the wastes of time that they are beautiful; they are not desirable because they are immortal but because they are irrevocably time-bound. One of the most profound truths is expressed in Sonnet 64: "Ruin hath taught me thus to ruminate/ That Time will come and take my love away./ This thought is as a death, which cannot choose/ But weep to have that which it fears to lose." The power of such lines goes far beyond the serene platitudes of Sonnet 116. At their most courageous, humans do not merely affirm, despite the forces of change and unpredictability that provide the ever-shifting centers of their lives; on the contrary, they discover their greatest strengths because of and within their own contingency. To accept rather than to deny time is to prove that humanity's deepest life ultimately does not recognize stasis but always craves growth, and that fulfillment is built not on the need for finality, for being "ever fixed," but on the need to violate apparent limits, to push forward or die.

Against a sonnet such as 116, some sonnets depict love not as a serene continuation of life but rather as a radical reorientation. Readers are asked not to dismiss, but to affirm fears of limitation. It is in the midst of contingency, when meditations are overwhelmed by the betrayals of the past, while "I sigh the lack of many a thing I sought,/ And with old woes new wail my dear Time's waste" (Sonnet 30), that love may open up the future as possibility, not as completion—so long as one accepts that it is time itself that offers such possibility, not any attempt to escape from it.

The typical Renaissance attitude to time and mutability was one of fear or resignation unless, as in Spenser, the traditional Christian context could be evoked as compensation; but for Shakespeare the enormous energies released by the Renaissance are wasted in trying to escape the burden of temporality. The drive to stasis, to repress experiences and meanings, is a desire to escape the burden of realizing that there are some transformations which love cannot effect. Ultimately, it is impossible to get inside a lover's soul no matter how much the flesh is seized and penetrated. The drive to possess and so to annihilate is a desire derived from the old Platonic ideal of original oneness, which only Shakespeare among the Renaissance poets seems to have seen as a clear and fearful perversion—it certainly haunts the lover of the Dark Lady sonnets and readers are invited to stand and shudder at the speaker's Augustinian self-lacerations. In Sonnet 144, the two loves "of comfort and despair,/ Which like two spirits do suggest me still" are not just a "man right fair" and a "woman, colour'd ill": They are also aspects of each lover's self, the two loves that a dualistic mind cannot affirm and by which people may be paralyzed.

Throughout this discussion of the sonnets, what has been stressed is that their power rests on the seemingly fragile basis not of Shakespeare's but of their readers' shifting and unpredictable experiences. They are offered not in certainty, but in hope. They invite affirmation while insisting that pain is the dark visceral element in which humans must live and struggle. Many of the Dark Lady sonnets are grim precisely because the lover can see no way to break through such pain. What they lack, fundamentally, is hope. By accepting that, for a time, "my grief lies onward and my joy behind" (Sonnet 50), the lover may be able, however temporarily, to make some commitment. Sonnet 124 is particularly suggestive, categorizing love as "dear," costly, not only because it is "fond," beloved, but also because it is affirmed in the knowledge of the world. Moreover, while it "fears not Policy" it is nevertheless "hugely politic." It is as if love must be adaptable, cunning, even deceptive, aware of the untrustworthiness of the world from which it can never be abstracted: "it nor grows with heat, nor drowns with showers." Finally, the poet affirms with a strong and yet strangely ironic twist: "To this I witness call the fools of Time,/ Which die for goodness, who have liv'd for crime."

As Stephen Booth notes, Sonnet 124 "is the most extreme example of Shakespeare's constructive vagueness," its key the word "it," which, "like all pronouns, is specific, hard, concrete, and yet imprecise and general—able to include anything or nothing." "It" occurs five times, each time becoming more indeterminate, surrounded by subjectives and negatives: In this sonnet "composed of precisely evocative words in apparently communicative syntaxes which come to nothing and give a sense of summing up everything, the word it stands sure, constant, forthright, simple and blank." The blankness to which Booth points has been filled very specifically by generations of readers to force the poem into a repressive argument like that of Sonnet 116. For example, the key phrase "the fools of time" is usually glossed as local, historical examples of political or religious timeservers—but the phrase contains mysterious reverberations back upon the lovers themselves. There

is a sense in which men are all fools of time. When Sonnet 116 affirms that "Love's not Time's fool," it betrays a deliberate and fearful repression; an unwillingness to acknowledge that Love is not able to overcome Time; time is something that can be fulfilled only as it presents opportunity and possibility to humans. People rightly become fools—jesters, dancers in attendance on Time, holy fools before the creative challenge of humanity's finitude—and people die, are fulfilled sexually, existentially, only if they submit themselves, "hugely politic," to the inevitable compromises, violence, and disruption which is life. People "die for goodness" because in a sense they have all "lived for crime." People are deceivers yet true; the truest acts, like the truest poetry, are the most feigning.

The twelve-line Sonnet 126 is conventionally regarded as the culmination of the first part of the sequence. Its serenity is very unlike that of 116. It acknowledges that, even if the fair youth is indeed Nature's "minion," even he must eventually be "rendered." Such realism does not detract from the Youth's beauty or desirability; it in fact constitutes its power.

Whether one considers the Fair Youth or the Dark Lady sonnets, or whether one attempts to see a "hidden" order in the sonnets, or even if one wishes to see a story or some kind of biographical origin "within" them, perhaps their greatness rests on their refusal to offer even the possibility of "solutions" to the "problems" they raise. They disturb, provoke, and ask more than merely "aesthetic" questions; read singly or together, they make readers face (or hide from) and question the most fundamental elements of poetry, love, time, and death.

Garry F. Waller

For Further Study

Ackroyd, Peter. *Shakespeare: The Biography*. New York: Nan A. Talese, 2005. An examination of the life and works of Shakespeare, including his poetry.

Bate, Jonathan. *Soul of the Age: A Biography of the Mind of William Shakespeare*. New York: Random House, 2009. A biography of Shakespeare that looks at his life and writings as they relate to the times in which he lived.

Bloom, Harold, ed. *The Sonnets*. New York: Bloom's Literary Criticism, 2008. A collection of essays that examine Shakespeare's sonnets, perhaps his best poetry.

Cheney, Patrick. *The Cambridge Companion to Shakespeare's Poetry*. New York: Cambridge UP, 2007. A collection of essays offering literary, historical, and cultural information on Shakespeare's poetry. Bibliographies and suggestions for further reading make this an invaluable source for those interested in Shakespeare's poetic work.

De Grazia, Margreta & Stanley Wells, eds. *The Cambridge Companion to Shakespeare*. New York: Cambridge UP, 2001. This work provides an extensive guide to Shakespeare's life and works.

Dobson, Michael & Stanley Wells, eds. *The Oxford Companion to Shakespeare*. New York: Oxford UP, 2001. An encyclopedic treatment of the life and works of Shakespeare.

Hart, Jonathan. *Shakespeare: Poetry, Culture, and History*. New York: Palgrave Macmillan, 2009. Hart looks at the poetry of Shakespeare and examines how culture and history influenced it and were influenced by it.

Heylin, Clinton. *So Long as Men Can Breathe: The Untold Story of Shakespeare's Sonnets*. Philadelphia: Da Capo Press, 2009. Heylin examines the history of the sonnets' publication and researches the possibility that Shakespeare never intended them to be published.

Hope, Warren & Kim Holston. T*he Shakespeare Controversy: An Analysis of the Authorship Theories*. 2d cd. Jefferson, NC: McFarland, 2009. The authors examines the various authorship controversies and theories surrounding Shakespeare's work. Although much of the discussion involves plays, it sheds light on the author himself.

Matz, Robert. *The World of Shakespeare's Sonnets: An Introduction*. Jefferson, NC: McFarland, 2008. Matz examines the sonnets in terms of the customs and beliefs that shaped them and with reference to Shakespeare's world.

Introduction to Shakespeare's Sonnets

Although Shakespeare's sonnets are generally considered to be among the most beautiful and most powerful poems in English literature, the attention of readers and scholars has more often centered on their possible biographical significance than on the literary qualities that give them their greatness. So little is known of the inner life of the poet, so little that helps to explain his genius, that it is not surprising to find critics minutely examining these lyrics that seem to reveal something of Shakespeare the man.

The sonnet sequence was one of the most popular poetic forms in the early 1590s; modeled originally on works by Dante Alighieri and Petrarch, the genre developed in sixteenth-century France and Italy and quickly reached England. Sir Philip Sidney's Astrophel and Stella (1591), written a few years before the poet's death in 1586, is a demonstration of how quickly the sonnet cycle achieved excellence in English. Edmund Spenser, Samuel Daniel, Michael Drayton, and many other well-known Elizabethan men of letters followed Sidney's example, paying tribute to the idealized ladies who inspired their almost religious devotion.

Shakespeare's poems, probably composed at intervals during the decade between 1590 and 1600, differ radically from the sonnets of his contemporaries in several ways. They are not based on the traditional Petrarchan theme of a proud, virtuous lady and an abject, scorned lover, and there is in them relatively little of the platonic idealism that fills such works as Spenser's Amoretti (1595), in which the poet's love for his lady lifts him above human weakness to contemplation of the divine. Shakespeare records a strangely ambiguous, tortured affection for a young nobleman; the emotions he expresses in his sonnets have a depth and complexity, an intensity, that can be encountered elsewhere only in the speeches of some of his greatest dramatic creations.

The narrative of Shakespeare's sequence is exceedingly sketchy. Scholars have, in fact, rearranged the poems many times in an attempt to produce a more coherent "plot" than appeared in the volume published, without the author's supervision, in 1609. It seems likely that the work as it now stands contains at least a few poems that were written as independent pieces, sonnets on popular Renaissance themes that have no real bearing on the subject of the sequence itself.

Three shadowy figures move through the reflections of the poet as he speaks in his sonnets. The most important is the "fair youth," the young nobleman. The fervor of the language with which Shakespeare speaks of his feelings for the youth has led to considerable discussion of the precise nature of the relationship. It must be remembered that the Renaissance regarded the friendship of man and man as the highest form of human affection, for within this relationship there could be complete spiritual and intellectual communication, unmarred by erotic entanglements.

The nobleman is initially idealized in much the same way that most poets envision their ladies, as the embodiment of beauty and virtue. Unlike the typical lady of more conventional sonnets, however, he proves to be false and deceptive, shifting his attention to a rival poet, whose identity has been the subject of much speculation. The sequence records the narrator-poet's despair at this betrayal and at the nobleman's affair with the "dark lady," the poet's mistress, who is, in a sense, his evil genius. It is not the loss of the lady he regrets, for he knows her character all too well, but that his friend has yielded to her corruption. Throughout the sonnets the reader feels the poet's agonized sense that there is nothing lastingly beautiful or virtuous.

While it is customary to speak of the "I" of the sonnets as Shakespeare, it is dangerously misleading to overlook the possibility that these poems are dramatic, that "I" is as vividly conceived a creature of Shakespeare's mind as Hamlet, and that the poet is projecting himself into an imagined situation rather than describing a personal experience. Whether the speaker of the sonnets is Shakespeare or not, it does not alter the essential value of the poems themselves.

The greatness of the sonnets lies in their intellectual and emotional power, in Shakespeare's ability to find exactly the right images to convey a particular idea or feeling and in his magnificent gift for shaping the diction and rhythms of ordinary human speech into expressions of the subtlest and deepest human perceptions. He also developed his own sonnet form, the Shakespearean sonnet form, with which Thomas Wyatt and Henry Howard Surrey experimented earlier in the century. Almost all of Shakespeare's sonnets are divided into three quatrains, each with alternately rhyming lines, followed by a concluding couplet. This form is technically less complex than the Italian pattern, in which the first eight lines are built around two rhymes, rather than four. The technical requirements of the two forms determine to a degree their organization. The Italian sonnet generally breaks down into two sections, with the statement of a problem in the octave and its solution in the sestet, while the form used by Shakespeare lends itself to a tripartite exposition followed by a brief conclusion in the couplet. Shakespeare was, however, capable of varying his development of his subject in many different ways; a thought may run through twelve lines with a surprise conclusion or shift of emphasis in the couplet; it may break into the eight-line, six-line division of the Italian sonnet; or it may follow one of many other patterns.

The organization of the sequence seems somewhat haphazard. Within it are several groups of poems that clearly belong together, but they do not form an entirely satisfying narrative. Shakespeare uses his half-untold story as a basis for poems upon many familiar Renaissance themes: love, time, mutability, the conflict of body and soul, passion and reason. The first eighteen poems, all addressed to the nobleman, are variations on the theme of the transience of youth and beauty and the need for the youth to marry and beget children in order to preserve his virtues of face and mind in them. Shakespeare draws upon nature for images to convey his sense of the destruction that awaits all beauty, referring to "the violet past prime," "winter's ragged hand," "summer's green all girded up in sheaves." Youth becomes more precious and the preservation of beauty more important still when the poet considers that "everything that grows holds in perfection but a little moment."

Shakespeare's sense of the ravages of time leads him to a second important theme: Poetry, as well as heirs, can confer immortality. Sonnet 18 is one of the most beautiful and clearest expressions of this idea:

Shall I compare thee to a summer's day?
Thou are more lovely and more temperate:
Rough winds do shake the darling buds of May,
And summer's lease hath all too short a date;
Sometime too hot the eye of heaven shines,
And often is his gold complexion dimm'd;
And every fair from fair sometime declines,
By chance, or nature's changing course, untrimm'd:
But thy eternal summer shall not fade
Nor lose possession of that fair thou ow'st;
Nor shall Death brag thou wander'st in his shade,

When in eternal lines to time thou grow'st;
So long as men can breathe or eyes can see,
So long lives this, and this gives life to thee.

The same idea forms the basis for another well-known sonnet, "Not marble nor the gilded monuments of princes," in which Shakespeare affirms the power of his verse to withstand the assaults of war, fire, and death. The sonnets making up the middle of the sequence deal with many aspects of the poet's feeling for the nobleman. Their tone is almost universally melancholy; the haunting language and clear visual images of Sonnet 73 make it perhaps the finest expression of this dominant mood:

That time of year thou mayst in me behold
When yellow leaves, or none, or few, do hang
Upon those boughs which shake against the cold,
Bare [ruin'd] choirs where late the sweet birds sang.
In me thou see'st the twilight of such day
As after sunset fadeth in the west,
Which by and by black night doth take away,
Death's second self, that seals up all in rest.
In me thou see'st the glowing of such fire
That on the ashes of his youth doth lie,
As the death-bed whereon it must expire,
Consum'd with that which it was nourish'd by.
This thou perceiv'st, which makes thy love more strong,
To love that well which thou must leave ere long.

The speaker pictures himself as a man aging, unworthy, despairing. Initially his friendship with the young nobleman provides his one comfort against the frustrations of his worldly state. At those moments, as in Sonnet 29, when he is most wretched,

Haply I think on thee; and then my state,
Like to the lark at break of day arising
From sullen earth, sings hymns at heaven's gate.
For thy sweet love remember'd such wealth brings
That then I scorn to change my state with kings.

A brilliantly conceived image, in Sonnet 33, communicates the impact of the poet's loss of confidence in the youth when the youth turns to the rival poet.

Full many a glorious morning have I seen
Flatter the mountain tops with sovereign eye,
Kissing with golden face the meadows green,
Gilding pale streams with heavenly alchemy;

Anon permit the basest clouds to ride
With ugly rack on his celestial face,
And from the forlorn world his visage hide,
Stealing unseen to west with this disgrace:
Even so my son one early morn did shine
With all triumphant splendour on my brow;
But out, alack! he was but one hour mine,
The region cloud hath mask'd him from me now.
Yet him for this my love no whit disdaineth;
Suns of the world may stain when heaven's sun
  staineth.

Many of the poems show the poet's attempts to accept the faithlessness, the fall from virtue, of the youth. While his betrayal cannot destroy the poet's affection ("Love is not love which alters when it alteration finds"), it represents the decay of all good, leaving the speaker filled with despair.

There are, toward the end of the sequence, approximately thirty poems addressed to or speaking of the "dark lady." The lighter of these lyrics are witty commentaries on her brunette beauty—in the sonnet tradition, the lady is fair: "Thine eyes I love, and they as pitying me,/ Knowing thy heart torment me with disdain,/ Have put on black, and loving mourners be,/ Looking with pretty ruth upon my pain."

The overworked Petrarchan metaphors about the charms of the sonneteer's mistress are parodied in another well-known poem.

My mistress' eyes are nothing like the sun;
Coral is far more red than her lips' red;
If snow be white, why then her breasts are dun;
If hairs be wires, black wires grow on her head.

Surrounding these relatively happy pieces are verses revealing the pain and conflict in the relationship between the poet and the lady. He knows that his feeling for her is primarily lustful and destructive; yet, as he says in Sonnet 129, he cannot free himself from her: "All this the world well knows; yet none knows well/ To shun the heaven that leads men to this hell."

Irony pervades the sonnets in which Shakespeare declares his full knowledge of her vices and her deceptions both of her husband and of him: "When my love swears that she is made of truth,/ I do believe her, though I know she lies." The poet's conflict is intensified by the lady's affair with the nobleman, and he tries to explain

his reaction in the little morality play of Sonnet 144.

Two loves I have of comfort and despair,
Which like two spirits do suggest me still:
The better angel is a man right fair,
The worser spirit a woman colour'd ill.
To win me soon to hell, my female evil
Tempteth my better angel from my [side],
And would corrupt my saint to be a devil,
Wooing his purity with her foul pride.
And whether that my angel be turn'd fiend,
Suspect I may, yet not directly tell;
But being both from me, both to each friend,
I guess one angel in another's hell.
Yet this shall I ne'er know, but live in doubt,
Till my bad angel fire my good one out.

The tremendous appeal of Shakespeare's sonnets through the centuries rests essentially on the same qualities that have made his plays immortal, his phenomenal understanding of the workings of the mind and his incredible ability to distill many aspects of human experience into a few lines. The sonnets are, in many ways, dramatic poetry; the reader is constantly aware of the presence of the poet, the "I" of the sequence, who addresses the nobleman and the dark lady forcefully and directly, not as if he were musing in his study. A brief perusal of the opening lines of the sonnets shows a remarkable number of questions and commands that heighten the reader's sense of a dramatic situation:

That thou hast her, it is not all my grief,
And yet it may be said I lov'd her dearly . . .
Being your slave, what should I do but tend
Upon the hours and times of your desire?
Farewell! thou art too dear for my possessing,
And like enough thou know'st thy estimate.

The compression of language; the vivid images drawn from nature, commerce, the theater, and many other aspects of life; the wordplay; and the flexibility of rhythms of speech that characterize Shakespeare's blank verse—all contribute to the greatness of the sonnets as well. In these poems, as in his plays, he was able to transform traditional forms and raise them to new heights.

Salem Press Editors

For Further Study

Blades, John. *Shakespeare: The Sonnets*. New York: Palgrave Macmillan, 2007. An introduction to the sonnets, providing textual analysis, discussion of themes, and critical history of these poems. Examines the development and characteristics of the sonnet form, Humanist themes, and early modern print culture.

Callaghan, Dympna. *Shakespeare's* Sonnets. Malden, MA: Blackwell, 2007. Comprehensive introduction, discussing the poems' structure, images, and themes of identity, beauty, love, numbers, and time. An appendix provides a summary of each sonnet with descriptions of their key literary figures.

Cheney, Patrick, ed. *The Cambridge Companion to Shakespeare's Poetry*. New York: Cambridge UP, 2007. Includes essays discussing Shakespeare and the development of English poetry; rhetoric, style, and form in his verse; the poetry in his plays; his poetry as viewed from a twenty-first century perspective; and "The Sonnets" by Michael Shoenfeldt.

Cousins, A. D. *Shakespeare's Sonnets and Narrative Poems*. New York: Longman, 2000. Divides the Sonnets into three parts, devoting a chapter to each and focusing on a particular aspect of each part. The discussion of Sonnets 1-19 is described as "The Young Man, the Poet, and Father Time"; Sonnets 20-126 are summarized as "The Poet, the Young Man, Androgyny, and Friendship"; and Sonnets 127-154 center on "The Poet, the Dark Lady, and the Young Man."

Green, Martin. *Wriothesley's Roses: In Shakespeare's Sonnets, Poems, and Plays*. Baltimore: Clevendon Books, 1993. Links historical records with poetic context in various sonnets in an interesting attempt to establish the identities of Shakespeare's fair young man and of the rival poet who seems to compete with Shakespeare's speaker for the affections of the dark lady. Provides a good historical background.

Hyland, Peter. *An Introduction to Shakespeare's Poems*. New York: Palgrave Macmillan, 2003. Discusses the characteristics of the Elizabethan sonnet and Shakespeare's contributions to this genre. Provides interpretive readings of the Sonnets. Places Shakespeare's poetry within the context of the politics, values, and tastes of Elizabethan England, arguing that he was a skeptical voice during this socially turbulent era.

Matz, Robert. *The World of Shakespeare's* Sonnets*: An Introduction*. Jefferson, N.C.: McFarland, 2008. Focuses on the social and cultural world in which Shakespeare lived and how this environment shaped his sonnets. Describes the sonnets as "brilliant, edgy expressions" of English Renaissance culture.

Ramsey, Paul. *The Fickle Glass: A Study of Shakespeare's Sonnets*. New York: AMS Press, 1979. A clearly written scholarly examination of critical problems, poetic techniques, and meaning in the sonnets. Explores questions of authorship, order, and date of composition. Excellent discussion of metrical rules and Elizabethan rhetoric in the sonnets.

Smith, Hallet. *The Tension of the Lyre: Poetry in Shakespeare's Sonnets*. San Marino, CA: Huntington Library, 1981. General discussion of the sonnets, beginning with an exploration of poetic voice and audience, and including an overview of Shakespeare's world as it is reflected in the sonnets.

Weiser, David K. *Mind in Character: Shakespeare's Speaker in the Sonnets*. Columbia: U of Missouri P, 1987. Thorough explication of the sonnets. Useful appendix classifies the sonnets by modes of address.

The Lasting Allure of Shakespeare's Sonnets

The name William Shakespeare doth bestride the world of literature like a colossus, omnipresent, unavoidable, sometimes delightful, sometimes overwhelming. Where, for example, is the student, whether in high school or in the college or university classroom, who has not read at least some of the man's works? Vanishingly hard to find, I'll warrant. Echoes of Shakespeare's verse reverberate up and down the long, twisty halls of culture high and low, from old leather-bound tomes dusty on library shelves to countless annotated "classics" texts riding in bright new nylon backpacks, in speech from erudite quotations to quips tossed off half-unknowing, in film from painstakingly faithful costume drama to purposefully anachronistic reimaginings.

Why, even in Ray Bradbury's bookless near-future of *Fahrenheit 451*, *Hamlet* is still "a faint rumor of a title" to the even most anesthetized television junkies (55), and the wryly depicted collectivist deep-future dystopias of Aldous Huxley's *Brave New World* and Yevgeny Zamyatin's *We* likewise cannot quite forget "a man called Shakespeare" (Huxley 51) or "the antediluvian times of all those Shakespeares and Dostoevskys, or whatever you call them" (Zamyatin 43). Writers simply cannot resist such drollery toward perhaps the most famous name in all of letters. Yet it is not merely highbrow authors and literary critics who keep Death from bragging that the Bard wand'reth in his shade, for in the world of today, except perhaps in the initial line of an encyclopedia entry, we scarcely even need bother label the man as *playwright* and *poet*, since of course he is these. Of course. Really, a first name is not even necessary. Say mere *Shakespeare*—'tis enough, 'twill do.

And while plays comprise the basis of the artist's legacy, nevertheless the sonnets are a very fine subject of study as well, both for students new to Shakespeare and for those already imbued with the sound and sense of his dramatic tragedies, comedies, and histories. The sonnets are intriguing yet approachable, after all, especially in relation to the significantly more substantial expenditure of effort, and time, required for the analysis of a major play. Once editors have attended to matters of changing vocabulary, syntax, and context, these fourteen-line poems can be comprehended without too much difficulty, and indeed with pleasure, with some pieces perhaps even being memorized now and then as the reader's fancy particularly chances to be struck. And it does seem likely indeed that even the most initially doubtful reader will find those moments of affinity, for although certain assumptions of gender, race, class, even humoral physiology and cosmology may have changed in the four-hundred-odd years since Shakespeare's time, the true fundamentals of the human condition have not. Love and desire, friendship and betrayal, the joy and uncertainty of life and the finality of death—these eternals shall not fade.

The Elizabethan Era

Understanding the sonnets entails realizing how vocabulary and syntax have shifted across the span of four full centuries, issues to which the contributors and editors of this text naturally will attend in following chapters. Our reading may be deepened as well by knowing something of the artist who penned the poems, and this introduction will touch upon that shortly. The era itself, however, naturally colors all, so it is here that we shall start.

Six years before the birth of William Shakespeare, Queen Elizabeth I ascended the throne of England in 1558 following the death of her Catholic half-sister Mary I. The world into which the future embodiment of English letters was to be born was different from our own in a host of ways, a place of change and conflict, and yet exciting newness as well. It should not be forgotten, for example, that the Americas had been unknown to Europeans scarcely three generations earlier and that the globe was not circumnavigated until Ferdinand Magellan's expedition of 1519 to 1522. Moreover, while Spain soon busied itself in the conquest of the Aztec and Inca empires and the merciless exploitation of the indigenous peoples and resources there, the English incursions into the Americas would not begin in earnest until the abortive Roanoke Colony in the 1580s and Jamestown in 1607. The world was still a very large place to Shakespeare and his contemporaries, one where wand'ring barks might sail out in all directions such that, to borrow historian J.R. Hale's beautifully wry phrase, "both God and mammon would be served" (62): by trade, by exploration and conquest, by imperial intrigue and wars of religion.

Religion of course was still a major force in empire and in everyday life as well. The splitting of the Church of England from the Roman Catholic Church by Henry VIII, for example, affected not just the governance of the State but also the operation of individual conscience, while Mary's persecution of Anglican reformers is legendary and was bloody indeed. Religion extended from the catechisms a youth might learn at school to the very shape of the universe. The shift from the old geocentric cosmology of Ptolemy to a heliocentric Copernican model may have re-centered the solar system, but it did not yet dispense with the notion that the planets were carried around the sun on crystal spheres, and even English astronomer Thomas Digges, whose 1576 book kept celestial spheres for sun and planets but put the "fixed" stars not on a final sphere but within a universe extending infinitely outward, still described that highest region as "the very courte of coelestiall angelles" and "the habitacle for the elect" (Harrison 79-80).

As historian E.M.W. Tillyard puts it, "sermons were as much a part of the ordinary Elizabethan's life as bearbaiting" (3), and everything, from God and the angels above to the animals, plants, and minerals below—and humanity in the middle—was seen as linked in a Great Chain of Being. All material objects were believed to be composed of the four elements of earth, water, air, and fire, with human disposition being governed by the corresponding humors of melancholy, phlegm, blood, and choler…oh, yes, and by the influence of the stars, too (Tillyard 68-69, 52-53). Correspondences, it appeared, were manifest everywhere, and it seemed obvious that society could exist without a reigning queen or king precisely as well as one could live without one's head. Thus when throughout Shakespeare's works we see portrayed the reality of supernatural spirits, the effect of humors and the stars on temperament, and notion of the body as State and vice versa, we see not mere poetic flourishes—we see the unquestioned commonplaces of Elizabethan thought.

Shakespeare's Family and Life

The man who understood so much of what it means to be human, and who portrayed it in verse that still rings true, was baptized on 26 April 1564 in Stratford-upon-Avon, in the county of Warwickshire, England. The exact date of his birth is unknown, though it likely would not be more than a few days before the 26th; in fact, the 23th often is supposed, both in light of Elizabethan baptismal customs and, perhaps, simply in symmetry with the date of his death. For after fifty-two years, Shakespeare died on 23 April 1616, back in Stratford, after a career in London that carried him from acting to sonnet-writing and the creation of the most lasting plays of the ages. In an era of aristocracy and abject poverty, of pastoral landscapes and plague-ridden city lanes, William Shakespeare's life included public success and yet also private tragedy, such as the death of his young son Hamnet. Some events are clearly documented, while some are conjectured, and others must remain unknown.

Shakespeare's father, John, was a dealer in wool and leather as well as a maker of gloves in Stratford in Warwickshire, and apparently a decently successful businessman at first, as even before his marriage to Mary Arden, daughter of a well-to-do landed family, he owned a house and other property. Sometime around 1556 or 1557 or so, John Shakespeare and Mary Arden wed, eventually producing eight children, of whom five survived to adulthood. William was the third, born in 1564.

The first two offspring of John and Mary, Joan and Margaret, baptized in September 1558 and December 1562, respectively, died in infancy, Joan at around a month in age, Margaret about a year. The Shakespeares' fifth child, Anne, born in 1571, also died young, at age eight. Of the five surviving children, Gilbert came next after William; baptized in October 1566, he lived until age 41, dying in February 1612. Another daughter Joan was baptized in 1569. Destined to live to age 77, this Joan married a man named William Hart and gave birth to four children; of the two who survived, William, born in 1600, became an actor and even performed in productions of his famous uncle's plays. John and Mary's son Richard was baptized in March 1574 and died in February 1613. The Shakespeares' last child, Edmund, was baptized in May 1580, ultimately became an actor in his brother's acting company, and died in December 1607.

Understandably enough for the era, little is known of the Shakespeares' personal lives, and the basic facts we do know come mainly from church and official records, supplemented by informed supposition and occasional hearsay. From the late 1550s onward, John Shakespeare held a number of respectable municipal posts, but eventually he fell into debt and occasional legal trouble in the 1570s and '80s, and hence had to withdraw from public service. Near the end of his life, however, perhaps due to the influence of his prominent playwright son, he was able to attain a coat of arms from the Crown. The ensuing hereditary title of gentleman which this brought may have been welcome to an old man, and perhaps just as much so to a son who had seen his father's fortunes fall and who now wished to restore his family's standing.

We may guess at the motivations of the early-middle-aged William Shakespeare in pursuing social status for his father, and of course for himself as well, but the artist's childhood is comparatively unrecorded. No school records exist, for example, although considering his father's standing at the time, "we need not doubt that Shakespeare received a grammar-school education" (Schoenbaum 63). What sort of curriculum would the local school in Stratford have offered? Young boys began with the alphabet and religious catechisms, naturally, but lessons also would have progressed into Latin grammar, forensics, and Classical literature. Clarice Swisher summarizes the situation adroitly:

> According to scholar and critic George R. Price, in Reading Shakespeare's Plays, "This education was at least comparable with a modern college major in classics." Years later, contemporary English playwright Ben Johnson disparagingly called Shakespeare's learning "small Latin and less Greek," but, by Johnson's standards, "much" learning would have meant a five-year study of Latin, ending with a master's degree.
>
> (14)

It may be difficult for twenty-first-century readers to imagine the equivalent of an undergraduate major in Roman oratory and drama for students so young, and yet those were indeed the standards of the day, at least for those able to attend such a school. Certainly Shakespeare's plays reflect a mind familiar with the history and literature of the Classical world.

Before Shakespeare wrote or even acted, however, at the end of November 1582 the eighteen-year-old married Anne Hathaway, a woman eight years his senior. Anne also was three months pregnant with young William's child, and in late May she gave birth to a child they named Susanna. The premarital pregnancy might have been somewhat scandalous, or it might have been fairly unremarkable; contemporary statistics suggest that pregnancy preceded the actual wedding for between ten and thirty percent of English married couples, and when the couple planned on marriage, such a situation was more accepted than modern readers otherwise might suppose (D'Emilio and Freedman 5). The age difference between William and Anne is more noticeable, however, and we can only speculate on whether and how it might have affected the pair.

In any event, William and Anne first lived with Shakespeare's family in Stratford. After their first child came twins Hamnet and Judith at the end of January or beginning of February 1585. Whereas Susanna was to live to the age of 66, and Judith to 77, Hamnet was to die at age eleven from causes not recorded. This personal tragedy still lay in the future, however, and 1585 also began the seven-year period known as Shakespeare's "lost years," for no details of his whereabouts during this time have come down to us. At a date unknown, for reasons to be supposed but never numbered or unraveled, and after matrimonial discussions surely intriguing yet just as surely lost to history, Shakespeare left Stratford for London sometime after the birth of his twins. He must have acted in plays and begun to write them as well, for in 1592 the university-educated Robert Greene's *Groats-Worth of Wit* criticized, in a now-infamous jibe, the "upstart crow" who not only acted but wrote. This was the first printed document linking Shakespeare with the stage.

Shakespeare's primary fame is as a playwright, of course. From at least the 1590s onward he authored some three-dozen dramas whose names stand as instantly recognizable monuments even four centuries later: *Romeo and Juliet*, *Richard III*, *A Midsummer Night's Dream*, *King Lear*, *Macbeth*, and others, many, many others. Shakespeare worked in London with a company of actors called the Lord Chamberlain's Men—after the death of Elizabeth I called the King's Men, and thence supported by James I—and eventually he owned a ten-percent share in the profits of the Globe Theater. The playwright's skill brought, aside from pleasure to contemporary playgoers and countless others since, fame to the talented artist, and quite a decent measure of wealth as well. It is not the dramas but the sonnets that this text investigates, however, so we will leave discussion of the plays and their various issues to a veritable army of other scholars and a small mountain of other books. The sonnets themselves will provide topic enough here.

Sonnets and "The" Sonnets

Shakespeare of course did not invent the sonnet form, although it may be his examples with which modern students of literature are most familiar. The rhyming fourteen-line poem broken into eight-line octave and six-line sestet first appeared first in Italy, and gained particular prominence in the work of fourteenth-century Italian scholar and poet Petrarch. A Petrarchan sonnet generally shows end rhymes of *abbaabba* in the octave and either *cdecde* or *cdccdc* in the sestet; the octave introduces some problem or situation that, after a volta, or turn, is resolved or concluded in the sestet. Shakespeare's contemporary, Sir Philip Sydney, wrote Petrarchan sonnets in English, as did, later, John Donne and John Milton.

While it thus is possible to craft a heavily rhymed Petrarchan sonnet in a language less melodious than Italian, shifting the number of rhymes from four or five to seven, as Shakespeare did, does indeed open up some more options, and, moreover, it prompts the poet to shift the structure from octave and sestet to three quatrains plus a concluding pair of rhymed lines called a couplet. The Shakespearean sonnet generally rhymes *abab cdcd efef* in three quatrains and then *gg* in its final couplet; thematically, then, the quatrains together present the problem, while the couplet wraps things up with a crispness accentuated by nearness of the volta and the brevity and unity of the final paired lines. This pattern of rhyme, again, is not an afterthought, not an affectation, not a literary conventional unwillingly inherited and grudgingly used—it is a choice purposefully made, and one that helps shape the theme of the work.

Perhaps just as immediately apparent as the rhyming structure of the Shakespearean sonnet, though, is its meter: iambic pentameter. An iamb is a metrical foot of two syllables, the first unstressed and the second stressed, and Shakespeare's general pattern in the sonnets is to write in lines of five feet, meaning roughly ten syllables. The lines may be end-stopped, with a natural pause at the end, or they may be enjambed, with both sound and sense continuing from the end of one line through the beginning of the next. Variations exist, certainly, with a stray syllable missing here and there or a stress shifting up and down the line now and then, but the basic pattern, one very well suited to many uses in the English language, holds.

To examine the structure and meter of a Shakespearean sonnet, let us choose one not already discussed in this text, Sonnet 12:

> When I do count the clock that tells the time,
> And see the brave day sunk in hideous night;
> When I behold the violet past prime,
> And sable curls are silvered o'er with white;
> When lofty trees I see barren of leaves,
> Which erst from heat did canopy the herd
> And summer's green, all girded up in sheaves,
> Borne on the bier with white and bristly beard;
> Then of thy beauty do I question make,
> That thou among the wastes of time must go,

> Since sweets and beauties do themselves forsake,
> And die as fast as they see others grow,
>   And nothing 'gainst Time's scythe can make defense,
>   Save breed, to brave him when he takes thee hence.

After this initial read of the poem above, then, below let us mark the sonnet for easy note of its structural features. On the left, the better to delineate the quatrains from one another and from the closing couplet, every fourth line is numbered. On the right, the scheme of end rhymes is spelled out, with *a* being the first sound awaiting a rhyme and each succeeding new sound being depicted with the next letter in the alphabet. Within the poem, each iambic foot is separated from the next with a vertical line, even at the rather unsightly expense of breaking words in two, and the stressed syllable in each foot is marked with an accent.

> When Í | do cóunt | the clóck | that télls | the tíme,   a
> And sée | the bráve | day súnk | in híd-|-eous níght;   b
> When Í | behóld | the ví-|olet | past príme,   a
> 4   And sá-|-ble cúrls | are síl-|-vered ó'er | with whíte;   b
> When lóf-|-ty trées | I sée | bárren | of léaves,   c
> Which érst | from héat | did cán-|-opy | the hérd,   d
> And súm-|-mer's gréen, | all gírd-|-ed úp | in shéaves,   c
> 8   Borne ón | the bíer | with white | and bríst-|-ly béard;   d
> Then óf | thy beaú-|-ty dó | I qués-|-tion máke,   e
> That thoú | amóng | the wástes | of tíme | must gó,   f
> Since swéets | and beaú-|-ties dó | themsélves forsáke,   e
> 12 And díe | as fást | as théy | see óth-|-ers gbrów,   f
> And nóth-|-ing 'gáinst | Time's scýthe | can máke |
>   defénse,   g
> Save bréed, | to bráve | him whén | he tákes | thee
>   hénce.   g

Not everything is of precise textbook regularity, of course. The final foot of Line 2, for example, is three syllables rather than two; it is difficult to desire the last syllable of *violet* in Line 3 to be marked with an accent merely so that we may call that foot an iamb; and we can debate whether *Borne on* in the first foot of Line 8 should be stressed more naturally on the first syllable or, instead following the meter, on the second syllable. Again, variations exist. None, however, jars or detracts from the simple flow of the reading, whether aloud or merely in one's head.

In addition—although these are not marked above, lest the poor poem begin to look like a football playbook—as long are we are noting end rhyme, perhaps we also should comment on Shakespeare's use of repeated consonant and vowel sounds within lines. Alliteration, the repetition of a consonant sound at the beginning of words, can be seen, for example, in the *count—clock* and *tells—time* of Line 1, *see—sunk* of Line 2, *sable—silvered* of Line 4, *Borne—bier* and *bristly beard* of Line 8, *Then—thy* of Line 9, *That thou* of Line 10, *Since sweets* of Line 11, and *breed—brave* of Line 14. Occasionally consonants at the end of a word also echo those at the beginning of a nearby word or even at its own beginning. Between the alliterative *sable* and *silvered* in Line 4, for example, comes the similar *z* sound that ends *curls*, while Line 13 shows mirroring *k* sounds in *can make*, and the tightly alliterative *Since sweets* of Line 11 shows an *s* sound at the end of each word as well as at the beginning, or four within a mere two syllables. On the other hand, assonance, the repetition of similar vowel sounds, can be seen in the long *a* sounds of *brave day* in Line 2, the long *e* sounds of *trees—see* in Line 5, and the long *i* sounds of *Time's scythe* in Line 13. None of these sonic devices is necessarily integral to the sonnet form as is end-rhyme, but all such things nevertheless also help weave the piece together into a more unified whole.

In any event, just as the reading of Sonnet 12 is good, pleasurable in sound and in image, the understanding is fairly easy, too, is it not? Perhaps one might have to hit the books—or consult the footnotes of a kind and thoughtful editor—to discover that *erst* means *formerly* or *previously*, that a bier is a stand for displaying a coffin before burial, that *save* in the final line means *besides* or *except for*, or that the verb *brave* immediately following means to defy or to shake one's fist at, with *him*, the object of the verb, being Time, or Death, which here is personified, rather traditionally, as one who cuts down human lives with a scythe in the same way mowers once cut down grass or crops. Such glosses clear up potential confusion quite quickly, though.

Even the now-unusual syntax of Line 9, with its *of thy beauty do I question make*, need not hold back the most inexperienced Shakespeare reader very long. The use of *do* for emphasis, even when appearing before *I*, the subject of the clause, is archaic or poetic but not unintelligible, and the now-uncommon inversion of verb and object at the end of the line can be puzzled through pretty shortly as well. Soon we will come to *I do make question of thy beauty*, meaning *I raise a question about*, *I question*, *I doubt*, or *I am uncertain about* the beauty of the person whom the speaker is addressing. The various

images of entropy—of the passage of time, of barrenness and decay, of death—show us that the question regards not whether the person actually is beautiful but instead this beauty's permanence and hence its true worth.

Intellectually, therefore, the theme of the piece is easily comprehensible: Like everything else in nature, even the most beautiful person dies, so producing offspring is the closest we have to defying the forces of time. Without this content—if, say, the piece merely presented images of flowers, butterflies, and sunshine, without any lasting meaning—even the prettiest poem would not be worth reading. Just as surely, however, without deftly chosen and skillfully balanced imagery supported by careful meter, rhyme, and other sonic devices, even the most profound piece of wisdom would not be a *poem*, a thing we read for the pleasures of interwoven sound and sense. We already have noted sound, so let us turn to the vocabulary and the imagery of which sense is made.

Shakespeare's use of language, both in vocabulary chosen and in images depicted, is fresh and therefore affecting. Even in the very first line, for example, note the rather striking use of the verb *count*. To *count the clock* strikes us as an archaism, of course, but while the phrase instantly connotes the tolling of a clock bell or chime, this is not the only way Shakespeare could have put it, and indeed it may not have been the first phrasing to come to mind. Verbs such as the flat *hear* or the slightly more forceful *note* would have been easy choices, for example. Neither, however, is as arresting as *count*, and in addition to catching our attention with the less expected word, the poet emphasizes the speaker's own very focused attention on the inexorable passing of time in a way that the other, more passive choices would have.

Similarly unexpected word choices may be seen throughout. The description of night as *hideous* in Line 2, for example, is surprisingly forceful. The strong verb in that line, *sunk*, is likewise well chosen. It is easy to imagine a handful of alternatives Shakespeare could have used in place of the ominous *sunk in*: *changed to*, *faded to*, *turned to*, *passing to*, *become*. These, after all, are the phrases of common speech. Yet their commonness is precisely why the good poet does not choose them. *Sunk* is so much more arresting.

And aside from the fact that alternatives like *turned to* show the necessary change of day into night but do not carry the connotation of entrapment or miring or menace that *sunk* does, we should note as well that the verb Shakespeare picked is, grammatically, a "strong verb." A weak, or regular, verb in English shows change of tense with an -ed ending: *I walk, I walked, I had walked.* A strong verb, however, is conjugated irregularly: *I sing, I sang, I had sung.* Strong verbs are a relic of the earliest Germanic roots of the English language and are now comparatively rare, with only 68 strong verbs from the Old English of a thousand years ago still remaining today, plus another two-dozen-odd verbs that either can be conjugated both ways or have changed from weak to strong (Baugh and Cable 164-65). This is not to say that *sunk* is an exotic or unusual work, of course, but it does have a subtle strength, and with this word Shakespeare avoids the obvious and common, brings in ominous connotations, and reinforces the latter with a bold verb that also ends in a hard, final consonant sound. In a composition only fourteen lines long, all elements of form support function.

Shakespeare's juxtaposition of unlike images is similarly fresh and arresting rather than expected—no *moon, June, spoon, croon* here. In Line 2, for example, *the brave day* is contrasted with *hideous night*, while *sable* and *white* face off in Line 4. The *thou* already described as beautiful stands against the exquisitely evocative *wastes of time* in Line 10, and the positive *sweets and beauties* of Line 11 are opposed by the negative *forsake.* Deft handling of personification here gives a similar pleasure of clichés avoided. Although portraying Time as an implacable figure with a scythe of course is far from new, Shakespeare in the middle of the poem unexpectedly turns the natural world to human by describing harvested crops as *girded*, or gathered up in a belt, as being carried on a *bier*, and as having a *beard.* It is easy to imagine how a poet of the era might create from these elements some fully developed metaphor running through the whole piece simply for the sake of the creation, something which to our eyes now might cloy and strangle. Shakespeare's technique, however, is sparing, and with his unexpected alternations—of natural and human, of light and dark, of positive and negative—he uses a subtle touch to keep the elements of form from overpowering the experience of the poem.

As we can see, in discussing the sonnets, Sonnet 12 is a useful place to begin. Verbally, it is understandable. Artistically, it is enjoyable. It reads well. It sounds clear and strong. It *speaks* to us. It is a fine example of poetic craft. Approaching the other sonnets with the techniques and tools we have used here—an understanding of form, an investigation of changing vocabulary, flexibility and imagination with unusual syntax, and, most perhaps importantly, an openness to the pleasures that even challenging poetry can bring to the appreciatively questing mind—may lead to further enjoyment and further recognition of what it means to be human.

One thing we have not discussed, however, is the question of whom the speaker of the poem is addressing. If reading only this sonnet, without context or other editorial apparatus, we might assume very easily that since the poet most likely is a man, the poem is speaking to a beautiful woman. Looking at Sonnet 12 within the sequence of the whole, however, suggests that the words instead address a young man. Yet is that which we call Sonnet 12 actually the twelfth because Shakespeare ordered it as such or merely because Thomas Thorpe, the original publisher of the works in 1609, did so? Did Shakespeare ever intend these sonnets, some of which seem so very personal and intimate, to be read by anyone but himself? And if this poem is indeed addressed to a man, as so many others of the sonnets clearly are, exactly what does or does not this reveal about the artist who wrote it? Really, even after 400-odd years, many puzzles still remain.

Unresolved Questions

Historian A.L. Rowse considers the sonnets to "offer us the greatest puzzle in the history of English literature" (vii), and of the subsequent puzzling-out, poet and critic W.H. Auden has observed, rather archly, that "more nonsense has been talked and written, more intellectual and emotional energy expended in vain…than on any other literary work in the world" (xvii). The latter is inevitable. The only thing we truly know about the sonnets, after all, aside from the fact that they are Shakespeare's, is that the collection first was published in 1609 by Thomas Thorpe. Exactly when were they written? To whom were they written, and why? Is their order Shakespeare's, or does the numbering of the one-hundred-fifty-four poems stem from Thomas Thorpe? Were these works truly intended for publication, or had Shakespeare desired them to remain private? None of these questions can be answered by real evidence rather than conjecture. Yet, neither, however, can we help wondering.

To discuss the various scholarly opinions on merely the composition of the sonnets would require a work larger than the entirety of the present text…and we still would not yet have begun on the poems themselves. Some brevity here, therefore, seems appropriate. It is natural enough to ascribe the sonnets to the early 1590s, when Shakespeare gained the patronage of Henry

Wriothesley, the Third Earl of Southampton, who was nine years younger than the actor-playwright, and possessed a delicate face perhaps described as correctly by the term *beautiful* as by *handsome*. Such connection with a titled aristocrat certainly can make life easier for an artist, and perhaps it may be somewhat flattering as well, especially when the recipient of the favors began his career as a comparative nobody from the country. During the period of 1593 and 1594, when the theaters of London were closed due to another outbreak of bubonic plague, Shakespeare turned his pen to poetry rather than drama. Both of his long narrative poems published then, *Venus and Adonis* and *The Rape of Lucrece*, were dedicated to Southampton, and "A Lover's Complaint," which was not published until Thorpe included it with the sonnets, may date from this period as well. It is therefore by no means unlikely that the sonnets, several of which praise a young man's beauty and urge him to marry and thereby produce offspring, were written during the Southampton patronage.

Even more tantalizing, though, are the issues of the sonnets taken as a whole. First, of course, were they actually presented by Shakespeare, or were they instead *taken* from him? While no direct historical evidence exists, it is difficult to disagree with W.H. Auden:

> How the sonnets came to be published—whether Shakespeare gave copies to some friend who then betrayed him, or whether some enemy stole them—we shall probably never know. Of one thing I am certain: Shakespeare must have been horrified when they were published.
>
> (xxxvi)

Indeed, what Auden terms "the impression of naked autobiographical confession" that runs through much of the work (xxxiv) makes it unlikely that the sonnets were written for a wide audience, and yet that impression will be diluted unless one reads a sizeable enough sampling of them and unless, moreover, one understands the shape of the collection as a whole. This text, of course, will provide both.

It is a truism that just as the intention to publish his sonnets likely was not Shakespeare's, neither was their order. This is not to say that anyone knows exactly how Shakespeare would have arranged the poems, only that there is no reason to assume their current numbering was necessarily the artist's choice. Nevertheless, the 154 sonnets fall into two broad blocks: Numbers 1 through

126, which are addressed to a young man, and Numbers 127 through 154, concerning a dark-haired woman who supposedly beguiles and betrays.

In the Young Man set, the first seventeen sonnets call for the beautiful youth to marry so that he may grace the world with an equally beautiful son. Others in this group speak further of the poet's love and longing for this young man: Sonnet 18, "Shall I compare thee to a summer's day?;" Sonnet 20, "A woman's face, with Nature's own hand painted;" and Sonnet 36, "Let me confess that we two must be twain," for example. Still others suggest torment at the way the youth strays from the poet, or takes a lady from the poet: Sonnet 40, "Take my loves, my love, yea take them all;" Sonnet 41, "Those petty wrongs that liberty commits;" and Sonnet 42, "That thou hast her, it is not all my grief," for example. Sonnets 78 through 86, on the other hand, seem to show jealousy in the way some rival poet has written about the young man.

The Dark Lady sonnets are rather more expected in their clearly heterosexual focus, though Ilona Bell is correct to suggest that we should not read the group too unquestioningly by "assuming either that the man is basically innocent and forgivable or that the dark lady is adulterous, promiscuous, deceitful, and thoroughly reprehensible" (294). Critics here and there over the centuries have tried to determine whether, presuming that the speaker is Shakespeare himself rather than a constructed character, the Young Man and the Dark Lady were real people as well. Regardless of identities, however, underlying it all is something more fundamental:

> [W]hat was their relationship to Shakespeare and to each other? Much of what happens in the dark lady sonnets and the intertwined young man sonnets is so intimate, so sexual, so fraught with desire and potential scandal that Shakespeare would rather not say—exactly. And to make matters even more baffling, there is a great deal he does not know and cannot understand about the man and the lady, and their relationship to each other…
>
> (Bell 295)

As Auden suggests, it is as silly to pretend "in defiance of common sense…that Shakespeare was merely expressing in somewhat hyperbolic terms, such as an Elizabethan poet might be expected to use, what any normal man feels for a friend of his own sex" as to make him, to quote a term I fervently hope has not been made too obscure by the fall of the Soviet Union, "a patron saint of the Hominterm" (xxix).

In short, there are no easy answers about the type, or types, of love being depicted in the sonnets—that is perhaps the greatest puzzle of them all. As the Bard predicted, however, since men, and women, still breathe and eyes still see, the sonnets' eternal lines to time still are read even four centuries later. And just as we continue to find delight and challenge and truth in these little fourteen-line marvels of image and emotion, it seems likely that so, too, will students in yet another four centuries as well, and another, and another.

Rafeeq O. McGiveron

Works Cited

Auden, W.H. "Introduction." *Shakespeare's Sonnets*. Ed. William Burto. 1965. New York: Signet, n.d. xvii–xxxviii.

Baugh, Albert C. & Thomas Cable. *A History of the English Language*. 3rd ed. Englewood Cliffs, NJ: Prentice, 1978.

Bell, Ilona. "Rethinking Shakespeare's Dark Lady." *A Companion to Shakespeare's Sonnets*. Ed. Michael Schoenfeldt. Malden, MA: Blackwell, 2007. 293-313.

Bradbury, Ray. *Fahrenheit 451*. 1953. New York: Del Rey, 1991.

D'Emilio, John & Estelle B. Freedman. *Intimate Matters: A History of Sexuality in America*. 1988. New York: Perennial, 1989.

Hale, J.R. *Renaissance Exploration*. New York: Norton, 1968.

Harrison, Edward R. *Cosmology: The Science of the Universe*. Cambridge: Cambridge UP, 1981.

Huxley, Aldous. *Brave New World*. 1932. New York: Harper, 1989.

Rowse, A.L., ed. *Shakespeare's Sonnets*. New York: Harper, 1964.

Schoenbaum, S. *William Shakespeare: A Compact Documentary Life*. New York: Oxford UP, 1977.

Swisher, Clarice, ed. *Readings on the Sonnets*. Greenhaven Literary Companions to British Literature Series. San Diego: Greenhaven, 1997.

Tillyard, E.M.W. *The Elizabethan World Picture*. New York: Vintage, n.d.

Zamyatin, Yevgeny. *We*. 1922. New York: Penguin, 1993.

For Further Study

Archer, John Michael. *Technically Alive: Shakespeare's Sonnets*. New York: Palgrave, 2012.

Baldwin, T.W. *Shakespeare's Small Latine and Lesser Greeke*. Urbana: U of Illinois P, 1944.

Bate, Jonathan. *Soul of the Age: A Biography of the Mind of William Shakespeare*. New York: Random, 2009.

Bearman, Robert. *Shakespeare in the Stratford Records*. Phoenix Mill, UK: Sutton, 1994.

Blades, John. *Shakespeare: The Sonnets*. Analysing Texts Series. Houndmills, UK: Palgrave, 2007.

Booth, Stephen. *An Essay on Shakespeare's Sonnets*. New Haven: Yale UP, 1969.

Evans, G. Blakemore, ed. *The Sonnets*. New Cambridge Shakespeare Series. Cambridge; Cambridge UP, 1996.

Green, Martin. *The Labyrinth of Shakespeare's Sonnets: An Examination of Sexual Elements in Shakespeare's Language*. London: Skilton, 1974.

Hammond, Gerald. *The Reader and Shakespeare's Young Man Sonnets*. London: Macmillan, 1981.

Herrnstein, Barbara, ed. *Discussions of Shakespeare's Sonnets*. Discussions of Literature Series. Boston: Heath, 1964.

Heylin, Clinton. *So Long as Men can Breathe: The Untold Story of Shakespeare's Sonnets*. Philadelphia: Da Capo, 2009.

Leishman, J.B. *Themes and Variations in Shakespeare's Sonnets*. 2nd ed. London: Hutchinson, 1963.

Matz, Robert. *An Introduction to the World of Shakespeare's Sonnets*. Jefferson, NC: McFarland, 2008.

Muir, Kenneth. *Shakespeare's Sonnets*. 1979. London: Allen, 2005.

Park, Honan. *Shakespeare: A Life*. Oxford: Oxford UP, 2000.

Pequigney, Joseph. *Such Is My Love: A Study of Shakespeare's Sonnets*. Chicago: U of Chicago P, 1985.

Price, George R. *Reading Shakespeare's Plays*. Woodbury, NY: Barron's, 1962.

Rowse, A.L. *Shakespeare the Man*. Revised ed. Houndmills, UK: Macmillan, 1988.

_____, ed. *Shakespeare's Sonnets*. New York: Harper, 1964.

Schiffer, James, ed. *Shakespeare's Sonnets: Critical Essays*. New York: Garland, 2000.

Schoenbaum, S. *William Shakespeare: A Compact Documentary Life*. New York: Oxford UP, 1977.

Schoenfeldt, Michael, ed. *A Companion to Shakespeare's Sonnets*. Malden, MA: Blackwell, 2007.

Swisher, Clarice, ed. *Readings on the Sonnets*. Greenhaven Literary Companions to British Literature Series. San Diego: Greenhaven, 1997.

Wait, R.J.C. *The Background to Shakespeare's Sonnets*. New York: Schocken, 1972.

Willen, Gerald & Victor B. Reed, eds. *A Casebook on Shakespeare's Sonnets*. New York: Crowell, 1964.

Historical & Literary Contexts

English Poetry in the Sixteenth Century

The poetry of the sixteenth century defies facile generalizations. Although the same can obviously be said for the poetry of other periods as well, this elusiveness of categorization is particularly characteristic of the sixteenth century. It is difficult to pinpoint a century encompassing both the growling meter of John Skelton and the polished prosody of Sir Philip Sidney, and consequently, past efforts to provide overviews of the period have proven unhelpful. Most notably, C. S. Lewis in his *English Literature in the Sixteenth Century Excluding Drama* (1954) contrived an unfortunate division between what he called "drab" poetry and "Golden" poetry. What he means by this distinction is never entirely clear, and Lewis himself further confuses the dichotomy by occasionally suggesting that his own term "drab" need not have a pejorative connotation, although when he applies it to specific poets, it is clear that he intends it to be damaging. Furthermore, his distinction leads him into oversimplifications. As Lewis would have it, George Gascoigne is mostly drab (a condition that he sees as befitting a poet of the "drab" mid-century) though blessed with occasional "Golden" tendencies, while Robert Southwell, squarely placed in the "Golden" period, is really a mediocre throwback to earlier "drab" poetry. Such distinctions are hazy and not helpful to the reader, who suspects that Lewis defines "drab" and "Golden" simply as what he himself dislikes or prefers in poetry.

The muddle created by Lewis's terminology has led to inadequate treatments of the sixteenth century in the classroom. Perhaps reinforced by the simplicity of his dichotomy, teachers have traditionally depicted the fruits of the century as not blossoming until the 1580s, with the sonneteers finally possessing the talent and good sense to perfect the experiments with the Petrarchan sonnet form first begun by Sir Thomas Wyatt early in the century. Students have been inevitably taught that between Wyatt and Sidney stretched a wasteland of mediocre poetry, disappointing primarily because so many poets failed to apply their talents to continuing the Petrarchan experiments begun by Wyatt. Thus, indoctrinated in the axiom that, as concerns the sixteenth century, "good" poetry is Petrarchan and "bad" poetry is that which fails to work with Petrarchan conceits, teachers deal in the classroom mostly with the poets of the 1580's and later, ignoring the other poetic currents of the early and mid-century. It has been difficult indeed to overcome Lewis's dichotomy of "drab" and "Golden."

Fortunately, there have been studies of sixteenth century poetry that are sensitive to non-Petrarchan efforts, and these studies deserve recognition as providing a better perspective for viewing the sixteenth century. In 1939, Yvor Winters's essay "The Sixteenth Century Lyric in England: A Critical and Historical Reinterpretation" focused on some of the less notable poets of the period, such as Barnabe Googe, George Turberville, and Gascoigne, who, until Winters's essay, had been dismissed simply because they were not Petrarchan in sentiment, and the essay also helped to dispel the notion that the aphoristic, proverbial content of their poetry was symptomatic of their simple-mindedness and lack of talent. By pointing out how their sparse style contributes to, rather than detracts from, the moral content of their poetry, Winters's essay is instrumental in helping the reader develop a sense of appreciation for these often overlooked poets. In addition to Winters's essay, Douglas L. Peterson's book *The English Lyric from Wyatt to Donne: A History of the Plain and Eloquent Styles* (1967), taking up where Winters left off, identified two major poetic currents in the sixteenth century: the plain style and the eloquent style. Peterson provided a more realistic and less judgmental assessment of the non-Petrarchans as practitioners of the "plain" rhetorical style, a term that was a welcome relief from Lewis's "drab." Thus, Winters's and Peterson's efforts were helpful in destroying the damaging stereotypes about the "bad" poets of the mid-century.

Poetry as craft

Despite the difficulties inherent in summarizing a century as diverse as the sixteenth, it is possible to discern a unifying thread running through the poetry of the period. The unity stems from the fact that, perhaps more than any other time, the sixteenth century was consistently "poetic"; that is, the poets were constantly aware of themselves as poetic craftsmen. From Skelton to Edmund Spenser, poets were self-conscious of their pursuits, regardless of theme. This poetic self-consciousness was manifested primarily in the dazzling display of metrical, stanzaic, and prosodic experimentation

Illustration 1. William Shakespeare performing before Queen Elizabeth and her court. (*Library of Congress*)

that characterized the efforts of all the poets, from the most talented to the most mediocre. In particular, the century experienced the development of, or refinement upon, for example, the poulter's measure (alternate twelve-and fourteen-syllable lines), blank verse, heroic couplets, rime royal, ottava rima, terza rima, Spenserian stanza, douzains, fourteeners—all appearing in a variety of genres. Characteristic of the century was the poet watching himself be a poet, and every poet of the century would have found himself in agreement with Sidney's assessment of the poet in his Defence of Poesie (1595) as prophet or seer, whose craft is suffused with divine inspiration.

Social context

This process of conscious invention and self-monitoring is one key to understanding the poetry of the sixteenth century. It is a curious fact that whereas in other periods, historical and social factors play a large role in shaping poetic themes, in the sixteenth century, such extraliterary influences did little to dictate the nature of the poetry. Surprisingly, even though Copernicus's theory of a heliocentric universe was known by mid-century, the poetry barely nodded to the New Science or to the new geographical discoveries. Certainly, the century experienced almost constant political and religious turbulence, providing abundant fare for topical themes; a less

apolitical period one can hardly imagine. It was the prose, however, more than the poetry, that sought to record the buffetings created by the fact that the official religion in England changed four times between 1530 and 1560.

It seems that the instability created by this uneasiness had the effect of turning the poets inward, rather than outward to political, social, and religious commentary (with the exceptions of the broadside ballads, pseudo-journalistic poems intended for the uncultivated, and the verse chronicle history so popular at the close of the century), bearing out the hypothesis that good satire can flourish only in periods of relative stability. For example, despite the number of obvious targets, the genre of political satire did not flourish in the sixteenth century, and its sporadic representatives, in particular anticlerical satire, a warhorse left over from the Middle Ages, are barely noteworthy. A major figure in Spenser's *The Faerie Queene* (1590, 1596) is Gloriana, a figure depicting Queen Elizabeth, but she is an idealized rendering, only one of many such celebrations in poetry of Queen Elizabeth, not intended to provide a realistic insight into her character.

Rise of vernacular languages

Thus, to the poet of the sixteenth century, the primary consideration of the poetic pursuit was not who or what to write about, but rather how to write. The reason for this emphasis on style over content is simple enough to isolate. By the middle of the sixteenth century, the English language was experiencing severe growing pains. In fact, throughout Europe the vernacular was struggling to overthrow the tyranny of Latin and to discover its essential identity. Nationalism was a phenomenon taking root everywhere, and inevitably, the cultivation of native languages was seen as the logical instrument of expediting the development of national identity. Italy and France were undergoing revolts against Latin, and Joachim du Bellay's La Défense et illustration de la langue française (1549; *The Defence and Illustration of the French Language*, 1939) proclaimed explicitly that great works can be written in the vernacular. In England, the invention of new words was encouraged, and war was waged on "inkhornisms," terms of affectation usually held over from the old Latin or French, used liberally by Skelton. Thus, George Puttenham, an influential critical theorist of the period, discusses the question of whether a poet would be better advised to use "pierce" rather than "penetrate," and Richard Mulcaster, Spenser's old headmaster, was moved to announce, "I honor the Latin, but I worship English."

It was no easy task, however, to legislate prescribed changes in something as malleable as language, and the grandeur of the effort nevertheless often produced comic results. Sixteenth century English vernacular, trying to weed out both Latin and French influences, produced such inelegant and uneasy bastardizations as "mannerlier," "newelties," "hable" (a hangover from Latin habilis), and "semblably," leading William Webbe in his *Discourse of English Poetry* (1586) to rail in a sneering pun about "this brutish poetry," with "brutish" looming as a veiled reference to "British." Although the sixteenth century was constantly discovering that the subtleties of perfecting a new language could not be mastered overnight, the effort was nevertheless sustained and paved the way for a future confidence in what the vernacular could achieve. Words that often strike the modern reader as outdated, stodgy pedantry are, in fact, the uncertain by-products of innovative experimentation.

Thus, to understand sixteenth century poetry is to ignore the stability of language, which is taken for granted in later centuries, and to understand the challenge that the poets experienced in shaping the new language to fit their poetry. Working with new words meant changes in the old classical syntax, and, in turn, changes in the syntax meant changes in the old classical versifications. These changes often resulted in frustration for the poet

(and for the reader), but, depending on the skills of the poet, the result of all this experimentation could mean new rhyme schemes, new meters, and new stanzaic structures. In the wake of all the excitement generated by this constant experimentation, the poets cannot be blamed for often judging innovations in content as secondary to the new prosody. The volatility and flux of the language siphoned all energies into perfecting new styles not into content.

Translations
The zeal for metrical experimentation that characterized the sixteenth century is manifested not only in the original poetry of the period but also in the numerous translations that were being turned out. The primary purpose of the translations was to record the works of the venerable authorities in the new vernacular, and it is significant that Webbe refers to these works not as being "translated" but as being "Englished." Vergil's Aeneid (c. 29-19 b.c.e.; English translation, 1553) was a favorite target for the translators, with Henry Howard, the earl of Surrey, publishing a translation in 1553, Thomas Phaer in 1558, and Richard Stanyhurst in 1582. Stanyhurst translated only the first four books, and he achieved a metrical monstrosity by attempting to translate Vergil in English hexameters, reflecting the tensions of cramming old subject matter into new forms. Ovid was another favorite of the translators. Arthur Golding translated the Metamorphoses (c. 8 c.e.; English translation, 1567) in 1567, and also in that year, Turberville translated the Heroides (before 8 c.e.; English translation, 1567), featuring elaborate experiments with the poulter's measure, fourteeners, and blank verse. Most of the translations of the period may be dismissed as the works of versifiers, not poets (with the exception of George Chapman's Homer, which has the power of an original poem), but they are valuable reflections of the constant metrical experimentations taking place and, subsequently, of the ongoing process of shaping the new vernacular.

Literary theory
An overview of the poetry of the 1500s would be incomplete without an introduction to the critical theory of the period and the ways in which it recorded the successes and failures of the new vernacular experimentations. Not surprisingly, critical theory of the age was abundant. An obvious representative is Sidney's Defence of Poesie. The elegance and polish of this argument for the superiority of poetry over any other aesthetic pursuit has made

it the most outstanding example of Renaissance critical theory. The easy grace of the work, however, tends to obscure the fact that the new experiments in prosody had created a lively, often nasty debate in critical theory between the guardians of the old and the spokespersons for the new. There were many other works of critical theory closer than the Defense of Poesie to the pulse rate of the arguments.

The turbulent nature of the critical theory of the period (and, by implications, the turbulence of the poetry itself) is reflected by Gascoigne, who in his "Certayne Notes of Instruction Concerning the Making of Verse" (1575) serves as a hearty spokesperson for the new vernacular, advocating a more widespread use of monosyllables in poetry and a rejection of words derived from foreign vocabularies so that "the truer Englishman you shall seem and the less you shall smell of the inkhorn," and decrying poets who cling to the old Latin syntax by placing their adjectives after the noun. In his Art of English Poesy (1589), Puttenham scolds those poets who "wrench" their words to fit the rhyme, "for it is a sign that such a maker is not copious in his own language." Not every critic, however, was so enchanted with the new experimentation. In his Art of Rhetorique (1553), Thomas Wilson called for continued practice of the old classical forms, and he sought to remind poets that words of Latin and Greek derivation are useful in composition. Contempt for new techniques in versification pervades Roger Ascham's The Schoolmaster (1570). He condemns innovations in rhyming, which he dismisses as derived from the "Gothes and Hunnes," and calls for renewed imitation of classical forms. In his Discourse of English Poetry (1586), William Webbe is even less charitable. He scorns the new experiments in prosody as "this tinkerly verse," and he campaigns for keeping alive the old, classical quantitative verse, in which the meter is governed by the time required to pronounce a syllable, not by accentuation. Clearly the severity of the critical debate needs to be kept in the forefront as one begins consideration of the poetry of the period; to fail to do so is to overlook what the poets were trying to accomplish.

Allegories and dream visions

The opening of the sixteenth century, however, was anything but a harbinger of new developments to come. Like most centuries, the sixteenth began on a conservative, even reactionary note, looking backward to medieval literature, rather than forward to the new century.

Allegories and dream visions written in seven-line stanzas, favorite vehicles of the medieval poets, dominated the opening years of the sixteenth century. Under Henry VII the best poets were Scottish—William Dunbar, Gavin Douglas, and Sir David Lyndsay—and they were devoted imitators of Geoffrey Chaucer. The first English poet to assert himself in the new century was Stephen Hawes, who published The Pastime of Pleasure in 1509 which represented uninspired medievalism at its worst. The work is constructed as a dream-vision allegory. An almost direct imitation of John Lydgate's work, The Pastime of Pleasure narrates the hero Grand Amour's instruction in the Tower of Doctrine, employing a profusion of stock, allegorical characters reminiscent of the morality plays. The old medieval forms, especially those combining allegory and church satire, were hard to die. In 1536, Robert Shyngleton wrote *The Pilgrim's Tale*, a vulgar, anticlerical satire directly evocative of Chaucer, and as late as 1556, John Heywood wrote The Spider and the Fly, a lengthy allegory depicting the Roman Catholics as flies, the Protestants as spiders, and Queen Mary as wielding a cleanig broom.

John Skelton

Another heavy practitioner of the dream allegory was John Skelton (c. 1460–1529), one of the most puzzling figures of the century. Skelton has long been an object of negative fascination for literary historians—and with good reason. He deserves a close look, however, because, despite his reactionary themes, he was the first metrical experimenter of the century. His paradoxical undertaking of being both metrical innovator and medieval reactionary has produced some of the oddest, even comic, poetry in the English language. His infamous Skeltonic meter, a bewildering mixture of short, irregular lines and an array of varying rhyme schemes, relies on stress, alliteration, and rhyme, rather than on syllabic count, and as a result, the reader is left either outraged or amused. His subject matter was inevitably a throwback to earlier medieval themes. He wrote two dream-vision allegories, *The Bowge of Court* (1499), a court satire, and *The Garlande of Laurell* (1523). Skelton is still read today, however, because of his fractured meter. The theme of his Collyn Clout (1522), a savage satire on the corruption of the English clergy (whose title, incidentally, was the inspiration for Spenser's Colin Clouts Come Home Againe, 1591), is of interest to the modern reader not so much for its content as for its versification. In the work, Skelton describes his own rhyme as being

"Tatterèd and jaggèd/ Rudely rain-beaten/ Rusty and moth-eaten." Skelton's rhyme arrives fast and furious, and it is possible to conclude that he may have been the object of Puttenhm's attack on poets who "wrench" their words to fit the rhyme.

Continental influences

Despite his original metrical experimentation, Skelton was still entrenched in inkhornisms and looked backward for his themes. Paradoxically, as is often the case, it can be the poet with the least talent who nevertheless injects into his poetry vague hints of things to come. Alexander Barclay wrote no poetry of the slightest worth, but embedded in the mediocrity lay the beginnings of a new respect for the vernacular. To the literary historian, Barclay is of interest for two reasons. First, he was the sixteenth century's first borrower from the Continent. Specifically, in his Certayn Egloges (1570), he was the first to imitate the eclogues of Mantuan, which were first printed in 1498 and which revolutionized the genre of the pastoral eclogue by making it a vehicle for anticlerical satire, although such satire was of course nothing new in England at that time. Barclay's second importance, however (and perhaps the more significant), lies in the fact that he was the first to use the vernacular for the pastoral.

Tottel's Miscellany

It was not until mid-century that English borrowings from the Continent were put on full display. In 1557, a collection of lyrics known as Tottel's Miscellany was published, and the importance of this work cannot be overemphasized. It was innovative not only in its function as a collection of poems by various authors, some of them anonymous, but also in the profusion of prosodic experimentation that it offered. Tottel's Miscellany represented nothing less than England's many-faceted response to the Continental Renaissance. In this collection, every conceivable metrical style (including some strange and not wholly successful experiments with structural alliteration) was attempted in an array of genres, including sonnets, epigrams, elegies, eulogies, and poems of praise and Christian consolation, often resulting in changes in the older Continental forms. Truly there is no better representation of poets self-consciously watching themselves be poets.

Nevertheless, unfair stereotypes about the collection abound. Perhaps because of Lewis's distinction between "drab" age and "Golden" age poetry, students are

often taught that the sole merit of Tottel's Miscellany is its inclusion of the lyrics of Wyatt and Surrey (which had been composed years earlier)—in particular, their imitations of the amatory verse of Petrarch. The standard classroom presentation lauds Wyatt and Surrey for introducing Petrarch and his sonnet form into England. Students are further taught that the long-range effects of Tottel's Miscellany proved to be disappointing since no poet was motivated to continue Wyatt's and Surrey's experiments with Petrarch for decades thereafter. Thus, Tottel's Miscellany is blamed for being essentially a flash-in-the-pan work lacking in any significant, literary influence. Such disappointment is absurdly unjustified, however, in view of what the publisher Richard Tottel and Wyatt and Surrey were trying to accomplish. Tottel published his collection "to the honor of the English tong," and in that sense the work was a success, as the conscious goal of all its contributors was to improve the vernacular. Furthermore, its most talented contributors, Wyatt and Surrey, accomplished what they set out to do: to investigate fully the possibilities of the short lyric, something that had never before been attempted in England, and, in Surrey's case, to experiment further with blank verse and the poulter's measure.

By no stretch of the imagination did Wyatt view himself as the precursor of a Petrarchan movement in England, and he made no attempt to cultivate followers. In fact, despite the superficial similarity of subject matter, Wyatt's poetry has little in common with the Petrarchan sonneteers of the close of the century, and he most assuredly would have resented any implication that his poetry was merely an unpolished harbinger of grander efforts to come. As Douglas L. Peterson has pointed out, Wyatt used Petrarch to suit his own purposes, mainly to perfect his "plain" style; and Yvor Winters maintains that Wyatt is closer to Gascoigne than Sidney. Whereas the sonneteers of the close of the century composed decidedly in the "eloquent" style, Wyatt expressed contempt for trussed-up images and pursued the virtues of a simple, unadorned style.

Plain style

Thus, far from attempting to initiate a new "movement" of Petrarchan eloquence, many of the poems in Tottel's Miscellany sought to refine the possibilities of the plain style. As Peterson defines it, the plain style is characterized by plain, proverbial, aphoristic sentiments. It is a style often unappreciated by modern readers because its obvious simplicity is often mistaken for simplemindedness. The practitioners of the plain style, however, were very skilled in tailoring their verse to fit the needs of the poem's message, the pursuit of simplicity becoming a challenge, not a symptom of flagging inspiration. Skelton unwittingly summarizes the philosophy of the plain style when, commenting on his rhyme in Collyn Clout, he instructs the reader: "If ye take well therewith/ It hath in it some pith."

Thus, a plain-style poet expressing disillusionment with the excesses of love or extolling the virtues of frugality, rather than adorning his poem with an abundance of extravagant images, he instead pared his sentiments down to the minimum, with the intense restraint itself illuminating the poet's true feelings about love or money. The desiderata of the plain style were tightness and disciplined restraint. In the hands of an untalented poet, such as Heywood, who wrote *A Dialogue of Proverbs* (1546, 1963), the aphoristic messages could easily become stultifying; but as practiced by a poet with the skill of Wyatt, the economy of rendering a truth simply could produce a pleasurable effect. Interestingly, near the close of the century, when the eloquent style was all the rage, Sir Walter Ralegh, Thomas Nashe, and Fulke Greville often employed the techniques of the plain style.

Further anthologies

The three decades following the publication of *Tottel's Miscellany* have been stereotyped as a wasteland when poetry languished desultorily until the advent of the sonneteers in the 1580s. Nothing could be more unfair to the poetry of the period than to view it as struggling in an inspirational darkness. Amazingly, such a stereotype manages to overlook the profusion of poetry collections that *Tottel's Miscellany* spawned. Though admittedly the poetry of some of these collections is forgettable, nevertheless the continual appearance of these collections for the next fifty years is an impressive indication of the extent to which Tottel's philosophy of prosodic experimentation continued to exert an influence.

The first imitation of Tottel to be published was *The Paradise of Dainty Devices* (1576), the most popular of the imitations. As its title would indicate, a number of amatory poems were included, but the predominant poems had didactic, often pious themes, which offered ample opportunity for further experimentation in the plain style. A number of reasonably accomplished poets contributed to the collection, including Sir Richard Grenville, Jaspar Heywood, Thomas Churchyard, and

Barnabe Rich. Another successful collection was Brittons Bowre of Delights (1591), interesting for its wide range of metrical experimentation, especially involving poulter's measure and the six-line iambic pentameter stanza.

Imitations of Tottel's works did not always prove successful. In 1577, *A Gorgeous Gallery of Gallant Inventions* appeared, a monotonous collection of poems whose oppressive theme was the vanity of love and pleasure, and it was as plagued with affectations and jargon as Brittons Bowre of Delights was blessed with fresh experimentation. Not everyone was pleased, however, with the new direction the lyric was taking after Tottel. In 1565, John Hall published his *Court of Virtue*, an anti-Tottel endeavor designed to preach that literature must be moral. In his work the poet is instructed by Lady Arete to cease pandering to the vulgar tastes of the public and instead to write moral, instructive lyrics, an appeal which results in the poet's moralizing of Wyatt's lyrics.

The experimental spirit of Tottel carried over into the works of individual poets, as well. From such an unlikely source as Thomas Tusser's *A Hundreth Good Points of Husbandry* (1557), an unassuming almanac of farming tips, explodes a variety of metrical experimentation, including Skeltonics, acrostics, and other complicated stanzaic forms. Despite his willingness to experiment, however, Tusser was not an accomplished talent, and thus there are three poets, Googe, Turberville, and Gascoigne, to whom one must turn to refute the stereotype of the mid-century "wasteland." Too often viewed as bungling imitators of Tottel, these poets deserve a closer look as vital talents who were keeping poetry alive during the so-called wasteland years.

Barnabe Googe

In his Eclogues, Epitaphs, and Sonnets (1563), Barnabe Googe's explicit poetic mission was to imitate Tottel. Working mostly in the didactic tradition, he wrote some epitaphs and poems in praise of friends, but his eclogues are of primary interest to the literary historian. He revived the Mantuan eclogue, which had been lying dormant in England after Barclay, and his eclogues were good enough to offer anticipations of Spenser's The Shepheardes Calender (1579). Another noteworthy work is his Cupido Conquered (1563), a dream-vision allegory, which Lewis dismissed as "purely medieval." The dismissal is unfair, however, because, despite the throwback to medieval devices, the plot, in which the languishing, lovesick poet is chided by his muses for his shameful lack of productivity, reveals Googe's self-consciousness of himself as craftsman, a characteristic pose for a poet of the sixteenth century.

George Turberville

George Turberville's dexterity with metrics in his translation of Ovid has already been mentioned. Like Googe, Turberville, in his *Epitaphs, Epigrams, Songs, and Sonnets* (1567), carried on with Tottelian experimentation, primarily in didactic poems employing poulter's measure and fourteeners written in the plain style.

George Gascoigne

George Gascoigne has been late in receiving the attention that he deserves, his poetry serving as the most impressive evidence disproving the existence of a post-Tottel wasteland. Predictably, Lewis describes him as a precursor of golden age poetry, ignoring Gascoigne's contributions to the plain style. In his *A Hundreth Sundrie Flowres Bounde up in One Small Poesie* (1573, poetry and prose; revised as The Posies of George Gascoigne Esquire, 1575), Gascoigne was the first to experiment with Petrarch and the sonnet form since Wyatt and Surrey, but he was no slavish imitator. Gascoigne's poetry is often coarser and more lewd than that of Petrarch, but he never sacrifices a robust wit. In addition, he is an interesting figure for his variations in the sonnet form, featuring the octave-sestet division of the Petrarchan form, but in an English, or abab rhyme scheme. Puttenham refers to his "good meter" and "plentiful vein."

Elizabethan poetry

Thus, the poetry of the latter part of the century, the great age of the eloquent style, must not be viewed as a semi-miraculous phoenix, rising from the ashes between Wyatt's experiments with Petrarch and the advent of Sidney. Nevertheless, it must be noted that the Elizabethan era ranks as one of the outstanding poetic periods of any century, its development of the eloquent style ranking as an outstanding achievement. A valuable representative of what the eloquent style was trying to accomplish is Sir John Davies' *Orchestra: Or, A Poeme of Dauncing* (1596, 1622). In his *Elizabethan World Picture* (1943), E. M. W. Tillyard analyzes the poem at length as a fitting symbol of the Elizabethans' obsession with cosmic order. Though accurate enough, Tillyard's discussion places too much emphasis on the poem's content and does not pay enough attention to the style in which the

message is delivered. In the poem, the suitor Antinous launches an elaborate discourse designed to persuade Penelope, waiting for her Odysseus to return, to dance. Through Antinous's lengthy and involved encomium to cosmic order and rhythm, Davies was not attempting a literal plea to Penelope to get up and dance. Rather, he was using Antinous as a vehicle for an ingenious argument, ostentatious in its erudition and profusion of images; in effect, Antinous's argument is the repository of Davies' experiments in the eloquent style. It is the dazzling display of the process of argumentation itself, not the literal effort to persuade Penelope, that is the essence of the poem. The way in which the poem is written is more important than its content, and in that sense (but in that sense only) the goal of the eloquent style is no different from that of the plain style.

Petrarchan and "eloquent" style

When one thinks of sixteenth century poetry and the eloquent style, however, one almost immediately thinks of the Petrarchan sonnet sequence, and one explanation for the almost fanatic renewal of interest in Petrarch was the inevitable shift of interests in poetic style. The plain style, so dominant for almost half a century, was beginning to play itself out, a primary indication being the decline in use of the epigram, whose pithy wit held little appeal for Elizabethan poets. The more skillful among them were anxious to perfect a new style, specifically the "eloquent" style, almost the total antithesis of the plain style. Not particularly concerned with expressing universal truths, the eloquent style, as practiced by Davies, sought embellishment, rather than pithy restraint, and a profusion of images, rather than minimal, tight expression. The eloquent style effected some interesting changes in the handling of the old Petrarchan themes, as well. It should be noted that in his experiments with Petrarch, Wyatt chafed at the indignities suffered by the courtly lover. By contrast, the sonneteers emphasized with relish the travails of the lover, who almost luxuriates in his state of rejection. In fact, there is no small trace of fin de siècle decadence in the cult of the spurned lover that characterized so many of the sonnets of the period, most notably Sidney's Astrophel and Stella (1591), and it decidedly signaled the end of the plain style.

Sonnets and sonnet sequences

The sonnet sequence, a collection of sonnets recording the lover's successes and failures in courting his frequently unsympathetic mistress, was practiced by the brilliant and mediocre alike. Of course, the two most outstanding poets of the century pioneered the form— Sidney in his Astrophel and Stella, who in the true spirit of the poetic self-consciousness of the century wrote sonnets about the writing of sonnets and wrote some sonnets entirely in Alexandrines, and Spenser in his Amoretti (1595), who, in addition to introducing refinements in the sonnet structure, also intellectualized the cult of the rejected lover by analyzing the causes of rejection.

In the next twenty years the contributions to the genre were dizzying: Greville's *Caelica* (wr. 1577, pb. 1633); Thomas Watson's *Passionate Century of Love* (1582); Samuel Daniel's *Delia* (1592); Henry Constable's *Diana* (1592); Thomas Lodge's *Phillis* (1593); Giles Fletcher's *Licia* (1593); Barnabe Barnes's *Parthenophil and Parthenophe* (1593); Bartholomew Griffin's *Fidessa* (1593); Michael Drayton's *Ideas Mirrour* (1594), noteworthy for its experiments with rhyme; *The Phoenix Nest* (1593), a collection of Petrarchan sonnets in a wide variety of meters by George Peele, Nicholas Breton, Thomas Lodge, and others—the list of accomplished poets and tinkering poetasters was almost endless.

By the close of the century, so many mediocre poets had turned out sonnet sequences, and the plight of the rejected lover had reached such lugubrious proportions that the form inevitably decayed. The cult of the masochistic lover was becoming tediously commonplace, and one of the major triumphs of the eloquent style, the Petrarchan paradox (for example, Wyatt's "I burn, and freeze like ice") lost its appeal of surprise and tension as it became overworked, predictable, and trite. The genre had lost all traces of originality, and it is interesting to consider the fact that the modern definition of a sonneteer is an inferior poet. As early as 1577, Greville in his Caelica had perceived how easily in the sonnet sequence numbing repetition could replace fresh invention, and to maintain some vitality in his sequence his subject matter evolves from the complaints of the rejected lover to a renunciation of worldly vanity and expressions of disappointment in the disparity between "ideal" love and the imperfect love that exists in reality. (For this reason, of all the sonneteers Greville is the only precursor of the themes so prevalent in seventeenth century devotional poetry.)

The success and subsequent decline of the sonnet sequence left it wide open to parody. Many of the sonnets of William Shakespeare, who himself revolutionized the sonnet structure in England, are veiled satiric statements on the trite excesses of Petrarchan images ("My mistress's eyes are nothing like the sun"), indicating his impatience with the old, worn-out sentiments. Davies' collection of Gulling Sonnets (c. 1594) was an explicit parody of Petrarchan absurdities and weary lack of invention, and, following their publication, the genre spun into an irreversible decline.

Mythological-erotic narrative

As the sonnet declined, however, another form of amatory verse was being developed: the mythological-erotic narrative. This form chose erotic themes from mythology, embellishing the narrative with sensuous conceits and quasipornographic descriptions. It was a difficult form to master because it required titillation without descending into vulgarity and light touches of sophisticated humor without descending into burlesque. Successful examples of the mythological-erotic narrative are Christopher Marlowe's Hero and Leander (1598; completed by Chapman), Shakespeare's *Venus and Adonis* (1593), Chapman's Ovid's *Banquet of Sense* (1595), Drayton's *Endimion and Phoebe* (1595), and Lodge's *Scillaes Metamorphosis* (1589). Like the sonnet, the mythological narrative fell into decline, as evidenced by John Marston's *The Metamorphosis of Pygmalion's Image and Certain Satires* (1598), in which the decadence of the sculptor drooling lustfully over his statue was too absurdly indelicate for the fragile limits of the genre.

Satiric and religious verse

As the mythological narrative and the sonnet declined, both social satire and religious verse experienced a corresponding upswing. The steady growth of a middle-class reading audience precipitated an increased interest in satire, a genre which had not been represented with any distinction since Gascoigne's *The Steele Glas, a Satyre* (1576). Understandably, though inaccurately, Joseph Hall labeled himself the first English satirist. Juvenalian satire flourished in his *Virgidemiarum* (1597), similar to Davies' *Gulling Sonnets*, followed by Everard Guilpin's *Skialetheia: Or, Shadow of Truth in Certain Epigrams and Satyres* (1598), which attacks the "wimpring sonnets" and "puling Elegies" of the love poets, and Marston's *The Scourge of Villainy* (1598).

Perhaps feeling reinforced by the indignation of the satirists, religious verse proliferated at the end of the century. Bedazzled by the great age of the sonnet, the modern reader tends to generalize that the latter decades of the century were a purely secular period for poetry.

Such a view, however, overlooks the staggering amount of religious verse that was being turned out, and it should be remembered by the modern reader that to the reader of the sixteenth century, verse was typified not by a Sidney sonnet, but by a versified psalm. Throughout the century, experiments with Petrarch ebbed and flowed, but the reading public was never without religious writings, including enormous numbers of sermons, devotional manuals, collections of prayers and meditations, verse saints' lives, devotional verse, and, of course, an overflow of rhyming psalters. Versifying the psalter had begun as early as the fourteenth century, but its popularity and practice went unsurpassed in the sixteenth. Although many excellent poets tried their hand at the Psalms, including Wyatt, Spenser, and Sidney, who saw them as legitimate sources of poetry, these versifications were led by the Thomas Sternhold and John Hopkins edition of 1549, and it represents a mediocre collection of verse. Nevertheless, the uncultivated reading public hailed it as an inspired work, and people who refused to read any poetry at all devoured the Sternhold and Hopkins edition. Popular collections among the Elizabethans were William Hunnis's *Seven Sobs of a Sorrowfull Soule for Sinne* (1583) and William Byrd's *Psalmes, Sonnets, and Songs of Sadnes and Pietie* (1588).

By the close of the century, attempts at religious verse by more accomplished poets were surpassing the efforts of hack versifiers. While the satirists were ridiculing the atrophied sonnet sequence on aesthetic grounds, other writers were attacking it on moral grounds, and perceptions of what poetry should be and do were shifting as the sonnet lost its influence. Having put a distance of four years between his *Astrophel and Stella* and the publication of his *Defence of Poesie*, Sidney authoritatively proclaimed in the latter work that poetry should celebrate God and Divine Love. Nashe attacks verse in which "lust is the tractate of so many leaves." Physical love was no longer au courant. In "A Coronet for his Mistress Philosophy," Chapman reflects the new vogue of Neoplatonism by carefully identifying the differences between divine and physical love, also investigated meticulously by Spenser in his Fowre Hymnes (1596). Joshua Sylvester's translations between 1590 and 1605 of the works of the French Huguenot poet Guillaume du Bartas helped to reinforce Protestant piety and further counteracted the Petrarchans. The most saintly poet of the period was Southwell, a Jesuit. In his preface to his Saint Peter's *Complaint, with Other Poems* (1595), Southwell laments that the teachings of Christ

Illustration 2. Edmund Spenser (*Library of Congress*)

go unheeded as poets would rather celebrate the glories of Venus. In Saint Peter's *Complaint*, Peter excoriates himself for his denial of Christ, and the fact that the work is oddly adorned with sensuous conceits is an interesting indication that Petrarchan images managed to survive stubbornly, even in works inimical to their spirit. Finally, in 1599, Davies published *Nosce Teipsum: This Oracle Expounded in Two Elegies*, whose theme was self-knowledge, rather than carnal knowledge of one's mistress, as well as the proper relationship between the soul and the body.

Edmund Spenser

The tug of war between the sonneteers and the religious poets was only one of several noteworthy poetic developments near the close of the century. Edmund Spenser, the most talented poet of the century, contributed to both sides of the battle (the Amoretti and Fowre Hymnes), but his versatility as a poet enabled him to transcend any one category. Spenser's early poetic career is not without its mysteries. No literary historian would have predicted that at a time when a new poetry was being refined by means of the sonnet form, someone would choose to revive the old medieval forms, but that is what

Spenser did. *The Shepheardes Calender* is a throwback to the Mantuan eclogues, at this point almost a century old, and *Colin Clouts Come Home Againe* is reminiscent of Skelton's anticlerical satires. His "Prosopopoia: Or, Mother Hubberd's Tale" is an imitation of a medieval beast fable, and even *The Faerie Queene*, his most famous work, is essentially a compendium of medieval allegory and Italian epic forms derived from Ludovico Ariosto and Torquato Tasso. Furthermore, many of Spenser's works were written in a deliberately archaic style.

Thus a major contribution to Spenser's fame is not the originality of his themes but the range of his metrical and stanzaic experimentations. In a century characterized by poets self-consciously aware of themselves exercising their craft, Spenser was the apotheosis of the poetic craftsman. Though his archaic diction violated the tenets of many critics who believed that the vernacular must grow, Spenser's experiments in versification furthered the cause of making English more vital. Despite its reactionary themes, *The Shepheardes Calender* explodes with experimentation in poetic forms. The "January" eclogue is written in the six-line ballad or "Venus and Adonis" stanza, "February" is written in Anglo-Saxon accentual verse, "March" is written in the romance stanza of Chaucer's "Sir Topaz," "July" is written in a rough, vulgar ballad meter, and "August" is a contrast of undisciplined folk rhythms and elegant sestinas. Though not Spenser's most famous work, *The Shepheardes Calender* is nevertheless a remarkable symbol and culmination of the poetic self-consciousness of the sixteenth century and a fusion of the experiments in poetic versification that had helped to shape English as a suitable vehicle for poetry.

Verse chronicles

As the century was drawing to a close, a popular genre flourishing outside the continuing battle between amatory and religious verse was the verse chronicle history. Of all the genres popular in the sixteenth century, the verse chronicle history is probably the most difficult for the modern reader to appreciate, probably because of its excruciating length; but more than any other genre, it serves as a repository for Elizabethan intellectual, historical, and social thought, especially as it reflects the Elizabethan desire for political order, so amply documented by Tillyard in his Elizabethan World Picture.

The first treatment of English history in poetry was the landmark publication of *A Mirror for Magistrates*

(1555, 1559, 1563). It was a collection of tragedies of famous leaders in the medieval tradition of people brought low by the turning wheel of Fortune and was written in rime royal, the favorite stanzaic vehicle of medieval narrative. The structure of its tragedies was imitated from John Lydgate's *Fall of Princes* (1494), and the constant themes of the tragedies were both the subject's responsibility to his king and the king's responsibility to God; if either the ruler or the subject should fail in his proper allegiance, disorder and tragedy would inevitably ensue. *A Mirror for Magistrates* was extraordinarily popular with a reading public desiring both entertainment and instruction. It went through eight editions in thirty years, with Thomas Sackville's "Induction" being considered at the time the best poem between Chaucer and Spenser.

The major importance of *A Mirror for Magistrates* is the fact that it fulfilled Sidney's mandate in his Defence of Poesie that the poet take over the task of the historian, and *A Mirror for Magistrates* exerted a powerful influence on the late Elizabethan poets. Pride in the royal Tudor lineage led not only the prose chroniclers but also the poets of the Elizabethan period to develop a strong sense of Britain's history. Shakespeare's history plays are widely recognized as reflections of England's growing nationalistic fervor, and because of the magnitude of the plays, it is easy to overlook the contributions of the poets to English history, or, perhaps more accurately, pseudohistory. The troublesome murkiness of Britain's origins were efficiently, if somewhat questionably, cleared up by exhaustive embellishments of the legends of Brut and King Arthur, legends that spurred England on to a sharpened sense of patriotism and nationalism. An obvious example is Spenser's chronicle of early British history at the end of book 2 of The Faerie Queene. In 1586, William Warner published his Albion's England, a long work ambitiously taking as its province all of historical time from Noah's Flood down to the execution of Mary, Queen of Scots.

The following years saw the publication of Daniel's The *First Fowre Bookes of the Civile Warres* (1595, 1599, 1601), whose books represented the apotheosis of all attempts at versified history. Like Shakespeare in his history plays, Daniel focused on a theme common in Elizabethan political theory, the evil that inevitably results from civil and moral disorder—specifically, the overthrow of Richard II. The modern reader has a natural antipathy toward the Elizabethan verse chronicles because of their length and because of the chroniclers' penchant for moral allegorizing, for their tedious accounts of past civil disorder as illustrative of present moral chaos, and for their far-reaching, interweaving parallels among mythological, biblical, and British history (for example, the Titans' defeat of Saturn being contrasted with the victory of Henry V at Agincourt in Heywood's "Troia Britannica," 1609). Nevertheless, these versified histories and their championing of moral order and nationalism constituted much of the most popular poetry of the Elizabethan period, and their impact cannot be overemphasized.

Growth and transition

In retrospect, it is indeed astonishing to consider precisely how much the poetry of the sixteenth century grew after Hawes's allegories first limped onto the scene in 1509. The pressing need for most poets at the beginning of the century was to imitate medieval forms as faithfully as possible. There was no question as to the superiority of the classical authorities, and there was no "English" poetry as such. In 1531, Sir Thomas Elyot mentions Ovid and Martial but not English poets, and, as late as 1553, Wilson was defending the rhetoric of the authorities Cicero and Quintilian. Gradually, however, by struggling with the new language and continuing to experiment with verse forms both new and original, poets were starting to shape a new English poetry and were achieving recognition as craftsmen in their own right. By 1586, Webbe respectfully addressed the preface to his Discourse of English Poetry to "the Noble Poets of England" and made mention of Skelton, Gascoigne, and Googe, finally recognizing Spenser as "the rightest English poet that ever I read." Thus, by the end of the century the question of whether there could be an English poesy had been replaced by the question of what were the limits of the great English poets.

Because of the struggle to shape the new vernacular, the sixteenth century differs from other centuries in that many innovations were coming from the pens of not particularly gifted poets. Thus, working in a period of volatility and flux in the language, such men as Barclay and Skelton could exert an impact on the shaping of the poetry and earn their place in literary history. The first half of the sixteenth century did not witness the formation of new genres. The old reliables, dream-vision allegories, anticlerical satires, pastorals, ballads, versified psalms, and neomedieval tragedies, were the favorite vehicles of most poets. The extraordinary development of this period was the metrical experimentation, which never stopped, no matter how limited the poet. Perhaps

more than any other period, therefore, the first half of the sixteenth century reveals as many noteworthy developments in its bad poets as in its talented ones.

After the publication of *Tottel's Miscellany*, poetry began to settle down somewhat from its pattern of groping experimentation as it gained confidence and stability working with the vernacular. Perhaps the surest indication that poetry had hit its stride in England was the parody of the Petrarchan sonnet. The parody of the first truly great lyric form in England was a significant landmark because only widely popular forms tend to serve as targets for parody. A further indication of the vitality of the poetry was the fact that its poets survived the parody and went on to create new forms. Furthermore, poetic tastes were flexible enough to produce a Spenser who, while forging ahead with prosodic experimentation, looked backward to the archaisms that English poetry had originally used.

As the sixteenth century waned and old genres, such as the sonnet, the pastoral, and the verse chronicle, faded, there were numerous hints of what the poets of the new century would be attempting. In particular, there were several suggestions of the Metaphysicals. The decline in popularity of the Petrarchan sonnet and its subsequent ridicule paved the way for John Donne's satires of the form in many of his secular lyrics. As was seen earlier, Greville's religious themes in his Caelica were a precursor of devotional poetry. The sensuous conceits of Southwell heralded the Baroque extravagances of Richard Crashaw. The pastoral, a favorite Elizabethan genre, was fast fading, as indicated by Ralegh's cynical response to Marlowe's "The Passionate Shepherd to His Love," a plea for living a romantic life in pastoral bliss. In his "Nymph's Reply to the Shepherd," Ralegh makes it clear that such idyllic bliss does not exist. The pastoral was being replaced, however, by a less idealized, more rational mode, the theme of self-contained, rural retirement, as embodied at the close of the century in Sir Edward Dyer's "My Mind to Me a Kingdom Is," a theme that became increasingly popular in the new century. Finally, the proliferation of songs and airs, found in such collections as Nicholas Yonge's *Musica Transalpina* (1588), John Dowland's *The First Book of Songs or Airs* (1597), and Thomas Campion's *A Booke of Ayres* (1601), created a vogue that influenced the lyrics of Ben Jonson and his followers.

The true worth of the poetry of the sixteenth century, however, lies not in the legacies that were inherited from it by the next century but rather in the sheer exuberance for the poetic undertaking that characterized the century from beginning to end. Because of the continuing process of shaping the new vernacular, the tools of the poetic craft are evident in every work, and in no other century did the poets better embody the original etymology of the word "poet," which comes from the Greek word for "maker." To use Webbe's term, they "Englished" the old poetry and proved to be untiring "makers" of a new.

Elizabeth J. Bellamy

For Further Study

Bell, Ilona. *Elizabethan Women and the Poetry of Courtship*. Illustrated ed. New York: Cambridge UP, 1999. Bell argues that women's voices can be heard not only in poems by women writers but also in the implied responses by women to poetry addressed to them. The book bears evidence of extensive research, combined with judicious analysis of the poems mentioned.

Blevins, Jacob. *Catullan Consciousness and the Early Modern Lyric in England: From Wyatt to Donne*. Farnham, Surrey, England: Ashgate, 2004. The purpose of this study is to demonstrate that like Catullus, some English poets departed from convention and used the lyric both to praise and to reject accepted cultural ideals, thus establishing a personal identity. The author is convinced that this process is essential to the creation of good lyric poetry. Bibliography and index.

Braden, Gordon. *Sixteenth-Century Poetry: An Annotated Anthology*. Hoboken, NJ: Wiley-Blackwell, 2005. Selections from a wide range of poets and from the major genres, including both sacred and political poetry. Fully annotated. Contains both a conventional table of contents and an alternate, thematic listing, as well as a chronology, an index of titles and first lines, a bibliography, and a topical index.

Cheney, Patrick, Andrew Hadfield & Garrett A. Sullivan, Jr., eds. *Early Modern English Poetry: A Critical Companion*. New York: Oxford UP, 2006. A collection of twenty-eight essays, three of them dealing with cultural changes and poetic theories, the rest suggesting new approaches to major poems. Contains a list of suggested readings at the end of each chapter and a chronology of Renaissance poetry.

Huntington, John. *Ambition, Rank, and Poetry in 1590's England*. Urbana: U of Illinois P, 2001. Huntington points out evidence of social protest in the works of writers of relatively humble origins, such as George Chapman, Christopher Marlowe, Ben Jonson, Edmund Spenser, Matthew Roydon, and Aemilia Lanyer. Huntington's close readings indicate that there is a need for reinterpretations of the poetry written during the period.

Kinney, Arthur F., ed. *The Cambridge Companion to English Literature, 1500–1600*. New York: Cambridge UP, 2000. Essays about such subjects as Tudor aesthetics, poetry and patronage, lyric forms, romance, the epic, and patriotic works. Bibliographical references and index.

Lewis, C. S. *Poetry and Prose in the Sixteenth Century*. Oxford, England: Clarendon Press, 1990. Originally published as *English Literature in the Sixteenth Century Excluding Drama*, Vol. 3 in *The Oxford History of English Literature* in 1954. A new version of Lewis's controversial work. Bibliography and index.

Mapstone, Sally, ed. *Older Scots Literature*. Edinburgh: John Donald, 2005. The second section of this volume consists of thirteen essays on sixteenth century writers and their works. One of the essays deals with the "female voice" in the poetry of the period, while others discuss ballads, comic verse, and the elegiac tradition. Writers who flourished both in the late sixteenth century and in the early seventeenth century are discussed in the third part of the volume. Bibliographical references and index.

Morotti, Arthur F. *Manuscript, Print, and the English Renaissance Lyric*. Ithaca, NY: Cornell University Press, 1995. The author of this important study examines the tradition of manuscript transmission of poetic works and explains how the change to print publication was effected. He also notes the ways in which the new process altered not only the creative process but also the cultural milieu. Bibliography and index.

Rivers, Isabel. *Classical and Christian Ideas in English Renaissance Poetry: A Student's Guide*. 2d ed. New York: Routledge, 1994. Contains a number of chapters on classical philosophies and Christian doctrines, as well as one chapter on theories of poetry. Lists of authors, an author index, and a bibliographical appendix.

Vickers, Brian, ed. *English Renaissance Literary Criticism*. 1999. Reprint. Oxford, England: Clarendon Press, 2003. This invaluable work presents thirty-six texts, each preceded by a biographical and textual headnote. Annotations with every selection. Includes suggestions for further reading, a glossary, an index of names, and an index of topics.

Whitney, Isabelle, Mary Sidney, & Amelia Lanyer. *Renaissance Women Poets*. New York: Viking, 2001. Considers the lives and works of three English women poets who wrote during the Renaissance. Though their social and cultural backgrounds were very different, all of them used their poetry to voice their convictions and to establish their identities as women and as talented, intelligent human beings.

Does Shakespeare's Life Matter?

Did people who lived a long time ago live different lives to the ones we live now? How much importance does historical context play when we are attempting to read a life? Do we think people are different just because the fragments of their lives survive in unfamiliar forms? Do we think they are different because the evidence of their lives is often fragmentary? These might seem very basic and banal questions, but they are fundamental ones that have to be asked by anyone who wants to think about what having a life means.

The questions are especially pressing if we consider the early modern period, c.1500–c.1700. There would appear to be a fundamental and unbridgeable divide between those who write biographies of early modern figures, and many who have been influenced by the impact of literary theories of various forms since the 1980s. While the former group write as if lives can be read transhistorically, and that humans are fundamentally the same once a degree of historical context has been considered, the latter argue that the early modern period witnessed the birth of the subject, a self-sufficient individual who has come to define modernity as we understand it. For the former group change is incidental and accidental in nature; for the latter it is a fundamental issue that defines the nature of human existence. A number of divisions exist, not simply between scholars who have their own disagreements about the significance and content of lives, or about the impact of specific historical changes, suggesting that there is a fundamental gulf between biographers and historicists.

Life and art

The relationship between life and letters is intensely problematic. Works should, of course, stand alone from the author behind the text. But how then do we deal with writing that is conspicuously autobiographical, or, more complex still, writing that we may not even realize is autobiographical, yet which draws on the author's experiences in ways that may or may not be apparent to certain groups of readers? What if certain readers were/are aware of the relationship between life and art? Does that make them better or more complete readers than those who are unable to understand such references and nuances? And, most difficult of all, perhaps, what if the author makes extensive use of his or her life in the text,

challenging the reader to make connections between the two that may or may not be there? My contention is that if we explore these issues in the early modern period, the literature of that era starts to seem more like modern literature than is generally assumed. Forms and styles may differ, but the substance starts to look the same.

Consider two relatively recent examples. In Martin Amis's memoir, *Experience* (2000), the author describes the horror he experiences when it dawns on him that his father's novel, *Jake's Thing* (1978), is far more autobiographical than he had ever realised, and represents his father's divorce from his step-mother, Elizabeth Jane Howard, in embarrassingly graphic detail. Martin asks Kingsley if he really went to all the sexual therapy sessions that Jake has to attend in the novel before his wife finally leaves him for a nicer, kinder man and finds that everything is based on fact. It is little surprise that Martin then informs us that, after this humiliation, Kingsley reined in his libido, abandoning women forever in favor of television and huge bags of boiled sweets.[1] Here, art is more truthful to life than had been realized.[2] Literary works sometimes represent the lives of their authors as they thought they lived them.

There are, of course, very different examples, a case in point being that of another conspicuously self-referential writer, Malcolm Lowry (1909–57). Lowry was a consummate and polished liar, often believing his own myth-making, especially when in his cups. Perhaps his most absurd boast was that he had been a junior national golf champion in his youth, a story believed by most of his friends, and repeated in the first full biography by Douglas Day. It was only when Gordon Bowker tracked down Lowry's brother, Russell, soon before he died that the truth emerged.[3] Lowry had, in fact, been entered for the competition but had rather overdone it the night before and missed the tournament, a fact that he did not allow to get in the way of a good story. Lowry's storytelling ability was easily transferred to his fiction. His first novel, *Ultramarine* (1933), narrates the coming of age of a young man, Dana Hilliot, on his first voyage at sea based on Lowry's own experience of sailing to the Far East as a deck hand between school and university. Hilliot is despised by his fellow sailors, whose good opinion he craves. He dreams of rehabilitating himself, at one point seeing a chance if he rescues the galley boy's carrier pigeon, which has fallen into shark infested waters, but fails to do so, an episode based on an incident in Lowry's life.[4] Despite such verisimilitude, Lowry has Hilliot eventually accepted by his fellow mariners at the end of the voyage, which was not how the voyage really ended.[5] Hence, sometimes literature is designed as a fantasy, making use of the material from a life only to distort or falsify that life.

That authors might use their lives in diametrically opposed ways is an obvious enough point, and many other examples from modern literary texts can easily be found, suggesting that authors play with the material of their lives, molding it into a variety of forms. In fact, one influential way of reading a great deal of modern writing is to point out how much more autobiographical many works are than even those who assume that authors obsessively use their own lives realize: think of T.S. Eliot, Virginia Woolf, Henry James, James Joyce, Marcel Proust. Equally significantly, it is notable how inconsistently such a notion is applied the further back one travels in literary historical time. Either works are assumed to reflect the life unproblematically, as in the vast array of biographies of Shakespeare of varying degrees of sophistication; or, the life and the work are prized apart, often because it is hard to write about the life when no records of it remain. But, just because no life remains does not mean that the work does not refer to it. As much research has demonstrated, in the days before the widespread use of the printing press, literature was often written for a small group who could decode its meaning which might remain opaque to other readers.[6] The stubborn refusal of the life to remain behind—after all, we know far more about the lives of politicians and the aristocracy than we do most writers who were not always from such exalted social ranks—may have further distorted our interpretations of literary works.

Public lives/private lives

When records of the life do survive, as is more often the case with aristocratic writers, especially if they were public figures, we can often see how closely related the life and the work are. The evidence suggests that, as now, writers took certain liberties, and did not always use experience in a straightforward manner, but played with an audience's expectations of who they were, what they had done and what they thought. The most obvious, well-recorded and analyzed example is Sir Philip Sidney (1554–86), whose life was recorded extensively in contemporary documents, and was also the subject

of a biography by his friend, Sir Fulke Greville (1554–1628).[7] Sidney based his sonnet sequence, *Astrophil and Stella* (c.1582), a work which had an enormous influence on subsequent poetry, on his failed courtship with Penelope Devereux, daughter of Walter Devereux, the first earl of Essex (1539–76).[8] The sequence clearly challenges the reader of the manuscript, who may well have been a friend or acquaintance of the author, to read the poems in terms of the author's life. Furthermore, there is a studied ambiguity as to whether the life in question is a publicly constructed one, or whether the poetry is providing privileged inside information. The reader has to play a cat and mouse game with the author, the game being to guess what the author actually intends. Astrophil is cast as an alter ego of Sidney himself, although he is often made to look ridiculous. Two sonnets, numbers 24 and 37, make a series of outrageous puns on the word 'Rich,' transparent satires of the wealthy man, Lord Robert Rich, who became Penelope's husband when the negotiations with the Sidney family broke down:

> Rich fooles there be, whose base and filthy hart
> Lies hatching still the goods wherein they flow;
> And damning their owne selves to Tantal's smart,
> Wealth breeding want, more blist, more wretched grow...
> that rich foole, who by blind Fortune's lot
> The richest gemme of Love and life enjoyes,
> And can with foule abuse such beauties blot;
> Let him, deprived of sweet but unfelt joyes,
> (Exil'd for ay from those high treasures, which
> He knowes not) grow in only follie rich.[9]
>
> (Sonnet 24)

Sidney does not make himself sound like a gracious loser in the game of love. No reader could possibly doubt that the text refers to the author's own life, but what does it actually tell us? Is Sidney describing his own feelings in verse, or playing on what people thought they knew about him? Can we believe what Astrophil says? If we compare Sonnet 24 to Sonnet 30, a rather different picture emerges. Six sonnets later Astrophil claims that he has no real interest in political events because he is so obsessed with Stella:

> Whether the Turkish new-moone minded be
> To fill his hornes this yeare on Christian coast;
> How Poles' right king meanes, without leave of hoast,
> To warme with ill-made fire cold Muscovy:
> If French can yet three parts in one agree;

What now the Dutch in their full diets boast;
How Holland hearts, now so good townes be lost,
Trust in the shade of pleasing Orange tree;
How Ulster likes of that same golden bit,
Wherewith my father once mad it halfe tame;
These questions busie wits to me do frame;
I, cumbred with good maners, answer do,
But know not how, for still I thinke of you.

For someone who is not interested in politics Astrophil clearly knows a great deal about contemporary developments. Moreover, the sonnet is a lengthy example of the rhetorical trope, paralipsis or occultatio, 'when one pretends to pass over a matter and so draws attention to it,' in itself, a means of warning the reader that this is a carefully crafted work and may not be quite what it seems.[10] As anyone who knew him would have realised, Sidney, even more than most courtiers, was closely interested in contemporary political events. Sonnet 30 pulls the reader in the opposite direction to 24, suggesting that Astrophil is not Sidney: rather, casting him as either the polar opposite of the author, or his ironic wraith. Readers are unsettled because the sequence makes use of Sidney's life in deliberately opposing ways, asking us to identify protagonist and author at one point and then denying that equation at another. Sidney's writings, which were instrumental in establishing the direction of English literary history for more than a generation, encourage authors to play games with their private and public selves, making the matter of their life, whether real or fictional, part of the literary experience.[11]

Erotic life

John Donne (c.1572–1631) is an equally complicated case, whose work draws on his life in diverse ways. His poetry, like Sidney's, also circulated in manuscript and hardly any was published in his lifetime. Donne's work appears to have been intended for private circulation among a small group of friends and he was reluctant to publish it.[12] In the absence of external evidence it is therefore hard to establish when most poems were written. Nevertheless, a number of assumptions are made about Donne's own life based on his work, partly confirmed by Izaac Walton's *Life of Dr. John Donne* (1675), partly by comments such as that of his contemporary, Richard Baker, that in his youth Donne was a 'great visiter of ladies.'[13] Not surprisingly perhaps, readers often make assumptions about Donne, based on the strong, masculine and overtly sexual style of his erotic poetry,

collected in *Songs and Sonnets* (1633). Donne's love poetry used to be admired, especially when Donne was rediscovered as a major poet early in the last century. However, Donne is again falling out of favour because he is now often perceived to have been a lecherous and misogynist young writer.[14]

But how much do these judgments depend on our using what we think we know about his life to read his poetry and what we think we then know about his poetry to read his life, as well as also making problematic assumptions about the readership in order to read the work? Donne wrote the overtly misogynist poem, 'Twickenham Garden' at some point after 1607 when his patron, Lucy, Countess of Bedford, acquired the grounds.[15] The poem's speaker is an embittered lover who fulminates against his fickle mistress and women in general. He contrasts his own miserable state to that of the burgeoning springtime and concludes in the final stanza that his mistress is paradoxically true to the nature of women because she is false to him:

Hither with crystal vials, lover come,
And take my tears, which are love's wine,
And try your mistress' tears at home,
For all are false, that taste not just like mine;
Alas, hearts do not in eyes shine,
Nor can you more judge woman's thoughts by tears,
Than by her shadow, what she wears.
O perverse sex, where none is true but she,
Who's therefore true, because her truth kills me.[16]

Read straightforwardly, this is a standard piece of anti-feminist rhetoric. John Carey, contrasting this poem with the obsequious verse letters that Donne wrote for his patron, comments that 'Donne's ego has taken over. He has become the centre of his own poem, and dropped his subservient role . . . Through its fiction, Donne regains his manhood.'[17] Carey reads 'Twickenham Garden' 'straight'—although he acknowledges its fictional nature—casting it as a male poem breaking free of women's influence. The unspoken assumption is that Donne writes best when he is most 'masculine', writing as a seducer or as a misogynist for other men. Carey employs a familiar version of Donne's life, his modes of address in his poetry and his readership to interpret the poem, even though none of these issues are explicitly stated. The logic is circular: the life explains the art and the art explains the life.

However, 'Twickenham Garden' reads very

differently if we assume that it was written for female as well as male readers, which, after all, the setting suggests. What if Lucy, Countess of Bedford had a robust sense of humor and could join in the joke of the lover scorning all women, making Donne's voice a way of exposing male attitudes rather than celebrating them? This would make 'Twickenham Garden' into quite a different sort of work, one that is ironic and aware of the ways in which women have been represented in literature and life. It also makes Donne another sort of writer and person, more like Sir Philip Sidney, who has long been cast as a man happy in the company of women.[18] The fact that 'Twickenham Garden' was written after 1607, when the Countess acquired Twickenham Garden, should also alert us to the problem of assuming that Donne wrote all his erotic poetry as a youth and then became more sober in middle age.

An even more striking case of the life and the work being inextricably entwined occurs in the much-anthologized 'The Flea,' which is often taken to be Donne's most characteristic poem, an example of the lecherous and witty young Jack Donne at his most knowingly suggestive.[19] But the voice in the poem is perhaps more subtle, witty, and personal than has often been realized. The poem begins dramatically *in media res*, forcing the reader to reconstruct the encounter between the speaker and his lady: 'Mark but this flea, and mark in this, / How little that which thou deny'st me is.' These opening lines make the situation clear enough. The speaker is a man who wishes to persuade a reluctant woman to go to bed with him. He uses the example of the flea to show her that surrendering her honor to him is not of great consequence so she might as well submit and enjoy the experience. The three stanzas reveal the speaker using a variety of strategies in response to dramatic developments in the situation. In the first stanza he claims that the insect has sucked the blood of both of them, so he argues that mingling their bodily fluids through sexual intercourse is of no greater consequence. In the second she has obviously threatened to kill the flea, so he argues that the flea represents their marriage. Therefore, killing it would be a sacrilege. In the final stanza she has killed the flea, so he argues that as the death of the flea has caused no serious consequences, neither will their making love.

Not only were such seduction poems so common that they formed a recognizable type of literature, but the 'flea' poem formed a distinct subgenre within this larger group.[20] Donne's poem is hardly a scandalous departure

from the norms and traditions of classical erotic poetry and its later European forms. It is the second stanza that makes the lyric both interesting and particularly distinctive:

> Oh stay, three lives in one flea spare,
> Where we almost, nay more than married are.
> This flea is you and I, and this
> Our marriage bed, and marriage temple is;
> Though parents grudge, and you, we 'are met,
> And cloistered in these living walls of jet.
> Though use make you apt to kill me,
> Let not to this, self murder added be,
> And sacrilege, three sins in killing three.

The second line has invariably been taken as a metaphor, with the poet addressing an un-named lady—real or fictional—as though she were his wife, simply as a means of gratifying his appetites. But it is surely more plausible to read this lyric as a witty marriage poem, one addressed by a fictionalized Donne to his wife, Ann. The Donnes, as is well known, were ruined by their secret marriage in December 1601. John had worked for Sir Thomas Egerton, the Lord Keeper of England, the brother of Ann's father, Sir George More, who was busy negotiating his wife's marriage at the time of her clandestine union. When he learned of the marriage, More had Donne dismissed from his brother's service and undoubtedly helped to close off other routes to preferment before Donne entered the ministry in 1615.[21] The circumstances of Donne's marriage may well explain the nature of many of his poems (which is not to seek to reduce his poetry to biography). The wit of the first four lines works best if we imagine that the speaker is addressing someone to whom he is not just pretending to be married. What seems like a hypothesis is actual fact. It is a device Donne employs when his speaker addresses God in 'Divine Meditation' seven, 'At the round earth's imagined corners,' a sonnet that, as the first line indicates, depends on the interplay between the fictional and the real. The last lines rely on the shock of the real: 'Teach me how to repent; for that's as good/As if thou hadst sealed my pardon, with thy blood'. The conditional 'if' is counter-factual because every reader would have known that God had died for man's sins, so making it possible for repentance to save the individual's soul.

The same may well be true of the lines 'This flea is you and I, and this/Our marriage bed, and marriage temple is,' referring to the poverty that the Donnes had to endure together. If so, then Donne has adapted a prominent form of seduction poem as a humorous and witty comment on his own fate—as well as that of his wife. The reason why the lady will not be shamed by surrendering to him is because there is nothing wrong with a husband and wife making love. Even more to the point perhaps, their marriage has already brought them a great deal of poverty and shame so advertising their love life will not make a lot of difference. It is significant that Donne refers to the 'parents' grudge' when it was Ann's father who objected most to the marriage, having the bridegroom dismissed from his job as sword bearer to his son, and having Donne imprisoned. The description of the lovers 'cloistered in these living walls of jet' is one of many images in Donne's poems of small rooms as an escape from a hostile world: again, the reader might infer that this applies to Donne's own life. The last line of the stanza, suggesting that the lady will commit 'three sins in killing three' could be taken to refer to her pregnancy, and the need for the couple to make the best of their circumstances.

It is, of course, possible that these references are less secure than such speculations suggest, just as 'Twickenham Garden' may well be a straightforwardly misogynistic poem. But it is hard to imagine that early readers did not make connections between the works and the life of the poet, considering the encouragement given in the text. Izaac Walton, whose *Life* was so important in establishing the critical reputation of Donne and the relationship of the verse to the life, makes little reference to the erotic poetry, encouraging the reader to think instead in terms of Donne's piety and religious sensibility, and his relationship with his wife. The only non-devotional verse that Walton mentions is 'A Valediction forbidding mourning,' which is cited to show the strength of Donne's devotion to his wife. Walton assumes that the poem was 'given by Mr. *Donne* to his wife at the time that he parted from her,' and commends its quality to the reader: 'I beg leave to tell, that I have heard some Criticks, learned, both in Languages and Poetry, say, that none of the Greek or Latine Poets did ever equal them.'[22] Walton reads the verse in terms of the life, valuing the poetry written to Ann above that written to other women, a verdict that has influenced Donne's critical and personal reputation ever since.[23] Walton's judgment may need qualification but he was reading the work in ways established within the texts, which, as in Sidney's poetry, encourage the reader to relate the work to the life.

Political life

Edmund Spenser (1552–99) is another Elizabethan poet who appears regularly in his own works and who invariably tells the reader when he does. In his early days, Spenser appears as a cheeky and cocksure young man, delighted to inform everyone that he is the future of English poetry. In his later years, he is a forlorn and embittered figure, invariably telling readers that he should have been the future of English poetry. Spenser generally casts himself as the plain spoken man of the people, Colin Clout, making use of the well-known satirical mask adopted by John Skelton, one of the few English poets taken seriously by English writers in Elizabeth's reign.[24] Towards the end of the final book of the published *Faerie Queene* Spenser poses the rhetorical question, 'Who knows not *Colin Clout*?'[25] The obvious answer he is expecting the reader to produce is 'Colin Who?'[26] This is a long way from the bravura performance in the letters and the *Calender*. The audience of these works is expected to expand, readers to take notice and help establish Spenser as the major figure in the English literary world. The audience of the later work is imagined as contracting, Colin Clout having become an obscure and isolated figure to whom no one listens.

Spenser reminds us frequently enough that he has been scandalously treated by those who rule in England.[27] *The Faerie Queene* ends with a lament for past misreadings and a plea for a sympathetic audience so that the author's verse will not become the target of the venomous Blatant Beast who misreads and slanders everything that comes his way:

Ne may this homely verse, of many meanest,
Hope to escape his venomous despite,
More then my former writs, all were they clearest
From blamefull blot, and free from all that wite,
With which some wicked tongues did it backbite,
And bring into a mighty Peres displeasure,
That neuer so deserued to endite.

Spenser is probably referring to the fact that his satire of William Cecil, Lord Burghley in *Mother Hubberds Tale* (1590), in which he represented the queen's first minister as a crafty and self-seeking fox, came to the attention of the peer in question, who was not amused.[28] Spenser had ample reason to be paranoid. The second edition of *The Faerie Queene* was read by James VI of Scotland who took particular exception to Spenser's representation of the execution of his mother, Mary

Queen of Scots. James wrote a series of furious letters to Elizabeth demanding that she punish the poet. Given that Spenser had portrayed Mary as Duessa, who elsewhere in the poem appears as the Whore of Babylon, James clearly had reason to be angry.[29]

Given this history, and the relationship between the personal and the political in Spenser's poetry, we should be wary of *not* reading Spenser's poetry in terms of his life and opinions, a reversal of the ways in which critics generally approach the relationship between life and art. The verse cited above establishes a complicated and tense relationship between author, intention, reader, and interpretation, teasing the reader to read the verse rightly or wrongly. The idea that *Mother Hubberds Tale* —assuming this is the work to which the lines refer—was 'clearest/From blamefull blot' is absurd, as it was clearly designed to wound its target, making the author's profession of innocence disingenuous. If so, this would suggest that Spenser wants his reader to be aware of who is writing, alerting us to the fact that he is likely to appear in the text himself at any given moment. The works contain, as might be expected, a number of key moments when either the author in persona appears within the text, or the passage in question adopts a register of truthful sincerity at odds with the fictional nature of the poem.

Spenser habitually relates the metaphysical nature of the universe, and the geopolitical situation of England, Britain and Ireland to his own life, establishing his authority as a poet to pass judgment on the world. Perhaps the most spectacular example of this occurs in the 'Two Cantos of Mutabilitie,' apparently a fragment of *The Faerie Queene*, Book VII, which the poet did not publish in his lifetime. The cantos describe the challenge that the Titaness Mutabilitie makes to Jove, who is the current ruler of the universe. Mutabilitie argues that the world is really chaotic and constantly changing so that she should be its rightful sovereign. Jove, who stands for the stability brought about by the right of conquest, resists her claims and the two agree to be judged by Nature on Arlo Hill, just by Spenser's house, in front of the assembled gods.[30] The personal does indeed meet the political.

Nature awards victory to Jove. However, his triumph is undercut in a number of ways. His representative on earth is the goddess, Cynthia, and we are given a graphic picture of the changes that she is undergoing. As Mutabilitie points out, rather cruelly:

Then is she mortall borne, how-so ye crake;
Besides, her face and countenance euery day
We changed see, and sundry forms partake,
Now hornd, now round, now bright, now brown & gray:
So that as changefull as the Moone men vse to say.

Cynthia, as Spenser makes clear elsewhere in the poem, is a representation of Elizabeth, the virgin queen, now coming to the end of her life and reign.[31] The lines point out that not merely was Elizabeth thought to be capricious and inconsistent, but that she was dying. In 1598, when these lines were probably written, Elizabeth was 65, which made her the oldest reigning English monarch for over four-hundred years, since Henry II, who died in 1189 (aged fifty-six). Her subjects were unsure who would replace her as the succession had not been sorted out and it was an offence to discuss it.[32] The most likely candidate was actually James VI of Scotland, the son of Mary Stuart, Mary Queen of Scots, who was executed while in exile in England in 1587.[33] Mary had been executed because of her apparent complicity in plots against Elizabeth that would place her on the throne, but now she would be triumphing posthumously as she had produced an heir whereas Elizabeth had not, which was indeed a change. Spenser had justified the execution in trenchant terms in *The Faerie Queene*, much to the chagrin of James. Now it looked as if Elizabeth had undone all the good work of the Protestants and allowed the son of an evil Catholic to rule England, her changeable nature proving Mutabilitie's point, and demonstrating that Cynthia/Elizabeth was no longer really fit to rule. Mutabilitie's challenge to Cynthia, makes her sound rather like Mary, given that she is a queen challenging another queen's right to rule, so Spenser's poem represents the battle between the two queens living in the British Isles.[34]

How does this poetry relate to Spenser's life? What part does Spenser himself play in these events? The 'Two Cantos' contain an allegory of Ireland, the setting for the debate over the fate of the universe, which in itself shows how important Spenser thought his adopted homeland was and that its vulnerability to a Catholic revolt against English rule was likely to spell the end of English Protestantism. Ireland was once the fairest of the British Isles where the goddess Diana—another name for Cynthia—would visit for her private pleasure. The cheeky god, Faunus, has an overwhelming desire to see her naked. He persuades one of her nymphs, Molanna, to lead him to her favourite bathing spot, hides in the bushes and is able to possess his heart's desire:

There Faunus *saw that pleased much his eye,*
And made his hart to tickle in his brest,
That for great ioy of some-what he did spy,
He could him not containe in silent rest;
But breaking forth in laughter, loud profest
His foolish thought. A foolish Faune *indeed,*
That couldst not hold thy selfe so hidden blest,
But wouldest needs thine owne conceit areed.
Babblers vnworthy been of so diuine a meed.

Who is Faunus? Faunus is another name for the god Pan, the god of flocks and shepherds who was always represented with his pipe.[35] Given Spenser's representation of himself as Colin Clout—always with his pipe—it is hard not to think that Faunus is a version of the poet himself. Like Spenser he is loquacious and in trouble with the authorities. Spenser would appear to be saying that he is the one who has seen the queen naked, exposed her for the fool that she really is, unable and unwilling to protect her true subjects from the ravages of time and mutability, a problem exposed most cruelly and dangerously in Ireland. But perhaps he is the real fool, for when exposed she flees and leaves the land to its unhappy fate. This may, of course, be a problematic reading of the passage, but the crucial point is that the reader is asked to make the connection between the poet's life and the serious issues represented in the works.

In case this seems too speculative, another example should make the possibility that Spenser might be Faunus more plausible. In an extraordinary moment Spenser merges the personal and the political as his marriage is consummated in the *Epithalamion*, the marriage hymn he wrote as the culmination of his courtship of Elizabeth Boyle, represented in the sonnet sequence, the *Amoretti* (both published in one volume in 1595). Spenser, in a pointed, discordant moment, imagines the queen peering through the windows in envy as she perceives the joy of the lovers:

Who is the same, which at my window peepes?
Or whose is that faire face, that shines so bright,
Is it not Cinthia, she that never sleepes,
But walkes about high heaven al the night?
O fayreset goddesse, do thou not envy
My love with me to spy:
For thou likewise didst love, though now unthought,
And for a fleece of woll, which privily,
The Latmian shephard once unto thee brought,
His pleasures with thee wrought.

Therefore to us be favourable now;
And sith of wemens labours thou hast charge,
And generation goodly dost enlarge,
Encline thy will t'effect our wishfull vow.
And the chast wombe informe with timely seed,
That may our comfort breed:
Till which we cease our hopefull hap to sing,
Ne let the woods us answere, nor our Eccho ring.

This can be read as an extraordinarily offensive stanza, especially given Spenser's track record, designed to provoke the queen—should she read it—and out of place in a marriage hymn.[36] The key word is 'envy,' given Elizabeth's virginity, and the reminder that she once loved (*The Shepheardes Calender* [1579] makes a number of references to the projected match with Francois, duke of Alenc,on, Elizabeth's last chance of marriage, which eventually led nowhere).[37] The queen is cast as a voyeur, peeping through the curtains, jealous of the joy of the lovers, an image that repeats the closing lines of the first edition of *The Faerie Queene* with Britomart gazing enviously at the joy of the hermaphrodite created by the lovers Amoret and Scudamore.[38] The narrative had already made it clear that Britomort would have her time when she married Artegall. Here we are told that Cynthia/Elizabeth has had hers, and needs to bless the lovers and stop her envy. Spenser would—again—appear to be commenting on her inability to govern Ireland, and her failure as a ruler of men and women who have sexual desires (Elizabeth was a notoriously jealous queen who could not bear her courtiers getting married, as Sir Walter Raleigh discovered to his cost when he secretly married Elizabeth Throckmorton, Elizabeth's maid-of-honor, in 1592, as *The Faerie Queene*, Book 4, canto 7, narrates in considerable detail).[39] The stanza is yet another *memento mori*, an attack on Elizabeth for failing to marry and produce an heir. Spenser has linked his own life and situation with that of the monarch, skillfully drawing together his main concerns. His personal life is seen at odds with, and more ordered than, the larger political state of affairs.

Shakespeare's life

We cannot always know the lives of the poets and, even if we do, reading literary works in terms of what we know is problematic and fraught with difficulties. Nevertheless, it may be a hermeneutic challenge that we have to face. Early modern writers, whether their work appeared in manuscript or print, deliberately played games with the ways in which their texts related to public and private lives, exactly like more recent writers. William Shakespeare is yet another case in point, his most ostensibly autobiographical work, the *Sonnets* (published 1609) teasing the reader into making ever more elusive identifications between the work and the life. Shakespeare does leave his signature in the *Sonnets*, through the extensive wordplay on his Christian name in sonnets, 134-6, a mini-sequence that concludes 'Make but my name thy love, and love that still, /And then thou lov'st me for my name is Will.'[40] The reader is directly confronted by the author who leaves his name in his text, precisely the sort of game that Sidney played in *Astrophil and Stella* with the puns on 'Rich,' an example Shakespeare may have copied. Shakespeare seems to have written his *Sonnets* within a recognizable tradition, giving us glimpses of his life, and daring us to read them as the truth.

If we read Shakespeare's sonnets as biography then we read the story of a man who has an intense relationship with a beautiful young man, then an overtly sexual relationship with a woman who both fails and refuses to conform to accepted standards of beauty.[41] In what may be the most scandalous poem in the collection, the poet reveals that he fears that the young man and the young woman have, in fact, also encountered each other:

> *Two loves I have, of comfort and despair,*
> *Which like two spirits do suggest me still.*
> *The better angel is a man right fair;*
> *The worser spirit a woman coloured ill.*
> *To win me soon to hell my female evil*
> *Tempteth my better angel from my side,*
> *And would corrupt my saint to be a devil,*
> *Wooing his purity with her foul pride.*
> *And whether that my angel be turned fiend*
> *Suspect I may, yet not directly tell,*
> *But being both from me, both to each friend,*
> *I guess one angel in another's hell.*
> * Yet this shall I ne'er know, but live in doubt,*
> *Till my bad angel fire my good one out.*[42]

(Sonnet 144)

This must surely be too bad—or too good—to be true. The sonnet declares that he will only know if his suspicions of his two lovers having sex are right if the young man catches venereal disease from the dark lady. In doing so, this may be telling a lie that is like the truth, because the concomitant position is that if the young man remains disease free then he is not having an affair with the lady. And, as everyone knows, the sonnets tease us with issues of truth and falsehood, notably in Sonnet 138, which opens, 'When my love swears that she is made of truth, /I do believe her though I know she lies, /That she might think me some untutored youth, / Unlearned in the world's false subtleties'. These lines contain a number of tantalizing phrases, starting with the lady 'made of truth'. Of course, we know that she only exists in the poem and may, or may not be, 'made of truth' in a different sense from the ostensible, literal meaning (exactly the sort of wordplay that the *Sonnets* rely on). The lady might think Shakespeare an 'untutored youth, /Unlearned in the world's false subtleties' because she thinks that he cannot detect her lies. But then again it may be that the reader is the naive one, believing the lady to exist in the first place—if she does not exist then she cannot be 'made of truth', and the poet knows that 'she lies'. Shakespeare is clearly not an 'untutored youth' to play such naughty games with his poor reader—the very fact that he says this again suggests that he is lying—or, at least, being economical with the truth.

As has often been noted, actors had a very bad reputation in the first few decades after the establishment of the commercial theatre in London. They were considered immoral and dangerous, especially difficult to place within the social order or to fix in one place or station in life. They were reputed to encourage debauched behavior, partly because playhouses existed outside the city walls in the midst of brothels (a connection that *Measure for Measure* exploits).[43] Shakespeare's *Sonnets* are especially scandalous, even more so if we remember that Shakespeare had already written one of the most popular erotic/pornographic poems of the age, *Venus and Adonis* (published 1593).[44] The *Sonnets* represent the author as bisexual, involved in a problematic love triangle. It is possible that they would have shocked readers because of their representation of homosexuality; it is equally possible that the representation of a lady whose breath reeked and was obviously a sexually voracious good-time girl in Sonnet 130, would have been more shocking still, given how women were usually represented in love poetry.[45] But the fact that they got it on together probably took this to another dimension still.

Perhaps Shakespeare was giving his readers a version of what they thought actors actually got up to. There is a famous anecdote in John Manningham's diary that Shakespeare managed to supplant his fellow thespian, Richard Burbage in the affections of a keen theatre fan when he overheard his rival being told 'to come that night unto her by the name of Richard the Third.' Shakespeare made sure he got there first so that when Burbage approached the lady's door he was told that 'William the Conqueror was before Richard the Third.' The truth of the anecdote would appear to matter less than its significance as an indication of the reputation of actors.[46] And, if this was your cultural reference point then the Sonnets will clearly not disappoint you. Authors controlled and manipulated the ways in which they were read, much like contemporary writers. Shakespeare's life matters, but it may not mean quite what you think.

Andrew Hadfield

Notes

1. Martin Amis, *Experience: A Memoir* (New York: Vintage, 2000), 229-30.
2. For further discussion, see Richard Bradford, *Kingsley Amis* (London: Arnold, 1989); id. Richard Bradford, *Lucky Him: The Biography of Kingsley Amis* (London: Peter Owen, 2001).
3. Gordon Bowker, *Malcolm Lowry Remembered* (London: BBC, 1987), 20.
4. Gordon Bowker, *Pursued by Furies: A Life of Malcolm Lowry* (London: Heinemann, 1994), 70-1.
5. Bowker, *Pursued by Furies*, 66-73.
6. See, for example, Harold Love, *Scribal Publication in Seventeenth-Century England* (Oxford: Clarendon Press, 1993); H. R. Woudhuysen, *Sir Philip Sidney and the Circulation of Manuscripts, 1558–1640* (Oxford: Oxford UP, 1996); Greg Walker, *Writing Under Tyranny: English Literature and the Henrician Reformation* (Oxford: Oxford UP, 2005).
7. Sir Fulke Greville's *Life of Sir Philip Sidney Etc., First Published 1652,* ed. Nowell Smith (Montana: Kessinger, 2007). There are numerous lives of Sidney, including Katherine Duncan-Jones, *Sir Philip Sidney: Courtier Poet* (London: Hamish Hamilton, 1991); Michael Brennan, *The Sidneys of Penshurst and the Monarchy, 1500–1700* (Aldershot: Ashgate, 2006); Roger Howell, *Sir Philip Sidney: The Shepherd Knight* (London: Hutchinson, 1968); Alan Stewart, *Philip Sidney: A Double Life* (London: Chatto, 2000); Malcolm M. Wallace, *The Life of Sir Philip Sidney* (New York, Octagon, 1967, rpt. of 1915).
8. For discussion see, for example, J. G. Nichols, *The Poetry of Sir Philip Sidney: An Interpretation in the Context of his Life and Times* (Liverpool: Liverpool UP, 1974); Duncan-Jones, Sidney, Ch. 9; Arthur F. Marotti, '"Love is not Love": Elizabethan Sonnet Sequences and the Social Order', *ELH* 49 (1982), 396-428; Ann Rosalind Jones and Peter Stallybrass, 'The Politics of Astrophil and Stella', *Studies in English Literature, 1500–1900*, 24 (1984), 53-68.
9. Maurice Evans, ed., *Elizabethan Sonnets* (London: Dent, 1977). All subsequent references to this edition. On Lord Rich, see Duncan-Jones, Sidney, 198-200.
10. Brian Vickers, *In Defence of Rhetoric* (Oxford: Clarendon Press, 1988), 496.
11. On Sidney's influence and afterlife, see Gavin Alexander, *Writing After Sidney: The Literary Response to Sir Philip Sidney, 1586–1640* (Oxford: Oxford UP, 2006).
12. For a recent discussion, see Benjamin Saunders, 'Circumcising Donne: The 1633 Poems and Readerly Desire,' *Journal of Medieval and Modern Studies 30* (2000), 375–99. See also J. W. Saunders, 'The Stigma of Print: A Note on the Social Bases of Tudor Poetry,' *Essays in Criticism 1* (1951), 139-64.
13. Cited in R. C. Bald, *John Donne: A Life* (Oxford: Clarendon Press, 1970), 72.
14. For discussion, see John Carey, *John Donne: Life, Mind and Art* (London: Faber, rev. ed., 1990), introduction; Andrew Mousley, ed., *John Donne: Contemporary Critical Essays* (Basingstoke: Macmillan, 1999); Rebecca Ann Bach, '(Re)placing John Donne in the History of Sexuality,' *ELH* 72 (2005), 259-89.
15. Bald, Donne, 172-5.
16. 'John Donne, 'Twickenham Garden,' lines 19-27. All references to John Donne, *The Complete English Poems* (Harmondsworth: Penguin, 1971).
17. Carey, Donne, 65-6.
18. Duncan-Jones, Sidney, 1-3, 182-6, passim; *The Collected Works of Mary Sidney Herbert, Countess of Pembroke*, ed. Margaret P. Hannay, Noel J. Kinnamon and Michael G. Brennan, 2 vols. (Oxford: Clarendon Press, 1998), introduction.
19. Thomas Docherty, John Donne, Undone (London: Methuen, 1986), 53-9; Carey, Donne, 32-3; James Winny, *A Preface to Donne* (London: Longman, 1970),126-8.
20. Donne, *Poems*, 376.
21. Bald, Donne, Ch. 7.
22. Izaak Walton, *Life of Dr. John Donne in The Lives of John Donne*, Sir Henry Wotton, Richard Hooker, George Herbert, Robert Sanderson (London: Oxford UP, 1927), 42.
23. For comment, see Saunders, 'Circumcising Donne,' 394,

footnote 9.

24. Anthony S. G. Edwards, *Skelton: The Critical Heritage* (London: Routledge, 1981), 56-66.

25. Edmund Spenser, *The Faerie Queene*, A. C. Hamilton (London: Longman, rev. ed., 2001), VI, 10, 16. All subsequent references to this edition in parentheses in the text.

26. Andrew Hadfield, *Literature, Politics and National Identity: Reformation to Renaissance* (Cambridge: Cambridge UP, 1994), 170-71.

27. See, for example, John D. Bernard, *Ceremonies of Innocence* (Cambridge: Cambridge UP, 1989); Thomas H. Cain, Praise in The Faerie Queene (Lincoln: Nebraska, 1978).

28. For recent comment, see James Norhnberg, 'Britomart's Gone Abroad to Brute-Land, Colin Clout's Come Courting from the Salvage Ireland: Exile and Kingdom in Some of Spenser's Fictions for "Crossing Over"', in J. B. Lethbridge, ed., *Edmund Spenser: New and Renewed Directions* (Madison: Farleigh Dickinson UP, 2006), 214-85, at 262-6.

29. Richard A. McCabe, 'The Masks of Duessa: Spenser, Mary Queen of Scots and James VI,' *ELR* 17 (1987), 224-42.

30. The locations are represented in A. C. Judson, *Spenser in Southern Ireland* (Bloomington: Principia Press, 1933).

31. For comment, see David Norbrook, *Poetry and Politics in the English Renaissance* (Oxford: Oxford UP, 2002, rev. ed.), 134-9.

32. Cyndia Susan Clegg, *Press Censorship in Elizabethan England* (Cambridge: Cambridge UP, 1997), 81-9.

33. For discussion and analysis, see 'Revenge Her Foul and Most Unnatural Murder? The Impact of Mary Stewart's Execution on Anglo-Scottish Relations,' *History* 85 (2000), 589-612; Susan Doran 'Gender, Religion, and Early Modern Nationalism: Elizabeth I, Mary Queen of Scots, and the Genesis of English Anti-Catholicism,' *AHR* 107 (2002), 739-67.

34. Andrew Hadfield, 'Spenser and the Stuart Succession,' Literature and History 13.1 (Spring 2004), 9-24.

35. On Faunus and Pan, see Jane Davidson Reid, ed., *The Oxford Guide to Classical Mythology in the Arts, 1300–1990s* (Oxford: Oxford UP, 1993), 802. Patricia Merivale, in her entry, 'Pan', fails to mention this vital link: A. C. Hamilton, ed., *The Spenser Encyclopaedia* (London & Toronto: Routledge: Toronto UP, 1990), 527.

36. For a splendid reading of the complex politics of the poem, see Christopher Warley, *Sonnet Sequences and Social Distinction in Renaissance England* (Cambridge: Cambridge UP, 2005), 116-22.

37. McLane, *Spenser's Shepheardes Calender*, Ch. 2.

38. See Lauren Silberman, *Transforming Desire: Erotic Knowledge in Books III and IV of The Faerie Queene* (Berkeley: U of California P, 1995), Ch. 3.

39. James P. Bednarz, 'Ralegh in Spenser's Historical Allegory,' *Spenser Studies*. 4 (1983), 49-70.

40. For further comment, see Marshall Grossman's essay in this volume.

41. For recent comment, see Park Honan, *Shakespeare: A Life* (Oxford: Oxford UP, 1998), 180-91; Katherine Duncan-Jones, *Ungentle Shakespeare: Scenes from His Life* (London: Thomson, 2000), 215-9.

42. All quotations from *William Shakespeare, The Complete Poems and Sonnets*, ed. Colin Burrow (Oxford: Oxford UP, 2002).

43. Andrew Gurr, *The Shakespearean Stage, 1574–1642* (Cambridge: Cambridge UP, 1992), Ch. 3; Ian W. Archer, 'Shakespeare's London,' in David Scott Kastan, ed., *A Companion to Shakespeare* (Oxford, Blackwell, 1999), 43-56.

44. See Sasha Roberts, *Reading Shakespeare's Poems in early Modern England* (Basingstoke: Palgrave, 2003), Ch. 2.

45. See Margreta de Grazia, 'The Scandal of Shakespeare's Sonnets,' *Shakespeare Survey* 46 (1994), 35-49.

46. Honan, Shakespeare, 263.

The Sins of the Sonnets

If Shakespeare's private correspondence fell out of an ancient cupboard tomorrow, with letters from "fair youth" and "dark lady" and reference to the "rival poet," their identities secure beyond doubt, it would not make much difference to reading the sonnets. Perhaps a few would seem more intimately biographical, fragments of the tangled private life of the Elizabethan and Jacobean courts laid bare; but interpretations depend little on whom the poems address and which boy or woman the poet wasted his feelings over.

Speculation about the missing identities has not lapsed for centuries; and centuries from now scholars will still be raking old ground, raising Southampton at Pembroke's expense, touting some Elizabethan nobody with the initials W. H., savaging scholars who hold deviant views. The scholars will get no more temperate (at least one critic has argued the dark lady *was* the fair youth, master-mistress Mrs. Shakespeare).

Shakespeare's *Sonnets* was printed in 1609 for Thomas Thorpe, who had published Jonson's *Sejanus* and *Volpone* and plays by Chapman and Marston (sometime rivals to Shakespeare and each other, though Shakespeare acted in *Sejanus)*. The print run, which may have been a thousand copies or so, was divided between two bookshops near St. Paul's (one at the sign of the Parrot— today, we would call it the Parrot Bookshop). Thirteen copies now survive.[1]

The sonnets had first been mentioned in print a decade before. In 1598 Francis Meres wrote in his field guide to current writers, *Palladis Tamia,* "The sweete wittie soule of *Ouid* liues in mellifluous & honytongued *Shakespeare,* witnes his *Venus and Adonis,* his *Lucrèce,* his sugred Sonnets among his priuate friends, &c." The following year two sonnets (138 and 144 in the 1609 Quarto) were printed by William Jaggard in a narrow volume titled *The Passionate Pilgrime,* "By W. Shakespeare." Jaggard included a lyric and two additional sonnets from the Quarto of *Love's Labour's Lost,* but the remaining fifteen poems were probably not by Shakespeare. There is evidence he was angry over the publication or deception.

The 1609 Quarto *Sonnets* (called Q) may have been authorized, but if so Shakespeare did not bother to read proof; it is littered with errors few authors could have ignored. Since no copy of any further printing exists, Q

was probably no rousing success, certainly not the success of *Venus and Adonis* (1593), the pillow book for young Elizabethans that had reached its tenth printing by 1609. The *Sonnets* was not reprinted until 1640, and then in corrupt and incomplete fashion.

Shakespeare's sonnets are divided into two groups, the first (1–126) addressed to a "fair youth," the much smaller second (127–152) to a "dark lady." These are not the poet's terms; but, having grown up in the criticism, they are now almost inseparable from it. These enigmatic figures might more accurately be named the "sweet boy" (or "lovely boy") and the "mistress." The sequence closes with two Anacreontic sonnets (153–154), often felt to be un-Shakespearean, followed by the poem "A Lover's Complaint," which may have had nothing to do with the sonnets, though recent critics have strongly argued the contrary. Thorpe dedicated the *Sonnets* to a Mr. W. H., "THE.ONLIE.BEGETTER. OF THESE.INSVING.SONNETS." Often identified as the fair youth, Mr. W. H. has provided literary criticism with one of its fondest mysteries.

Shakespeare's rhetoric was not well adapted to the sonnet. His signature violence of language, the images spinning like plates on poles, rarely survives the sonnets' casuistic wrangle of heartbreak and passion. Auden thought only forty-nine of them perfect. By my count, twenty-three have changed English literature (our language wouldn't be the same without them); there are twenty-five others I'd sell my soul for, and dozens of strange but fragmentary achievement (Shakespeare's humiliations are a poetry in themselves). As other critics have recognized, many of the concluding couplets attach only weakly to the preceding quatrains, as if Shakespeare had bought them in a job lot. The most memorable sonnets are often those most thickly and flamboyantly stuffed with images: their scarcity implies how cramped Shakespeare found the sonnet for his rhetorical flourish.

No one grinds out one-hundred-fifty-four sonnets on a whim; no one writes so possessively unless a little possessed. Some critics have proposed that Shakespeare was commissioned to write the first seventeen sonnets, which urge the fair youth to marry and have children. They do read as if an anxious parent had paid a guinea a throw. Whether the incentive came first from emolument or emotion matters little now; whatever the soiled inspiration for sonnets, emotion soon spills into them. It's not enough that when Shakespeare was young the form was popular, or that poets on the make (or on the take) feel the urge to exceed their rivals in some form in public favor. The sonnets obtained an immediate if perhaps small private audience, so they must have been passed around (and yet not far around—Donne's poems were widely copied, but no contemporary manuscript copy of any of Shakespeare's sonnets has been discovered).

Neither pride in his achievement nor envy of other poets (each a lively component in the sonnets' structure of deadly sins) is a sufficient motive. I would suggest two necessary ones. The sonnets must have been largely autobiographical: there must have been private reasons, a desire to please or punish, to cajole or anger or praise the fair youth and dark lady. The biographical motive may be suspect, but when a poet writes compulsive love poems there is almost always a real lover in view. The facts may be false, the emotions worked up or over, the speaker may have sung his lines at various distances from the breathing Shakespeare; yet the controlling impulse, the fraught drive through pentameter, seems to derive from strong feeling toward a wayward mistress and a wayward friend.

There must have been private longings; and there must have been entanglement in the form, some satisfaction beyond the satisfaction of writing to lover or friend. It's hard to compose over and over in a form as tightly knotted as the sonnet without an addict's grace and consolation. The narrative of the sonnets must partly be that of their rhetoric, the pleasure of taking possession of the form in words.

In the sonnets, as transiently in the plays, Shakespeare can be darkly chaotic, his language impacted beyond rescue of grammar or sense. Not every obscurity can be blamed on myopic scribes or the all-thumbs compositors—the confusion is intimate to the style. Stephen Booth has argued that Shakespeare sometimes abandoned lines to their disorder. This would make him irresponsible. Among the additions to the manuscript of *The Book of Sir Thomas More,* the loose, hurried pages almost certainly in Shakespeare's hand are never clumsy or incompetent. If there was disarray beyond manuscript or printing house, a writer of tortuous invention in the grip of emotion perhaps could not, finally, see the strain in his syntax or the angle of his ambiguities (and he would have had no actor in rehearsal to lift an eyebrow and ask what the hell he meant). Because the sonnets

were addressed to those who knew him, perhaps he did not need to.

❧

The Arden edition of the *Sonnets* and a long commentary by Helen Vendler inherit the tradition begun by Thorpe and continued by John Benson in 1640. (Benson was the sonnets' first interpreter. Because sonnets by then seemed out of date, he lumped many together as longer poems and, by slyly changing pronouns, at times made the lovely boy a lovelier girl.) The Arden series has been without a new *Sonnets* since World War I. Neither Leslie Hotson nor Winifred Nowottny completed editions announced in their names. Nowottny, whose *The Language Poets Use* displayed her precision and good sense, was named editor in the early sixties for an edition still being promised when the second series was closed, with some chagrin, twenty years later. It was with fine hubris that the complete set of the Arden sold in the eighties was never advertised as *Shakespeare's Complete Works, Unfortunately Missing the Sonnets.*

Katherine Duncan-Jones's treatment of the sonnets is mostly loyal, no-stone-unturned scholarly work, ferreting meaning and snaring allusion, patching up bad lines (or not patching them and telling why), keeping one eye on past critics and one on contemporary argument. All editors of Shakespeare rely on centuries of dead scholars; the shrewdness of the present owes much to the sound practice of the past. Duncan-Jones's edition gives the sonnets the full Arden treatment, with a collation of readings from prior editions, lavish *en face* notes (a sensible departure from normal Arden layout), and a thorough if idiosyncratic introduction. This Arden is three times as long as C. Knox Pooler's of 1918, and Duncan-Jones's exhaustive notes show how much scholarship has been lavished on the poems in our studious century. (In a strange fit of scholarly laziness, the editor has collated just a dozen earlier editions—after Q and Benson, only Capell and Malone before this century. Her collation is therefore misleading about the origin of many readings.)

This edition is based on a number of provocative theories, cogently argued if not always convincing or even plausible. Duncan-Jones thinks the *Sonnets* was authorized (that is, Shakespeare contracted with the publisher and provided copy, but never read proof); that writing and revision of the poems proceeded in stages, from early in Shakespeare's career to months before publication;

that, driven to find income during plague years when the playhouses were shut, Shakespeare almost came to publish the work once before; that the Earl of Southampton's identification as Mr. W. H. is probably untenable; that the Earl of Pembroke is a stronger candidate than ever; and that Shakespeare was homoerotic (if not homosexual) and a sickening misogynist.

Editors of the sonnets take pride in their innovations, and Duncan Jones opens her edition with perhaps the most trivial claim ever made: hers is the "first edited text . . . to include the two pairs of empty parentheses which follow the six-couplet poem numbered 126." It's easy to distrust a scholar who finds Francis Meres's mention of the sonnets a "mouthwatering account" (and later a "succulent reference"), who boasts that "homoeroticism is here confronted positively" (whatever that means—it sounds like kiss and tell), who calls the sonnet an "almost uniquely contained, delimited form of versification" (all poetic forms are "delimited" and "contained"), and who resorts to coercive rhetoric like "He could scarcely have failed to notice" and "Having noticed that, Shakespeare surely also took note of . . ." One of her first notions is that the *"&:c."* that ends Meres's passage might be an allusion to vaginas.

Her most contentious arguments concern Shakespeare's "misogyny" and "homoeroticism." Misogyny seems a peculiarly misguided characterization, given Shakespeare's devoted portrayal of women good and ill, high and low, comic and tragic. In the comedies, the women are more stung with sense than the men; in the tragedies and romances, they are tempered into triumphs of our literature (Ophelia, Lady Macbeth, Cordelia, Desdemona, Miranda, Juliet, Portia, Cleopatra). Has any playwright created women more fascinating, or more fascinating women? Only in the histories, because of genre and source, are women mere shadows. If Shakespeare was a misogynist, what does that make other men?

Duncan-Jones writes fixed in feminist outrage, and outrage is a poor recommendation for dispassionate scholarship. She reads the dark-lady sonnets as "backhanded praise of a manifestly non-aristocratic woman who is neither young, beautiful, intelligent nor chaste," a harsh and willful distortion of Shakespeare's portrait. The poet celebrates her "in swaggering terms which are ingeniously offensive both to her and to women in general." He wants "to brag to other men in his audience that he can make satisfactory sexual use of a woman too stupid to realize that she is also being set up as the butt

of his wit." The dark-lady sonnets are "sheer nastiness" and "outrageous misogyny."

This is as patronizing to the dark lady as it is to Shakespeare. That Shakespeare shared the assumptions of his age is a commonplace; not being psychic, he never intuited our decade's protective and puritanical view of women, for whom even a man's gaze may be violent: Petrarch's flatteries have been equated with the butchery of *Titus Andronicus*—both "dismember" women. "Misogyny" offers a deforming vision of sonnet 130 ("My mistress' eyes are nothing like the sun"), with its darkly loving picture of a lover whose flesh refuses the cold conceits of Petrarchan beauty—and who therefore becomes more powerfully erotic. If her lips were not as red as coral nor her cheeks the tints of an English rose, if her hair was black rather than blonde or her breath not sweet as perfume ("reeks" at this period, as Duncan-Jones notes, meant nothing unpleasant), Shakespeare might have been honest in his confession, not sparing her faults in art in order not to bring lies to life: "I think my love as rare / As any she belied with false compare." To Duncan-Jones, this means "all that is necessary is that the object of desire is female and available." Her Shakespeare is without irony.

To Duncan-Jones, the dark lady is merely stupid. The speaker of "A Lover's Complaint" is a victim of "sexual harassment," a term that would have had no meaning for Elizabethans and that describes a situation very different from that of the seduced and abandoned maid (in harassment, the victim has no choice; in seduction, the choice may be regretted—in "A Lover's Complaint," it is not even wholly regretted). Duncan-Jones is so ticklish about sex, she thinks if Shakespeare uses a word like "rise" or "use," it must always conceal sexual motive. "Spend" is an allusion to masturbation ("why dost thou spend / Upon thyself thy beauty's legacy," sonnet 4); "treasure" is semen (6); "nothing" the space between a woman's legs ("And nothing 'gainst time's scythe can make defence," 12); the repetition of feminine rhymes in "-ing" "hints at 'ingle,' = a boy favourite, a catamite" (87). That some of these words are in bawdy use elsewhere, usually an elsewhere clear in context (Ophelia: "I think nothing, my lord." Hamlet: "That's a fair thought to lie between maids' legs"), moves Duncan-Jones to see them everywhere. Like Freud, she finds a phallus around every corner.

Sonnet 126, six couplets short a seventh, may have been a mistake, or a self-conscious shortening to mark the end of the fair-youth sonnets. When printed in Q, its length was tricked out with two pairs of widely spaced parentheses. These are almost surely printing-house devices to reassure the reader the amputation was not in error—such graphic devices are unlikely to have been authorial. For Duncan-Jones, they deserve a lengthy note, nearly her longest, stressing that the sonnet's incompleteness "is reinforced by the empty parentheses which follow, as if they figure the emptiness which will ensue." Well, not quite emptiness, since what "ensues" are the dark-lady sonnets. To her whimsical imagination, the parentheses suggest "marks in an account-book enclosing the final sum, but empty." (I've looked at Elizabethan ledgers and account books without seeing this symbol, but in modern accounts parentheses mark a loss. Perhaps an immeasurable loss, then?) Or, "since these brackets enclose an expected couplet, they may image a failure to 'couple.' "If Shakespeare had wanted to "image" the fair youth's indolent desires, he probably could have found words enough. While making heavy weather of such marks, Duncan-Jones quotes approvingly recent scholars who thought them the "shape of an hourglass, but one that contains no sand," or the "silence (quiet) of the grave," or "little moons" that "image a repeated waxing and waning of the moon, pointing to fickleness and frailty." The fancies of critics are better than poetry. If such symbols were in the foul papers, they could only have been to remind Shakespeare he was a couple of lines short. You half expect a critic to remark that the inked page looks like a dirty "sheet" or that a book is shaped like a bed.

Such readings rise to the comedy of paranoia. In sonnet 129 ("Th' expense of spirit in a waste of shame"), Duncan-Jones uses an old association between sexual ejaculation and failing eyesight to suggest that the "speaker's eyesight may have been damaged by sexual activity"—which might explain, she adds, why the speaker thinks the dark lady is beautiful! But it might also explain why he thinks the dark lady is dark—this is bad medicine and worse criticism. (She believes the leafless trees in sonnet 73 may refer to Shakespeare's bald head—after all, he says, "That time of year thou mayst *in me* behold.") There is more venereal disease in her sonnets than any reader would have thought possible. Her perverse readings are not merely sexual: in sonnet 33 she decides that Q's phonetic spelling of "alchemy" as "alcumy" hints at "all comers," and in sonnet 45 that the "extra-metrical syllable in *melancholy* reinforces the sense of congestion." The twenty-eight (actually, twenty-six) sonnets to the dark lady mark the "lunar month

or menstrual cycle." Lest the reader believe such a numerical "allusion" neutral, it confirms the "suspicion of some preoccupation with the negative connotations of menstruation" and reveals a "male disgust." Shakespeare must also have had something against the moon.

The equation implicit beneath the accusation of misogyny is that Shakespeare hated women because he was a repressed homosexual. (Duncan-Jones never quite says this, though sometimes there's an Orwellian slogan behind her remarks: one penis bad, two penises good, no penis best.) How queer was Shakespeare, exactly? The question has troubled editors, perhaps from the beginning. (Why else was Benson so eager to castrate the fair youth?) Did Shakespeare like to take it . . . *there*? Did he get on his knees and . . . *you* know? A century ago, editors were defending him against the charge; now they can't welcome him to queer studies fast enough. Though prurient curiosity is profoundly human, the urge to make Shakespeare *just like us* (or some of us) is as wistful as it is sadly mawkish. Every age remakes Shakespeare in its own image; but every age gets the Shakespeare it deserves, turning whatever was contrary to cliché.

We know little about Elizabethan sexual life. Men and women made love (there were children to prove it), and men apparently made love to men (otherwise it wouldn't have been a capital crime); yet we have only an eclipsed idea of the codes and comedies of their intimacies, what they proposed erotically and disposed carnally. What was dangerous under Elizabeth might have been de rigueur under James, just as the mores of the sixties are not those of today, and the mores of the forties were not those of the sixties. It doesn't alter the sonnets if Shakespeare liked to insert his privates into the privates of men, or women, or both indifferently. We are unlikely ever to know where and how thoroughly he took his joys.

Today only a homosexual would write the fair-youth sonnets. Auden said, "The homosexual reader, . . . determined to secure our Top-Bard as a patron saint of the Homintern, has been uncritically enthusiastic about the first one hundred and twenty-six of the sonnets, and preferred to ignore those to the Dark Lady in which the relationship is unequivocally sexual, and the fact that Shakespeare was a married man and a father." Duncan-Jones uses a quiet piece of tattle to call this a "characteristic instance of Auden's cowardice," a curious thing to say of a man who went to drive an ambulance in the Spanish Civil War, only to be foiled by bureaucrats, and who wrote frankly of Shakespeare's possible homosexuality (in an edition used by high-school students) when criticism was still mired in its euphemisms. According to Robert Craft, Auden didn't think 1964—as it happened, the four-hundredth anniversary of Shakespeare's birth—the time "to admit that the top Bard was in the homintern." (The scholar quoting Craft found the evidence ambiguous—Auden might have been playing to his audience. Craft and the Stravinskys.) Auden loved to provoke conversation, but he was serious about his scholarship. He didn't recant when he collected his introduction to the *Sonnets* in *Forewords and Afterwords* the year he died (1973), though feelings toward homosexuality were by then very different and it was no longer illegal in Britain.

Duncan-Jones uses the slippery word "homoerotic" about the fair-youth sonnets, which seems craven itself. (It means Shakespeare was aroused by boys but didn't necessarily fiddle with them.) She offers strong if circumstantial evidence that the sonnets unsettled readers in 1609; but this may only support Auden's notion that they were so unusually and disturbingly autobiographical, Shakespeare would never have shown most of them to the fair youth or dark lady and would never have approved their printing.

If past critics were too eager to remove the possibility of gay sex from Shakespeare, critics now are too eager to put it back. It seems beyond their imagination that men could have intimate, sentimental friendships without physical arousal (though we see its distant kin in the bluster and butt-slapping of football players). Duncan-Jones knows how rare such poems by a man were (in English, if not in French) and how strangely and nervously the sonnets have been received. We don't see such skittishness again until *In Memoriam*. There are men, usually around eighteen or twenty, so beautiful that if they were women other men would long to possess them. To most men who desire women, however, the presence of a penis is a powerful disincentive, no matter the beauty of the beheld. Shakespeare and the youth might have liked women so well their language of mutual affection was allowed teasing latitude—such language (we will never know what the language meant *to them)* might deny homoerotic passion in the very terms of that passion. The bantering exaggeration of the sonnets often seems of this sort.

Because the sonnets were private documents, not public dramas, the tone can be elusive, as it often is in letters. The sonnets are so subject to irony that the "rival poet," one critic has proposed, might have been

preposterously bad, Shakespeare's mean humblings mockingly insincere. We recall from childhood the passion, and betrayals, without sex for the same sex. Was it not possible, in a different society and atmosphere (a whole anthropology of difference), that male friendship and its jealousies were equally fevered? That whatever intimacy Shakespeare gained from his friend, it was threatened by the disparity in social class? If the fair youth was a lord, he could act (was no doubt taught to act) in a manner all too casual and high-handed; and bonds of intimacy could be as easily broken as made by a rich, careless, pretty youth.

The sonnets may record only the relations they claim: an affair with an unfaithful mistress and passionate, resentful friendship with a young man. Shakespeare never speaks of the youth with the rapture of physical longing reserved for the dark lady—until Shakespeare grows jealous, the friendship sounds like a Sunday afternoon tea. One of the few places he swaggers is when he says, "And when a woman woos, what woman's son / Will sourly leave her till he have prevailed?" (41) (To eliminate the swagger, many editors, following Malone, emend "he" to "she.") Duncan-Jones finds the amusing tongue-in-cheek of sonnet 20 "embarrassingly anatomical." She assumes anyone who denies the homoerotic nature of the sonnets wants to exonerate Shakespeare from the "suspicion of pederasty."

The case for William Herbert, Earl of Pembroke, as the "fair youth" fits her speculations about dating the poems. Gorgeous as a young man, Pembroke hated the idea of marriage and was, in the words of Clarendon (as Duncan-Jones quotes), "immoderately given up to women." The sonnets may have predated Pembroke's inheritance of title: perhaps "Mr. W.H." (I admit this is a wild guess) was a term of intimacy between the two men even afterward. (The editor thinks some of the early poems might have been to Southampton, most of the later to Pembroke; but, if the dedicatee was one of the two, he would have known that ONLIE.BEGETTER was then a lie.) Despite her promise to place the sonnet in the "homosocial" world of James I's court, Duncan-Jones can dredge up only a bit of gossip from a Venetian account of the coronation, at which Pembroke "actually kissed his Majesty's face, whereupon the King laughed and gave him a little cuff."

While not claiming that Pembroke was anything but a womanizer, the editor calls this kiss "enthusiastic participation in the homosocial familiarities of James and his minions." Indeed, she argues that the "outrageous

misogyny" of the later sonnets as well as what she hap-
lessly terms the "homoerotic thrust" of the early ones
may have been attempts to curry favor in James's court,
revealing nothing about Shakespeare the "man." Her
case for misogyny and the homoerotic starts to leak
away here, though soon she's describing what must have
been, in French fashion, no more than a brush on the
cheek as a "full-frontal kiss."[2]

Shakespeare may have been a garden-variety married
homosexual, or a look-but-don't-touch, all-play-but-no-
business homoerotic with a hard-on, or something we
have no name for. We should not attempt to fit what
may have been struggling or confused or individual into
modern pigeonholes that would seem bizarre to Elizabethans. We don't necessarily understand the Elizabethans
better than the Elizabethans did—they would not be so
strange to us, otherwise.

Duncan-Jones's bad arguments don't make Shakespeare's sex life any clearer. She's condescending to
scholars less quick to judge than herself, including the
editors of the three best editions of the last half century,
W. G. Ingram and Theodore Redpath (1964), Stephen
Booth (1977), and John Kerrigan (1986). She doesn't
understand why her nastiness is comic and misguided—
she mocks scholars who "devoted large parts of their
lonely lives" to pursuing the identity of the dark lady.
(Fruitless quests sometimes lead to rich scholarship.)
Referring to the movie *Sense and Sensibility* (1995),
she rages at the "fantasy in which shared appreciation of
Shakespeare's Sonnets serves to reinforce heterosexual
attraction." This recklessly ignores the psychology of
reading: fair-youth sonnets like "Shall I compare thee
to a summer's day?" and "Let me not to the marriage of
true minds / Admit impediments" have deceived more
than one female heart. They are among the poems most
often read at weddings.

The wild excesses of Duncan-Jones's criticism do
injustice to the handsome, unshowy analysis in many
sonnets, the edgy discriminations in her notes; but such
careful work is vitiated when she cries wolf (or sexual
harassment) at the least opportunity. Suggestiveness is
everywhere turned to certainty—the reader has to fend
off as many readings as he accepts. A scholar so careless
of her opportunities, and heedless of her responsibilities, has prepared a dry document for our sexual wars.
Eager to criticize other scholars for "such careful pro-
paganda," for failing to analyze their prejudices, she is
blind to her own. In her last note on the sonnets, she
suggests the FINIS beneath sonnet 154 "may hint at an

allusion to the miraculous draught of fishes in St John's
Gospel." The finality of that FINIS might have brought
into doubt any tie to "A Lover's Complaint," which immediately follows. (To me, it has always seemed giddy,
insubstantial work, as likely a political allegory as a romantic interlude.) I had to read her note twice to realize
she meant FINIS had something to do with fins and fish.

❧

Helen Vendler's *The Art of Shakespeare's Sonnets* is
a masterpiece of reader's attention, a painstaking, and
sometimes painful, dissection of the sonnets' smallest
formal structures. Critical discussion since Empson has
focused on tremors of verbal meaning and the embar-
rassments of ambiguity (a tradition Duncan-Jones snide-
ly labels the "critical cult of ambiguity and word-play").
Ignoring Shakespeare's local meanings for the autopsy
of his sentences, of the poems as *poems,* Vendler examines pronouns, verb tense and mood, syntax, prosody,
chiastic structure, comparatives and superlatives, repetition, anagrams, assonance and consonance, time frames,
and enjambment, only rarely embracing metaphor or
etymology in the New Critics' old-fashioned way. In his
grammatical orders, she argues, Shakespeare turns language to dramatic mimesis.

Vendler's analysis is heavily indebted to Continental structuralists like Roman Jakobson (a bridge to the
Russian formalists) and Roland Barthes (especially in
S/Z). Like the structuralists, Vendler includes a lot of
nifty charts and diagrams. Though such attentions to the
cogs and gears of the sonnets have been proposed before (Jakobson's and L. G. Jones's essay "Shakespeare's
Verbal Art in 'Th' Expence of Spirit" is full of crazed,
niggling comprehension), no one has been so dedicated
to the microscopic view. I admire her enterprise while
thinking it wrong-headed, grand in its ambition but
awry in its particulars. Much future study of the sonnets
will argue with these short essays, just as current verbal
analysis must confront Stephen Booth's Polyphemus-
like commentary.

Vendler is at odds with current criticism, that tar
pit of vengeance and half-baked philosophy. She takes
too much pleasure in the language of the sonnets, their
intimacies and emotional torsions, to put up with the
dismissive strictures of recent critics (she quotes some
hilarious examples). Her immersion in poetry has been
the mark of her scholarly life: Vendler says she has the
sonnets by heart.

The introduction to *The Art of Shakespeare's Sonnets* is full of good sense, a quality no longer in long supply. Vendler doesn't much like calling the dark lady the dark lady, but notes that we must respect historical conventions of the language. She dismisses charges of misogyny as anachronistic, arguing that Shakespeare's duty was to accuracy of feeling, not our tender sensibilities. The wish to have Shakespeare model for modern behavior (or, where he fails, to keelhaul him by feminist codes) is part of criticism's new preciousness. Vendler is brutal to complaints that the dark lady and fair youth have been "silenced" in the sonnets; their gagging is a condition of the lyric, not the author's sadistic nature. A sonnet's inner voice is not a parliamentary debate.

In fact, Vendler believes the sonnets record traces of fictional speech by youth and lady. She argues that many sonnets reply to some a priori complaint or criticism, and her elaboration of these dramatic scenes is sweetly absurd. Sonnet 82 ("I grant thou wert not married to my Muse") is therefore Shakespeare's reply to the fair youth, who, irritated by the poet's jealousy, might have said, "I'm not *married* to *your* Muse." It's not clear whether Vendler believes he did, or whether Shakespeare only imagined for the sake of; her point is that the sonnet incorporates the language of such complaint. Her reading of sonnet 116 finds such fossils of imagined conversation everywhere:

> *Let me not to the marriage of true minds*
> *Admit "impediments": love is* not *love*
> *Which "alters when it alteration finds,"*
> *Or "bends with the remover to remove,"*
> *O no!*

O no! indeed. There's a lot of brattish behavior by youth and lady in these scenarios—you wonder why the poet would put up with it. Are such closet dramas necessary? A poet already lives in the silence of projection and displacement: he's answering not something fictionally (or actually) said but a tension roused in the poem's logic by the silent imagination of private affairs. The poem is the expression of ends for which no means have been spoken. Vendler would make these sonnets grumpy arguments with a voice offstage rather than figments of self-explanation. Her "reply sonnets" aren't unlikely so much as irrelevant: the poet can raise complaints against himself without the fiction of prior speech.

Poems have a speaker; and critics sometimes make heavy weather of the speaker's identity, berating the reader who thinks it might be the poet—the poet of biography, with birth date and death date in parenthesis, with callouses, a bald spot, and a shrewish wife. No reader is quite that innocent. Vendler cares little for biography, but one danger of her analysis is her sober disintegration of the speaker's wholesome identity: "Shakespeare" is the man who wrote the poems in ink, the "speaker" the man who fictionally says them, unless he wants to be a poet, whereupon he becomes "the poet." The dramatis personae are ever more disordered, since Vendler believes the lyric, unlike novel or play, is a script for the reader to recite *to himself,* so the "speaker" is in trust the reader, except when the reader decides to be "the poet." This is a recipe for schizophrenia. For most poets, the self is more fluid and less multiple. Every trace of biography may be murdered for a rhyme, but poets begin by writing themselves into their lyrics.

If lyrics weren't scripts, Vendler claims there'd be no point to writing them down. In my experience, alas, a poet writes to see what he says; the words, even the feelings, don't exist until cast on the page—poems embody what may have been shadow without substance. By ancient custom, the poet cannot be held to account for his words. (Other poets therefore thought Auden odd to suppress "Spain" and "September 1, 1939.") Only unwary biographers, of which there are many, draw the facts of life from the fakes of art—for readers as well as poets, the lyric pretends to the inner thoughts of the poet, not "the poet." Vendler fails the author's detachment: the reader knows the dumb show, knows the author may aim irony at himself the truths of the heart fall from lies of the tongue. When a new sonnet was delivered, Mr. W. H. didn't stutter, "I wonder who the speaker is?" He thought the speaker was Shakespeare. (In sonnet 82, Vendler imagines an unreal speaker speaking to a real patron—hardly a way to endear oneself to the patron.)

The sonnets are fractions in rhetoric, their sums larger than their fictions. Vendler's sensitivity to a poem's struggle toward meaning, though it can make raw accident seem overcooked intention, saturates her description of the sonnets' complexity:

> When God saw his creatures, he commanded them
> to increase and multiply Shakespeare, in this first
> sonnet of the sequence, suggests we have internal-
> ized the paradisal command in an aestheticized
> form: *From fairest creatures we desire increase.*
> The sonnet begins, so to speak, in the desire for an
> Eden where beauty's rose will never die; but the

fall quickly arrives with *decease* (where we expect, by parallel with *increase*, the milder *decrease*). Unless the young man pities the world, and consents to his own increase, even a successively self-renewing Eden is unavailable.

Such critical writing sustains itself with self-renewing insight—it's not just the sonnet that has an "aesthetic investment in profusion." Vendler's gift is to show how many approaches have the virtue of their responsibilities.

In her discussion of the opening sonnet (so rightly in place, she notes, it might have been written much later), she brings to the surface Shakespeare's range of tones, the interpénétration of his metaphors, his "contrastive taxonomy" (the pairing of ideas), his use of the organic versus the inorganic, his deluge of speech acts ("appeal to the *consensus gentium . . .,* exemplum . . . direct address . . . narrative . . . paradoxes . . . reproach . . . exhortation . . . prophetic threat"), even his own status as a father (one of her rare concessions to biography). Her balanced discussion of the sonnet's unbalanced structure and the "shadow sonnet" beneath it reveals how structure and language are indivisible in their use of expectation:

> If Shakespeare (and the social *world* linking the
> third quatrain and the couplet) are [sic] here the
> owners and deployers of judgmental language,
> the young man is the sovereign over descriptive
> usage: he compels it to be beautiful, even when it is
> describing a sinner.

These sharp insights make it easy to forgive the occasional grammatical error or lapse into critical cant (whether "different rhetoricity" or the "social norm of reproduction").

Vendler's discussion of sonnet 30 is a similar tour de force, tracking the speaker through five "panels" of time. The beauty of English tenses lies in their fastidious erection of the past, their loyalty to the prim order of events, an inheritance from the intricacy of Indo-European verb forms. In this sonnet, famous for remembrance ("When to the sessions of sweet silent thought"), Vendler takes the subtle regrets of memory through their implicated chronology, their shifting periods deep in the verbal gestures—gestures so guarded, she gets confused herself (on one page, T3 is the time of grief, T2 loss, T1 happiness or neutrality before loss; on the next, T3 is the loss, T2 happiness, and T1 neutral prehappiness). We

have perhaps become too familiar with Shakespeare's language to appreciate the knowing complications of his art.

Vendler's "many-paneled past" would be just clever insight (which is all too often abuse of insight) if the invocation of the past didn't lead to restoration of the present. This poem of memory shapes the construction of memory; where it becomes "rawly new," old grief is grieved again. The "sweet" sessions turn sour despite their pleasures: "To be able to find pleasure in resummoning griefs that were once anguishing indicates, in itself[,] a loss of perceptual freshness." Vendler never forgets how fluid the sonnet is, or how confidently Shakespeare marshals the divisions of grammar. She has the witty thought, given the Renaissance muddling of *sigh* with *sight,* of having discovered an unknown strong verb: *sigh, sight, sought.* Vendler thinks Shakespeare particularly fond of chiasmus (the rhetorical figure a:b::b:a) and often finds chiastic structure in the poems. She has thereby clarified a problematic reading in sonnet 99, in which Shakespeare compares the youth to various plants. The line "And buds of marjoram had stol'n thy hair" has given scholars fits, because it's not clear whether Shakespeare meant the smell, the color, or the texture. Vendler believes the comparisons through the lines culminating in that image were laid out "odor:hue::hue: odor" and therefore the boy's hair must be sweet-smelling as marjoram (rather than, say, dense as a thicket). It's odd that this line has proven so difficult—Shakespeare must have thought the metaphor immediate and unambiguous. If scholars kept herb gardens now, they'd know the scent of sweet marjoram is richly unmistakable ("sweet" meant "scented").

Such lively discussions recall the strengths of New Criticism, open to all the relevant evidence a literary form itself presents. Truffling for metaphors in sonnet 34 (which produces one of the book's most ingenious charts) or dye-marking pronouns in sonnet 42, Vendler demonstrates that in every line a critic must be alive to her medium. We've never had so thorough an account of the architecture of the sonnets (an account that revels in the wiring and plumbing); her commentary values the democracy of insight even more than the tolerance of hindsight.

The means of Vendler's analysis are as various as Shakespeare's technique—her methods are stimulating rather than exhaustive, cross-sections not panoramas (she believes most sonnets respond to variant analysis). Sometimes, the poor sonnet is left looking like an exploded-parts diagram. For this critic, every change in feeling must be guaranteed in the style. No one would deny that changes in feeling often resonate in the form; but to argue that "every significant change of linguistic pattern represents a motivated change in feeling" is disingenuous, if the critic gets to decide what's significant. She sees intention behind every tense shift, and her Shakespeare buries puns like nuts for winter. (In sonnet 3, you might see the husband in *husbandry,* but is there really age in *tillage* and *image* and old in *golden?)*

Vendler is fascinated by what she calls Key Words (words appearing in each quatrain and the couplet) and Couplet Ties (words in both the body of the poem and the couplet). In a tangled form like the sonnet, obsession is likely to appear obsessively, to bind in structure what's bound into rhetoric. Vendler's Key Words don't explain very much (she's otherwise eager to know where argument violates the quatrains), and she's put to critical contortions explaining why in some quatrains they're missing—or, worse, why they appear in code. As Frank Kermode has pointed out, she wins both ways: if key words are present, they're present for a reason; if absent, they're absent for an even better reason ("This may be a DEFECTIVE KEY WORD poem: LOVE is missing from Q2, perhaps to represent the speaker's fear that he will *not* be loved after his death").

Vendler lives for the minutiae of the sonnets, especially the music in the minutiae. She warns against discovering in a sonnet more than is there, but her definition of *there* is elastic. Her batlike ear for consonance and assonance is so acute, it becomes too acute. In sonnet 54, for example, there's an echo between "canker blooms" in one line and "perfumed tincture" in the next, but hardly one that warrants this critical arabesque:

> Summer's "honey" breath . . . momentarily sweetens the canker blooms by borrowing for its lines the very sound of the rose's perfume (the K:-sound of the preceding *tincture*) in *maskèd* and *discloses.* Early on, the poem had represented its own confusion between canker roses and real roses by melding their naming sounds Now, as the summer's breath does duty for the (missing) perfumèd tincture, the shared *canker/tincture* /K-sound reappears in *discloses* and *maskèd,* with overtones of *damasked.*

I like the "very sound of the rose's perfume." Vendler's true passion is phoneme hunting; though much of her

detective work reveals the delicacy and persistence of sound in the sonnets, she's all too eager to find "hidden" anagrams, like a dotty Scrabble player: "The *mira* of *miracle* may have appealed to Shakespeare as an anagram of *rima* (rhyme)," *"created* contains *read, breathers* conceals 'hearers,' and *earth* and *rehearse* contain 'hear.' Of their respectively eight and nine letters, *rehearse* and *breathers* have seven in common." Phoneme hunting begins in innocence, but ends in Javert-like experience.

No cryptographer could be more diligent. In sonnet 20 ("Bizarre as it may appear," Vendler says), the letters *h-e-w-s* or *h-u-e-s* are found scrambled in almost every line. "A man in hew all Hews in his controwling," though an entrancing line, is one of the least important in the sonnet; and Shakespeare didn't spell his *hews h-u-e-s.* If he were going to make a game of it, he'd play by stricter rules (the letters *h-e-w-s* occur in only eight lines other than the line above).

Such cryptograms, even if real, wouldn't tell us much. You could say, for example, the letters in *rose* (an anagram of *eros* and *sore)* have been jumbled sixteen times in twelve lines of sonnet 94, that they appear in five different words *(worse, sourest, sommers* [also *sommer], others, owners)* and three phrases, that the poem is about summer flowers ("The summer's flower is to the summer sweet"), though it names only lilies. You could then say the roses lie hidden and that, following the last line of the previous sonnet ("If thy sweet virtue answer not thy show"), the false show here conceals the love *(eros),* the pain *(sore),* and the thorny symbol of both. Indeed, "rose" blooms from concealment in the next sonnet, and in sonnet 98 roses and lilies at last appear together. You could say these things and be a clever Mad Hatter of a critic. Vendler says none of them, but in sonnet 68 finds five words containing the letters *r-o-s-e* (a "bouquet of five invisible roses"). As cryptographers know, these are two of the three most common vowels, two of the four most common consonants. More than one line, like "Devouring time blunt thou the Lyons pawes" or "And from the forlorne world his visage hide," contains the scrambled letters *h-e-l-e-n v-e-n-d-l-e-r,* the latter even conceals the letters *h-e-l-e-n v-e-n-d-l-e-r h-i-d t-h-i-s.* Shakespeare played language games, but not perhaps these games.

You might think a musical ear would attract Vendler to prosody. Though the sonnets are the most metrically timid of Shakespeare's works, their use of meter is more flexible and fluent than Marlowe's, whose mighty line is often just a line, end-stopped to extinction. (Shakespeare drives conversation into the meter.) Vendler avoids meter, she says, "not yet having found an acceptably subtle and yet communicable theory of scansion." That may seem a peculiar thing for a critic to say, since the basic principles of scansion (at least the sort poets actually use) are fairly simple; but in sonnet 39 her scansion gives birth to monsters. According to Vendler, the following are "two metrically irregular lines":

```
-  /  -    -  -  /  -    -    -  /
O absence // what a / torment / wouldst thou / prove
 -  /  -  /  /   /  /  -    /   /    /
Were it not I thy sour I leisure I gave sweet I leave
```

The second line may be a little tricky (if "were it" were elided as "were't," "sour" would be a disyllable, as it is in *The Comedy of Errors*; "This week he hath been heavy, sour, sad" [5.1.45]), yet few poets would think these anything but regular iambic pentameter, without even much by way of variation:

```
 -  /   -    /   - /  -   /     -   /
O ab-/ sence what / a tor- / ment wouldst / thou prove
 -  /   -  /  - /  -   /     /   /
Were't not / thy so-/ ur lei- / sure gave / sweet leave
```

or

```
  -  /  - /      /  -  /    /  /
Were it / not thy / sour lei- / sure gave / sweet leave
```

Vendler seems to scan according to the rhythms and phrases (even verbal identities) of the line, not its metrical value. This confuses rhythmic properties with metrical stress. In her reading of sonnet 126, keeping the words intact within metrical feet creates this gorgeously shipwrecked scansion:

```
  -  / -    /   -  /   - - -      /
If Nature // sovereign / mistress / over / wrack
 -   /  -  - / /     /  -   /    - /
As thou / goest onwards / still will / pluck thee / back
  - /   -  -  /   /  -    -  -    /
She keeps thee / to this / purpose // that her / skill
 -   /    -  -  /  -   /  - / -    /
May Time / disgrace // and wretched / minutes / kill
```

Here, poor regular iambs have been tortured into amphibrachs, one-syllable feet, and other gruesome deformities.

Vendler often goes too far, which is only sometimes better than not going far enough. Her fancies are easy enough to dismiss, but I find myself arguing with her arguments. The readings in the commentary are illuminating, though often arch or strained—not just wrong in the details, but wrong because of the details. In sonnet 64, for example, there's a watchful quatrain on the sea and shore:

> *When I have seen the hungry ocean gain*
> *Advantage on the kingdom of the shore*
> *And the firm soil win of the wat'ry main*
> *Increasing store with loss, and loss with store.*

The last line's chiasmus ties together this zero-sum game: the ocean wins at the shore's expense, the shore at the ocean's (what Shakespeare in the following line calls "interchange of state")—it's an old battle, familiar to those who live along beaches. Perhaps Shakespeare had heard of the medieval village slipping into the sea off Suffolk; the image need call up only the advance and withdrawal of wave or tide. Vendler interprets:

> The speaker manifests his horror at this purposeless exchange of terrain by his unparaphrasable summary line. *Increasing store with loss, and loss with store*. Loss is added to store; and loss is increased by store. Loss wins in both cases. It is of course impossible to increase abundance with loss, and equally impossible to increase loss by adding abundance to it. Behind such a line . . . one sees Time's purposeless playing at ruin.

Horror may be too strong for regret (even rage) at such inevitable and dispassionate natural processes, but "Loss wins in both cases" misses the point. You could just as easily say, "Store wins in both cases"—the line is balanced and logical, even heartless, yet hardly unparaphrasable. The ocean's estate is increased by whatever the shore loses, and the ocean's loss exactly measured by the increasing shore. Vendler seems to have forgotten the old saw "My loss is your gain."

Though every reader of the sonnets must be allowed mistakes, it's disturbing that a critic good at attentions is so guilty of inattention. The second quatrain of sonnet 96 is an elaborate metaphor for the youth's sins—what might seem "faults" in others are made "graces" in him:

As on the finger of a thronèd queen
The basest jewel will be well esteemed
So are those errors that in thee are seen
To truths translated, and for true things deemed.

Vendler, in contrived fashion, sees this as a metaphor not just for the youth but for style in sonnets:

> The queen is a respectable queen, whose essence is unimpugnable; but her ornament is contemptible, both in itself and in its effect. One might say that analogically the queen represents estimable matter adorned with debased tropes. The underlying question is why the queen would lend herself to such a hoodwinking of her subjects, who think her ring valuable only because it is on her finger.

The queen isn't necessarily "respectable" or "estimable"—she's only "thronèd." Her power, not her qualities, makes an otherwise worthless jewel esteemed. Neither can she be said to "hoodwink" her subjects; she's not responsible for how they value her jewels. Similarly, the youth, enthroned in the power of youth (later in the sonnet, the poet says, "If thou wouldst use the strength of all thy state"), may cause silly idiots to overrate his qualities, or to judge as qualities what are defects. Dethrone the queen (the youth will eventually be overthrown by age), and the jewels will be judged by their carats, not their caretaker. Besides, a queen may perhaps have good reason for wearing a cheap jewel—it may have sentimental value.

Vendler turns this, and the metaphor on "wolf" in the following quatrain, into an indictment of metaphor (it is ironic that the metaphors serve to damn their kind): "If bad, like the queen's ring, *they may* degrade virtue; if attractive, they may adorn vice." If so, the metaphors have outwitted her—revealing these faults, they've shown that metaphors have moral effect (we couldn't have seen these points except through the metaphors). The sonnet easily subverts her reading. Self-reflexive readings, where the poem seems to speak about poetry, are clever in the classroom; but on the page they're often self-indulgent.

Another problem with *The Art of Shakespeare's Sonnets* is the free-fall descent of the prose. For a critic so enamored of style, Vendler is curiously given to passages of cheerful gobbledygook:

> We now come [in sonnet 116], pursuing a reading for difference, to a reinscription in the poem of a previous pattern: the third quatrain repeats, in briefer form, the pattern of negative refutation followed by positive assertion which the preceding two quatrains had initiated. In this way, as reinscription, this quatrain initiates our sense of the poem as repetitive—as something that is reinscribing a structure which it has already used once . . . . But of course the hyperbolic, transcendent, and paradigmatic star is the casualty of the refutational reinscription contained in the third quatrain. The vertically conceived star cannot be reinscribed in the matrix of the métonymie hours and weeks of linear sublunary mortality.

The writing is much worse than the thinking, but the thinking is muddled by such writing. Part of what might be called her "vision statement" suggests that these poetic substructures "enact, by linguistic means, moves engaged in by the human heart and mind." *Moves? Moves engaged in?* Vendler has shown her eloquence often enough, but her recent style has too often become a critic's porridge. Even the passages beyond style can be airless and choked with information:

> The technical aim of the sonnet [151] is to enact appetite and orgasm The point of *orgasm—prize/ proud/pride*—especially needs concatenation. The *p's* obtrude themselves, beginning in *prove* and *part*, climaxing at *point, prize, proud,* and *pride*, and falling off in *poor* (with graphic reinforcement of *p* in *triumph* and *triumphant)*. The unstoppability of orgasm is certainly imitated here, with "ejaculation" occurring in the redundancy of *proud of this pride*; and orgasm is reinforced by the flurry of sounds reinforcing the phonemes of "rising," "raise," and "ride." . . . Detumescence is represented not only by the semantic decline from *proud* to *poor* but also from *tr-iu-mph* to *dr-udge*, words which, with their initial double consonants, triple final letters and common u in the middle, seem to be some sort of graphic cousins. Post-coital quiet comes in *con/[cunt]/ tented* . . .

This sonnet hardly lacks sexual play, but Vendler's overreading makes it an orgy. My quarrels with Vendler are not an indictment of method; bad methods may give good readings, and good methods hopeless ones. I'm grumbling because she wants to load every rift of the sonnet with meaning, to find meaning even among its accidents—in sonnet 27, for example, she invents the speaker's "jealousy" because she hears *jealous* as a "shadow-word" beneath *zealous* (a critic has pointed out to me that in the sonnets as elsewhere in Shakespeare the word is actually jealious). I'm grumbling because she makes meaning complex even when Shakespeare is simple—some of Shakespeare's richness is in his simplicity. In sonnets 66, and 71, and 92, Vendler decides the speaker wants to commit suicide. Suicide? When Shakespeare says, "Tired with all these, for restful death I cry" (66) and "No longer mourn for me when I am dead" (71), he's only expressing the Elizabethan version of Weltschmerz. A world-weary longing for death is not a suicide note—Vendler hears suicide threats almost as often as Duncan-Jones diagnoses venereal disease.

Vendler is hardly the first critic to find more in the sonnets than Shakespeare wrote—these poems have haunted our literature. Authors have trolled them for titles, and their phrases are the clichés of love: if an anxious parent did commission them, the children born would populate whole Londons. It may seem unfair that Shakespeare's sonnets have been re-edited dozens of times this century when you can't buy even one decent edition of poor Drayton's. The world is sonnet-mad only to the degree it is Shakespeare-mad. Poets still write sonnets, grim and even grand sonnets; but they know in their hearts their sonnets will never be as good as Shakespeare's.

For all their flaws and provocations, Shakespeare's sonnets remain one of the heroic achievements in the language, undertaken (like many heroic acts) for furtive, private reasons, unlike the rest of his public art. Each is only a hundred words or so, yet their compressive repetition exposes the poet's passion and fixation—we see in drama the tragedy of emotion over time (or its comedy through time), not the seeping, corrosive acid of emotion repeated (*Othello* comes closest). Dramas are directed toward one crucial act; but the sonnets act again and again, until we are exhausted by them, as the poet is exhausted by his varied loves. The pleasure of reading the sonnets is partly the pleasure of putting them down again, of leaving their cloistered interiors. The poems remind us how glorious the extremes of love can be and how relieved we are to abandon them.

Four Emendations and a Reading

Every critic should risk his judgment. Except as noted, none of the conjectures below is offered or defended in the standard editions, though it wouldn't be surprising if they had appeared, unknown to me, in

the vast secondary literature on the sonnets.

❧

And sable curls or siluer'd ore with white

This famous crux is usually emended "And sable curls all silvered o'er with white" (Booth, Kerrigan, Blakemore Evans, Duncan-Jones). This was Malone's emendation, though others have rung the changes: "o'er-silvered all," "are silvered o'er," "o'er-silvered are" (the line does not want a verb). Among recent editors, only Martin Seymour-Smith kept the Q reading, interpreting the line to mean the "golden tints in black hair silvered over with white" ("or" meaning gold in heraldry—but who before peroxide had black hair with gold tints?). "Ore" is the usual Q spelling of "o'er" (often in verb compounds: "ore-take," "ore-greene"), so the problems have been whether "or" is a misreading (of "are" or "all") and whether the two words were by accident transposed. Interpretation of the line in Q has foundered on heraldic use of "sable" and "or." Yet what if Shakespeare had in mind only a lump of silver ore (a spelling of "ore" being "or" in this period), brought back from Spanish mines in the Americas? "Ore" was not associated only with gold; it referred indifferently to ores of lead, brass, silver, and other metals (*OED:* "The oure that the Almaines had diged in a mine of silver," 1552). Shakespeare never used "or" in the heraldic sense; but in *All's Well That Ends Well* (3.6.40) we find "to what metal this counterfeit lump of ore will be melted" and in *Hamlet* "like some ore / Among a mineral of metals base." This reading would be less strained than Seymour-Smith's, the line meaning "black hair gone gray, like dark ore threaded with silver."

Read: *And sable curls ore silver'd o'er with white*

❧

But why thy odor matcheth not thy show.
The solye is this, that thou doest common grow.

The usual emendation is "soil" ("soyle"), first adopted by Benson in 1640. The transposition would be an easy mistake for the compositors, who reversed letters fitfully in Q; but the reading is awkward. There is no evidence of "soil" used as a noun to mean "explanation" or "answer," though there was the noun "assoil" (Shakespeare could just as easily have written, "Th' assoil is this . . .."). "Soil" has an attractive resonance with botanic terms, reaching allusively toward "stain" and "earth." Other emendations, to "solve" and "sole," are not convincing. Dover Wilson once proposed "sully" (in *The Manuscript of Shakespeare's Hamlet),* though he did not adopt it in his Cambridge edition of the sonnets. The extra syllable creates a problem. The sonnets are very conservative metrically: except for feminine endings, they don't admit extra syllables. The line would be possible only if read "The sully's this," on the analogy of 27.4 ("To work my mind, when body's work's expired") or 97.14 ("That leaves look pale, dreading the winter's near"). The conjecture has usually been dismissed because "sully" is not an attractive reading. Perhaps the manuscript read "folye," the crux due to a type-case error, a long *s* confused among the fs (the reverse of what apparently occurred at 152.14, which reads "fo" for "so"). "Folye" is a period spelling of "folly" (cf. "Haplye" at 29.10). If the previous line ended with a question mark (punctuation especially at line end being the concern of the printing house), the meaning would be obvious: "Why must you look gorgeous but stink of corruption? The folly is, you're growing common." The passage is reminiscent of 102.12 ("And sweets grown common lose their dear delight"), 121.12 ("By their rank thoughts my deeds must not be shown"), and particularly—note the rhymes—93.13-14 ("How like Eve's apple doth thy beauty grow, / If thy sweet virtue answer not thy show"). It would *be* folly for the young aristocrat, if such he was, to grow common by the common report of common tongues. Shakespeare's irony implies the folly is, their reports are *right*

Read: *But why thy odor matcheth not thy show? / The folly's this, that thou dost common grow.*

ꝫ

Bare rn'wd quiers, where late the sweet birds sang

This was emended by Benson in 1640 to what may be the most beautiful line in the sonnets, "Bare ruin'd choirs, where late the sweet birds sang." (Benson's spelling was "quires.") It may seem foolish to hazard any correction to a line altered to perfection, but the change assumes three errors by the compositor: misreading minims so *ui* was mistaken for *w,* transposing *n* and *w,* and misplacing the apostrophe (or two errors if he displaced *w* by

two characters). Alternatives long abandoned include "Barren'wed quiers" (Lintott) and "Barren'd of quires" (Capell). Perhaps the line actually read "Bare renewed choirs," which requires only a missed *e* by the compositor ("Bare r[e]n'wd quiers"). The *e* in the terminal "-ed" is often suppressed when unaccented (note especially "borrow'd," 153.5). For cases of dropped medial es, compare "lowrst" for "lower'st" at 149.7 and "scond" for "second" at 68.7. The spelling of "renewed" at 111.8 is "renu'de," scarcely less peculiar that "rn'wd." *Othello* (2.1.81) has the word in the same metrical position: "Give renew'd fire to our extincted spirits!" The line could still refer to ruined churches: the boughs year by year helplessly repeat the destruction and stripping of the monasteries. A less likely conjecture, because requiring more mistakes, would be "Barren wood choirs," the "wood" remarked because "choirs" (as opposed to choir stalls) were made of stone.

Read: *Bare renew'd choirs, where late the sweet birds sang*

ꝫ

Poore soule the center of my sinfull earth.
My sinfull earth these rebbell powres that thee array

Here, the compositor has made nonsense of the second line by repeating the last words of the first. Many corrections have been proposed, none particularly satisfying. Ingram and Redpath noted the four conditions for a successful emendation (two syllables, good sense, good Shakespearean sense, the words preferably used elsewhere by Shakespeare in the sense demanded here). They found nearly a hundred possibilities in Shakespeare's vocabulary. Past solutions have included "Fool'd by those" (Malone), "Starv'd by the" (conjecture, Steevens), and "Foil'd by" (Palgrave). Some editors, like Booth and Kerrigan, choose not to alter the line, replacing the repeated words with brackets or ellipsis. "Feeding," adopted by Vendler and Duncan-Jones, makes uninteresting sense, dissipating the sonnet's tensions by telegraphing the ending. ("Feeding" was originally a conjecture by Sebastian Evans and, later. Pooler. Duncan-Jones mysteriously attributes it to Vendler.) The feeding, finally a feeding on death in the couplet, is more dramatic if delayed. The lines require a word that anticipates the lexical solutions of the poem without merely duplicating them. The initial question ought to have more mystery—it's the mystery that keeps us reading. The missing word might imply collaboration with the rebel powers, connivance or fraternization with the enemy (the "rebel powers" besiege the soul). The meaning might be "Why are you mollifying these rebels surrounding you? Why spend resources prettying up the outside of your house for your enemy, when you're starving inside?" "Array" is cunningly ambiguous, calling up military siege and flare of fashion. (As if the soul were responding to one pretty "array" by painting her walls to match.) I suggest "Flattering," included by Ingram and Redpath among the scores of Shakespearean words that make sense in context. This word complicates the opening, clarifies the surrounding lines by an action sinful and gaudy, and delays the notion of "feeding" until the next quatrain.

> Read: *Poor soul, the center of my sinful earth, /*
> *Flatt'ring these rebel powers that thee array*

≈

> *And yet this time remou'd was sommers time.*
> *The teeming Autumne big with ritch increase.*
> *Bearing the wanton burthen of the prime*

The lines have caused much comment. Winter is invoked in the sonnet's opening ("How like a winter hath my absence been"); but the poet says that, though it felt like winter, the time of absence was "summer's time." Critics have had trouble aligning the various invocations of summer, autumn, and spring ("prime"). If the "teeming Autumn" is in apposition to "summer's time," the seasons are not quite themselves. Duncan-Jones claims the whole period from spring to harvest was considered summer and that summer is therefore autumn, too. Kerrigan argues that "summer's time" is not "summertime," but the "time when summer laboured to bear offspring," that is, autumn. (For Ingram and Redpath, who do not see the terms in apposition, the time of removal was by the calendar summer; the poet is writing in autumn, amid the bounty that summer promised.) What has been overlooked is that summer is personified as male (11: "For Summer and his pleasures wait on thee") and autumn as female, ready to give birth—they must have a differential relation. Summer and Autumn are not just seasons; they're personified mythological figures

who mated in spring. Summer's "time" is merely an epithet for Autumn—the season loved or taken sexually by Summer, possessed as a wife is possessed. Autumn *is* Summer's wife—they lie next to each other—but, when Autumn gives birth. Summer is gone, literally as a season but figuratively as a husband. Therefore Autumn is

> *Bearing the wanton burden of the prime,*
> *Like widowed wombs after their lords' decease:*
> *Yet this abundant issue seemed to me*
> *But hope of orphans, and unfathered fruit,*
> *For summer and his pleasures wait on thee.*

Autumn becomes a widow, and the children born after Summer is dead are "unfathered" orphans (they still have a mother). But Summer isn't really dead—he's off attending the fair youth. The sonnet manages wittily to invoke all the seasons in a small morality play, while looking toward the chill disappointment of winter.

William Logan

Notes

1. Catherine Duncan-Jones argues that, because only four copies of the 1609 Quarto of Troilus and Cressida survive, it "was three times as popular" as the Sonnets. This is an oddly mechanical argument. If, reading by reading, the rough hands of readers mash up a popular book (though rag-paper books can prove surprisingly durable) they also preserve books held in esteem and callously treat books despised. Numbers may tell us nothing: print runs may have been different, or some copies unsold or destroyed (fire, flood). Copies that survive usually survive by accident. Even if survival varied inversely with popularity, the few books remaining and the numerous variables would make precise estimate impossible. By her argument, most popular of all would be the Quarto of *Love's Labour's Won*, of which no copy survives.

2. The attending lords were meant to kiss ring or crown, so the kiss on the face (an amusing breach of decorum) was worth mentioning, as was the king's good nature. A kiss on the lips would have been so shocking, my correspondent Dr. Claude Luttrell believes that lips would then *certainly* have been mentioned. As lips were *not* mentioned, the kiss was probably, like a social kiss, to the cheek.

Reprinted from *Parnassus: Poetry in Review* 24, No. 1, pp. 250-280 by William Logan. Copyright © 1999 Parnassus.

Shakespeare (Not?) Our Contemporary: His Sonnets and More Recent Examples

Surely it is largely thanks to William Shakespeare that the sonnet has so long remained such a vital form not only of, but also in, English poetry. Shakespeare, after all, has long enjoyed more prestige than any other English–language author. Some might argue (and some indeed *have* argued) that his status results mainly from mere tradition: he is famous because he is famous. Others have maintained that he is widely valued because his status serves the interests of the powerful, who have long rejected more supposedly "subversive" voices. Most people would claim, however, that Shakespeare is so widely valued because his works are so valuable *as literature*—as writing interesting and powerful as writing. When we read Shakespeare, we often feel that he does things with the English language that few other authors can do or have done. Little wonder, then, that he has long inspired such enthusiasm among critics, scholars, teachers, students, and "ordinary" readers and audiences. For whatever reasons, Shakespeare often seems a still-living author—an idea implied in the title of Jan Kott's famous book *Shakespeare Our Contemporary*.

Shakespeare's status as a writer of sonnets is similar to his status as a writer of plays. If we search Google Books for the word "sonnet," Shakespeare's sonnets—editions, commentaries, companions, even "translations" into modern English—immediately appear. His sonnets are still widely read, both inside and outside the classroom. Contemporary poets who write sonnets are perhaps especially cognizant of Shakespeare's precedent as a sonnet-writer. It is hard to write a sonnet without thinking of Shakespeare's. Contemporary playwrights have many more recent models and precedents to follow and/or reject. But anyone today who sits down to compose a "modern" sonnet is very likely aware of *Shakespeare's* sonnets, which are by far the most famous and influential sonnets in English. As modern sonnet-writers compose their works, Shakespeare is always leaning over their shoulders. It is hard to ignore his looming presence.

I.

How have modern writers of sonnets coped with this situation? How have they responded to Shakespeare's influence and to their knowledge that their potential readers, as well as other modern poets, are likely to be highly familiar with Shakespeare the sonnet-writer?

One way to answer this question is to examine the sonnets reprinted in major modern anthologies of the sonnet form. Various such collections exist. They include (for instance) *The Making of a Sonnet: A Norton Anthology* (edited by Edward Hirsch and Eavan Boland). This book, more than five hundred pages long, unsurprisingly includes more sonnets by Shakespeare than by any other writer (only William Wordsworth even comes close to Shakespeare's total). The same is true of *The Penguin Book of the Sonnet* (edited by Phillis Levin). It includes three times as many sonnets by Shakespeare as are included in the Norton collection. In major recent anthologies of the sonnet, then—that is, in books specifically designed for readers with a strong interest in the sonnet form—Shakespeare remains the major voice.

The Penguin collection is especially valuable because it often reprints multiple sonnets by major modern writers, whereas the Norton anthology more typically reprints only one poem per modern poet. Thus, in the Norton collection, Marilyn Hacker is represented by a single poem, whereas in the Penguin anthology six of her sonnets appear. Likewise, in the Norton collection, Gwendolyn Brooks is represented by just one sonnet; in the Penguin collection, she is represented by seven. The Norton anthology reprints three poems by E. E. Cummings; the Penguin collection prints thirteen. The Penguin anthology, therefore, provides an especially useful overview of what has been happening to, with, and in sonnets lately and of how those developments are relevant to the precedents Shakespeare set.

II.

One fact most people know about Shakespeare's sonnets is that they have a distinctive rhyme scheme. Earlier sonnets, written and influenced by the Italian poet Francesco Petrarca (Petrarch), were divided into two parts consisting of eight lines and six lines. The rhyme scheme of the opening "octave" contained very few rhymes: a/b/b/a/a/b/b/a. (The "sestet" was more flexible, although it contained just three more rhymes, often organized as follows: c/d/e/c/d/e.) It is easier in Italian to use just a few rhymes than it is in English, and so Shakespeare's major innovation in the sonnet form was to loosen that form—to add more rhymes and to organize the poem into three four-line units (quatrains) followed by a closing couplet: a/b/a/b c/d/c/d/ e/f/e/f g/g. Yet however much Shakespeare departed from Petrarch both in rhyme scheme and in stanza structure, he—like Petrarch—stuck firmly to the rules he had set for himself. Rhyme strictly organized is crucial to Shakespearean sonnets.

Some modern poets have themselves consciously employed the Shakespearean sonnet form. By doing so, they have implicitly paid tribute both to Shakespeare and to other "Shakespearean" sonnet writers, even as they have also involved themselves in a kind of competition with these very same predecessors. By structuring their sonnets as Shakespeare structured his, they have set themselves a difficult challenge—one that fewer and fewer major modern poets have wanted (for various reasons) to confront.

If we examine the Penguin anthology and focus on the sonnet-writers it includes who were born in 1900 or later, we can see that relatively few of them have chosen to follow the strict rules of a Shakespearean sonnet. Although most of the older poets in this grouping do use rhyme schemes of some sort, only a handful obviously imitate Shakespeare. Edwin Denby (born 1903) does so in his sonnet titled "Air" (Levin 208), and so does Patrick Kavanagh (born 1904) in his sonnet titled "Canal Bank Walk" (Levin 209). Denby makes his echoes of Shakespeare especially apparent by using spacing to make the three quatrains and a couplet inescapably obvious. Like Kavanagh, however, Elliot Coleman (born 1906) uses the Shakespearean form in his sonnet "In a May evening" without calling any special attention to it (Levin 210). The same is true of the African American poet Countee Cullen (born 1903) in his sonnet "At the Wailing Wall in Jerusalem" (Levin 208).

A pattern that quickly emerges, however, involves the sheer number of writers who seem *at first* to be following the Shakespearean model but who then veer off in other directions. Thus, Roy Campbell (born 1907) writes

a sonnet titled "Luis de Camões" that begins in standard Shakespearean fashion: a/b/a/b c/d/c/d. But the sonnet then suddenly breaks with this familiar pattern: e/f/g/e/ f/g (Levin 206). Similarly, Countee Cullen's sonnet "Yet Do I Marvel" also echoes Shakespeare at first before breaking from him: a/b/a/b c/d/c/d e/e/ f/f/ g/g (Levin 207). Yet if the Penguin anthology is any indication, the really prominent modern poet who most enjoyed playing on (and playing with) the Shakespearean rhyme scheme was W. H. Auden (born 1907). Auden is represented by eight different sonnets in Levin's collection, all of which begin by seeming at first to echo Shakespeare (a/b/a/b). Sometimes the expected second quatrain appears (c/d/ c/d), but sometimes the second quatrain already shows significant variations (including c/d/d/c in "Montaigne" and a/c/c/a in "The Door" [Levin 211, 213]). It is in his final six lines, however, that Auden seems most restlessly inventive. "Who's Who" ends with e/f/g/g/f/e; "Our Bias" and "Montaigne" end with e/f/e/g/f/g; "Rimbaud" ends with e/f/g/f/e/g; "Brussells in Winter" (which combines Petrarchan and Shakespearean patterns in its first eight lines) ends with e/f/g/g/e/f; and the poem beginning "And the age ended" has an unusual pattern all the way through: a/b/b/a/c/d/d/c/e/f/e/g/g/e (Levin 210-14). On the evidence of these sonnets, Auden was one of the most consistently experimental of the major twentieth-century sonnet writers who chose to use rhyme. Auden often begins by glancing over his shoulder at Shakespearean precedents and then quickly moves off in new directions all his own.

If the Penguin anthology is a reliable guide, then relatively few significant sonnet-writers born in the twentieth century who have used rhyme have used a purely Shakespearean rhyme scheme. Thom Gunn (born 1929) uses it in "Keats at Highgate" (Levin 252); Robert Mezey (born 1935) uses it in a poem titled "Hardy" (Levin 264); June Jordan (born 1936) uses it in "Sunflower Sonnet Number Two" (Levin 266); and Henry Taylor (born 1942) uses three quatrains and a couplet in "Green Springs the Tree" (although his rhymes are near rhymes rather than exact [Levin 287]). Eavan Bolland writes a beautiful near-Shakespearean sonnet in "Yeats in Civil War" (Levin 290). Ironically, then, an Irish poet writes about another Irish poet in a poem about Ireland while using the standard "English" sonnet rhyme scheme.

Marilyn Nelson (born 1946) uses a basically Shakespearean rhyme scheme (sometimes rejecting exact rhymes) in three sonnets reprinted in the Penguin collection (Levin 296-97). Molly Peacock (born 1947) definitely uses the scheme in one sonnet ("Desire") of the five sonnets by her reprinted by Levin, and she uses it with some significant (and effective) variation in another of the five ("The Lull"; Levin 298-300). Floyd Skoot (born 1947) also uses it (Levin 301). But the last major modern poet in the Penguin anthology who is represented by a Shakespearean sonnet is Carol Ann Duffy (born 1955). Her splendid poem titled "Prayer" is even broken, on the page, into three quatrains and a couplet (Levin 322). The fact that England's current poet laureate saw fit at one point in her career to write a Shakespearean sonnet somehow seems highly appropriate.

III.

Why have relatively few major modern poets used the Shakespearean rhyme scheme? Several possible reasons suggest themselves. Perhaps that rhyme scheme is *so* familiar to *so many* readers that using it might seem hackneyed and uninventive. Perhaps to write as Shakespeare wrote might seem to risk what Harold Bloom has famously called "the anxiety of influence"—the worry that one can never measure up to a famous predecessor's accomplishments, especially if that predecessor is Shakespeare. Neither of these concerns, however, seems to have prevented a surprising number of major modern poets from using the Petrarchan rhyme scheme. John Berryman, for instance, uses the Petrarchan pattern in each of the six selections from *Berryman's Sonnets* that are included in the Penguin anthology (Levin 221-23). The same is true (allowing for just a bit of inexact rhyme) in five of the six sonnets by Hayden Carruth that Levin reprints (234-37). Sylvia Plath's sonnet titled "Mayflower" is Petrarchan (Levin 262). Three of the six sonnets by Marilyn Hacker included in Levin's collection follow a clear Petrarchan pattern (278-81). Finally, one of the three poems reprinted from Mark Jarman's *Unholy Sonnets* is Petrarchan (the other two are not [Levin 312-13]).

In short, if Levin's anthology is anywhere close to being representative, Petrarch's rhyme scheme has been almost as attractive to modern English-language poets as Shakepeare's rhyme scheme has been (if not more so, if whole sequences, such as Berryman's, are included). These results seem counter-intuitive. After all, isn't Shakespeare's scheme useful precisely *because* it is harder to rhyme in English than in Italian? Isn't Petrarch's form even *more* demanding and restrictive than

Shakespeare's? Why, then, is Petrarch's form so commonly used by major modern English-language poets?

One suspects that the trouble may involve the Shakespearean sonnet couplet—the way Shakespeare's sonnets end with two rhyming lines that, even in Shakespeare's poems themselves, can sometimes seem too tidy and neat, too emphatically conclusive. By contrast, Petrarch's six-line sestet can seem more flexible and open, less formulaic. And if there is any trend that seems reflected in most of the modern sonnets included in Levin's collection, it is a trend toward flexibility, freedom, and a rejection of conventional restrictions, both in structure and in subject matter. Ironically, if Petrarch has sometimes seemed a surprisingly attractive model for modern sonneteers, it may be because the final Shakespearean couplet seems too tight and tidy. Modern sonnet writers (like modern poets in general) tend to emphasize the complexities, complications, ambiguities, and sheer messiness of life in ways that may make a quick, abrupt summary or epigrammatic commentary often seem inappropriate.

IV.

The most pertinent fact about the formal features of the "modern" sonnets Levin reprints is how varied their forms often seem. Many of the poems do not rhyme at all; some rhyme only in part; some rely on rhymes that are only approximate or inexact. In the twentieth and twenty-first centuries, sonnet writing has been a far more flexible and open-ended, far less restrictive and restricted kind of writing than it had been in the past. If the modern age has been the age of individualism, freedom, and personal self-expression, those traits have definitely been reflected in the sonnets the age has produced. Shakespeare, like most poets of his age, set himself a specific challenge and then went about meeting the demands he had embraced. In his use of rhyme as well as in his use of meter, he played by a certain set of clear, conventional rules. Doing so was part of the whole point of writing poetry in his day. To write sonnets without using a definite rhyme scheme and meter would probably have struck Shakespeare much as using free verse struck Robert Frost, who likened it to playing tennis with the net down. The rhyme scheme and meter of a Shakespearean sonnet (or of any other kind of traditional sonnet) make the poet's job fairly exacting. Simply put, more modern poets have usually wanted more freedom. Many of them have not wanted to follow rigid rules.

If we examine the Penguin anthology for sonnets written by poets born in 1900 or later, certain patterns quickly emerge. First is the enormous number of rhyme schemes invented or employed; second is the fact that many poets abandoned rhyme altogether; third is a tendency to vary the lengths of sonnets, often going beyond the conventional fourteen lines; and fourth is a tendency to vary even the lengths of lines themselves, using either more or less than the standard ten syllables per line, sometimes in fairly unpredictable ways.

Yvor Winters is the first poet included in Levin's collection who was born in 1900. Although Winters is often considered a highly conservative writer, the sonnet by him included by Levin ("To Emily Dickinson") follows neither the Shakespearean nor the Petrarchan rhyme schemes (a/b/b/a a/c/c/a d/e/d/e/f/f [Levin 206]). A sonnet by Merrill Moore (born 1903) is even more idiosyncratic (a/a b/b/c c/d c/a d/d/e/e/d/d/d [Levin 208]), and a sonnet by Stephen Spender (born 1909) is also obviously inventive (a/b/a/b/c/a/c/a/d/e/d/e/d/e [Levin 216]). The same is true of a sonnet by Elizabeth Bishop (born 1911: a/b/a/c/d/b/c/e/d/f/e/f/f/f), and the sonnet that immediately follows that work (as part of the same poem) is even less conventional (a/b/a/c/d/b/e/c/f/e/d/f/g/h). It would be easy to continue listing an extraordinary number of different kinds of rhyme schemes that have been adopted or invented by sonnet writers of the twentieth century and beyond, and it would be even easier to list the number of modern sonnet writers who have abandoned rhyme altogether. This, then, is the major difference between Shakespeare's sonnets and more recent ones: he lived in an age in which poets demonstrated their talent by mastering conventions; we live in an age in which conventions are often seen as dull, stifling, or bothersome. They often seem to fail to do justice to the complexities of actual experience. Of course, *some* modern poets (as has already been demonstrated) do employ conventional forms, but the choice to do so is entirely theirs. They are under no great cultural pressure to use obvious patterns. Lyric poets in Shakespeare's age were generally expected to use rhyme and other clear formal devices; poets today are under no such obligations, and indeed, rhyme, meter, and other predictable designs have often been considered (at least by some) retrograde or reactionary—signs not of talent or skill but of mere uninventiveness.

V.

The major modern poets who *have* imitated or echoed Shakespeare in their own sonnets provide us with the opportunity not only to assess their own achievements but also to compare and contrast their works with his.

One very important writer of modern sonnets was E. E. Cummings. Although born before 1900 (in 1894), he seems worth discussing here for several reasons. First, he wrote many, many sonnets and clearly labeled them as such. Few modern poets have been more openly interested in the sonnet form than Cummings. Second, Cummings was one of the most self-consciously radical and experimental of all modern poets. Although much older than a poet like, say, Richard Wilbur (born 1921), Cummings seems far more "youthful" in the sense of being unconventional, innovative, and daring, both in content and especially in form. Third, although Cummings is technically a "modern" poet, he might easily be described as "postmodern": his innovations continue to seem so path-breaking (if not even sometimes bizarre) that he seems almost an honorary citizen of the twenty-first century, even though he died in 1962.

One of Cummings' most famous "Shakespearean" sonnets is this untitled poem:

> i carry your heart with me(i carry it in
> my heart)i am never without it(anywhere
> i go you go,my dear;and whatever is done
> by only me is your doing,my darling)
>   i fear
> no fate(for you are my fate,my sweet)i want
> no world(for beautiful you are my world,my true)
> and it's you are whatever a moon has always meant
> and whatever a sun will always sing is you
>
> here is the deepest secret nobody knows
> (here is the root of the root and the bud of the bud
> and the sky of the sky of a tree called life;which grows
> higher than soul can hope or mind can hide)
> and this is the wonder that's keeping the stars apart
>
> i carry your heart(i carry it in my heart)

Many aspects of this poem seem "Shakespearean" besides its clearly Shakespearean rhyme scheme (although Cummings' rhymes are often deliberately inexact). Like many of Shakespeare's sonnets, this one deals prominently with the topic of love. It relies, as

Shakespeare's poems often do, on emphatic repetition of words and phrases in general as well as on the use of anaphora (repetition of words and phrases at the very beginnings of lines). The phrasing and syntax here are less confusing, more straightforward, more obviously "logical" than is often the case in Cummings' poems, and so this poem resembles Shakespeare's in those respects more than is often the case in Cummings' verse. The typographical oddities in this poem are so minor and relatively meaningless that they almost seem affectations: does it really matter much that Cummings omits spaces between some words and some punctuation marks? It is as if Cummings wanted this poem to seem stranger and more unusual in its incidentals than its rather straightforward meanings would justify. The poem is far more conventional in what it says than in how it is made to appear. In its wordplay, wittiness, coherence, and ultimate symmetry, it is quite Shakespearean indeed. There are moments, in fact, when we wonder if Cummings is perhaps pulling our legs (especially in the phrases "my dear," "my darling," "my sweet," and "my true")—as if he is engaged in self-mockery and parody rather than being completely serious. This effect, however, seems part of the poem's over-all wit, and wit is a very typical feature of many of Shakespeare's own sonnets.

It would be hard to imagine poets more different than E. E. Cummings and Gwendolyn Brooks. Cummings was white, privileged (his father was a Harvard professor and prominent minister), well-connected, and Harvard-educated. Brooks was black, poor (her father was a janitor), relatively isolated socially, and a graduate of Wilson Junior College. Yet Brooks, like Cummings, was an innovative poet who nevertheless turned sometimes to Shakespeare as an inspiration when she wrote sonnets. Some of her most intriguing efforts in the sonnet form are poems from a sequence of sonnets titled *Gay Chaps at the Bar*, written to commemorate the return of American soldiers—especially black soldiers—from World War II. One of these poems is titled "my dreams, my works, must wait till after hell:"

> *I hold my honey and I store my bread*
> *In little jars and cabinets of my will.*
> *I label clearly, and each latch and lid*
> *I bid, Be firm till I return from hell.*
> *I am very hungry. I am incomplete.*
> *And none can tell when I may dine again.*
> *No man can give me any word but Wait,*
> *The puny light. I keep eyes pointed in;*

> *Hoping that, when the devil days of my hurt*
> *Drag out to their last dregs and I resume*
> *On such legs as are left me, in such heart*
> *As I can manage, remember to go home,*
> *My taste will not have turned insensitive*
> *To honey and bread old purity could love.*

As in the Cummings poem already quoted, the rhymes here are inexact, but the Shakespearean rhyme scheme is nevertheless clear. By using Shakespeare's scheme without committing themselves to precise rhymes, Cummings, Brooks, and other modern poets allude to Shakespeare's practice while allowing themselves far more flexibility and freedom than Shakespeare himself enjoyed. Cummings, Brooks, and other such poets thus seem simultaneously conventional and innovative: aware of tradition but not bound to it in any slavish ways.

The fact that Brooks uses her poem to adopt the voice of a male soldier already suggests one way in which modern Shakespearean sonnets often differ from the sonnets written by Shakespeare himself. Shakespeare's poems are often read as if they are autobiographical, as if he speaks in his own voice. Whether or not this assumption makes sense, it has certainly seemed plausible to many readers. Cummings' poem (already quoted) can also be read as a personal expression of Cummings himself. Brooks, however, in these "*Gay Chaps* poems," clearly adopts a voice or voices that are not her own. She also innovates in her subject matter. Cummings' poem, after all, is a poem (like so many of Shakespeare's) about love. Brooks, however, writes from the perspective of a man (a *black* man) at war. In this respect her poem illustrates the ways in which many modern poets have used the sonnet form in general (and the Shakespearean sonnet form in particular) to write about practically *anything*, using practically any imaginable voice or point of view. Brooks's *Gay Chaps* sonnets are, in this sense, far more obviously "dramatic" than the sonnets written by the world's greatest dramatist. Modern sonnet writers are bound to no traditional topics, stances, meanings, or moods. They can write Shakespearean sonnets about literally anything, in ways that Shakespeare himself (ironically) could not. Shakespeare, for instance, could never have written a sonnet openly espousing atheism or conversion to Islam (or even Catholicism, for that matter). He lived in a society in which there were clear limits to self-expression. Poets today, writing in the style of Shakespeare, are far freer to say whatever they want to say.

Eavan Boland, another modern author very interested in sonnets, also sometimes writes in the Shakespearean sonnet style. Boland combines some of the personal traits of both Cummings and Brooks while also, of course, having her own distinctive identity. A woman born into an Irish family, Boland is in both senses a member of "minority" groups. Yet her family was socially prominent and she herself was well educated in ways not true of Brooks. As a self-consciously Irish writer, Boland is precisely the sort of poet who would interest so-called "post-colonial" critics. Thus it is not surprising that the single poem by her included in the Penguin anthology is titled "Yeats in Civil War." It alludes to Ireland's greatest twentieth-century poet and the battles the Irish fought amongst themselves in 1922-23 after having just achieved independence from Britain.

> *In middle age you exchanged the sandals*
> *Of a pilgrim for a Norman keep*
> *in Galway. Civil war started. Vandals*
> *Sacked your country, made off with your sleep.*
>
> *Somehow you arranged your escape*
> *Aboard a spirit ship which every day*
> *Hoisted sail out of fire and rape.*
> *On that ship your mind was stowaway.*
>
> *The sun mounted on a wasted place.*
> *But the wind at every door and turn*
> *Blew the smell of honey in your face*
> *Where there was none.*
>   *Whatever I may learn*
> *You are its sum, struggling to survive—*
> *A fantasy of honey your reprieve.*

Unlike Cummings and Brooks, Boland's rhymes are almost completely perfect and exact (except in the final couplet). She breaks the poem clearly into quatrains (although here again there is some slight variation, in line 12). Using a form associated with perhaps the greatest English poet, she pays tribute to perhaps the greatest Irish poet. She explores the irony that this great Irish writer was, in a sense, victimized by some of the Irish people he had done so much to serve, both in his literature and through his outspoken political efforts. Boland's poem is public and political in ways that Shakespeare's sonnets never are. Addressing Yeats, she implicitly criticizes an earlier generation of Irish people

in ways that are perhaps relevant to continuing conflicts among some Irish people (especially Catholics and Protestants) during her own lifetime. In any case, her poem shows how Shakespearean sonnets in the modern period might explicitly address political and historical issues in ways that Shakespeare's own sonnets tended not to do.

Finally, one last modern author of a contemporary Shakespearean sonnet seems worth mentioning. Carol Ann Duffy is not only the first female English poet to be appointed Poet Laureate (one of the nation's highest honors) but is also the first lesbian poet to enjoy that distinction. Duffy is widely considered one of the pre-eminent contemporary poets writing in English. Duffy's single poem in the Penguin collection is clearly formatted as a Shakespearean sonnet and is indeed the only "Shakespearean" sonnet really examined here to use a perfectly exact rhyme scheme. The final line alludes to the "shipping forecast." This has been broadcast daily on the BBC radio since the 1920s. It is essentially a list of weather conditions in various regions of the sea, but many Britons apparently find listening to it hypnotically soothing.

> *Some days, although we cannot pray, a prayer*
> *utters itself. So, a woman will lift*
> *her head from the sieve of her hands and stare*
> *at the minims sung by a tree, a sudden gift.*
>
> *Some nights, although we are faithless, the truth*
> *enters our hearts, that small familiar pain;*
> *then a man will stand stock-still, hearing his youth*
> *in the distant Latin chanting of a train.*
>
> *Pray for us now. Grade 1 piano scales*
> *console the lodger looking out across*
> *a Midlands town. Then dusk, and someone calls*
> *a child's name as though they named their loss.*
>
> *Darkness outside. Inside, the radio's prayer—*
> *Rockall. Malin. Dogger. Finisterre.*

Doing justice to this poem would require much space, but one can briefly note its solid structure, especially the way the second quatrain echoes, with variations, the content and organization of the first). Like many of Shakespeare's own poems, this one is controlled by a central idea (prayer) while also seeming continually inventive. It is a meditative poem, providing further evidence—if any were needed—that the Shakespearean sonnet can be used today for almost any purpose and can be written in almost any style. The final couplet, far from seeming neat and tidy, suddenly seems to expand the geographical range of the poem far beyond a predictable English landscape. It also plays one final clever variation on the idea of prayer. The words of the final line can seem so random as to seem pointless in ways that was never true of traditional prayers. But those words can also seem deeply comforting to those who know the tradition to which Duffy alludes.

Surely Shakespeare himself would be proud of a poem like this and of the rich legacy he bequeathed to English verse and the many rich works his example has inspired and continues to evoke.

Robert C. Evans

Works Cited

Bloom, Harold. *The Anxiety of Influence: A Theory of Poetry.* 2nd ed. Oxford: Oxford UP, 1997.

Hirsch, Edward and Eavan Boland. *The Making of a Sonnet: A Norton Anthology.* New York: Norton, 2008.

Levin, Phillis, ed. *The Penguin Book of the Sonnet: 500 Years of a Classic Tradition in English.* New York: Penguin, 2001.

Close Readings of 25 Sonnets

Sonnet 1

From fairest creatures we desire increase,
That thereby beauty's rose might never die,
But as the riper should by time decease,
His tender heir might bear his memory:
But thou contracted to thine own bright eyes,
Feed'st thy light's flame with self-substantial fuel,
Making a famine where abundance lies,
Thy self thy foe, to thy sweet self too cruel:
Thou that art now the world's fresh ornament,
And only herald to the gaudy spring,
Within thine own bud buriest thy content,
And, tender churl, mak'st waste in niggarding:
   Pity the world, or else this glutton be,
   To eat the world's due, by the grave and thee.

Abstract

Sonnet 1 introduces the conventional themes of beauty, love, aging, reproduction, and legacy, which reemerge as central themes in Shakespeare's entire sonnet sequence. Yet, by addressing a beloved young man and encouraging procreation over chastity, Sonnet 1 departs from the sonnet conventions of Shakespeare's time.

Keywords

- Abundance
- Age
- Beauty
- Confessional Poetry
- Contrast
- Desire
- Iambic Pentameter
- Marriage
- Mortality
- Procreation

Context

The first sonnet in Shakespeare's 154-sonnet sequence is in many ways thoroughly conventional and yet deeply subversive. The poem's central themes and images invoke such well-known Western literary tropes as love, beauty, mortality, and aging. Yet, by addressing the sonnet to a beloved but then encouraging him to marry another and procreate, the sonnet subverts the conventions that characterized love poetry of the time.

Both structurally and thematically, the sonnet proceeds through contrasts. In the first quatrain, the speaker praises the man's beauty and claims that human desire for reproduction is intensified in the face of the "fairest creatures" (line 1), whose beauty implies a privileged evolutionary status but also a greater duty to reproduce, so that "his tender heir might bear his memory" (4). In the second and third quatrains, the speaker shifts his tone to criticize the beloved for failing to act upon this reproductive imperative. The speaker accuses his beloved of self-absorption, stating, "But thou, contracted to thine own bright eyes, / Feed'st thy light's flame with self-substantial fuel" (5-6). The beloved here is likened to a candle whose lifetime is waning and who is selfishly consuming his own life essence. This image launches a series of contrasts; the outcome of his refusal to procreate is famine in the context of abundance, making him a cruel foe to his own sweet self. The speaker reminds the young man that although he is now "the world's fresh ornament" (9), with time, his beauty will wither within him without being passed on to future generations. He then warns the young man that he is selfishly hoarding his beauty to himself and, paradoxically, "makest waste in niggarding" (12) by saving his chastity. The final couplet counters the earlier mention of famine by saying that, should the beloved choose not to pity the world and never produce offspring, he is nothing more than a glutton eating what he owes to the world, "the world's due" (14).

The themes of beauty, love, aging, reproduction, and legacy and their accompanying images reappear throughout the sonnet sequence, so that this first sonnet acts as an introduction to the whole collection, particularly the first seventeen sonnets, which are collectively known as the "procreation sonnets." The related themes of procreation and mortality were well established in the English literary tradition by Shakespeare's time. The biblical book of Genesis, for example, commands humans to increase and multiply. The speaker's accusations of gluttony and covetousness also refer to the capital vices, which are based in Christian theology.

The praise of a beloved's beauty and exhortation to act properly are central elements of the French and Italian courtly lyric tradition that Shakespeare inherited. This inheritance is evident in details such as the sonnet's conventional address of "beauty's rose" in the first line.

The sonnets of fourteenth-century Italian poet Frances Petrarch, which alternately praise and blame his beloved, Laura, popularized the sonnet form throughout Western Europe. These sonnets heavily influenced Shakespeare's poetry, particularly Sonnet 1, with its paradoxical contrasts as noted above, which were a prominent feature in the love poetry of Petrarch. By Shakespeare's time, the love sonnet was well established in English literature by writers such as Thomas Wyatt and the Earl of Surrey. Philip Sidney, with his sonnet sequence *Astrophel and Stella*, also popularized the genre in the 1590s.

In this context, however, Shakespeare's treatment is remarkably unconventional in that the speaker addresses a beloved young man rather than a woman and urges him to marry another. While the sonnet introduces the whole sequence, it also belongs to its own subgroups. The first 126 sonnets in Shakespeare's sonnet sequence are all addressed to an unnamed young man, known as the "Fair Youth," and in Sonnets 1 through 17, the speaker urges the young man to marry and have children. This exhortation to procreate was a surprising one for the time and for the genre, given that sonnets typically praised beauty and urged chastity. Moreover, as literary critic Helen Vendler points out in her book *The Art of Shakespeare's Sonnets*, the images used to describe the man also derive from different categories: while the terms "foe," "glutton," and "churl" all imply a human, the rose and bud are organic and the candle's light fed by its own fuel implies an inorganic metaphor (48). This deliberate use of dissonant metaphors "presses the reader into reflection; and this technique, recurrent throughout the sonnets, is the chief source of their intellectual provocativeness" (Vendler 48).

The themes of beauty, mortality, and reproduction have been popular throughout the ages, but procreation has taken on particularly rich significance in twentieth-century literature. In particular, the refusal to procreate has flourished as a theme in modern poetry, perhaps most notably in T. S. Eliot's 1922 poem *The Waste Land*, whose central theme of barrenness evolves into a metaphor for the despair of modernity. Contemporary poets such as Sharon Olds have moved on to treat the theme of procreation in the context of female sexuality and in more celebratory terms. Shakespeare's work thus provided an important model for modern artists who address timeless themes with original perceptions and inventive approaches.

Ashleigh Imus

Works Cited

Evans, G. Blakemore, ed. *The Riverside Shakespeare*. Boston: Houghton, 1974.

Schoenfeldt, Michael. *A Companion to Shakespeare's Sonnets*. Malden: Blackwell, 2007.

Vendler, Helen. *The Art of Shakespeare's Sonnets*. Cambridge: Belknap, 1997.

For Further Study

Bloom, Harold, ed. *William Shakespeare's Sonnets*. New York: Chelsea, 1987.

Callaghan, Dympna. *Shakespeare's Sonnets*. Malden: Blackwell, 2007.

Schiffer, James, ed. *Shakespeare's Sonnets: Critical Essays*. New York: Garland, 1999.

Sonnet 18

Shall I compare thee to a summer's day?
Thou art more lovely and more temperate:
Rough winds do shake the darling buds of May,
And summer's lease hath all too short a date:
Sometime too hot the eye of heaven shines,
And often is his gold complexion dimmed,
And every fair from fair sometime declines,
By chance, or nature's changing course untrimmed:
But thy eternal summer shall not fade,
Nor lose possession of that fair thou ow'st,
Nor shall death brag thou wander'st in his shade,
When in eternal lines to time thou grow'st,
  So long as men can breathe, or eyes can see,
  So long lives this, and this gives life to thee.

Abstract

Perhaps the most famous love poem in English literature, Sonnet 18 is a powerful poem on the ability of art to preserve beauty through the ages. Beauty in the natural world fades with time, but artists through the ages have celebrated the ability of their work to capture life's most fleeting and alluring moments, rendering them unchanging and eternal in art.

Keywords

- Age
- Art/Artists
- Beauty
- Eternity
- Hyperbole
- Iambic Pentameter
- Mortality
- Poetry

Context

One of the best-known sonnets, Sonnet 18 is concerned both with the beauty of the young man it addresses and the poem's ability to capture and preserve his beauty. The sonnet begins with the suggestion of a whimsical comparison—that the youth looks as lovely as a summer's day. This comparison, however, is found lacking; the young man is said to be even fairer than the idealization of summer, as summer days inevitably grow shorter and harsher as the season ends. This comparison establishes the structure of the first twelve lines of the poem, as the fanciful first thought is heightened into hyperbole until the speaker broaches the subject of death. With the coming cold of winter acknowledged, the closing couplet asserts that the youth is in fact superior to summer because his beauty will last forever, as it has been captured by and preserved in the sonnet. As long as people live, the final couplet claims, this verse will keep the young man's allure alive. The sonnet itself, then, is able to undo the progression toward death that began with the first dreamy comparison.

Sonnet 18 is categorized with the first 126 sonnets in Shakespeare's sonnet sequence, which all address an unnamed young man known as the Fair Youth. However, Sonnet 18 marks an important turning point in the sonnet sequence's treatment of the Fair Youth, who is suddenly regarded with a more romantic love than in the first seventeen poems, which are known collectively as the "procreation sonnets." Sonnets 1 through 17 consistently argue the merits of marriage and fatherhood, urging the young man to find a wife and to continue his legacy and preserve his beauty in future generations through procreation. In Sonnet 18, however, the speaker himself finds a way for the young man's legacy and beauty to endure through poetry.

This impassioned belief in the lasting power of art was a popular theme in the work of nineteenth-century Romantic poets, whose poetry was often characterized by hyperbolic statements similar to that which Shakespeare employs in Sonnet 18. For example, John Keats's "Ode on a Grecian Urn" (1819), one of the most famous Romantic poems, focuses on the questions raised by art's eternal potential. The poem's speaker praises the scenes painted on an urn both because of their beauty and because that beauty, made permanent on the vase, will never fade. The art is superior to nature, as he declares, "Ah, happy, happy boughs! that cannot shed / Your leaves, nor ever bid the Spring adieu" (lines 21–22). As with Sonnet 18, the joy here is twofold. In part, it rises from enjoying the beauty of the object itself (the Fair Youth and the urn). Yet, as enthralled as both poets are with beauty, they are perhaps more excited that they have managed to find a way to make that beauty endure. Keats and other Romantics (such as Percy Bysshe Shelley in his 1818 poem "Ozymandias") did consider some potential downfalls to this sense of eternal art—flaws that are not explored in the amorous Sonnet 18. However, the joy and ecstasy of beauty, particularly the artist's satisfaction at capturing or replicating beauty in art or literature, remain consistent.

Just as Shakespeare and Keats suggest art can make beauty eternal, so too do artists working the modern medium of filmmaking use their work to preserve the glamour and allure of young love. For example, the trilogy of romantic films titled *Before Sunrise* (1995), *Before Sunset* (2004), and *Before Midnight* (2013) also play off of this idea. In the first film, a young man and a young woman meet while on vacation and decide to spend one romantic day together, enraptured by the optimism of their youth and each other's beauty. In the sequel, however, nine years have passed without them seeing each other, and the young man has written a book about their affair. Reconnected, the romantic story he captured forever in the book must face the reality of the actual woman, now older and changed by her life.

In Sonnet 18, the Fair Youth is still like the main characters of these films, with his innocence and beauty idealized. The beloved in the sonnet and these films ultimately do change, shaken by the "rough winds" (3) of life. Even so, the works of art remain, and just as the sonnet's couplet promises, the beauty of the Fair Youth continues to inspire today, his flawless good looks only outdone by the gorgeous sonnet that keeps his memory alive.

T. Fleischmann

Works Cited

Before Sunrise. Dir. Richard Linklater. Perf. Ethan Hawke and Julie Delpy. Castle Rock Entertainment, 1995. Film.

Booth, Stephen, ed. *Shakespeare's Sonnets*. By William Shakespeare. New Haven: Yale UP, 1977.

Keats, John. "Ode on a Grecian Urn." *John Keats: The Complete Poems*. New York: Penguin, 1997.

Shakespeare, William. "Sonnets 18." *Complete Works of William Shakespeare*. Fairbanks: Project Gutenberg Literary Archive Foundation, 2006. *Literary Reference Center*. Web. 10 Apr. 2014. <http://search.ebscohost.com/login.aspx?direct=true&db=lfh&AN=22968934&site=ehost-live>.

Thorp, Burt. "Ode on a Grecian Urn." *Masterplots*. 4th ed. Ed. Laurence W. Mazzeno. Pasadena: Salem, 2010. *Literary Reference Center*. Web. 10 Apr. 2014. <http://search.ebscohost.com/login.aspx?direct=true&db=lfh&AN=103331MP423919820000708&site=ehost-live>.

For Further Study

Lord, Russell. "Sonnet 18." *Masterplots II: Poetry* (2002): 1–2. *Literary Reference Center*. Web. 10 Apr. 2014. <http://search.ebscohost.com/login.aspx?direct=true&db=lkh&AN=103331POE21389650000609&site=lrc-plus>.

Vendler, Helen. *The Art of Shakespeare's Sonnets*. Cambridge: Belknap, 1999.

Sonnet 19

Devouring Time, blunt thou the lion's paws,
And make the earth devour her own sweet brood;
Pluck the keen teeth from the fierce tiger's jaws,
And burn the long-lived phoenix in her blood;
Make glad and sorry seasons as thou fleet'st,
And do whate'er thou wilt, swift-footed Time,
To the wide world and all her fading sweets;
But I forbid thee one most heinous crime:
O! carve not with thy hours my love's fair brow,
Nor draw no lines there with thine antique pen;
Him in thy course untainted do allow
For beauty's pattern to succeeding men.
  Yet, do thy worst old Time: despite thy wrong,
  My love shall in my verse ever live young.

Abstract

Sonnet 19, like many of his early sonnets, deals with the threat time and change pose to human beauty and love. This essay describes the speaker's responses to time, his efforts to defeat time by writing poetry, and the poem's implied concession that however much one may resist time's passage, its forward march is inevitable.

Keywords

- Age
- Beauty
- Death
- Love
- Time
- Youth

Context

Mutability is a theme common to sixteenth-century literature and Shakespeare's sonnets in general. Sonnet 19 in particular focuses on the idea that all physical things, including human beings, are subject to constant, often negative change. No earthly thing can escape change, and such change often involves deterioration and even death. In the grouping of sonnets addressed to a young man known as the Fair Youth—of which Sonnet 19 is a part—the speaker emphasizes mutability partly because the sonnets are designed to urge the young man to marry and have children. Doing so, the speaker maintains in these early sonnets, is one way to escape mutability, cheat death, and ensure that the young man's

beauty lives on through another generation. By Sonnet 19, however, the speaker has also begun to promise the young man a different kind of immortality: the immortality that comes with being celebrated in the speaker's poetry.

The speaker begins by personifying Time and describing it as "devouring" (line 1), suggesting already its destructive tendencies, almost as if it is a dangerous animal that feeds on its prey. Time, however, does not attack swiftly; rather, it poses a gradual danger. Through the change that comes with aging, the speaker implies, Time blunts a lion's paws, makes the earth kill the things that live upon it—its "own sweet brood" (2)—and plucks teeth from the jaws of fierce tigers. Even the mythical phoenix, the speaker laments, cannot escape the ravages of Time.

After the violent language of the first quatrain, the language of the second seems more subdued. Line 5 seems to allude to the passage from spring and summer to fall and winter. Time itself is described as quick-footed (it "fleet'st" [5]), but it also works gradually through the passage from one season to another—a "fading" (7) that involves the slow loss of the rich colors of life. In this second quatrain, Shakespeare suggests one of the paradoxes associated with time: its passage seems both slow and ever-quickening.

In the third quatrain and the concluding couplet, the speaker's metaphors mainly involve marking of various kinds, whether carving, drawing, or writing. The speaker asks Time to refrain from carving wrinkles or drawing lines of age in the young man's forehead (9). Although carving and drawing are often associated with the creation of beautiful works of art, in this case, carving or drawing would deface what is already beautiful.

Yet the speaker knows, as does the reader, that this request—or demand—is pointless. As with the immediately preceding sonnets, Sonnet 19 ends with a promise to immortalize the complete young man (not merely his beauty) through poetry. Time is itself dismissed as an "old" criminal (13), while the emphatic and significant final word of the poem is "young" (14).

Part of the irony of this poem is that the speaker spends much more time discussing Time and its destructive effects than describing the beauty of the young man. All the reader knows is that the youth is good-looking:

the speaker reveals no further details of his appearance. Thus, even as the poem dismisses Time, it also concedes Time's power. It implies the fear most humans have of mortality even while claiming that that fear can be defeated by great art. The speaker is in no real position to "forbid" (8) Time from marring the young man's appearance; instead the speaker can only compensate, in his art, for the damage Time will inevitably inflict upon the young man's beauty.

Defeating time has always been—and still remains—a major human concern and a key theme of much literature and art. Cosmetics are the most obvious means humans use as a kind of art intended to prevent the loss of beauty; dieting and physical workouts are two others. For centuries, people have relied on the visual arts of painting, sculpture, and photography to leave some permanent record of their youthful beauty. Shakespeare is perhaps the greatest literary artist ever to claim that beauty could be preserved through superb writing, though English poet Edmund Spenser made similar claims in some of his late *Amoretti* sonnets. The last three words of Shakespeare's sonnet almost foreshadow three modern pop songs (all titled "Forever Young") by Bob Dylan, Rod Stewart, and German synthpop group Alphaville, which express similar themes.

Robert C. Evans

Works Cited

Booth, Stephen, ed. *Shakespeare's Sonnets*. New Haven: Yale UP, 1977.

Duncan-Jones, Katherine, ed. *Shakespeare's Sonnets*. London: Nelson, 1997.

Edmondson, Paul, and Stanley Wells. *Shakespeare's Sonnets*. Oxford: Oxford UP, 2004.

Evans, G. Blakemore, ed. *The Sonnets*. By William Shakespeare. Cambridge: Cambridge UP, 1996.

Vendler, Helen. *The Art of Shakespeare's Sonnets*. Cambridge: Harvard UP, 1997.

For Further Study

Jungman, Robert E. "'Untainted' Crime in Shakespeare's Sonnet 19." *ANQ* 16.2 (2003): 19–21. *Literary Reference Center*. Web. 28 Apr. 2014. <http://search.ebscohost.com/login.aspx?direct=true&db=lfh&AN=9426538>.

Shakespeare, William. "Sonnet 19." *Shakespearian Sonnets. Poetry Reference Center*. Web. 28 Apr. 2014. <http://search.ebscohost.com/login.aspx?direct=true&db=prf&AN=23064424>.

Welsh, James M., and Jill Stapleton-Bergeron. "Sonnets of Shakespeare." *Magill's Survey of World Literature*. Rev. ed. Ed. Steven G. Kellman. Pasadena: Salem, 2009. Literary Reference Center. Web. 28 Apr. 2014. <http://search.ebscohost.com/login.aspx?direct=true&db=lfh&AN=103331MSW23359850001334>.

Sonnet 20

A woman's face with nature's own hand painted,
Hast thou, the master mistress of my passion;
A woman's gentle heart, but not acquainted
With shifting change, as is false women's fashion:
An eye more bright than theirs, less false in rolling,
Gilding the object whereupon it gazeth;
A man in hue all hues in his controlling,
Which steals men's eyes and women's souls
amazeth.
And for a woman wert thou first created;
Till Nature, as she wrought thee, fell a-doting,
And by addition me of thee defeated,
By adding one thing to my purpose nothing.
  But since she prick'd thee out for women's plea-
sure,
  Mine be thy love and thy love's use their treasure.

Abstract

Sonnet 20 grapples with same-sex love, offering an origin myth of how Nature created the beloved as female but then changed her to be male after finding herself smitten with her creation. The poem attempts to resolve the speaker's resulting conflict over same-sex attraction by separating love and sex.

Keywords

- American Romanticism
- Cross-Dressing
- Gender
- Love
- Nature
- Origin Myth

Context

As part of the first 126 sonnets dedicated to the Fair Youth (also known as the young man), Sonnet 20 presents a myth about the young man's origin, which explores the themes of love, sex, and gender in remarkably explicit terms. In the preceding sonnets, the speaker expresses love for the young man with increasing openness; through a fantasized myth about the young man's gender, this sonnet wrestles with the speaker's same-sex love attachment.

The sonnet's first two lines describe the young man's feminine appearance: "A woman's face with nature's own hand painted, / Hast thou the master mistress of my passion" (lines 1–2). The speaker then moves on quickly in the second part of the quatrain to the beloved's heart, which he says is gentle like a woman's, but "not acquainted / With shifting change as is false women's fashion" (3–4). The second quatrain continues this comparison; the speaker claims the young man's eyes are brighter than women's and "less false in rolling" (5), and his beauty "steals men's eyes and women's souls amazeth" (8). The third quatrain elaborates the speaker's fantasy of how Nature created the young man first as a woman, but then Nature fell in love with the new female and so, ostensibly to enable her love, she decided at the last moment to change the female to a male. And so the speaker declares that Nature has left him defeated: "And by addition me of thee defeated, / By adding one thing to my purpose nothing" (11–12). However, the final couplet proposes that the young man reserve his emotional love for the speaker: "But since she pricked thee out for women's pleasure, / Mine be thy love, and thy love's use their treasure" (13–14).

The speaker's myth of the young man's gender-bending origin is an aggressive fantasy that serves to negotiate his frustration that the young man is not a woman whom he can possess. At the same time, however, the poem also denigrates women and suggests the young man's male superiority. The speaker attempts to resolve this frustration by dividing love and sex: he can still love the young man even if he decides that he cannot consummate his love physically. Although Nature changes her creature's sex to justify her attraction, the poem frankly portrays both Nature's and the speaker's same-sex passion. There was, in Shakespeare's, time a well-established context for the themes of origin and same-sex love. Origin myths flourished in ancient Greek and Latin mythology, particularly Ovid's *Metamorphoses*, which presents stories like that of Pygmalion, an artist who sculpts the perfect woman and then convinces Venus to make her human; other myths show gender changes as part of the metamorphoses, as in the story of the prophet Tiresias, and same-sex love is prominent in ancient myths involving the god Apollo, Orpheus, and other male characters.

Shakespeare also renders Nature as a type of artist or maker of forms in other sonnets, such as Sonnet 11, but he was even more fascinated with gender ambiguity, which his work reflects frequently through the popular Renaissance plot device of cross-dressing characters. Many of Shakespeare's plays include characters that cross-dress, and several plays make cross-dressing a central part of the plot, particularly female characters who dress as men. In *As You Like It*, Rosalind dresses as a male shepherd so that she can pursue her love for Orlando. Portia, in *The Merchant of Venice*, disguises herself as a lawyer so that she can help her lover Bassanio resolve his financial troubles. In *Twelfth Night*, Viola disguises herself as a man after she is shipwrecked on an island and decides to protect herself by entering the service of Duke Orsino. The Renaissance fascination with gender-bending began not with Shakespeare, but in earlier narratives, particularly the Italian short stories of Giovanni Boccaccio, whose *Decameron* is one of the most important prose collections in the early Renaissance period.

The ideas of same-sex love and gender ambiguity present a particularly rich context for more recent narrative and poetry, particularly in the nineteenth and twentieth centuries. In the American Romantic tradition, one of the most prominent celebrations of male love is Walt Whitman's "Calamus" poems from his collection *Leaves of Grass*, written in the second half of the nineteenth century. Many poets in the twentieth century, from May Swenson to Mark Doty, have also written of same-sex love, as have writers in other genres, including playwright Tony Kushner, whose 1993 play *Angels in America* won the Pulitzer Prize. But there is also the implicit theme of changing one's gender. Films such as *Boys Don't Cry* (1999) and *Brokeback Mountain* (2005) explore the experience of same-sex love in modern American life, with the former featuring a transgendered protagonist based on the real-life story of Brandon Teena. From ancient myths to modern films, the themes of love, sex, and gender ambiguity have flourished, providing a rich tradition on which Shakespeare relied and to which he contributed in both his sonnets and his plays.

Ashleigh Imus

Works Cited

Evans, G. Blakemore, ed. *The Riverside Shakespeare*. Boston: Houghton, 1974.

Poets.org. "LGBTQ Poetry." *Poets.org*. Academy of American Poets, n.d. Web. 14 Apr. 2014. <https://www.poets.org/page.php/prmID/608>

Martin, Philip J. T. *Shakespeare's Sonnets: Self, Love, and Art*. Cambridge: Cambridge UP, 1972.

Shakespeare, William. "Sonnet 130." *Shakespearian Sonnets* (2006): 6. *Literary Reference Center*. Web. 14 Apr. 2014. <http://search.ebscohost.com/login.aspx?direct=true&db=prf&AN=23066401&site=prc-live>.

Vendler, Helen. *The Art of Shakespeare's Sonnets*. Cambridge: Belknap, 1997.

For Further Study

Bromley, James M. *Intimacy and Sexuality in the Age of Shakespeare*. Cambridge: Cambridge UP, 2011.

Gajowski, Evelyn. *Presentism, Gender, and Sexuality in Shakespeare*. New York: Palgrave, 2009.

Wells, Stanley. *Shakespeare, Sex, & Love*. Oxford: Oxford UP, 2010.

Sonnet 29

When in disgrace with fortune and men's eyes
I all alone beweep my outcast state,
And trouble deaf heaven with my bootless cries,
And look upon myself, and curse my fate,
Wishing me like to one more rich in hope,
Featured like him, like him with friends possessed,
Desiring this man's art, and that man's scope,
With what I most enjoy contented least;
Yet in these thoughts my self almost despising,
Haply I think on thee, and then my state,
Like to the lark at break of day arising
From sullen earth, sings hymns at heaven's gate;
*   For thy sweet love remembered such wealth brings*
*   That then I scorn to change my state with kings.*

Abstract

Sonnet 29 presents the theme of love's redemptive power, a central belief in many Western cultures. By framing nature and society as opposing realms, the poem structures the speaker's mental shift from despair to hope as he contemplates his beloved.

Keywords

- Christianity
- Despair
- Iambic Pentameter
- Love
- Middle Ages
- Nature
- Redemption
- Society

Context

Of the 154 sonnets Shakespeare wrote, Sonnet 29 is among the best known, perhaps because its theme of love's redemptive power has long been a central belief in many Western cultures, with roots in the Bible's Gospel of John. The theme has, however, evolved in various ways since its inception, especially in modern narratives. Shakespeare's treatment of the subject in Sonnet 29 represents a secular belief in the redemptive power of love and is somewhat unusual in its focus on the individual lover rather than on the beloved.

In this poem, generally categorized with the 126 poems in which the speaker addresses an unnamed young man known as the Fair Youth, the first two quatrains present a moment of despair in which the speaker declares his "disgrace with fortune and men's eyes" (line 1). His initial reaction to society's disfavor is to bemoan his "outcast state" (2), offer useless complaints to heaven, and feel envious of those who are more hopeful or talented or who have better social connections and opportunities. In line 8, the speaker has a moment of self-reflection in which he reveals that in this state of despair, the things that he usually most enjoys paradoxically please him least. The third quatrain marks a shift, as the speaker begins to realize the fruitlessness of his self-hatred, which prompts positive thoughts of his beloved in line 10 ("Haply I think on thee"). This in turn prompts him to compare his "state" with that of a lark singing at daybreak: now, rather than complaining uselessly to "deaf heaven" (3), he can "sing hymns at heaven's gate" (12). In the final rhyming couplet, the memory of his beloved's "sweet love" (13) brings a wealth that allows him to scorn even the wealth and power of kings.

As literary critic Helen Vendler points out in her book *The Art of Shakespeare's Sonnets*, Sonnet 29 dramatizes the end of the speaker's despair by presenting and then fusing two hierarchies: the hierarchy of human society and the hierarchy of nature (161). The speaker is an outcast and envious of everyone above him in the social hierarchy, but by entering the hierarchy of nature, which he achieves by remembering the strength of his love and by comparing himself to the lark, he recasts heaven and himself as part of nature's hierarchy, in which he is able to rise up from his lowly position on the "sullen earth" (12) and ascend toward heaven. In this way, he relocates himself, as it were, in a new hierarchy, which enables him to redirect his scorn for himself toward the social realm and to look down upon the wealth and power of his social superiors. For twenty-first-century readers, these social and natural contexts—which go beyond individual love—for the speaker's redemption are important to understand because they point toward the cultural roots of the poem's themes of despair and redemption through love. The idea that love could have redemptive power derives from Christian theology, specifically from the notion that God's boundless love for the world prompted him to send to earth and sacrifice his only son, Jesus, in order to redeem humanity's sins. Christian

teachings, particularly Jesus's radical new command-
ment in the Gospel of John to "love one another," model
this type of redemptive love for Christian followers.

In the twelfth and thirteenth centuries, this idea of
love's spiritually transformative powers evolved to become an essential theme of courtly love poetry. This
poetry idealized aristocratic, unattainable ladies and
presented their admirers as men who served them and
became worthy through suffering in love. The Italian
poet Dante Alighieri took this idea much further by
presenting the beloved as an aspect of God, thereby
making romantic love a vehicle for becoming a more
devout Christian. Thus, in Dante's *Divine Comedy* (ca.
1310s), the lady Beatrice, whose historical counterpart
Dante in fact loved when she was alive, guides the character Dante through heaven, channeling his romantic
love into spiritual fulfillment. Dante's innovation concerning romantic love also helps to explain the Western belief in the power of love to heal despair, which
characterizes the fictional Dante's state when he begins
his otherworldly journey. Despair also characterizes
Shakespeare's speaker in Sonnet 29, and even though
this despair is not rooted in a crisis of religious faith as
it is for Dante, both protagonists redeem their psyches
through the power of romantic love.

With its enduring theme of love's redemptive force,
Sonnet 29 has appeared in many modern contexts and
been quoted in a wide range of works, from T. S. Eliot's
1930 poem "Ash Wednesday" to the 1990 film *Pretty
Woman*. The idea that romantic love for another person
can redeem one's spirit is now an unquestioned theme in
high and low art. Because the theme has become something of a cliché, many artists have sought new ways
to embrace the idea. In "Love after Love" (1986), for
example, poet Derek Walcott explores redemption from
the perspective of regaining a sense of self-love after a
failed relationship. Donald Hall's moving 1998 collection of poetry, *Without*, chronicles the illness and death
of his beloved wife, fellow poet Jane Kenyon, in effect
making the act of writing about love a redemptive force
in the face of despair over love's loss. The influence of
this theme, which Shakespeare's Sonnet 29 helped to re-
establish in Western literature and culture as a secular
and personal process, exemplifies a belief so ubiquitous
that the idea has endured and evolved over the centuries.

Ashleigh Imus

Works Cited

Evans, G. Blakemore, ed. *The Riverside Shakespeare*. Boston: Houghton, 1974.

Ramsey, Paul. *The Fickle Glass: A Study of Shakespeare's Sonnets*. New York: AMS, 1979.

Shakespeare, William. "Sonnet 29." *Shakespearean Sonnets. Poetry & Short Story Reference Center*. Web. 4 Apr. 2014. <http://search.ebscohost.com/login.aspx?direct=true&db=prf&AN=23064694&site=prc-live>.

Vendler, Helen. *The Art of Shakespeare's Sonnets*. Cambridge: Belknap, 1997.

Waller, Gary F. "William Shakespeare." *Critical Survey of Poetry*. 4th ed. Ed. Rosemary M. Canfield Reisman. Pasadena: Salem, 2011. *Poetry & Short Story Reference Center*. Web. 4 Apr. 2014. <http://search.ebscohost.com/login.aspx?direct=true&db=prf&AN=103331CSPBIC11630108000261&site=prc-live>.

For Further Study

Booth, Stephen. *Shakespeare's Sonnets*. New Haven: Yale UP, 1977.

Martin, Philip J. T. *Shakespeare's Sonnets: Self, Love, and Art*. Cambridge: Cambridge UP, 1972.

Sonnet 30

When to the sessions of sweet silent thought
I summon up remembrance of things past,
I sigh the lack of many a thing I sought,
And with old woes new wail my dear time's waste:
Then can I drown an eye, unused to flow,
For precious friends hid in death's dateless night,
And weep afresh love's long since cancelled woe,
And moan the expense of many a vanished sight:
Then can I grieve at grievances foregone,
And heavily from woe to woe tell o'er
The sad account of fore-bemoaned moan,
Which I new pay as if not paid before.
   But if the while I think on thee, dear friend,
   All losses are restor'd and sorrows end.

Abstract

Through memory, the loss and pain of the speaker's past overwhelm him with despair in Sonnet 30. In the sonnet's final couplet, however, the thought of a beloved friend brings relief. The theme of the emotional highs and lows of memory is also explored as a major influence in literature.

Keywords

- Alienation
- Grieving
- Memory
- Sorrow

Context

Although beginning with what seems to be a pleasant recollection of the past as the speaker is lost in "sweet silent thought" (line 1), Sonnet 30 quickly gives way to a deluge of regret and anxiety over the loss and pain of the past. Shakespearean sonnets follow a set pattern, progressing through three quatrains that build off of each other until the sonnet reaches a concluding couplet, which usually summarizes the preceding lines and offers some new way of viewing them. In Sonnet 30, the quatrains present the sorrows of the speaker's past as it increasingly encroaches on the present. The deaths of friends and the loss of old lovers become so painful to remember that the final line of the third quatrain declares them to be as distressing now as when they first occurred. Suddenly, however, the couplet offers a way to soothe this pain, declaring, "If the while I think on thee, dear friend, / All losses are restored and sorrows end" (13–14). Even though the speaker is not at this moment with the friend, the simple recollection of this person is enough to release the pain, and the speaker is no longer alone in the haunted past.

Sonnet 30 appears in a cluster of sonnets during which temporary separation from this friend (the Fair Youth, a young man to whom the majority of Shakespeare's sonnets are written) becomes a source of depression. While these poems are some of the most despairing of all Shakespeare's sonnets, they are also consistently written in praise of the youth, and so they regularly culminate in final moments in which his love (although absent for a moment) is enough to end even the darkest sorrow. Among these similar poems, Sonnet 30 has proven over time to be a favorite of many readers, because of both Shakespeare's strikingly beautiful language and his ability to address several emotions in only fourteen brief lines.

Memory's ability to confront human beings with the extremes of emotion, from overwhelming loss to deep joy, has been a recurring theme in literature. It is not surprising that the title of one of the greatest works of literature associated with memory, French writer Marcel Proust's seven-volume novel *À la recherche du temps perdu*, has been translated into English as *Remembrance of Things Past*, a phrase from line 2 of Sonnet 30. This expansive novel begins with the main character eating a madeleine, a small sponge cake. When he dips the cake in tea, a rush of memories from his childhood come back to him, including the memories of waiting for his mother to kiss him goodnight and the beginning of a love affair as a young adult. These memories are both painful and wonderful to the aged narrator, and he lingers over the recollection of loss and memory of joy while he sits in the dark, quiet room of his adult life (much like the "sweet silent thought" of Sonnet 30). At the place of Sonnet 30 in Shakespeare's sonnet cycle, the speaker is still able to overcome his sorrow by remembering the one he loves. For the narrator of *Remembrance of Things Past*, however, memory must be treated with some caution, for the unhappiness he feels in the present is never totally ameliorated through his recollections.

This tension between the sorrow and the joy of memory is also explored through the contemporary tools of fantasy in the 2004 film *Eternal Sunshine of the Spotless Mind*. In the film, a man and a woman meet and are immediately drawn to one another, and they begin a relationship. They learn, however, that they had loved one another in the past, and although their chaotic relationship ended, the pain of the breakup was too much to endure. They employed a man with an invention that promised to erase selected memories, wanting to ensure they would never again remember or feel the past pain. The two characters then begin a journey of slowly reconstructing their memories, remembering the initial joy of their romance as well as the incredible pain of their separation. In Sonnet 30, new affection does prove strong enough to eclipse the pain of "grievances foregone" (9). The characters in the film cautiously arrive at a similar belief, deciding to come together once more and risk the pain of loss in order to experience the joy of love again.

One of the most striking qualities in Sonnet 30 is that such highs and lows fit comfortably together in one sonnet. This is also, however, the truth of memory. The sorrow that builds through the first three quatrains is like the sorrow Proust's narrator knows when looking back on his own losses, all the death and failed romances suddenly available at once through the magic of recollection. However, Shakespeare's speaker ultimately focuses on the joy that memory can provide, demonstrating that the bliss of recollecting the one he loves is more powerful than any loss he has endured.

T. Fleischmann

Works Cited

Eternal Sunshine of the Spotless Mind. Dir. Michel Gondry. Focus Features, 2004. Film.

Grau, Christopher. "Eternal Sunshine of the Spotless Mind and the Morality of Memory." *Journal of Aesthetics and Art Criticism* 64.1 (2006): 119–33. *Academic Search Premier*. Web. 9 Apr. 2014. <http://search.ebscohost.com/login.aspx?direct=true&db=aph&AN=19977605>.

Oliver, Kenneth. "Remembrance of Things Past." *Masterplots*. 4th ed. Ed. Lawrence W. Mazzeno. Pasadena: Salem, 2010. *Literary Reference Center*. Web. 9 Apr. 2014. <http://search.ebscohost.com/login.aspx?direct=true&db=lfh&AN=103331MP426679330000288>.

Proust, Marcel. *In Search of Lost Time*. New York: Modern Library, 2003.

Shakespeare, William. "Sonnet 30." *Shakespearian Sonnets*. *Literary Reference Center*. Web. 9 Apr. 2014. <http://search.ebscohost.com/login.aspx?direct=true&db=lfh&AN=23064703>.

For Further Study

Adams, Howard C. "Sonnet 30." *Masterplots II: Poetry*. Rev. ed. Ed. Philip K. Jason. Pasadena: Salem, 2002. *Literary Reference Center*. Web. 9 Apr. 2014. <http://search.ebscohost.com/login.aspx?direct=true&db=lfh&AN=103331POE21409650000611>.

Vendler, Helen. *The Art of Shakespeare's Sonnets*. London: Belknap, 1999.

Sonnet 31

Thy bosom is endeared with all hearts,
Which I by lacking have supposed dead;
And there reigns Love, and all Love's loving parts,
And all those friends which I thought buried.
How many a holy and obsequious tear
Hath dear religious love stol'n from mine eye,
As interest of the dead, which now appear
But things removed that hidden in thee lie!
Thou art the grave where buried love doth live,
Hung with the trophies of my lovers gone,
Who all their parts of me to thee did give,
That due of many now is thine alone:
  Their images I loved, I view in thee,
  And thou (all they) hast all the all of me.

Abstract

Sonnet 31 is a paradoxical poem whose basic argument is that a beloved youth symbolically reconciles life and death, spirit and flesh, and present and past for the poem's speaker and for others who love him. The youth symbolizes the ideal union of the spiritual and physical elements that matter most to the speaker.

Keywords

- Death
- Desire
- God
- Eternity
- Love
- Paradox
- Physicality
- Spirituality
- Time

Context

Love is one of the crucial themes of Sonnet 31, as it is in much of the literature of Shakespeare's time and indeed English-language literature in general. In Shakespeare's era, the word *love* had various connotations, including not only emotional affinity and physical desire but also spiritual devotion and affection. Most of Shakespeare's contemporaries believed that the source and model of all true love was God, according to Christian theology. They believed that God loved all creatures, that all creatures should love God, and that the love of humans for one another should mirror such divine and absolute spiritual affection. All these different kinds of love—spiritual, physical, and emotional—are implied, at one point or another, in Sonnet 31. Indeed, various forms of the word *love* are used seven times in the space of fourteen lines.

The argument of the poem is straightforward. The sonnet addresses the unnamed young man known as the Fair Youth, to whom the first 126 sonnets of Shakespeare's 154-sonnet sequence are addressed. In Sonnet 31, the speaker asserts that his beloved is all the more valued because he was beloved by persons, now dead or departed, whom the speaker also loved. In a sense, these dead or departed loved ones live on in the beloved young man. The poem essentially dissolves the distinctions between the speaker, the youth, and the dead or departed loved ones; all are united in and through their love for the beloved youth. By loving the young man, the speaker feels the love of all their mutual but absent friends, who are kept alive in the youth.

Yet the sonnet achieves unity not only through its strong emphasis on the theme of mutual love but also by its repeated stress on the contrast between the physical and the spiritual. Love is the means by which distinctions of body and soul are dissolved. By loving the soul of the physical youth, the speaker also loves the souls of those who are now physically dead or absent but who still live spiritually in and through the young man.

The words "bosom" and "hearts" in line 1 can have both physical and spiritual connotations. The youth's "bosom" is literally his physical chest, but it is also figuratively the seat of his emotions, just as the word "hearts" suggests the literal physical organs that pump blood and the loving feelings that the organ symbolizes. Line 2 reinforces the physical/spiritual emphasis: the friends alluded to by the word "hearts" are dead or departed, but they are also somehow spiritually alive and present in the living youth. Love—stressed in three separate ways in line 3—is also both physical and spiritual. Love lives on in the bosom of the youth, thereby intensifying the speaker's love for the youth as well as for the physically departed friends.

In lines 4 and 5, "tears" symbolize earthy and physical love, just as the adjective "holy" implies the spiritual while the balancing adjective "obsequious" implies mourning for the dead. The dead now lie "hidden" in the living youth (8), who symbolically reconciles life and death, spirit and flesh, present and past, and others, himself, and the speaker. The youth symbolizes the ideal union of everything spiritual and physical that matter most to the speaker.

As befits such claims, the sonnet describes the youth in paradoxical terms. He is both a grave and a source of life, another manifestation of the physical/spiritual theme (9). He solely possesses what once belonged to many (12), yet by possessing their love he makes that love accessible to others, especially the speaker. The physical images the speaker recalls when he thinks of his dead and departed friends are now spiritually present when the speaker views the youth (13). Finally, line 14 echoes line 3 in structure, phrasing, and meaning; however, whereas line 3 emphasizes the word "love" three times, line 14 instead emphasizes the word "all" three times. The youth somehow embodies all their dead and departed friends, even as he enjoys the complete affection of the speaker.

This, then, is a poem rooted in paradoxes: the dead are somehow alive; the past is somehow present; the physical and the spiritual are reconciled; and the youth is simultaneously himself, the dead friends, and the speaker combined. By loving the youth, the speaker loves and is loved by their mutual departed friends. The poem begins by mentioning the youth ("thy bosom") and ends by mentioning the speaker ("all of me"), but in the space between the poem's beginning and end, any distinctions between the youth and the speaker collapse. By being united with the youth, the speaker is reunited with the friends, now dead, whom the youth and speaker had in common. The youth's ability to resurrect the dead and departed friends through love evokes Christian theology, which holds that Jesus Christ died out of love for all people and was resurrected by God to bring eternal life to all who love Jesus and God. According to Christian theology, only Jesus could truly and literally resolve the paradoxes that this poem explores. The beloved youth can do so only through the speaker's intense and somewhat hyperbolic praise.

Robert C. Evans

Works Cited

Booth, Stephen, ed. *Shakespeare's Sonnets*. New Haven: Yale UP, 1977.

Duncan-Jones, Katherine, ed. *Shakespeare's Sonnets*. London: Nelson, 1997.

Edmundson, Paul, and Stanley Wells. *Shakespeare's Sonnets*. Oxford: Oxford UP, 2004.

Evans, G. Blakemore, ed. *The Sonnets*. Cambridge: Cambridge UP, 1996.

Vendler, Helen. *The Art of Shakespeare's Sonnets*. Cambridge: Belknap, 1997.

For Further Study

Schoenfeldt, Michael, ed. *A Companion to Shakespeare's Sonnets*. Malden: Blackwell, 2010.

"Sonnets of Shakespeare." *Masterplots*. 4th ed. Ed. Laurence W. Mazzeno. Pasadena: Salem, 2010. *Literary Reference Center*. Web. 28 Apr. 2014. <http://search.ebscohost.com/login.aspx?direct=true&db=lfh&AN=103331MP428589560000853&site=lrc-live>.

Welsh, James M., and Jill Stapleton-Bergeron. "Sonnets of Shakespeare." *Magill's Survey of World Literature*. Rev. ed. Ed. Steven G. Kellman. Pasadena: Salem, 2009. Literary Reference Center. Web. 28 Apr. 2014. <http://search.ebscohost.com/login.aspx?direct=true&db=lfh&AN=103331MSW23359850001334&site=lrc-live>.

Sonnet 53

What is your substance, whereof are you made,
That millions of strange shadows on you tend?
Since every one hath, every one, one shade,
And you but one, can every shadow lend.
Describe Adonis, and the counterfeit
Is poorly imitated after you;
On Helen's cheek all art of beauty set,
And you in Grecian tires are painted new:
Speak of the spring, and foison of the year,
The one doth shadow of your beauty show,
The other as your bounty doth appear;
And you in every blessed shape we know.
  In all external grace you have some part,
  But you like none, none you, for constant heart.

Abstract

In this sonnet, Shakespeare's Fair Youth is so beautiful that every gorgeous thing recalls his looks, with even the masculine Adonis and the feminine Helen of Troy becoming reminiscent of his mien. Androgyny as an extreme of beauty is further considered in the poetry of Aphra Behn and the 1992 film adaptation of Virginia Woolf's novel *Orlando*.

Keywords

- Androgyny
- Aphra Behn
- Beauty
- Hyperbole
- Shakespearean Sonnet
- Virginia Woolf

Context

Sonnet 53 takes as its subject a youth so beautiful that he is seen in every gorgeous moment and prepossessing object on earth. The sonnet's first quatrain deals with this shape-shifting quality as an abstraction, asking what this youth could possibly be made of, as people have only one shadow, yet all shadows seem to be cast by him. This somewhat strange compliment is then clarified in the second quatrain, which explains that either a description of Adonis or a painting of Helen (both legendarily beautiful) would end up simply looking like the youth. Indeed, the third quatrain explains, even trying to speak of the beauty of the seasons will only result in

speaking of the youth again. This progression increasingly stresses that the youth's fair features are of a universal beauty, too great to be confined by any one form, for he is "in every blessed shape we know" (line 10). Following this hyperbolic statement, the sonnet's closing couplet explains the one way in which the youth is different from all things. While everything else might fade or leave, he has a "constant heart" and so is endlessly devoted to the speaker. This couplet adds a final element of superiority to the youth while also enhancing his charms beyond the physical and into the realm of emotional devotion.

Sonnet 53 is one of the many sonnets about the Fair Youth. A young man who is the object of desire, longing, and praise, the Fair Youth is absent from the speaker's life in Sonnets 43–58. This separation causes a great amount of pain, and the resulting intensification of longing can be seen in Sonnet 53. With that in mind, the final lines in which the speaker praises the Fair Youth's "constant heart" might be more wishful thinking than actual compliment, the speaker hoping the youth will return even if he is not quite convinced himself.

Just as Shakespeare describes the youth as androgynous, being both like the masculine Adonis and the feminine Helen, so too does the poet Aphra Behn describe great beauty as something that transcends gender and form. Writing in the middle of the seventeenth century, Behn is often considered to be the first professional woman writer, her work influencing the courses of fiction, drama, and poetry. Behn's "To the Fair Clarinda, Who Made Love to Me, Imagined More than Woman" is an ode of love to the eponymous Clarinda. In it, the speaker describes Clarinda by oscillating between masculine and feminine attributes, as "without blushes I the youth pursue, / When so much beauteous woman is in view" (lines 7–8). This Clarinda, like the Fair Youth of Shakespeare, has a "deluding form" (10), able to appear as all things and so to entrance all people. In both instances, much of the value of beauty is placed in its ability to escape traditional forms, to be more powerful and more valuable than constructions such as gender or human bodies. Likewise, just as Shakespeare's speaker finds in his Fair Youth an ultimate virtue, devotion, that is even more important than physical beauty, so too does Behn's speaker find a greater virtue in her

beloved, as "the noblest passions do extend / The love
Hermes, Aphrodite the friend" (23–24). Clarinda is at
once made male and female, lover and friend, but ultimately "noble."

In the modern day, writers and filmmakers continue
to play with the idea that beauty can be so great as to
transcend gender, form, and even time. The 1992 film
Orlando, based on Virginia Woolf's modernist classic
novel of the same name, tells the story of an androgynous youth born in Elizabethan England. The youth is
so beautiful and so striking that Queen Elizabeth offers
him riches and land on the condition that he agrees to
never let his androgynous beauty fade. The film's story
then continues for hundreds of years, the youth even
becoming a woman at one point (although her appearance remains the same). Just as the hyperbolic praise
of Shakespeare's speaker is firmly rooted in the Fair
Youth's appearance, then extended to a higher ideal, so
too does Orlando begin the film simply as an incom-
parable beauty. It is only through time and through the
experiences afforded by that beauty that Orlando becomes something more, just as only time and devotion
can bring the Fair Youth to his highest virtue.

The hyperbole at the heart of Sonnet 53, the claim
that a single person's beauty might transcend all else on
earth, might almost seem trite in its extremes. Yet it is
exactly that expansiveness—the Fair Youth as Adonis
and Helen, Clarinda as youth and lady, and Orlando
transcending time and gender—that allows these writers to reach a greater truth. Often, one in love cannot
help but see his or her beloved in every fair object and
likewise cannot help but ascribe to such beauty a higher
virtue, a greater purpose than the common beauty of the
mundane world.

T. Fleischmann

Works Cited

Archer, Stanley. "Aphra Behn." *Magill's Survey Of World Literature, Revised Edition* (2009): 1–5. *Literary Reference
Center*. Web. 24 Mar. 2014. <http://search.ebscohost.com/
login.aspx?direct=true&db=lfh&AN=103331MSW103598
50000034&site=ehost-live>.

Behn, Aphra. Oroonoko, The Rover, *and Other Works*. New
York: Penguin, 1993.

Bloom, Harold, ed. *Shakespeare's Poems and Sonnets*. New
York: Chelsea, 1999.

Orlando. Dir. Sally Porter. Perf. Tilda Swinton, Billy Zane,
and Quentin Crisp. Adventure Pictures, 1992. Film.

Shakespeare, William. "Sonnet 53." *Shakespearian Sonnets*
(2006): 14. *Literary Reference Center*. Web. 24 Mar. 2014.
<http://search.ebscohost.com/login.aspx?direct=true&db=l
fh&AN=23065220&site=ehost-live>.

For Further Study

Atkins, Carl D., ed. *Shakespeare's Sonnets: With Three Hundred Years of Commentary*. Cranbury: Associated UPs,
2007.

Vendler, Helen. *The Art of Shakespeare's Sonnets*. Oxford:
Belknap, 1999.

Sonnet 54

O! how much more doth beauty beauteous seem
By that sweet ornament which truth doth give.
The rose looks fair, but fairer we it deem
For that sweet odour, which doth in it live.
The canker blooms have full as deep a dye
As the perfumed tincture of the roses,
Hang on such thorns, and play as wantonly
When summer's breath their masked buds discloses:
But, for their virtue only is their show,
They live unwoo'd, and unrespected fade;
Die to themselves. Sweet roses do not so;
Of their sweet deaths are sweetest odours made:
And so of you, beauteous and lovely youth,
When that shall vade, my verse distills your truth.

Abstract

Through an extended metaphorical description of a rose, this sonnet praises the beauty of the Fair Youth. Shakespeare praises this beauty's truth and its ability to endure the changes of time through verse. The transcendental potential of truth and beauty are explored in the poetry of Emily Dickinson and in Walt Disney animated features.

Keywords

- Beauty
- Death
- Emily Dickinson
- Mortality
- Shakespearean Sonnet
- Truth
- Walt Disney

Context

A simple comparison between two flowers is drawn into an extended and powerful metaphor in this sonnet. Shakespeare begins Sonnet 54 by laying out the conceit that beauty is even more "beauteous" (line 1) when it is truthful. The sonnet then declares that the truth of a rose lies not in its sight, but in its scent. The second quatrain continues this metaphor, explaining that a canker bloom (a wild flower) is visually equal to a rose. However, the third quatrain reinforces the original conceit, claiming that the canker blooms' "virtue only is their show" (9)— that is, the canker bloom does not have a scent—and therefore offers only beauty without truth. In contrast, the rose might die but will leave behind its odor, a gorgeous smell that is the distilled truth of the flower. With this metaphor completed, the sonnet closes with a final couplet, which redirects the praise of the rose to that of the beloved youth. The youth might, like the rose, fade in beauty some day, but the speaker promises that "my verse distills your truth" (14), the poem itself lasting like the scent of the flower and providing virtue to the youth's good looks.

Within the sonnet sequence, Sonnet 54 is one of many praising the beauty of the Fair Youth, a young man to whom the speaker is devoted. While the qualities of the youth are certainly present here, however, the sonnet wrestles with the tension between immortal virtues and fleeting beauty. Although at times the obsession with beauty will dominate a single sonnet, in this instance, the poet prefers virtue, even as he somewhat selfishly gives himself (and his sonnet) all of the credit.

In Sonnet 54, the greatest height of beauty is truth, an abstract essence that exists beyond the physical form. Poets often bring these ideals together into one transcendent moment, as in early American writer Emily Dickinson's "I died for beauty, but was scarce." The poem presents the speaker after death, her life having been somehow lost to the greater concept of beauty. She is not alone in the tomb, however; another deceased person is placed beside her, "one who died for truth" (3). Both the speaker and the companion quickly acknowledge that they have, in fact, died for the same thing, as "the two are one; / We brethren are" (7–8). Like Shakespeare, Dickinson does not make clear why, exactly, truth and beauty become the same once they reach death. Instead, her poem concludes with the two deceased people speaking in the grave, their voices going on until the moss of the tomb covers their lips. In both instances, the transcendence of beauty and truth, when brought together, allows the artistic moment to extend beyond death. The scent of the rose and the poeticized good looks of the Fair Youth are more romantic versions of this transcendence, but even in Dickinson's dark tomb, the ideals of truth and beauty live beyond the end of the physical body.

Physical beauty as a route to transcendence and truth is also a common theme in many modern animated films by the Walt Disney Company. Many of these films center on a beautiful young woman, often a princess, who is placed in danger yet able to find truth and sometimes even eternal life because of her fair looks. This can be seen in the film *Sleeping Beauty*, in which an evil witch curses the princess Aurora into an eternal sleep. A prince, however, is so taken by Aurora's beauty that he resolves to rescue her, using a weapon called the Sword of Truth to battle the witch. When truth is able to defeat the witch, he kisses Aurora, which causes her to rise from her sleep. The powers of truth and beauty come together to bring Aurora back from death, just as Shakespeare promises the right combination of truth and beauty through verse will allow the beloved's existence to extend beyond his mortal life. A similar theme appears in *Beauty and the Beast*, where the woman Belle is forced to live with a fearsome, cursed Beast. When the Beast is on the verge of death, however, Belle realizes her love for him, and this love both restores him to his true form—that of a handsome prince—and brings him back to life. As in Sonnet 54, the concepts of beauty and truth are largely left metaphorical and abstract yet, when idealized and brought together, are able to transcend the death and evil of the world.

By the concluding couplet of Sonnet 54, truth and beauty are no longer realized as distinct qualities, but rather brought together through the metaphor of the rose, each an idealized part of the other. It is this idealization that allows the speaker of Emily Dickinson's poem to continue beyond death and that rescues the cursed lovers of so many Disney films, bringing them back from their curses and their eternal sleeps. Even in the dark tomb of Dickinson's work, then, these portrayals remain optimistic and inspiring, suggesting that the truth of life is itself unendingly beautiful and powerful.

T. Fleischmann

Works Cited

Beauty and the Beast. Dir. Gary Trousdale & Kirk Wise. Perf. Paige O'Hara, Robby Benson, & Richard White. Walt Disney Pictures, 1991. Film.

Benoit, Raymond. "Dickinson's 'I Died for Beauty' and Shakespeare's 'The Phoenix and the Turtle.'" ANQ 19.4 (2006): 31–33. *Literary Reference Center*. Web. 27 Mar. 2014. <http://search.ebscohost.com/login.aspx?direct=true&db=lfh&AN=23675724&site=ehost-live>.

Dickinson, Emily. *The Complete Poems of Emily Dickinson*. Ed. Thomas H. Johnson. New York: Back Bay, 1976.

Shakespeare, William. "Sonnet 54." *Shakespearian Sonnets* (2006): 14–15. *Literary Reference Center*. Web. 27 Mar. 2014. <http://search.ebscohost.com/login.aspx?direct=true&db=lfh&AN=23065223&site=ehost-live>.

Sleeping Beauty. Dir. Clyde Geronimi. Perf. Mary Costa & Bill Shirley. Walt Disney Productions, 1959. Film.

For Further Study

Atkins, Carl D., ed. *Shakespeare's Sonnets: With Three Hundred Years of Commentary*. Cranbury: Associated UPs, 2007.

Vendler, Helen. *The Art of Shakespeare's Sonnets*. Oxford: Belknap, 1999.

Sonnet 57

Being your slave what should I do but tend
Upon the hours, and times of your desire?
I have no precious time at all to spend;
Nor services to do, till you require.
Nor dare I chide the world without end hour,
Whilst I, my sovereign, watch the clock for you,
Nor think the bitterness of absence sour,
When you have bid your servant once adieu;
Nor dare I question with my jealous thought
Where you may be, or your affairs suppose,
But, like a sad slave, stay and think of nought
Save, where you are, how happy you make those.
  So true a fool is love, that in your will,
  Though you do anything, he thinks no ill.

Abstract

While romantic love is often treated as a source of heightened joy, in Sonnet 57 Shakespeare instead likens it to slavery, the speaker powerless in his devotion. The hyperbolic situation in which one loses all agency to love is further explored in the novel *Great Expectations* and in the pop music of Britney Spears.

Keywords

- Britney Spears
- *Great Expectations*
- Hyperbole
- Love
- Shakespearean Sonnet
- Sorrow
- Suffering

Context

Inspired in equal measure by love and self-pity, Shakespeare's Sonnet 57 compares romantic feelings to the experience of enslavement. The poem opens with this exaggerated conceit, the speaker declaring that he has no duties except to please his beloved. While this devotion is sincere, however, the sonnet reveals that the beloved is actually absent. The second quatrain then begins a needy rhetorical game—the speaker explains the ways that the absence makes him unhappy, yet in listing the miseries he claims not to suffer, he simultaneously manages to suggest them. He does not think the "bitterness of absence sour" (line 7), nor does he wonder with a "jealous thought" (9) where the beloved is. Making these claims suggests that he is, in fact, jealous and bitter, despite protesting otherwise. This is affirmed with the final couplet, which, in Shakespearean sonnets, often provides commentary on what came before. The sonnet closes by making the broad declaration that a lover "thinks no ill" (14) of anything the beloved does, no matter how hurtful. This thought completes the initial comparison, love being such a totalizing form of slavery that the lover cannot even acknowledge his own happiness.

A majority of Shakespeare's sonnets detail the speaker's romantic longing for a figure called the Fair Youth, a beautiful young man who remains the object of the speaker's obsession. Sonnet 57 appears alongside a series of poems in which the Fair Youth is absent, the distance between him and the speaker only causing that longing to grow more pronounced. As with many of its neighboring sonnets, the speaker of Sonnet 57 seems as interested in his own emotions and self-deceits as he is in the beloved, his suffocating emotional state being the sonnet's actual topic.

Extreme romantic yearning can often make an individual feel as though she or he has lost freedom, as happens to the character of Miss Havisham in Charles Dickens's 1860 novel *Great Expectations*. Focusing on the life of an orphan named Pip in Victorian London, the novel explores a range of colorful characters who are all attempting to navigate the social and economic forces of their era. Miss Havisham is one of the most tragic of these figures. Falling in love at a young age with a man named Compeyson, she learns minutes before her wedding that he had been lying to her all along and stealing her money; he then abandons her at the altar. Miss Havisham is unable to truly face this rejection, and in response, she spends the rest of her life locked away in her home, never removing her wedding dress and leaving her wedding cake to rot alongside her. Miss Havisham certainly knows she has been abandoned, just as the speaker of Sonnet 57 on some level knows that his beloved is off romancing others, but neither of them, however, is able to break free of that devotion. They are instead trapped in prolonged yearning and dissatisfaction and are slaves to romantic longing.

Despite the tragic tone that both Shakespeare and

Dickens imbue in their respective works, an omnipotent love capable of enslaving them to its desires can also be paradoxically appealing. Modern pop music regularly makes use of these extreme desires, celebrating the devotion that turns the speaker of Sonnet 57 into a "sad slave" (11). Pop artist Britney Spears's 2001 song "I'm a Slave 4 U," for instance, describes a person enslaved by love who declares, "I just can't help myself," while feelings build until she proclaims, "I'm a slave for you . . . I won't deny it; I'm not trying to hide it." As in Sonnet 57, Spears describes an absence of controlled emotions and an abandonment of one's identity and individual needs in favor of all-encompassing love for another. Shakespeare's speaker, by the end of Sonnet 57, suggests that his own obsessive devotion might not be as pure and joyous as he would like it to be. For Spears, however, and in songs with similar themes, enslavement of the self to love for another is portrayed as acceptable and commonplace and is justified because of the appearance of happiness that love brings.

The use of slavery as a metaphor for love speaks to the control it can have over someone in love. It is also a vivid commentary on the loss of power and individual identity to which many are susceptible when in the throes of extreme longing. Unchecked devotion often reveals itself as too strong a force, driving the lover into self-deceit and misery through the promise of ever-lasting happiness.

T. Fleischmann

Works Cited

Dickens, Charles. *Great Expectations*. New York: Dover, 2001.

Mittleman, Leslie B. "Great Expectations." *Masterplots, Fourth Edition* (2010): 1–4. *Literary Reference Center*. Web. 26 Mar. 2014. <http://search.ebscohost.com/login.aspx?direct=true&db=1-fh&AN=103331MP418099320000106 >.

Leishman, J. B. *Themes and Variations in Shakespeare's Sonnets*. London: Routledge, 2010.

Riley, Dick, and Pam McAllister. "The Fair Youth, a Rival Poet, and the Dark Lady—the Sonnets as Soap Opera." *Bedside, Bathtub & Armchair Companion to Shakespeare* (2001): 62–70. *Literary Reference Center*. Web. 26 Mar. 2014. <http://search.ebscohost.com/login.aspx?direct=true&db=lfh&AN=24016794 >.

Shakespeare, William. "Sonnet 57." *Shakespearian Sonnets* (2006): 15. *Literary Reference Center*. Web. 26 Mar. 2014. <http://search.ebscohost.com/login.aspx?direct=true&db=lfh&AN=23066354 >.

Spears, Britney. "I'm a Slave 4 U." *Britney*. Jive, 2001. CD.

For Further Study

Schoenfeldt, Michael Carl. *A Companion to Shakespeare's Sonnets*. Malden: Blackwell, 2010.

Vendler, Helen H. *The Art of Shakespeare's Sonnets*. London: Belknap, 1999.

Sonnet 73

That time of year thou mayst in me behold
When yellow leaves, or none, or few, do hang
Upon those boughs which shake against the cold,
Bare ruined choirs, where late the sweet birds sang.
In me thou see'st the twilight of such day
As after sunset fadeth in the west;
Which by and by black night doth take away,
Death's second self, that seals up all in rest.
In me thou see'st the glowing of such fire,
That on the ashes of his youth doth lie,
As the death-bed, whereon it must expire,
Consumed with that which it was nourish'd by.
  This thou perceiv'st, which makes thy love more strong,
  To love that well, which thou must leave ere long.

Abstract

The aging of the speaker directs Sonnet 73, one of Shakespeare's most famous. Metaphors of death, including dying trees and the onset of night, lead the speaker to celebrate the little time that remains with his beloved. Similar themes of enjoying a moment despite its impermanence are explored in the poetry of Percy Bysshe Shelley and in the film *Harold and Maude*.

Keywords

- Age
- *Harold and Maude*
- Mortality
- Percy Bysshe Shelley
- Seasons
- Shakespearean Sonnet

Context

Old age upon him, the speaker of Sonnet 73 addresses his young beloved, describing the brevity of his life in order to praise the youth's love and devotion. The three quatrains of the sonnet are each structured along a metaphor. The speaker first describes his life as being like a tree with yellowing and falling leaves, then as the twilight of a day before night falls, and finally as a fire turning to ashes. In all three metaphors, the speaker focuses on himself rather than the beloved. The images are dark and disparaging, such as describing the branches of the tree as being like "Bare ruined choirs" (line 4) and the site of the fire a "deathbed" (11). The

quick encroachment of death on these natural images, however, gives way to the final stanza, in which the beloved finally takes a substantive presence. The speaker knows that the beloved sees these signs of death—in acknowledging them, he realizes their love is made stronger, not weaker, for it is a powerful thing "To love that well, which thou must leave ere long" (14). Death might make love fleeting, but in its brevity it can only be more intense.

As in many of the sonnets addressed to the Fair Youth, Shakespeare seems as preoccupied with the differences in age and class between the speaker and the youth as he does in the youth's beauty. The speaker and the beloved are not equals. Instead, the difference in their age causes both anxiety and heightened affection for the speaker (in several Fair Youth sonnets, he anguishes over whether the youth might leave him). Here, those contradictory emotions are brought together, the speaker's vain fears of aging and death ultimately feeding that romance.

The Romantic poet Percy Bysshe Shelley (1792–1822) believed firmly in the inspirational power of nature and art and in idealized moments of blissful love and romance, yet he also situated these moments as temporary and fleeting. His 1821 poem "Mutability," like Shakespeare's Sonnet 73, begins by using metaphors from nature to explore the inevitability of aging and death, opening with the simple statement "The flower that smiles to-day / To-morrow dies" (1–2). From here, Shelley's speaker catalogues a number of joyous and revelatory aspects of life, from deep friendship to gorgeous clear skies, while repeatedly noting their eventual end. Even love, the speaker claims, can only end in "proud despair" (11). "Mutability" is filled with these desperate and dark moments, ending on the claim that every happy experience is but a dream from which all must eventually "wake to weep" (21), just as Shakespeare's speaker spends all but the final couplet of Sonnet 73 detailing the death and decay of the body. Despite this, however, the message of "Mutability" remains in line with Sonnet 73, urging the reader to "Make glad the day" (18) and to enjoy these temporary pleasures because their brief nature is all the more reason to treasure them.

Knowledge of impending death often heightens emotions, including emotions that are based in romantic love, which is at the heart of the 1971 dark comedy

Harold and Maude about a young man obsessed with death. Harold meets seventy-nine-year-old Maude, who, despite her age and evitable death, is able to enjoy the pleasures of life for what they are, reveling in nature and art. The connection between the two develops into a romance, despite Maude's insistence that she will die once she turns eighty. When her birthday comes and she commits suicide by taking sleeping pills, Harold is left permanently changed because he has found an appreciation for life's pleasures. Harold's journey through the film in many ways reflects the progression of Sonnet 73—both the sonnet's speaker and Harold are initially obsessed with death and morbidity; they then develop an understanding of the permanence of death and the importance of incorporating bliss and pleasure into one's life, regardless of how much life one has left to experience.

Although Shakespeare uses other sonnets to rally against death and to seek immortality through art, in Sonnet 73 he redirects that energy away from eternal aspirations and into the present moment. Like Shelley's, his speaker sees no reason to hide from mortality. Instead, he embraces change as a reason to more fully live in the present, the Fair Youth's love made all the more wondrous in the context of an aging world.

T. Fleischmann

Works Cited

Harold and Maude. Dir. Hal Ashby. Perf. Ruth Gordon and Bud Cort. Paramount Pictures, 1971. Film.

McLean, John L. "Percy Bysshe Shelley." *Magill's Survey of World Literature, Revised Edition* (2009): 1–7. *Literary Reference Center*. Web. 27 Mar. 2014. <http://search.ebscohost.com/login.aspx?direct=true&db=lfh&AN=103331MSW13219850000320>.

Prince, John S. "Shakespeare's Sonnet 73." *Explicator* 55.4 (1997): 197. *Academic Search Premier*. Web. 27 Mar. 2014. <http://search.ebscohost.com/login.aspx?direct=true&db=aph&AN=9710063090>.

Shakespeare, William. "Sonnet 73." *Shakespearian Sonnets* (2006): 19. *Literary Reference Center*. Web. 27 Mar. 2014. <http://search.ebscohost.com/login.aspx?direct=true&db=lfh&AN=23066370>.

Shelley, Percy Bysshe. "Mutability." *Shelley's Poetry and Prose*. New York: Norton, 2002.

For Further Study

Lord, Russell. "Sonnet 73." *Masterplots II: Poetry, Revised Edition* (2002): 1–3. *Literary Reference Center*. Web. 27 Mar. 2014. <http://search.ebscohost.com/login.aspx?direct=true&db=lfh&AN=103331POE21459650000614 >.

Vendler, Helen. *The Art of Shakespeare's Sonnets*. London: Belknap, 1999.

Sonnet 90

Then hate me when thou wilt; if ever, now;
Now, while the world is bent my deeds to cross,
Join with the spite of fortune, make me bow,
And do not drop in for an after-loss:
Ah! do not, when my heart hath 'scaped this sorrow,
Come in the rearward of a conquered woe;
Give not a windy night a rainy morrow,
To linger out a purposed overthrow.
If thou wilt leave me, do not leave me last,
When other petty griefs have done their spite,
But in the onset come: so shall I taste
At first the very worst of fortune's might;
 And other strains of woe, which now seem woe,
 Compared with loss of thee, will not seem so.

Abstract

Sonnet 90 examines the theme of loss, as the speaker urges his beloved to reject him sooner rather than later, after the speaker has already suffered countless woes at the hands of Fortune. Through the use of structural irony, the poem creates a fresh approach to this enduring topic.

Keywords

- Courtly Love
- Irony
- Loss
- Repetition
- Suffering
- Troubadours

Context

Sonnet 90 belongs to the first 126 poems in Shakespeare's sonnet sequence, which are dedicated to a young man known as the Fair Youth, but it is also a subset of poems 87–90, which all center on the beloved's rejection of the speaker. The first line of Sonnet 90, "Then hate me when thou wilt, if ever, now," refers to the last line of sonnet 89, "For I must ne'er love him whom thou dost hate" (14). In this concluding line of Sonnet 89, the abject speaker vows to hate himself, since he has surmised that his beloved now hates him. In the beginning of Sonnet 90, the speaker first tells his beloved to hate him "when thou wilt" but then immediately exhorts him to do so "now, / Now while the world is bent my deeds to cross; / Join with the spite of Fortune, make me bow" (1–3). Here, the speaker introduces what will become, as the poem progresses, an extended complaint about his "woes," which he says result from the world countering his efforts at every turn. He invites the lover to "join with the spite of Fortune" and defeat him, as Fortune has done, but soon rather than after Fortune has already laid him low, "in the rearward of a conquered woe" (6), which would simply prolong his misfortunes.

In the third quatrain, the speaker begins to explain why he wants the beloved to act soon: "so shall I taste / At first the very worst of Fortune's might" (11–12). The final couplet states that the result of experiencing the worst loss is that "other strains of woe, which now seem woe, / Compared with loss of thee will not seem so" (13–14). The poem thus presents a contrast between its structure and the message of the concluding lines. The sonnet emphasizes almost obsessively for the first ten lines the speaker's other woes, in phrases such as "deeds to cross," "spite of Fortune," "this sorrow," "conquered woe," and "petty griefs." Yet ultimately the purpose of obsessing over the "other strains of woe" (13) is to show how little they mean compared with "loss of thee" (14), the beloved's rejection. In this way, the poem enacts structural irony, or a distance between what the structure implies and what the speaker finally asserts.

The theme of devastating loss in love that drives Sonnet 90 had been long established by Shakespeare's time, and it informs many of his own tragedies written for the stage, such as *Romeo and Juliet*. The idea of failed romantic love emerged in twelfth-century French and Italian lyrics of courtly love, in which troubadours idealized the beauty of noble ladies but also lamented their love as unattainable and sometimes even attacked the ladies as haughty and cruel. Thus, for many medieval and subsequent poets, an undertone of aggression complicates and even comes to define aspects of the angelic, idolized lady. The experience of loss in love is part of the human experience, which is why the theme was still popular in Shakespeare's day and, for that matter, why it remains popular. Yet, by the sixteenth century, the medieval courtly model of this poetry had become stale; Shakespeare's use of structural irony in Sonnet 90 thus represents one way that he maintained the theme's artistic currency. Other artists treated the theme with humor, such as Shakespeare's contemporary Sir John Suckling, whose poem "Loving and Beloved" offers a playful, bawdy take on the hopelessness of achieving true and lasting love.

This aesthetic challenge remains in more recent efforts, as writers addressing the topic of failed love must be alert to the risk of falling into sentimentality, self-absorption, or self-pity. The best treatments thus find ways to avoid these dangers. The high emotion surrounding the tragic love story of the 1950s musical *West Side Story* succeeds in part because the story also boldly addresses social and ethnic conflict in New York City, marking a turning point in American theater. In poetry, the formal approach of Elizabeth Bishop in her famous poem "One Art" transforms its theme of pervasive loss into an elegant, restrained meditation on how human beings negotiate such loss. In this way, she resists the dangers of both self-pity and numbing despair. Part of the lesson of Sonnet 90 is that the experience of pain in love is universal, and for artists who seek to represent this loss, it is also fraught with particular risks, which is why the best artists mobilize strategies to temper or complicate the theme's intensity.

Ashleigh Imus

Works Cited

Evans, G. Blakemore, ed. *The Riverside Shakespeare*. Boston: Houghton, 1974.

"Poems about Heartache and Difficult Love." *Poetry Foundation*. Poetry Foundation, n.d. Web. 9 Apr. 2014. <http://www.poets.org/viewmedia.php/prmMID/20042>.

Shakespeare, William. "Sonnet 90." *Shakespearian Sonnets. Poetry & Short Story Reference Center*. Web. 9 Apr. 2014.

"Sir John Suckling." *Poetry Foundation*. Poetry Foundation, n.d. Web. 9 Apr. 2014. <http://www.poetryfoundation.org/bio/sir-john-suckling>.

Vendler, Helen. *The Art of Shakespeare's Sonnets*. Cambridge: Belknap, 1997.

For Further Study

Booth, Stephen. *Shakespeare's Sonnets*. New Haven: Yale UP, 1977.

Burrow, Colin. *The Complete Sonnets and Poems, William Shakespeare*. New York: Oxford UP, 2002.

Sonnet 94

They that have power to hurt, and will do none,
That do not do the thing they most do show,
Who, moving others, are themselves as stone,
Unmoved, cold, and to temptation slow;
They rightly do inherit heaven's graces,
And husband nature's riches from expense;
They are the lords and owners of their faces,
Others, but stewards of their excellence.
The summer's flower is to the summer sweet,
Though to itself, it only live and die,
But if that flower with base infection meet,
The basest weed outbraves his dignity:
 For sweetest things turn sourest by their deeds;
 Lilies that fester, smell far worse than weeds.

Abstract

Sonnet 94, like many of his sonnets, concerns an appealing young man often referred to as the Fair Youth, but this poem suggests that the youth's moral beauty may possibly be at risk and may not match his physical attractiveness. The poem uses a variety of literary devices to make readers experience a series of alternating feelings, but the final point of the sonnet seems to be that the youth must resist any temptation that would make him seem ethically ugly, however physically handsome he may be.

Keywords

- Beauty
- Nature
- Pentameter
- Sin
- Youth

Context

William Shakespeare's Sonnet 94 is addressed to the Fair Youth mentioned in so many of the other poems in Shakespeare's sonnet sequence, a young man whose identity remains unknown. The purpose of the poem seems to be to remind the young man of the importance of self-control—of resisting the kind of temptations and corruption emphasized in the sonnet's final lines. The young man is given credit for possessing physical beauty, but his moral beauty may be somewhat in doubt. The final couplet reminds the reader that ugliness is especially repulsive in anything that had originally seemed attractive.

One of the advantages of sonnet sequences is that they allow poets to explore rapid alterations in topics and moods. The very brevity of a sonnet means that a particular feeling, thought, tone, or atmosphere can be forcefully expressed in just a few lines, and the next sonnet can either develop such emphases or shift to emphases that significantly differ.

Sonnet 94 is especially interesting because it explores so many changes of tone within a single lyric, especially in the first two quatrains. As Stephen Booth notes in *Shakespeare's Sonnets*, the "sentences wander from attribute to attribute in such a way that a reader's response to 'them' who are the subject of lines 1–8 swings repeatedly back and forth between positive and negative" (305). The poem is at least as interesting, then, for the effects it has on readers as for any meaning that can easily be paraphrased.

Consider, for instance, the opening line. As Booth notes, "*They that have pow'r to hurt* invites a negative response; the addition of *and will do none* invites a dramatically opposed positive response" (305). Such alternations characterize much of the rest of the poem. They capture the variable moods of the speaker and create the same in the reader. Significantly, the poem opens with an unexpected use of meter. The speaker does not employ the standard iambic pentameter pattern one might have predicted—a pattern in which odd syllables are unstressed and even syllables are stressed. Instead, the meter not only catches the reader by surprise but also accentuates all the line's crucial words: "they," "power" (read as a monosyllable), "hurt," and "do." Part of the effectiveness of Shakespeare's poems results from his subtle use of music and rhythm, and certainly the first line here reveals his skill at quite literally stressing the words that matter most.

The alternating pattern of positives and negatives mentioned by Booth is present in the first four lines. Line 1 begins with negative implications and then switches to positive; line 2 is entirely positive; the first half of line 3 is positive, but the second half seems negative; and the first two words of line 4 are negative while the rest have a positive connotation. These positive overtones are then reinforced in lines 5 through 7, while line 8 has slightly negative overtones. Lines 9 and 10 revert to positive; lines 11 and 12 introduce negative connotations again; and the same seems true of the final couplet. Thus the overall movement of the poem is from positive to negative, but that movement is marked by steady but unpredictable fluctuation. The accumulative effect is to make the reader experience and feel the duality of the speaker's own mind and emotions.

Alongside the alteration of tones, however, is a striking amount of repetition of words, syntactical patterns, and sounds. The repetition of "do" in line 2 has already been mentioned. Also noteworthy, however, is the way "stone" (3) echoes the same vowel sound as "show" (2); the way "inherit heaven's graces" is paralleled by "husband nature's riches" (5–6); the way "owners" (7) once more picks up the long *o* sound already stressed in "show," "stone," and "slow" (2–4); and the way this same echo appears again in "though" and "only" (10). Part of the effect of all this echoing (which involves many consonants as well as many vowels, not to mention whole words, such as "summer" and "flower") is to give the sonnet a particularly thick texture of sound. The complications created by the poem's alternating tones are made more complex by the constant repetitions of similar sounds. Also noteworthy and contributing to the sense of alternation is the somewhat paradoxical phrasing of the first three lines and of the final couplet.

The main theme of this poem—that humans have ethical and spiritual obligations and must resist corruption—is as old as Longinus's treatise *On the Sublime* and as recent as the film *Mean Girls*, in which a kind and genuine high schooler betrays herself and her friends in an effort to become part of the popular crowd. Countless stories feature pure and beautiful characters who are made ugly by their unethical behavior. The radiant innocence and beauty of youth can be dulled by the more devious forces in nature, which the speaker of Sonnet 94 laments within. The poem both opens and closes, then, with a strong emphasis on opposites ("sweetest" / "sourest"; "lilies" / "weeds" [13–14]), but the worry implied in the closing two lines is that the clear distinctions those delineations emphasize may collapse, and that the physically beautiful Fair Youth may turn out to be ethically ugly and unreliable.

Robert C. Evans

Works Cited

Booth, Stephen, ed. *Shakespeare's Sonnets*. New Haven: Yale UP, 1977.

Duncan-Jones, Katherine, ed. *Shakespeare's Sonnets*. London: Nelson, 1997.

Edmondson, Paul, and Stanley Wells. *Shakespeare's Sonnets*. Oxford: Oxford UP, 2004.

Evans, G. Blakemore, and Anthony Hecht, eds. *The Sonnets*. By William Shakespeare. Cambridge: Cambridge UP, 1996.

Vendler, Helen. *The Art of Shakespeare's Sonnets*. Cambridge: Harvard UP, 1997.

For Further Study

Schoenfeldt, Michael, ed. *A Companion to Shakespeare's Sonnets*. Oxford: Blackwell, 2010.

"Sonnets of Shakespeare." *Masterplots*. 4th ed. Ed. Laurence W. Mazzeno. Pasadena: Salem, 2010. *Literary Reference Center*. Web. 28 Apr. 2014. <http://search.ebscohost.com/login.aspx?direct=true&db=lfh&AN=103331MP428589560000853&site=lrc-live>.

Welsh, James M., and Jill Stapleton-Bergeron. "Sonnets of Shakespeare." *Magill's Survey of World Literature*. Rev. ed. Ed. Steven G. Kellman. Pasadena: Salem, 2009. Literary Reference Center. Web. 28 Apr. 2014. <http://search.ebscohost.com/login.aspx?direct=true&db=lfh&AN=103331MSW23359850001334&site=lrc-live>.

Sonnet 97

How like a winter hath my absence been
From thee, the pleasure of the fleeting year!
What freezings have I felt, what dark days seen!
What old December's bareness everywhere!
And yet this time removed was summer's time;
The teeming autumn, big with rich increase,
Bearing the wanton burden of the prime,
Like widow'd wombs after their lords' decease:
Yet this abundant issue seemed to me
But hope of orphans, and unfathered fruit;
For summer and his pleasures wait on thee,
And, thou away, the very birds are mute:
  Or, if they sing, 'tis with so dull a cheer,
  That leaves look pale, dreading the winter's near.

Abstract

Sonnet 97 explores the tension between perception and reality as the speaker compares the beloved's absence to winter while simultaneously acknowledging that it is actually summer. Going beyond this simple contrast, the poem reveals the power of the speaker's subjective perspective.

Keywords

- Absence
- Perception
- Seasons
- Sorrow
- Subjectivity
- Time

Context

Part of the 126-sonnet sequence addressing an unnamed young man known as the Fair Youth, Sonnet 97 compares the speaker's absence from his beloved to winter even as he emphasizes that in reality, the separation occurs in summer. The poem explores the competing perspectives of the speaker's experience of reality and his overpowering emotions. This basic contrast is clear enough, but the speaker's perspective often shifts abruptly in ways that demand careful reading and that ultimately suggest the power of subjective perception as the poem's central theme, which the poem relates to the connection between love and the seasons.

The first quatrain establishes the poem's central comparison as the speaker's perception of reality is blurred by his emotions. The absence of his beloved has been like winter, and he asserts, "What freezings have I felt, what dark days seen! / What old December's bareness every where!" (lines 3–4). The second quatrain counters this perception by emphasizing that the absence in fact is occurring during summer, when growing crops are producing a "teeming autumn big with rich increase, / bearing the wanton burthen of the prime" (6–7). As literary critic Helen Vendler elucidates in her book *The Art of Shakespeare's Sonnets*, the fact that the speaker's reference to summer is immediately followed by the mention of autumn signals that the speaker is conflating his subjective perception with reality even as he affirms that reality, a deliberate confusion already implicit in his earlier claim to have felt cold and seen dark days in the midst of summer (416). The conflation becomes explicit in line 8, when the speaker compares the bounty of summer's crops to "widowed wombs after their lords' decease" (8)—that is, to a widow giving birth after the recent death of her husband. In the speaker's eyes, summer's "abundant issue" (9) has been diminished to the "hope of orphans, and unfathered fruit" (10), and the poem concludes with the speaker's final assertions that in the speaker's absence, either the "birds are mute," or their singing is so dull "that leaves look pale, dreading the winter's near" (14). These shifting perceptions never settle on a final reality but assert the power of the speaker's subjectivity, as they reveal how his mind restlessly constructs and revises his point of view (Vendler 417). In this way, the sonnet connects the speaker's shifting emotions and perceptions to the changing seasons.

The association of the seasons with individual emotions and experiences, particularly the link between spring and happy romantic love, was well established in medieval and Renaissance courtly love lyric poetry, but there were also examples that disrupted this association. English poet Geoffrey Chaucer's fourteenth-century poem *The Canterbury Tales* links the coming of spring not with romance but with a pilgrimage, and the poem's pilgrims represent a late-medieval world that is increasingly defined by church corruption, the growth of capitalism, and social turmoil brought on by the plague and other changes, which translates into a growing gap between the ideal and the actual, between perception and reality. Shakespeare's connection between subjective experience and the seasons eventually became a fully realized poetic theory in the Romantic period, which privileged nature in terms of subjective emotion as one of the most worthy poetic topics, albeit with very different emphases than Shakespeare's Sonnet 97. Samuel Taylor Coleridge's "Work without Hope," for example, describes the speaker's hopelessness in opposition to the teeming life of early spring, in a way that privileges nature as the higher reality.

The celebration of nature and subjectivity defines much twentieth-century poetry as well, such as in Robert Frost's "Stopping by Woods on a Snowy Evening," in which a winter scene comes to reflect the speaker's haunting contemplation of life and death. Later in the century, the poet Louise Glück conflates fraught emotions regarding sexuality with a specific flower in her famous poem "Mock Orange." The tension between perception versus reality is also explored in novels, perhaps most famously George Orwell's 1949 dystopian novel *Nineteen Eighty-Four*, and in drama, notably in Edward Albee's *Who's Afraid of Virginia Woolf?* (1962), in which an aging couple grapples with the destructive illusions they create based on their inability to have children. The 1999 science-fiction film *The Matrix* imagines a society in which machines create a simulated reality as a way of controlling humans. All of these examples suggest an intriguing evolution of this enduring theme over five centuries. Whereas medieval and early modern writers were fascinated by the human processes of perception and subjectivity, modern artists instead imagine the larger social dangers of the gap between perception and reality, particularly in the contexts of technology and ideology.

Ashleigh Imus

Works Cited

Duncan-Jones, Katherine, ed. *Shakespeare's Sonnets*. London: Nelson, 1997.

Edmondson, Paul, and Stanley Wells. *Shakespeare's Sonnets*. Oxford: Oxford UP, 2004.

Evans, G. Blakemore, ed. *The Riverside Shakespeare*. Boston: Houghton, 1974.

"Sonnets of Shakespeare." *Masterplots*. 4th ed. Ed. Laurence W. Mazzeno. Pasadena: Salem, 2010. *Literary Reference Center*. Web. 28 Apr. 2014. <http://search.ebscohost.com/login.aspx?direct=true&db=lfh&AN=103331MP42858956 0000853&site=lrc-live>.

Vendler, Helen. *The Art of Shakespeare's Sonnets*. Cambridge: Belknap, 1997.

For Further Study

Baldwin, T. W. *On the Literary Genetics of Shakespeare's Sonnets*. Urbana: U of Illinois P, 1950.

Booth, Stephen. *Shakespeare's Sonnets*. New Haven: Yale UP, 1977.

Cousins, A. D., and Peter Howarth. *The Cambridge Companion to the Sonnet*. Cambridge: Cambridge UP, 2011.

Sonnet 98

From you have I been absent in the spring,
When proud pied April, dressed in all his trim,
Hath put a spirit of youth in every thing,
That heavy Saturn laughed and leapt with him.
Yet nor the lays of birds, nor the sweet smell
Of different flowers in odour and in hue,
Could make me any summer's story tell,
Or from their proud lap pluck them where they grew:
Nor did I wonder at the lily's white,
Nor praise the deep vermilion in the rose;
They were but sweet, but figures of delight,
Drawn after you, you pattern of all those.
　Yet seemed it winter still, and you away,
　As with your shadow I with these did play.

Abstract

The romantic and lush imagery of spring is brought to life and contrasted with the speaker's sadness at his beloved's absence in Sonnet 98. The use of springtime imagery to explore the themes of love and romance in the poetry of Robert Herrick and in popular music of the twentieth century is also considered.

Keywords

- Absence
- Love
- Seasons
- Sorrow
- Time
- Understatement

Context

In Sonnet 98, the beauty of spring is rendered powerless to make the speaker happy in light of the beloved's absence. The speaker begins by firmly establishing traditional metaphors of spring, with the "spirit of youth" (line 3) animating everything. However, the speaker also declares himself absent from his beloved. This absence drives the second quatrain, which lists the specific wonders of springtime, from "lays of birds" (5) to "different flowers in order and in hue" (6). Rather than celebrate these sights, however, the speaker negates their power, prefacing each one with "nor" in order to stress his inability to appreciate them. These descriptions are also charged with sexual imagery, particularly the images of flowers. At the conclusion of the third quatrain, the speaker reveals that he is unable to appreciate these experiences because each one is "drawn after you" (12), asserting the superiority of the beloved. The concluding couplet extends the seasonal metaphor, declaring that it is always winter for the poet when the beloved is gone. This couplet also echoes the opening line, in which the speaker states "from you I have been absent in the spring" (1), yet the final lines reference only winter, darkness, and shadows, demonstrating the completeness of the speaker's despair at his lover's absence.

Sonnet 98 is a part of the first 126 poems in the 154-sonnet sequence known as the Fair Youth sequence, which are addressed to an unnamed beloved young man. Within the overall sonnet sequence, Sonnet 98 is bookended by two similar poems. Like Sonnets 97 and 99, Sonnet 98 describes the speaker's sorrow while the Fair Youth is absent for an extended period of time, and the speaker turns to imagery from the seasons and nature to express his sadness. Sweetly melancholy, these poems also come after many sonnets in the sequence that are driven by seasonal imagery, such as the comparison of the youth to a "summer's day" in Sonnet 18. His appearance is regularly likened to the beauty of flowers and sunlight throughout the sequence.

Shakespeare is making use here of seasonal imagery that has maintained a fairly regular prominence through the history of English literature, in which spring is commonly associated with sexuality, beauty, and rebirth. The seventeenth-century lyric poet Robert Herrick, for instance, made frequent use of springtime imagery in his romantic verse, including the 1648 poem "Corinna's Going A-Maying" (sometimes rendered as "Corina's Going A-Maying"). In it, the speaker implores a young woman, Corinna, to come out into the May morning and join him in the romantic and idealized natural world. The poem draws on a tradition of pastoral poetry in which the countryside is presented as an idyllic place, both visually gorgeous and able to inspire romance. It is, in Herrick's description, filled with "dew-bespangling Herbe and Tree" (6), spring having thrown "fresh-quilted colours through the aire" (4). Herrick also makes this landscape sexualized, filling it with kisses and even claiming that it is a sin to refrain from enjoying these pleasures. In the entirety of "Corinna's Going

A-Maying," the speaker uses this imagery in an attempt to persuade his lover to join him, the wonders of the season being an excuse to enjoy the pleasures of nature and of the flesh. For Sonnet 98, however, this imagery is presented in stark contrast to the speaker's feelings, as even the wondrous experience of pastoral spring is not enough to bring him out of the metaphorical winter caused by his beloved's absence.

Spring remains strongly linked to romance and beauty in contemporary popular culture, and the poetic treatment of springtime images and romance is a regular feature of twentieth-century popular music. Elvis Presley's song "Spring Fever," for instance, tells a lover (in the style of Herrick's speaker in "Corinna's Going A-Maying") that "the sky is full of butterflies" and "the world's in love," using the joys of spring to urge his beloved to join him in the day. Frank Sinatra's classic hit "Suddenly It's Spring" likewise makes feelings of romance inseparable from the season. Simply looking at his beloved transports him into a metaphorical springtime, his "heart dancing" and his spirit "high on a hilltop." Just as the speaker of Sonnet 98 is unable to enjoy springtime because of his beloved's absence, Sinatra is able to experience spring at any time of year when he is with his beloved. The Billie Holiday song "Some Other Spring," however, falls in line with Shakespeare's inability to appreciate the season. Holiday sings about a recent heartbreak, one that hurts so deeply that, despite the warmth of the season, "deep in my heart it's cold as ice." Some of the most popular and respected American musicians of all time, Presley, Sinatra, and Holiday all made use of the same springtime imagery and associations Shakespeare played with centuries before in Sonnet 98.

T. Fleischmann

Works Cited

Blake, Robert G. "Corinna's Going A-Maying." *Masterplots II: Poetry*. Rev. ed. Ed. Philip K. Jason. Pasadena: Salem, 2002. *Literary Reference Center*. Web. 28 Apr. 2014. <http://search.ebscohost.com/login.aspx?direct=true&db=lfh&AN=103331POE12849650000135>.

Herrick, Robert. "Corina's Going A Maying." *Selection from the Lyrical Poems of Robert Herrick*. London: Macmillan, 1888. *Literary Reference Center*. Web. 28 Apr. 2014. <http://search.ebscohost.com/login.aspx?direct=true&db=lfh&AN=23003445>.

Holiday, Billie. "Some Other Spring." *Lady Sings the Blues*. Clef Records, 1956. LP.

Presley, Elvis. "Spring Fever." *Girl Happy*. RCA Victor, 1965. LP.

Shakespeare, William. "Sonnet 98." *Shakespearian Sonnets*. *Poetry & Short Story Reference Center*. Web. 28 Apr. 2014. <http://search.ebscohost.com/login.aspx?direct=true&db=lfh&AN=23066395>.

Sinatra, Frank. "Suddenly It's Spring." *Best of Frank Sinatra*. United Multi Consign, 2001. CD.

For Further Study

Hart, Jonathan. *Shakespeare: Poetry, History, and Culture*. New York: Palgrave, 2009.

Vendler, Helen. *The Art of Shakespeare's Sonnets*. Cambridge: Belknap, 1999.

Sonnet 102

My love is strengthened, though more weak in seeming;
I love not less, though less the show appear;
That love is merchandized, whose rich esteeming,
The owner's tongue doth publish every where.
Our love was new, and then but in the spring,
When I was wont to greet it with my lays;
As Philomel in summer's front doth sing,
And stops his pipe in growth of riper days:
Not that the summer is less pleasant now
Than when her mournful hymns did hush the night,
But that wild music burthens every bough,
And sweets grown common lose their dear delight.
  Therefore like her, I sometime hold my tongue:
  Because I would not dull you with my song.

Abstract

The strength of love to last through time is celebrated through the metaphor of a nightingale in this sonnet. The speaker argues that just as a songbird sings less in the summer, he praises his beloved less than when they first met but loves him more deeply. The theme of enduring love is also explored in the play *Cyrano de Bergerac* and the film *The Princess Bride*.

Keywords

- Hyperbole
- Love
- Nature
- Paradox
- Shakespearean Sonnet

Context

Beginning with the paradox that the speaker's love is both "strengthened" and "more weak in seeming" (line 1), Sonnet 102 explores the tensions between love felt and love professed in an ongoing romance. Addressed to a figure called the Fair Youth, the speaker of Shakespeare's sonnet acknowledges that he does not sing his beloved's praise as often as when they first met. To explain why this is, the second quatrain presents the metaphor of a Philomel, a nightingale. The bird will sing often when spring begins, yet only occasionally once the full warmth of summer sets in. The third quatrain continues the metaphor, showing that the Philomel sings less not because she cares less, but because "sweets grown common lose their dear delight" (12)—that is, too much praise ceases to please. With the concluding couplet, Shakespeare's speaker directs the metaphor and the paradox back to his beloved, declaring that, like the bird, he refrains from singing the Fair Youth's praise because he "would not dull you with my song" (14). The youth, then, becomes like the summer, overwhelmed with praise, and the speaker forced to recognize the uselessness of his compliments.

Of Shakespeare's 154 sonnets, the first 126 are addressed to the Fair Youth. By Sonnet 102, then, the lover and the beloved have gone through a wide range of emotions, from hyperbolic praise to overwhelming insecurity. The sonnet's placement so close to the conclusion suggests that the speaker is confronting the inevitable changes in a relationship over time. Rather than take these as signs of a diminishment in the relationship, he insists again on their love, providing one more sonnet even as he falsely protests that the time for praise has passed.

The paradox between the infatuations and constant praise of early love and the quieter (yet more deeply felt) experiences of lasting love is one of the central tensions in the play *Cyrano de Bergerac*. Based on a real writer, the 1897 play tells the fictional account of de Bergerac's unrequited love for a woman named Roxane. De Bergerac is a poet and a swordsman, although his thoughts are more often occupied with his deep longing for Roxane, whom he believes will never love him because of his unattractive appearance. De Bergerac writes Roxane a poetic and emotional note, declaring his love for her, but when he intends to pass the note along, she tells him that she is in love with a man named Christian before he has the chance. De Bergerac then begins writing love notes for Christian to woo Roxane, pouring his flowery praise onto her through another. When Christian dies, de Bergerac spends fifteen years visiting Roxane at her convent without revealing his true feelings. Like the speaker in Shakespeare's sonnet, love for de Bergerac is stronger after the initial infatuation and hyperbolic emotions. It is "Not that the summer is less pleasant now" (9), but rather that the strength of de Bergerac's love is shown through his long devotion, the year where he refrains from burdening Roxane with his praise knowing that she has heard enough.

The story of early hyperbolic romance transitioning into a stronger and more lasting love has become so popular that it is even parodied in the 1987 film *The Princess Bride*. The movie combines romance, fantasy, and adventure into a spoof on all the genres. It focuses on the story of Buttercup, a young lady who falls in love with her farmhand, Westley. The two young lovers share the heights of romance, repeating their chosen phrase, "As you wish," as a constant reminder of their love and basking in the beautiful light of their country home. When Westley departs to earn a fortune, however, his ship is attacked by pirates and he is presumed dead. Years later, when Buttercup is in danger, a mysterious man in black returns to rescue her. He risks his life and fortune for Buttercup before finally revealing that he is Westley in disguise, still in love with her after all the years. The peaceful and idyllic moments of early romance, their countryside home like the landscape of which the Philomel sings, gives way to something even stronger and more devoted. As with Sonnet 102, the strength of Westley's love is not proven by his proclamations and compliments, but by his long commitment, including a period in which he does not praise his love or even reveal his identity to her.

Love at its strongest is the not the love of first sight, but one that endures. Paradoxically, as Shakespeare shows with his lovely metaphor, this lasting love often remains unspoken. Just as de Bergerac visits Roxane and Westley saves Buttercup while keeping their loves silent, so too does the speaker of Sonnet 102 understand that he must refrain from complimenting the Fair Youth. Rather than framing this with sadness, however, Shakespeare manages to elevate it, revealing that the prepossessing moments of late romance are ripe enough with beauty that the speaker can rest confidently, knowing his romance to be true.

T. Fleischmann

Works Cited

Bloom, Harold, ed. *The Sonnets*. New York: Chelsea, 2008. Print. Bloom's Shakespeare through the Ages ser.

Marlowe, Jean G. "Cyrano De Bergerac." *Masterplots, Fourth Edition* (2010): 1–3. *Literary Reference Center*. Web. 28 Mar. 2014. <http://search.ebscohost.com/login.aspx?direct=true&db=lfh&AN=103331MP414429560000163&site=ehost-live>.

The Princess Bride. Dir. Rob Reiner. Perf. Cary Elwes and Mandy Patinkin. Act II Communications, 1987. Film.

Rostand, Edmond. *Cyrano de Bergerac*. Trans. Brian Hooker. New York: Bantam Classics, 1950. Print.

Shakespeare, William. "Sonnet 102." *Shakespearian Sonnets* (2006): 26–27. *Literary Reference Center*. Web. 11 Apr. 2014. <http://search.ebscohost.com/login.aspx?direct=true&db=lfh&AN=23066399&site=ehost-live>.

For Further Study

Schoenfeldt, Michael. *A Companion to Shakespeare's Sonnets*. Malden: Blackwell, 2010.

Vendler, Helen. *The Art of Shakespeare's Sonnets*. Oxford: Belknap, 1999.

Sonnet 104

To me, fair friend, you never can be old,
For as you were when first your eye I ey'd,
Such seems your beauty still. Three winters cold,
Have from the forests shook three summers' pride,
Three beauteous springs to yellow autumn turned,
In process of the seasons have I seen,
Three April perfumes in three hot Junes burned,
Since first I saw you fresh, which yet are green.
Ah! yet doth beauty like a dial-hand,
Steal from his figure, and no pace perceived;
So your sweet hue, which methinks still doth stand,
Hath motion, and mine eye may be deceived:
*   For fear of which, hear this thou age unbred:*
*   Ere you were born was beauty's summer dead.*

Abstract

Sonnet 104 wrestles with the speaker's perception of his beloved's timeless youth and beauty, a perception that initially seems to signify devotion, but gradually it becomes clear how deeply transient the young man's beauty is.

Keywords

- Age
- Beauty
- Perception
- Repetition
- Time
- Transience
- Youth

Context

Sonnet 104 belongs to the group of 126 poems relating to the Fair Youth and, specifically, to those sonnets addressing the beloved's extraordinary youth and beauty. The poem begins with the speaker's perception of the young man's seemingly eternal youth but concludes by offering something of a reality check, as the speaker begins to realize the transience of beauty, after all. The first quatrain establishes the speaker's sweet perception that his "fair friend . . . never can be old" (line 1) because he seems just as beautiful as he was when they first met. The speaker then offers three successive accounts of the time that has passed since he met his beloved. First, he says that "three winters cold" (3) have shaken the leaves from the forest's trees. Next, in the second quatrain, he says that he has seen "Three beauteous springs to yellow autumn turned" (5). Finally, he says, "Three April perfumes in three hot Junes burned, / Since first I saw you fresh, which yet are green" (7–8). At first glance, these statements might all seem to simply indicate in various ways that three years have passed, but each statement implies an earlier endpoint in the year: the leaves drop from the trees in October and November, but they turn yellow prior to this, and fading scent of spring flowers occurs much earlier than either of the first two processes.

These increasingly early points of the year imply acceleration in the pace of nature's transience (Vendler 442), and this in turn gives readers a hint about where the speaker's perception is headed. In the third quatrain, he acknowledges that his beloved's beauty has in fact changed but that he cannot perceive this change: "So your sweet hue, which methinks still doth stand / Hath motion, and mine eye may be deceived" (11–12). Once the speaker has realized that his perception is flawed, he draws the startling conclusion that his beloved's beauty in fact lasted the briefest time. The speaker then calls out to generations yet to come, warning them that beauty has died before they could even be born. This astonishing, definitive realization implies transience as a theme that ultimately overpowers the other central themes of eternal youth and beauty.

The context for the theme of transience is especially rich in Western ancient and medieval cultures. Awareness of transience underlies one of the most famous poems by the Roman poet Horace, whose verses in *Odes* 1.11 urge readers to "carpe diem," or "seize the day," which in that context does not mean to simply enjoy life, but to act sooner rather than later and to prepare wisely because the future is unknown. In the Middle Ages, the concept of transience defined the world for Christians who believed the earth to be inherently transient, a sort of intermediary zone defined by the drudgery and suffering of human life—a necessary burden to be endured prior to entering the eternal time of the afterlife. Representing this belief is the Old English philosophical poem *The Wanderer*, which tells of a man who roams the earth in exile and sorrow after the loss of his lord and comrades in battle, learning to accept his sufferings as necessary aspects of existence on earth. In the seventeenth century, the theme of transient youth and beauty appear in Andrew Marvell's poem "To His Coy Mistress," whose speaker urges his beloved to grant her love before time steals her beauty. Here, Marvell advocates the more popular sense of "carpe diem" as "enjoy life now while you can."

Twentieth-century American artists take up the theme of transient youth, beauty, and fortune in various ways, from Edith Wharton's 1905 novel *House of Mirth*—whose protagonist Lily Bart tragically fails to understand the transience of her youth and social status—to the 1950 film *Sunset Boulevard*, which tells the story of aging silent-film star Norma Desmond, whose inability to accept her lost youth leads her to live a bizarre and haunting life of illusion that ultimately ends in madness. In poetry, Robert Frost's "Nothing Gold Can Stay" remains a classic example of lyric mastery, whereas Allen Ginsberg's "The Baggage Room at Greyhound" offers a totally different type of meditation on transience versus eternity, featuring Ginsberg's conversational, irreverent style. One persistent idea in these modern sources and their artistic precedents is how difficult it can be to accept the reality of the fleeting nature of youth, beauty, love, or status. Shakespeare's Sonnet 104 offers a moving dramatization of the restlessness and courage required to accept the transience of being.

Ashleigh Imus

Works Cited

Bloom, Harold, ed. *The Sonnets*. Bloom's Shakespeare through the Ages series .New York: Chelsea, 2008.

Evans, G. Blakemore, ed. *The Riverside Shakespeare*. Boston: Houghton, 1974.

Martin, Philip J. T. *Shakespeare's Sonnets: Self, Love, and Art*. Cambridge: Cambridge UP, 1972.

Shakespeare, William. "Sonnet 102." *Shakespearian Sonnets* (2006): 27. *Literary Reference Center*. Web. 11 Apr. 2014. <http://search.ebscohost.com/login.aspx?direct=true&db=prf&AN=23066401&site=prc-live>.

Vendler, Helen. *The Art of Shakespeare's Sonnets*. Cambridge: Belknap, 1997.

For Further Study

Duncan-Jones, Katherine, ed. *Shakespeare's Sonnets*. London: Thomson Learning, 1997.

Evans, Gwynne Blakemore, ed. *The Sonnets*. By William Shakespeare. Introd. Anthony Hecht. Cambridge: Cambridge UP, 1996.

Kerrigan, John, ed. The Sonnets *and* A Lover's Complaint. By William Shakespeare. London: Penguin, 1999.

Sonnet 106

When in the chronicle of wasted time
I see descriptions of the fairest wights,
And beauty making beautiful old rhyme,
In praise of ladies dead and lovely knights,
Then, in the blazon of sweet beauty's best,
Of hand, of foot, of lip, of eye, of brow,
I see their antique pen would have expressed
Even such a beauty as you master now.
So all their praises are but prophecies
Of this our time, all you prefiguring;
And for they looked but with divining eyes,
They had not skill enough your worth to sing:
*   For we, which now behold these present days,*
*   Have eyes to wonder, but lack tongues to praise.*

Abstract

Sonnet 106 deals with the problem of capturing and conveying true beauty in words. Like many of the other sonnets, it is a poem about poetry, and in particular it is about the difficulties of using literature to do justice to genuine beauty. The poem is structured in ways that emphasize the passage of time and that possibly suggest distinctions between physical and spiritual beauty.

Keywords

- Art/Artists
- Beauty
- The Divine
- History
- Time
- Youth

Context

Sonnet 106 emphasizes a number of themes that can be found throughout his extensive sonnet sequence as a whole. These include the passage of time, the appeal of beauty, and the ways a poet can immortalize beauty by writing verse about persons or things. Like many of the earlier sonnets in the series, this one is addressed to a handsome young man (known as the Fair Youth) whose beauty—sometimes physical, sometimes ethical, sometimes both—the speaker celebrates and seeks to preserve in his poems.

The very first word of the poem ("When") emphasizes the crucial theme of time—a theme acknowledged explicitly in the last word of line 1. The word "When" also initiates a long series of dependent clauses (a device Shakespeare often uses in these sonnets). As readers wait for the main noun and verb to arrive, they are made to feel the effect of time's passage as they wonder what essential statement the speaker plans to make. That noun and that verb do not appear in the poem until line 7, so that half the sonnet has passed before the speaker reveals the main point of the work. It is not until line 8 that the first period arrives, and so the poem is more than halfway completed before the whole of its first statement is realized. Shakespeare thus makes the reader endure the lengthening passage of time even as he explores that passage as a theme. The opening sentence creates tension and examines the past while lengthening a crucial moment in the present.

Shakespeare emphasizes the theme of time in other subtle ways as well. For instance, by using the phrase "fairest wights" (that is, most attractive persons) in line 2, he deliberately chooses an archaic-sounding noun. There is something equally old-fashioned about conjuring images of "ladies" and "knights" and calling the latter "lovely" (4). It is as if the speaker is invoking bygone days of medieval romance (much as sixteenth-century English poet Edmund Spenser does in his *Faerie Queene*). In contrast to this nostalgic language, Shakespeare's speaker can be blunt in emphasizing time's passage. The beautiful ladies, after all, are quite frankly "dead" (4)—an adjective that has the power to shock and bring the reader back to hard, cold facts. Beauty as an abstract quality (a Platonic idea) may be eternal, and such beauty can be expressed and preserved in poems, but beautiful persons inevitably die.

Line 6, in particular, emphasizes the physical beauty of the body. Each noun is pushed to the forefront and emphasized by repeated commas: "Of hand, of foot, of lip, of eye, of brow." The general movement here is upward, arriving at the eye (associated with the soul, perception, and insight) and then finally at the brow (seat of the brain and mind). Yet the main focus of this poem, as of others in the sequence, is not on the young man's beautiful character, impressive intellect, or admirable soul, but on his physical appearance.

This fact makes the comparison implied in the final six lines all the more intriguing, and perhaps even a bit unsettling. As many commentators have noted, the concluding six lines implicitly compare the young man to Jesus Christ. Just as the Old Testament prophets dimly foretold the coming of a savior they themselves would never see, so, the poem argues, poets of the past, when celebrating beautiful persons of the past, without knowing it, foretold or prefigured the coming of the handsome youth.

Beyond the Fair Youth's superficial beauty, there is a hint of the youth's moral, spiritual value in the word "worth" in line 12, but that hint is left undeveloped in this poem. Instead, the poem ends by emphasizing—as if to complete the list in line 6—two more body parts: "eyes" and "tongues" (14). Here as in so many of Shakespeare's other sonnets, the speaker is at least as much concerned with himself and his poetry as he is with the handsome young man. Ultimately, he suggests that no poet—whether of the present or the past—had, has, or could have the power to celebrate adequately the beauty of the handsome youth.

This idea—that no words can do real justice to true beauty—is especially common in religious writings, from works as old as Dante's *Divine Comedy* to ones as recent as the writings of C. S. Lewis. But anyone who has ever seen something overwhelmingly beautiful, be it the Grand Canyon or a spectacular sunset, will know firsthand that mere words cannot express or convey the real power of true beauty.

Robert C. Evans

Works Cited

Booth, Stephen, ed. *Shakespeare's Sonnets*. New Haven: Yale UP, 1977.

Duncan-Jones, Katherine, ed. *Shakespeare's Sonnets*. London: Nelson, 1997.

Edmondson, Paul & Stanley Wells. *Shakespeare's Sonnets*. Oxford: Oxford UP, 2004.

Evans, G. Blakemore, ed. *The Sonnets*. By William Shakespeare. Cambridge: Cambridge UP, 1996.

Vendler, Helen. *The Art of Shakespeare's Sonnets*. Cambridge: Harvard UP, 1997.

For Further Study

Schoenfeldt, Michael, ed. *A Companion to Shakespeare's Sonnets*. Oxford: Blackwell, 2010.

"Sonnets of Shakespeare." *Masterplots*. 4th ed. Ed. Laurence W. Mazzeno. Pasadena: Salem, 2010. *Literary Reference Center*. Web. 24 Apr. 2014. <http://search.ebscohost.com/login.aspx?direct=true&db=lfh&AN=103331MP428589560000853>.

Welsh, James M., and Jill Stapleton-Bergeron. "Sonnets of Shakespeare." *Magill's Survey of World Literature*. Rev. ed. Ed. Steven G. Kellman. Pasadena: Salem, 2009. Literary Reference Center. Web. 24 Apr. 2014. <http://search.ebscohost.com/login.aspx?direct=true&db=lfh&AN=103331MSW23359850001334>.

Sonnet 109

O! never say that I was false of heart,
Though absence seemed my flame to qualify,
As easy might I from my self depart
As from my soul which in thy breast doth lie:
That is my home of love: if I have ranged,
Like him that travels, I return again;
Just to the time, not with the time exchanged,
So that myself bring water for my stain.
Never believe though in my nature reigned,
All frailties that besiege all kinds of blood,
That it could so preposterously be stained,
To leave for nothing all thy sum of good;
 For nothing this wide universe I call,
 Save thou, my rose, in it thou art my all.

Abstract

In Sonnet 109, the poem's speaker defends himself against any allegation that he has been untrue to his beloved simply because he has been physically distant. The speaker uses simple words, simple sentence structure, and a homely image to emphasize his loyalty to the youth, although ultimately the poem seems to say more about the speaker himself than about his beloved.

Keywords

- Absence
- Alienation
- Betrayal
- Change
- Friendship
- Hypocrisy
- Love
- Metaphor
- Mutability
- Paradox

Context

Sonnet 109 has been categorized as one of the 126 sonnets that are addressed to an unnamed young man commonly known as the Fair Youth. In this poem, the speaker insists that he not only has been but also remains loyal to the youth, even if he has been physically absent from him. The speaker defends his true commitment to the young man and to their relationship.

The poem's very first word—"O"—immediately establishes the strength of the speaker's emotions and convictions. The speaker then defends himself against charges that he has been "false of heart," a phrase that implies the speaker may have been unfaithful (line 1). The next line reveals, however, that the speaker has merely been physically absent from his beloved. Physical absence, the speaker suggests, does not necessarily imply emotional distance. His "flame" (a word that suggests heat, light, and intensity) still burns bright for the youth (2).

In the next two lines, the speaker relies on paradoxes to emphasize the strength of his attachment. Paradoxes are common in Shakespeare's writing, partly because they merge apparent illogic with apparent good sense. They therefore catch the reader's attention to emphasize the speaker's points and demonstrate his wit. Thus the speaker claims in lines 3 and 4 that the youth and he are somehow the same person and that the speaker's soul resides in the youth's breast. These ideas might seem a bit cliché, but then the speaker invents what is easily the most brilliant metaphor of the poem: he calls the young man's breast "my home of love"—a wonderfully suggestive image. It implies domesticity, comfort, intimacy, privacy, rest, relaxation, nourishment, security, and sexuality. A word such as "place" would have the same general meaning but none of the specific connotations of "home" just listed. The Greek philosopher Aristotle argued that the ability to create effective metaphors was the key talent of a true poet, and by creating this particular metaphor, Shakespeare illustrates his genuine creativity.

As the sonnet develops, the speaker asserts again that physical distance does not change either him or his regard for the youth. In another striking metaphor, he maintains that he brings "water" (perhaps implying tears) to clean his own "stain" (8). Does such phrasing imply sexual infidelity, as literary scholar Stephen Booth suggests in his book *Shakespeare's Sonnets* (351–53)? If so, the speaker fails to make that idea especially clear. It seems safer to say that the poem instead stresses the speaker's emotional loyalty to the youth. The poem seems all the more emphatic because of its plain, straightforward sentence structure and because most of its diction consists of simple, one-syllable words. Thus the word "preposterously" (11) stands out all the more when the speaker claims that he would never "eave for nothing all thy sum of good" (12).

In general the poem's phrasing sounds strongly self-defensive (note how many times the words "I" and "my" appear in just fourteen lines), and although the speaker proclaims his unchanging, unchangeable attachment to the youth, this poem, like so many of the other sonnets, ultimately reveals more about the speaker himself than about the beloved young man.

Sonnet 109 bears a striking thematic resemblance to English poet John Donne's famous poem "A Valediction Forbidding Mourning" (1611), in which the poem's speaker urges his beloved not to weep at their parting because the strength of their love will sustain them through an extended separation. The speaker in Donne's poem asserts that he and his beloved share a connection that is far superior to "dull sublunary lovers' love / —whose soul is sense" (13-14), arguing that their love for one another is strong enough to extend beyond their sensual desires and physical absence. In the next lines, Donne's speaker admonishes other lovers who "cannot admit / of absence, 'cause it doth remove / the thing which elemented it" (14-16), thereby dismissing those whose love depends upon a physical connection to be sustained. Instead, the speaker argues that because he and his beloved are "inter-assured of the mind" (19), his departure from his beloved does not represents "a breach, but an expansion, / like gold to aery thinness beat" (23-24). Like Shakespeare's Sonnet 109, Donne's "A Valediction Forbidding Mourning" affirms the superiority and strength of love that is based on a spiritual and emotional connection regardless of physical proximity.

Robert C. Evans

Works Cited

Booth, Stephen, ed. *Shakespeare's Sonnets*. New Haven: Yale UP, 1977.

Donne, John. "A Valediction Forbidding Mourning." *Collected Classic Poems, Coleridge to Gascoigne. Poetry & Short Story Reference Center*. Web. 28 Apr. 2014.

Duncan-Jones, Katherine, ed. *Shakespeare's Sonnets*. London: Thomas Nelson, 1997.

Edmondson, Paul, and Stanley Wells. *Shakespeare's Sonnets*. Oxford: Oxford UP, 2004.

Evans, G. Blakemore, ed. *The Sonnets*. Cambridge: Cambridge UP, 1996.

For Further Study

Schoenfeldt, Michael, ed. *A Companion to Shakespeare's Sonnets*. Oxford: Blackwell, 2010.

"Sonnets of Shakespeare." *Masterplots*. 4th ed. Ed. Laurence W. Mazzeno. Pasadena: Salem, 2010. *Literary Reference Center*. Web. 28 Apr. 2014.

Welsh, James M., and Jill Stapleton-Bergeron. "Sonnets of Shakespeare." *Magill's Survey of World Literature*. Rev. ed. Pasadena: Salem, 2009. Literary Reference Center. Web. 28 Apr. 2014.

Sonnet 116

Let me not to the marriage of true minds
Admit impediments. Love is not love
Which alters when it alteration finds,
Or bends with the remover to remove:
O, no! it is an ever-fixed mark,
That looks on tempests and is never shaken;
It is the star to every wandering bark,
Whose worth's unknown, although his height be taken.
Love's not Time's fool, though rosy lips and cheeks
Within his bending sickle's compass come;
Love alters not with his brief hours and weeks,
But bears it out even to the edge of doom.
  If this be error and upon me proved,
  I never writ, nor no man ever loved.

Abstract

One of best-loved sonnets, Sonnet 116 attempts to define the nature of true love, using both negation and positive metaphor. However, the poem's placement in the sonnet sequence and certain stylistic features have led some readers to find a more complicated message than typical readings suggest.

Keywords

- Beauty
- Eternity
- Love
- Metaphor
- Rebuttal
- Time

Context

One of the most famous love poems in the English canon, William Shakespeare's Sonnet 116 has also been the subject of lively critical debate. The poem offers a clear and masterful declaration of true love's nature, but some readers have felt that aspects of its style and its position in the overall 154-sonnet sequence suggest that Sonnet 116 might act as a rebuttal. The first quatrain asserts the eternal nature of true love and attempts to define true love in terms of negation: "Love is not love / which alters when it alteration finds, / or bends with the remover to remove" (lines 2–4). Here, the speaker asserts that love does not diminish or change simply because something about a lover or situation has changed. The second quatrain shifts to define love in positive terms through a nautical metaphor. Love is an "ever-fixèd mark" (5), which could be a lighthouse or a star that guides "every wand'ring bark" (7).

The third quatrain shifts back to the negative model of defining what "love is not," as did the first quatrain, but the sonnet here specifies in physical terms the abstract "impediments" that were referred to in line 2: love is not subject to time, says the speaker, even though the passing of time eventually destroys the "rosy lips and cheeks" (9) of young lovers. In lines 11 and 12, the speaker echoes line 3 by again denying that love "alters," but he now describes love in more human terms as someone who "bears it out even to the edge of doom" (12). The final couplet insists on the speaker's authority by setting up a counterfactual statement: if he is proved wrong, then he never wrote, and no man ever loved. Because both these consequences are manifestly untrue, the implication is that the speaker must be right.

Sonnet 116 appears toward the end of the group of the 126 poems dedicated to the unnamed young man known as the Fair Youth. Previous sonnets, such as Sonnet 90 and others, address the failure of the speaker's relationship with the young man, and sonnets 126–154 address another lover known as the Dark Lady. In addition, Sonnet 116 speaks relatively impersonally of love, which is unusual compared to the other sonnets in the sequence, and it contains many negative words, with repetitions of "not," "no," and never," suggesting a conflicted tone. The poem's context in the sonnet sequence and these stylistic details suggest to scholars such as Helen Vendler that the poem should be understood as the speaker's rebuttal to the young man's (imagined) claim that "impediments" now prevent him from remaining steadfast in love (488–93). With this interpretation, the sonnet's first sentence, "Let me not to the marriage of true minds / admit impediments" (1–2), would emphasize "me," as the speaker responds to the end of his relationship with the young man by insisting that *he* would never agree with such flawed views of love. Yet, other readers have argued that Shakespeare's intended order of the sonnet sequence is not absolutely certain, and because the poem does not explicitly address a specific person, the rebuttal interpretation is not reliable.

The thematic context of the poem has a rich history

in art and literature both before and after Shakespeare's time. The characterization of "true" romantic love emerged in the songs of twelfth-century troubadours, who called this love *fin amor*, or pure love, and developed an elaborate system of beliefs, attitudes, and literary practices regarding it. The thirteenth-century poem *The Romance of the Rose*, written by Guillaume de Lorris and expanded upon by Jean de Meun, is a dream vision intended to teach the art of *fin amor*, which was then reserved for the aristocracy. By Shakespeare's time, this idealized characterization of true romantic love was firmly rooted in Western European culture. For example, the poem "A Farewell to False Love," by Shakespeare's contemporary Sir Walter Raleigh, describes false love in acid terms, comparing it to "a poisoned serpent covered all with flowers" (7).

More recently, scores of poems, songs, plays, novels, and films have been dedicated to defining and exploring the nature of true love. This theme in fact is the central focus of one of the very first novels written in the English language, *Pamela*, composed by Samuel Richardson and first published in 1740. Subsequent classics, such as Jane Austen's nineteenth-century novel *Pride and Prejudice*, have celebrated the struggles of true love in the contexts of class and other social constraints. This theme eventually developed into a popular genre in the twentieth century, in which writers specialized in stories of tragic, passionate love that endures in spite of cruel obstacles, fueling the ever-strong market for romance novels. Popular films such as *Gone with the Wind* (1939) and *Titanic* (1997) overlay the human tragedy of the American Civil War and the famous shipwreck with stories of true love lost. The intensity and vulnerability of individuals within the thrall of romantic love help to explain the Western cultural obsession, from the Middle Ages to the present, with stories about the nature of true versus false love. With its insistence on true love as eternal and unchanging, Sonnet 116 remains an especially prized example in this tradition.

Ashleigh Imus

Works Cited

Evans, G. Blakemore, ed. *The Riverside Shakespeare*. Boston: Houghton, 1974.

Kinney, Arthur F., ed. *The Oxford Handbook of Shakespeare*. New York: Oxford UP, 2012.

Murphy, Garry. "Shakespeare's Sonnet 116." *Explicator* 39.1 (1980): 39–41.

Shakespeare, William. "Sonnet 116." *Shakespearian Sonnets. Poetry & Short Story Reference Center*. Web. 30 Apr. 2014. <http://search.ebscohost.com/login.aspx?direct=true&db=prf&AN=23066413&site=prc-live>.

Vendler, Helen. *The Art of Shakespeare's Sonnets*. Cambridge: Belknap, 1997.

For Further Study

Burt, Stephen & David Mikics. *The Art of the Sonnet*. Cambridge: Belknap, 2010.

Landry, Hilton. *New Essays on Shakespeare's Sonnets*. New York: AMS, 1976.

Sonnet 129

The expense of spirit in a waste of shame
Is lust in action: and till action, lust
Is perjured, murderous, bloody, full of blame,
Savage, extreme, rude, cruel, not to trust;
Enjoyed no sooner but despised straight;
Past reason hunted; and no sooner had,
Past reason hated, as a swallowed bait,
On purpose laid to make the taker mad.
Mad in pursuit and in possession so;
Had, having, and in quest to have extreme;
A bliss in proof, and proved, a very woe;
Before, a joy proposed; behind a dream.
  All this the world well knows; yet none knows well
  To shun the heaven that leads men to this hell.

Abstract

In Sonnet 129, Shakespeare describes lust as an irresistible and overpowering force characterized by the emotional extremes of terrible longing, ecstatic fulfillment, and inevitable regret. Similar literary depictions of the extremes of lust, such as in Dante's *Divine Comedy* and Vladimir Nabokov's *Lolita*, are compared to Shakespeare's treatment of the subject.

Keywords

- Desire
- Eroticism or sexuality
- Extremity
- Lust
- Passion
- Regret
- Suffering

Context

Passionate, physical desire and lust dominate the focus of Sonnet 129, one of the most impersonal poems in Shakespeare's sonnet sequence in that it does not appear to address anyone in particular. There is a familiar chronology of lust referenced here, in which one is overcome by desire, experiences the joy of consummation, and finally feels shame for the sexual act. Rather than structure the sonnet along this pattern, however, the speaker darts around the chronology frantically. The result is dizzying and, in the speaker's word, "extreme" (line 10). It is an experience filled with illogical decisions, with extremity and volatility marking every moment, and once the lust has been satisfied, it is "hated as a swallowed bait" (7). Like the lows, the pleasures of lust recur, and single lines within the sonnet reference the passion as both "enjoy'd" and "despised" (5), as a "bliss" and a "woe" (11). Because the speaker plays with the chronology in this way, he is able to reach a realization in the final couplet that lust can only truly be understood by looking at all of its aspects. Everyone is familiar with this experience, the speaker claims, but still are unable "to shun the heaven that leads men to this hell" (14). In effect, all the contradictions are true at once, with lust irresistibly offering both heaven in its pursuit and hell in its fulfillment.

In the sequence of sonnets, Sonnet 129 is the third in which the speaker's focus switches from the young man known as the Fair Youth to the woman known as the Dark Lady. These latter poems are marked by more extreme physical passion than the earlier Fair Youth sonnets, and the speaker in Sonnet 129 is already trying to make rational sense out of this irrational affair. This Dark Lady represents a force of sexual energy to whom the speaker is powerfully drawn. In this way, the impersonal tone of the poem is significant, as the speaker attempts to step back from his passionate feelings and use his intellect to understand an experience that defies logic.

The rough desire of lust, driving humans to both emotional highs and the depths of despair, is also a major theme in the epic poem *Inferno*, written by the Italian poet Dante in the fourteenth century as part of his masterpiece, the *Divine Comedy*. In it, the poet imagines himself on a journey through hell, which he describes as being divided into nine circles, with each circle devoted to a particular sin. Carnal sins dominate the second ring. Those in this circle are being punished for "subjecting reason to the rule of lust" (5.39), and their punishment is to be thrown violently back and forth by the winds of an unending and terrible storm. The circle is occupied by historical persons and characters from classical mythology, such as Helen of Troy and Cleopatra, whom Dante presents as having given in to lust during their lifetimes and, therefore, facing disastrous consequences in the afterlife. The violence and rapidly shifting nature of this punishing wind are similar to the rapid and unpredictable movement of Sonnet 129, while the root of the sin (allowing physical desire to overpower reason) is exactly the challenge that Shakespeare addresses in the sonnet. Even though the sonnet's speaker knows that he should "shun the heaven that leads men to this hell," the sonnet itself shows that resisting the temptation of one's most primal urges may be all but impossible.

The idea that the extremes of both heaven and hell could be engendered by lust is the driving theme of twentieth-century writer Vladimir Nabokov's novel *Lolita* (1955). Written from the perspective of a literary scholar, Humbert Humbert, Nabokov's novel details the older man's sexual obsession with a twelve-year-old girl, his stepdaughter, whom he nicknames Lolita. The particular form of lust is an extreme of disgrace, truly, in Shakespeare's words, "perjured, murd'rous, bloody, full of blame" (3). Nabokov's psychological exploration of Humbert is often concerned with the buildup of lust and the overwhelming temptation that one feels cannot be resisted, no matter the costs or consequences. Humbert deceives himself, as he knows the risks that he takes and the inappropriateness of his actions and as he experiences the physical bliss he desires. Finally, he is overcome by guilt for his indefensible actions. Much of *Lolita*'s strength lies in the careful description of Humbert's interior thoughts, as the man (like the speaker of Sonnet 129) attempts to reason and justify his way through a lust that consumes him.

Sonnet 129 depicts lust as a universal experience "the world well knows" (11), even as only a few are able to overcome its temptations and resist its tumultuous highs and lows. The extreme winds of hell's second circle and the desperate and despicable physical yearning of Humbert Humbert fit easily into the tortured state of mind that this sonnet describes, one in which not even a simple chronology can hold steady when subjected to the forces of lustful longing and regret. Inevitably, Shakespeare's sonnet sequence continues on the long, passionate affair with the Dark Lady, just as Humbert meets his downfall from pursuing the object of his desire and the souls of the *Inferno* find themselves in the eternal storm for their carnal sins.

T. Fleischmann

Works Cited

Adams, Michael. "Lolita." *Masterplots*. 4th ed. Ed. Laurence W. Mazzeno. Pasadena: Salem, 2010. *Literary Reference Center*. Web. 4 Apr. 2014. <http://search.ebscohost.com/login.aspx?direct=true&db=lfh&AN=103331MP421209820000153&site=ehost-live>.

Alighieri, Dante. *Inferno*. Trans. Allen Mandelbaum. New York: Bantam, 2004.

Bloom, Harold. *Shakespeare's Poems and Sonnets*. Broomall: Chelsea House, 1999.

Nabokov, Vladimir. *Lolita*. New York: Vintage, 1989.

Raffa, Guy P. *The Complete Danteworlds: A Reader's Guide to the Divine Comedy*. Chicago: U of Chicago P, 2009.

Shakespeare, William. "Sonnet 129." *Shakespearian Sonnets. Poetry & Short Story Reference Center*. Web. 4 Apr. 2014. <http://search.ebscohost.com/login.aspx?direct=true&db=lfh&AN=23066426&site=ehost-live>.

For Further Study

Atkins, Carl D., ed. *Shakespeare's Sonnets: With Three Hundred Years of Commentary*. Madison: Fairleigh Dickinson UP, 2007.

Vendler, Helen. *The Art of Shakespeare's Sonnets*. Cambridge: Belknap, 1999.

Sonnet 130

My mistress' eyes are nothing like the sun;
Coral is far more red, than her lips red:
If snow be white, why then her breasts are dun;
If hairs be wires, black wires grow on her head.
I have seen roses damasked, red and white,
But no such roses see I in her cheeks;
And in some perfumes is there more delight
Than in the breath that from my mistress reeks.
I love to hear her speak, yet well I know
That music hath a far more pleasing sound:
I grant I never saw a goddess go,
My mistress, when she walks, treads on the ground:
*   And yet by heaven, I think my love as rare,*
*   As any she belied with false compare.*

Abstract

Sonnet 130 mocks the exaggerated praise of beauty that flourished in the poetry of Shakespeare's time. Rather than supporting this type of praise, the speaker celebrates his lady as she is, implying his honesty as evidence of a more credible and authentic love.

Keywords

- Beauty
- Blazon
- Courtly Love
- Hyperbole
- Women
- Satire

Context

With its rejection of the hyperbole that had become standard in late medieval and early modern love poetry, Sonnet 130 is a mock-blazon that remains as relevant today as when Shakespeare wrote it. The poem belongs to the later sequence of Shakespeare's sonnets (numbers 127 through 152) that involve an irresistible, promiscuous woman whom scholars now refer to as the Dark Lady, in part based on the description offered in this sonnet. A simple reading might suggest that the speaker of Sonnet 130 denigrates his mistress by criticizing her ugly appearance, but the literary tradition and context of the poem as well as its final couplet clarify the intended effect of praise more worthy than that of other models.

The first quatrain presents a series of comparisons that subvert the clichés of conventional love poetry: the lover's praise of the beloved's eyes, lips, breasts, and hair. Here, the speaker proclaims that his lover's eyes "are nothing like the sun" (line 1), that "coral is far more red" (2) than her lips, that her breasts are dark rather than snowy, and "if hairs be wires, black wires grow on her head" (4). The second quatrain sustains this repudiation, as the speaker claims to find no roses in his mistress's cheeks and no aromatic scent on her breath. He asserts in the third quatrain that he loves to hear her speak, "yet well I know, / That music hath a far more pleasing sound" (10–11). Next, he admits that he has never seen a goddess walk (and therefore cannot reasonably offer a point of comparison) but notes, "My mistress when she walks treads on the ground" (12). The final couplet presents the key contrast to these apparent insults, as the speaker declares that his beloved is in fact rare, perhaps even more so than those lovers subject to false comparisons.

The poem's theme of exaggerated beauty becomes much clearer if one understands certain aesthetic values of the medieval and early modern cultures that informed Shakespeare's thought and work. Ideal female beauty in Shakespeare's time called for blonde hair, blue eyes, red lips, and fair skin with rosy cheeks. This image derived from the courtly love lyrics of twelfth-century French and Italian poets and musicians, who established it as a standard feature of the genre. In particular, the sonnets of fourteenth-century Italian poet Francesco Petrarca, better known as Petrarch, established both the figure of the angelic lady and the sonnet form as literary norms throughout Western Europe. In his poems, Petrarch idolizes his beloved, a golden-haired lady named Laura, whose unattainable love brings him both immeasurable joy and suffering.

Thomas Watson's late sixteenth-century collection of sonnets, *Hekatompathia or Passionate Century of Love*, represents an excellent English example of the tropes inspired by Petrarch and others. In the seventh sonnet in the *Hekatompathia*, Watson portrays his beloved as a "sainte I serve" (1) and claims that "her yellowe locks exceed the beated goulde" (2), that her sparkling eyes deserve a place in heaven, that her words "are musicke all of silver sounde" (5), that roses and lilies lie on her cheeks, that her "breath is sweete perfume" (9), and that her lips are redder than coral (Vendler 558). In Sonnet 130, Shakespeare upends most of these images and metaphors because they had become stale and meaningless; for the speaker, when it comes to his actual experience of love, these tropes no longer have cultural or aesthetic currency, so he exposes them for the silly exaggerations they really are. The poem thus seems to disparage the beloved, but in fact it defends and even celebrates her real self as superior to the ideals that no human woman can possibly approximate.

In the eighteenth century, English poet Alexander Pope mined the comic potential of hyperbole in *The Rape of the Lock*, which satirizes the triviality of aristocratic culture by elevating the theft of a lady's lock of hair to the level of an epic transgression such as the abduction of Helen of Troy. The poem thus portrays the potentially absurd consequences of idealizing aristocratic female beauty in the courtly tradition. The subversion or parody of idealized beauty, of course, does not mean that such ideals no longer exist in society, but it reveals a cultural awareness of the artificiality of such ideals.

With the rise of educational and artistic opportunities for women in the modern age, questioning ideals of beauty has become commonplace, and the artistic responses have become increasingly varied. Rather than using exaggeration to subvert the ideal, many writers have mobilized various forms of irony. For example, twentieth-century writer Anne Sexton's confessional poem "Snow White and the Seven Dwarfs" undermines conventional ideals of beauty to create a disturbing revision of the classic fairy tale that effectively conveys the destructive force of such ideals. Other modern narratives eschew irony to create more positive representations of female characters, portrayals that abandon or diminish society's emphasis on beauty. One notable example is Ethel Johnston Phelps's *Tatterhood and Other Tales*, a 1978 collection of classic folk and fairy tales that present strong heroines whose worth is not defined primarily by their appearance. This seminal collection inspired the publication of many subsequent volumes designed to shift values regarding the cultural importance placed on female beauty. Although this approach is totally different from Shakespeare's in Sonnet 130, both recognize in their own ways the crucial fact that unrealistic ideals become meaningless at best in the face of real human relationships.

Ashleigh Imus

Works Cited

Bloom, Harold, ed. *The Sonnets*. New York: Chelsea House, 2008.

Evans, G. Blakemore, ed. *The Riverside Shakespeare*. Boston: Houghton, 1974.

Martin, Philip J. T. *Shakespeare's Sonnets: Self, Love, and Art*. Cambridge: Cambridge UP, 1972.

Shakespeare, William. "Sonnet 130." *Shakespearian Sonnets. Literary Reference Center*. Web. 11 Apr. 2014. <http://search.ebscohost.com/login.aspx?direct=true&db=prf&AN=23066401&site=prc-live>.

Vendler, Helen. *The Art of Shakespeare's Sonnets*. Cambridge: Belknap, 1997.

For Further Study

Brewer, Leighton. *Shakespeare and the Dark Lady*. Boston: Christopher, 1966.

Lanyer, Aemilia & A. L. Rowse. *The Poems of Shakespeare's Dark Lady—Salve Deus Rex Judaeorum*. New York: Potter, 1979.

Rackin, Phyllis. *Shakespeare and Women*. Oxford: Oxford UP, 2005.

Sonnet 141

In faith I do not love thee with mine eyes,
For they in thee a thousand errors note;
But 'tis my heart that loves what they despise,
Who, in despite of view, is pleased to dote.
Nor are mine ears with thy tongue's tune delighted;
Nor tender feeling, to base touches prone,
Nor taste, nor smell, desire to be invited
To any sensual feast with thee alone:
But my five wits nor my five senses can
Dissuade one foolish heart from serving thee,
Who leaves unswayed the likeness of a man,
Thy proud heart's slave and vassal wretch to be:
*   Only my plague thus far I count my gain,*
*   That she that makes me sin awards me pain.*

Abstract

Sonnet 141 is one of a number of the later sonnets in which the speaker confesses, and regrets, his infatuation with the woman known as the Dark Lady. He finds it impossible to resist her or to control his own feelings, even though the poem makes it abundantly clear that he finds her physically unattractive. Paradoxically, by condemning her alleged physical ugliness he reveals his own moral shortcomings. Again paradoxically, by so openly revealing his own irrationality and his own flaws of mind and character, he implies that he still retains at least some moral and intellectual good sense.

Keywords

- Body
- Desire
- Ethics
- Infatuation
- Love
- Madness
- Morality
- Paradox
- Sin
- Soul
- Women

Context

Sonnet 141 is one of a number of sonnets from late in his sonnet sequence that address the mysterious woman known as the Dark Lady, who is presented as a source of unfortunate sensual temptation.. Frequently, the tone used when addressing her is mocking and even sardonic. In the present poem, for instance, she is depicted as far from physically beautiful but is still a source of irrational attraction to the speaker. The speaker's mind, common sense, and even physical senses tell him that his infatuation with her is foolish, but his heart persists in its misguided love for her.

The poem's opening line might at first seem to suggest a deep, spiritual affection rooted in love of the woman's character and soul rather than in her mere physical appearance, but the next few lines humorously undermine any such suggestion. The speaker is acutely aware that the woman is not beautiful, but the fact that he "despise[s]" (line 3) the "thousand errors" (2) he notes in her physical appearance reveals that physical appearance is in fact very important to him. Rather than ignoring or overlooking her physical flaws, he dwells on them in an outrageously comic manner. The poem is largely a list of insults directed at the woman he supposedly loves. He is in the paradoxical position, then, of being attracted to a woman he finds ugly even as he cares very little about her personality, morality, or spiritual traits.

The speaker "despise[s]" the woman's physical appearance (3), yet despite this fact he still "dote[s]" (4) on her—a word that suggests foolish attraction. This is a common theme of the later sonnets: the speaker in a sense despises himself for being attracted to a woman he finds, in many ways, despicable. In the present poem the tone is largely humorous as he finds ever more inventive ways to suggest that the woman is physically repulsive. Yet although he presents an unattractive picture of her, inevitably he presents a far from attractive picture of himself, suggesting his own shallow values even as he condemns her allegedly ugly appearance. The speaker is fully aware of the paradoxes of his relationship with this woman (as Sonnet 138 makes abundantly clear), but he feels powerless to end it.

Using a technique known as anaphora, in which successive lines begin with the same word or phrase—in this case "Nor" (5–7)—the speaker emphasizes that none of his five senses find the woman attractive. Nor do his "five wits" find her appealing (9): not his common sense, nor his imagination, nor his fantasy, nor his true estimation, nor his memory (Booth 487). This further emphasizes the speaker's irrationality in continuing to love her regardless. The final lines of the poem state that the speaker's attraction to the woman is sinful and that he suffers "pain" as a result (14). Is the pain, in part, the pain of venereal disease, as Booth suggests (488)? Such a reading makes sense in light of other sonnets (such as 144). In any case, the poem ends with a typical paradox: because the speaker admits to sin and believes he deserves pain as punishment, he paradoxically seems more spiritually worthy in the final, self-condemning line than he has seemed at any other point in the sonnet.

The theme that mere physical desire is often irrational is common in much medieval and Renaissance poetry. For instance, "The Miller's Tale," one of fourteenth-century English poet Geoffrey Chaucer's *Canterbury Tales*, features three men whose passion for a beautiful but faithless woman makes fools of them. All three are aware that pursuing the lovely Alison is not sensible: her older husband knows that she is young and wild and he cannot keep up with her, her lover Nicholas knows that she is married to a very jealous man, and her thwarted suitor Absalon knows that she does not care for him at all. Still, they are so overcome by desire for her that they woo her anyway, and all three end up worse off for it, just as the narrator in Sonnet 141 is "award[ed] pain" for his senseless desire for the Dark Lady. In contemporary popular culture, the pain caused by irrational love or desire is a frequent subject of song lyrics, though the treatment of the subject is often less self-aware than Shakespeare's is. Robert Palmer's famous song "Addicted to Love" has similar themes to Shakespeare's sonnet, but it lacks the irony and self-criticism Shakespeare's poem implies.

Sonnet 141's hyperbolic self-contradictions may be comical, but the speaker cannot be dismissed as simply an object of ridicule; many people have had the experience of realizing that something they do makes no sense even as they persist in doing it, or of craving something even though they are aware that it is not good for them. Both the humor and the pain of such situations have fueled fiction, poetry, and music from Chaucer's day to Shakespeare's to the twenty-first century.

Robert C. Evans

Works Cited

Booth, Stephen, ed. *Shakespeare's Sonnets*. New Haven: Yale UP, 1977.

Chaucer, Geoffrey. *The Canterbury Tales*. Trans. Nevill Coghill. New York: Penguin, 2003.

Duncan-Jones, Katherine, ed. *Shakespeare's Sonnets*. London: Nelson, 1997.

Edmundson, Paul & Stanley Wells. *Shakespeare's Sonnets*. Oxford: Oxford UP, 2004.

Evans, G. Blakemore, ed. *The Sonnets*. By William Shakespeare. Cambridge: Cambridge UP, 1996.

For Further Study

Schoenfeldt, Michael, ed. *A Companion to Shakespeare's Sonnets*. Oxford: Blackwell, 2010.

"Sonnets of Shakespeare." *Masterplots*. 4th ed. Ed. Laurence W. Mazzeno. Pasadena: Salem, 2010. *Literary Reference Center*. Web. 30 Apr. 2014. <http://search.ebscohost.com/login.aspx?direct=true&db=lfh&AN=103331MP428589560000853>.

Welsh, James M., and Jill Stapleton-Bergeron. "Sonnets of Shakespeare." *Magill's Survey of World Literature*. Rev. ed. Ed. Steven G. Kellman. Pasadena: Salem, 2009. Print. Literary Reference Center. Web. 30 Apr. 2014. <http://search.ebscohost.com/login.aspx?direct=true&db=lfh&AN=103331MSW23359850001334>.

Sonnet 146

Poor soul, the centre of my sinful earth,
... ... these rebel powers that thee array
Why dost thou pine within and suffer dearth,
Painting thy outward walls so costly gay?
Why so large cost, having so short a lease,
Dost thou upon thy fading mansion spend?
Shall worms, inheritors of this excess,
Eat up thy charge? Is this thy body's end?
Then soul, live thou upon thy servant's loss,
And let that pine to aggravate thy store;
Buy terms divine in selling hours of dross;
Within be fed, without be rich no more:
*   So shall thou feed on Death, that feeds on men,*
*   And Death once dead, there's no more dying then.*

Abstract

The pleasures of the body and the virtue of the soul are placed in tension with one another in Sonnet 146. Shakespeare argues that the body is like a "sinful earth" in which the soul is trapped and that attention to bodily pleasures come at great cost to the spirit.

Keywords

- Beauty
- Body
- Death
- Pleasure
- Soul

Context

At times referred to as Shakespeare's "Christian sonnet," Sonnet 146 addresses the speaker's soul in a rather despondent moment. It opens by questioning the soul, which the speaker describes as existing at " the centre of my sinful earth" (line 1). This metaphor, with the intangible soul existing in the real, physical form of the body, continues through the remainder of the poem. It is this tension between the physical and the spiritual that the sonnet seeks to resolve, asking why the soul would place itself in a body when the decoration and pleasures of that body come only at the expense of the soul. In the third quatrain, the sonnet ceases to question the soul and instead implores it, urging it to " within be fed, without be rich no more" (12)—that is, to take care of spiritual concerns rather than wasting energy on physical riches and pleasures. Ultimately, Shakespeare's speaker argues that a pure devotion to spiritual matters and rejection of the physical body might be a way to overcome death itself, for in such an ideal spirituality the soul will " feed on death, that feeds on men" (13). In the end, then, the metaphor of the sonnet's opening still stands, the body always destined to be a " sinful earth" in which the soul must live, the caring for the physical form possible only at the expense of the spiritual self.

Within the larger sequence of Shakespeare's sonnets, Sonnet 146 comes near to the conclusion. Following the romantic and spiritual love felt for the young man known as the Fair Youth and the outpouring of lust and bawdy attraction felt for the woman known as the Dark Lady, the subjects of many of Shakespeare's sonnets, Sonnet 146 finds Shakespeare's speaker in a somewhat pensive mood. He has spent a great majority of the sonnets praising the physical beauty of his two loves. Now, turning inward, he questions the worth of the body and attractiveness, realizing that he should scorn such preoccupations if he wishes to fulfill his soul.

The body and the soul are regularly portrayed as being in such tension in Western literature, with the pleasures of bodily beauty coming at great cost to the spirit. British writer Oscar Wilde's gothic novel *The Picture of Dorian Gray* (1890) takes this tension as one of its prime themes. The story follows young Dorian Gray, a gorgeous man who inspires the artist Basil Hallward. Hallward paints a picture of Gray, and when Gray is overcome by sadness with the realization that he will not always look so young, the will of his narcissism is able to summon supernatural results. As Gray goes on to lead a life driven by passion, bodily desire, and cruelty, he finds that his physical body stays youthful while the picture ages and grows ugly. Just as Shakespeare argues that the pleasures of the body cannot be pursued without some spiritual cost, the portrait of Gray stands as testament to all the man's wicked and indulgent ways, growing uglier with every evil deed. This contrast is the same as that which initiates the sonnet's questioning, Shakespeare wondering why a soul would take residence in a body when that body's beauty and perfection (like the fair looks of Gray) can be no more than a lie, a " sinful earth."

Just as the striking beauty of Gray is shadowed by

his hideous portrait, the gleaming and terrifying figure of Darth Vader in the science-fiction film franchise *Star Wars* hides a hideous and dying form. In the films, Darth Vader is the evil leader of a galactic empire. While he wears a black suit of technological armor, shining and perfect, inside he is a damaged and weak man. As Shakespeare imagines that one might spend great energy perfecting his or her body only to damage the soul, Darth Vader is revealed to " pine within and suffer dearth" (3). *Star Wars* further references the idea that such a split between exterior and interior might exist in the rare moment when Darth Vader appears without his helmet on. Having battled his estranged son, a dying Vader removes his helmet in one of his only kind moments, revealing that a soul (although dying) lives inside and separating himself from the façade of the armor.

Must the body and the soul be in strict opposition, the pursuit of physical pleasure only available at great cost to the spiritual self? This is not always the dominant theme in Shakespeare's sonnets, yet following the lustful longing and praise of beauty of the sequence, Sonnet 146 presents a speaker who doubts the values of those pleasures he so often pursues. In the end, while total devotion to the body might be desirable to some, the ideal beauty of a portrait or the perfectly gleaming exterior of a suit of armor almost always comes at a great expense to the spirit.

T. Fleischmann

Works Cited

Adcock, Patrick. " The Picture of Dorian Gray." *Masterplots*. 4th ed. Ed. Lawrence W. Mazzeno. Pasadena: Salem, 2010. *Literary Reference Center*. Web. 14 Apr. 2014. <http://search.ebscohost.com/login.aspx?direct=true&db=lfh&AN=103331MP425279320000264>.

Goldsmith, Robert Hillis. " Shakespeare's Christian Sonnet, Number 146." *Studies in the Literary Imagination* 11.1 (1978): 99. *Academic Search Premier*. Web. 14 Apr. 2014. <http://search.ebscohost.com/login.aspx?direct=true&db=aph&AN=6881439>.

Shakespeare, William. " Sonnet 146." *Shakespearean Sonnets*. *Literary Reference Center*. Web. 14 Apr. 2014. <http://search.ebscohost.com/login.aspx?direct=true&db=lfh&AN=23066445>.

Star Wars: Episode IV – A New Hope. Dir. George Lucas. Twentieth Century Fox, 1977. Film.

Wilde, Oscar. *The Picture of Dorian Gray*. New York: Dover Thrift, 1993.

For Further Study

Atkins, Carl D., ed. *Shakespeare's Sonnets: With Three Hundred Years of Commentary*. Madison: Fairleigh Dickinson UP, 2007.

Vendler, Helen. *The Art of Shakespeare's Sonnets*. Oxford: Belknap, 1999.

Sonnet 151

Love is too young to know what conscience is,
Yet who knows not conscience is born of love?
Then, gentle cheater, urge not my amiss,
Lest guilty of my faults thy sweet self prove:
For, thou betraying me, I do betray
My nobler part to my gross body's treason;
My soul doth tell my body that he may
Triumph in love; flesh stays no farther reason,
But rising at thy name doth point out thee,
As his triumphant prize. Proud of this pride,
He is contented thy poor drudge to be,
To stand in thy affairs, fall by thy side.
   No want of conscience hold it that I call
   Her love, for whose dear love I rise and fall.

Abstract

Bawdy puns and jokes abound in Sonnet 151, a poem in which the speaker wrestles between his physical desires and his conscience. The role of sexual puns in literature and art is further explored.

Keywords

- Physicality
- Puns
- Sexuality

Context

Bawdy and at times bordering on vulgar, Sonnet 151 uses the metaphor of an erect penis to explore the physical relationship between the speaker and his subject, a woman known as the Dark Lady. The sonnet opens with the declaration that the personification of love (a reference to Cupid) is too young to know the difference between right and wrong, yet all people know that "conscience is born of love" (line 2). From there, the sonnet quickly moves through a number of sexual puns and declarations of indecent behavior. The Dark Lady is a "gentle cheater" (3) and the speaker a man driven by his bodily needs. By the second quatrain, the puns come to dominate the verse, as his "nobler part" (6), a reference to his penis, is betrayed to the rest of his body. The soul regularly tries to rise, conscience taking hold again, but the speaker quickly falls back into the sexual puns, the phallus "rising at thy name" (9) and, in a reference to sex, quick to "stand in thy affairs, fall by thy side" (12).

The final couplet finally responds to the opening declaration by bringing the speaker's morality and sexuality together, insisting that he should not be judged for lacking a conscience just because he will "rise and fall" (14) for the Dark Lady.

The struggle between the body and the soul is a regular topic in Shakespeare's sonnet sequence. At this late point in the sequence, however, only a few sonnets before the close, it appears the body might be winning out. While Shakespeare's earlier sonnets, addressed to a young man known as the Fair Youth, emphasize a purer and more spiritual love, those focused on the Dark Lady are overtaken by sexual passion. Adulterous, bawdy, and crude, as the sequence comes to a close, the touching romances of early sonnets seem a distant memory.

Sexual puns have been common for centuries, even in the most sophisticated literature, and have appeared as important devices in everything from the work of Latin poet Catullus to the foundational literary masterpiece *The Canterbury Tales*. Shakespeare, however, arguably remains the master of the double entendre and bawdy pun, even in his most romantic works. *Romeo and Juliet*, for instance, is widely regarded as one of the most touching love stories of all time, yet its story is overflowing with crude puns. When Romeo struggles to find love, for instance, his friend Mercutio suggests that he should find a woman who is "an open arse, and thou a poperin pear." While "open arse" was the common name for a fruit at the time, a "poperin pear" did not even exist and is used here only for the crude pun on "pop 'er in." In effect, then, at the height of Romeo's romantic sorrows, his best friend suggests he find a woman who will have anal sex. Juliet is also subject to these bawdy jokes when her nurse repeats a story in which the young Juliet, having fallen on her face, is told that she will "fall backward when thou has more wit" (1.3.46), suggesting that she will soon lie down for sex. All of these puns are not out of place in the romantic play but rather, as in Sonnet 151, serve to emphasize the role of sexuality in love. Romeo and Juliet might wish to praise their sincere and soulful love, and the speaker of Sonnet 151 struggles with questions of conscience, but the bawdy puns reveal that they are all as fixated on sex as they are on romance.

Of course, crude sexual puns are also often funny, a quality that allows them to entertain audiences while challenging the distinction between sex and love. Such puns have become a regular feature of the James Bond series of adventure films. Bond is an action hero and spy as well as a suave seducer. Throughout the films, obvious puns are used to highlight his role as a legendary lover and to make fun of his obsession with sex. In the film *Moonraker* (1979), for instance, Bond defeats an evil villain aboard a spaceship, and in the moments after victory, he seduces a woman named Dr. Holly Goodhead. When his allies attempt to check on him, one claims that Bond is "attempting reentry," a pun on the spaceship reentering earth's atmosphere and on intercourse. Similarly, in the film *Tomorrow Never Dies* (1997), Bond's romance with a Scandinavian language teacher is met with the comment that he is a "cunning linguist," a play on the word *cunnilingus*. In the many sexual puns in Bond films, the hero is always both celebrated and teased for his amorous ways, just as Shakespeare struggles to reconcile his own physical passions with his faltering conscience.

Puns and crude jokes are often looked on as "low" forms of humor, yet they have had a significant role in literature. Puns such as "rising at thy name" and "cunning linguist" might be groan-inducing jokes, but they also help subtly comment on the characters themselves. Human beings might claim their concerns are based in higher, more spiritual matters or that Romeo and Juliet's love is the purest form of romance, but the sexual pun endures as a reminder that just as often, people are simply looking for some physical passion.

T. Fleischmann

Works Cited

Atchity, Kenneth John. "Romeo and Juliet." *Masterplots*. 4th ed. Ed. Lawrence W. Mazzeno. Pasadena: Salem, 2010. *Literary Reference Center*. Web. 9 Apr. 2014. <http://search.ebscohost.com/login.aspx?direct=true&db=lfh&AN=103331MP427149560000790>.

Moonraker. Dir. Lewis Gilbert. MGM, 1979. Film.

Shakespeare, William. *Romeo and Juliet*. Ed. Barbara A. Mowat & Paul A. Werstine. New York: Pocket, 1992.

Shakespeare, William. "Sonnet 151." *Shakespearian Sonnets*. *Literary Reference Center*. Web. 9 Apr. 2014. <http://search.ebscohost.com/login.aspx?direct=true&db=lfh&AN=23066455>.

Tomorrow Never Dies. Dir. Roger Spottiswoode. MGM, 1997. Film.

For Further Study

Hart, Jonathan. *Shakespeare: Poetry, History, and Culture*. New York: Palgrave, 2009.

Vendler, Helen. *The Art of Shakespeare's Sonnets*. Oxford: Belknap, 1999.

Critical Readings 1:
Form & Technique

The Form of Shakespeare's Sonnets

Here we shall discuss the overall form as it relates to the arrangement of Shakespeare's Sonnets and its subsections and argue that the poems are more properly regarded as a collection than as a sequence. They do not hang together on the thread of a single narrative or by virtue of a single addressee. Almost all of the mare love poems in the sense that they address a loved person or spring out of the poet's shifting relationship with such a person, and changes in the relationships hint at an underlying narrative, but it can scarcely be called a story.

As the collection was first printed it falls into two major divisions. The first one-hundred-twenty-six poems include none that are clearly addressed to, or concern, a woman, along with all the ones that are clearly addressed to, or primarily concern, a male. The sonnets from 127 onwards include all the poems that are overtly addressed to, or primarily concern, a female. This is clearly a deliberate and careful division. But it should not be assumed that the first part does not include any poems which might be addressed to a woman, and vice versa. As Colin Burrow writes, in these poems "one is not quite sure who is male and who is female, who is addressed or why, or what their respective social roles are." Nor should it be taken for granted that all the poems in the first part refer to a man, however likely this may seem. Some of the poems in the first part are regularly reprinted in anthologies as non-specific love poems. In particular, Sonnet 18, "Shall I compare thee to a summer's day?," is often taken to refer to a woman, and Sonnet 116, "Let me not to the marriage of true minds," is a popular choice for reading at heterosexual weddings and funerals. Table 1 shows more clearly how the collection can be gendered, depending on questions of context and ordering.

The last poem of the first group, beginning "O thou, my lovely boy," is not a strict sonnet, being a series of six rhyming pentameter couplets, as if the sonnet were entirely made up of conclusions. There are then only twelve lines in the poem in which the poet relinquishes the power of his love to the inevitability of Time. Because of its placing and its formal irregularity this poem is sometimes described as an envoi—a farewell, or closing poem. It marks a clear end to the first major part of the collection. In the 1609 Quarto two open, line-long empty brackets paradoxically emphasize the

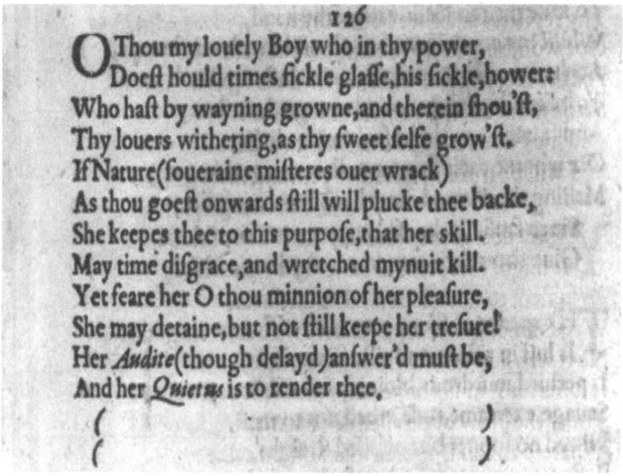

Image 1. The empty brackets printed after the twelve lines of Sonnet 126 have provoked much speculation about their significance.

absence of lines 13 and 14, suggesting perhaps that they have been erased by Time making "Her audit (though delayed)"—presumably over one-hundred-twenty-five sonnets.

Though the poem has something of the typical sonnet structure, in its original printing it is followed enigmatically by two pairs of brackets. Although for many years the general assumption was that the parentheses were simply a printer's aberration, or his way of indicating that the poem appeared to be incomplete, more recently they have been relentlessly interrogated, yielding an extraordinary range of interpretations which must derive rather from the reader than from the author. They have been compared to the (empty) marks in an account book; to the shape of an hourglass that contains no sand; to little moons that "image a repeated waxing and waning of the moon, pointing to fickleness and frailty"; to representations of a grave; and—because they stand in for a couplet—to the image of a failure to couple. They may be seen as marking a breathing space before the reader embarks on the second part; in their suggestion of curtailment they may indicate that the male/male relationship of the first part has petered out in insterility; they may even invite readers to contribute a couplet of their own devising.

Table 1. *Sexing the Sonnets: Male and Female addressees*
Sonnets which suggest a male addressee

1	33
3	39
6	41
7	42
9	63
13	67
16	68
19	101
20	108
26	126

Sonnets which might imply a male addressee, either because of their context, or because of their subject matter, but which could imply either a male or a female, if read independently

2	36
4	54
5	79
8	80
10	81
11	82
12	83
14	84
15	85
34	86
35	

Sonnets which suggest a female addressee

127	141
130	145
138	151
139	

Sonnets which might imply a female addressee, either because of their context, or because of their subject matter, but which could imply either a male or a female, if read independently

93	134
119	135
131	136
132	147
133	152

Sonnets which refer to male and female subjects

41	106
53	144

By our count, only twenty of the poems, all in the first group (Sonnets 1–126), can confidently be said, on the evidence of forms of address and masculine pronouns, to be addressed to, or to concern, a male, while seven, all in the second group (Sonnets 127–52), are clearly about a female. Other sonnets which might seem definite about the gender of their addressees rely on context, or subject matter, rather than pronouns (see Table 1). Some of the poems in the earlier group relate to the poet's relationship with a woman, and four of those in the later part—Nos. 133, 134, 135, and 144—show the poet anguishing about his relationship between a man and a woman; in the last of these, Sonnet 144—"Two loves I have, of comfort and despair"—he is torn between a man and a woman, and pretty clearly prefers the man, his "better angel." All the rest of the poems in the collection (those not listed individually on Table 1) could in theory be addressed to, or be about, either a male or a female. Some of the most intense love poems, such as Sonnets 27, 43, and 61, could, considered on their own, be addressed either to a male or to a female.

Of the one-hundred-fifty-four poems in the collection, one-hundred-twenty-three are addressed to an individual, whether male or female. The remaining thirty-one vary in their degree of relevance and connection to those that surround them. So, for example, Sonnet 5 when considered on its own is a meditation on the effects of time on human and natural beauty, concluding with the reflection that they can be countered by 'distillation.' But it leads straight into the following poem which, beginning 'Then let not . . .," applies to an individual the moral implied in the preceding one. The structure of the two poems taken together resembles that of Sonnet 12, where a generalized reflection on the effects of time is applied to an individual; in Sonnets 5 and 6, however, the generalization takes up one sonnet and its application another. These poems form a double sonnet which is essentially a single poem. Others are linked through contradiction (and 74). Some sonnets without personal addressees are linked to their neighbors in that, though they do not address anyone in particular, they write about a specific individual in the third person, for example Nos. 63–8—a mini-sequence in the first three of which the poet reflects upon the effects of time on his love, followed by three in which world-weariness is redeemed only by thought of the beloved. Other short sequences within the collection are linked by theme or subject matter, for example Nos. 100–3, in which the poet is searching for and responding to his muse. Many small groupings may be suggested within the collection as a whole; more are listed in Table 2.

Three poems have no obvious thematic connections with the sequence and could have been printed independently as generalized meditations. First is Sonnet 94, the enigmatic 'They that have power to hurt and will do none . . . ,' which in subject matter seems out of place in a collection of love poems (though the imagery of flowers in its sestet looks forward to the sonnet that follows). It comes in the midst of a sequence of loosely connected poems, stretching back at least as far as Sonnet 79, in which initially the poet expresses jealousy of a rival poet. There is nothing in any of the 'rival poet' poems to show that they are addressed to a male; the assumption that they are derives from the fact that they are in the first part of the collection and from their link with the love triangle revealed in Sonnets 133–6 and 144. Increasingly the poet resents the beloved's love of praise,

regretting his own incapacity to supply it. Sonnet 87 is a poem of renunciation—'Farewell, thou art too dear for my possessing'—and in the following three the still-loving poet declares himself not merely guilty of any faults that his lover may find in him but willing to take disgrace upon himself if it will help to justify his lover in joining with the rest of the world to spite him (Sonnet 90). There is a little relief in Sonnet 91, where the relationship seems to have been partly resumed though it is still precarious: 'thou mayst take | All this away, and me most wretched make.' In Sonnet 92 he fears that the beloved may 'be false, and yet I know it not,' and this

Table 2. *Groups of sonnets*
Note: Identifying groups of sonnets within the collection will always be, to some extent, subjectively inflected. This table has no claim to exhaustiveness in its search for links between one sonnet and another/others.

Small groups of sonnets and sequences within Shakespeare's collection	Reason for linkage: a keyword, or theme
1-17	Persuasion to procreate
5 and 6	*Then*
9 and 10	*shame* (last line of 9, first line of 10)
15, 16, and 17	Writing for eternity
23 and 24	Eyesight
27 and 28	Insomnia
33 and 34	Weather and relationship
40, 41, and 42	Attacking, love triangle
44 and 45	The four elements
46 and 47	*Eye* and *heart*
50 and 51	*Thus* and journey
55-60	Different experiences of Time when in love

57 and 58	Slave of love
63, 64, 65, 66, 67, 68	Time and beauty
67 and 68	Thus
69 and 70	Blame
71 and 72	*World*
73 and 74	*But*
78, 79, 80, 82, 83, 84, 85 and 86	Rival poet/s
88, 89 and 90	*Against myself*/hate
91, 92 and 93	*But*, falsity
97, 98 and 99	Seasons
100, 101, 102 and 103	Muse sonnets (Muse also mentioned in others)
106, 107, 108 and 109	Echoes on writing, peace, and time (Kerrigan, pp. 8-9)
109 and 110	Contradiction of constancy and falsity
111 and 112	Pity
113 and 114	*Mind*
118 and 119	Sickness/Fever
125 and 126	*Render*
129 and 130	Stand alone sonnets, work almost antithetically, unusual so close together
131, 132 and 133	Groaning sonnets
131, 132, 133, 134, 135 and 136	Love triangle

134, 135 and 136	*Will*
140, 141 and 142	*Eyes* and *sin*
(137), 138, 139, 140, 141 and 142	Lies, dishonesty
153 and 154	Classical allusions, Cupid, translations

leads into Sonnet 93 in which he imagines himself 'like a deceivèd husband.' (This is the only phrase in the whole mini-sequence which might be taken to imply that the poet is addressing a male; he could not feel *like* a husband if he were addressing his wife, and it would seem odd to use this phrase of a mistress.) This poem anticipates Sonnet 138, which is clearly about a woman, in its willingness to accept false appearances as reality. The idea that the beloved's beauty is such that, 'whate'er thy thoughts or thy heart's workings be, | Thy looks should nothing thence but sweetness tell' (Sonnet 93) provides at least a hint of a context for the otherwise independent Sonnet 94, which is about people who are 'lords and owners of their faces.' It's not, however, the same—in Sonnet 93 the person addressed simply cannot express anything but 'sweetness,' whereas in Sonnet 94 he or she has and exercises the ability to keep his or her features under complete control. But perhaps it's enough to plant a seed from which Sonnet 94 may have sprung. It may also be relevant that the ability to control facial expression is a virtue in members of the acting profession to which Shakespeare belonged.

The enigma in this poem resides partly in these lines:

The summer's flower is to the summer sweet,
Though to itself it only live and die,
But if that flower with base infection meet,
The basest weed outbraves his dignity:
 For sweetest things turn sourest by their deeds;
 Lilies that fester smell far worse than weeds.

What exactly is it saying? The first two lines refer to people who restrain themselves from causing hurt even if they 'show' the desire to do so. The next two indicate, however, that these people remain impassive even while 'moving others'—to what? Then we are told that these people 'rightly do inherit nature's graces,' as if the qualities we have been told they display deserve reward, which is not entirely evident. Lines 7 and 8 seem as if they should sum up what has so far been said: 'They are the lords and owners of their faces, | Others but stewards of their excellence.' Is impassivity a virtue? In what sense are people who cannot control their expressions 'stewards of their excellence'? Are they stewards of their own excellence, or of the excellence of those who are 'lords and owners of their faces'?

The rest of the sonnet is more straightforward. Metaphorically it says that beauty ('the summer's flower') is sweet even if it does not propagate itself ('Though to itself it only live and die'), but if it becomes infected it is worth no more than 'The basest weed.' What is the tenor of the metaphor? And the couplet appears to be trying to make a link with the octave: 'For sweetest things turn sourest by their deeds. | Lilies that fester smell far worse than weeds.' (This last line is found also in the anonymous play, attributed at least in part to Shakespeare, *Edward III*. Though proverbial in tone, it has not been found elsewhere.) But what exactly is the link? The poem struggles to give an impression of profundity but its excessive use of generalization and metaphor inhibits communication.

The next poem that lacks clear links to its companions, though it is relevant enough as a withdrawal from the particular to the general in a love sequence, is Sonnet 116, 'Let me not to the marriage of true minds,' an eloquent tribute to the power of love which nevertheless has a sting in its tail: 'If this be error and upon me proved, | I never writ, nor no man ever loved.' Does this mean that it is not an error, or that it is an illusion to which all lovers are susceptible? And, for that matter, do the last words stand independently as 'no man ever loved' or refer back to 'I' to mean 'I never loved any man'? And is the poem a tribute to the power of love in general, or of love of man to woman (as generally supposed) or of man for man, as the context might suggest?

Most detached of all is the great but damaged Sonnet 146, which would be more at home in a religious than in an amatory sequence. It may be significant that it immediately follows the Anne Hathaway sonnet (Sonnet 145), which also seems irrelevantly imported into the collection. The antithesis between soul and body has occurred earlier, and will be repeated in a grosser context in Sonnet 151. It is a Renaissance topos; *Love's Labour's Lost* might be regarded as an extended dramatization of it. Shakespeare develops it here with consummate skill in a perfectly formed poem, marred only by the textual dislocation in its second line. The couplet is worthy of

John Donne ('Death, thou shalt die,' *Holy Sonnets*, 6) and anticipates Dylan Thomas's 'Death, thou shalt have no dominion' (itself biblical in origin): addressing his soul, Shakespeare writes

So shalt thou feed on Death, that feeds on men,
And Death once dead, there's no more dying then.

(Sonnet 146)

The Chronology of the Collection

Discussion of the form of the collection cannot avoid consideration of whether it was written as a whole, and if not, when individual poems were composed. This is a highly contentious topic. Although the Sonnets were not initially written in the order in which they are printed in the 1609 text, there are a few fixed points. The irregular Sonnet 145, with its puns on Hathaway, is probably the earliest, dating from around 1581–2. Francis Meres's reference to Shakespeare's 'sugared sonnets' in 1598 shows that some of them were written by then (curiously, the phrase 'sugared sonnets' also occurs in Barnfield's *Greene's Funerals*, of 1594: Sonnet 9—a poem in the six-line stanza form of *Venus and Adonis*—Meres declares himself a friend of Barnfield's, who was a fan of both Marlowe and Shakespeare; it looks if they may have formed something of a poetic circle). There is no absolute certainty that these sonnets are among those printed in 1609; and 'sonnets' could mean simply lyrics. But in 1593 versions of two sonnets, Sonnets 138 ('When my love swears that she is made of truth') and 144 ('Two loves I have, of comfort and despair'), appear as Shakespeare's in *The Passionate Pilgrim*. As this is an unauthorized publication, we must suppose that they were printed from a privately circulated manuscript, presumably released by an indiscreet 'private friend.' Both are among Shakespeare's more intimate poems; maybe this, as much as the fact that they were printed without authority, was what caused Shakespeare's sense of offence with the publisher. And both, obviously, were finally printed in the later part of the collection. The latest datable sonnet may be Sonnet 107, in which the line 'The mortal moon hath her eclipse endured' may, but does not certainly, refer obliquely to the death of Queen Elizabeth in 1603.

The poems may then have been written over a period of some twenty years, and some could even date from as late as the year in which the collection first appeared; this is in itself an argument against the supposition, once current, that they were conceived as a sequence. Beyond this, attempts to date them have to rely principally on evidence from literary context and style, neither of which is infallible. The vogue for sonnet sequences initiated by the publication of Sidney's *Astrophil and Stella* in 1591 climaxed around 1596. Shakespeare's use of the form in plays extends as far as *Cymbeline*, written about 1610, but is most apparent in *Love's Labour's Lost* and *Romeo and Juliet*, of around 1595. This is in any case the period during which Shakespeare makes most use of lyric forms in his plays—*A Midsummer Night's Dream* is another example—so it would not be surprising to find him writing sonnets at the same time. Readers who know Shakespeare's plays may easily be tempted to see a broad resemblance between the stylistic development apparent in them and that between the earliest and latest printed poems in the collection. Shakespeare's earliest plays are those that display the greatest formality of style. The first seventeen of the Sonnets, which all play variations on the theme of procreation and are relatively distanced in their use of the sonnet form, may seem to belong to the same world as the early comedies.

The later sonnets include some of the most intense poems, resembling some of the anguished self-revelations of characters in the plays. The common impression that the latest printed poems were also the last to be written is based on a subjective reaction—not necessarily any the worse for that, but in contradiction to the results of recent, more scientifically based studies. Some of these rely on analyses of the Sonnets' vocabulary in relation to that of the plays (whose chronology itself is also, it has to be admitted, far from certain). They identify words that occur rarely within the canon as a whole, and within plays that are close in date of composition. Occurrence of such words within the Sonnets is taken to indicate composition around the same date. Studies carried out by MacDonald P. Jackson suggest that most of the sonnets from 1 to 103, and 127 to the end, were written from 1593 to 1599 (when the vogue for the sonnet form was at its height), that most of the so-called 'Dark Lady' sonnets are among the earliest, and that most of the sonnets from 104 to 126 were written in the seventeenth century. Jackson believes it is unhelpful to think of the Sonnets as chronologically homogeneous and that Burrow's edition represents the dating of the Sonnets too tidily. Burrow suggests, for example, that the latest sonnets were finished by 1604. We believe that, on balance, there can be no immediate objection to the proposition that Shakespeare was still writing or revising Sonnets up until their publication in 1609. The fairly recent

theory that the differences between Sonnets 138 and 144 as printed first in *The Passionate Pilgrim* in 1599 and later in 1609 result from revision rather than corruption in the earlier publication encourages the idea that individual sonnets may have been subject to some degree of revision at the time that they were assembled as a collection, presumably by Shakespeare himself. Other poets did the same kind of thing: Michael Drayton, for instance, reworked his sequence, first published as *Idea* in 1594, over a period of twenty years until it appeared in its final form as *Idea's Mirror* in 1619. It seems clear, then, that at some point in the early seventeenth century someone, presumably Shakespeare himself, arranged a pre-existing set of poems in which smaller groupings exist and in which connections concerned with dates of composition can be identified.

Within the two major divisions a number of other groupings may be discerned. Most clearly, the first seventeen poems as printed include all those that implore a young man to marry and to have children. Another mini-sequence of poems about separation and absence preluded by Sonnet 39—'let us divided live'—is taken up by Sonnets 41 and 42 in which it is linked with the theme of the youth's infidelity with the poet's mistress, and continues to Sonnet 52—'So am I as the rich . . . .' It is interrupted by the nevertheless not unrelated Sonnet 49, in which the poet meditates on how he might feel if the youth deserted him. Within this subgroup come pairs of sonnets which together virtually constitute a single poem. Sonnet 44's concern with two of the elements, earth and water, is picked up in the first line of Sonnet 45, 'The other two, slight air and purging fire.' Then Sonnet 46, beginning 'Mine eye and heart are at a mortal war,' is followed by one beginning 'Betwixt mine eye and heart a league is took.' Sonnets 79 to 80 and 83 to 86 concern the poet's rivalry with another poet for the young man's favors; the preceding sonnet—Sonnet 78—may be regarded as a prelude since in it the poet writes of how 'every alien pen' has found inspiration in his friend's beauty.

Some of the links between sonnets discussed above may result from contiguity of composition. Indeed certain linked sonnets may also be regarded as 'double sonnets,' or two-part poems. Other links may be the result rather of reorganization after the initial act of composition. It is often argued that the placing of certain sonnets has numerological significance. The numbering of Sonnet 60, with its emphasis on minutes and hours, is clearly appropriate. And the number 12 fits well with the ticking rhythm of that sonnet's opening line—'When I do count the clock that tells the time.' The physical effects of time on the lover are discussed in both Sonnet 63, the age at which the human body was thought to face its major crisis in development, or 'grand climacteric,' and Sonnet 49, the age at which a 'minor climacteric' was believed to occur. It is difficult to know whether to ascribe esoteric significance to the matches between number and content or to put them down to coincidence. They may be no more than a sophisticated kind of game with the reader, or a way of adding a few grace notes by way of decoration. If they are intentional the numbering must be Shakespeare's own, which might otherwise be doubted: the poems may have been unnumbered in the manuscript, and numbers may have been added either by a scribe or by a compositor.

Beliefs about the date of the Sonnets have critical consequences. The possibility that they were written over a long period of time, as well as the fact that they are not necessarily printed in the order in which they were composed, is a reason for questioning whether there may have been more than one friend, more than one lover. So, if the Sonnets are 'about' specific individuals, possibly commissioned or presented as gifts to Shakespeare's 'private friends,' there may have been more than two of them. At least four kinds of persons, three males and one female, figure in the collection. One is the poetic voice (and this may be re-imagined as female); another is a male addressee. A third is a poet who is amorously entangled with both a male addressee and the fourth person, a 'black' woman who is the initial poet's lover. Various characteristics which could be attributed to these personae may be identified, and an attempt to do this may help to illuminate a particular dimension of the sequence. The shifting impressionism of the poems' characterization creates a desire for a precision which the poems themselves deny. So we must emphasize that since the addressees may not remain constant throughout the collection, these characteristics may not inhere in any single individual, whether real or imaginary.

The Poet's Voice

The poet—or perhaps we should say the shifting persona of the poet—reveals a few aspects of himself relevant to the implied narrative at different points in the collection. The poet never states that he is married; he even goes so far as to suggest that his relationship to the male friend resembles that of a wife to her husband: 'So shall I live, supposing thou art true, | Like a deceivèd husband' (Sonnet 93). He has, however, a female partner, not only in the second but also in the first part; Sonnet 41, for instance, rebukes the friend for breaking a 'two-fold troth: | Hers, by thy beauty tempting her to thee, | Thine, by thy beauty being false to me.' In some of the poems the poet is older than the friend, most obviously in Sonnet 73:

> That time of year thou mayst in me behold
> When yellow leaves, or none, or few do hang
> Upon those boughs which shake against the cold,
> Bare ruined choirs, where late the sweet birds sang.

In Sonnet 62 he describes himself as 'Beated and chapped with tanned antiquity,' and in Sonnet 138 says that his mistress 'knows [his] days are past the best.' Though some of the poet's expressions of unworthiness ('Being your slave . . . ,' Sonnet 57) may simply be poetic tropes, at various points he expresses a sense of being victimized: 'Now, while the world is bent my deeds to cross, | Join with the spite of Fortune' (Sonnet 90), 'O, for my sake do you with Fortune chide, | The guilty goddess of my harmful deeds' (Sonnet 111). He is the victim of an unspecified 'vulgar scandal' (Sonnet 112). A sense of his own unworthiness in comparison with the beloved is a recurrent theme. Some unspecified cause, a 'separable spite' (Sonnet 36), often keeps him apart from his friend—is this disparity of rank?—geographical separation?—the poet's married state?—the fact that they are both male?; a number of the Sonnets express grief and longing in absence. He loves both the friend and a woman who is 'black' in appearance and in character, and is torn between them. And the poet's name is Will[iam] (Sonnets 135–6, and possibly Sonnet 143).

The Young Man (or Men)

A beloved is not certainly named, though it is possible to infer from the puns throughout Sonnets 135 and 136 that he, too, is a Will. He is certainly unmarried in some of the poems, and none of the others contradicts this. Early poems in the collection address a man in loving terms while criticizing, sometimes harshly, his selfishness in failing to marry and so to defy time by passing his beauty on to posterity.

One feature of Shakespeare's collection that differentiates it from all others is that the beloved, though frequently idealized in the first part, is nevertheless faulty: 'for the first time in the entire history of the sonnet, the desired object is *flawed*.' This is true of both parts of the collection. Sonnet 35—and, in conjunction with it, the preceding two poems—alludes to an unnamed 'trespass,' a 'sensual fault' which the poet forgives; Sonnet 41 speaks of 'pretty wrongs that liberty commits' and clearly implies that the friend has offended sexually with the poet's mistress:

> yet thou mightst my seat forbear,
> And chide thy beauty and thy straying youth,
> Who lead thee in their riot even there
> Where thou art forced to break a two-fold truth:
> Hers, by thy beauty tempting her to thee,
> Thine, by thy beauty being false to me.

The poem that follows (Sonnet 42) says that, though the poet loved the woman dearly, 'That she hath thee is of my wailing chief, I A loss in love that toucheth me more nearly.' Yet in a later, or at least later numbered, poem (Sonnet 53) the poet can write of his beloved's 'constant heart.' In Sonnet 67 a young man is apparently accused of keeping bad company. Sonnet 70 defends him against unspecified slander to his 'pure unstainèd prime.' Sonnets 78–80 and 81–6 are those concerned with the 'rival poets.' There is an implication in the couplet of Sonnet 88 that the poet is willing to take responsibility for his friend's wrongs (it is not clear whether the 'faults concealed' of line 7 are the friend's as well as the poet's), and this poem is followed by others such as Sonnets 93, 95–6, and 120 which show a troubled sense of the friend's transgressions.

In spite of his rebukes, the poet, as in sonnet sequences of the period addressed to women, shows a determination to idealize the beloved.

A Woman—or Some Women

As we have seen, it is common in sonnet sequences of the period for the woman addressed to bear a romantic, often classically derived name—Laura, Diella, Celia, Idea, Diana, Zepheria, and so on. No woman's name, whether romantic or ordinary, attaches itself to the woman (or women) of Shakespeare's sonnets. She is spoken of or addressed only generically as, for instance, 'my mistress' (Sonnets 127; 130), 'my music' (Sonnet 128, not specifically addressed to a woman), 'my love' (Sonnet 130), and 'Dear heart' (Sonnet 139). The term 'dark lady,' which in popular and even in critical usage has attached itself to the Sonnets, is an imposition upon them. 'Lady' is not found, and 'dark' only

once (Sonnet 147). Even 'black' occurs in only five of the sonnets (Sonnets 127, 130, 131, 132, and 147). In three of them it is the occasion for praise: the woman's (natural) blackness of eyes and brows shames those who make fair 'the foul with art's false borrowed face' (Sonnet 127); though (paradoxically) 'black wires grow on her head' yet the lover thinks her 'rare I As any she belied with false compare' (Sonnet 130). Her black eyes demonstrate her mourning for his 'pain'; and if her heart would mourn for his too, he would 'swear beauty herself is black, I And all they foul that thy complexion lack' (Sonnet 132). In two of the poems, however, 'black' provides an occasion for bitter wordplay on the word's literal and metaphorical senses. 'Thinking on' her 'face' he regards her 'black' as 'fair,' but she is 'black' in her 'deeds' (Sonnet 131). His 'thoughts' and 'discourse' are 'as madmen's are' because he has 'sworn thee fair, and thought thee bright, I Who art as black as hell, and dark as night' (Sonnet 147). In Sonnet 152, though she is not explicitly 'black,' the poet has falsely 'sworn [her] fair,' and in Sonnet 144 she is 'coloured ill.'

There are, then, only seven among the second group of twenty-eight sonnets in which a woman is explicitly or implicitly dark in coloring. There are, however, other poems in which a woman whom the poet loves is reviled as dark in character. Although Sonnet 129—'Th'expense of spirit in a waste of shame'—could, considered on its own, be unrelated to the rest of the collection, in context it reads like a poem of self-condemnation for the poet's subjugation to sexual desire. The difficult Sonnet 133 curses 'that heart that makes my heart to groan I For that deep wound it gives my friend and me.' Not only has the woman betrayed the poet, she has also enslaved his 'sweet'st friend,' his 'next self,' so that 'Of him, myself, and thee I am forsaken.' Nothing is left: he is bereft of himself, of the 'sweet'st friend' who is his 'next self, , and of the woman herself. His heart is imprisoned in her 'steel bosom'; he pleads that she will at least let his own heart stand bail for his friend's so that he can be the friend's prison-warder. The friend means even more to him than the woman.

Sonnet 134 runs straight on to beg the 'covetous' woman to restore his 'kind' friend to him. But there is no hope: 'Him have I lost; thou hast both him and me; I He pays the whole, and yet am I not free.' Then, in Sonnet 135, he puns tortuously and despairingly on the word 'will.' The word occurs thirteen times in this sonnet; on seven of these occurrences in the Quarto it is both italicized and capitalized; the same is true of three of its seven occurrences in Sonnet 136 and of its single one in Sonnet 143, where again a pun is clearly intended. Although such details could derive from the compositor, some at least of these are likely to have been marked in the manuscript.

So many senses of the word are pertinent in Sonnet 135 that it is often difficult to say which is uppermost, or even whether particular ones are present at any given point. Of course they may be present in the reader's mind even if they were not in the poet's. And we cannot be sure at what points capitalization should be used in a modern text to indicate the personal name. In the opening lines the name seems to be dominant: 'Whoever hath her wish, thou hast thy will, | And Will to boot, and Will in overplus'—that is, Will (the poet) is subjugated to her will (in the primary sense of sexual desire). The idea that she has 'will' in overplus may, in view of the following line—'More than enough am I that vex thee still'—act simply as an apology for continuing to trouble her, but could also imply that she is oversexed, and must surely also suggest that this is the name of his friend. If this is agreed it strengthens the case for a real-life addressee. In the following lines 'will' in the senses successively of vagina and penis dominates:

Wilt thou, whose will is large and spacious,
Not once vouchsafe to hide my will in thine?
Shall will in others seem right gracious,
And in my will no fair acceptance shine?

Then in the sestet multiple meanings proliferate: 'So thou, being rich in will'—that is, in sexuality, and the organs of the lovers named Will—'add to thy Will | One will of mine to make thy large Will more'—that is, if she agrees to his demands she will increase her sexual appetite (with a possible, however improbable, secondary sense of 'enlarge her vagina by enclosing his penis in it along with all the others'). Sonnet 152 implies not simply infidelity but adultery in that she has broken her 'bed-vow'—in other words, that she is married.

Other Poets

Along with the poet, the male friend (or friends), and the woman (or women) of the second group of sonnets, there is at least one additional though shadowy player in the drama, often known as 'the rival poet.' (While context suggests that the relevant poems—Sonnets 78–86—are about male friends, as is always assumed, it has to be admitted that so far as their content goes they could be

136

IF thy foule check thee that I come fo neere,
Sweare co thy blind foule that I was thy *Will*,
And will thy foule knowes is admitted there,
Thus farre for loue, my loue-fute fweet fullfill.
Will, will fulfill the treafure of thy loue,
I fill it full with wils, and my will one,
In things of great receit with eafe we prooue,
Among a number one is reckon'd none.
Then in the number let me paffe vntold,
Though in thy ftores account I one muft be,
For nothing hold me, fo it pleafe thee hold,
That nothing me, a fome-thing fweet to thee.
  Make but my name thy loue, and loue that ftill,
  And then thou loueft me for my name is *Will*.

Image 2. Printers in Shakespeare's time felt free to alter details of the way texts were presented in their manuscripts, including capitalization and italicization; and the manuscript used for the Sonnets may not have been in Shakespeare's hand. Nevertheless, it is difficult not to attribute significance to the use of italics and capitals for seven of the thirteen instances of the word 'will' in Sonnet 135; Sonnet 136 (above) ends with the words 'my name is *Will*.'

addressed to a woman. Likewise, depending on how the Sonnets are spoken or the context in which they are reproduced, some could be imagined as being from a female to a female.) In Sonnet 79 the poet complains that his 'sick Muse' has had to give way to another, and plays with the conceit that his rival's praise is worthless because all the qualities he (the rival) ascribes to the friend were there already. Sonnet 80 sees the poet panicking because a 'better spirit' is praising his friend, Sonnet 83 refers to 'both your poets;' Sonnet 84 has a conceit similar to that of Sonnet 79 while rebuking the friend for being 'fond on praise;' in Sonnet 85 the poet claims to be 'tongue-tied' in face of the rival's praise, while asking the friend to respect him for his 'dumb thoughts,' and Sonnet 86 again expresses humility in face of the 'proud full sail' of the rival's 'great verse.'

Little more can be deduced about this poet. He appears to be regarded as learned: the friend's eyes have 'added feathers to the learned's wing' (Sonnet 78; the friend is 'all my art, and dost advance | As high as learning my rude ignorance' (Sonnet 78), and Sonnet 86 speaks mysteriously of 'his spirit, by spirits taught to write | Above a mortal pitch,' of 'his compeers by night | Giving him aid,' and of 'that affable familiar ghost |

Which nightly gulls him with intelligence.'

There are then scattered gestures towards an impressionistic narrative that could lie behind the Sonnets. The poet loves one or more young men, and/or women, and his love is to some degree reciprocated. The poet also loves a 'black' woman. Another poet also loves the person or persons, who respond to his praise. One or more women has an affair with one or more young men which the poet deeply resents. There is no resolution to the situation.

The Sonnets conform to no predetermined formal structure. The collection is like a patchwork composed of separately woven pieces of cloth, some bigger than others, some of them re-stitched, rearranged from time to time and finally sewn together in a composition that has only a deceptive, though at times satisfying, unity. It is as if Shakespeare were providing us with all the ingredients necessary to make our own series of narratives about love. To insist on one story alone is to misread the Sonnets and to ignore their will to plurality, to promiscuity. To seek for a tidy pattern in these loosely connected poems is like trying to control or tidy the inevitable mess and freedom that love itself creates.

Paul Edmondson and Stanley Wells

Vocabulary and Chronology: The Case of Shakespeare's Sonnets

In the course of his career as playwright and poet, Shakespeare used a vast number of different words. Some appear in every play he wrote: *the, have, good, sir, love,* and *fair,* for example. Others appear only within early works, or only within late works, or are much more frequently used in the first or second halves of his writing life. Some are limited to a specific period of three or four years; or instances of their use tend to cluster within such a period. The noun *goodness,* for example, occurs only five times in the twenty-two plays written before *Hamlet* (1600–1), and no fewer than fifty-one times in the fifteen plays from *Hamlet* to *Henry VIII* (1612–13).[1] The fact that the only poems in which *goodness* is found are Sonnets 118 and 124 suggests that these may have been composed in the seventeenth century. The adjective or noun *particular* is used sixty-five times in Shakespeare's works, but the first fourteen plays and the two early narrative poems, *Venus and Adonis* (1592–93) and *The Rape of Lucrece* (1593–94), account for only one of these instances. *Particular* becomes an obsession with Shakespeare during the period of his great tragedies. Its presence in *A Lover's Complaint* and in Sonnet 91 affords a scrap of evidence for assigning both those poems to Shakespeare's maturity.[2] The verb *to ban* (meaning 'to curse'), by contrast, is used only in *1 Henry VI* (1589–90), *2 Henry VI* (1590-1, twice), *Venus and Adonis,* and *The Rape of Lucrece,* unless we accept the dubious instance of 'banning' in the Quarto (1622) of *Othello,* where the more authoritative Folio text reads 'foaming' (II. i. 11).

In short, every item of Shakespeare's lifetime word store was not equally accessible to him at any given moment. Not only were items added to his active vocabulary, or effectively dropped from it, but his personal development took place within a changing linguistic environment. The English lexicon was itself undergoing extraordinary expansion. A word for which the *Oxford English Dictionary's* first citation is 1600 is obviously much less likely to be encountered within a sixteenth-century Shakespeare work than within a seventeenth-century one.[3] The opposite holds for words that the *OED* indicates to have been falling into disuse around the turn of the century.

A tendency for the rarer items in Shakespeare's vocabulary to be used in works composed at about the same time has been demonstrated in elaborate statistical detail by Eliot Slater, who, checking all words that occur in at least two Shakespeare plays but not more than ten times within the canon as a whole, compiled tables enumerating each play's links with every other play.[4] Most plays show a significant excess of lexical links with at least some of their chronological neighbors and a significant deficiency of links with plays from which they are chronologically more distant. Slater's research has helped establish the likely date of composition of plays for which other evidence is indeterminate.

Analysis of vocabulary has been applied to the vexed problem of the date of Shakespeare's sonnets. One hundred years ago, Gregor Sarrazin, examining words that occurred only twice or thrice in the Shakespeare canon, found a surplus of links between the sonnets and plays written around 1593–8.[5] Slater himself showed that the sonnets exhibited a significant excess of lexical links with a cluster of four chronologically proximate plays, *Love's Labour's Lost* (1594–5), *Romeo and Juliet* (1595–6), *Richard II* (1595), and *A Midsummer Night's Dream* (1595–6), and also with the chronologically adjacent pair *Much Ado About Nothing* (1598–9) and *Henry V* (1599). He concluded that the sonnets belonged to 'the second quarter' of Shakespeare's career.[6] These two studies were useful, but suffered from one serious flaw: each treated the 1609 Quarto sequence as a homogeneous unit, lumping its individual components together.[7]

A. Kent Hieatt, Charles W. Hieatt, and Anne Lake Prescott have recently taken a different approach.[8] They came to doubt 'that Shakespeare had essentially completed composition of *Sonnets* in the first half of the fifteen-nineties,' realizing that—like his contemporaries Samuel Daniel and Michael Drayton, who kept revising, supplementing, and rearranging sonnet sequences over many years—he may have continued to compose or recast sonnets until shortly before publication of the Quarto, which they judge to have been fully authorised.[9]

They therefore undertook an investigation of all words occurring in the sonnets and in at least three but not more than seven other Shakespeare works, concentrating on those lexical items that were used only within the first half of Shakespeare's career, from *1 Henry VI* (1589–90) to *As You Like It* (1599), or only within the second half, from *Hamlet* (1600–1) to *The Two Noble Kinsmen* (1613).[10] They discovered that twenty-four of the rare words in the sonnets, or 3.62 percent were 'late rare words,' whose usage was otherwise restricted to the second half of the Shakespeare canon. *The Rape of Lucrece* (1593–4) and *Richard II* (1595) each had twelve late rare words, and *2 Henry IV* (1598) had twenty-seven, yielding percentages of late rare words (in relation to all rare words) of 1.46, 1.07, and 2.17. They concluded that 'Shakespeare was occupied with *Sonnets* at a date posterior to 1598.'

Hieatt, Hieatt, and Prescott found that the late rare words were more unevenly distributed in the sonnets than in *2 Henry IV,* where absence of late rare words from long stretches of the text could, in any case, be related to a general scarcity of rare words in the dialogue of 'rhetorically unskilled speakers,' such as Mistress Quickly, Shallow, Silence, and Doll Tearsheet. But the sonnets also yielded fifty-four 'early rare words.' On the basis of the distribution of both these and the late rare words, they divided the Quarto into four 'zones.' Zone 1 (Sonnets 1–60) contained twenty early rare words (12.3 percent of the total of rare words), and seventeen late rare words *(*10.4 percent). For Zone 2 (Sonnets 61–103) the figures were twenty-two early (14.8 percent) and three late (2 percent); for Zone 3 (Sonnets 104–26), three early (4.5 percent) and three late (4.5 percent); and for Zone 4 (Sonnets 127–54), nine early (15.2 percent) and none late (0 percent). They deduced that Zones 1, 2, and 4 had been written mainly during the first half of the 1590s, but that Zone 1 had been subject to seventeenth-century revisions or additions, perhaps as late as 1608 or 1609. Zone 3 they tentatively assigned to 'around the turn of the century.'

The work of Hieatt, Hieatt, and Prescott represents a big step forward. They have established beyond reasonable doubt that Shakespeare's involvement with the sonnets extended beyond the mid-1590s. But some of the refinements in their theories are not adequately supported by the evidence they adduce—which is not to say that they are necessarily mistaken. Three control *texts—The Rape of Lucrece, Richard II,* and *2 Henry IV—*are very few from which to draw inferences about Shakespeare's

practices, and numbers of late rare words are too small for us to be sure that their slightly more uneven distribution in the sonnets than in *2 Henry IV* is genuinely significant, requiring an altogether different explanation.[11] Hieatt, Hieatt, and Prescott seem wrong to claim that there is no relation in the sonnets between the frequency of late rare words and the frequency of all rare words. The thirteen sonnets that contain late rare words but no early ones average 3.77 'generally rare words' (words that occur in the sonnets and three to seven other works, but are used in both chronological halves of the canon), while the ninety-three sonnets that contain neither late nor early rare words average only 1. 97 generally rare words.

More importantly, Hieatt, Hieatt, and Prescott offer no information about the number and distribution of *early* rare words in *2 Henry IV or* their other control texts, so we have no means of assessing whether the mix of early and late rare words in Zone 1 sonnets might have arisen in work that Shakespeare composed once and for all close to the mid-point of his career. It would be surprising if extended passages in some 'middle' plays did not yield roughly even numbers of early and late rare words, along with many whose usage spanned both halves of the canon. Marked preponderance of early over late rare words certainly suggests sixteenth-century composition,[12] and marked preponderance of late over early rare words suggests seventeenth-century composition, but an approximately equal incidence of items from both categories is less readily interpreted.

Another pertinent point is that 'earliness' and 'lateness,' as Hieatt, Hieatt, and Prescott define them, are very broad concepts. The periods within which rare words classed as early or late may occur are extensive: ten years covering twenty-four works, and thirteen years covering nineteen works. And yet a substantial proportion of all the rare words—those appearing in the sonnets and in at least three but no more than seven other Shakespeare works—is associated exclusively or mainly with works written neither towards the beginning nor towards the end of Shakespeare's career, but in the middle. For example, the word *hymn,* classified as 'early,' is absent from Shakespeare's first twelve works, appearing, outside the sonnets, only in *King John* (1594–6) *Romeo and Juliet* (1595-6), *A Midsummer Night's Dream* (1595–6), *The Merchant of Venice* (1596-7), and *Much Ado About Nothing* (1598-9), while *aggravate,* also classified as 'early,' is confined to *Richard II* (1595), *A Midsummer Night's Dream* (1595–6), *The Merry Wives of Windsor*

Table 1. Totals and percentages of early, middle, and late rare words in four different 'zones' of Shakespeare's sonnets

	Early		Middle		Late	
	Total	%	Total	%	Total	%
Zone 1 (1-60)	20	12.3	15	9.2	17	10-.4
Zone 2 (61-103)	22	14.8	21	14.1	3	2.0
Zone 3 (104-26)	3	4.5	7	10.4	3	4-.5
Zone 4 (127-54)	9	15.2	4	6.8	0	0-.0

[a] Percentages are of 'all rare words' as defined by Hieatt, Hieatt, and Prescott, 'When Did Shakespeare Write Sonnets 1609?,' from which data have been extracted.

(1597), and *2 Henry IV* (1598), all written within the brief period 1595–8. The verb *o'erturn/overturn* is used only in the successive histories, *1 Henry IV* (1596-7), *2 Henry IV* (1598), and *Henry V* (1599).[13] So it seems worth extracting from the Hieatt-Prescott tables all the rare words whose use is restricted to the twenty-one works written after the first twelve and before the last ten, and so falling within an intermediate range, comparable in length to the early and late ranges, between *King John* (1594-6) and *Macbeth* (1606).[14]

Table 1 displays the results, alongside the Hieatt-Prescott figures for early and late rare words in the four suspected zones. The overall picture remains much the same. Indeed, the data for 'middle rare words' provide some support for Hieatt, Hieatt, and Prescott's interpretation of their figures for early and late rare words. In Zone 1 there are fairly similar numbers and percentages in all three columns. In Zone 2 early and middle rare words strongly predominate. In Zone 3 the figures are too small for confident interpretation, but the total for middle rare words exceeds the combined total for early and late ones. Zone 4 is heavily weighted with early rare words, and is the zone with the smallest percentage of middle rare words, besides being devoid of late ones.

There is a notable cluster of middle rare words in Sonnets 77–87, a series that includes tile 'Rival Poet' sonnets. There are eleven middle rare words in eleven sonnets, 84 and 85 each having two and 83 and 86 being the only two with none. An even tighter cluster of middle rare words occurs in Sonnets 100–3, which have nine.

More light can be shed on the subject by a new analysis of Sarrazin's century-old data, in terms of the Hieatt-Prescott zones. Slater demonstrated that the rarest words within the canon exhibit the strongest tendency to cluster according to chronology: thus words occurring in at least two plays and only twice or thrice in the canon are more apt to link plays of about the same date than words occurring nine or ten times.[15] Sarrazin's twice-used and thrice-used words, which he termed 'dislegomena' and 'trislegomena,' ought therefore to be quite sensitive indicators of chronological position. And in fact they are. In *Studies in Attribution: Middleton and Shakespeare,* I have shown that counts of Sarrazin link-words assign almost every Shakespeare play to the right one of four groups of plays formed according to Karl Wentersdorf's modified version of E. K. Chambers' standard chronology.[16] Only two plays failed to have the largest (or equal largest) number of Sarrazin links with the chronological group to which they rightly belonged, and in neither case was the evidence seriously misleading: *A Midsummer Night's Dream,* the last play in Group 1, had three more links with Group 2 than with Group 1 (but considerably fewer with Groups 3

Table 2. Rare-word links between different zones' of Shakespeare's sonnets and four chronological groups of plays

	Group 1	Group 2	Group 3	Group 4
Zone 1 (1-60)	15	15	12	9
Zone 2 (61-103)	11	13	10	5
Zone 3 (104-26)	8	6	14	11
Zone 4 (127-54)	3	10	3	8

[a] Links are for words used twice and thrice in the canon, as calculated from the tables of Gregor Sarrazin.

and 4);[17] *Much Ado About Nothing,* belonging to Group 2, had four more links with Group 1 than with Group 2 (though, again, fewer with Groups 3 and 4). Worth noting is that for some of the plays written late in the sixteenth century, such as *Henry V* (1599) and *As You Like It* (1599), the number of links with each of the four groups is much more even than for the plays that are decidedly early or late.

Also, for each play, a calculation of the percentage of Sarrazin links with the third and fourth groups combined served as a simple index of 'lateness.' When plays were ranked according to the size of this percentage, the order correlated quite strongly with Wentersdorf's chronological order. For thirty-one of the thirty-seven plays (84 percent) a dating arrived at by reading their position on the vocabulary order as a position on Wentersdorf's chronological order was not more than three years out, and half were correct to within a single year. For middle plays such as *Henry V* and *As You Like It* this way of handling the data tended to clarify the indistinct findings of the four-group analysis.

For *Venus and Adonis* the Sarrazin links with the four groups are 58 : 38 : 29 : 27, giving a percentage of 36.84 links with the last two. The evidence points overwhelmingly to composition within the first quarter of Shakespeare's career, and the actual index of 36.84 percent places the poem at exactly the right point, for a date of 1592-3.[18] The figures for *The Rape of Lucrece* are similar: 84 : 47 : 44 : 34, with an index of 37.32, for a correct date of 1593-4. *A Lover's Complaint* affords a striking contrast. The figures are 5

: 11 : 22 : 24, with an index (or percentage of links with the third and fourth groups) of 74.19 percent, which is higher than for any play (*Antony and Cleopatra* representing the peak of 63.7). The Sarrazin links thus confirm other vocabulary studies that assign its composition to the seventeenth century.[19] The closest parallel to the four-group pattern of *A Love's Complaint* is furnished by Shakespeare's share of *Henry VIII* (18 : 17 : 29 : 31), though the proportions for several other plays from *Hamlet* onwards are somewhat similar.

The Sarrazin links for the sonnets are presented in Table 2. The most notable feature is the sharp distinction between Zone 3, where Group 3 links predominate and links with Group 4 provide the second highest total, and the other three zones, in which the majority of links are with the first two groups. The percentages of second-half links (with Groups 3 or 4) are: Zone 1, 41.2, Zone 2, 38.5, Zone 3, 64.1, and Zone 4, 45.8. The raw figures for Zone 4 are too low, and thus too likely to have been subject to chance factors for the anomalous pattern, in which the highest and next-highest totals are for Groups 2 and 4, to be confidently interpreted. The pattern for Zone 1 is most closely matched by plays near the end of Group 1 and the beginning of Group 2, and the index ,would also suggest a date of around 1595-6. The slightly lower index for Zone 2 would place it in 1594–5: though it has two more links with Group 2 than with Group 1, it is more notably deficient in Group 4 links than is Zone 1. The evidence seems to indicate that Zone 3 was composed in the seventeenth century: the ·index of 64.1, associating it with the very last plays, cannot be taken too seriously, but Shakespeare's involvement ·with sonnets in this zone in the early Jacobean years is probable, and those scholars who have associated Sonnet 107 with Queen Elizabeth's death and King James's peaceful succession in 1603 are unlikely to have dated this particular sonnet too late.

As far as links formed by Sarrazin's dislegomena and trislegomena go, results for Zones 1, 2, and 4 might reasonably be added together, to give the following pattern of links with the four groups of plays: 29: 38: 25: 22. This quite closely matches such plays as *1 Henry IV, The Merry Wives of Windsor,* and *Henry V* in the period 1596-9, though the index of 41.2 would point to 1595-6. But of course these are merely dates upon which a period of several years' composition might centre. There is no clear support in the Sarrazin figures for the theory that Zone 1 was subjected to late revision and supplementation: though the proportion of links with the final group of plays is marginally higher than that for Zone 2, it is much lower than for Zone 4, and the four-group distribution would be quite normal for work written in the years 1595–7, for example.

One minor detail of possible significance is that Zone 3 has two Sarrazin links, with the early narrative poems *Venus and Adonis* and *The Rape of Lucrece* and two with the much shorter, and evidently late, poem *A Lover's Complaint,* whereas the total links for the other three zones are nine with the two early poems and one with the late one (2: 2 versus 9: 1). This gives a modicum of support to the conclusion that Zone 3 'was written appreciably later than most of the remainder of the sequence. Another small point is that the pattern of links for Sonnets 1-17, the 'marriage sonnets,' is 3 : 5 : 2 : 2. Although the figures are very low, they hint at composition in the second quarter of Shakespeare's career, rather than in the earliest period of 1588-94.

A little more information may be extracted from Hieatt, Hieatt, and Prescott's data. In an appendix to their article they record every instance of an early or generally rare ,word within each individual sonnet, together with a list of the other Shakespeare ,works in which it occurs. Supplementing this list, with their similar, but far shorter, list of late rare words, we can chart the number of links between each sonnet and the four chronological groups of plays used for my analysis of Sarrazin's twice-used and thrice-used words. The Hieatt-Prescott rare words—apart from those that are early, middle, or late—are unlikely to be such good indicators of chronology as Sarrazin's words, since they are found in up to

seven plays, and presumably several times in some of these plays. But one might expect them to behave rather like Slater's words that occur six to ten times in the canon. I have tallied Group 1, 2, 3, and 4 links wit11 each sonnet. For thirty-six of the sonnets that have at least ten links, Groups 3 or 4 yield the highest or equal highest tota1.[20] The pattern of Sarrazin links for these sonnets is 5 : 8 : 17: 10, which represents a surprising measure of agreement. For the fifty-nine sonnets that have at least ten links, but with the highest or equal highest total being with plays of Groups 1 or 2, the pattern of Sarrazin links is 16: 16: 9: 8, which is again in accord with the Hieatt-Prescott data.

If we calculate for each zone the number of sonnets that have their highest or equal highest total of Hieatt-Prescott links with Groups 1, 2, 3, or 4, we obtain the following results: for Zone 1 the pattern is 9 : 12 : 10 : 7; for Zone 2 it is 14 : 9 : 7 : 1; for Zone 3 it is 4 : 4 : 4 : 3; and for Zone 4 it is 8 : 4 : 3 : 3.[21] This tends to confirm that Zones 1 and (probably) 3 are 'later' than Zones 2 and 4, and the almost complete absence from Zone 2 of sonnets connecting most strongly with Group 4 is notable. But the Zone 1 pattern is perhaps marginally more suggestive of composition mainly within the early middle period than of very early composition and very late revision and augmentation.

Another set of relevant data concerns each zone's Hieatt-Prescott links with the three poems, *Venus and Adonis, The Rape of Lucrece,* and *A Lover's Complaint.* For Zone 1 the figures are (for links with each of the above poems in turn) 12 : 33 : 7; for Zone 2 they are 16 : 28 : 3; for Zone 3 they are 7 : 17 : 7; and for Zone 4 they are 10 : 12 : 1. On the basis of the size of the three poems, one would expect 33.5 percent of the links to be with *Venus and Adonis,* 56.5 percent to be with *The Rape of Lucrece,* and 9.9 percent to be with *A Lover's Complaint.*[22] The most striking deviation from these expectations is Zone 3's figure for links with *A Lover's Complaint,* which works out at 22.6 percent. Zone 1 also has a higher proportion of *A Lover's Complaint* links than expected, 13.5 percent, while percentages for Zones 2 (6.4 percent) and 4 (4.3 percent) are below expectation. Zones 1 and 3 have, proportionally, the fewest links with *Venus and Adonis,* 23.1 percent and 22.6 percent, while Zone 4 has more than expected, 43.5 percent. Zone 1 has the highest percentage of links with *The Rape of Lucrece,* 63.5 percent. *Venus and Adonis* was published in 1593, *The Rape of Lucrece* in 1594, and there is now general agreement that *A Lover's Complaint* was written in the seventeenth century. The pattern of sonnet links with the three poems is thus in accord with other indications that Zone 3 (Sonnets 104–26) especially, and Zone 1 (1–60), are later, or contain more late writing, than Zones 2 (61–103) and 4 (127–54).

It is possible to tally all the Hieatt-Prescott links with all the plays, and check observed frequencies against expected frequencies calculated according to the size of each play's vocabulary in proportion to the sum of these vocabularies.[23] A summary of the main points emerging from such an analysis may be useful. For Sonnets 1–103 to the Young Man (combining Zones 1 and 2) the notable result is the highly significant excess of observed over expected links with *A Midsummer Night's Dream* (1595–6) and *Henry V* (1599). *King John* (1594–6), which in the Riverside chronological order falls in between the other two plays, and which Chambers dated 1596–7, exhibits a less startling, but still statistically significant, excess, as does *Othello* (1604).[24] The high numbers of links with *A Midsummer Night's Dream, Henry V,* and *Othello* are partly due to the fact that the word 'muse,' which in the dramatic canon occurs only in these three plays, is used no fewer than fourteen times within Sonnets 1-103. But even if we "were to disregard all instances of 'muse,' the excess of links with *A Midsummer Night's Dream* and *Henry V* would still be statistically significant, though that with *Othello* would disappear. It is perhaps not surprising that love sonnets should have close affinities in their vocabulary with a romantic comedy such as *A Midsummer Night's Dream,* but *Henry V* belongs to an altogether different genre, as does *King John,* so that these data would hint at a period of composition for the main body of the sonnets to the Young Man of, say, 1596–9. For each of the last eleven plays, from *All's Well That Ends Well* to *Henry VIII,* the number of links is below expectation, which suggests little, if any, Shakespearian involvement with this portion of the sequence during the last quarter of his playwriting career.

The Dark Lady sonnets (127–52), in contrast, have statistically significant links with *2 Henry VI* (1590–1), *The Comedy of Error's* (1592–4), and *Richard II* (1595). For the cluster of plays comprising *2 Henry VI, 3 Henry VI, Richard III,* and *The Comedy of Errors* there are forty-two links, where twenty-five would be expected. The relative earliness of Zone 4 thus seems confirmed. For Zone 3 (104–26) there are no statistically significant results: the links are fairly evenly distributed.[25]

Hieatt, Hieatt, and Prescott freely admit that the borders between their zones are doubtful, and that even 'within a given zone one can speak of no more than a tendency. Individual sonnets probably have histories of their own.' I have already noted the cluster of 'middle rare words' in Sonnets 77–87, which include those on the theme of the Rival Poet. The Sarrazin links for this series run 2 : 6 : 2 : 0. Eight of the ten links are with plays between *1 Henry IV* (1596–7) and *Measure for Measure* (1604). The complete set of Hieatt-Prescott links between Sonnets 77 and 87 and my four chronological groups runs 55 : 59 : 64 : 25. This also suggests a 'middle' period of composition, and a closer inspection of the results, play by play, strengthens the impression. The total of links with Group 1 is swollen by the large number (fourteen) with *A Midsummer Night's Dream,* which is the last play in the group. With all other Group 1 plays the links are below, or (in three cases) virtually at, chance expectation, but for *A Midsummer Night's Dream* they are three times as great as chance would dictate. This excess is only partly explained by the fact that the noun *muse* four times links these sonnets with *A Midsummer Night's Dream.*[26] Positive sums for 'observation minus expectation' tend to predominate in plays of the second and, especially, third groups—in Group 3 only one of the eight plays has a number of links slightly below expectation—and then with everyone of the Group 4 plays the number of links is lower than expected. There are appreciably more links than would be expected with *King John* and with *Henry V,* but statistically the greatest excess of observed over expected links, apart from that for *A Midsummer Night's Dream,* is with the three-play cluster *Othello, All's Well That Ends Well,* and *Timon of Athens,* which form a sequence in Wentersdorf's chronology (1603–4 to 1604–5).[27] Again, statistical significance would remain even if we were to discount the four links formed by the presence of *muse* in *Othello.* Certainly the period bordered by *A Midsummer Night's Dream* (1595–6) and *Timon of Athens* (1606–7) is clearly indicated.[28] This is broader than the range implied by the more sensitive Sarrazin indicators, but supports their evidence, so that sometime between 1596 and 1604 seems probable for the composition of Sonnets 77-87. The pattern of links is particularly notable in certain of these sonnets. For example, sixteen of Sonnet 77's twenty links are with plays between *A Midsummer Night's Dream* and *Timon of Athens,* as are twenty-two of Sonnet *87's* thirty, while thirteen of Sonnet 83's sixteen are with plays between *A Midsummer Night's Dream* and *All's Well That Ends Well.*

As noted above, the Sarrazin links for the 'marriage sonnets' (1–17) relate to my four chronological groups as follows: 3 : 5 : 2 : 2. The Hieatt-Prescott links fall into a similar pattern: 50 : 60 : 36 : 52. The total of links with Group 1 as a whole closely matches chance expectation (51). For the thirteen plays extending from *Romeo and Juliet* (1594–5) at the beginning of Group 2 to *Hamlet* (1600-1), the third of Group 3, there is a marked excess of observed links over expected links (81/58), and this is followed by a marked deficit of links (17/34) in the plays from *Troiluss and Cressida* (1601-2) to *King Lear* (1605-6) at the beginning of Group 4.[29] For the remaining plays in Group 4, *Macbeth* (1605-6) to *Henry VIII* (1613), the number of links is slightly, but only slightly, above chance expectation (50/43). This suggests that these sonnets were written in the *second* half of the 1590s.

Hieatt, Hieatt, and Prescott consider, very tentatively, the evidence for dating other short series of sonnets or individual sonnets. The series 66–70 they judge to be early. The Hieatt-Prescott links support this view: 42 : 43 : 30 : 18. But again the 'earliness' seems not to be extreme earliness, since the largest number of links, though only just, is with Group 2 plays. The sole evidence from Sarrazin link-words comes in Sonnet 66, which has *strumpeted* linking with *The Comedy of Errors* and *restful* linking with *Richard II,* and Sonnet 68, with *tresses* linking to *1 Henry VI* and *King John;* so each has a Group 1 and a Group 2 link.[30] Hieatt, Hieatt, and Prescott think that the presence in Sonnet 67 of 'seven rare words, of which two are early, five general . . . suggests composition in the first half of the nineties.' But a closer scrutiny of their data casts doubt on this deduction. The four-group pattern runs 10 : 17 : 8 : 4. One of the two 'early' words, exchequer, occurs only in *The Two Gentlemen of Verona* (1594), *Richard II* (1595), *The Merry Wives of Windsor* (1596–7), *1 Henry IV* (1596–7), and *Henry V* (1599), and the other, *bankrupt,* occurs only in *The Rape of Lucrece* (1593–4), *The Two Gentlemen of Verona, Richard II, A Midsummer Night's Dream* (1595–6), and *Henry V.* So even these 'early' words are associated more firmly with the second half of the 1590s. Five of the sonnet's seven Hieatt-Prescott contact-words are found in *Henry V,*[31] which also affords the only Shakespearian parallel (in the Epilogue) to the sonnet's opening rhyme of *live* with *achieve.* Neither of the two earliest instances of the Sonnet 67 contact-word *lace* as a verb (in *The Taming of the Shrew* and *The Two Gentlemen of Verona)* is used, as in all the others, in the

figurative sense of 'adorn': in the former the lacing is literal, of a boot, and in the second the reference is to 'laced mutton,' a cant term for a prostitute.

Since Sonnet 107 has one late rare word, Hieatt, Hieatt, and Prescott are inclined to accept the arguments for supposing that it refers to the historical events of 1603. The full set of Hieatt-Prescott links has the following relation to my four chronological groups: 5 : 9 : 12 : 9. This is certainly consistent with 1603, and the three Sarrazin links are with *Othello* (1604, *balmy* twice) and *The Winter's Tale* (1610–11, *uncertainties).* Hieatt, Hieatt, and Prescott point out that the powerful Ovidian treatment of mutability, Sonnet 60, has no fewer than 'four late rare words represented in all three quatrains' and no early rare words (p. 94). The links to each chronological group work out at 7 : 5 : 14 : 13, which clearly indicates seventeenth-century composition, and the two Sarrazin links (*delve* linking with *Hamlet* [1600–1] and *Cymbeline* [1609–10]) add further support.

This is important, because Sonnet 60's numbering bears an unmistakable relationship to the content of its opening lines, as René Graziani pointed out: 'Like as the waves make towards the pebbled shore, | So do our minutes hasten to their end.'[32] He assumed that Shakespeare, having written fifty-nine numbered sonnets, headed up the next with a '60,' and that the figure prompted the idea of minutes in an hour. Katherine Duncan-Jones, noting other cases of the appropriateness of the head number to the material, judges it far more likely 'either that sonnets already written were subsequently carefully located, or that some were specially written or revised for particular positions in the sequence.'[33] Since Sonnet 60, in its present form, was probably written in the seventeenth century, and many of the Young Man sonnets that follow (as well as many of those in the Dark Lady section) were probably written several years earlier, Duncan-Jones seems right to draw a firm distinction between the order of original composition and 'the order of the sonnets as finally arranged in Q,'[34] even within the Young Man section, and to argue for Shakespeare's involvement in the arrangement of the sequence at a fairly late stage.

We must beware, however, of exaggerating the efficacy of the vocabulary evidence adduced so far. Hieatt, Hieatt, and Prescott rightly caution against placing much faith in even fairly decisive-seeming data for single sonnets: mere fourteen-line units are subject to far too much random fluctuation. Also, different sonnet themes necessarily call forth different vocabularies, which will be linked to different groups of plays: genre, subject-matter, tone, and so on, can all be seen to influence inter-play links, and doubtless also affect the statistics for various groups of sonnets.[35] Sonnet 60 is one of the strongest in the sequence, and when Shakespeare was writing at the height of his powers he may well have tended to use a more inventive diction that would recur in later works. Slater's tables show *Hamlet,* for example, linking, in its rare-word vocabulary, with later rather than earlier plays. They also show several instances of a kind of pattern of links exemplified by Me*asure for Measure* (1604). It has statistically significant associations, in 'two- to six-fold link words,' with the tight chronological series (1600–3), *Hamlet, Troilus and Cressida,* and *All's Well That Ends Well.* But it also has a highly significant excess of observed over expected links with *The Winter's Tale* (1610–11). We are not, however, forced to conclude that Shakespeare revised *Measure for Measure* towards the end of his playwriting career.[36] *The Taming of the Shrew* (1593–4) is firmly linked to several of the earliest plays, but also to *1 Henry IV* (1596–7).

The case of *The Phoenix and Turtle* is instructive. We know that Shakespeare had finished work on it by 1601, because in that year it was published as one of several 'new compositions' appended to Robert Chester's *Love's Martyr.* It is usually assumed to have been written shortly before it reached print. The vocabulary is heavily weighted towards Shakespeare's seventeenth-century plays. For example, usages that have only one or two parallels in the canon are as follows: *obey to* occurs only in *Troilus and Cressida* (1601–2); *surplice* only in *All's Well That Ends Well* (1602–3); *requiem* only in *Hamlet* (1600–1); *gender* meaning 'race' or 'kind' only in *Hamlet* and *Othello* (1604); *commence* as an intransitive verb only in *Timon of Athens* (1607–8) and *Macbeth* (1606); and *twain* substantively to mean 'pair' or 'couple' only in *Antony and Cleopatra* (1606–7) and *The Tempest* (1611).[37] In relation to my four chronological groups, this works out as 0 : 0 : 6 : 3. The links are predominantly with plays written after *The Phoenix and Turtle.* The poem, with its curious mix of intense abstraction, Cock Robin bird lore, incantation, wordplay, paradox, and personification of Property and Reason (not to mention its Chinese-box narrative structure), is so concentrated in thought and feeling that it is not surprising to find Shakespeare employing for the first time several words that he was later to reuse. Among *The Phoenix and Turtle's* Hieatt-Prescott contact words, which include only

those that also occur within the sonnets, are two 'late rare words' (*session* and *rarity*) and six 'generally rare words.' On this kind of evidence, Hieatt, Hieatt, and Prescott would tend to pronounce a sonnet or group of sonnets 'late,' meaning to imply composition or revision beyond the first few years of the seventeenth century. The Hieatt-Prescott links might seem to support such a conclusion concerning *The Phoenix and Turtle,* since they fall into the four-group pattern: 6 : 6 : 8 : 11. But it was in print by 1601.

For these reasons, I am unsure whether Hieatt, Hieatt, and Prescott are right in suspecting that Shakespeare continued to work on his sonnet sequence right up until 1609, with the implication that he authorized Thomas Thorpe's Quarto publication. Evidence for Shakespeare's substantial involvement with the sequence in the 'plague years 1603–4 is much more compelling.

However, if I am correct in thinking that the 'marriage sonnets' are no earlier than the second half of the 1590s, they cannot have been commissioned to overcome any reluctance of Henry Wriothesley, earl of Southampton, to marry. As John Padel has demonstrated, 'there is no time after 1590 appropriate for their composition' in the interests of such a project.[38] On Southampton's sixteenth birthday, 6 October 1589, his guardian William Cecil, Lord Burghley, proposed that the youth marry Burghley's eldest granddaughter, Elizabeth Vere. Southampton refused, and, despite pressure as he turned 17, continued in his refusal, knowing that when he came of age Burghley, to whom he meanwhile had to submit in all matters concerning the management of his estate, would exact a large sum in compensation, as he duly did. Payment of £5,000 impoverished Southampton for several years. Before he was 22 he had fallen in love with Elizabeth Vernon, whom he married in 1598. As Padel points out, if the marriage sonnets belonged to the four-year period in which Southampton and Burghley were estranged, 'the young man, still a minor, could marry nobody without his guardian's consent and was awaiting Burghley's savage bill of 1594. Shakespeare could have written them only advocating marriage with Elizabeth Vere and there would have been no surer way to alienate Southampton,' who would have reviled the poet as Burghley's hireling. On the other hand, 'If they belonged to 1594-5, it would have been a mockery of the young Earl, who could not now afford to marry and before his twenty-second birthday was in love with Elizabeth Vernon.'[39] As recipient of Sonnets 1–17, Henry Herbert, eventual earl of Pembroke, notoriously unwilling to accept as bride Elizabeth Carey in 1595-6, Bridget Vere in 1597, or a niece of Charles Howard in 1599, and even in 1600-1 refusing to marry Mary Fitton, whom he had made pregnant, would—if we are willing to believe that there is any sort of biographical base to the sonnets' cast of characters—provide a much better chronological fit.[40]

Similarly, if the Rival Poet sonnets were written sometime between 1596 and 1604, they cannot in any literal way relate to Christopher Marlowe, who was dead by 1593, but might have something to do with Samuel Daniel, George Chapman, or Ben Jonson.

There is a good deal more that might yet be done by way of analysis of the sonnets' vocabulary. Eliot Slater's words 'occurring from two to ten times in more than one Shakespeare play'—of which he gives a complete list—might be traced within the sonnets and related to particular groupings.[41] More significantly, attempts might be made to identify words like *particular* and *goodness* that occur quite frequently within the canon but are strongly associated with (though not confined to) one chronological half of it or with a restricted period, Also, with the help of Schmidt's *Lexicon,* it is possible to make distinctions between senses and kinds of usage that are included under a single headword. The verb *invite,* for example, is common, but it is used absolutely only in Sonnet 124, *A Lover's Complaint,* and *Othello,* with *Othello's* 'an inviting eye' more closely paralleling the sonnet's 'the inviting time.' The noun *child,* also very common, is used figuratively only in Sonnet 124, *Love's Labour's Lost, 1 Henry IV, Macbeth, Antony and Cleopatra,* and *Henry VIII.* Statistical analysis of phrasal collocations, methodically collected with the help of a concordance, can also be revealing, as Gary Taylor demonstrated in an article on *1 Henry VI.*[42] Even very common ones can have value for dating. For example, the phrase *cannot choose but,* used in the couplet of Sonnet 64, appears nineteen times in the plays, in the four-group pattern 3 : 6 : 6 : 4; moreover, there is a close parallel between the sonnet's 'cannot choose | But weep' and Ophelia's memorable 'I cannot choose but weep to think they would lay him i'th' cold ground' in *Hamlet,* IV. v. 69-70.

Meanwhile, the vocabulary evidence put forward in this article supports and clarifies some of the Hieatt-Prescott findings and muddies others. The main conclusion, which is unlikely to be overturned, is that the majority, if not all, of the last, twenty-odd of the sonnets to the Friend were written in the seventeenth century.[43] A

few other sonnets, in both the Friend and the Dark Lady series, may have been written equally late, but the bulk of them belong to the 1590s. Except that Sonnets 104–26 include many that are among the latest, the sonnets to the Friend are less likely to be in exact chronological order of original composition than to intermingle clusters of relatively early and relatively late work. The Dark Lady sonnets are mostly to be associated with the earliest among those to the Friend. The traditional notion that the sonnets were essentially completed in the period 1593-6 is certainly mistaken: the time-span, even for Sonnets 1–103 and 127–54, must be extended forwards at least another three or four years, and it is probable that very few were composed as early as 1593. Evidence for 'early' original writing and 'late' revision or supplementation of Sonnets 1-60 is somewhat ambiguous, and in any case the vocabulary data link this portion of the sequence, considered as a whole, predominantly with plays of the second quarter of Shakespeare's career.[44]

MacD. P. Jackson

Notes

1. Unless otherwise stated, the dates here assigned to Shakespearian works are those of *The Riverside Shakespeare,* ed. G. B. Evans (Boston, Mass., 1974), 47-56. Line references are to this edition.

2. MacD. P. Jackson, *Shakespeare's 'A* Lover's *Complaint'; Its Date and Authenticity* (Auckland, 1965), 27.

3. 'Much less likely,' but of course the *OED* is far from infallible in its recording of first and last usages.

4. E. Slater, *The Problem of 'The Reign of King Edward III'; A Statistical Approach* (Cambridge, 1988). This book is the culmination of Slater's research, but many of his findings had been published in articles listed in his bibliography.

5. G. Sarrazin, 'Wortechos bei Shakespeare,' *Shakespeare Jahrbuch,* 33 (1897), 121-65, and 34 (1898), 119-69.

6. E. Slater, 'Shakespeare: Word Links between Poems and Plays,' *Notes & Queries,* 220 (1975), 157-63.

7. Each author realized, however, that the sonnets may have been written, over a long period of time. A valuable contribution was also made by J. M. Nosworthy, 'All too Short a Date: Internal Evidence in Shakespeare's Sonnets,' *Essays in Criticism,* 2 (1952), 311-24. But Nosworthy's use of lexical data was somewhat impressionistic.

8. 'When Did Shakespeare Write *Sonnets* 1609?,' *Studies in Philology,* 88 (1991), 69-109. Page references to this article are given in the text.

9. This is the view taken by Katherine Duncan-Jones in

'Was the 1609 *Shakespeare's Sonnets* Really Unauthorized?' *Review of English Studies,* 34 (1983), 151-71, and in her Arden edition of *Shakespeare's Sonnets* (London, 1997).

10. They followed the Riverside chronology, as set out on p. 76 of their article, which is why I have chosen to adopt it.

11. In 2 *Henry IV* the average interval (expressed in hundreds of words) between occurrences of late rare words is 9.22, with a standard deviation of 8.09; the largest intervals are 2.39 and 2.21 standard deviations from the mean. In the sonnets the figures are: average 7.04, standard deviation 8.15, largest intervals 3.16 and 2.82 standard deviations from the mean. In *Richard II* the largest interval is 2.71 standard deviations from the mean. The differences are not very remarkable.

12. This is true only if the total number of 'early rare words' (as defined in the Hieatt-Prescott article) in the Shakespeare canon is roughly the same as the total number of 'late rare words.' In an internet communication in the 'SHAXPER' controversy, Donald Foster asserts that Shakespeare's early rare words appreciably outnumber his late rare words, which would imply that late rare words are stronger indicators of late composition than early rare words are indicators of early composition.

13. Hieatt, Hieatt, and Prescott list all 'early' and 'general' rare words and their contacts in an appendix (pp. 99-109), italicizing the 'early' ones, and all 'late' rare words in a table (p. 79). For some reason, presumably oversight, they do not mark o'*erturn/overturn* as an 'early rare word,' though it meets their criteria.

14. A few 'middle' rare 'words also qualify as 'early' or 'late' rare words. The list, with the sonnets in which the 'middle rare words' occur is: 2 *thriftless,* 6 *self-willed,* 20 *whereupon* (= 'upon which'), 21 *muse* (n.), 24 *perspective,* 26 *totter/tatter* (v., 'to make ragged'), 29 hymn (n.), 32 *muse* (n.), 35 *eclipse* (n.), 38 *muse* (n.) (three times), 41 *twofold,* 55 *o'erturn/overturn,* 60 *eclipse* (n.), 77 *mouth* (v.), 78 *muse* (n.), 79 *muse* (n.), 80 *wilfully,* 81 *o'er-read/over-read,* 82 *muse* (n.), 84 *penury,* 84 *copy,* 85 *muse* (n.), 85 *hymn* (n.), 87 *patent* (n.), 95 *habitation,* 100 *muse* (n.) (three times), 101 *truant* (adj.), 101 *muse* (n.) (three times), 102 *hymn* (n.), 103 *muse* (n.), 107 *prophetic,* 107 *eclipse* (n.), 109 *preposterously,* 110 *motley* (n.), 113 *latch* (v.), 118 *anticipate* (v.), 125 *rent* (n.), 140 *slanderer,* 142 *rent* (n.), 146 *aggravate,* 148 denote.

15. Slater, *Problem,* 88: 'The rarest words show . . . the greatest tendency to cluster.'

16. MacD. P. Jackson, *Studies in Attribution: Middleton and Shakespeare* (Salzburg, 1979), 148-58 and 211-12. K.

Wentersdorf 'Shakespearian Chronology and the Metrical Tests,' in W. Fischer and K. Wentersdorf (edd.), *Shakespeare-Studien. Festschrift für Heinrich Mutschmann* (Marburg, 1951). The groups are: (1) *Ti.,1H6, Err., 2H6, 3H6, Shr., R3, TGV, LLL, MND;* (2) *Rom., R2, Fn., MV, 1H4, 2H4, Wiv., Ado, H5, FG;* (3) *AYL, TN, Ham., Tro., MM, Oth., AWW, Tim.; (4) Lr., Mac., Ant., Per., Cor., Gym., WT, Tmp., H8.* My analysis excluded Fletcher's share of *H8,* according to the traditional Spedding-Hickson division, and the first two acts of *Pericles.* Sarrazin's tables are not perfect, but one or two obvious errors are easily corrected, and his data are accurate enough to furnish results that are trustworthy as far as their broad import is concerned.

17. The Riverside chronology would place *A Midsummer Night's Dream* after *Romeo and Juliet, Richard II,* and *King John.*

18. See Jackson, *Studies in* Attribution, 212, for the relevant table. Data for the narrative poems have since been extracted from Sarrazin, 'Wortechos.'

19. Jackson, Shakespeare's *'A Lover's Complaint';* K. Muir, '"A Lover's Complaint": A Reconsideration,' in Edward A. Bloom (ed.), *Shakespeare 1564-1964* (Providence, RI, 1964), repr. in Muir, *Shakespeare the Professional and Related Studies* (London, 1973), 204-19; Slater, 'Word Links'; A. K. Hieatt, T. G. Bishop, and E. A. Nicholson, 'Shakespeare's Rare Words: "Lover's Complaint", *Cymbeline,* and *Sonnets,'Notes & Queries,* 232 (1987), 219-25. The 17th-cent. composition of 'A Lover's Complaint' has been accepted by recent editors of the sonnets, such as John Kerrigan (Harmondsworth, 1986), G. Blakemore Evans (Cambridge, 1996), and Katherine Duncan-Jones (London, 1997), and by John Roe in his edition of *The Poems* (Cambridge, 1992). Hieatt, Bishop, and Nicholson agree with Slater that Shakespeare drafted the poem about 1600-3 and revised it 1608-9. In my own statistical analysis of data presented in *Shakespeare's 'A Lover's Complaint'* the poem's strongest lexical associations were with *All's Well That Ends Well* and *Timon of Athens,* which are adjacent in Wentersdorf's chronology (1604-5); there are also significant links with *Hamlet* and *Troilus and Cressida* (1600-2), and with *Cymbeline* and *Coriolanus (1607-9).*

20. Sonnets for which the highest or equal highest total of links is with Group 1 or 2 are: 2, 6, 8, 11,13, 15, 18,19, 21, 23, 25, 26, 27, 29, 32, 37, 46, 50, 53, 55, 61, 64, 65, 66, 67, 68, 70, 76, 78, 80, 82, 83, 85, 89, 90, 94, 95, 96, 97, 100, 101, 102, 105, 113, 118, 120, 122, 124, 125, 127, 133, 137, 138, 139, 140, 146, 147, 148, 151; sonnets for

which the highest or equal highest total of links is with Group 3 or 4 are: 3, 4, 12 22, 23, 25, 30, 35, 38, 43, 49, 56, 58, 59, 60, 62, 74, 77, 81, 83, 84, 87,98, l06, 107, 108, 110, 116, 117, 126, 137, 140, 141, 148, 153,154. Sonnets listed twice have equal highest totals of links with Group 1 and/or 2 and with Group 3 and/or 4.

21. Links with the poems and with *The Two Noble Kinsmen* have simply been left out of account, since my four-play chronological groupings ignored these works.

22. The 'size' of the poem is here based on the number of words cited three to ten times in Shakespeare's plays, according to Slater's table 1 in 'Word Links,' 159. Expected percentages reckoned from the total number of different words ('types') per poem, as given in M. Spevack, *A Complete and Systematic Concordance to the Works of Shakespeare,* 9 vols. (Hildesheim, 1968-80), would be similar: 29.4 for *Venus,* 58.8 *Lucrece,* and 11.8 for *Complaint.*

23. 'Expected' frequencies were calculated using Slater's method in *Problem,* 158-96. Slater relies on Alfred Hart's counts of the numbers of different words per play. The data are not available for a more 'correct' calculation, and Slater's approximations are adequate for the purpose. Presentation of the calculations and tables on which the results reported in this and the next paragraph are based would take up more space than is warranted, but the relevant data may all be extracted from the Hieatt-Prescott article.

24. The chi-square values are 26.586 for *A Midsummer Night's Dream* (58 links instead of an expected 29.836) and 25.771 for *Henry V* (72/39.924). *King John* yields 6.45 (52/36.629), and *Othello* 6.857 (53/38.068). These values cannot, strictly speaking, be translated into statistical probabilities, but the two higher ones, especially, are extremely unlikely to have occurred by chance. For a professional statistician's review of Slater's methods see .M. W. A. Smith, 'Shakespearian Chronology: A New Approach to the Method of Word-Links,' *Notes & Queries,* 235 (1990), 198-204.

25. Total Hieatt-Prescott links relating zones to my four groups are: Zone 1: 169 : 189 : 151 : 166; Zone 2: 195 : 186 : 161 : 89; Zone 3: 87 : 82 : 81 : 72; Zone 4: 78: 68 :41 : 46. These gross figures succeed only in blurring most of the significant points. But the relatively even distribution in Zones 1 and 3 is notable, as is Zone 2's marked dearth of links with Group 4. The totals at least confirm that Zones 2 and 4 are earlier, or contain a much larger proportion of early material than Zones 1 and 3.

26. When a word occurs once in a sonnet and more than once in a play, Hieatt, Hieatt, and Prescott count only one contact with that play, whereas if one instance of one of Sarrazin's thrice-used words occurs in a sonnet and two instances in a play this constitutes two 'Sarrazin links' between sonnet and play.

27. The total of links with this group is 29, instead of the expected 16.149, yielding a chi-square value of 10.227.

28. The *Timon of Athens* date is the Riverside's. Wentersdorf's chronology would place it in 1604-5.

29. In this paragraph, dealing with my four chronological groups based on Wentersdorf's chronology the dates are necessarily Wentersdorf's. The Riverside edition would place *Romeo and Juliet* in 1595-6, *King Lear* in 1605, and Macbeth in 1606.

30. However, in *1 Henry VI, tresses* comes in the third line, and Act I may well have been written by Thomas Nashe. (See Taylor, as in n. 42 below.) This would leave two of the three links falling within the chronologically adjacent *King John* and *Richard II* in the period 1594-6.

31. No other play or poem has more than three of the seven words.

32. R. Graziani, 'The Numbering of Shakespeare's Sonnets: 12, 60, and 126,' *Shakespeare Quarterly,* 35 (1984), 79-82.

33. *Shakespeare's Sonnets,* ed. Duncan-Jones, p. 16.

34. Ibid.

35. Slater's tables in *Problem,* 158-96, clearly reveal associations by genre as well as chronology.

36. However, Gary Taylor and John Jowett argue in *Shakespeare Reshaped 1606-1623* (Oxford 1993), 107-236, that Thomas Middleton made small contributions to the text after Shakespeare's death.

37. I have relied on A. Schmidt, *Shakespeare Lexicon* (Berlin, 1902; repr. New York, 1971).

38. J. Padel, *New Poems by Shakespeare: Order and Meaning Restored to the Sonnets* (London, 1981), 16. Padel's reordering of the sequence is unconvincing, but he makes some good points on the Southampton versus Pembroke debate.

39. Ibid.

40. Padel's discussion (ibid. 17-21) may be supplemented by J. Dover Wilson, *An Introduction to The Sonnnets of Shakespeare* (Cambridge, 1963), 59-74, and *Shakespeare's Sonnnets,* ed. Duncan-Jones, pp. 53-69.

41. For the list see Slater, *Problem, 136-57.*

42. G. Taylor, 'Shakespeare and Others: The Authorship of *Henry the Sixth, Part One,'* *Medieval and Renaissance Drama in England,* 7 (1995), 145-205, esp. pp. 189-94 and 198.

43. This conclusion was foreshadowed in Jackson, *Shakespeare's 'A Lover's Complaint,'* 13 n. 15, where he also declared that the sonnets had been 'written over a long period.'

44. D. W. Foster, 'Reconstructing Shakespeare Part 2: The Sonnets,' *Shakespeare Newsletter* (Fall 1991), 26-7, reaches somewhat different conclusions, based on his research with the electronic database SHAXICON. He assigns Sonnets 97-115 to 1602-4 and Sonnets 116-26 to 1608; but he also assigns the remaining sonnets, divided into groups, to periods from 1598-9 to 1608. But he has not yet published full details of his evidence.

Sound and Meaning in Shakespeare's Sonnets

More has been written about the Sonnets than any of Shakespeare's works except *Hamlet*. Surprisingly, however, practically nothing in this vast secondary literature offers a comprehensive answer to the most fundamental question of poetics, whether the sounds of the Sonnets are an echo of the sense. George T. Wright's bibliographical overview (1985:371-72) singles out two studies—Masson (1954) and Booth (1969: 66-79 et passim)—which investigate the Sonnets' phonetic structure in some detail, but neither of these authors has much of systematic purport to say beyond noting Shakespeare's obvious use of alliteration, assonance, and consonance in the service of syntactic and semantic parallelism.[1] Indeed, with respect to alliteration, the following might well function as an indirect characterization of the status of research on this problem:

> If Roman Jakobson had analysed [Sonnet] 55, one of the things he would have noticed in its first strophe is the high incidence of alliteration on 'm,' 'p,' and 's,' which is repeated in the third strophe. That Shakespeare 'affects the letter' in these strophes, and that they are thereby linked at the phonetic level is not in question. Our question is what performative relation this purely formal linkage at the level of the signifier might bear to the sonnet's signification, its 'contents' as Shakespeare equivocally puts it. Here Jakobson can be of little help, taking as he notoriously does, meaning or content for granted or reducing it to the received ideas of other commentators. In terms of his analysis, the most the empirical fact of alliteration can be is an earnest of poetic power, alerting us that some extra-communicative intention may be at work; in itself it cannot be a source or explanation of that power. Occurring as it does within a semantic field that the alliteration does not itself generate, the function of alliteration cannot be causal or integral to signified meaning. Rather, it operates here as what Puttenham would call a figure of 'ornament' of the kind Shakespeare designates and illustrates as such in the previous sonnet ('O how much more doth beauty beauteous seem / By that sweet ornament . . .'). As ornament or decoration, alliteration bears the same superficially attractive but functionally

inessential relation to the poem as 'gilt' does to the 'monuments / O princes' mentioned at the outset. Gilding is to monumental sculpture as alliteration is to the sonnet.

> (Felperin 1985:176-77).

If alliteration is largely irrelevant to understanding the significance of the sound pattern, what else, then, could there be of phonetic relevance in Sonnet 55? That a systematic answer to this question might exist has been obscured, first and foremost, by the lack of an appropriate methodology. We need to pose questions about the data that presuppose abandoning the fruitless atomism of previous approaches while addressing the phonetic structure in terms of GROUPS of sounds and their possible alignment with meanings. More positively, we need to face squarely the problem that sound-meaning correspondences, where they can be shown to exist, always involve the crossing of ontological domains—there being no 'natural' connection between any sound and any meaning in isolation. Sets of sounds have relational values vis-à-vis each other, in the same sense as when we say that sets of meanings are structured relationally. The correspondences between sounds and meanings in poems are grounded in the RELATIONAL VALUES of these units in the structure of the language that serves as the raw material for the poetry.

In this light, a natural beginning to a methodological answer lies by way of an appeal to some general principles of linguistic structure. The sound patterns of all languages past and present are characterized by one fundamental division, that between sonorants and obstruents. The class of sonorants includes all vowels and vowel-like sounds, i.e. nasals, liquids, and glides (sometimes called semi-vowels); the class of obstruents includes all other sounds, i.e. the 'true' consonants (cf. Hymes 1960:116).[2] In contemporary English, as in Early Modern English, the sonorants are (using orthography instead of phonetic transcription) the nasals *m, n, ng;* the liquids *l, r ;* and the glides *h, y w.*

Sonority is typically defined as the relative loudness of a given sound vis-à-vis other sounds with the same length, stress, and pitch; alternately, it is defined as the position of a sound on a scale that reflects the degree of openness or unobstructedness of the vocal apparatus.

Sonorants are more 'singable' than nonsonorants and may thus contribute to the perception of mellifluousness when found in nondiscursive implementations of speech (see n. 8 below). A synoptic view of both aspects—loudness and unobstructedness—is encompassed by the concept of the relative amount of acoustic energy produced by a sound. A sonority hierarchy based on these phonetic characteristics can consequently be established, going from most sonorous to least sonorous sounds: vowels are ranked as most sonorous, followed in diminishing order of sonority by glides, liquids, nasals, and obstruents.

For our purposes, which have to do with the contexture of verse, it is enough to distinguish sonorants from obstruents. Only one further point needs to be taken into account: since the smallest phonetic domain of verse structure is that of the syllable,[3] my analysis will concern sounds at the syllabic margins (onsets and codas) of words. All sequences of two sonorants count as what will henceforth be called a sonorant unit (SU); intervening vowels are ignored; a sequence of n sonorants is equal to $n-1$ SUs. Correspondingly, any cluster of two or more obstruents—whether it occurs within a word or at word boundaries without an intervening pause—counts as what will be called an obstruent unit (OU).[4]

Returning to Sonnet 55, here is a demonstration of the method of reckoning sonorant and obstruent units (single and double underscores mark SUs, dotted underscores mark OUs):

(1) Not marble nor the gilded monuments
Of princes shall outlive this powerful rhyme,
But you shall shine more bright in these contents[5]
Than unswept stone, besmeared with sluttish time.
When wasteful war shall statues overturn,
And broils root out the work of masonry,
Nor Mars his sword nor war's quick fire shall burn
The living record of your memory.
'Gainst death and all oblivious enmity
Shall you pace forth; your praise shall still find room
Even in the eyes of all posterity
That wear this world out to the ending doom.
So, till the judgement that yourself arise,
You live in this, and dwell in lovers' eyes.[6]

A count of the number of SUs yields forty-seven. There are one-hundred-forty syllables (ten per line times fourteen lines) in the sonnet.[7] Dividing the number of SUs by the number of syllables, one gets .336: this is the sonority quotient (SQ) of the poem. A perusal

of the values of all sonnets (Appendix 1) reveals the fact that Sonnet 55 is one among only six whose SQs are above .300, making them the most sonorous in the entire sequence. The other five—all but one more sonorous than 55—are 13, 33, 71, 72, and 81 (see Appendix 2).

A corresponding count of the OUs in Sonnet 55 yields the number 28, which when divided by 140 results in an OQ of .200. The range of OQ's goes from .357—the least sonorous (in Sonnet 73)—to the most sonorous .100 (in Sonnet 72). This means that .357 is relatively neutral with regard to obstruency. In the relation between SQs and OQs, the SQ is normally more significant as a measure of a given sonnet's sonority than is its OQ.[8] In the case of Sonnet 55, then, whatever its OQ, an SQ of .336 is unattenuated as an indicator of high sonority.

The question arising at this point, of course, is the relevance of the sonnet's high sonority to its meaning. Sonnet 55 in its barest outlines is an assertion of the liberating power, via their incorporeality, of words ('rhyme,' i.e. verse), as contrasted with the limitations inherent in monuments and other static objects. The renewed life the subject will gain is construed not only as a value in itself but as a dynamic liberation from oblivion in the course of time ('Gainst death and all oblivious enmity / Shall you PACE FORTH' [emphasis added]). This idea—whose compass in the Sonnets includes even Cupid, 'a boy who is warned that he must in due course succumb to Time's inexorable law of death' (Pooler 1918:xxx)—is punctuated in the first line of the couplet, where 'judgement' refers to the Day of Judgement: the addressee of the sonnet, will 'arise' from the dead, but more importantly for the semantic dominant, will thereby achieve eternal freedom.

The sound pattern of 55 can thus be accounted for in terms of its isomorphism with the poem's meaning, where meaning in Shakespeare's sonnets is uniformly understood—for the purposes of evaluating the sound-meaning nexus—as being subtended in its most abstractly fundamental sense by the OPPOSITION BETWEEN FREEDOM AND CONSTRAINT. There is a particular appropriateness to this isomorphism that bears emphasis. Let us recall the nature of sonority in phonetic terms: sonorants are the freest sounds, those produced with the least amount of obstructedness in the vocal tract. With this in mind, one can see the relationship between sound and meaning in the sonnet to be natural and iconic, not arbitrary and emblematic.

Further to this point, it is instructive to take two

sonnets that are immediately contiguous (but not linked in the sense to be developed later). Sonnets 33 and 34 contrast markedly in their SQs, which are respectively .371 and .179. In 33 the metaphor of the sun being obscured by clouds leads to the assertion of the sun's primacy as it emerges from the base obscurity which represents the beloved's dissipations. Smith (1981:19, citing Puttenham for his definition) points out that the sonnet exemplifies a rhetorical figure (PARADIASTO-LE) that moderates and abates the force of a bad thing 'by craft and for a pleasing purpose.' Sonnet 34 has a more 'severe' message, addressed straightforwardly to the beloved, with a possible 'link between the raindrops on the poet's face and the tears on the Friend's' (Smith, 20), and the image of a wound that might be cured by a salve but leaves a disgrace behind. This sonnet in turn has a relatively high OQ: .264.

This leaves moot, for the time being, whether a sonnet with low sonority can implement the meaning of freedom; and conversely, whether high sonority can cooccur with the meaning of constraint. As a matter of actual fact there are no such cases of mismatches between sound and sense in the Sonnets. At the extreme ends of the spectrum, the match is complete: high sonority is isomorphous with the meaning of freedom, low sonority with that of constraint. At intermediate points, not unexpectedly, given the aesthetic nature of the object of study, what one observes is either a loose correlation between sonority and freedom or no conclusive linking one way or the other.

This might be the moment to distinguish between musicality and sonority. Any poetic text labeled song might be expected to be full of sonorants and relatively unencumbered by obstruent clusters, which factors, separately and together, would seem to render the poetry musical. But this intuitive guess turns out to be wrong, at least as far as Shakespeare is concerned, For instance, the Clown Feste's song in *Twelfth Night* ('O mistress mine, where are you roaming?'), which spans 95 syllables, has SQ and OQ values of .210 and .189, respectively—not especially sonorous by the standards of the Sonnets. Or take Thomas Gray's *Elegy Written in a Country Churchyard* ('The curfew tolls the knell of parting day'), which consists of forty-syllable stanzas (except for 'The Epitaph' at the end, whose three stanzas are each 120 syllables). Its four-stanza spans of 160 syllables have SQ values in the .231 to .300 range, except for the opening quartet, whose SQ is .375. Coleridge's *Kubla Khan,* often held up as a model of musicality,[9]

has an SQ of .264 and an OQ of .161 over its span of 485 syllables—neither of which is notable in terms of sonority.

Taking the other end of the range from Sonnet 55, I examine Sonnet 4, whose SQ of .086 (only 12 SUs!) renders it the least sonorous in the entire corpus:

(2) Unthrifty loveliness, why dost thou spend
    Upon thyself thy beauty's legacy?
    Nature's bequest gives nothing, but doth lend,
    And being frank she lends to those are free.
    Then, beauteous niggard, why dost thou abuse
    The bounteous largess given thee to give?
    Profitless usurer, why dost thou use
    So great a sum of sums yet canst not live?
    For having traffic with thyself alone
    Thou of thyself thy sweet self dost deceive;
    Then how when Nature calls thee to be gone,
    What acceptable audit canst thou leave?
    Thy unused beauty must be tombed with thee, .
    Which, usèd, lives th'executor to be.

This poem bristles with the imagery of money, money lending, and inheritance, already familiar as constituent strands of a main theme in some of Shakespeare's most prominent nonhistorical dramas (e.g. *Love's Labour Lost, The Merchant of Venice*)—economic limitations on freedom. The sonnet is 'built almost entirely upon the idea of spending, saving, hoarding, lending, giving, bequeathing, and the like' (Smith, 95). Smith points out that 'live' in line 8 suggests both 'gain a livelihood' and 'survive after death,' heightening the connotations of constraint imposed by usury. The fourth and fifth lines convey this semantic dominant while playing on the meaning of 'lend': 'Nature's bequest gives nothing, but doth lend, / And being frank she lends to those are free.'

After Sonnet 4 the least sonorous, based on its SQ of .100 (OQ = .221), is 67.

(3) Ah, wherefore with infection should he live
    And with his presence grace impiety,
    That sin by him advantage should achieve
    And lace itself with his society?
    Why should false painting imitate his cheek
    And steal dead seeming of his living hue?
    Why should poor beauty indirectly seek
    Roses of shadow, since his rose is true?
    Why should he live, now Nature bankrupt is,
    Beggared of blood to blush through lively veins,
    For she hath no exchequer now but his,
    And, 'prived of many lives upon his gains?
    O, him she stores, to show what wealth she had
    In days long since, before these last so bad.

This sonnet accuses the beloved of artificiality and reflects the 'bias against cosmetics and extravagant dress which seems almost a personal trait of Shakespeare' (Smith, 21). In the terms of the conflict of freedom and constraint, elaboration and ornament impede the emergence of the beloved 's true beauty. According to John Kerrigan's commentary, 'this poem—especially in the wake of 66, with its self-pitying lament—marks a crucial stage in the poet's account of the youth' (Shakespeare 1986:257).[10] The linkage of 66 and 67 is reinforced by their unusually low SQs—.136 and .100, respectively. If one acknowledges, with Kerrigan, that Sonnet 68 continues the argument of 67, and that 69 anticipates 70 within a group extending from 66 through 70, then the unique clustering of low SQs becomes a motivated fact of poetic design . At no other point in the whole sonnet sequence does one encounter a set of five poems with three SQs below .200, as happens here.

Table 1: Sequence of 5 sonnets with SQ's below .200.

Sonnet	SQ	OQ
66	.136	.207
67	.100	.221
68	.186	.150
69	.143	.293
70	.164	.314

The average SQ in this quintuplet is .146—unmatched for any set of five contiguous sonnets. Note also the high obstruency of 69 and 70.

This group also 'uniquely anticipates (if 5, resolved by 6, is excepted) the issues of 94' (Shakespeare 1986:257), an 'elusive poem . . . perhaps the most discussed in the collection' (Shakespeare 1986:290).[11] It is situated in a group of six contiguous sonnets, 91-96, that share thematic issues or emphases (see Appendix 4) and constitute—like 66 through 70—what might be thought of as a POETIC MACROCONTEXT, defined as three or more linked poems.[12] From the standpoint of sonority, this set is held together by the functionally equivalent

Table 2. Poetic macrocontext (= set of linked sonnets).

Sonnet	SQ	OQ
91	.300	.200
92	.129	.207
93	.114	.193
94	.186	.314
95	.157	.286
96	.207	.300

factors of low sonority and high obstruency, alternating between subsets of two and three contiguous poems, respectively.

While 91 is somewhat neutral with respect to sonority, an SQ of .300 not being significant by itself,[13] the SQ's and the OQ's of the remaining five—as an ensemble—both signify low sonority. It would be tempting to stop at the notion of a binding function for low sonority in this quintuplet, similar topics being echoed by similar sound patterns tout court. But on closer analysis, sonnets 92-96 reveal a sound-meaning nexus that conforms to the iconic function of low sonority, namely a diagrammatic representation of constraint.

Sonnet 92 opens with the statement that the beloved is perpetually constrained to belong to the lover despite any attempt at escape (1-2) and goes on to draw an apparent equivalence: his life in turn relies for its continuance on this love. The two are thus inextricably intertwined (5-6). Freedom lies only in death, the escape from vexation (7-9). The legal right of ownership, or 'title' (Shakespeare 1986:278), signifies a strict bond. However, the equivalence is spurious, a fact which further increases constraint: 'happy to have thy love' (12) is unambiguous but ambiguated at the end (14: 'and yet I know it not'). 'Happy to die' (12) would ensue only from loss and misery. The uncertainty here is also a bind in itself.

Sonnet 93 continues the theme of knowledge and ignorance or truth and falsehood in love. The lover compares himself potentially to a deceived husband (2) constrained to ignorance of his wife's duplicity between 'looks' and 'heart' (4). The negative is entirely exluded from his lover's face, just as—conversely—'moods and frowns and wrinkles' are ineradicable from the faces of others (6-8). The beloved is forced by the 'decree' of 'heaven' (9) always to seem affectionate; the same decree constrains his 'thoughts' and 'heart's workings.' The lover, in turn, might be like Adam, possibly about to be 'betrayed'—again , like the deceived husband of line 2, who remains in the same bind as in Sonnet 92. Masks such as this constrain the truth, but the lover makes no move to uncover false temptation.

In 94 the unmoved move others (4), like godly powers. Their concealed hypocrisy involves constraint. Although the beloved is detached, he might not be free. At lines 5-7 comparisons based on finance, property, and contract law recur. Line 6 can be paraphrased: 'protect the riches of nature (here mainly beauty and charm) from wasteful expenditure by means of prudent management' (Shakespeare 1986:291). The beloved has 'complete control' over his features (Shakespeare 1986:292), gaining his freedom only through constraint, for self-possession involves great effort and loneliness; one is forced into one's own sole company. The flower (11) benefits others, not itself, by its beauty and its fragrance (9-10); and if its nature becomes corrupted, is necessarily reduced to greater baseness than any lowly weed in the eyes of others.

In Sonnet 95 even bad rumor (which is typically very free; cf. *Aeneid* 4, 'fama volat'), is constrained to turn positive when it concerns the beloved (1-8), again because of its beauty. The 'tongue that tells the story' (5) has its criticism converted to praise; the beloved's 'name' (8) determines every outcome. 'Vices' (8) may live under a 'veil' (11) in this 'mansion' (9) or 'habitation' (10), which makes seeing believing (12). Good judgment is constrained—more than encouraged—by the evidence of one's eyes. But the lover warns the beloved to rein in deceptive behavior or scheming at the risk of losing his 'edge' (14)—the power to constrain others.

Finally, 96 asserts that the lover 'owns' everything essential of the beloved (14), including a part of his reputation ('mine is thy good report'). The main preoccupation is again the contrast between an unknown truth about the beloved and a superordinate rule of representation: appearances constrain opinion ('Thou mak'st faults graces' [4]; also, 'So are those errors . . ./To truths translated' [7-8]). Context or contiguity work in supplementary ways to help determine judgment; thus a 'base' jewel (6) looks precious because it is contiguous to a queen's hand. 'Translated' (8) and 'translate' (10) mean forced movement and extreme

distortion from error to truth and from wolf to lamb, which is in the power of physical beauty.

The dyad of freedom and constraint may eclipse even that of unity and duality in the broad literary context known to Shakespeare. It pervades contemporary instances of the nature-versus-culture debate (translatable into the terms of Fate and Ability, *fortuna* and *virtu,* submission and release). A few outstanding examples have to suffice here. The vigorous Hoby translation of Castiglione's *Book of the Courtier,* which proved a basic text for Elizabethan 'self-fashioning,' exemplified both thematically and in its conversational form the constraint/freedom dyad. Throughout the four volumes, speaking characters with finely nuanced opinions strive to define a just midpoint between nonchalance *(sprezzatura)* and decorum in manners, language, and art, which they characterize as grace. It is the movement away from constraint towards freedom that motivates the famous section concerning the 'best' Italian language. They agree that it is to be based on a literary precedent derived from history but receptive to input from all parts of the country (in contradistinction to persistent latinizing and to the dominance of Tuscany), to foreign language terms, even neologisms. In keeping with the search for emotional and aesthetic equilibrium, the characters in the *Courtier* agree or are explicitly instructed to avoid extremist arguments or privative oppositions—a state of intersubjective and mutual constraint. Poetic diction of the time, however, is quite another matter. In Castiglione, Thomas More, Montaigne, and Rabelais 'the vertical flexibility of man becomes virtually a structural principle' (Greene 1968:255).

The conventions of pastoral lyric—with its dyad of nature versus culture, paradisiacal freedom versus earthly servitude—make it an obvious instance of the freedom-constraint dyad throughout the sixteenth century and into the next. The stringent demands of courtiership inform much production in this genre. But in lyric poetry a strong revision of Petrarchan conventions and their subtending humanist anthropology, at the same time, created a poet such as Michelangelo, who instantiates the drive for self-creation over and above all determinism, be it transcendental idealism or the obdurate indifference of a lover. Like Shakespeare Michelangelo was considered an anti-Petrarchan: an Italian tercet (by Francesco Berni) celebrates Michelangelo's directness and lack of artifice in this vein. Berni's view, of course, depends on a prior link with Petrarch, their common features being taken generally for granted. The series of existential crises that infuse many of Michelangelo's poems depict attempts to 'break free of emotional weight or even from an overweight content that strains the limitations of poetic form' (Shapiro 1980:214). He refers variously to heroic Christianity in Dante, or to the divided will of the speaker in Petrarch's Italian lyrics, now analogized to the contest between 'virtue' and 'fortune.' The poems often take their departure from a problem of act or form expressed as the striving of individual human action against the priority of rule-governed motion.

Shakespeare is 'not so much concerned to reforge and refashion himself as to escape [existence], transcend it, leave it behind' (Leishman 1966:132). The perennial themes of the constraints of time, the unwanted dominance of the calendar and the seasons, the desire to experience nature as the affirmation of one's innate character rather than as fate and destiny infuse the lyric of as conventional a poet as Torquato Tasso and betray themselves as diversionary preoccupations in his epic. Like the Spanish Golden Age, Tasso's work is shot through with liberating dreams of the New World. He praises exploration for its very transgression of ancient boundaries. Worn-out rhetorical topics such as lists of desired things are transformed by strong negatives.[14] An outstanding example of such revision in Shakespearean lyric is Sonnet 130 ('My mistress' eyes are nothing like the sun'), which arrogates to itself complete freedom from Petrarchan conventions of praise. The SQ here is actually on the high side (.264), meaning that the sonority correlates well with the content, freedom from the pressures of tradition.

Sonnets 91-96 seem to constitute the largest commonly acknowledged macrocontext but not the only one. Using the Kerrigan commentary as a convenient guide, and adhering to the definition of a macrocontext stipulated earlier (three or more linked poems), one can discern four other such loci (in addition to 66-70): 100-103, 106-109, 144-146, and 147-149:

Table 3. Four further sets of linked sonnets

Sonnet	SQ	OQ
100	.136}	.350
101	.136}	.243
102	.279}	.207

Sonnet	SQ	OQ
103	.286}	.157
106	.157	.257
107	.236	.350
108	.164}	.243
109	.164}	.193
144	.214}	.200
145	.214}	.196
146	.174}	.210}
147	.171}	.236}
148	.179	.221}
149	.157	.229}

The values linked by braces lend support to the unity of these macrocontexts. But the matter of linked poems might need to be reexamined entirely in light of the data in Appendix 1, where one finds THIRTY-THREE clusters of poems—some of which overlap—for which the SQs or the OQs are in the same numerical range (defined as beginning with an identical digit):[15] Sonnets 4-6, 7-9, 10-12, 15-18, 18-20, 19-21, 22-24, 23-26, 32-37, 38-40, 42-44, 48-52, 56-59, 57-59, 63-67, 66-70, 78-80, 79-81, 82-86, 88-90, 89-92, 92-95, 102-104, 108-110, 109-112, 115-117, 121-127, 127-129, 132-134, 137-142, 139-141, 146-151, and 146-154. It remains for further research to determine whether these sets also form macrocontexts, but the overlap in sound patterns is suggestive. So far I have concentrated on the SQ of a poem as the significant measure of the alignment of sound and meaning. This emphasis conforms to the idea that SQ's are more important than OQ's as an indicator of sonority. But the OQ's also play a role, albeit a subsidiary one. This can be seen from two contiguous poems, Sonnets 71 and 72, that are highly sonorous and, notably, continuous (share a theme) with each other. These two sonnets have the lowest degree of obstruency in the entire sequence, with OQs of .136 and .100, respectively.16 Correspondingly, Sonnet 71 has the

(4)   71

No longer mourn for me when I am dead
Than you shall hear the surly sullen bell
Give warning to the world that I am fled
From this vile world with vilest worms to dwell.
Nay, if you read this line, remember not
The hand that writ it, for I love you so
That I in your sweet thoughts would be forgot
If thinking on me then should make you woe.
O, if, I say, you look upon this verse,
When I, perhaps, compounded am with clay,
Do not so much as my poor name rehearse,
But let your love even with my life decay;
Lest the wise world should look into your moan,
And mock you with me after I am gone.

(5)   72

O, lest the world should task you to recite
What merit lived in me that you should love
After my death, dear love, forget me quite;
For you in me can nothing worthy prove,
Unless you would devise some virtuous lie
To do more for me than mine own desert,
And hang more praise upon deceasèd I
Than niggard truth would willingly impart.
O, lest your true love may seem false in this,
That you for love speak well of me untrue,
My name be buried where my body is
And live no more to shame nor me nor you;
For I am shamed by that which I bring forth,
And so should you, to love things nothing worth.

Table 4: Inverse correlation of SQs and OQs

SQ Range	Average OQ
.086-.099	.279
.100-.199	.241
.200-.299	.223
.300-.393	.172
OQ Range Average	**sQ**
.100-.199	.222
.200-.299	.197
.300-.357	.189

and OQs, respectively, that span one digit, there is a patterned relation between the averages such that higher sonority is always associated with lower obstruency and vice versa. The complete set of relevant data covering the entire sequence is to be found in Appendices 2 and 3. Table 4 is an abbreviated version that places the relationship in relief.[17]

As the sonority increases, the average obstruency decreases, and vice versa—from a low average obstruency of .172 characterizing sonnets in the high sonority range of .300-.393, to a high average obstruency of .279 characterizing those in the low sonority range of .086-.099. When the 77 sonnets in the .100-.199 SQ range are combined with the lone sonnet (4) in the .086-.099 range, the combined average OQ is .242. The intermediate averages are progressively more obstruent: .241 > .223. Data derived from the converse of the above comparison bear out the overall validity of the pattern. When OQ ranges differing by one digit are used to group poems, the SQ averages also array themselves by progressive sonority (full data in Appendix 3). Again, as the obstruency rises, the sonority falls and vice versa.

Shakespeare's use of these correspondences stands out in a comparison with other contemporary authors. Shakespeare's evidently deliberate placement of a sonnet sequence in a collection with a long poem, *A Lover's Complaint,* appears to have been part of a literary vogue in the 1590s which received its main impetus from Samuel Daniel's *Delia* (1592).[18] It was immediately followed

highest sonority of all the poems—.393; this makes it the single most sonorous sonnet in the whole group, when both the sonority and the obstruency quotients are considered in tandem. Here, again, the iconic function of the sounds mentioned earlier is confirmed. The poet is allowing his addressee complete freedom to forget him after he is dead. Nothing will constrain the beloved: no requirement of mourning, no need of remembrance. According to Smith (17), the beloved is also being liberated from potential 'social embarrassment or disgrace,' for 'the "wise world" [might] mock him for caring about one so lowly.' Sonnet 72 continues in the same vein: the SQ is .307, reinforcing the maximally low OQ of .100.

Sound-meaning coherences of this kind lend credence to the reality of the iconic function of sonority in Shakespeare's Sonnets. Reinforcing this is the negative relationship between sonorant in the sequence and obstruent quotients over all the sonnets in the sequence. When the sonnets are grouped by the numerical ranges of SQs

Table 5. Mean SQ.

Bacon	.161
Barnfield	.170
Fletcher	.181
Daniel	.197
Shakespeare	.203
Spenser	.238
Linche	.236
Lodge	.243

by five similar collections: Thomas Lodge's *Phillis* (1593), Giles Fletcher's *Licia* (1593), Edmund Spenser's *Amoretti* (1595), Richard Barnfield's *Cynthia* (1595), and Richard Linche's *Diella (1596).*

Ten sets of sonnets chosen at random from modern editions of these collections were subjected to the same analysis as Shakespeare's sonnets. For further comparison, twenty stretches of 141-230 syllables selected at random from Book One of Francis Bacon's *The Advancement of Learning* (1605) were included as well.[19]

Among these authors, Shakespeare falls clearly in the middle of the range in the matter of sound-meaning correspondences: SQ .16 to .24 vs. Shakespeare's .20; OQ .19 to .25 vs. Shakespeare's .23. Statistical analysis (analysis of variance) sets Shakespeare's SQs apart from a high-sonority group composed of Linche, Spenser, and Lodge and a low-sonority group composed of Bacon, Barnfield, Daniel, and Fletcher; the same analysis fails to distinguish any difference among the authors in their average OQs. However, as Figures 1 and 2 show, the negative relationship of SQ and OQ within Shakespeare is notably absent in the other authors.

Statistical testing confirms this relationship: SQ and OQ are negatively correlated within the corpus of Shakespeare's Sonnets (correlation—.312; probability of similar or stronger result by chance—less than .001), and are not correlated within the corpus of the other authors (correlation—.16; probability of similar or stronger result by chance—.17, failing usual statistical criteria for significance).

In addition to underscoring the uniqueness of Shakespeare's poetic technique as regards sonority in the Sonnets, the difference seen between Shakespeare and the other authors demonstrates that the negative relationship between SQ and OQ in Shakespeare is not, as might be guessed, a structural feature of text (SQs and OQs are negatively correlated because textual places occupied by sonorant units are thereby made unavailable for obstruent units). In fact, although obstruents and sonorants are mutually exclusive and jointly exhaustive, OUs and SUs are not jointly exhaustive and, therefore, SQ does not in principle vary inversely with OQ.[20]

Table 6. Mean OQ

Fletcher	.195
Bacon	.203
Spenser	.204
Barnfield	.220
Daniel	.221
Shakespeare	.228
Linch	.231
Lodge	.245

Shakespeare's achievement, against this background, is to be located in his unwaveringly motivated implementation of sonority. The judiciousness of his poetic technique in this respect merits special attention. Just as there are Shakespeare Sonnets that eschew alliteration or other forms of paronomasia, so sonority or obstruency quotients can be neutral vis-à-vis the poem's semantics, neither confirming nor disconfirming the meaning. However, when these quotients are significantly high or low, within the statistical parameters of the entire sonnet sequence, one finds a uniquely Shakespearean sonority that is never deployed indiscriminately: without fail the poet's ear gives warrant to a sound pattern that is an icon of the sense.

Michael Shapiro

Sonority vs. Obstruency: Shakespeare's sonnets

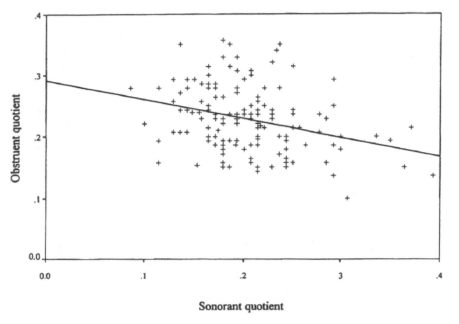

FIGURE 1

Sonority vs. Obstruency: Other texts

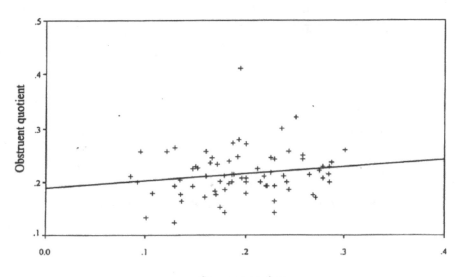

FIGURE 2

APPENDIX 1: PROFILE OF SQS AND OQS IN SHAKESPEARE'S SONNETS

SONNET	TOTAL SYLLABLES	SONORANT QUOTIENT	OBSTRUENT QUOTIENT	SONNET	TOTAL SYLLABLES	SONORANT QUOTIENT	OBSTRUENT QUOTIENT
1	140[a]	0.221	0.279	28		0.193	0.228
2		0.192	0.186	29		0.214	0.257
3	142	0.148	0.239	30		0.171	0.186
4		0.086	0.279	31		0.193	0.193
5		0.214	0.236	32		0.171	0.264
6		0.143	0.207	33		0.371	0.214
7		0.207	0.157	34		0.179	0.264
8		0.229	0.321	35		0.143	0.279
9		0.229	0.229	36		0.250	0.243
10		0.114	0.279	37		0.136	0.271
11		0.179	0.329	38		0.207	0.186
12		0.186	0.350	39		0.207	0.157
13		0.350	0.193	40		0.221	0.250
14		0.150	0.293	41		0.179	0.193
15		0.186	0.193	42		0.236	0.200
16		0.293	0.136	43		0.179	0.229
17		0.179	0.150	44		0.193	0.271
18		0.207	0.186	45		0.164	0.193
19		0.293	0.293	46		0.214	0.264
20		0.293	0.250	47		0.207	0.307
21		0.171	0.200	48		0.157	0.257
22		0.243	0.164	49		0.164	0.286
23		0.200	0.243	50		0.214	0.214
24		0.214	0.243	51		0.279	0.236
25		0.193	0.221	52		0.171	0.229
26		0.171	0.229	53		0.250	0.157
27		0.214	0.150	54		0.164	0.300

[a] In these appendices, wherever a sonnet has the standard 140 syllables, this datum will be omitted and is to be assumed.

APPENDIX 1: PROFILE OF SQS AND OQS IN SHAKESPEARE'S SONNETS

SONNET	TOTAL SYLLABLES	SONORANT QUOTIENT	OBSTRUENT QUOTIENT	SONNET	TOTAL SYLLABLES	SONORANT QUOTIENT	OBSTRUENT QUOTIENT
55		0.336	0.200	105		0.179	0.186
56		0.179	0.179	106		0.157	0.257
57		0.243	0.150	107		0.236	0.350
58		0.250	0.157	108		0.164	0.243
59		0.236	0.171	109		0.164	0.193
60		0.193	0.329	110		0.186	0.193
61		0.193	0.221	111		0.243	0.193
62		0.214	0.143	112		0.214	0.186
63		0.236	0.200	113		0.164	0.279
64		0.193	0.236	114		0.164	0.314
65		0.250	0.236	115		0.200	0.293
66		0.136	0.207	116		0.164	0.214
67		0.100	0.221	117		0.229	0.236
68		0.186	0.150	118	144	0.153	0.153
69		0.143	0.293	119		0.171	0.279
70		0.164	0.314	120		0.293	0.186
71		0.393	0.136	121	142	0.155	0.239
72		0.307	0.100	122		0.221	0.214
73		0.179	0.357	123		0.164	0.200
74		0.143	0.243	124		0.186	0.236
75		0.214	0.221	125		0.236	0.200
76		0.179	0.157	126	120	0.217	0.217
77		0.207	0.229	127		0.193	0.221
78		0.171	0.286	128		0.164	0.300
79		0.114	0.157	129		0.164	0.250
80		0.179	0.171	130		0.264	0.186
81		0.364	0.150	131		0.164	0.279
82		0.207	0.236	132		0.243	0.179
83		0.229	0.150	133		0.236	0.279
84		0.200	0.179	134		0.207	0.250
85		0.250	0.314	135		0.300	0.179
86		0.214	0.200	136		0.243	0.157
87		0.171	0.186	137		0.207	0.229
88		0.207	0.164	138		0.171	0.264
89		0.243	0.200	139		0.286	0.229
90		0.250	0.214	140		0.200	0.236
91		0.300	0.200	141		0.200	0.236
92		0.129	0.207	142		0.129	0.293
93		0.114	0.193	143		0.193	0.307
94		0.186	0.314	144		0.214	0.200
95		0.157	0.286	145	112	0.214	0.196
96		0.207	0.300	146	138	0.174	0.210
97		0.171	0.200	147		0.171	0.236
98		0.257	0.214	148		0.179	0.221
99	150	0.233	0.340	149		0.157	0.229
100		0.136	0.350	150		0.193	0.279
101		0.136	0.243	151		0.136	0.207
102		0.279	0.207	152		0.221	0.279
103		0.286	0.157	153		0.129	0.257
104		0.229	0.243	154		0.279	0.236

APPENDIX 2: PROFILE OF SONNETS BY SQ RANGES AND OQ AVERAGES

A. SQ = .300–.393 (8 sonnets = 5%)

13	.350	.193
33	.371	.214
55	.336	.200
71	.393	.136
72	.307	.100
81	.364	.150
91	.300	.200
135	.300	.179

AVERAGE OQ = .172

B. SQ = .200–.299 (68 sonnets = 44%)

1	.221	.279	84	.200	.179
5	.214	.236	85	.250	.314
7	.207	.157	86	.214	.200
8	.229	.321	88	.207	.164
9	.229	.229	89	.243	.200
16	.293	.136	90	.250	.214
18	.207	.186	96	.207	.300
19	.293	.293	98	.257	.214
20	.293	.250	99	.233	.340
22	.243	.164	102	.279	.207
23	.200	.243	103	.286	.157
24	.214	.243	104	.229	.243
27	.214	.150	107	.236	.350
29	.214	.257	111	.243	.193
36	.250	.243	112	.214	.186
38	.207	.186	115	.200	.293
39	.207	.157	117	.229	.236
40	.221	.250	120	.293	.186
42	.236	.200	122	.221	.214
46	.214	.264	125	.236	.200
47	.207	.307	126	.217	.217
50	.214	.214	130	.264	.186
51	.279	.236	132	.243	.179
53	.250	.157	133	.236	.279
57	.243	.150	134	.207	.250
58	.250	.157	136	.243	.157
59	.236	.171	137	.207	.229
62	.214	.143	139	.286	.229
63	.236	.200	140	.200	.236
65	.250	.236	141	.200	.236
75	.214	.221	144	.214	.200
77	.207	.229	145	.214	.196
82	.207	.236	152	.221	.279
83	.229	.150	154	.279	.236

AVERAGE OQ = .223

C. SQ = .100–.199 (77 sonnets = 50%)

2	.192	.186	78	.171	.286
3	.148	.239	79	.114	.157
6	.143	.207	80	.179	.171
10	.114	.279	87	.171	.186
11	.179	.329	92	.129	.207
12	.186	.350	93	.114	.193
14	.150	.293	94	.186	.314
15	.186	.193	95	.157	.286
17	.179	.150	97	.171	.200
21	.171	.200	100	.136	.350

	OQ	SQ		OQ	SQ
25	.193	.221	101	.136	.243
26	.171	.229	105	.179	.186
28	.193	.228	106	.157	.257
30	.171	.186	108	.164	.243
31	.193	.193	109	.164	.193
32	.171	.264	110	.186	.193
34	.179	.264	113	.164	.279
35	.143	.279	114	.164	.314
37	.136	.271	116	.164	.214
41	.179	.193	118	.153	.153
43	.179	.229	119	.171	.279
44	.193	.271	121	.155	.239
45	.164	.193	123	.164	.200
48	.157	.257	124	.186	.236
49	.164	.286	127	.193	.221
52	.171	.229	128	.164	.300
54	.164	.300	129	.164	.250
56	.179	.179	131	.164	.279
60	.193	.329	138	.171	.264
61	.193	.221	142	.129	.293
64	.193	.236	143	.193	.307
66	.136	.207	146	.174	.210
67	.100	.221	147	.171	.236
68	.186	.150	148	.179	.221
69	.143	.293	149	.157	.229
70	.164	.314	150	.193	.279
73	.179	.357	151	.136	.207
74	.143	.243	153	.129	.257
76	.179	.157			

AVERAGE OQ = .241

D. SQ = .086–.099 (1 sonnet = 1%)

	OQ	SQ
4	.086	.279

APPENDIX 3: PROFILE OF SONNETS BY OQ RANGES AND SQ AVERAGES

A. OQ = .100–.199 (46 sonnets = 30%)

	OQ	SQ		OQ	SQ
2	.192	.186	72	.307	.100
7	.207	.157	76	.179	.157
13	.350	.193	79	.114	.157
15	.186	.193	80	.179	.171
16	.293	.136	81	.364	.150
17	.179	.150	83	.229	.150
18	.207	.186	84	.200	.179
22	.243	.164	87	.171	.186
27	.214	.150	88	.207	.164
30	.171	.186	93	.114	.193
31	.193	.193	103	.286	.157
38	.207	.186	105	.179	.186
39	.207	.157	109	.164	.193
41	.179	.193	110	.186	.193
45	.164	.193	111	.243	.193
53	.250	.157	112	.214	.186
56	.179	.179	118	.153	.153
57	.243	.150	120	.293	.186
58	.250	.157	130	.264	.186
59	.236	.171	132	.243	.179
62	.214	.143	135	.300	.179
68	.186	.150	136	.243	.157
71	.393	.136	145	.214	.196

AVERAGE SQ = .222

B. OQ = .200–.299 (91 sonnets = 59%)

1	.221	.279	86	.214	.200
3	.148	.239	89	.214	.200
4	.086	.279	90	.250	.214
5	.214	.236	91	.300	.200
6	.143	.207	92	.129	.207
9	.229	.229	95	.157	.286
10	.114	.279	97	.171	.200
14	.150	.293	98	.257	.214
19	.293	.293	101	.136	.243
20	.293	.250	102	.279	.207
21	.171	.200	104	.229	.243
23	.200	.243	106	.157	.257
24	.214	.243	108	.164	.243
25	.193	.221	113	.164	.279
26	.171	.229	115	.200	.293
28	.193	.228	116	.164	.214
29	.214	.257	117	.229	.236
32	.171	.264	119	.171	.279
33	.371	.214	121	.155	.239
34	.179	.264	122	.221	.214
35	.143	.279	123	.164	.200
36	.250	.243	124	.186	.236
37	.136	.271	125	.236	.200
40	.221	.250	126	.217	.217
42	.236	.200	127	.193	.221
43	.179	.229	129	.164	.250
44	.193	.271	131	.164	.279
46	.214	.264	133	.236	.279
48	.157	.257	134	.207	.250
49	.164	.286	137	.207	.229
50	.214	.214	138	.171	.264
51	.279	.236	139	.286	.229
52	.171	.229	140	.200	.236
55	.336	.200	141	.200	.236
61	.193	.221	142	.129	.293
63	.236	.200	144	.214	.200
64	.193	.236	146	.174	.210
65	.250	.236	147	.171	.236
66	.136	.207	148	.179	.221
67	.100	.221	149	.157	.229
69	.143	.293	150	.193	.279
74	.143	.243	151	.136	.207
75	.214	.221	152	.221	.279
77	.207	.229	153	.129	.257
78	.171	.286	154	.279	.236
82	.207	.236			

AVERAGE SQ = .197

C. OQ = .300–.357 (17 sonnets = 11%)

8	.229	.321	94	.186	.314
11	.179	.329	96	.207	.300
12	.186	.350	99	.233	.340
47	.207	.307	100	.136	.350
54	.164	.300	107	.236	.350
60	.193	.329	114	.164	.314
70	.164	.314	128	.164	.300
73	.179	.357	143	.193	.307
85	.250	.314			

AVERAGE SQ = .189

APPENDIX 4: POETIC MACRDCONTEXT

91

Some glory in their birth, some in their skill,
Some in their wealth, some in their body's force,
Some in their garments, though new-fangled ill,
Some in their hawks and hounds, some in their horse;
And every rumour hath his adjunct pleasure,
Wherein it finds a joy above the rest.
But these particulars are not my measure;
All these I better in one general best.
Thy love is better than high birth to me,
Richer than wealth, prouder than garments ' cost,
Of more delight than hawks or horses be;
And, having thee, of all men's pride I boast—
  Wretched in this alone, that thou mayst take
  All this away, and me most wretched make.

92

But do thy worst to steal thyself away,
For term of life thou art assured mine;
And life no longer than thy love will stay,
For it depends upon that love of thine.
Then need I not to fear the worst of wrongs,
When in the least of them my life hath end.
I see a better state to me belongs
Than that which on thy humour doth depend.
Thou canst not vex me with inconstant mind,
Since that my life on thy revolt doth lie.
O, what a happy title do I find,
Happy to have thy love, happy to die l
  But what's so blessed-fair that fears no blot?
  Thou mayst be false, and yet I know it not.

93

So shall I live, supposing thou art true,
Like a deceived husband; so love's face
May still seem love to me, though altered new,
Thy looks with me, thy heart in other place.
For there can live no haired in thine eye;
Therefore in that I cannot know thy change.
In many's looks, the false heart's history
Is writ in moods and frown and wrinkles strange,
But heaven in thy creation did decree
That in thy face sweet love should ever dwell:
What 'er thy thoughts or thy heart's workings be,

Thy looks should nothing thence but sweetness tell.
  How like Eve's apple doth thy beauty grow,
  If thy sweet virtue answer not thy show.

94

They that have power to hurt and will do none,
That do not do the thing they most do show,
Who, moving others, are themselves as stone,
Unmoved, cold, and to temptation slow;
They rightly do inherit heaven's graces
And husband nature's riches from expense;
They are the lords and owners of their faces,
Others but stewards of their excellence.
The summer's flower is to the summer sweet,
Though to itself it only live and die:
But if that flower with base infection meet,
The basest weed outbraves his dignity:
  For sweetest things turn sourest by their deeds;
  Lilies that fester smell far worse than weeds.

95

How sweet and lovely dost thou make the shame
Which, like a canker in the fragrant rose,
Doth spot the beauty of thy budding name!
O, in what sweets dost thou thy sins enclose!
That tongue that tells the story of thy days,
Making lascivious comments on thy sport,
Cannot dispraise but in a kind of praise;
Naming thy name blesses an ill report.
O, what a mansion have those vices got
Which for their habitation chose out thee,
Where beauty's veil doth cover every blot,
And all things turns to fair that eyes can see!
  Take heed, dear heart, of this large privilege;
  The hardest knife ill-used doth lose his edge.

96

Some say thy fault is youth, some wantonness,
Some say thy grace is youth and gentle sport;
Both grace and faults are loved of more and less;
Thou mak'st faults graces that to thee resort.
As on the finger of a thronèd queen
The basest jewel will be well esteemed,
So are those errors that in thee are seen

To truths translated and for true things deemed.
How many lambs might the stem wolf betray,
If like a lamb he could his looks translate;
How many grazers might'st thou lead away,
If thou wouldst use the strength of all thy state!
　But do not so; I love thee in such sort
　As, thou being mine, mine is thy good report.

APPENDIX 5: PROFILE OF SQs AND OQs IN SONNETS BY SHAKESPEARE'S CONTEMPORARIES

Bacon

PASSAGE	TOTAL SYLLABLES	SONORANT QUOTIENT	OBSTRUENT QUOTIENT
1	144	0.174	0.153
2	194	0.160	0.211
3	170	0.241	0.200
4	147	0.218	0.211
5	177	0.147	0.192
6	157	0.134	0.204
7	141	0.170	0.177
8	156	0.179	0.186
9	150	0.187	0.273
10	141	0.135	0.177
11	146	0.178	0.212
12	230	0.152	0.226
13	179	0.196	0.207
14	170	0.129	0.124
15	151	0.166	0.245
16	148	0.095	0.257
17	191	0.147	0.225
18	185	0.092	0.200
19	151	0.225	0.245
20	158	0.101	0.133

Barnfield

SONNET	TOTAL SYLLABLES	SONORANT QUOTIENT	OBSTRUENT QUOTIENT
1	144	0.188	0.214
2	140	0.129	0.264
12	140	0.150	0.229
13	146	0.192	0.247
14	140	0.200	0.271
15	142	0.225	0.218
16	142	0.169	0.183
17	142	0.183	0.197
19	142	0.085	0.211
20	142	0.183	0.239

Daniel

SONNET	TOTAL SYLLABLES	SONORANT QUOTIENT	OBSTRUENT QUOTIENT
1	144	0.174	0.201
2	145	0.159	0.172
3	140	0.229	0.243
4	142	0.268	0.176
8	144	0.160	0.257
9	140	0.193	0.279
57	140	0.271	0.264
58	140	0.271	0.143
59	140	0.207	0.279
60	140	0.150	0.250

Fletcher

SONNET	TOTAL SYLLABLES	SONORANT QUOTIENT	OBSTRUENT QUOTIENT
1		0.200	0.207
5		0.229	0.193
6		0.271	0.171
11		0.214	0.200
12		0.200	0.207
15		0.136	0.164
16		0.107	0.179
31		0.200	0.179
32		0.129	0.193
38		0.121	0.257

Linche

SONNET	TOTAL SYLLABLES	SONORANT QUOTIENT	OBSTRUENT QUOTIENT
1		0.236	0.300
2		0.264	0.214
3		0.250	0.321
8		0.200	0.200
9		0.286	0.229
15		0.186	0.214
16		0.257	0.250
35		0.229	0.164
36		0.186	0.200
38		0.264	0.214

Lodge

SONNET	TOTAL SYLLABLES	SONORANT QUOTIENT	OBSTRUENT QUOTIENT
1	150	0.220	0.193
2	146	0.301	0.260
3	144	0.285	0.215
12	144	0.194	0.410
13	147	0.238	0.211
17	153	0.275	0.222
18	146	0.171	0.233
19	142	0.211	0.225
20	146	0.288	0.237
40	140	0.186	0.293

Spenser

SONNET	TOTAL SYLLABLES	SONORANT QUOTIENT	OBSTRUENT QUOTIENT
1		0.279	0.229
2		0.164	0.236
3		0.286	0.200
4		0.279	0.207
5		0.221	0.193
15		0.257	0.243
16		0.179	0.143
20		0.243	0.186
21		0.243	0.257
30		0.229	0.143

Notes

1. A curiosity of the history of scholarship on this subject are two articles by B. F. Skinner (1939, 1941). Skinner's conclusion about alliteration in the first of these, that 'Shakespeare might as well have drawn his words out of a hat' (1939: 191), was countered in detail in Goldsmith 1950. See also Pirkhofer 1963:3-14. Hymes 1960 is a good example of a more ramified approach to the problem of the sound-meaning nexus in twenty sonnets (ten each) by Wordsworth and Keats which utilizes the concept of the 'summative word,' i.e. reckons the repetition of certain sounds to be anagrammatically related to a particularly significant ('dominant') word in a given poem. Tsur 1992 addresses the general problem of sound-meaning correspondences and includes some analysis of Shakespeare's poetry.

2. Since the analysis of sonority in Shakespeare's sonnets does not deal with vowels, all further reference to sonorants is meant to include only nasals, liquids, and glides.

3. The syllable as the gestalt domain of phonetic contexture in poetry is matched at the metrical level by the foot, which is the context for ictuses (stresses).

4. This conception of the sound structure of poetry as fundamentally dependent on sonority and obstruency was first advanced in Shapiro & Shapiro 1993.

5. Line ends are assumed to be immune to ligature with line beginnings (despite enjambment), so there is no OU here; ditto between lines 10-11, where an SU would otherwise appear ('room/Even in' [contracted form of even]). Cf. lines 7-8 in Sonnet 4 below.

6. All texts of the Sonnets are cited from The New Penguin Shakespeare edition (1986), general editor T. J. B. Spencer, associate editor Stanley Wells. This edition is in the series of Shakespeare texts now used—and recommended as authoritative—by the Royal Shakespeare Company. The New Cambridge Shakespeare edition of the Sonnets (1996), just published under the editorship of G. Blakemore Evans, does not in any way supersede the Penguin Shakespeare; in fact, Evans specifically acknowledges his debt to it and to its editor, John Kerrigan (ix). The most detailed commentary is still that of Booth (1977); but see also Vendler 1997. In determining sonorant and obstruent units, Shakespeare's speech is presupposed on the basis of Kökeritz 1953 and Cercignani 1981. One major assumption is that the speech of poetry in Shakespeare's time did not drop r's before consonants or in auslaut (even though there is plenty of evidence that r-less dialects already existed in Early Modern English). Another is that diphthongs were phonological units—as generally analyzed in contemporary English—not combinations of vowel + off-glide. Word boundaries are routinely disregarded when no pause between contiguous words is obligatory in an allegro tempo (conversational) reading of the lines.

7. Strictly speaking, there are 140 metrical positions (MPs), which are equivalent to the number of vowels that are actually pronounced. A word like powerful in this poem counts as disyllabic, not tri syllabic, reflecting the pronunciation with syncope of the medial vowel; similarly syncopated are oblivious (3 MPs) and Even (1 MP). In compiling the statistical profiles of the sonnets, only MPs were considered relevant. The main thrust of the argument is in fact unaffected by the asymmetries between MPs and syllables; hence for the purposes of this study they and any related local problems of pronunciation are ignored as immaterial. It should be noted that of the 154 Sonnets, there are seven with something other than 140 syllables: #3 (142), #99 (150), #118 (144). #121 (142), #126 (120), #145 (112), and #146 (138).

8. This follows from the phonotactics and syllable structure of English, a language abundant in both sonorant and obstruent clusters. Where both sonority and nonobstruency are possible measures of sonority, it is primarily the sonorant units that determine poetic sonority—for the simple reason that (ontologically) the positive realization of the category by which something is measured is by definition its primary realization, the realization of its negated opposite being secondary. But in languages like French or Italian containing few obstruent clusters, the reverse is true, and it is the OQ that is the prime indicator of poetic sonority via nonobstruency. For example, a Baudelaire sonnet like the famous 'Correspondances' ('La Nature est un temple où de vivant piliers') has only 12 obstruent clusters over its 168-syllable span, yielding an OQ of .071 (its SQ is .125—only 21 SUs). Mallarmé's 'Sonnet' ('Sur les bois oublié quand passe l'hiver sombre'),with 27 SUs and a resultant SQ of .161, has only 5 obstruent clusters, hence an OQ of .030!' Petrarch's sonnets typically have OQs going as low as the .058 range.

9. A different sense of this term—essentially the repetitions and reversals characteristic of the design of classical music rather than tonality—is used by Kenneth Burke (1957) to examine the sound structure of Coleridge's poem.

10. Since Kerrigan's commentary is relied on in more than one instance, perhaps it ought to be mentioned that there is nothing exceptionable in what is attributed to him. The interpretations supplied in this paper tally with those of numerous other sources besides Kerrigan, of which for obvious reasons only a representative few can actually be cited here.

11. Among eminent critics who have crossed swords over this

poem are William Empson and John Crowe Ransom.

12. Kerrigan re marks (Shakespeare 1986:290): 'The section of the book within which 94 falls is peculiarly connective: 92 follows 91 with But, and 93 picks up with So; 95 is essentially a development from the couplet of 94, and 96 continues to worry at the faults discussed in all these poems. If it is read in this light, 94 looks like an intense meditation on the issues raised in 92 and confronted in 93.'

13. As the data of Appendixes 2 and 3 show, there are eight sonnets (5%) with SQs in the .300s. with an average OQ of .172. and 91 sonnets (59%) with OQs in the .200s, with an average SQ of .197. Sonnet 91 appears in these respects to be indeterminate as to the function of low sonority.

14. Leishman (187-88) compares Petrarch, Ronsard, and Shakespeare in this respect.

15. Admittedly, this may be less than the optimal way of defining 'same numerical range,' since, for example, .501 and .599 are much further apart than are .499 and .501 or .599 and .601; also some of the cases discussed in detail have identical SQs (100-1, 108-9, and 144-45). At this point in my research, no conception of numerical range that would accommodate some middle ground has been found.

16. Sonnet 16 shares with 71 the OQ .136, but only 72 has a lower obstruency (.100).

17. These statistics may have a bearing on the old question of Shakespeare scholarship as to whether the order of the Sonnets in the so-called Quarto edition of 1609 (the editio princeps—abbreviated Q—underlying all modern editions) is correct. Two modern books that argue anew for a reordering of the poems are Stirling 1968 and Padel 1981. But their analyses (like earlier ones) ought to be scrutinized in the light of the present one, specifically as concerns the statistical data presented herein, which, together with the evidence of the linked poems analyzed earlier, tend to substantiate the authoritativeness of the order in Q.

18. Kerrigan, Introduction (Shakespeare 1986: 12-13).

19. The range goes beyond 140 syllables because the principle of counting used was: 140 syllables + number of syllables to the end of the sentence. See Appendix 5.

20. It follows (a) that one might think of a high ratio of OUs to syllables as the opposite of sonority but (b) that sonority as measured by 1/SQ is NOT the same as sonority as measured by OQ.

Works Cited

Bacon, Francis. The Advancement of Learning. ed. G. W. Kitchin. London: Dent, 1958.

Barnfield, Richard. The Complete Poems. ed. George Klawitter. Selinsgrove: Susquehanna UP, 1990.

Booth, Stephen. An Essay on Shakespeare's Sonnets. New Haven: Yale UP. 1969.

_____, ed. Shakespeare's Sonnets. New Haven: Yale UP, 1977.

Burke, Kenneth. "On Musicality in Verse." The Philosophy of Literary Form: Studies in Symbolic Action. 2nd ed. New York: Vintage Books, 1957.

Cercignani, Fausto. Shakespeare's Works and Elizabethan Pronunciation. Oxford: Clarendon, 1981.

Daniel, Samuel. The Complete Works in Verse and Prose, Vol. 1. ed. Alexander B. Grosart. New York: Russell & Russell, 1963.

Felperin, Howard. Beyond Deconstruction: The Uses and Abuses of Literary Theory. Oxford: Clarendon, 1985.

Fletcher, Giles. The Elder. The English Works. ed. Lloyd E. Berry. Madison: U of Wisconsin P, 1964.

Goldsmith, Ulrich K. "Words Out of a Hat?: Alliteration and Assonance in Shakespeare's Sonnets." Journal of English and Germanic Philology 50.33-48, 1950.

Greene, Thomas. The Flexibility of the Self in Renaissance Literature. The Disciplines of Criticism: Essays in Literary Theory, Interpretation, and History. ed. Peter Demetz, Thomas Greene & Lowry Nelson, Jr., 241-64. New Haven: Yale UP, 1968.

Hymes, Dell. Phonological Aspects of Style: Some English Sonnets. Style in Language. ed. Thomas A. Sebeok, 109-31. Cambridge, MA: MIT Press, 1960.

Kokeritz, Helge. Shakespeare's Pronunciation. New Haven: Yale UP, 1953.

Leishman, J. B. Themes and Variations in Shakespeare's Sonnets. 2nd ed. New York: Harper & Row, 1966.

Linche, Richard. xPoems. Occasional Issues of Unique and Very Rare Books, Vol. 4. ed. Alexander B. Grosart. Manchester: Charles E. Simms, 1877.

Lodge, Thomas. Complete Works, Vol. 2. New York: Russell & Russell, 1963.

Masson, David I. Free Phonetic Patterns in Shakespeare's Sonnets. Neophilologus 38.277-89, 1954.

Padel, John. New Poems by Shakespeare: Order and Meaning Restored to the Sonnets. London: Herbert Press, 1981.

Pirkhofer, Anton M. "A pretty pleasing pricket" — On the use of alliteration in Shakespeare's sonnets. Shakespeare Quarterly 14.3-14, 1963.

Pooler, C. Knox. Introduction to The Works of Shakespeare: Sonnets. ed. C. Knox Pooler. vii–xxxviii. London: Methuen, 1918.

Shakespeare, William. The Sonnets and A Lover's Complaint. ed. John Kenigan. London: Penguin, 1986.

_____. The Sonnets. ed. G. Blakemore Evans. Cambridge: Cambridge UP, 1996.

Shapiro, Marianne. Hieroglyph of Time: The Petrarchan Sestina. Minneapolis: U of Minnesota P, 1980.

_____ & Michael Shapiro. Pushkin and Petrarch. American Contributions to the Eleventh International Congress of Siavists. ed. Robert A. Maguire & Alan Timberlake, 154-69. Columbus, OH: Siavica, 1993.

Skinner, B. F. The Alliteration in Shakespeare's Sonnets: A Study in Literary Behavior. The Psychological Record 3.186-92, 1939.

_____. A Quantitative Estimate of Certain Types of Sound-Patterning in Poetry. American Journal of Psychology 54.64-79, 1941.

Smith, Hallett. The Tension of the Lyre: Poetry in Shakespeare's Sonnets. San Marino, CA: Huntington Library, 1981.

Spenser, Edmund. Works: A Variorum Edition, vol. 2: The Minor Poems. ed. Charles Grosvenor Osgood, Edwin Greenlaw & Frederick Padel Ford. Baltimore: Johns Hopkins Press, 1947.

Stirling, Brents. The Shakespeare Sonnet Order: Poems and groups. Berkeley: University of California Press, 1968.

Tsur, Reuven. What Makes Sound Patterns Expressive?: The Poetic Mode of Speech Perception. Durham, NC: Duke UP, 1992.

Vendler, Helen. The Art of the Sonnets. Cambridge, MA: Harvard UP, 1997.

Wright, George T. "Shakespeare's Poetic Technique." William Shakespeare: His World, His Work, His Influence, Vol. 2: His Work. ed. John F. Andrews, 363-87. New York: Charles Scribner's Sons, 1985.

Ambiguous Speaker and Storytelling in Shakespeare's Sonnets

The nature of a sonnet sequence as a poetic art form is essentially two-fold: it contains self-sufficient, prosodically complex poems, each seeking to develop an idea to its conclusion; but it also typically functions as a *sequence,* an integrated work in which poems have been ordered, and characters fashioned, to make sense when the work is read from beginning to end. It seems hardly necessary to point this out; yet, while the sonnets of the Petrarchan discourse receive what appears to be continuous critical attention, acknowledgment of their "sequentiality" is rare and at best tacit. There is a need to turn critical attention to mechanisms that sonneteers employ to foster a perception of cohesion, as well as to acknowledge that such preoccupations betray the presence of novelistic thinking.

The sonnet sequence genre constructs a double sense of immediacy: drawing on the lyricism of its constituent sonnets, it also often generates a perception of a personal narrative when the sequence is read from beginning to end. Sonneteers use many speaker figures or voices in the sonnets that constitute a sequence; one of the more striking examples is certainly Petrarch's giving of the first-person plural voice to "little animals" in his sonnet 8.[1] Yet varied uses of voice in individual sonnets detract little, if at all, from the impression created in the mind of the reader that they are reading a love story told in the first person. The disjointed nature of the sonnet sequence "voice" is an important part of its effect. Thus, talking about the birth of the sonnet sequence vogue, Jacques Barzun writes: "[Petrarch] fashioned into a shapely quasi narrative work, a kind of allusive autobiography . . . Sonnet sequences like Petrarch's or Shakespeare's make possible a narrative-by-episode; the poet need not versify any connective matter as he must in an epic. Rather, he anticipates by five or six hundred years the technique of film and television";[2] and Roland Greene considers the history of Petrarchism from the fourteenth to the twentieth century representative of the staged development of the sequence's "fictional" mode.[3] As such, it is a rare literary genre to offer first-person fictions to the medieval and early modern reader, and for a long time the only one to deal with erotic subject matter in the first person.[4]

The link between medieval first-person genres and Dante and Petrarch, originators of the genre, is clear: St. Augustine's *Soliloquia* and *Confessions,* and Boethius's *Consolatio Philosophiae* are considered to be standard sources for Dante's work as well as Petrarch's *Secretum.*[5] The public letter, another one of Petrarch's favorite genres, also relies on the first-person voice and self-fictionalization, a unique, creative process of authored selfhood based on literary and cultural subtext, as well as the essentially documentary processes such as self-betrayal, self-representation, self-fashioning, and auto-ethnography.[6] Petrarch's decision to remove the first-person prose surrounding the poems in Dante's *La Vita Nuova,* the resulting complexity of his *Il Canzoniere,* and the subsequent popularity of the Petrarchan (proseless) sonnet sequence model may all have had implications for the development of first-person narration.

The context within which individual sonnets in a sequence are considered is a question of importance where sequences initially circulated in manuscript form (yet carefully numbered by their authors), such as Petrarch's *Il Canzoniere* and Sir Philip Sidney's *Astrophil and Stella,* are concerned. It is equally important for linear and circular sequences; seemingly disjointed or frequently revised sequences, such as Michael Drayton's *Idea;* as well as those sequences, such as Shakespeare's *Sonnets,* that have the best of both worlds: printed to be read in a linear manner yet, as James Schiffer has suggested, potentially brilliantly constructed to make the collection *seem* as if it originally had an exclusive primary audience.[7] Whether read more or less linearly, the voices of the sonnet sequence speakers are constructed by their authors, and it is methods used to construct them in a way that generates reader interest, sympathy, and involvement that deserve closer attention.

Perhaps, however, a caveat is in order. I have structured my analysis outside the current scholarly debate on whether all English sonnet sequences follow a tripartite, "Delian" structure that unites a sequence of sonnets, Anacraeontics, and a longer narrative poem—usually a complaint, or in Edmund Spenser's case,

Epithalamion—into an integral work in which each section plays a carefully orchestrated role.[8] I have made Shakespeare's sonnet sequence itself my primary concern for two main reasons: first, ambiguous characterization and its role in reader involvement can be traced back to Petrarch, a poet who worked two hundred years before the "Delian structure"; and second, narrativity of the complaints and the *Epithalamion* is not a category that warrants contesting.

Despite occasional mentions in critical literature of tension as an important mainstay of a sonnet sequence, little attempt has been made to examine the role that ambiguous characterization plays in building this tension. Spenser studies provide a good example. As early as 1956, J. W. Lever noted the characterization shifts in *Amoretti,* but dismissed them as "structural inconsistencies."[9] Similarly, Kenneth Larsen acknowledged the "unease" present in some of the sonnets, but ascribed this to insufficient poetic skill.[10] Carol Kaske noted the ambiguity of Spenser's speaker's character, but explained it in terms of character development, of "emotional progression from sexual conflict to Christian-humanist resolution of Epithalamion."[11] While Donna Gibbs saw irony (an invitation to the reader to sub-read) as the structural principle of *Amoretti,* she denied a division between the historic author and his first-person speaker, and thus the primacy of self-fictionalization over autobiography.[12] Roger Kuin acknowledged the role of characterization in promoting the narrativity of the sequence, but viewed the dynamic between the two main characters, "the unstable space (gap) between them," as the main narrative motor. He also suggested the presence of two plots in *Amoretti,* one based on the fidelity/cruelty topos, and the other on a "love conformable to . . . the bold equation of *eros* and *agape,*" yet ambiguous characterization, which clearly forms the basis for both of these "plots," remains unexplored.[13] Lisa Klein saw the clash of "irreconcilable ethics—love as domination versus love as freely chosen submission"— as the "main conflict in Spenser's poetic tribute," but sought to examine this conflict for the insight it might provide into the author's philosophical standpoint rather than its potential for reader involvement.[14]

Perhaps unlike any other aspect of the discussion on Shakespeare's sequence, there appears to be little critical disagreement that the character of Shakespeare's speaker is indeed ambiguous. He has been described in terms of his "anomaly" and "unpredictability,"[15] his "claims undercut by slippery language"[16] and defiance

of "sequential logic,"[17] as well as a "poetics of narcissism" that emerges from "relationships between consecutive sonnets that are bewilderingly unstable."[18] Yet the link between the speaker's contradictions and sonnet sequence integrity has not, to my knowledge, been explicitly made. Because I wish to suggest character ambiguity as the aspect bridging the space between lyric and fictional aspects of a sonnet sequence, in this essay I will look at how an ambiguous character has been built out of remodeled myth, interactions of disparagement and praise, and sophisticated voice-gendering. Then, seeking to show how character ambiguity relates to reader involvement and a sense of sonnet sequence integrity, I will propose that ambiguous characterization in a sonnet sequence triggers an intellectual and emotional response I would call splintered identification, whereby the reader simultaneously sympathizes with some of the speaker's aspects while resenting others. This process generates tension, but what may be called catharsis is never reached, so the reader's mind is recruited to connect individual lyrical units into an integral work. Instantiated by Petrarch, the mechanism draws on the tendency of a reader's narrative consciousness to make up logical connections where they appear to be missing, and is ideally suited to an environment with no conventional narrative, informed by the complexity, polarity, and viscosity of the first-person voice.[19]

As I have argued elsewhere, ambiguous speakers appear and perform their integrating functions in Petrarch's as well as all the major sonnet sequences of the Elizabethan period.[20] However, the difference between Shakespeare's and other great Elizabethan sonnet sequences lies in the degree and complexity of his main character's ambiguity, as well as in the skill with which this complexity is managed. Shakespeare's contradictory speaker stands as one of the most important elements of the artistic impact and lasting vitality of the sequence. His never-resolved ambiguities provide thematic links between the two parts of the work, inducing the reader to question the speaker's motives. This silent questioning acts as a fictional motor, fostering the perception of the sequence as an integral work with the (disjointed and contradictory) speaker at its center. The constant shifting of Shakespeare's speaker's voice could thus be seen to betray what Mikhail Bakhtin called "creative disorder and the plurality of voices" or "narrative polyphony," a sign of a novelistic principle at work within a genre.[21]

The question of Shakespeare's authorization of the order of the *Sonnets* is implicit in any discussion that treats his sequence as a whole. As is well known, Shakespeare's authorization of the sequence is questioned by many, on various grounds;[22] more often than not, questioning authorization implies questioning the ability of the sequence to function as a work of fiction. Yet many of these doubts are presented in contradictory terms, probably due to the unease that excessive biography making of the *Sonnets* has inspired. For instance, according to Heather Dubrow, "Critics impose a narrative and dramatic framework on a sequence that resists those modes," but she subsequently proposes a variant reading that offers an alternative fiction.[23] Paul Ramsay denies the *Sonnets* authorization and integrity, to reaffirm them shortly afterward: "Had Shakespeare invented a story to build poems on, it would have been more . . . realized . . . What else are we to think? . . . That Shakespeare wrote some 500 sonnets creating a full story, and that only these 154 remain, sonnets 1–126 somehow having preserved chronological order?"[24] (What he seems to be saying is that a story is present but unfinished, and that chronological development can be perceived in sonnets 1–126.[25]) Helen Vendler argues, on one hand, that a lyric poem is judged memorable if the reader's "self" can seamlessly inhabit the poem's "I" (a definition of the lyric that in itself seems dangerously close to identification—a fictional, rather than lyrical, reader response usually linked to characterization), yet she also predicates the success of the sequence on Shakespeare's ability to sustain "feelings in form over 154 sonnets," which would imply a sense of integrity as crucial to the effect of the sequence.[26]

On the other hand, recent scholarship demonstrates a growing confidence in the idea of authorization. In the 2003 Arden edition of Shakespeare's *Sonnets,* Katherine Duncan-Jones puts forward a seemingly incontrovertible case in favor of authorization,[27] and the traditional, bipartite structure of the sequence is also, more or less apologetically, supported or implied by many Shakespearean critics and editors since Edmond Malone.[28] Evidence demonstrating that Shakespeare's sonnets were not in fact written in the order in which they appear in Thomas Thorpe's 1609 edition also supports the idea of order-related authorial intent,[29] as does the internal evidence of deliberation, notorious for defying attempts at reordering.[30] Most important, exciting as it is to imagine a discovery of Shakespeare's autograph different from Thorpe's 1609 text, such a discovery would not change the cultural influence that Shakespeare's sequence exerted over the past 450 years or diminish its value as a

field of study.[31] On balance, in this article I will consider the order of the poems in Shakespeare's *Sonnets* to be based on Thorpe's 1609 text and indicative of authorial intent.

Even the briefest and most general of attempts to summarize Shakespeare's *Sonnets* reveals more characters than a reader of sonnet sequences is accustomed to, deployed with elements of plot and suspense. Despite the paucity of gendered pronouns,[32] the first part of the sequence gives the impression of being concerned primarily with the young man, and the text allows for a possibility of a homoerotic reading. The second, shorter story maps the speaker's attempts to comprehend the continued and profound emotional impact of a consummated relationship with a female protagonist. The two "stories" also have complications: jeopardy to loyalty, the rival poet, the periodic absences and suggested dalliances, and, last but not least, the speaker's devastating suspicion of an affair between his two beloveds. Both "stories" remain unresolved, and the sequence ends at the highest point of the reader's intellectual and emotional involvement, leaving a lasting impression of the speaker's emotional turmoil. It also leaves a sense that an integral work has been read.

Rather than showing neglect for the depth of Shakespeare's themes or the volumes of criticism attesting to them, this rudely brief synopsis underpins my conviction that not unlike his plays, Shakespeare's sequence works to enhance the intellectual impact of its themes by underwriting them with the emotional engagement of the audience.[33] Granted, a summary of a poem sequence is nothing but a snapshot of an individual receptive consciousness at work. However, it is precisely our ability to summarize—as well as the points of similarity that inevitably arise between individual retellings of Shakespeare's *Sonnets*—that suggests that the connective ability of our minds has been successfully recruited to piece a story out of 154 distinct, self-contained lyrical poems, most of which employ classic second-person address or explore complex material not directly related to the "plots." This is a remarkable feat—and one, I would like to suggest, achieved by the presence in the *Sonnets* of original decisions that are essentially novelistic. Shakespeare's sequence has two plots, combined into an overarching third story: a voice that fosters a sense of intimacy with the reader and foils its richly polyvalent subtexts; and the absence in the sequence of a professed erotic rhetorical goal, which results in a focus on the speaker's emotional outcomes beyond the pursuit of consummation.

All of these aspects of Shakespeare's sequence involve ambiguous characterization of the speaker, and none of them are to be found at the same level of development in other contemporaneous sequences.

Although his final result circuitously reclaims a fundamentally Petrarchan purpose (to tell a story of the journey of the speaker's writing self as he is abased and ennobled by a multifaceted experience of love), Shakespeare arrives at this purpose by non-Petrarchan means. Reading the *Sonnets,* the reader recognizes the speaker's frustration, which is crucial to the genre; yet its objective of sexual gratification, which the sonnet sequence reader has come to expect, is missing. Both of Shakespeare's "stories" contain non-Petrarchan elements, connected by formal means (characters recur in both "stories," the second foreshadowed in the first) as well as thematically (by themes employed in both stories). Remodeling of myth, ambiguous gendering of the speaker's voice, as well as the interaction of disparagement and praise are all such elements; they have been used to highlight the aimlessness of the sequence and dramatize the speaker's inner fluctuations between authority and weakness, enhancing the appeal of the character.

Shakespeare's speaker applies to a man what by now have become commonplaces of Petrarchan misogynist insult. Purporting to praise the addressee's beauty, he implies in the man an inability to love (10.4), an obsession with deceitful appearances (53.5–8), vacuity, lack of constancy (53.13–14), and insufficient intelligence or vanity (84.9–14). Embedded in a sonnet of praise, disparaging couplets are revealed only once the alternating rhymes have been removed:

> *Look in thy glass, and there appears a face*
> . . . .
> *Dulling my lines, doing me disgrace.*
> . . . .
> *And more, much more, than in my verse can sit*
> *Your own glass shows you when you look in it.*
>
> (103.7–14)

Ostensibly expressing idolatrous sentiment akin to the Trinitarian rhetorical formulas of the Athanasian Creed,[34] the speaker could also be accusing the young addressee of promiscuity:

> *Fair, kind and true have often lived alone,*
> *Which three, till now, never kept seat in one*
>
> (105.13–14)

At this point Shakespeare had already used "seat" to suggest female sexuality in the *Sonnets* ("Ay me, but yet thou mightst my seat forbear" [41.9]), and Samuel Daniel used it in similar way in *Delia* ("There my soules tyrant ioyes her, in the sack / Of her owne seate, whereof I made her guide" [39.5–8]).[35] The feminine focus of the metaphor also allows for the possibility that the accusation to the young man quietly employs an element of misogyny.

The speaker has similar motives in appropriating the Ovidian figure of Philomela, semantically inseparable from the ideas of rape and speaking out by alternative means after a violent silencing:[36]

> *As Philomel in summer's front doth sing,*
> *And stops her pipe in growth of riper days*
> . . . .
> *Therefore, like her, I sometime hold my tongue,*
> *Because I would not dull you with my song.*
>
> (102.8–14)

Here, "Philomel" has been employed to project tension between inspiration and loathing, and by "stoping her pipe" the speaker is revealed as his own violator. First, the seemingly misaligned pronouns in my previous sentence will already have called attention to the gender ambiguity of Shakespeare's image. The ambiguity does not seem to arise solely from the uncertainty that surrounds the use of pronouns in the quarto, where the text reads "stops his pipe" (120.9) ("her pipe" is an emendation favored by Katherine Duncan-Jones, based on the clash with Q "Therefore, like her" [120.13] and a proposal that the Q "his" is a misreading of the manuscript "hir,"[37] whereas C. Knox Pooler, Stephen Booth, and Gwynne Blakemore Evans all retain "stops his pipe"[38]) but primarily from Shakespeare's decision to use a female figure for his speaker. Gwynne Blakemore Evans unwittingly acknowledges this even as he proposes a factual error on Shakespeare's part ("The error may well be Shakespeare's," he writes, "who . . . is thinking of himself as Philomel"[39]). And second, the speaker's self-imposed silence is supremely ambiguous. In one possible reading the speaker is submissive and "holds his tongue," because he does not wish to "dull," or bore, the addressee; in another, he assumes ironic authority and suggests that his tongue could render the addressee dull.[40] Lest the latter meaning of the verb "dull" escape the reader, it is reemployed in the very next sonnet, which purports to praise the addressee's glorified indescribability:

> ....*a face*
> *That overgoes my blunt invention quite,*
> *Dulling my lines, and doing me disgrace.*
>
> (103.6–8)

Even when it claims Petrarchan *sobramar,* "love which surpasses speech"[41] (102.3–4), the speaker's silence could imply contempt. By the same token, calling the youth a "pattern" for all human flowers (98)[42] acquires a deeply ironic meaning when we consider Shakespeare's variations on the Petrarchan comparison of the beloved with flowers. These variations involve, among other things, using the lily (94.14)—a flower that elicits a dual response in the contemporary imagination as a symbol of purity, but also toxicity linked to malodorous putrefaction and disease,[43] as well as terms of criminality, unease, and threat:

> *The forward violet thus did I chide:*
> . . . .
> *the purple pride*
> . . . .
> *in my love's veins thou hast too grossly dyed.*
> . . . .
> *The roses fearfully on thorns did stand,*
> *One blushing shame, another white despair;*
> *A third, nor red, nor white, had stol'n of both,*
> . . . .
> *But for his theft, in pride of all his growth,*
> *A vengeful canker ate him up to death.*
>
> (99)[44]

Indeed, insult to the young man, concealed beneath the rhetoric of respect, often draws on the subversion of social norms. Having presented his young addressee with a notebook (77), the speaker scornfully rejects his reciprocal gift of tables (a hand-bound notebook) and reports having given it to someone else (122). Although written in a way that stages submission, such rejection breathes disrespect as it contravenes Elizabethan decorum of patronage, founded on the reciprocal Senecan theory of gift giving.[45] Signaling offense and, particularly, giving away the addressee's gift are rude and potentially dangerous gestures. By making them the speaker rejects socially sanctioned reciprocity out of hand. The device quietly but effectively implies that the speaker's need for equality has reached a desperate stage. The speaker's rudeness repels, his despair attracts; splintered identification leaves the reader's reactions divided.

Some of the speaker's most powerful expressions of disparagement depend on the reader's recognition of subtext. Sonnet 20 offers a prime example of this. The poem begins by describing the addressee as both male and female. This is presented as perfection, yet this sonnet has a long history of eliciting unease in its readers.[46] A cultural duality surrounds androgynous myths: the laudatory "layer" works by association with the "positive" androgynous figures, such as Androgynos, a Platonic being of near-divine perfection, power, and hubris;[47] Hermaphroditus, a symbol of unity in marriage;[48] *Phoebus Kitharoidos* or *Apollo Citaredo* (Apollo with the Lyre), a personification of complete poetic consciousness;[49] *Venus biformis,* a figure of generative self-sufficiency;[50] and many other mythical figures symbolizing greatness, with ambiguous gender as a subsidiary characteristic.[51] The "disparaging" layer, on the other hand, draws on the "negative" associations that androgynous figures evoke: Ovid's contempt for Hermaphroditus (*Met,* IV.379) finds many echoes in early modern iconography,[52] and some contemporary writers represent androgyny as a monstrosity to be scrupulously concealed.[53] These dualities aside, however, Shakespeare's concealed insult should be sought in the way Nature is shown to have created the addressee: she suddenly becomes so taken with her creation that she cannot resist turning her into a man. The sonnet presents this process as a compliment to the speaker's beauty:

> *And for a woman wert thou first created,*
> *Till Nature as she wrought thee fell a-doting*
>
> (20.9–10)

Yet a compliment this can never be. By representing a man hastily created from a woman, Shakespeare is consciously mocking three crucial subtextual frameworks: God's creation of Man in the book of Genesis; the myth of Nature's creation of (the male) Man, a process that was seen to symbolize the panegyric precisely because of the associated painstaking effort, care, and forethought it involved;[54] and the widely circulated Aristotelian and Galenic commonplaces of the defectiveness female-yielding gestation, clearly known to Shakespeare:

> [S]ince nature always intends and plans to make things most perfect, she would constantly bring forth men if she could; and that when a woman is born, it is a defect and mistake of nature, . . . as is . . . one who is born blind, or lame, or with some

other defect . . . A woman can be said to be a creature produced by chance and accident.

(Castiglione, *The Courtier*, III.11)[55]

Macbeth: *Bring forth men-children only!*
For thy undaunted mettle should compose
Nothing but males.

(*Macbeth*, I.7.73–75)[56]

It is clear that instead of praise, sonnet 20 actually offers
a two-pronged insult: not only has the addressee been
created at whim and without forethought, but also by
repairing a woman, a "defect of nature" and a product of
a natural "accident."

As has been shown, the sonnets to the young man
conceal disparagement under the guise of praise. Sonnets to the dark lady mirror this approach: they conceal
praise under the guise of disparagement. The lady's appearance is the first example of this. The sonnets to the
dark lady begin with an apology that "in the old age
black was not counted fair" (127.1), which suggests
that the lady's looks, as well as the speaker's taste in
women, diverge from the Petrarchan norm. Nevertheless, the first descriptions of the lady seem carefully orchestrated to suggest beauty; the lady's hair or skin will
not have been mentioned for another three sonnets, and
black eyes have no claim to historic novelty—they *are*
the norm. The sum of contemporary precepts of female
beauty, Federico Luigini da Udine's *Libro della bella
donna,* printed in Venice in the 1540s, defines ideally
beautiful eyes as "black, like mature olives, pitch, vel-
vet or coal, for such are the eyes that belong to Laura,
Angelica, Alcina and the beloveds of Propertius, Horace
and Boccaccio," [57] and, as Shakespeare no doubt knew,
to Sidney's Stella. Golden locks and florid cheeks may
have been fashionable, but it was not entirely anomalous
to think a dark woman beautiful, as the reputation of
Mary Queen of Scots attests.[58] The speaker is, in fact,
circuitously claiming some legitimacy for his taste.

Yet the speaker does not seem attracted to the lady
because of her physical, intellectual, or moral excellence. On the contrary, much care has been taken to
represent this attraction as self-generated, with no basis in "reality." Shakespeare's speaker's schizophrenic
division occurs, remarkably, outside the classically
Petrarchan standoff between the body (pro) and mind
(contra); his self appears conflicted between intellectual
and sensual reluctance pitched against an inexplicable
emotional craving:

Nor taste, nor smell, desire to be invited
To any sensual feast with thee alone;
But my five wits, nor my five senses, can
Dissuade one foolish heart from serving thee

(141.7–10)

Nor is the speaker's frustration caused by the lady's un-
availability, for she is clearly available. Sonnet 129, the
third sonnet of the dark lady group, acknowledges consummation as soon as plausible. What, then, is the reason for the speaker's frustration? What is Shakespeare's
purpose in remodeling the Petrarchan convention of sty-
mied desire?

The sequence represents two accounts of emotional
subjugation lodged in aware (as opposed to frustrated)
thralldom. Shakespeare's focus on the impact of real
relationships, superimposed on the Petrarchan poetics
of unsatisfied desire, represents a genuine development
in the history of first-person speech in the sonnet sequence genre. By moving his focus away from a time
when a relationship is imagined and into the forum of
real relationship/s, Shakespeare demonstrates that longing does not represent the end of a sonnet sequence, and
that consummation does not represent the end of narrative. In fact, he demonstrates that the sonnet sequence
genre in its original form is no longer sufficient unto
itself. The strongest bid the *Sonnets* make to independence from Petrarchism is also one of their important
contributions to literary history. It rests on the unlikely
distinction of not having a rhetorical goal.[59] Unlike the
other Petrarchan speakers, Shakespeare's speaker does
not seek to overcome a status quo; instead, the author's
focus is firmly on the speaker's emotional outcomes.
Frustration has moved away from external sources and
become firmly rooted in the speaker's consciousness.

Shakespeare's placement of his speaker's infatuation with the dark lady at a time in the "story" that
follows consummation, as well as the un-Petrarchan
loathing with which he describes the event, render the
subsequent pleas for the attention of the lady—the one
already won and loathed—all the more striking. In fact,
begging for the same lady's exclusive attention, Shakespeare divides the reader's loyalties by superimposing
the "feminine" rhetoric of entreaty ("dear heart," "forbear") on the patriarchal ideal of chaste female eyes
directed only at their lord (139.4–5).[60] To a contemporary reader, the contrast projects an image of embattled
masculinity, a character whose emotional needs pull
in the opposite direction from social expectations. The

technique can involve considerable ethical ambiguity, as when the speaker's frustration finally erupts in a curious merging of the "feminine" rhetoric of entreaty with the "masculine" rhetoric of threat:

> *Be wise as thou art cruel; do not press*
>
> (140.1)

> *For if I should despair, I should grow mad*
>
> (140.9)

Similar fluctuations in the gendering of the voice are observable in the section to the young man. When the speaker feels that the young man's absences are sapping his strength, he reclaims his authority in a "masculine" voice that hints at inconsequential infidelities of his own:

> *Yet seemed it winter still, and, you away,*
> *As with your shadow I with these did play.*
>
> (98.13–14)

The speaker uses this "masculine" voice to say he is uninspired and bored, or to threaten that the addressee's role in his life could be temporary:

> *do not kill*
> *The spirit of love with perpetual dullness*
>
> (56.7–8)

> *From thee, the pleasure of the fleeting year!*
>
> (97.2)

The speaker also uses his "masculine" voice to imagine that the addressee is listening to his words from the perspective of "feminine," receptive docility:

> *This is my home of love: if I have ranged,*
> *Like him that travels I return again*
>
> (109.5–6)

> *For nothing this wide universe I call,*
> *Save thou, my rose*
>
> (109.13–14)

> *And worse essays proved thee my best of love(*
>
> 110.7–8)

> *Mine appetite I never more will grind*
> *On newer proof*
>
> (110.10–11)

> *Then give me welcome, next my heaven the best,*
> *Even to thy pure and most most loving breast.*
>
> (110.13–14)

The last example uses the rhetorical figure of *ploce*, where a word is repeated to show that the opposite is meant:[61] the speaker's praise, once again, implies disparagement—even tacit violence.

The "masculine" voice is also used to describe the addressee in Petrarchan terms that are traditionally associated with female sexual or procreative appeal. Thus the addressee's "beauty's rose" must be opened and distilled,[62] his "fresh ornament" preserved, time's action to "dig deep trenches" in the addressee's "beauty's field" prevented—either by persuading the speaker to procreate or by immortalizing him in poetry. Each image appears to have been especially selected for its ability to elide the sexual and the autopoetic, as well as to imply in the addressee an enabling, "feminine" function for the speaker's "masculine" authority and creativity.

By contrast, the speaker also constructs a "female" voice, predicated on characteristics that are traditionally associated with women, such as submission or proneness to wiles in the context of seduction. The speaker uses his "female" voice when he employs the language of injured ownership to describe his feelings ("take," "robb'ry," "mine/thine," "usest," "bear" "hast/had," "steal"),[63] when he "forgives" the addressee's transgressions in a way that accuses him, or when he stages submission in order to determine the outcome of the dynamic:

> *I do forgive thy robb'ry, gentle thief,*
> *Although thou steal thee all my poverty*
>
> . . . .
>
> *Lascivious grace, in whom all ill well shows,*
> *Kill me with spites; yet we must not be foes.*
>
> (40)

It is also in his "feminine" voice that Shakespeare's speaker claims ignorance where it is obvious that he is skilled, and the one in which he protests his emotional and sexual magnanimity:

But thou art all my art, and dost advance
As high as learning, my rude ignorance.

(78.13–14)

Mine be thy love, and thy love's use their treasure.

(20.14)

Here, the speaker promises to the young man that he can tolerate his infidelities if he can refrain from being deliberately cruel toward him. The theme is echoed in the dark lady sonnets (140.14) and is exceptionally effective in portraying thralldom. Another similarly effective technique is that used in sonnet 144, which shows the speaker at once angered by the beloveds' suspected infidelity and voyeuristically attracted to it:

Suspect I may, but not directly tell;
. . . .
I guess one angel in another's hell.

(144.10–12)[64]

Other interactions of disparagement and praise also offer thematic links between the two parts of the sequence. In both instances, love is represented as an addiction or an incurable disease (118.14, 147.1–2), and both of the beloveds possess the devil-like ability to make sin and corruption irresistibly attractive (95.1, 9; 150.6–8). Yet another such link, crucially, serves to signal that the speaker has seen through the deceit of both:

And to the painted banquet bids my heart

(47.6)

Feeding on that which doth preserve the ill

(147.2)

Ambiguous characterization underpins the thematic links that turn the speaker into the focus of the sequence and enhance the perception of the sonnet sequence as an integral work of fiction.

The speaker's ambiguous autopoetics add to the reader's fascination. Where the English Petrarchan convention dictates gentle disparagement of other poets to position oneself as original, Shakespeare's speaker achieves the same purpose by employing the opposite strategy. On one hand, he pretends to disparage his own style in a way that reads suspiciously like bragging:

Why write I still all one, ever the same,
. . . .
That every word doth almost tell my name

(76.5–7)

On the other, by this stage the speaker has already voiced insecurity in terms more genuine and profound than Petrarchan staged modesty:

For I am shamed by that which I bring forth
And so should you, to love things nothing worth.

(72.13–14)

Similarly, Shakespeare's speaker promises to immortalize yet also explicitly claims the self-reflexive value of his praise (39.2). The speaker's subtle schizophrenic divisions attest to the author's characterization skill. The fluctuations of the speaker's tone from "masculine" to "feminine," his tenor from authority to self-abasement, his claims of grandeur undercut by dread, the intensity of his attempts to destabilize his beloveds with no apparent purpose; the intensity of his efforts is, in fact, inversely proportionate to hope.

By replacing consummation, the traditional sonnet sequence goal, with the addressee's and the lady's attention, loyalty, and thralldom—all elusive, emotional categories, not easily "pursued"—Shakespeare simultaneously harkens back to the Platonic and Neoplatonic ideas of wooing of the soul by rhetorical means, and heralds modern first-person writing and its quest to portray the multiplicity of personal reality. Self-contradicting characterization elicits splintered identification in the reader; this response generates interest and reader involvement, causing "narrative" responses ("What happens next? I wonder what will happen to him? Will he be all right?") rather than only lyrical ones ("How true—it could be me saying this"). Shakespeare's divided character promotes reader involvement and fosters perception of his sequence as an integral work.

Danijela Kambaskovi-Sawers

Notes

1. Francesco Petrarch, *The Canzoniere; or, Rerum vulgarium fragmenta,* ed. and trans. Mark Musa (Bloomington: Indiana UP, 1996).
2. Jacques Barzun, *From Dawn to Decadence: Five Hundred Years of Western Cultural Life* (New York: HarperCollins, 2000), 49 and 51.
3. In Roland Greene's view, the "fictional" and "lyrical"

modes characterize the genre, and their prevalence within the sequence marks the direction in which the genre will develop. Roland Greene, *Post-Petrarchism: Origins and Innovations of the Western Lyric Sequence* (Princeton, NJ: Princeton UP, 1991).

4. As I have argued elsewhere, five "great" English sonnet sequences of the Elizabethan and Jacobean periods (Sir Philip Sidney's *Astrophil and Stella,* Edmund Spenser's *Amoretti,* Samuel Daniel's *Delia,* Michael Drayton's *Idea,* and William Shakespeare's *Sonnets*) show important thematic links with emerging narrative genres exploring the pseudo-authenticity of the first-person voice. Foremost among them are the complaint (such as sonneteer Samuel Daniel's *Complaint of Rosamond*), emerging epistolary first-person narratives (such as sonneteer Michael Drayton's *Heroicall Epistles*), and narrative poems or popular romances. The latter two are, of course, not first person genres, but can contain segments written in the first person. See also my book, *Character Ambiguity and the Novelistic Impulse in the Petrarchan Sonnet Sequence* (Lewiston, NY: Edwin Mellen Press, 2008).

5. See, for instance, *Petrarch's Secretum,* ed. and trans. with an introduction by Davy A. Carozza and H. James Shey (New York: Peter Lang, 1989), 9–11, and Victoria Kahn, "The Figure of the Reader in Petrarch's Secretum," in *Petrarch: Modern Critical Views,* ed. Harold Bloom (New York: Chelsea House, 1989), 141.

6. For representative discussions, see Stephen Greenblatt, *Renaissance Self-Fashioning from More to Shakespeare* (Chicago: University of Chicago Press, 1980); Henk Dragstra, Sheila Ottway, and Helen Wilcox, eds. *Betraying Our Selves: Forms of Self-Representation in Early Modern English Texts* (London: Macmillan Press, 2000); and James Buzzard, "On Auto-Ethnographic Authority," *Yale Journal of Criticism* 16, no. 1 (2003): 61–91. Also relevant is Steven Shurtleff, "The Archpoet as Poet, Persona and Self: The Problem of Individuality in the Confession," *Philological Quarterly* 73, no. 4 (Fall 1994): 373.

7. James Schiffer, "The Incomplete Narrative of the Sonnets," in *A Companion to Shakespeare's Sonnets,* ed. Michael Schoenfeldt (Malden, MA: Blackwell, 2007), 47–56, esp. 50.

8. *The Sonnets and A Lover's Complaint,* ed. John Kerrigan (London: Penguin, 1986), 13–14; Katherine Duncan-Jones, ed. *Shakespeare's Sonnets* (1997; London: Arden Shakespeare, 2003), 45; Colin Burrow, ed. *The Complete Sonnets and Poems* (Oxford:Oxford UP, 2002), 140; *The Sonnets and A Lover's Complaint,* ed. Martin Dodsworth

(London: Charles E. Tuttle, 1995), xvii; *The Sonnets and "A Lover's Complaint,"* ed. Walter Cohen, in *The Norton Shakespeare,* gen. ed. Stephen Greenblatt (New York: Norton, 1997), 1916, which, unless otherwise specified, I will be using to cite Shakespeare's work other than the *Sonnets*; Margreta de Grazia, "Revolution in Shakespeares Sonnets," in *Companion to Shakespeare's Sonnets,* ed. Schoenfeldt, 57–70; and Heather Dubrow, "'Dressing old words new?' Re-evaluating the 'Delian Structure,'" in *Companion to Shakespeare's Sonnets,* ed. Schoenfeldt, 90–103.

9. J. W. Lever, *The Elizabethan Love Sonnet* (1956; London: Methuen: 1966), 94 and 101.

10. Kenneth J. Larsen, *Amoretti and Epithalamion: A Critical Edition* (Tempe: Arizona State University, 1997), 25.

11. Carol V. Kaske, "Spenser's Amoretti and Epithalamion of 1595: Structure, Genre, and Numerology," *English Literary Renaissance* 3 (Autumn 1978): 271–95, esp. 273.

12. Donna Gibbs, *Spenser's Amoretti: A Critical Study* (Aldershot, UK: Scolar Press, 1990), 30 n.19.

13. Roger Kuin, "The Gaps and the Whites," in *Spenser Studies: A Renaissance Poetry Annual VIII,* ed. Patrick Cullen and Thomas P. Roche (Brooklyn: AMS Press: 1987), 251–85.

14. Lisa M. Klein, "*Let us love, deare love, lyke as we ought*: Protestant Marriage and the Revision of Petrarchan Loving in Spenser's Amoretti," *Spenser Studies* 10 (1989): 109–37, esp. 110. In addition, even where ambiguous characterization and the resulting tensions have been noted, they are not studied as important aspects of a reader's experience of the sequence as a whole. Neil Rudenstine, *Sidney's Poetic Development* (Cambridge: Harvard UP, 1967); David Kalstone, *Sidney's Poetry: Contexts and Interpretations* (Cambridge: Harvard UP, 1965).

15. Lever, *Elizabethan Love Sonnet,* 173.

16. Katherine Duncan-Jones, "Playing Fields or Killing Fields: Shakespeare's Poems and Sonnets," *Shakespeare's Quarterly* 54, no. 2 (Summer 2003): 127–41.

17. Frank Bernhard, "Shakespeare's Sonnet 73," *Explicator* 62, no. 1 (Fall 2003): 3–4.

18. Jane Hedley, "Since first your eye I eyed: Shakespeare's Sonnets and the Poetics of Narcissism," *Style* 28, no. 1 (Spring 1994): 1.

19. My thinking on character ambiguity has been influenced by Elizabeth Fowler's proposal that the early modern reader had the ability to "read" characters that contained several, often contrasting "social personae." Elizabeth Fowler, *Literary Character: The Human Figure in Early English Writing* (Ithaca, NY: Cornell UP, 2003). I am also

indebted to the thought of David Buchbinder on the "models" of the sonnet sequence. David Buchbinder, "True-Speaking Flattery: Narrativity and Authenticity in the Sonnet Sequence," *Poetics* 17 (1988): 37–47. In viewing character ambiguity as essential for the creation of captivating characters, I build on William Empson's *Seven Types of Ambiguity* (London: Chatto and Windus, 1956).

20. In my articles "*Never Was I the Golden Cloud*: Ovidian Myth, Ambiguous Speaker, and the Narrative in the Sonnet Sequences by Petrarch, Sidney, and Spenser," *Renaissance Studies* 5, no. 21 (November 2007): 637–61, and "*Carved in Living Laurel*: The Sonnet Sequence and Transformations of Idolatry," *Renaissance Studies* 3, no. 21 (June 2007): 379–94.

21. M. M. Bakhtin, "From the Prehistory of Novelistic Discourse," in *The Dialogic Imagination,* ed. Michael Holquist (Austin: University of Texas Press, 1994), 41–84. And while one could no doubt argue that any lyric is dialogic, in that the voice of the speaker communicates with the reader, I am primarily interested in the inherent plurality of a contradictory first-person voice and the tension translated into involvement that such characterization generates.

22. J. W. Lever denies the 1609 folio any credibility because of the "chances of coincidental dissarangement." Lever, *Elizabethan Love Sonnet,* 170–71. W. H. Auden discredits both authorization and narrativity. W. H. Auden, *William Shakespeare, The Sonnets* (New York: Signet Classic Shakespeare, 1964), xxi and xxxvi. Roderick Eagle also rejects authorization. Roderick Eagle, *The Rival Poet and the Dark Lady: The Secrets of Shakespeare's Sonnets* (London: Mitre Press, 1965).

23. "What if we were to admit the possibility that one of the highly erotic poems after 126 refers to the Friend?" Heather Dubrow, "'Incertainties now crown themselves assur'd': The Politics of Plotting Shakespeare's Sonnets," *Shakespeare Quarterly* 3, no. 47 (Fall 1996): 301. In her earlier writings Dubrow upholds the idea of sonnet sequence narrativity. *Captive Victors: Shakespeare's Narrative Poems and Sonnets* (Ithaca, NY: Cornell UP, 1987), 171–90.

24. Paul Ramsay, *The Fickle Glass: A Study of Shakespeare's Sonnets* (New York: AMS Press, 1979), 18–19.

25. At the other end of the spectrum, James Schiffer argues that it is precisely the incompleteness of the narrative that makes the *Sonnets* what it is, "a kind of Goldilocks's bed, neither too big nor too small, but just right: big enough to enable dramatic and lyric moments to develop, yet not so big as to disrupt or dilute lyric intensity." Schiffer, "Incomplete Narrative," 49.

26. Helen Vendler: *The Art of Shakespeare's Sonnets* (Cambridge: Harvard UP, 1998).

27. Duncan-Jones, Arden *Sonnets,* 29–45. I have used this edition to quote from Shakespeare's *Sonnets.*

28. For example, Hilton Landry, *Interpretations in Shakespeare's Sonnets* (Berkeley: University of California Press, 1963), 4–5; Stephen Booth, ed. *Shakespeare's Sonnets* (New Haven, CT: Yale UP, 1977), 430; Margreta de Grazia, *Shakespeare Verbatim: The Reproduction of Authenticity and the 1790 Apparatus* (Oxford: Clarendon Press, 1991); William Empson, "They That Have the Power," postscript to William Shakespeare, *The Sonnets* (New York: Signet Classic Shakespeare, 1964), 201; and Richard A. Levin, "Shakespeare's Sonnets 153 and 154," *Explicator* 1, no. 53 (Fall 1994): 11. Some attempts to negotiate with the binary division include Lever's use of the word "sequence" to mean "group" (Lever, *Elizabethan Love Sonnet,* 170–171) and proposal of a fourpartite design (Katherine Duncan-Jones, "Was the 1609 Shakespeares Sonnets Really Unauthorized?" *Review of English Studies* 34 (1983): 151–71, esp. 62. Later, in her edition of the *Sonnets,* she changes her mind, presenting a strong case in favor of binary division (Duncan-Jones, Arden *Sonnets,* 363). Like Katherine Duncan-Jones but a year earlier, Roy Neil Graves had also argued for authorization based on the "empty couplet" at the end of sonnet 126. Roy Neil Graves, "Shakespeare's Sonnet 126," *Explicator* 4, no. 54 (Summer 1996): 203.

29. Such as the appearance of sonnets 138 and 145 in *The Passionate Pilgrim* (1598); the interpretation of "hate away" of 145.13; and "and" of 145.14 as referring to Anne Hathaway. Andrew Gurr, "Shakespeare's First Poem: Sonnet 145," *Essays in Criticism* 21 (1971): 221–26.

30. For an excellent history of reordering (also in favor of authorization), see MacDonald P. Jackson, "Shakespeare's Sonnets: Rhyme and Reason in the Dark Lady Series," *Notes and Queries* 2, no. 46 (June 1999): 220–22.

31. See Peter Stallybrass, "Editing as Cultural Formation: The Sexing of Shakespeare's Sonnets," *Modern Language Quarterly* 54 (1993): 91–103; Michael Keevak, "Shakespeare's Queer Sonnets and the Forgeries of William Henry Ireland," *Criticism* 2, no. 40 (Spring 1998): 167–89; and, above all, Margreta de Grazia, "The Scandal of Shakespeare's Sonnets," in *Shakespeare and Sexuality,* ed. Catherine M. S. Alexander and Stanley Wells

(Cambridge: Cambridge UP, 2001), 146–67.

32. De Grazia, "Scandal," 149.

33. James Schiffer has argued that the absence of narrative resolution enhances lyrical attentiveness. Schiffer, "Incomplete Narrative," 52.

34. Duncan-Jones, Arden *Sonnets,* 320.

35. *Samuel Daniel's Poems and a Defence of Ryme,* ed. Arthur Colby Sprague (Chicago: University of Chicago Press, 1965), 30.

36. Shakespeare remodels the myth of Philomela also in *Lucrece* (ll.1465): moved by a tapestry that shows Hecuba's grief but gives it no "tongue," Lucrece's (imagined) speech assumes the role of Philomela's weaving.

37. Duncan-Jones, Arden *Sonnets,* 314.

38. C. Knox Pooler, ed., *The Works of Shakespeare: Sonnets* (London: Arden Shakespeare, 1918), 211; Stephen Booth, ed. *Shakespeare's Sonnets* (New Haven, CT: Yale UP, 1977), 330, and Gwynne Blakemore Evans, ed. *The Sonnets* (1996; Cambridge: New Cambridge Series, 2003), 211.

39. Evans, *Sonnets,* 211.

40. The reading is close to *OED* 8, "to tarnish."

41. Gordon Braden, *Petrarchan Love and the Continental Renaissance* (New Haven, CT: Yale UP, 2000), 27.

42. Possibly a reference to Spenser's Adonis: "Yet is eterne in mutability, And by sucession made perpetual, / Transform'd oft, and chang'd diversely; / For him the father of all forms they call." Edmund Spenser, *The Fairie Queene* III.vi.47, facsimile of the 1596 edition published by W. Posonbie, London, intro. by Graham Hough (London: Scolar Press, 1976).

43. "[T]he flowers, leaves and rootes are used in medicine, but not in the kitchen . . . They are a great ornament to a garden or in a house, yet the smell of them is discommended and accounted ill for the plague." Thomas Cogan, *The Haven of Health* (London: Printed by Henrie Midleton, for William Norton, 1584). See also Duncan-Jones, "Playing Fields," 127–41, esp. 138.

44. The word "pride," which appears twice in sonnet 99, carries a phallic connotation in 103.2 and 144.8.

45. The theory stipulates that upon receiving a gift, one thanks the giver, praises the gift, and seeks to reciprocate in kind. A. D. Cousins, *Shakespeare's Sonnets and Narrative Poems* (London: Longman, 2000), 167.

46. For a cogent historic recapitulation of critical views voicing disgust with this sonnet and a useful guide of early modern medical attitudes toward sex transformation and bisexuality and interpretation of bisexual myths in the sixteenth century, see Raymond B. Waddington, "The Po-

etics of Eroticism: Shakespeare's Master Mistress," in *Eros and Anteros: The Medical Traditions of Love in the Renaissance,* ed. Donald A. Beecher and Massimo Ciavolella (Ottawa: Dovehouse Editions, 1992), 177–92.

47. Plato, *Symposium* 189 e and 190 d, translated into English by Michael Joyce, in *Plato: Collected Works,* ed. Edith Hamilton and Huntington Cairns (1961; Princeton, NJ: Princeton UP, 1989).

48. William Keach,"The Epyllion and the Poetry of the 1590s: Alternatives to the Spenserian Synthesis," in *Elizabethan Erotic Narratives* (New Brunswick, NJ: Rutgers UP, 1977), 231.

49. Apollo's ambiguous gender is described positively by Elizabethan mythographers. "By Apollo is meant the Sunne, and being withoute a Beard, Lustines of youth," writes Stephen Batman, *The Golden Booke of the Leaden Gods,* London 1577, folio 2 dorso (New York: Garland, 1976). "The auncients . . . shaped [Apollo] with a very youthfull countenance, beardlesse, and young-yeard . . . in the shape of a beauteous Nimph, with her apparel exquisitely well wouen, excelling in curious worke of foliature, hauing her [sic] temples bound about, and instrophiated with sweet'smelling garlands, resembling much the goddesse Flora," writes Richard Lynche, *The Fovntaine of Ancient Fiction,* "Alciatus," London 1599 (New York: Garland, 1976), without pagination. Magnificent gender-ambiguous Roman representations of Apollo as god of poetry (*Phoebus Kitharoidos* or Apollo Citaredo, Apollo with the Lyre), dating from the third century BC to the first century AD, are now kept in the Capitolline Museum, Palazzo Alle Terme, Galleria Villa Borghese, Palazzo Altemps, and the Vatican Museum in Rome, as well as the British Museum in London. All statues have a woman's head (sometimes also breasts) and male genitalia. Gender-ambiguous representations are reserved for Apollo as god of poetry; they are rarely used to represent Apollo in his guises as god of sun or, after the Laconian tradition, the God of hunting.

50. *Venus biformis* is recalled by Keach ("Epyllion and the Poetry"), as well as Graham Atkin, *"Both kinds in one / both male and female": Ate, Lust, and hermaphroditic Venus in Book IV of Edmund Spenser's* The Faerie Queene (Chester, UK: Chester College of Higher Education, 1996).

51. Jupiter, Orpheus, Narcissus, Amor, Hermaphroditus, Thiresias, and Dionysius all play different roles in the Ovidian universe, but have ambiguous sexuality as their common denominator. How Petrarch uses this in the building of his speaker has been suggested in my article

"*Never Was I the Golden Cloud.*"

52. Waddington, "Poetics of Eroticism," 182 and 190.

53. As Spenser hides the statue of Venus in *The Faerie Queene*: "Nor any blemish, which the worke mote blame; / But for, they say, she hath both kinds in one, / Both male and female, both under one name." Spenser, *Fairie Queene*, IV.x.41. See also Luc Brisson, *Sexual Ambivalence, Androgyny, and Hermaphroditism in Graeco-Roman Antiquity*, trans. Janet Lloyd (Berkeley: University of California Press, 2002).

54. For a summary of Bernard de Silvestris's *De Universitate Mundi* (written between 1145 and 1153), a work that provides the account of Natura/Nous' creation of a perfect (male) Man, see Ernst Robert Curtius, *European Literature and the Latin Middle Ages*, trans. Willard R. Trask (1953; New York: Harper & Row, 1963), 110–11.

55. Baldesar Castiglione, *The Book of the Courtier* (1528), trans. Charles S. Singleton (Garden City, NY: Doubleday, 1959). Also "Young parents, and those who are older too, tend to produce female offspring rather than parents which are in their prime; the reason being that in the young their heat is not yet perfected, in the older, it is failing. [Producing females] is due to a deficiency of natural heat." Aristotle, *The Generation of Animals* IV.ii.766a, trans. A. L. Peck (London: William Heinemann, 1943), 397.

56. William Shakespeare, *Macbeth*, ed. Kenneth Muir (London: Routledge, 1994), 44.

57. Federico Luigini da Udine's *Libro della bella donna* (p. 236), cited by Naomi Yavneh in "The Ambiguity of Beauty: Tasso and Petrarch," in *Sexuality and Gender in Early Modern Europe*, ed. James Grantham-Turner (Cambridge: Cambridge UP, 1993), 136–38. It is not known whether the other beauty precepts summarized by the Luigini's *Libro*—the "curly, luxurious, long, golden" hair, and cheeks combining the "white of lilies with the vermillion of the rose or the purple of the hyacinth"—were directly known to Shakespeare and his contemporaries, but there is no doubt that they too find their echoes in Shakespeare's *Sonnets*, remodeled in ways that subtly mock Petrarchan excesses of the day. ("Or from their proud lap pluck them where they grew; / Nor did I wonder at the lilies white / nor praise the deep vermillion of the rose" (98.9–10); also, "If hairs be wires, black wires grow on her head / I've seen roses damask'd, red and white / But no such roses see I in her cheeks" (130.3–5). Clearly, Shakespeare uses the motif indiscriminately of gender. See also, "And in his blood, that on the ground lay spill'd / a purple flower sprung up, chequer'd with

white / resembling his fair cheeks"(*Venus and Adonis*, 1167–70). Shakespeare's image of Adonis's flower combines elements taken from Ovid's descriptions of Hyacinthus and Adonis. (Hyacinthus: "A flower rose / Gorgeous as Tyrian dye, in form a lily, / Save that a lily wears a silver hue, / the richest purple." Adonis: "A blood-red flower arose, like the rich bloom / of pomegranates which in a stubborn rind / conceal their seeds." Ovid, *Metamorphoses*, X.209–13 and 735–36, trans. A. D. Melville (Oxford: Oxford UP, 1986).

58. Some contemporary portraits show Mary, Queen of Scots, to have been of dark coloring, notably the portrait by a follower of Francis Clouet, kept in Victoria and Albert Museum, London. (Other portraits show a lighter coloring.) The beauty of Mary, Queen of Scots, was universally acclaimed. Pierre de Ronsard lauded it; a Venetian ambassador thought her "the most beautiful in Europe"; and even John Knox thought her features and deportment "pleasing." Alison Weir, *Mary, Queen of Scots and the Murder of Lord Darnley* (London: Jonathan Cape, 2003), 30.

59. I am referring to the main Petrarchan rhetorical goal of seeking to woo the beloved and overcoming the status quo of lovelessness, which provides a sonnet sequence with a narrative purpose. Shakespeare's sequence retains a few minor rhetorical goals (such as, for instance, immortalizing or persuading the addressee to procreate) yet dispenses with the fundamental one.

60. Throughout this essay, the words "masculine," "feminine," "male," and "female," used in quotation marks, signify contemporary cultural constructs of gender, not biological determinants. (Male) troubadour and Petrarchan poets, of course, routinely appropriate "feminine" (submissive) speech, but not to relate to a lady already won and loathed.

61. See discussions of the "perversity" of this sonnet by Booth, *Shakespeare's Sonnets*, 354, and Duncan-Jones, Arden *Sonnets*, 330. Shakespeare also uses the figure in sonnet 90.

62. See the commentary on *Roman de la Rose* by Georges Duby, *Love and Marriage in the Middle Ages*, trans. Jane Dunnett (Cambridge: Polity Press, 1994), 91. Ovid uses rosebuds to signal Orpheus's conversion to homosexuality following Eurydice's death (*Metamorphoses* X.88–90).

63. For a detailed discussion of theft as metaphor, see Heather Dubrow, "In Thievish Ways: Tropes and Robbers in Shakespeare's Sonnets and Early Modern England, *Journal of English and Germanic Philology* 4, no. 96 (Octo-

ber 2003): 514–44.

64. The word "hell" suggests endless suffering and culpabil-
ity, here distributed equally between the lady and the
young man (Booth, *Shakespeare's Sonnets,* 499–500).
The word also draws on the common identification of hell
with the vagina, first made in Boccaccio's *Decameron,*
3.10. Compare Shakespeare's sonnets 129.14 and 144.12
and *King Lear* IV.6.129. Duncan-Jones, Arden *Sonnets,*
373.

Reprinted from "Three themes in one, which wondrous scope
affords: Ambiguos Speaker and Storytelling in Shakespeare's
Sonnets" by Danijela Kambaskovi-Sawers in *Criticism: A
Quarterly for Literature and the Arts*, Vol. 49, No. 3. Copyright © 2007 Wayne State University Press. Reprinted with
permission of the Publisher.

Secrets of the Dedication to Shakespeare's Sonnets

TO.THE.ONLIE.BEGETTER.OF.
THESE.INSVING.SONNETS.
Mr. W. H. ALL.HAPPINESSE.
AND.THAT.ETERNITIE.
PROMISED.

BY.

OVR.EVER-LIVING.POET.

WISHETH.

THE.WELL-WISHING.
ADVENTVRER.IN.
SETTING.
FORTH.

T. T.

TO HIS KIND, AND TRVE FRIEND:
EDWARD BLVNT.

Blount: I purpose to be blūt with you, & out of my dulnesse to encounter you with a Dedication in the memory of that pure Element all wit Chr. Marlow; whose ghoast or Genius is to be seene walke the Churchyard in (at the least) three or foure sheets. Me thinks you should presently looke wilde now, and growe humorously frantique

Thine in all rites of perfect friendship,

THOM. THORPE.

There it is, so familiar, and so obscure: what an amazing production! There's nothing remotely like it anywhere else in Elizabethan or Jacobean literature. What does it mean, for a start? What is it trying to tell us? The opening phrase is so well-known, "To the onlie begetter," but how many people know that the spelling of "onlie" is very rare indeed? It could have been, in its tiny way, a clue to something quite unsuspected until very recently. Surely there is rather more in the Dedication than first meets the eye. Just to show you how peculiar it is, here is a look at one of Thorpe's other dedications. You can see that it has a heading, the text is in lower-case italics, some words have capitals, and several words are in Roman type for emphasis. This is absolutely typical of most dedications of the period, often with the Roman and italic fonts interchanged. Now compare it with the Sonnets' Dedication. They couldn't be more different!

I first became aware of it in 1964, the 400th anniversary of the birth of a certain gentleman from Stratford. It was therefore seized upon as a milestone in Shakespearean studies, and it did not go unnoticed by the publishing fraternity. According to the *London Sunday Times*, his birthday was "the peak of the biggest literary bonanza in history." Over four-hundred books dealing with Shakespeare were published to commemorate the event, and among them, none was more eagerly awaited than one with the title "Mr. W. H.," by the great Shakespeare scholar Leslie Hotson, who claimed to have finally determined, once and for all, the identity of the mystery person to whom the *Sonnets* were dedicated. Such was the hype surrounding this book that I found myself buying a copy as soon as it was published. I still recall the excitement I felt when I took the book home and devoured it eagerly. Here was the solution to the biggest literary mystery of all time! (Bar one, I would now add.)

I found it completely convincing. It is a marvelous book, full of wonderful things, and I strongly recommend it to anyone interested in Shakespeare, or in the mechanics of self-deception—for its main thesis is completely wrong. But at the time I didn't know that.

Hotson, I don't need to remind you, had a tremendous reputation. At the age of twenty-six or so he had discovered in the Public Record Office the report of the inquest on Christopher Marlowe, whose death up till then had been shrouded in mystery. (The fact that it has subsequently been shrouded in still more mystery is another story.) This coup started him on a golden trail of further discoveries, this time about Shakespeare, of injunctions naming him, and details of his friends—not always very desirable characters, it must be said—and in 1949 he hinted for the first time that he had discovered who "Mr. W. H." was. With such a track record, whatever he said was listened to very seriously. He delved away for the next fifteen years or so, and by 1964 (pure coincidence of course), all could be revealed.

It was a marvelous discovery. Practically every Elizabethan of suitable age, with initials W.H. or H.W., had already been put forward as the young man, but Hotson managed to find a new one. This was a certain William Hatcliffe, admitted to Gray's Inn as a law pupil in 1586 and the next year elected Prince of Purpoole, the title given to the student who had been chosen to act as a kind of temporary *Lord of Misrule*, or *Lord of Liberty*, to preside over the festivities of the Christmas season.

This position, Hotson explains, was one of enormous prestige and dignity. In effect, the "Prince" was expected to act like a Prince of royal blood, and, for the brief period of his reign, would be accorded all the respect and deference such a Prince would command. Both for him and for the other students it was a kind of practice run for life at the Court of Queen Elizabeth, since many of the students were of good family, and might well find themselves in exalted circles in later life. And indeed, his installation ceremony was magnificent, modeled on that of a Coronation, with a procession of over two-hundred students and others taking part, each with a defined role to play, shadowing the various Officers of State and other dignitaries.

Why, then, was Hotson's theory so appealing? For a start, it explained simultaneously both the "Mr." of Mr. W. H., and all the references in the *Sonnets* to the high status of "the Fair Youth." In various sonnets he is addressed as "Lord," "prince," "sovereign," "king," while elsewhere he is referred to obliquely as "the Sun," "a God," "the Ocean," all—as Hotson shows—terms applied to royalty. Many scholars thought that the youth must be a lord, such as Henry Wriothesley, Third Earl of Southampton, or William Herbert, Third Earl of Pembroke. But Hotson argued like this: had he been a real Lord, he could hardly be addressed in the Dedication as "Mr." but if he was a "Mr.," he could have been a temporary Prince. Then there was Hotson's masterstroke, which comes from "Sonnet 125," which starts:

> Were it ought to me I bore the canopy,
> With my extern the outward honoring.

Hotson shows by numerous quotations from contemporary documents that a "canopy" could only, by law, be carried over the Sovereign. Hence, if the canopy in the sonnet is a real canopy, carried on poles by four distinguished people at a public ceremony, then the sonnet must either be addressed to the Sovereign, or to someone

TO THE HONORABLEST
PATRON OF MVSES AND
GOOD MINDES, LORD
William Earle of Penbroke,
*Knight of the Honourable
Order, &c.*

Ight gracious and gracefull Lord, your late imaginary, but now actuall Trauailer, then to most conceited *Virginia*, now to almost-concealed *Virginia* ; then a light, but not lewde , now a sage and allowed tranflator; then of a scarce knowne nouice, now a famous *Father* ; then of a deuised Country scarse on earth, now of a desired *Citie* sure in heauen ; then of *Vtopia*, now of *Eutopia* ; not as by testament, but as a te-

Tb. Tb.

elected to a temporary position where they are treated like one—in other words, someone like Hatcliffe, Prince of Purpoole.

I was completely captivated by Hotson's theory. It seemed to solve so many of the problems associated with the Sonnets, such as the affection between the poet and the young man, and their sharing the same mistress—hard to understand as between commoner and Earl, but readily believable as between poet and law student, so much closer in station. I read the book two or three times over the next few years, still with great enjoyment—and I do seriously recommend it—but with gradually increasing disbelief, until eventually I realized that of genuine evidence connecting Shakespeare with Hatcliffe there was nothing at all. In particular, Hotson's evidence about the canopy was self-defeating, since elsewhere in the book he quotes a long passage from an account (the Gesta Grayorum) of the procession which took place a few years later, and this makes it quite clear that no canopy was carried over the Prince of Purpoole. Through some unaccountable oversight, Hotson failed to point this out.

Only one piece of evidence remained which appeared to connect Hatcliffe with Shakespeare, and that was in the Dedication, which Hotson boldly declared was a cryptogram. It is indeed a very odd and strange production, completely different from Thorpe's other dedications. The Blount dedication shows Thorpe's efforts to

be witty and entertaining, at least by Elizabethan standards, and actually it is quite funny. "Blount, I purpose to be blunt with you," and so on, while the dedication to Pembroke is full of sophisticated word-play of the most excruciating kind, witty and tedious, totally different from the Dedication to the *Sonnets*. "Most-conceited" is contrasted with "almost-concealed"; Viraginia with Virginia—very skilful word play; *Utopia* versus *Eutopia*—there's a subtle difference which I had to look up. Both these dedications are so different from the *Sonnets'* Dedication, that it is hard to believe that all were written by the same person.

Now let's return to Hotson's claim that the Dedication was a cryptogram. He gave a number of reasons for this idea, such as the layout, the capital letters, the full-stops, but his chief reason is that the sentence is back-to-front. What we would expect is:

> To the only begetter of these insuing sonnets, Mr. W. H., the well-wishing adventurer T. T. (in setting forth) wisheth all happiness, and that eternity promised by our ever-living poet.

In other words, what we expect is: "To Mr. W. H., the publisher T. T. wishes all happiness" and so on. Hotson gives examples of nine similar dedications, all of which have this sort of word order, that is, "To Sir A. B., X. Y. wishes happiness." But the Sonnets' Dedication has the order "To Mr. W. H., happiness wishes the publisher." Hotson states that it is unique, and that he has never seen another dedication like it. In fact, he calls it "preposterous," a good word, I think. (It is the more extraordinary, in that it could so easily have been amended to read "To Mr. W. H., happiness is wished by the publisher T. T." It would then have seemed perfectly normal, at least in this respect.) Peculiar wording, Hotson goes on to say, is often a pointer to some cryptic intention, and he proceeds to solve the cryptogram as follows:

He starts with "Mr. W. H." in line 3, moves down to pick up the H in the next line, chooses HAT from this word, then drops down to line 7, and picks up LIV from EVER-LIVING. In this way he obtains HATLIV, a reasonably good shot at "Hatcliffe" (or so he tells us). I accepted this unthinkingly to begin with, but on the third or fourth reading of the book, in about 1967, I happened to reach this passage late at night, around 11 o'clock, and it suddenly became clear to me that it was

nonsense—utter nonsense. There are too many arbitrary steps; one could find several different names made up from a syllable near the beginning and a syllable towards the end. Cryptography is systematic and scientific, and picking out syllables at random is not the way to solve a genuine cipher; there must be some kind of regular pattern (or algorithm). It is this pattern which gives the solver reason to think that he has found the right solution. Hotson's solution has nothing even approaching a regular pattern—it is all far too flimsy! In any case, it is obvious that Hotson was very strongly biased towards the result he claimed to find. It is not a good idea to have preconceptions in this kind of endeavor.

If the piece was a cryptogram (as Hotson had argued so strongly), then it was clear to me that it must be concealing something else. As it was so late, I decided to give myself five minutes to find the solution, and if it didn't work out, I would forget the whole thing.

One of the oddest features of the Dedication is the full-stops after every word. Puzzling over this, at about 11.01, it suddenly occurred to me that they suggest counting words. One can imagine someone with a pen or pencil touching the point on the paper after each word as it is counted. The stops and hyphens tell one to count the two compound words separately, it would seem, and that "Mr. W. H." counts as three items, not one. If we have to count words, the obvious thing to do is to see whether every third word, or fourth or fifth and so on, yields a message. It takes very little time to do this, and the result in every case is rubbish. For example, every fifth word gives this message: OF. W. THAT. EVER. WELL. FORTH., not very promising. It was now about 11.02.

The next simplest thing to do, still sticking with counting words, is to alternate two numbers, and for example to take the third word, followed by the fifth, and then the third, and so on. But if the scheme is like this, trial and error would get us nowhere, as there are so many possible combinations of two small numbers. Indeed, if we try and guess two numbers, we might well end up with two or more possible messages, and be unable to decide between them. If the cryptographer was working along these lines, it would be obvious to him (just as it is obvious to us) that he must tell us what the two numbers are, either directly, or hidden in some simple fashion. It is now 11.03.

There are no numbers in the Dedication, and nothing to suggest two numbers. But if we have to count words, there must be numbers somewhere. Time was running out. I was about to give up. 11.04. Then I suddenly focused in on another peculiarity. The text is laid out in three blocks, which might suggest three numbers. The number of lines in each block is something that the cryptographer would have had under his control. The lines in the three blocks give us the three numbers: 6-2-4. Perhaps this is the clue to the hidden information? Remember, I was after "Mr. W. H." Counting through, using these numbers as the key, I found the following:

THESE. SONNETS. ALL. BY. EVER. . . .

This message started off in quite an interesting fashion, but sadly it ended up as rubbish, just as the other attempts at a solution had. I had never heard of any Elizabethan poet called EVER, and it sounded very unlikely as a name anyway. Obviously the Dedication was not a cryptogram, after all, so I put the book down, feeling a little disappointed, and went off to sleep. In any case, like Hotson, I was looking for a clue to the identity of "Mr. W. H.," and had never doubted that the gentleman from Stratford was the author of the Sonnets and everything else. Incidentally, I would like to suggest that perhaps Hotson's heart was really in the right place, all along, since after analyzing many of the sonnets, he says finally, "If one had to put the *Sonnets* into one word, that word would be *Truth*."

I forgot all about this discovery, or rather non-discovery, for the next two or three years, until having time to spare in a big library I decided (on an impulse) to look at the article on Shakespeare in the *Encyclopedia Britannica*. I leafed idly through it until towards the end, when I found a section headed "Questions of Authorship." I was rather surprised to find anything on such a fringe topic (my apologies all round), but duly read the general argument and a paragraph on Francis Bacon, until I was amazed to come upon the following two sentences.

A theory that the author of the plays was Edward de Vere, seventeeth earl of Oxford, receives some circumstantial support from the coincidence that Oxford's known poems apparently ceased just before Shakespeare's works began to appear. It is argued that Oxford assumed a pseudonym in order to protect his family from the social stigma then attached to the stage, and also because extravagance had brought him into disrepute at Court.

I immediately recalled the rubbish message of a few years back, since obviously EVER could now be read as E. VER or *Edward Vere*. A strange coincidence, not to

say a thought-provoking one. But I still remained very skeptical, and was sure that chance was the most likely explanation of this odd result.

Books on Edward deVere were not easy to find in those days, but I did read the book by Hilda Amphlett, and found it very far from convincing. It seemed to me that the coincidences between Oxford's life and the plots of *Hamlet*, or *All's Well*, or the Gad's Hill episode, could all be explained if Shakespeare spent some time in Oxford's household, or had a friend who had. I emerged from the book an even stronger Stratfordian than before. I did however make a mental note to look into the authorship question when I had more time, partly I think because I had noticed something which Hilda Amphlett doesn't mention—a strong resemblance between the portrait of the young deVere and the Droeshout engraving in the First Folio. Another odd coincidence.

We now skip some fifteen years, and in the fullness of time, Charlton Ogburn's book was duly published in the UK. I read it with much the same excitement as I'd experienced reading Hotson's book twenty-odd years earlier. But despite the fact that I had the (dubious) solution to the Dedication cipher at the back of my mind while reading it, again I was left unconvinced. Stratford still held the day.

Although Shakespeare seemed to have left very few signs of his impact on the theatrical world, it seemed far more extraordinary that Oxford had left so few. A commoner could work in the theatre unobserved, but surely not a great lord? Seventy years after he had been first put forward, surely more evidence should have come to light? Why the complete silence by his contemporaries? Why continue the cover-up twenty years after his death, when the *First Folio* was published? And the specialized knowledge that the plays exhibited was just the sort of knowledge that a clever lad, up from the sticks, might pick up from his aristocratic patrons, or from casual acquaintances in taverns.

True to form, I re-read Ogburn's book again two or three times, and I won't bore you with what it was which made me change my mind, but it finally dawned on me that it was important to try to see whether the message in the Dedication might actually be genuine, and not just an accident of chance. With this in mind, I read numerous books on codes and ciphers, and attempted to find out what was known about Elizabethan cryptography.

I discovered that this type of cryptogram is called an *innocent letter code*, since the objective is to distribute the words of the secret message systematically throughout the words of what seems like a normal letter. It is a method often used by people locked up, wanting to communicate secretly with friends in the outside world. It was frequently used to good effect by prisoners of war in World War II, notably those in Colditz Castle sending information about the German war effort back to the UK.

In order to indicate the key to the hidden message, various schemes can be used. For example, the ten letters in "Dear George" could indicate every tenth word, and the twelfth in "My Dear George" every twelfth word; or the date "September 5th" could indicate the key 9-5, that is, take the ninth and fifth words alternately throughout the letter, September being the 9th month. These tricks are all described in books on elementary codes and ciphers, such as are published quite often nowadays. So the idea of hiding the key in the text is a commonplace today, and would certainly have been as obvious to the Elizabethans as it is to us.

But what I was really hoping to find was examples of Elizabethan ciphers. This took quite a long time, basically because there aren't any. None have survived, although several people at the time did describe various useful techniques which might have been used, for all we know. (Strictly speaking, one should class acrostics as very simple ciphers. The Elizabethans were certainly fond of them, and quite a lot do survive, especially in poetry.) The only example of a cipher I was able to find was in a biography of John Dee, the Elizabethan savant and astrologer (he was instructed by Robert Dudley to choose an auspicious day for the Queen's Coronation, and many people would agree that he did a good job). Here is the example his biographer gave to illustrate a described by John Dee. This reads, going down and method up the columns, "The Spanish ships have sailed." The message would be sent off, reading across, as T H S S A H S H E I. . . . To someone intercepting it, it would obviously proclaim itself as a coded message and to decode it, all one has to do is to count the number of letters—twenty-five—and write it out again in a five by five square. It is amusing to learn that Dee regarded this as "a childish

```
T H S S A
H S H E I
E I I V L
S N P A E
P A S H D
```

```
E R F D L E E L L T
I E T O O S W I I H
L S U U H H S N T E
P H O T O A V C S P
P A H T T L T R H E
U N T H E L S E T S
S D I E L N G A O T
Y S W S B O N S D I
D P E I A T O E C L
E E G E E B M A N E
```

cryptogram such as eny man of knowledge shud be able to resolve."

Another similar example (right) is given by Bishop John Wilkins, in a book published in 1641, with the splendid title, *Mercury*, or the *Secret and Swift Messenger*, which described all the cryptographic methods he knew of which he thought might be useful in the Civil War. Here one has to start reading from the top right-hand corner, "The pestilenc[e] doth still increase . . .," etc. Again it would be sent off in the form: E R F D L E E L L T. . . , and so on. Incidentally, it is interesting to see that in order to get the message into a perfect 10 by 10 square, the word *pestilence* is spelt without the final e. Clearly what one has to do when receiving this kind of cipher, nowadays called a *transposition cipher*, is to set out the letters of the code into an array, either a square or a rectangle.

Now I can't recall what made me think of doing this to the Dedication, but I do remember that I put it off for months, because I thought that it would take hours, if not days, of hard work—and also because I thought the chance of finding anything was vanishingly small. Eventually I got down to it, and started by counting the number of letters—one-hundred-forty-four, which rang a very loud bell, as it is twelve squared, and has many other factors.

I then wrote the Dedication out into arrays, starting with a square having 12 rows of 12 letters, then rectangles with rows of fifteen letters, eighteen, twenty-one, twenty-four, and so on. Thankfully, one doesn't have to write out all possible arrays, as words can be read out diagonally as well as up and down. For example, from the twelve by twelve array, one can inspect arrays with eleven letters and thirteen letters in each row by reading diagonally, while the array with fifteen letters in each row also allows one to inspect the arrays having fourteen and sixteen letters per row, and so on. So far from taking days, this took about twenty minutes, which was a relief.

The first thing I noticed was in the array with fifteen letters in each row:

```
T O T H E O N L I E B E G E T
T E R O F T H E S E I N S V I
N G S O N N E T S M r W H A L
L H A P P I N E S S E A N D T
H A T E T E R N I T I E P R O
M I S E D B Y O V R E V E R L
I V I N G P O E T          etc
```

HENRY! It is evident that the letters of the name are all equally spaced—every fifteenth letter starting from the H spells out the name. This is sufficiently unusual to suggest that it might have been deliberately arranged by a cryptographer. But Henry who? For some weeks I thought it might possibly be the name of the man who had (perhaps) hidden the message about EVER in the Dedication, though it didn't seem to me that he deserved to immortalize himself in this way. Perhaps his name was "Henry Oliver," the surname being indicated by the letters OLVR which follow on down from HENRY, and I did look in various books to see if such a person flourished at the time, without success.

Eventually the penny dropped. In the array with eighteen letters in each row (below) I had repeatedly overlooked something. There, split up into three bits, is the name WR-IOTH-ESLEY, spelt perfectly, just as it was always spelt officially. I first noticed the letters

```
T O T H E O N L I E B E G E T T E R
O F T H E S E I N S V I N G S O N N
E T S M r W H A L L H A P P I N E S
S E A N D T H A T E T E R N I T I E
P R O M I S E D B Y O V R E V E R L
I V I N G P O E T W I S H E T H T H
E W E L L W I S H I N G A D V E N T
V R E R I N S E T T I N G F O R T H
```

ESLEY in the middle column, and almost immediately the letters IOTH in the one next to it. At that moment I knew with absolute certainty that I would find the letters WR somewhere, and there they are, at the bottom of the second column. Moreover this is a perfect rectangle, where the cryptographer would naturally try to hide the most important information, since perfect rectangles are where a cryptanalyst would look first of all for something hidden. And if "onlie" had been spelt with an e between the *n* and the *l*, as was usual, the number of letters would have been one-hundred-forty-five, with the wrong factors, so that particular e had to be omitted.

It is interesting that the three sections of the name read down-up-down, rather as in the examples I gave earlier. All the same, I feel sure that the cryptographer would have liked to have got WR joined up with IOTH, to make WRIOTH, in the column next to ESLEY. Presumably he just couldn't find the right words for the last two lines of the text to achieve this, and had to be content with leaving them offset. If only he had succeeded, it would now be self-evident that the full name had been deliberately ciphered into the Dedication. By the way, if you are thinking that the name HENRY may be somewhat suspect because it doesn't appear in a perfect rectangle, it can also be found along a diagonal in an array with nine rows of sixteen letters—a perfect rectangle.

The big question, of course, is whether the name HENRY WRIOTHESLEY (or indeed the five-word message) really is the genuine solution of a genuine cryptogram, or some strange accident of chance. It may be that we are just reading something out of these arrays that isn't really there, rather as Hotson convinced himself that HATLIV had been coded into the text. I will just give two lines of approach which suggest that the name HENRY WRIOTHESLEY really was deliberately encoded into the Dedication.

The first is to examine all the arrays, from six letters wide to thirty, and see how many words there are of various lengths. Reading downwards in these arrays, there are one-hundred-eighty three-letter words, forty-two four-letter words, but only three five-letter words, ie HENRY, WASTE, and TRESS, plus the obvious five-letter segment ESLEY. So out of these four five-letter words or segments, two are used in the full name HENRY WRIOTHESLEY. This is very strong evidence for deliberate concealment. It seems that the cryptographer realized that the segments had to be as long as possible, to ensure both that the name would be recognized and that it would be taken seriously. Three- or four-letter segments would have been no use for his purpose, because the name might then never get spotted, and even if it were spotted, it would be impossible for the solver to tell whether chance was at work or a cryptographer.

The other method concerns the odds of the full name turning up accidentally. Without going into the details, the odds of HENRY turning up in any array are about one in one thousand, and the odds of WRIOTHESLEY turning up in any three fragments similar to (and including) ESLEY, WR, IOTH, all in the same array, are about one in twenty thousand. So the chances of the full name turning up accidentally in these two arrays is the product of the separate odds, i.e. one in twenty million.

These odds would be much the same for any name consisting of a five-letter first name and an eleven-letter second name, split up in a similar way—just for example, FELIX MENDELSSOHN (rather ahead of his time). But we are considering the proposition that the Dedication might be a cryptogram, and so the fact that the name found is the person most scholars already believe to be "the Fair Youth" of the *Sonnets* and "Mr. W. H.," makes it much more probable that it really does contain a genuine cipher. Chance would have had to work extra hard (as it were) to get by far the most likely person into the text. With a very vague figure of one in one hundred on this part of the argument, we arrive at an overall figure of very roughly one in two billion for the very small possibility that the result is an accident of chance.

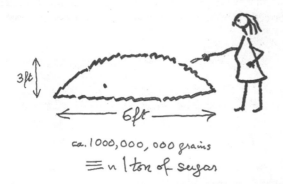

ca. 1000,000,000 grains
= n 1 ton of sugar

It is quite hard to envisage what this means, so after grappling with a packet of sugar and some letter scales, I worked out that a ton of sugar contains about one billion grains, and it forms a heap about six feet across and three feet high. Now imagine that one of the grains is colored red, you are given a pair of tweezers, and you have to pick out the red grain at your first attempt.

(I forgot to say that you are also blindfolded.) That represents odds of one in one billion. As for HENRY WRIOTHESLEY in the Dedication, there are two such piles. First you will have to choose the right pile—and then find the red grain.

There is now, in my view, no doubt whatever that the name of Henry Wriothesley, Third Earl of Southampton, was deliberately recorded in the Dedication, and very little room for doubt that this was in order to record the fact that he was indeed "the onlie begetter . . . Mr. W. H." and "the Fair Youth" of the Sonnets. It could be argued that his name was recorded in the Dedication for some other reason, but that seems to me to be highly unlikely. The *Sonnets* promise the Fair Youth immortality in several sonnets, and yet they offer no clue as to who he was; one even gets the impression that any sonnet which came close to revealing his name would have been dropped from the printed series. Consequently, it seems entirely appropriate that the Dedication should supply what is missing from "these insuing Sonnets." The young man's name was presumably put there by someone who was determined that he would eventually be identified, to claim at long last the immortality the poet had conferred upon him. Personally, I find it very satisfying that one of the chief mysteries of the *Sonnets* should find its solution in the Dedication, printed between the title page and the first sonnet.

But perhaps the Dedication has another mystery folded within it. What about the five-word message we started out with? What is the likelihood that that is authentic? The message was found, as we saw, by counting words, the idea of counting being suggested by the full-stops after every word. The only other explanation ever offered for the full-stops is that they are there in imitation of a Roman inscription chiseled into a stone slab. But if one examines Roman inscriptions, they differ from the Dedication layout in several ways. This is how the Dedication would look if it were laid out as a Roman monumental inscription (next page). You can see that the full-stops are in the middle of the type area, rather than on the printing line, and there are stops at the beginning as well as at the end of each line. This suggests that the full-stops in the Dedication are not there in imitation of a Roman stone monument, and may be there for some other purpose. As I mentioned before, when I first had the idea of counting words, it seemed intuitively obvious that the stops were there to indicate that each word and letter was to be counted separately. Thus "Mr. W. H." counted as three words, not one, and

```
•TO•THE•ONLIE•BEGETTER•OF•
•THESE•INSVING•SONNETS•
•Mr•W•H•ALL•HAPPINESSE•
•AND•THAT•ETERNITIE•
•PROMISED•
•BY•

•OVR•EVER-LIVING•POET•
•WISHETH•

•THE•WELL-WISHING•
•ADVENTVRER•IN•
•SETTING•
•FORTH•

                    T. T.
```

"ever-living" and "well-wishing" each counted as two. Without the stops, one would probably count each of these as one word each, and so miss the message.

Now, the message was found by counting through using the key 6-2-4, derived from the layout, which produced a short but (dare I say) intriguing message. When I first did this, I thought that it must be quite common to find possible messages in this sort of way, and that was why I was so ready to believe that the message was simply a chance sequence of words. Eventually I decided to put this to the test. I started counting through paragraphs of books I happened to be reading, every now and then, in order to see how often 6-2-4 turned up a meaningful five-word sentence or remark, not knowing whether it would be one in ten or one in one hundred or whatever.

Well, after several years, and many thousands of paragraphs, probably well over twenty thousand, I have only found one sentence that even remotely made any sense at all. I will give it to you for your edification: "London was not built before." It comes out of Boswell's *Life of Johnson*, and has not the slightest relevance to the rest of the paragraph. Using this experimental evidence as a basis, I worked out that the odds that the message was a chance finding were roughly one in one hundred million. Not as remote a possibility as finding the name *Henry Wriothesley*, but still pretty remote.

But I had overlooked something, which reduces the odds by a factor of 100, to one in ten billion. Take yet another look at the Dedication. Does the layout perhaps remind you of anything? If you look at the acrostic poem by Anthony Munday, (right, next page), you will immediately see that the 6-2-4 layout of the Dedication corresponds exactly to the name *Edward de Vere*.

```
TO.THE.ONLIE.BEGETTER.OF.
THESE.INSVING.SONNETS.
Mr.W.H.  ALL.HAPPINESSE.
AND.THAT.ETERNITIE.
PROMISED.

BY.

OVR.EVER-LIVING.POET.

WISHETH.

THE.WELL-WISHING.
ADVENTVRER.IN.
SETTING.
FORTH.
```

So it seems that our cryptographer chose the name *Edward de Vere* as his keyword (in modern cryptographic parlance), and derived from it the three numbers 6-2-4 to provide the numerical key to the ciphered message. In this simple way, it would appear, he provides us with confirmation that we have correctly deciphered the message, and correctly identified EVER with E. Ver, Edward deVere.

E xcept I should in freendship seeme ingrate,
D enying duty, where to I am bound;
W ith letting slip your Honour's worthy state,
A t all assayes, which I have Noble found.
R ight well I might refrayne to handle pen:
D enouncing aye the company of men.

D owne dire despayre, let courage come in place,
E xalt his fame whom Honour doth imbrace.

V ertue hath aye adornd your valiant hart,
E xampled by your deeds of lasting fame:
R egarding such as take God Mars his part,
E che where by proofe, in Honnor and in name.

As an aside, I am sometimes asked why it is that the Dedication—which looks so like a cipher that one expert remarked that it cannot possibly be one!—has not been solved until now. Part of the answer must lie in the fact that editors, both in the past and at the present time, have felt free to alter the spelling, layout, and punctuation of the text in a wide variety of ways. That this has resulted in the destruction of essential aspects of the ciphers, rendering their solution impossible, is shown by the examples given on the following pages.

In conclusion, I would like to suggest (no more) that the mysterious Dedication to *Shake-speare's Sonnets* is a masterpiece of cryptography, and records for posterity two tremendous secrets: the name of the true poet, and the name of the young man he was so certain he had immortalized in his verse, before the indifference of history decreed otherwise.

TO THE ONLIE BEGETTER
OF THESE ENSUING SONNETS,
MR. W.H.
ALL HAPPINESS,
AND THAT ETERNITY PROMISED
BY OUR EVER-LIVING POET,
WISHETH THE
WELL-WISHING ADVENTURER
IN SETTING FORTH,

T. T.
Edmond Malone, 1790

TO THE ONLIE BEGETTER OF THESE INSUING
SONNETS,

MR. W.H.

ALL HAPPINESS AND THAT ETERNITY
PROMISED BY OUR EVER-LIVING POET
WISHETH THE
WELL-WISHING ADVENTURER IN SETTING
FORTH

T. T
W. Harvey, 1825

TO
THE ONLY BEGETTER OF THESE ENSUING
SONNETS,
MR. W.H.,

ALL HAPPINESS,
AND
THAT ETERNITY PROMISED BY OUR EVER-
LIVING POET,
WISHETH
THE WELL-WISHING ADVENTURER
IN SETTING FORTH,

T. T.
Charles Knight, 1844

TO THE ONLIE BEGETTER OF
THESE INSUING SONNETS
MR. W.H. ALL HAPPINESSE
AND THAT ETERNITIE
PROMISED BY
OUR EVER-LIVING POET
WISHETH
THE WELL-WISHING
ADVENTURER IN
SETTING
FORTH

T. T.
F. T. Palgrave, 1879
Michael O'Mara, 1988

To the only begetter of
these ensuing sonnets
Mr. W. H all happiness
and that eternity
promised
by
our ever-living poet
wisheth
the well-wishing
adventurer in
setting
forth

T.T
A. L. Rowse, 1964, 1973

TO THE ONLY BEGETTER OF
THESE ENSUING SONNETS
MR. W.H. ALL HAPPINESS
AND THAT ETERNITY
PROMISED
BY

OUR EVER-LIVING POET
WISHETH
THE WELL-WISHING
ADVENTURER IN
SETTING
FORTH

T. T.
Pelican, 1956, 1969

TO. THE. ONLIE. BEGETTER. OF.
THESE. INSUING. SONNETS.
MR. W.H. ALL HAPPINESSE.
AND. THAT. ETERNITIE.
PROMISED.
BY.
OUR EVER-LIVING POET.
WISHETH.
THE. WELL-WISHING.
ADVENTURER. IN.
SETTING.
FORTH.

T. T.
Kenneth Muir, 1979

To the Only Begetter of These Ensuing Sonnets
MR. W. H
*All Happiness and That Eternity Promised
by Our Ever-living Poet
Wisheth the Well-wishing Adventurer in
Setting Forth*

T. T.
David Bevington, 1994

Postscript

In reviewing my paper, "Secrets of the Dedication," after several years, it seems to me that there is good news and bad news. First, the bad news. The likelihood of the message "These sonnets all by ever . . ." occurring by chance in the Dedication to the Sonnets was certainly small (very small!), but not zero. It is a matter of probabilities, as I outlined in my paper in the *Elizabethan Review* (1997, vol. 5, no. 2, pp. 93-122), where I specifically said that the *interpretation* of the odds is 'up to each individual' to decide. The odds by themselves decide nothing other than the *possibility* of a cipher, and a mathematical friend of mine has pointed out that, in assessing a cipher solution, once the odds of a chance

result are less than one in (say) three thousand, it hardly matters whether they are less than one in thirty thousand or one in three million; little extra significance can be attached to decreasingly small odds. The two coincidences ("EVER" = Edward de Vere = 6-2-4) are highly suggestive, but the human mind is always on the lookout for coincidences, which may just be the random workings of chance. The Friedmans imply (in *The Shakespearean Ciphers Examined*, p. 22) that a sentence needs to be reasonably long before it can be confirmed as the solution of a possible cipher. Though the five words found may be grammatical (allowing for ellipsis), the fact that they lack a verb (e.g. "made" or "written") is sufficient to cast doubt on the validity of the proposed solution.

It is now clear to me that a three-element key such as 6-2-4 is far too ingenious or complex for the Elizabethan or Jacobean period. Extensive reading carried out both before and after writing the paper has found only one similar instance. It occurs in the Friedmans' book (p. 39), and was designed (in 1888) as an example of what *could* be done, not an example of something that had *actually* been done by someone for genuine concealment purposes; the key was 10, 18, 27. For the record, it is documented that two-element keys were used (by prior arrangement) in letters sent home by a few people captured as prisoners in WW2.

I still think that the names 'Henry' and 'Wr-ioth-esley' were almost certainly deliberately concealed in the Dedication, and if 'Wriothesley' had been in two segments, 'Wrioth-esley,' I think almost everyone would agree; there has to be some explanation for the fractured text of the Dedication. Transposition ciphers (such as produce Henry Wr-ioth-esley) were described in print by Bishop Wilkins in 1641, as mentioned in my paper, and were probably familiar to a number of people several decades earlier.

The main point is that even when the odds against a chance occurrence are high, chance cannot be ruled out. Every time a player at bridge picks up a hand, the odds against it occurring are 635,013,559,600 to 1, yet there it is in front of them. An unverifiable cipher solution, employing techniques not recorded as having been used until the twentieth century, is unlikely to be the genuine solution of a hypothetical cryptogram dating from 1609.

John M. Rollett

Critical Readings 2:
Main Themes

Four Pivotal Sonnets: Sonnets 20, 62, 104, 129

In this chapter we have selected four sonnets for special consideration, as taken together they illuminate the Poet's most prevalent concerns, including his horror of aging and his bisexuality.

If we allow ourselves to assume that the "I" of the sonnets is a single character (whether that is Will Shakespeare himself or a character of his creation doesn't matter) we can connect seemingly disparate material into a revealing, coherent picture. By so doing we are well aware that we have ventured beyond the relatively safe harbor of the psychoanalytic hour where a living patient can confirm the analyst's insights and we recognize that what seems evidence to us may not be convincing to some readers. But the approach has one certain benefit: by following it we will gain access to the major themes of the sonnets and get to know this astonishing body of poems very well.

The Poet of the Sonnets, being a man of the Renaissance, made full use of classical mythology but was also capable of coining new myths of his own making and creating an imagery so beautiful that, once comprehended, it remains with us even if we do not share the Poet's interior psychic conflicts.

Sonnet 20

A woman's face with nature's own hand painted,
Hast thou the master mistress of my passion,
A woman's gentle heart but not acquainted
With shifting change as is false women's fashion,
An eye more bright than theirs, less false in rolling:
Gilding the object whereupon it gazeth,
A man in hue all hues in his controlling,
Which steals men's eyes and women's souls amazeth.
And for a woman wert thou first created,
Till nature as she wrought thee fell a-doting,
And by addition me of thee defeated,
By adding one thing to my purpose nothing.
  But since she pricked thee out for women's pleasure,
  Mine be thy love and thy love's use their treasure.

In the first five lines the feminine aspects of the Young Man are stressed, as is his superiority over women. The next three lines will emphasize his masculine aspects. In line 6, this androgynous man-woman is compared to the sun: "Gilding the object whereupon it gazeth." The act of gilding, as distinguished from gilded, appears only twice in Shakespeare's work, in this sonnet and in Sonnet 33:

Kissing with golden face the meadows green,
Gilding pale streams with heavenly alchemy
                        (Sonnet 33, lines 3-4)

In mythology the sun is usually a masculine symbol, whereas the "pale" moon is experienced as feminine; the use of the term gilding emphasized the masculine aspect of this bisexual youth.

A gender change is introduced in line 7, when the Young Man is addressed as "A man in hue, all hues in his controlling." The word "hue" had in Shakespeare's time many connotations, such as appearance, bearing, and grace. In these lines, the Poet seems eager to counteract the feminine impression he conveyed in the first six lines. "Masculine" means being in control of all his hues so that nothing that emanates from him is beyond his control. In Sonnet 94 a similar praise appears: "They are the lords and owners of their faces," meaning that those whose face does not betray what they feel are masculine. Commentators have also noted that "controlling" in line 7 contains a pun on "cunt." In that case the faint echo of "his cunt" in "his controlling" increases the sense of the Young Man as hermaphroditic.

Line 8 affirms the Young Man's appeal to both men and women: "Which steals men's eyes and women's souls amazeth." We note that the appeal is not equal on both genders. The Young Man evokes admiration from men, "stealing their eyes," implying taking men's eyes away from women. The Young Man has an even deeper effect on women, whose "souls he amazes." Blackmore Evans believes that the asymmetry is intended to convey that men responding with their eyes are more intellectual, while women, responding with their souls are more richly endowed with emotions. However, we will see that the eye is often the principal sexual organ in Shakespeare's sonnets—perhaps because it is the organ used to read them—so to "steal men's eyes" has sexual undertones.

The third quatrain introduces a legend that Shakespeare created for this occasion. Nature was engaged in creating a woman when she "fell a-doting"—that is, in love with the woman she was creating. Being heterosexual, Nature decided to add a penis for her own sexual pleasure. The Poet suggests that he was ready to love the woman nature was creating, but nature defeated him by the addition of the penis, making a sexual relationship between the Poet and the Young Man impossible. Hence, "me of thee defeated." Nature can have him but the Poet cannot. The verb "painted," found in the first line, appears in Shakespeare's work 58 times and is mostly used as a metaphor, often to connote the opposite of genuine as in "your painted counterfeit" in Sonnet 16. In this sonnet, when nature paints a woman, the woman comes to life, and when she adds a penis the woman becomes a bisexual person.

The term "a-doting" appears only in this sonnet. In the quarto edition, the line reads: "fell a doting." In Sonnet 131 the Poet speaks of "my dear doting heart." In Sonnet 141 the Poet tells us that his heart is "pleased to dote." And in Sonnet 148 the Poet speaks of "my false eyes dote." In these sonnets, as well as in other works of Shakespeare, doting means loving to excess, or loving foolishly. However, to be the recipient of such a love may not be undesirable. Thus, in *Much Ado About Nothing* we are told that Beatrice loves Benedick with an "enraged affection." Don Pedro muses "I would she had bestowed this dotage on me" (Act II, Scene III). An extreme form of dotage takes place in *A Midsummer Night's Dream* when Titania tells Bottom, transformed into an ass, "Oh, how I love thee; how I dote on thee." Oberon comments, "Her dotage now I begin to pity." Dotage can be a painful emotion.

Who is this nature so charmingly anthropomorphized? If we turn to other sonnets to discover who nature is, we will find, in Sonnet 4, that "Nature's bequest gives nothing, but doth lend," meaning that the loveliness of the Young Man was not given to him as a permanent right, but only lent to him by "nature," obliging him to pass on his beauty to the next generation. In Sonnet 18 we are told that "nature" is far from constant: "nature's changing course untrimmed." In Sonnet 60 "nature" can be in conflict with time, when time "Feeds on the rarities of nature's truth." In Sonnet 67 "nature" can be experienced as bankrupt, and when that happens there is no reason to live on. Depressing is also that "nature" uses the Young Man as a kind of souvenir of times now past. In Sonnet 126 "nature" is described as "sovereign mistress over wrack." At times "nature" is equated with life itself, a ruler over destruction, as for example in Sonnet

122: "so long as brain and heart/Have faculty by nature to subsist." Nature can be playful and goddesslike; she sometimes helps and at other times hinders our effort. Basically, in this sonnet, nature is portrayed by the Poet as narcissistic and irresponsible, pursuing her own ends indifferent to human wishes. In other sonnets discussed in Chapter 2 she is a sort of stand-in for the Poet himself, keeping the Young Man youthful as a souvenir of the beauty she had long ago. This idea seems strange but we will come to know it well, beginning with the discussion of Sonnet 62 later in the chapter.

There is a bawdy play on words in line 12: "adding one thing" is a reference to the penis; "to my purpose nothing" is the opposite of "one thing" and a reference to the vagina. It is likely that line 14 in Sonnet 8—"Thou single wilt prove none"—is also a reference to the female genital. There is a famous scene in *Hamlet* that can also be cited as confirmation of the Elizabethan equation between vagina and nothing:

Hamlet: Lady, shall I lie in your lap?
Lying down at Ophelia's feet.
Ophelia: No, my lord.
Hamlet: I mean, my head upon your lap?
Ophelia: Ay, my lord.
Hamlet: Do you think I meant country matters?
Ophelia: I think nothing, my lord.
Hamlet: That's a fair thought to lie between maids' legs.
Ophelia: What is, my lord?
Hamlet: Nothing

(Act III, Scene II, 119-28.)

In the third quatrain of Sonnet 136, (a sonnet we do not otherwise include in this book) we read:

Among a number one is reckoned none.
Then in the number let me pass untold,
Though in thy store's account I one must be.
For nothing hold me, so it please thee hold
That nothing, me, a something sweet to thee.

(lines 8-12)

The Poet asserts that one is no number, and that one is to be reckoned as none. That one is none is a proverb in many languages. For example, the German "Einmal (once) ist Keinmal (never)." A favorite strategy used by seducers is to persuade that one intercourse is no intercourse. "Store's account" contains an allusion to cunt. "Nothing" in line 11 can be read as "no thing" and therefore again as a reference to the vagina. The psychoanalyst Bertrand Lewin (1948), without reference to Shakespeare stated, "When a patient in analysis says he is thinking of nothing, he or she will soon be talking about the female genital."

The Poet has fallen in love with a very attractive and effeminate young man, but the Poet knows that homosexual relationships are forbidden under Elizabethan law. He may also share the abhorrence for homosexual activities, or may only be careful not to express them. In any case, he hopes homosexual love that does not lead to homosexual activity can be made acceptable to the reader. No wonder, then, that in subsequent years this poem evoked controversy, some using it to prove Shakespeare's homosexuality while others employed it as a proof that he was not. It is hardly surprising: an overt homosexual would never have written this sonnet, but neither would it have occurred to a heterosexual man.

The Young Man in this poem represents a solution to a particular problem that the Poet experiences. The Young Man is as beautiful as a woman but, being a man, is free from the character defects that the Poet attributes to women. The Poet of the Sonnets leads us to believe, at least in his case, that love and sexuality run along different tracks: the Poet's feelings of love are easily and unselfconsciously directed towards a man, but his feelings of sexual attraction remain directed towards women. Both feelings are presented as natural, so as to require no explanation to the reader.

In Sonnet 20, the beauty of women is regarded as self-evident, as the poem begins by attributing to the man "a woman's face." Written in an exuberant mood with a great deal of humor, many original ideas, and unexpected puns, this sonnet is a charming fable. One would have expected that it would rank among Shakespeare's more popular sonnets, but only one anthology included it. We suspect that it did not fare well because in spite of the Poet's denial so charmingly stated, the implicit homosexuality was too disturbing to many readers. To our knowledge, Sonnet 20 is unique in celebrating love based on the bisexual appeal of the person chosen.

In real life there are heterosexual women who love their female friends, and enjoy their company and have much more in common with them than they do with their heterosexual mates. The reverse is equally common: men who spend most of their time and pleasure in the company of other men and yet seek sexual gratification from a woman or from more than one woman. In psychoanalytic terms such solutions are called compromise formations between homo- and heterosexual wishes. Many masculine women and feminine men exert a special fascination on their partners, appearing bisexual; as both man and woman, they represent a possible solution to a conflict between homo- and heterosexual wishes. As a rule, however, the perceived bisexuality of the partner remains unconscious. However in Sonnet 20, this knowledge has not only become conscious but was transformed into a highly original poem. Sonnet 20 is an attempt at compromise formation based on love for a man who seems to the Poet to possess the attributes of both genders; the Poet admits openly that it is the bisexuality of the Young Man that is attractive, but denies that the Young Man is sexually attractive. Bisexuals attract for the same reason that narcissists are attractive: they are or at least appear self-sufficient. Psychoanalysts often discover that both envy and jealousy often interfere with the capacity to love, but love for a bisexual person who is believed to have within her or his orbit all that is the best in both genders must evoke also a great deal of envy. Falling in love with a hermaphrodite, as the Young Man is experienced in Sonnet 20, contains an obstacle. Anyone experienced in fantasy as hermaphroditic fantasy is bound to seem self-sufficient and therefore incapable as well as unwilling to love the other.

On the surface, this sonnet is in praise of a young man the Poet adores, or to use Shakespeare's term, "dotes upon." There are many sonnets in praise of this or another young man, but the nature of the praise bestowed in this sonnet is unique. The Young Man is exalted because he has androgynous qualities; because he combines masculine and feminine tendencies, being both master and mistress is proclaimed to be unique. This dual nature is captured in the second line: "the master mistress of my passion." In Shakespeare's time, the term "mistress" had not yet acquired the connotation it has for us—that of a "kept woman," or a woman who belongs to a man, usually married, who is financially supporting her. The term "master" here refers to a person endowed with the right to command. A note of submission to this hermaphroditic creature is introduced.

Shakespeare's commentators have interpreted that "but not acquainted" puns as not having a cunt. Whether this interpretation is accepted or not, it is clear that a strong anti-femine attitude is present when the Young Man's eyes are seen as "less false in rolling," namely, more loyal than woman's eyes. This belief in the lover's constancy will not be sustained in the subsequent sonnets. Patrick Mahony (1979) noted that the syntactical structure of Sonnet 20 contains many inversions (changes in the words' order), ellipses (omission of words necessary to complete the sentence), paralaxis (change in direction), and hypotaxis (subordinate clauses). The sonnet is unique in having fourteen hypermetric lines (exceeding the established meter of the sonnets). The bisexuality is also reflected in the binarity of the lines, two different ideas being pressed into the same line. He noted that to be accepted with the reverse side, or back side, is a reference to anal eroticism, so prominent in homosexuality. What Mahony discovered is a connection between the style of the poem and what the Poet tried to repress. What is repressed in the content, the anal homosexual wish, resurfaces in the style.

In psychoanalytic practice, one occasionally encounters men and women who have fallen in love with someone of their own gender, but this love or even sexual attraction notwithstanding, they insist that they are not homosexuals. As the Poet declares in Sonnet 20, they only happen to have fallen in love with this particular person. With humor and irony some people wear a button that says, "I'm not gay, my lover is."

One of the important contributions of psychoanalysis to the understanding of homosexuality was the insight that in addition to overt homosexuality, two other types have to be added: latent homosexuality, where homosexual wishes, insufficiently held back by repression, require fear and hatred of homosexuals to contain the homosexual wishes in a state of repression. Latent homosexuals rely heavily on projection (attributing their feelings to others, not themselves) and reaction formation (feeling repelled by what unconsciously attracts them) to keep their homosexuality repressed. Another diagnostic group comprises desexualized homosexuality; such men and woman have passionate love relationships with members of their own gender, including jealousy when the loved one prefers someone else, but the relationship does not include direct sexual wishes. In Sonnet 20 desexualized homosexuality is the Poet's ideal. It is possible to read all the love sonnets to the Young Man as examples of desexualized homosexuality, but the heterosexual sonnets, including the painful triangle, cast doubt on the fact that the desexualization idealized in this sonnet was actually achieved.

In the Poet's unconscious there was a choice: he could desire the Young Man's penis as a woman would and find that he is a homosexual. Or he could ask for friendship based on admiration but devoid of sexual interest, thus sublimating homosexual wishes into a

"mere" friendship. Unwilling to accept the implication of homosexuality, the Poet created Sonnet 20. Resigned to the fact that nature "pricked" the man he loves, that is, endowed him with a penis for woman's pleasure, he asks only for the Young Man's love and suggests the Young Man's sexuality, here called "love's use," should go to women. What the Poet advocated was a radical separation between love and sexuality; as we will see in other poems, sexless love also implies loveless sexuality.

Sonnet 20 and the classical past

Shakespeare very likely wrote under the influence of the Roman poet Ovid, who in his famous book *Metamorphoses* told the story of the sculptor Pygmalion, who fell in love with and caressed the statues of a young woman he had created. Venus granted is prayer that the statue come to life and become his wife. In psychoanalytic terms both Shakespeare's Nature and Ovid's Pygmalion are not capable of loving a real person and fall in love with what they themselves have created.

Whether Shakespeare read Ovid in the original in his student years or whether he read it in the Golding translation that had just appeared in 1565 is not clear, but the bisexuality was described by Golding thus:

Her countenance and her grace was such as in a boy might well be called a wench's face, and in a wench be called a boy's

(Golding 10:429-36)

Ovid's story of Salmachis and Hermaphroditus is also relevant to Sonnet 20. The water nymph Salmachis did not enjoy the hunt, preferring to look at herself in the water mirror and comb her lovely hair (we will meet her masculine equivalent as Narcissus). Hermaphroditus, the son of Hermes and Aphrodite, was a beautiful lad fifteen years old. He came to a pool translucent to the very bottom and it was the pool that Salmachis was using as mirror to her self-love. She sees Hermaphroditus, admires his beauty, desires him and pleads for kisses. Hermaphroditus is reluctant. Salmachis lures him into the water and once there, serpentlike, she coils herself around him. She prays to the gods, "May no day ever come to separate us." Her prayer was answered. Their bodies merged, becoming one person, both man and woman. "Two beings and no longer man and woman but neither and yet both" (Ovid *Metamorphoses*, 4:285-388, Humphries translation).

"Master mistress of my passion" goes even further

back to the fable told in Plato's *Symposium*. The best-known part of the *Symposium*, the one that has influenced Western culture most profoundly, is the legend told by Aristophanes to explain the nature of love: originally mankind was com posed of double creatures, having two heads, four arms, four legs, and two genitalia. Some were double-males, others double-females, and still others were composed male and female. These creatures threatened the gods because being self-sufficient they felt no need to sacrifice to the gods and the gods were in turn desperately dependent on human sacrifices. So the gods decided to cut each creature in half and since then the two halves are yearning to be reunited.

The legend told in the *Symposium* explained also why some people are heterosexual and others homosexual: sexual orientation depends on the gender of the person with whom we were originally united. We should note the wisdom of this legend. The hermaphrodite is self-sufficient and does not need the help of the gods, and therefore will feel no need to sacrifice to the gods. Being self-sufficient themselves, these gods nevertheless "need" the sacrifices offered by mortals for their own gratification; therefore they have a narcissistic relationship with mortals. These gods are interested in mortals only as sacrificers.

Our analysis of Sonnet 20 leads us to believe that this sonnet has been underestimated by the commentators and anthologizers. There is first the original use of the classical heritage and its transformation beyond what had been transmitted by the tradition. But there is more; whenever in the course of psychoanalysis sexual or love wishes for someone of one's own gender emerge, anxiety of becoming homosexual or bisexual surfaces. Shakespeare was capable of taking this anxiety-laden subject and treating it lightly and with humor; a taboo subject was given permission to become articulated. A weight of guilt and shame was lifted, if only for the time it takes to read this sonnet.

In Sonnet 20 we encounter the Poet who can bring to life the classical past, but is capable of creating a personal myth modeled on the classical past. Shakespeare's humor goes beyond Ovid; his nature is not a goddess-like Aphrodite who grants the sculptor's wish. She herself falls a-doting and for her own sexual satisfaction adds the penis the Poet claims not to need. We can look upon this sonnet as a compromise between homo- and heterosexual wishes. If the Poet had succeeded to live up to this division we would not have had the conflicts that animate the other sonnets. Because the sonnet is an erudite and funny compromise it remains inherently unstable. An unstable compromise is a wonderfully promising dramatic premise and since the rest of the sonnets show that the compromise of Sonnet 20 did not lead to a permanent resolution, we selected this poem as the gateway to one of the Poet's major inner struggles.

Sonnet 62

Credit for the discovery of self-love as a third form of love after heterosexual and homosexual love goes to Ovid. This love still carries the name of his legendary character Narcissus and is called narcissism. Ovid, being a poet and not a systematic thinker, created a legendary character, not a psychological concept.

According to Ovid, Narcissus was a youth of wondrous beauty. Perceptively, Ovid made him not the child of a loving couple but of the nymph Leiriope, who was ravished by the river god Cephisus, who encircled her with his winding streams. Leiriope consulted the prophet Tiresias as to whether Narcissus would reach old age; the prophet replied, "Only if he never knows himself." It has been pointed out that the seer's answer was Ovid's ironical reversal of the Greek ideal "know thyself," inscribed on Apollo's temple in Delphi. Beautiful youths, men, women and nymphs fell in love with Narcissus but he rejected them all. In response to a rejected lover, Nemesis, the goddess of vengeance, inflicted upon Narcissus the pain he caused others, to love without being loved. Exhausted from the hunt, Narcissus reaches a fountain whose waters are unruffled. In the silvery waters he is smitten by love for the image that stares at him from the water. Narcissus cannot tear himself away and dies gazing at his image.

Among those who fell in love with Narcissus was the nymph Echo, who was punished by Juno to be unable to have independent speech and was capable only of repeating what she was told.

> Out of the woods she came with arms all ready
> to fling around his neck, but he retreated. "Keep
> your hands off," he cried, "and don't touch me.
> I would die before I would give you a chance at
> me." "I'd give you a chance at me," was all that
> poor Echo could reply
>   (Ovid Metamorphoses 3, Humphries' translation)

This story, in our opinion, shows how profound a psychologist Ovid was. Milder narcissists may not be able to love an independent person but at least they can find a partner who mirrors them, who, echo-like, reflects back what they are. That Narcissus could not even love Echo doomed him to utter loneliness.

With these preliminaries behind us, we turn to Sonnet 62.

> *Sin of self-love possesseth all mine eye,*
> *And all my soul, and all my every part;*
> *And for this sin there is no remedy,*
> *It is so grounded inward in my heart.*
> *Methinks no face so gracious is as mine,*
> *No shape so true, no truth of such account,*
> *And for my self mine own worth do define,*
> *As I all other in all worths surmount.*
> *But when my glass shows me my self indeed*
> *Beated and chopped with tanned antiquity,*
> *Mine own self-love quite contrary I read:*
> *Self, so self-loving were iniquity.*
>   *'Tis thee (my self) that for my self I praise,*
>   *Painting my age with beauty of thy days.*

The very first words of the sonnet are a surprise. Why is self-love a sin? There is hardly a passage in the Bible where self-love is denounced with such vehemence. What has usually been condemned is the sexual expression of self-love, masturbation. True, during the Middle Ages vanity had the status of a sin. But there is little evidence that the author of the sonnets was a believing Christian.

"Self-love possesseth all mine eye" tells us that the eye is the crucial organ in self-love. This self-love permeates the Poet's soul and every part of him. The expression "possesseth" implies that self-love, like other forms of love, can overwhelm the person in love, who has the feeling of being taken captive by the love. To feel possessed implies that love is experienced passively as something that overwhelms us, not actively as something we choose to do. This self-love first conquered the eye, then the soul and then "every part." This self-love is so grounded in the Poet's heart that there is no remedy for it. The first quatrain is stated as an overwhelming fact; the second quatrain opens with "Methinks." It is not as absolute as the first quatrain, for "Methinks"—the equivalent of "it seems to me"—mitigates the absoluteness of the first quatrain. It was this all-conquering self-love that made the Poet think that "no face so gracious is as mine/ No shape so true, no truth of such account." The last statement is of special interest because even if something is believed to be truth it can be held weakly

or uncertainly, or, as it happened to the Poet, so strongly that no other truth compares to it and is of similar account. The second quatrain ends with the declaration that the Poet feels he surmounts, or surpasses, everybody else.

In the first two quatrains the Poet, like Narcissus, is in love with himself. Regarding self-love as a sin, he knows no cure for it. In the third quatrain, however, the remedy for self-love is discovered. The same mirror that trapped Narcissus has a sobering effect on the Poet.

Shakespeare transformed Ovid's tale. The very glass that trapped Narcissus awakens the Poet out of his narcissistic slumber. His age, in this sonnet called "tanned antiquity," causes him to fall in love with someone who reminds him of his own now-lost self-love while he was young. This is expressed metaphorically in the last line, "Painting my age with beauty of thy days."

It is only when he happens to look in the mirror ("but when my glass shows me myself indeed" sounds like something that happens, not like something that happened once) he is suddenly reminded that he is praising the Young Man. The Poet moves beyond his self-love when he can no longer maintain it because of aging. This moment allows him to write uniquely because he gained some distance from his self-love.

Thus for all its debt to Ovid, Sonnet 62 tells the story of a "Narcissus" who became a lover of someone else. The young man who looks at his reflection and falls in love has become an old man who loves himself until he sees his reflection and then finds a young man to love instead (this idea is the inspiration for the drawing on the cover of this book). Where a more ordinary mind would have had the Poet roused from his narcissism by the beauty of another (one, perhaps, who reminded him of himself), Shakespeare gives us a story of self-love that is thwarted by the Poet's horror of old age. This is of great importance, for the relationship because the man the Poet loves will himself age, which, in other poems, will raise the question of whether the Poet will be able to love him as he gets older.

The term "self love" appears in Sonnet 62 three times: in lines 1 and 11, and in line 12 as "self loving." In all of Shakespeare's writing, "self love" appears eight times and "self loving" three times. In Sonnet 3 "Who is so fond will be the tomb/Of his self love to stop posterity." Sonnet 62 alone would have assured for Shakespeare a prominent role in the Western understanding of the nature of narcissistic love. Love is a dominant theme in all poetry, but self-love has rarely been seen as a worthy topic for poetry. Poetry communicates one's love to the other; as a communication to the self it seems cumbersome.

'Tis thee (my self) that for my self I praise,
Painting my age with beauty of thy days.

This couplet can be read in two different ways depending on how we interpret "thee." Most commentators think that "thee" refers to the Young Man. In this interpretation the Poet used the Young Man as a kind of deceptive mirror to persuade himself that he was young. But the parentheses around the word myself suggests another and deeper possibility: that it refers to the self-love of the Poet as a Young Man. The cunning poet may have wished to convey the two interpretations simultaneously, obliterating the difference in the state of love between himself and the Young Man.

Vendler believes that the Poet created this delusory self-image in order to be able to believe in the Young Man's affections for him. We, by contrast, believe that the Poet fell in love with the Young Man in order to prolong or recapture the illusion of his own youth and beauty. The love of the Young Man was in the service of the Poet's restoration of his own narcissism.

It was in 1914 that Freud recognized that self-love, or as he preferred to call it "narcissism," can give rise to a special kind of love, which he called "narcissistic love." In that love, we love someone else who reminds us of ourselves either as we are or as we had once been or as we wished to have been. It is a love that is based on converted envy. When we read Sonnet 62, we can see that Shakespeare had this insight three hundred years before Freud. But, because the Poet condemned his own self-love, he also condemned his narcissistic love for the Young Man. Only Auden included this sonnet in his anthology. From a psychoanalytic perspective, the transformation of narcissism into a narcissistic love as depicted by the Poet is a milestone in the understanding of self-love.

Sonnet 104

Sonnets 62 and 104 have in common the fear of aging. In Sonnet 62 aging forced the Poet to change his self-love for the love of the Young Man. In Sonnet 104 the Poet is amazed that his love for the Young Man lasted for three years without his lover showing signs of aging.

To me fair friend you never can be old,
For as you were when first your eye I eyed,

Such seems your beauty still: three winters cold,
Have from the forests shook three summers' pride,
Three beauteous springs to yellow autumn turned,
In process of the seasons have I seen,
Three April perfumes in three hot Junes burned,
Since first I saw you fresh which yet are green.
Ah yet doth beauty like a dial hand,
Steal from his figure, and no pace perceived,
So your sweet hue, which methinks still doth stand
Hath motion, and mine eye may be deceived.
For fear of which, hear this thou age unbred,
Ere you were born was beauty's summer dead.

The poem has a unique structure. The first two lines are addressed to the Young Man, assuring him that he can never be old. The next six lines are a description of three years and their respective seasons, implying the Poet's amazement that the youth did not appear to have aged in the last three years. In the third quatrain this peculiar certainty has gone; the Poet has become suspicious: time is compared to a "dial hand" that moves so slowly that beauty can be stolen from the Young Man's figure without the pace being "perceived," that is, without us noticing that the shadow on the sun dial has moved at all. In line 11 what was a certainty in the first lines has been reduced to a mere "methinks;" the Poet suggests that the Young Man has aged in these three years but the Poet's eyes have been deceived.

The couplet is addressed to future generations, here called "age unbred," and the Poet tells them that even before they were born "beauty's summer," a reference to the Young Man, beauty had died. The couplet thus takes back what the poem tried to affirm.

The traditional division of the sonnet into three quatrains in contrast as well as in communication with each other has not been observed. Instead, the theme of the second quatrain extends over six lives, giving the changes of the season extra power.

The second line brings in the role the eye plays in the Poet's falling in love. Love took place literally at the first sight, when "your eye I eyed." Once more we can confirm that the main sexual organ for the Poet is the eye and this displacement from the penis to eye helped the Poet separate love from sexuality. When the eye takes over the function of the genital, psychoanalysis uses the term "displacement." Already in Sonnet 20 the lover was praised as having "an eye more bright than theirs/Less false in rolling;" and in Sonnet 62, "sin of self love possessed my eye." There are a number of other sonnets in which the eye plays a prominent role in the love feelings of the Poet. For example in Sonnet 1: "But thou contracted to thine own bright eyes;" Sonnet 14: "But from thine eyes my knowledge I derive;" Sonnet 47: "Mine eye is famished for a look;" Sonnet 49: "Scarcely greet me with that sun, thine eye;" Sonnet 61: "It is my love that keeps mine eye awake;" Sonnet 93: "There can live no hatred in thine eye;" Sonnet 139: "Wound me not with thine eye, but with thy tongue."

Nature, we note, is experienced as both active and hostile as well as passive and enduring. Active forces playing havoc alternate with passing events that could not be prevented, "three winters cold" is experienced as the aggressor, who "shook three summers' pride." In the fifth line, "beauteous spring to yellow autumn turned" without anyone actively bringing this change about. The next metaphor is a powerful one, "three April perfumes in three hot Junes burned," implying that April perfumes linger until they are burned up by the hot June. The Poet repeats that these changes have taken place three times since the two have met. In the third quatrain, the Young Man himself is introduced into the cycles of nature. Three years ago, he was green, but unlike nature human life is not cyclical and subject to the power of time.

In line 9, a major shift takes place. What impresses the Poet now is not nature, but the clock.

The word dial appears in Shakespeare's work nine times, the word dial's four times, and dials twice. The full term sundial was not used by Shakespeare. Two references to dial appear in Sonnet 77:

Thy glass will show thee how thy beauties wear,
Thy dial how thy precious minutes waste.

And again,

Thou by thy dial's shady stealth mayst know
Time's thievish progress to eternity;

The phrase "dial's shady stealth" refers to the fact that in the shade the dial cannot register the changing hours, and this is how time can steal. In psychoanalytic terms, the dial is a symbolic representation of the superego; it admonishes the Poet to note how precious moments are wasted, but it is also an instrument used by time as in "thievish progress to eternity," where time allegedly steals from us our hours. The reference to eternity is one of the few places where the Poet speaks in religious language. The metaphor used by the Poet in

line 10: "Steal from his figure, and no pace perceived;" is of special interest because it illustrates how a creative poet can use the paranoid idea of stealing and transform it into poetry. Beauty is compared to a "dial hand" (sundial) that moves so slowly that no movement is noticed, expressed as "no pace perceived." Beauty itself, in line 10, is accused of stealing from the figure of the Young Man. Beauty also fades imperceptibly like the dial hand. What the Poet means is that because aging takes place, the beauty of the Young Man is stolen from him, a striking example of how a paranoid idea can become transformed into an original metaphor. Because the idea is paranoid, lines 9 and 10 are difficult to decipher logically. To make sense of them, we have to divide the thoughts that have become condensed. Beauty is accused of stealing (sneaking away) from the Young Man's figure and treated like a possession that can be stolen. Another metaphor is then added: beauty behaves like a dial hand that moves so slowly that we did not ever perceive the motion. The Poet frequently used the metaphor of stealing to connote lack of legitimacy; for example, in Sonnet 63 time is described as "Stealing away the treasure of his spring."

As we reach line 11, the certainty of the first line has vanished. The bold statement "you never can be old" has become the hesitant "methinks still doth stand." The metaphor of the dial hand in line 9 is still animating line 12. The dial can deceive the eye by moving in such a way that the motion itself is not noticed. The Young Man can age without the Poet noticing it. The fear of not noticing the effect of time grips the Poet. The Young Man was never supposed to age, and by loving him the Poet would also stay young. This was beyond the power of Eros to achieve. The Young Man may still be "green," but the Poet knows that he will not stay young forever. The Poet cannot accept that beauty is transient. "Sweet hue" in line 11 refers to the Young Man's complexion. "Hue," as we saw in Sonnet 20, is a word the Poet usually uses to describe masculinity. The Poet is no longer sure that a Young Man's "sweet hue…still doth stand." He begins to feel that his eyes, which have not noticed aging, may have deceived him. What the Poet feared becomes a certainty in the couplet. With "thou age unbred" the Poet addresses future generations and tells them (us) that with the aging of his lover, "beauty's summer" died. Thus the personal tragedy of the Poet, seeing the Young Man he loves aging, becomes a universal tragedy because his beauty will never be replicated. The coming generation will no longer know the beauty that died with the summer. Future generations should know that when the Poet's Young Man aged, summer's beauty died.

What is striking, particularly to older readers, is that three years seems such a long time to the Poet. In Sonnet 116, Shakespeare expressed the opposite feeling that love is "not time's fool, though rosy lips and cheeks within his bending sickle's compass come." In Sonnet 104, the mere anticipation of aging frightens the Poet. He does not explain this sonnet and we cannot be sure that we grasped it fully, but a hypothesis does come to mind. There are three years that make a very big difference: these three years may have been so crucial if they embrace the years during which the Young Man will have reached puberty. This hypothesis cannot be entirely dismissed because we encounter in real life people who can love either boys or girls as long as they are pre-pubescent (Charles Dodgson's desexualized love for Alice Liddell gave us *Alice in Wonderland).* If this was to any de gree true of the Poet of the Sonnets, we gain a new understanding of the procreation sonnets which begin the sonnets in the traditional published sequence and which we describe in Chapter 5. They are addressed to the Young Man the Poet loved who is now reaching sexual maturity. If this was the case we can also understand better the enmity between the Poet and time. It is normal to have difficulty in accepting aging, but if love is confined to the few years before pubescence sets in, there will be a deeper reason to be at war with the destructive power of time. Sonnet 104 leads to the hypothesis that the Young Man the Poet loved was not only young but not yet a man.

Sonnet 129

The three sonnets we have looked at so far cover a wide range of variations on falling in love, and what we think of as normal or at least typical falling in love ("boy meets girl" in American popular culture) is noticeably absent. Absent, too, is the theme of sexual desire or the fulfillment of love through the sexual act.

Sonnet 129, by contrast, concerns itself directly with desire and lust and ranks among Shakespeare's best-known sonnets and was chosen by five anthologies. The sonnet has its own unique structure but it is also one of the most savage ones. The word "lust" did not at first have the sinister connotation it has in this sonnet; though a deadly sin in the Christianity of the Middle Ages it was synonymous with pleasure and delight. However, by the time the sonnet was written the word lust acquired the meaning of strong, excessive or

inordinate desire followed, once gratified, by loathing.

When a minister in one of his sermons fulminates against lust, we are not surprised. It is, so to speak, his métier. But Shakespeare? There is nothing in the other sonnets to prepare us for the vehemence with which lust is denounced in this sonnet, except the similar denunciation of self-love in Sonnet 62.

Sonnet 129

Th' expense of spirit in a waste of shame
Is lust in action, and till action, lust
Is perjured, murd'rous, bloody full of blame,
Savage, extreme, rude, cruel, not to trust;
Enjoyed no sooner but despised straight,
Past reason hunted, and no sooner had,
Past reason hated as a swallowed bait,
On purpose laid to make the taker mad:
Mad in pursuit and in possession so,
Had, having, and in quest, to have, extreme;
A bliss in proof and proved, a very woe,
Before a joy proposed behind a dream.
    All this the world well knows yet none knows well,
    To shun the heaven that leads men to this hell.

"Th' expense of spirit," the opening words in this sonnet, are as striking as they are puzzling. The word expense was used by Shakespeare 19 times and only this once in the sonnets. It is the only place in his work where the word is used metaphorically rather than concretely. Commentators interpreted "Th' expense of spirit" as waste of vital energy, which results in a "waste of shame." By putting the two words "waste" and "shame" under the same yoke the Poet created a term that never existed before.

Something more can be learned from Shakespeare's use of the word waste, which appears in his works 51 times. Words can be wasted, breath can be wasted, and also memory, and above all the treasure of time can be wasted by idle hours. Man can waste time but time can also waste the man. One can also make "waste in brief mortality (*Henry V,* I.ii.28)." Because the Poet was, as we shall demonstrate in the next chapter, at war with time, he was highly sensitive to any waste. In the sonnets the word waste appears seven times, as for example in Sonnet 30, "And with old woes new wail my dear time's waste," or Sonnet 77, "Thy dial how thy precious minutes waste."

"Waste of shame" evokes the image of desolate

territory—a desert inhabited by shame, possibly a non-flattering reference to the vagina. Lust is an action; it lasts only as long as the action lasts. The third and the fourth lines are lines of invectives; altogether nine invectives are hurled against lust. These invectives tell us what happens after lust has passed. The second quatrain repeats explicitly what was implicit in the second line. It emphasizes the brevity of the enjoyment and the guilt feelings that follow after consummation, expressed as "despised straight." In lines 6 through 8, the use of "past reason hunted" and "past reason hated" portray the double nature of lust. One feels first hunted by it and then overcome by hatred of it. Reason cannot explain either the haunting quality of lust nor why it is so powerfully hated after consummation. "Past reason" is repeated in lines 6 and 7; it is the Poet's term for what we call the "irrational." The Poet then goes on to compare the person seized by a lust to a fish that swallowed bait—a highly compressed metaphor, the word fish being eliminated. A person overtaken by lust is struggling like a fish that just swallowed bait, struggling in vain to free itself from the bait.

In line 8 a paranoid idea emerges. Lust has the character of conspiracy imposed upon us by some mysterious evil designer "to make the taker mad." The couplet emphasizes human helplessness in avoiding lust, even though we know full well its destructive power.

The Poetic impact of the sonnet is due in part to its structure: four nouns in line 1; the repetitive reversal of the words "lust" and "action" in line 2; three adjectives in line 3, followed by four adjectives in line 4. Together, they give the first quatrain a strong declarative and impersonal quality.

The second quatrain is constructed differently. It contains one sentence per line, but each sentence contains two ideas. The third quatrain is structurally similar to the second; all lines until the couplet consisting of six to nine words, while the couplet is longer, consisting of ten words. However, it is the content, the savage denunciation of lust that is most striking.

We are fortunate to have the analysis of Sonnet 129 by the distinguished linguist Roman Jakobson (in collaboration with Lawrence Jones, quoted by Rosen). In his analysis of that sonnet, Jakobson relied on the principle of binary opposition, which played so fundamental a role in his systematization of the study of sound structure in language. This binary opposition highlights the collision of pairs that provides a linguistic representation of the collision of two bodies in the act of fulfilling lust. And since, to Shakespeare, lust was the opposite of love, the structure of the sonnet captures and repeats the enmity between these two emotions.

Inserting vertical lines into the sonnet emphasizes the binary opposition.

I   *Th' expense of Spirit / in a waste of shame*
    Is lust in action, / and till action, lust
    Is perjured, murd'rous, / blouddy full of blame,
    Savage, extreame, rude, / cruel, not to trust,
II   *Injoyd no sooner / but dispised straight,*
    Past reason hunted, / and no sooner had
    Past reason hated / as a swallowed bayt,
8   *On purpose layd / to make / the taker mad.*
III   *Mad[e] in pursuit / and in possession so,*
    Had, having, and in quest, / to have extreame,
    A blisse in proofe / and provd, / a[nd] very wo,
    Before a joy proposd / behind a dreame.
IV   *All this the world / well knows / yet none knowes well,*
    To shun the heaven / that leads / men to this hell.

(Rosen, p. 199)

As the vertical lines show, the binary opposition is maintained until line 8. In the first seven lines the grammatical parallelism has been maintained, while line 8 is built on five dissimilar grammatical forms. Equally striking for Jakobson is the fact that this sonnet alone among the 154 contains no personal or possessive pronouns, giving the sonnet an abstract structure, making it possible for Jakobson to speak of the "poetry of grammar." The impersonal structure of Sonnet 129 is in sharp contrast to the most personal theme of fornication and its bitter aftermath. Even the fornicator is never referred to directly, except in dependent clauses. Charles Rosen, who quoted Jakobson's work in a chapter entitled "Concealed Structures," noted that "the ability of the grammatical structure of language to assume a poetic life of its own is fundamental to music, which imitates this aspect of language."

After quoting Jakobson, Rosen also suggested an alternate analysis. He noted that the four consonants of s.p.r.t. dominate the first 12 lines.

1 Expence, Spirit, waste (sp sp st)
2 lust, lust (st st)
3 Is perjurd (s p r r)

4 Savage, extreame, trust (s str tr st)
5 despised straight (sp s str t)
6 Past reason hunted (p st r s t)
7 Past reason hated (p st r s t)

Rosen differentiates between what he calls the canonical interpretation, which deals with the interrelationship between the three quatrains and the couplet, and the "microscopic analysis," to which Sonnet 129 was subjected by Jakobson. If Shakespeare had attempted to achieve both kinds of symmetries, it would require an enormous amount of work and concentration. It is therefore likely that Shakespeare was so sensitive to language that such hidden structures occurred to him effortlessly and even unintentionally. Words occur to the Poet the way melodies occur to the composer.

A biblical passage is probably the oldest text to describe the pernicious effect of lust. Amnon, one of King David's sons, was so vexed by his desire for his half sister, Tamar, that he fell sick: "For she was a virgin; and Amnon thought it hard for him, to do anything to her." Following the advice of a lecherous friend, he pretended to be sick, and when King David visited him, he asked as a special favor that Tamar come and cook for him so that he can recover. King David complied, and Tamar came and cooked for him. Amnon then sent away all servants and when the two of them were left alone, the following happened.

(11) *And when she had brought them unto him to eat, he took hold of her, and said unto her, Come lie with me, my sister.*

(12) *And she answered him, "Nay, my brother, do not force me; for no such thing ought to be done in Israel: do not thou this folly.*

(13) *And whither shall I cause my shame to go? And as for thee, thou shalt be as one of the fools in Israel. Now therefore, I pray thee speak unto the King: for he will not withhold me from thee.*

(14) *Howbeit he would not hearken unto her voice: but, being stronger than she, forced her and lay with her.*

(15) *Then, Amnon hated her exceedingly; so that the hatred wherewith he hated her was greater than the love wherewith he had loved her. And Amnon said unto her, Arise, be gone.*

(16) *And she said unto him, there is no cause: this evil in sending me away is greater than the other that thou didst unto me, but he would not hearken unto her.*

(17) *Then he called his servant that ministered unto him, and said, Put now this woman out from me, and bolt the door after her*

(Samuel II, Chapter 13)

In the biblical passage, the essence of lust is an overwhelming desire before consummation, followed by an even more powerful disgust after the sexual act has been completed. The Bible offers no explanation for the radical shift in mood.

One of the influences of Freud's ideas on our way of feeling is that we no longer feel as inimical to lust as earlier generations were. We know today that the main enemies of love are more likely to be hatred or jealousy rather than lust. The term lust connotes a powerful sexual attraction driven by hostility that takes hold of a person after the sexual act has been completed. Lust can take place between two consenting partners but is more commonly experienced in isolation. It is usually a powerful sexual attraction to a person considered a forbidden partner, as when incest is involved, or as in happened in *The Winter's Tale*, where the coveted woman was the wife of the childhood friend. (However, there is no evidence that Polixenes actually lusted after Hermione, wife of his childhood friend Leontes. Rather, the sexual attraction between the two appears to be a product of Leontes' paranoid imagination.) Within the Freudian sphere of influence, lust takes place within the sexual sphere of narcissism, where the partner's needs are ignored; if the welfare of the partner is taken into account, lust will not be the word chosen. Lust is the sexuality of those who cannot love.

Wilson (1966) noted that unlike most sonnets, this sonnet was not written in quatrains, conveying to us the impression of being written in one breath, the form imitating the content. Wilson also put forth the idea that Sonnet 129 comprises all the different stages of lust: the after-lust period (had), the actual experience of lust (having) and the anticipation of lust (in quest) and that the extremes of lust are felt—all these stages (to have extreme). He credits Laura Riding and Robert Graves for this observation. In the biblical account that we presented, this chronological order was followed, but it ended in disgust, avoiding repentance. In psychoanalytic terms, if the capacity for repentance is present, the person who succumbed to lust is functioning on a higher psychological level of development than the one who stops at the level of disgust.

The psychoanalyst André Green (1975) differentiated between the object of need and the object of desire. In a relationship in which need predominates the gratification of the need leads to a loss of interest in the object. In a relationship of this kind once the sexual need has been gratified the other is of no further interest. If, however, the partner is the object of desire, gratification does not lead to satiety, and no one knew this difference better than Shakespeare.

Cleopatra is clearly the object of desire and not an object of need in *Antony and Cleopatra*. As Enobarbus puts it:

> *Age cannot wither her, nor custom stale*
> *Her infinite variety; other women cloy*
> *The appetites they feed, but she makes hungry*
> *Where most she satisfies; for vilest things*
> *Become themselves in her, that the holy priests*
> *Bless her when she is riggish.*
>
> (II.iii.240-246)

To our knowledge no one equaled Shakespeare in describing the object of desire. What is astonishing is that the same man who wrote Sonnet 129 knew also of the bliss of which Enobarbus speaks.

The place of Sonnet 129 among Shakespeare's sonnets is a puzzle. Why should a cycle of love poems be interrupted to make room for a vehement denunciation of lust? If religious scruples, ideas of hell and punishment after death, were in the Poet's mind, surely this was the sonnet in which to express them. But there is no hint of religious feelings in this sonnet.

It therefore seems to us that Sonnet 129 was the result of the Poet's inability to maintain the split between love and "love's use" that the Poet tried to maintain in Sonnet 20. In our view the Poet would not have written Sonnet 129 had he been able to keep his sexual wishes out of the relationship with the Young Man. The sonnet suggests that the Poet could neither abstain nor accept his homosexual wishes.

Sonnet 129 has been placed within the series of the heterosexual sonnets devoted to the Dark Lady. The general tendency of the Poet to direct his feelings of love to the Young Man and his sexual feelings to the Dark Lady support a heterosexual reading of the poem as does phrase "waste of shame" in the first line suggesting an unflattering reference to the vagina. But if Sonnet 129 documents a moment when the Poet's deep love of the Young Man finally overcame his inhibition against desiring his beloved, then the failure of the avowal of sexual disinterest in Sonnet 20 could well account for the bitterness, rage and linguistic violence that permeate the poem. The sonnet itself gives us scant evidence as to whether lust was experienced in a homo- or heterosexual relationship, but makes it clear that sex and desire were not, for the Poet of the Sonnets, happy components of life.

We have selected these four sonnets for special consideration because they seem to us, individually and taken together, to yield an introduction to the major themes of the sonnets. We will see the Poet's war with time played out with astonishing richness. No man, one would think, can win the battle against time, but time was a worthy adversary for a pen as great as Shakespeare's and it will be left to the reader to judge who is winning. The Young Man's self-love will haunt many other poems, as will the Poet's attempt to love people other than himself. Nature, too, will return again and again, not as the goddess of Sonnet 20 but as the object of the Poet's immense affection as he describes trees, flowers and sunlight with great tenderness. In fact, we will see that it is the Poet's indisputable love of nature that makes us believe him when he says he loves the Young Man and the Dark Lady.

Martin Bergmann and *Michael Bergmann*

Shakespeare's Sonnets and the History of Sexuality

Most readers of Shakespeare's sonnets today first encounter the poems in the form of a paperback book. Even a moderately well stocked bookstore is likely to offer a choice. Some of these editions are staid academic affairs. Others, however, package the sonnets as ageless testimonials to the power of love. A particularly striking example is *Shakespeare in Love: The Love Poetry of William Shakespeare*, published by Hyperion Press in 1998. The title says it all. The book was published as a tie-in to Marc Norman and Tom Stoppard's film of the same name, also released in 1998. There on the cover is Joseph Fiennes passionately kissing Gwyneth Paltrow. Other photographs from the film illuminate scenes and speeches from selected plays, along with the texts of sixteen of the 154 sonnets first published as Shakespeare's in 1609. These sixteen sonnets, presented to the unwary buyer as "*the* love poems of William Shakespeare," have been carefully chosen and cunningly ordered. The first two selections, sonnets 104 ("To me, fair friend, you never can be old") and 106 ("When in the chronicles of wasted time / I see descriptions of fairest wights"), give to the whole affair an antique patina. Next comes that poem of ten thousand weddings, sonnet 116 ("Let me not to the marriage of true minds / Admit impediments"). Two sonnets explicitly referring to a woman, 130 ("My mistress' eyes are nothing like the sun") and 138 ("When my love swears that she is made of truth, / I do believe her"), then establish a thoroughly heterosexual, if not altogether conventional, context for the eleven sonnets that follow (18, 23, 24, 29, 40, 46, 49, 57, 71, 86, 98), even though all eleven of these poems in the 1609 Quarto form part of a sequence that seems to be addressed to a fair young man. All told, the paperback anthology of *Shakespeare in Love* participates in the same heterosexualization of the historical William Shakespeare that Norman and Stoppard's film contrives (Keevak 2001: 115–23).

Contrast that with the earliest recorded reference to Shakespeare's sonnets. Francis Meres included in his book of commonplaces, *Palladis Tamia, Wit's Treasury* (1598), a catalog of England's greatest writers, matching each of them with a famous ancient writer. "The soul of Ovid," Meres declares, "lives in mellifluous and honey-tongued Shakespeare, witness his *Venus and Adonis*, his *Lucrece*, and his sugared sonnets among his private

friends" (Meres 1938: fols. 280v-281).[1] It was a high compliment. For Renaissance writers and readers, Ovid was the greatest love poet of all time: witness his how-to manual (*Ars Amatoria*), his love lyrics (*Amores*), and his encyclopedia of violent transformations wrought by love (*Metamorphoses*). The love Ovid wrote about was not, however, the sort that led to the marriage of true minds. Shakespeare's narrative poems *Venus and Adonis* and *The Rape of Lucrece* share with Ovid's *Metamorphoses* a fascination with the violence of desire. Venus's predatory lust for Adonis ends in the young man's being gored by a wild boar. Tarquin's brutal violation of the chastity of his friend's wife ends in her sheathing a knife in her breast. Of the one-hundred-fifty-four sonnets included in *Shake-speare's Sonnets Never Before Imprinted* (1609), fully half express disillusionment or cynicism. The first editions of both of Shakespeare's narrative poems bear dedications to Henry Wriothesley, Earl of Southampton. The "private friends" mentioned by Meres as the first readers of Shakespeare's sonnets may have included the other young men who counted Southampton as friend and patron. The nature of the books dedicated to Southampton, as well as the testimony of at least one eyewitness, suggest that the earl was, in Katherine Duncan-Jones's words, "viewed as receptive to same-sex amours" (Duncan-Jones 2001: 79). With this group of readers Joseph Fiennes and Gwyneth Paltrow sort very oddly indeed. The distance from Southampton House on The Strand in the 1590s to *Shakespeare in Love* at the local Cineplex in the 1990s points up the need for a reception history of Shakespeare's sonnets.

Meres's allusion to Ovid likewise suggests the need for a history of sexuality. In describing the various configurations of erotic desire in Ovid's poems we are apt to say that the poems imply a certain sexuality, or perhaps a certain range of sexualities. Sexual acts between man and boy, sexual acts between woman and woman, sexual acts between woman and beast, sexual acts between father and daughter all find places in Ovid's *Metamorphoses*. With what authority, however, can we speak of "sexuality" in connection with Ovid's poems? Or Shakespeare's? "Sexuality," after all, is a relatively recent word. It was coined about 1800 as a strictly biological term, as a name for reproductive activity that involves male and female apparatus. In fact, the earliest recorded application of the word in English refers specifically to the reproductive processes of plants (*OED* "sexuality" 1). It was not until the later nineteenth century that the word came to mean manifestations of a sexual "instinct" and not until the early twentieth century, with the publication of Sigmund Freud's works, that the subjective experience of sexual desire was added to the ensemble of meanings (Smith 2000b: 318-19). (Curiously, both of these later meanings are absent from the *OED*, even in its revised 1989 edition.) "Sexuality" and "sexual" are not in Shakespeare's vocabulary. The word "sex" occurs in Shakespeare's plays twenty-one times but only in the anatomical sense of female as distinguished from male. "You have simply misused our sex in your love prate," Celia chides Rosalind after she has said unflattering things about women to Orlando (*As You Like It* 4.1.185 in Shakespeare 1988).[2]

To describe stirrings of feeling in the genitals the word that Shakespeare and his readers would have used instead was "passion." Sonnet 20, for example, addresses the speaker's beloved as "the master mistress of my passion" (20.2). The word "passion" in this context carries a quite specific physiological meaning. According to the ancient Greek physician Galen and his early modern disciples, light rays communicating the shape and colors of another person's body enter the crystaline sphere of the eyes, where the sensation is converted into an aerated fluid called *spiritus*. *Spiritus* conveys the sensation to the brain, where imagination receives the sensation and, via spiritus, sends it to the heart. The heart then determines whether to pursue the object being presented or to eschew it (Wright 1988: 123). Whichever the choice, the body's four basic fluids undergo a rapid change. If the heart decides to pursue the object, quantities of choler, phlegm, and black bile are converted into blood. The person doing the seeing experiences this rush of blood as passion. What a person told himself or herself was happening when a good-looking person excited feelings of desire was thus different in the 1590s from how the same experience would be explained today. What causes a person to feel desire for genital contact with another body? A sudden flux of blood, or release of the infantile id? The very question proves the validity of Michel Foucault's claim that sexuality is not a natural given. Sexuality has a history: "It is the name that can be given to a historical construct: not a furtive reality that is difficult to grasp, but a great surface network in which the stimulation of bodies, the intensification of

pleasures, the incitement to discourse, the formation of special knowledges, the strengthening of controls and resistances, are linked to one another, in accordance with a few major strategies of knowledge and power" (Foucault 1980: 105-6).

In the course of his multi-volume *History of Sexuality*, left unfinished at his death, Foucault suggests several points when major paradigm shifts occurred, but for the purposes of Shakespeare's sonnets the crucial change came about in the eighteenth century. It was during the Enlightenment that sexuality was isolated as an object of rational inquiry. What had been an ethical concern in Shakespeare's time ("Two loves I have, of comfort and despair, / Which like two spirits do suggest me still," declares sonnet 144) became in Diderot's time a medical concept (Foucault 1980: 23-4). In the course of the nineteenth century the medical concept became a psychological concept. It is Freud who is responsible for the modern conviction that sexuality is a core component of self-identity. We have, then, two histories to consider in these pages: the history of how Shakespeare's sonnets have been read and interpreted and the history of how men and women have experienced and articulated feelings of bodily desire. We can trace these interrelated histories in four broad periods, each defined by a major event in the publishing history of Shakespeare's sonnets: 1590–1639, 1640–1779, 1780–1888, and 1889 to the present.

The Man of Two Loves: 1590–1639

Each word in Meres's reference to Shakespeare's "sugared sonnets among his private friends" is worthy of scrutiny. Of the six words, "sugared" may be the oddest. In the days before coffee and tea had reached England, what was most likely to be "sugared" was wine. Biron in *Love's Labor's Lost* mentions three varieties, "metheglin, wort, and malmsey," in one of his verbal games with the Princess (5.2.233). In 1 *Henry IV* Poins adds a fourth when he hails Falstaff as "Sir John Sack and Sugar" (1.2.112-13). But the adjective is still puzzling. By the 1590s "sonnets" were a well-established verse form, perfectly devised for expressing both sides of being in love, the pleasures and the pains, thanks to the *volta* or "turn" that typically divides the fourteen lines into two parts. Shakespeare's sonnets, taken as a whole, are rather longer on the pains than the pleasures. Metheglin, wort, malmsey, and sack might be appropriate ways of describing Michael Drayton's sonnets or Edmund Spenser's or Sir Philip Sidney's but hardly the piquant, often bitter poems that make up most of the 1609 Quarto of *Shakespeare's Sonnets*. Combined with the reference to "melliﬂuous [literally, "honeyﬂowing"] and honey-tongued Shakespeare," Meres's taste metaphor may have less to do with the poems' content than with the feel of Shakespeare's words in the mouth. In his own time Shakespeare was known, not as a creator of great characters, but as a writer of great lines, and lots of them.

"Sugared" may also refer to the way the sonnets were circulated, "among his private friends." In 1598, when Meres was writing, Shakespeare's collected sonnets were eleven years away from publication in print. Before then, they seem to have been passed around in manuscript, probably in single copies or in small groups rather than as a whole one-hundred-fifty-four-poem sequence. The word "among" suggests the way manuscript circulation in the sixteenth and early seventeenth centuries served to establish and maintain communities of readers who shared a certain place of residence, institutional affiliation, profession, religion, or political purpose (Love 1993; Marotti 1995). The word "his" confirms Shakespeare's already recognized status as an author unmistakable for anyone else; the words "private" and "friends," the close-knit, even secretive character of the readers who passed his sonnets from one to another. This sharing of poems, Meres implies, was like sharing a cup of sweetened wine, perhaps like kissing on the lips. Ben Jonson catches the scenario in a famous lyric: "Drink to me only with thine eyes, / And I will pledge with mine; / Or leave a kiss but in the cup, / And I'll not look for wine" (Jonson 1985: 293). Reading Shakespeare's sonnets in manuscript, Meres seems to imply, was in itself an act of passion.

Be that as it may, reading Shakespeare's sonnets in manuscript was an act of identity-formation, both for individuals and for the social group to which they belonged.

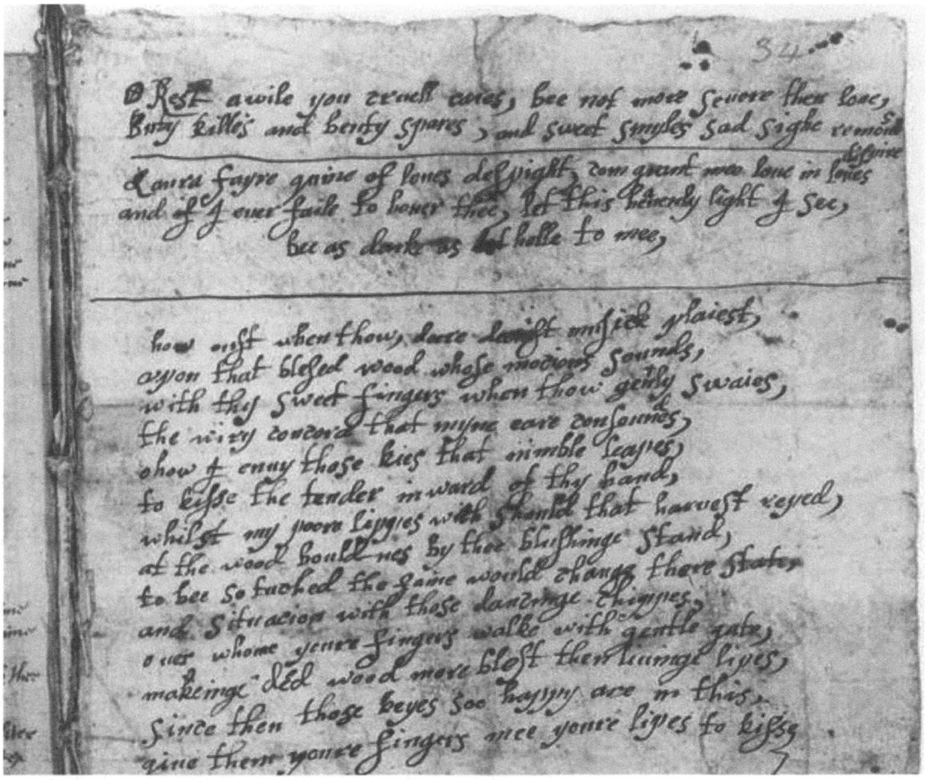

Figure 1. Sonnet 2 in Manuscript Circulation, Bodleian MS Rawlinson Poetic 152, fol. 345 (1625–40)

To judge from surviving manuscripts, erotic desire figured prominently in that process of identity-formation. No manuscripts of the sonnets from Shakespeare's own time have survived, but a single sheet of paper, datable to 1625–40 and bound up a century or so later in Bodleian Library MS Rawlinson Poetic 152, gives us some idea of how Shakespeare's sonnets may have circulated as individual poems in the 1590s.[3] On the six-by-six-inch sheet, five poems – all of them about the pains and the pleasures of love – have been written out in a neat italic hand. Vertical and horizontal creases in the paper suggest how it might once have been folded for passing from hand to hand. In the sequence of poems two stanzas from John Dowland's song "Rest awhile, you cruel cares" precede a version of the Shakespeare sonnet that figures as number 128 in the 1609 Quarto ("How oft, when thou my music music play'st"), which is in turn followed by two more love poems, "This is love and worth commanding, / Still beginning, never ending" and "I bend my wits and beat my brain / To keep my grief from outward show" (MS Rawlinson Poetic

152, fols. 34-34v). Neither Dowland nor Shakespeare is credited with the first two poems, even though the source in each case was almost certainly a printed book that prominently displayed the author's name on the title page: *Songs or Ayres . . . Composed by John Dowland* (1597) and *Shake-speare's Sonnets* (1609). Instead, the writer has appropriated the poems: he has given them his own voice, imbued them with his own passion. (It is not impossible, of course, that the sheet was written out by a woman, especially considering that italic hand was commonly taught to women.) Shakespeare's sonnet takes its place in a veritable litany of ever mounting desire. The first Dowland stanza asks for smiles; the second wants 8 Bruce R. Smith Sonnet 2 in Manuscript Circulation, Bodleian MS Rawlinson Poetic 152, fol. 345 (1625–40) more: "Come grant me love in love's despair." Shakespeare's sonnet continues the progression toward physical closeness: the speaker uses a phallic pun ("saucy jacks") to fantasize about kissing first "the tender inward" of the lady's hands and then her lips. The third poem carries the erotic fantasy even further: "twining arms, exchanging kisses, / Each partaking other's blisses, / Laughing, weeping, still together / Bliss in one is mirth in either." If the third poem represents consummation, the final poem finds no release from the writer's desires: "I force my will, my senses I constrain / To imprison in my heart my secret woe, / But musing thoughts, deep sighs, or tears that flow / Discover what my heart hides all in vain."

The transcription of sonnet 2 demonstrates graphically how Shakespeare's sonnets, for the poems' earliest readers, were not part of a sequence that came equipped with its own narrative implications. Copied out by hand, each poem became the writer's poem and the reader's poem; the passions of the poem became the writer's passion and the reader's passion. That became even more true when certain sonnets were copied, along with diverse other poems, into blank books like the "tables" mentioned in sonnet 122 ("Thy gift, thy tables, are within my brain / Full charactered with lasting memory"). Aside from the single sheet in MS Rawlinson Poetic 152, all nineteen other survivals of Shakespeare's sonnets in early seventeenth-century manuscripts occur in this form. Many of these books belonged to single individuals, even if the poems came from a common repertory; others show marks of joint compilation. The earliest is a miscellany of poems put together by George Morley (1597–1684) while he was a student at Christ Church, Oxford, between 1615 and 1621, just a few years after Shakespeare's death in 1616. Morley went on to become Bishop of Winchester, and his manuscript resides today in the library of Westminster Abbey. The poem that Morley copied is a version of the sonnet that appears as number 2 in the 1609 Quarto, "When forty winters shall besiege thy brow." No fewer than thirty-one variations in Morley's version from the one-hundred-dred-sixteen words in the Quarto text suggest to Gary Taylor that Morley may have been copying from a manuscript of an earlier version of the poem than the 1609 Quarto presents, especially since the variations betray parallels with scripts that Shakespeare was writing in the 1590s (Taylor 1985). Morley does not provide an attribution. Like the writer of the single sheet in MS Rawlinson Poetic 152, he seems to be less interested in who originally wrote the poem than in his own uses for it.

What Morley has done is to imagine the sonnet as a seduction device very much of a piece with the other poems he has copied: he entitles it "To one that would die a maid." Now, "maid" in early modern English could refer to a virgin of either sex, male as well as female, but the other poems in Morley's collection suggest that it was a female recipient he had in mind. Morley's version of sonnet 2, Taylor has demonstrated, is likely the exemplar for four other surviving manuscript copies of sonnet 2, all of which repeat the title "To one that would die a maid" (Taylor 1985: 217). One other manuscript, from the 1630s, heads the poem "A lover to his mistress" (Beal 1980: 452-4). The title suggests that the copyists thought of sonnet 2 more as an ingenious argument for getting someone into bed than as a persuasion to marry and beget children. The "you" of the poem is assumed to be a woman, not the fair young man implied by the first nineteen sonnets in the 1609 Quarto. Among the poems collected in Morley's manuscript is Donne's elegy "On his mistress going to bed" (Westminster Abbey MS 41, fols. l4v-15). The tone of the entire collection can be gathered from the poem that immediately precedes Shakespeare's sonnet, an epigram on an old woman who has worn her teeth away with talking too much, and the poem that follows it, a memorial tribute to a fart inadvertently let out by a speaker in parliament (fols. 49-49v).

Another group of manuscript copies of sonnet 2 comes closer to the context created in the 1609 Quarto. In four of the surviving table-books the poem bears the title "*Spes Altera*," "Another Hope," which implies that the collectors took the sonnet's third quatrain quite seriously: "O how much better were thy beauty's use / If thou couldst say, 'This pretty child of mine / Saves my account and makes my old excuse,' / Making his beauty by succession thine" (2.9-12 as transcribed in Taylor 1985: 212). The title "*Spes Altera*," as Taylor points out, comes from the last book of Virgil's *Aeneid,* where Aeneas's son Ascanius is praised as "*magnae spes altera Romae*" (12.168), "great Rome's other hope," just before the decisive battle in which Aeneas defeats Turnus, wins the hand of Lavinia, and secures the lands that become the site of Rome. In political terms this scenario resembles the context provided for sonnet 2 in the 1609 Quarto, where it appears second in a sequence of poems advising a noble young man to marry and beget heirs. In sexual terms the emphasis falls, not on the genital pleasure of a single night, but on a vision of fecundity that spans time and space. In this respect, "Spes Altera" is not unlike the moment of sexual consummation that Edmund Spenser imagines for himself and his bride in the *Epithalamion* he wrote for his own wedding day. First Spenser invokes Juno, goddess of marriage, then

> glad Genius, in whose gentle hand
> The bridal bower and genial [i.e., generative] bed remain
> Without blemish or stain,
> And the sweet pleasures of their loves' delight
> With secret aid does succor and supply
> Till they bring forth the fruitful progeny.
> (lines 398–403 in Spenser 1989: 678)

Similar images color the marriage-night blessing that Puck pronounces at the end of *A Midsummer Night's Dream.* The curtains and hangings on early modern bedsteads, richly embroidered with plants and animals, suggest that Spenser's and Shakespeare's contemporaries, some of them at any rate, liked to imagine themselves in just such settings of procreative plenitude when they had sex (Smith 1996: 95–121).

Yet another sexual scenario is set in place by the first book in which any of Shakespeare's sonnets appeared in print, *The Passionate Pilgrim,* published by William Jaggard in either 1598 or 1599. Only fragments of that first edition survive; the title page is not among them. A second edition followed in 1599 and a third in 1612, both proclaiming the entire book to be "*by W. Shakespeare.*" Despite that claim, only five of the twenty verses in the first and second editions can be attributed to Shakespeare on the basis of other evidence: the two poems that lead off the collection, "When my love swears she is made of truth, / I do believe her" (the poem that became sonnet

138 in the 1609 Quarto) and "Two loves I have, of comfort and despair" (144 in the 1609 Quarto), versions of two sonnets that are incorporated into the dialogue of *Love's Labour's Lost* ("Did not the heavenly rhetoric of thine eye / . . . / Persuade my heart to this false perjury?" [4.3.57–70] and "If love make me forsworn, how shall I swear to love?" [4.2.106–19]), and a song that likewise figures in that play ("On a day – alack the day – / Love whose month is ever May / Spied a blossom passing fair / Playing in the wanton air" [4.3.99–118]). The other fifteen selections include, without any attributions, Christopher Marlowe's lyric "[Come] live with me and be my love," followed by Sir Walter Raleigh's reply, as well as poems by Richard Barnfield and Bartholomew Griffin. All in all, *The Passionate Pilgrim* reads like a sheaf of leaves taken from a manuscript table-book.

More than Shakespeare's sonnets, it is Marlowe's poem, printed here for the first time, that establishes the tone of the whole affair: "Live with me and be my love, / And we will all the pleasures prove / That hills and valleys, dales and fields, / And all the craggy mountains yield" (Shakespeare 1939: sig. D5). The implicit setting for all twenty poems is the pastoral dream world that Shakespeare and his contemporaries knew as a *locus amoenus* (literally, a "delightful place"), a landscape of flowers and fields where the season is always May and the only occupations are being in love and writing poems about being in love. In this context, "When my love swears she is made of truth" is drained of all the acerbic cynicism it has in the 1609 Quarto. In the final couplet of *The Passionate Pilgrim* version the speaker simply abandons himself to voluptuous pleasure: "Therefore I'll lie with love, and love with me, / Since that our faults in love thus smothered be" (sig. A3). Compare that with the wincing pun on "lie" in the 1609 version: "Therefore I lie with her, and she with me, / And in our faults by lies we flattered be" (138.13-14 in Shakespeare 1977).[4] If there is a story line to *The Passionate Pilgrim* it is provided by four sonnets, dispersed through the first half of the collection, that recount Venus' attempted seduction of Adonis. The tremendous popularity of Shakespeare's narrative poem on the same subject, first published five years earlier and already reprinted four times, made it plausible for readers in 1598 to imagine that he had written these four sonnets, too. A smirking sensuality pervades the four *Venus and Adonis* sonnets: to warn Adonis of the thigh-wounds he might receive from hunting the boar, "She showed hers, he saw more wounds than one" (Shakespeare 1939: sig. B3). Amid the bowers of bliss erected in *The Passionate Pilgrim* the sonnet "Two loves I have, of comfort and despair" becomes no more than a conventional lament about unsatisfied desire, or perhaps a boast that the sonneteer enjoys not one love but two.

By 1609, when Thomas Thorpe published *Shakespeare's Sonnets Never Before Imprinted*, quite a few of the poems had, therefore, a sexual history already—and a remarkably varied one at that. The addition of a substantial number of other sonnets in the 1609 volume and their arrangement into a one-hundred-fifty-four-poem sequence reconfigured the place of the sonnets in the history of sexuality once again. Shakespeare's personal connection with the 1609 publishing venture is a controversial issue (Duncan-Jones 1983). Whoever may be responsible for the arrangement of the poems, the 1609 Quarto does suggest several groupings. Sometimes the connections are imagistic, as in the many pairs of sonnets that ask to be read as a diptych. In sonnet 27, for example, the speaker first specifies an occasion — "Weary with toil, I haste me to my bed" (27.1)—and then describes how he cannot rest from the cares of the day, how his thoughts "intend a zealous pilgrimage to thee" (278.6). The beloved's "shadow" appears to him "like a jewel hung in ghastly night" (27.11). Sonnet 28 follows as a natural conclusion—"How can I then return in happy plight / That am debarred the benefit of rest" (28.1-2)—and repeats the images of night, starlight, journey, and oppression. Other groupings are thematic. Sonnets 1–19, all seemingly addressed to the same young man, are concerned with securing immortality, either through the begetting of children or, later in the group, through the verses that the poet writes. Sonnet 20 introduces erotic desire by addressing the recipient as "the master mistress of my passion" (20.2), praising his woman-like beauties (20.1, 5), celebrating his manly constancy (20.3-6) and skin coloring (20.7-8), and making punning sport with his penis (20.11-14). Still other groupings seem situational. Sonnets 33–42 contain dark allusions to some offence that the beloved has committed, possibly by stealing the poet's mistress ("That thou hast her, it is not all my grief" [42.1]). A rival poet is implied in sonnets 78–86. Finally there is the question of whom the poet addresses or whom he is thinking about from poem to poem. Sonnets 1–19 and 20–1 clearly imply a male recipient. Sonnet 126 ("O thou, my lovely boy, who in thy pow'r / Dost hold time's fickle glass, his sickle hour"), with its male addressee, is followed by a poem that abruptly introduces a dark-hued woman as the subject of most of the ensuing poems: "In the old age black was not counted fair" (127.1). Read in isolation, many of the sonnets seem ambiguous with respect to the subject's gender (Dubrow 2000: 113-34).

What do they imply when read in sequence? Thorpe mystifies the question by providing a dedication that looks on the page like an epigram engraved on stone. It reads like a riddle. Who is "M[aste]r W. H.," identified by Thorpe as "the only begetter" of the sonnets? Who, for that matter, is "the well-wishing adventurer" who is "setting forth"? Syntactically he has to be Thomas Thorpe, who is setting forth the poems in print, but many readers of the collected sonnets have felt themselves to be cast in the role of adventurer or explorer amid the sonnets' cryptic allusions. By connecting Master W. H. with "that eternity promised by our ever-living poet," Thorpe's dedication prepares the reader to assume that the ensuing sonnets, the first nineteen of them at least, are addressed to Master W. H. Nothing explicitly challenges that assumption until sonnet 127. Do the poems, then, fall into a group addressed to the man right fair and a group addressed to the woman colored ill? At the least we can say that all the sonnets explicitly addressed to a male subject occur before sonnet 126, while all those explicitly addressed to a female subject occur after 127.

Whether that distinction applies to *every* poem before 126 and after 127 is harder to tell. Certainly sonnet 20 is not the only sonnet in the first group to speak of the man right fair in erotic terms. Sonnet 106 ("When in the chronicle of wasted time / I see descriptions of the fairest wights") takes Petrarchan poetry's conventional blazon of a lady's hand, foot, lip, eye, and brow and applies it to "ev'n such a beauty as you *master* now" (106.8, emphasis added). The sentiment voiced in the couplet of sonnet 106—"For we which now behold these present days, / Have eyes to wonder, but lack tongues to praise" (106.13–14)—is typical of the way the poems addressed to the fair young man preserve the idealism of the Petrarchan sonnet tradition, even as the gender of the subject changes from female to male. Contrast with the sexual cynicism bruited in many of the poems addressed to the woman colored ill could hardly be sharper.

What sonnets 20 and 106 do *not* register is anxiety over erotic appreciation of the fair young man's beauty. Aristotle's valuation of bonds between male and male over all other human ties, marriage included, was maintained in early modern ethics. Such bonds, after all, cemented the political power of patriarchy. The fact that male–male bonds could be celebrated in erotic images, in the very terms that might be read as signs of sodomy, constitutes one of the central ironies of early modern culture (Bray 1994: 40–61). In their own time, Margreta de Grazia (2000) has argued, the real "scandal" of Shakespeare's sonnets was to be found in the poems addressed to the woman colored ill, not in the poems addressed to the man right fair. All the distinctions on which the edifice of early modern society was founded—not just sexual difference but social rank, age, reputation, marital status, moral probity, even physical availability—are undermined by sonnets 127–52: "It is Shakespeare's gynerastic longings for a black mistress that are perverse and menacing, precisely because they threaten to raze the very distinctions his poems to the fair boy strain to preserve" (106). Sonnet 144 confirms such a reading: "Two loves I have of comfort and despair / Which like two spirits do suggest me still; / The better angel is a man right fair, / The worser spirit a woman colored ill" (144.1-4).

The circulation of Shakespeare's sonnets in manuscript from the 1590s through the 1630s, the printing of two of them in *The Passionate Pilgrim* in 1598–9, and the appearance of a collected edition in 1609 point up a fundamental fluidity, not only in what the poems could mean to different readers, but in what those readers' passions made them desire in other people. Our need to have an authorized fixed text and our need to typecast people according to "sexual orientation" are both revealed to be anachronistic back-projections.

The Cavalier Poet: 1640–1779

The most telling evidence of how people read the 1609 Quarto of Shakespeare's sonnets is to be found in manuscript table-books of the 1620s and 1630s, in which poems from the printed edition passed back into the manuscript culture from which they had originally emerged. Aside from sonnet 2, which seems to have circulated independently of the Quarto, the surviving manuscripts include single instances of sonnets 8, 32, 71, 116, 128, and 138. The only sonnet to be copied more than once, number 106, shows the same personal appropriation that we have noticed already with respect to sonnet 2. The two collectors who copied out "When in the chronicle of waste time, / I see descriptions of the fairest wights" in MS Pierpoint Morgan MA 1057 and Rosenbach MS 1083/16 seem not to have noticed the gender of the verb in the phrase "Even such a beauty as you master now"; both of them entitle the poem "On his mistress" (Beal 1980: 452-4). At least two readers of the 1609 Quarto,

however, seem to have picked up on the homoeroticism of many of the first 126 sonnets. A copy of the Quarto in the Rosenbach Library in Philadelphia bears the comment after sonnet 154, "What a heap of wretched infidel stuff," with the word "infidel" capitalized and tricked out in fresh ink (Shakespeare 1998b: 69). "Infidel" may refer to Shakespeare's apostasy before the court of love; it may also have specific reference to Moors, who were infamous as sodomites (Hutcheson 2001). A more appreciative response to the sonnets' erotic ambidexterity is registered in Sir John Suckling's play *Brennoralt* (written ca. 1640), in which lines adapted from sonnets 33, 99, 104, and 140 are given to a woman who lives her life disguised as a man (Shakespeare 1998b: 73-4).

In 1640, the very year that Suckling was writing his play, there appeared a revised edition of the sonnets that smoothed over any awkward questions about erotic feelings being addressed to a man. In his preface to *Poems Written by Wil. Shake-speare, Gent.* the editor, John Benson, claims to be giving the reader "some excellent and sweetly composed poems, of Master William Shakespeare, which in themselves appear of the same purity, the author himself then living avouched" (Shakespeare 1640: sig.*2). Now, "purity" may refer to the style Benson attributes to the sonnets—later in the preface he calls them "serene, clear, and elegantly plain" (sig.*2v)—or perhaps to the accuracy of the texts he has edited. To "avouch" purity, however, seems to be making some kind of moral claim. By rearranging the order of the poems from the 1609 Quarto Benson destroys any sense of a narrative that involves a man right fair and a woman colored ill. Generic titles invite the reader to regard the book as the kind of random miscellany that more up-to-date poets like Thomas Carew were publishing in the 1640s (Baker 1998). Thus "Two loves I have" becomes "A Temptation"; "When my love swears she is made of truth" becomes "False belief." Thematically related sonnets get grouped into threes that are printed as new 42-line poems (albeit with the three concluding couplets of each sonnet indented). The sonnets numbered 1, 2, and 3 in the 1609 Quarto, for example, become "Love's cruelty." Interspersed with the 1609 are poems from the 1612 edition of *The Passionate Pilgrim*, including the amorous sonnets on *Venus and Adonis*. Through it all, a conventional male-to female eroticism is insinuated.

Whether Benson set out to censor the homoeroticism in the 1609 Quarto or whether he was simply trying to turn Shakespeare into a "cavalier" poet like Carew is open to question (de Grazia 2000). Serene, clear, and elegantly plain, cavalier poetry typically strikes a politer, more public tone than Shakespeare's anguished, idiosyncratic sonnets (Baker 1998). On three occasions, but just three, Benson supplies titles that specify a female addressee for poems that the 1609 Quarto groups among those addressed to the fair young man; on three other occasions Benson alters the texts of the poems themselves so that "he" becomes "she." At the same time, however, Benson retains intact sonnet 20 ("A woman's face") and gives it a title, "The Exchange," that calls witty attention to Nature's substitution of penis for vagina in lines 9-12. In context, the poem could be read as spoken by Venus, since it is preceded, first by one of the Venus and Adonis sonnets from *The Passionate Pilgrim*, then by one of the Petrarchan sonnets from *Love's Labour's Lost*, "If love make me forsworn." It is followed by a particularly passionate amalgam of three sonnets, "The disconsolation," made up of "Weary with toil, I haste me to my bed," "How can I then return in happy plight," and "When in disgrace with Fortune and men's eyes."

At least one early reader of the 1640 edition was not distracted by Benson's coy title for sonnet 20. In a copy of the book in the Folger Shakespeare Library the reader has provided, as he does for many of the poems, an alternative title: "The m[ist]ress masculine" (Shakespeare 1640: sig. B4). Does this imply that the reader has taken the poem's "master mistress" to be a manly woman? Perhaps. On the other hand, the reader may be echoing Thersites in *Troilus and Cressida* when the straight-talking satirist taunts Patroclus as "Achilles' male varlet," his "masculine whore" (5.1.14, 16). By 1640 the phrase *masculus amor*, "masculine love," had emerged as a code word for male–male eroticism (Cady 1992: 9-40). Benson may have attempted to forestall such sodomitical readings by grouping under the title "The benefits of friendship" three sonnets from the young man group: "When to the sessions of sweet silent thought / I summon up remembrance of things past," "Thy bosom is endearéd with all hearts," and "If thou survive my well-contented day." Worth noting is the fact it was precisely during these years, during the 1630s and 1640s, that increasing prudery about female homoeroticism began to be registered in English translations of Ovid's heroical epistle from Sappho to Phaon. The implication is that writers and readers were newly aware of sexual behavior that had passed without comment fifty years before (Andreadis 2001: 30-7). The very phrase *masculus amor* means that, in the 1620s and 1630s, something new was being recognized that now required

a name. Was that something the very thing that Benson wished not to name?

Benson's edition had staying power. It formed the basis for every reprinting of Shakespeare's sonnets for 126 years. An edition of *Venus and Adonis*, *The Rape of Lucrece*, and Shakespeare's "miscellany poems" printed in 1709 retains Benson's texts and titles, even as it breaks up the amalgamated poems into their three-sonnet constituent parts (Shakespeare 1709: title page). Bernard Lintott's edition of about two years later returns to the 1609 Quarto text but bills the entire sequence as "One hundred and fifty sonnets, all of them in praise of his mistress" (Shakespeare 1998b: 43). Lintott's title page—*A Collection of Poems in Two Volumes . . . Being All the Miscellanies of Mr. William Shakespeare, Which Were Published by Himself in the Year 1609*—stresses the diffuseness of the poems and does not encourage readers to look for any sort of plot, much less one that involves a male beloved. It was just in the years that these editions were being printed that the sex of the bodies one desired was beginning to be taken as an index of one's own gender identity. Randolph Trumbach has pointed out how the rake-figure in comedies of the 1660s, 1670s, 1680s, and 1690s, with his mistress on one arm and his boy-lover on the other, came to be bifurcated: the rake who prefers men and the rake who prefers women (Trumbach 1990: 105-24). In the sixteenth and early seventeenth centuries erotic desire itself was felt to be effeminating, regardless of the sex of the bodies a man might desire. Hearing of Mercutio's murder, Romeo exclaims, "O sweet Juliet, / Thy beauty hath made me effeminate / And in my temper softened valour's steel" (3.1.113-15). By the early eighteenth century it was only men who desired other men who were identified as effeminate (Bray 1982: 81-114; Trumbach 1989: 129-40; 1998: 49-65). In such a culture, to declare "Two loves I have" was to invite criminal charges. The isolation of the man who desires other men made him an easier target not only for satire but for legal prosecution. The eighteenth century witnessed a huge increase in prosecutions for sodomy (Crompton 1985: 12-62).

The National Bard: 1780–1888

Authenticity was the watchword that guided Edmund Malone, the first great Shakespeare scholar, in editing Shakespeare's sonnets in 1780. Malone's edition appeared as a supplement to Samuel Johnson and George Steevens's edition of Shakespeare's plays, published two years earlier. Where editors and publishers since the seventeenth century had been content to reprint the most recent edition of Shakespeare's texts, Johnson, Steevens, and Malone returned to the earliest texts. Malone in particular brought to the project an historian's sense of the cultural distance that separated late eighteenth-century readers from the texts they were reading (de Grazia 1991). When it came to the sonnets, Malone's quest for authenticity ran into problems. The public and conventional cast that Benson and his successors had given to the sonnets disappeared when Malone took the 1609 Quarto as his copy text. Above all, there was the problem of the first 126 sonnets. It is to Malone that readers ever since have owed the conviction that sonnets 1–126 all concern a man and sonnets 127–54 a woman. Steevens, for his part, made no attempt to hide his repugnance at the first group. For Malone's 1780 edition Steevens supplied this note on sonnet 20: "It is impossible to read this fulsome panegyric, addressed to a male object, without an equal mixture of disgust and indignation" (Vickers 1981: 288). To leave no question about what he was talking about, he cited the term "male varlet" from *Troilus and Cressida*.

Malone, in the first edition, seems to have agreed. When Steevens complained, in a note to sonnet 127, that the sonnet form in general was not to his taste, Malone conceded that Shakespeare's sonnets do seem to have two "great defects": "a want of variety, and the majority of them not being directed to a female, to whom alone such ardent expressions of esteem could with propriety be addressed" (Vickers 1981: 294). For the edition of 1783 Malone went further: he tried to explain away these "ardent expressions of esteem" by appealing to history. In reply to Steevens's note on sonnet 20 Malone wrote, "Some part of this indignation might perhaps have been abated if it had been considered that such addresses to men, however indelicate, were customary in our author's time, and neither imported criminality, nor were esteemed indecorous" (Vickers 1981: 551). And to prove the point he cites Shakespeare's use of the word "lover" in contexts that are clearly not sexual. In a note on sonnet 32 Malone repeats his assertion about historical difference and goes on to note that Shakespeare's age "seems to have been very indelicate and gross in many other particulars besides this, but certainly did not think themselves so" (Vickers 1981: 552). That, basically, has been the dodge adopted ever since by critics who feel uneasy about the first 126 sonnets. Steevens remained unconvinced. In his 1793 edition of Shakespeare's plays Steevens spoke for many eighteenth-century readers in

dismissing the sonnets, along with *Venus and Adonis* and *The Rape of Lucrece*, as essentially unreadable works: "We have not reprinted the sonnets etc. of Shakespeare, because the strongest act of Parliament that could be framed, would fail to compel readers into their service; nothwithstanding these miscellaneous poems have derived every possible advantage from the literature and judgement of their only intelligent editor, Mr. Malone" (quoted in Shakespeare 1998b: 75).

With respect to sexuality, Malone's notes on the sonnets display two rather contradictory aims: on the one hand to extirpate suspicions of sodomy by thoroughly historicizing the poems and, on the other, to get at the authentic Shakespeare by reading the poems autobiographically. Thus Malone can seize on lines from one of the sonnets addressed to the young man—"So shall I live, supposing thou art true, / Like a deceived husband" (93.1–2) —and put them forward as proof that the historical William Shakespeare knew sexual jealousy from the inside: "he appears to me to have written more immediately *from the heart* on the subject of jealousy than on any other; and it is therefore not improbable that he might have felt it" (Vickers 1981: 291, emphasis original). When Malone amplified this opinion in the 1783 edition, he insisted that jealousy "is a passion which it is said 'most men who have ever loved have in some degree experienced'" (Vickers 1981: 554). Malone is caught here between his desire that Shakespeare be understood in historically informed terms and his desire that Shakespeare be regarded as just such a man as Malone and his eighteenth-century contemporaries would have him be. Key to both concerns is Shakespeare's imputed sexuality. No better evidence than Malone's notes could be found of Foucault's contention that sexuality emerged as a distinct domain of knowledge in the late eighteenth century. In speculating about Shakespeare's sexuality Steevens and Malone are not just talking about certain physical actions that a man might make with his body; they are talking about a whole way of *being* as a person. They desperately want Shakespeare to share their middle-class values. Among the Shakespearean forgeries that William Henry Ireland concocted in the 1790s was a love-letter from "Willy" to his wife "dearest Anna," enclosing a lock of his hair. "I pray you," the letter goes, "perfume this my poor lock with thy balmy kisses, for then indeed shall kings themselves bow and pay homage to it" (Folger MS W.b.496, fol. 93). Michael Keevak has suggested that Ireland's forgery was a response to imputations of sodomy in Malone's notes to the sonnets

(Keevak 2001: 23-40). Shakespeare's ethical probity was important in the eighteenth century because it was precisely then that Shakespeare was being constructed as "the national poet" of Great Britain (Dobson 1992).

Malone's desire to read Shakespeare's sonnets autobiographically touched off two centuries of speculation about who Master W. H. might have been (William Herbert, Earl of Pembroke? Wriothesley, Henry? William [Shakespeare] Himself?), not to mention the dark lady (Anne Hathaway? Mary Fitton? Emilia Lanyer?) (Schoenbaum 1991: 314-30, 376-7). It also anticipates an early nineteenth-century shift in what readers ever since have understood poetry to be. Well into the eighteenth century poets could still aspire to speak in the public voice that Milton had assumed or, in matters of the heart, with the smooth urbanity that John Benson tried to impose on Shakespeare's sonnets. With the Romantic revolution in style and sensibility came the conviction that the very reason for poetry's existence is to express the writer's private, subjective experience. Shakespeare's sonnets, with their insistent "I," seemed, to Romantic readers, to be just poems. By one count, forms of the first-person singular pronoun—"I," "me," "my," "mine"—constitute the single most frequently recurring word group in Shakespeare's sonnets: 1,062 instances in all (Spevack 1968, 2: 1255–87). Writers of Wordsworth's generation grew up with the eighteenth-century's contempt for the sonnet as an artificial, un-English verse form. By 1827, however, Wordsworth had changed his mind, at least with respect to Shakespeare. In a sonnet called "Scorn not the sonnet" Wordsworth gave Shakespeare's sonnets the highest praise a Romantic poet could give: "With this key / Shakespeare unlocked his heart" (Wordsworth 1981, 2: 635). What nineteenth-century readers found in Shakespeare's heart, especially if they read the sonnets in sequence, did not match their own notions of sexual propriety.

For Wordsworth, the cynical sonnets to the dark lady were the problem; for Coleridge, it was the poems to the young man (Stallybrass 2000: 75–88). In 1803 Coleridge made private notes about the thoughts he had on reading Shakespeare's sonnets, in particular the thoughts he had on reading sonnet 20. He imagines his infant son Hartley reading the poem many years later. He realizes that Hartley will need some knowledge of Greek history and "the Greek lovers." Coleridge instances "that Theban band of brothers over whom Philip, their victor, stood weeping." "This pure love," Coleridge writes to himself, "Shakespeare appears to have felt—to have been in

no way ashamed of it—or even to have suspected that others could have suspected it." And yet, surely, Shakespeare would have realized that "so strong a love would have been more completely a thing of permanence and reality, and have been more blessed by nature and taken under her more especial protection, if this object of his love had been at the same time a possible object of desire—for nature is not soul only" (quoted in Stallybrass 2000: 81–2). Coleridge recognizes sonnet 20 as a poem of homoerotic desire but denies the possibility that such a love could ever really exist.

Thirty years later he came back to the issue in *Table Talk*. Sonnet 20, he decided, was "a purposed blind." The sonnets "could only have come from a man deeply in love, and in love with a woman" (quoted in Stallybrass 2000: 82–3). Reasons for such denial were viscerally immediate: prosecutions for sodomy in England reached an alltime high in the early nineteenth century (Crompton 1985: 12–62). Peter Stallybrass has summarized the dilemma: "Steevens and Malone between them had constructed and passed down an impossible legacy: a legacy from Malone of the *Sonnets* as crucial documents of the interior life of the national bard; a legacy from Steevens of that interior life as one that would destroy the life of the nation" (Stallybrass 2000: 84). Coleridge speaks for many later nineteenth-century readers of the sonnets in knowing what the poems are about and yet willfully *not* knowing what they are about. Henry Hallam, the ardent friend of Tennyson and the subject of "In Memoriam," lamented the "circumstances" of the sonnets' production and concluded, "It is impossible not to wish that Shakespeare had never written them" (quoted in Stallybrass 2000: 83).

Hostage in the Culture Wars: 1889–present
For many readers in the eighteenth and nineteenth centuries, probably for most readers in fact, the sexuality implied by Shakespeare's sonnets was not an issue for the simple reason that those readers encountered the poems as scattered items in anthologies and not as a one-hundred-fifty-four-poem sequence. That remains true for most readers today, the readers of *Shakespeare in Love* included. Alexander Chalmers, who collected the works of major British poets in the early nineteenth century and published them in multivolumed sets, speaks for received opinion about Shakespeare's non-dramatic poems when he almost apologizes for printing all one-hundred-fifty-four sonnets. Chalmers quotes Steevens's judgment about Shakespeare's non-dramatic

poems needing more than an act of parliament to make them popular. "Severe as this may appear," Chalmers concludes, "it only amounts to the general conclusion which modern critics have formed. Still it cannot be denied that there are many scattered beauties among the sonnets" (Chalmers 1810: 15). Looking for "scattered beauties" permitted editors to avoid questions of sexuality altogether.

A major example is the selection of Shakespeare's sonnets printed in Francis Turner Palgrave's *The Golden Treasury of the Best Songs and Lyrical Poems in the English Language*, first published in 1861. Put together with advice from Tennyson, Britain's Poet Laureate from 1850 to 1892, the anthology was frequently reprinted and extended throughout the nineteenth and twentieth centuries. In 2001 the sixth edition was still in print. Palgrave's principles of selection and arrangement for the original edition are specified in the preface. Individual poems have been chosen simply because they constitute "the Best" (Palgrave 1890: vii, capitalization original); within the chronological limits of the anthology's four books, the poems have been arranged "in gradations of feeling or subject." Poems by different authors are interspersed with each other. The result, Palgrave trusts, will be "a certain unity, 'as episodes,' in the noble language of Shelley, 'to that great Poem which all poets, like the co-operating thoughts of one great mind, have built up since the beginning of the world' " (ibid: ix, capitalization original). Within Book One, which covers the years 1525 to 1616, Palgrave notes a progression from the "simplicity" of the earlier poems, through "pastoral fancies and Italian conceits," to "the passionate reality of Shakespeare" (ibid: 417).

With respect to sexuality, Shelley's one great mind turns out to have thoroughly predictable and anodyne thoughts. In the 1890 edition of Palgrave's *Golden Treasury* Book One contains 80 poems, 34 of which are by Shakespeare, a little more than 40 percent of the whole. Palgrave's notion of what constitutes "the Best" can be suggested by a tally of poems by other poets: William Drummond of Hawthornden seven, Thomas Campion six, Sir Philip Sidney five, Ben Jonson zero, John Donne zero. The predominance of Campion, the writer of lute-songs, is telling: fully 14 of the 34 Shakespearean selections are songs from the plays. Of the 20 sonnets that are printed, only 2 come from the group numbered 126 to 154 in the 1609 Quarto. Lifted out of their context in the Quarto, neither sonnet 146 ("Poor soul, center of my sinful earth") nor 148 ("O me! what eyes hath love

put in my head, / Which have no correspondence with true sight!") gives any idea of the tortured relationship between the speaker and the dark lady. Neither poem makes any explicit reference to the lady, her darkness, or her sexual treachery.

What of the fair young man? He, too, is absent. Although 18 sonnets from the group 1–126 are included in *The Golden Treasury*, not a single one refers explicitly to the young man. The context in which the reader is expected to view the sonnets is created by the first six poems in Book One. Thomas Nashe's rollicking lyric "Spring" leads off the collection; then comes a poem by Drummond that has been given the title "A Summons to Love." The first two Shakespeare sonnets, the Quarto's number 64 ("When I have seen by Time's fell hand defaced / The rich proud costs of outworn buried age") and 65 ("Since brass, nor stone, nor boundless sea, / But sad mortality o'ersways their power"), are grouped together under the title "Time and Love." The poems that follow, Marlowe's "Come live with me and be my love" and the anonymous song lyric "Fain would I change that note / To which fond love has charmed me," maintain the amorous cast of the episode but keep it utterly nonspecific. Throughout *The Golden Treasury* generic titles reminiscent of Benson's edition of 1640 maintain this public character. For example, Shakespeare's sonnets 18 ("Shall I compare thee to a summer's day?") and 106 ("When in the chronicle of wasted time / I see descriptions of the fairest wights") are printed successively under the same repeated title: "To his love." The effect is to invite the reader to project his or her own sexuality onto the poems. And that sexuality is plainly assumed to be the sexuality of middle-class Britons of the mid-to-late nineteenth century. "The passionate reality of Shakespeare" turns out to be the quotidian reality of the Victorian reader. The moral cast of the whole affair is suggested by Book One's final episode, which is concerned with death. The last three Shakespeare sonnets in Palgrave's sequence are numbers 71 ("No longer mourn for me when I am dead"), 146 ("Poor soul, center of my sinful earth"), and 66 ("Tir'd with all these, for restful death I cry"). Through it all Palgrave displays an absolute unwillingness to see homoeroticism, even when it is staring him in the face in sonnet 106's celebration of "such a beauty as you master now."

Oscar Wilde changed all that. Alan Sinfield has argued that it was Wilde's arraignment for gross indecency with Lord Alfred Douglas in 1895 that solidified the notion of "the male homosexual" that still has wide currency (Sinfield 1994: 1-24). Before the trial many of Wilde's associates could accept his effeminate manner and his aesthetic interests without ever entertaining the idea that he had pursued sexual relations with other men. After the trial it was hard not to make that connection. We can see that process of identity-formation in Wilde's story "The Portrait of Mr. W. H.," printed in *Blackwood's Magazine* in 1889 and enlarged (though not republished) four years later. Although a piece of fiction, the story amounts to a scholarly case that Master W. H. was a boy actor named Willie Hughes. All the competing theories of Mr. W. H's identity from the eighteenth century and after are considered. The reluctance of commentators since Malone to push the question of Shakespeare's sexuality too far is registered even by the character in the story who concocts the theory, Cyril Graham. The first-person narrator of the story hears about Cyril's theory second hand, from Cyril's friend Erskine. "The problem he pointed out," Erskine tells the narrator,

> was this: Who was that young man of Shakespeare's day who, without being of noble birth or even of noble nature, was addressed by him in terms of such passionate adoration that we can but wonder at the strange worship, and are almost afraid to turn the key that unlocks the mystery of the poet's heart? Who was he whose physical beauty was such that it became the very corner-stone of Shakespeare's art; the very source of Shakespeare's inspiration; the very incarnation of Shakespeare's dreams?
>
> (Wilde 1994: 56)

Cyril goes so far as to pay an artist to forge a portrait of Willie Hughes. Pictured with his right hand resting on an open copy of the sonnets, the boy presents an intriguingl ambiguous appearance with respect to gender:

> He seemed about seventeen years of age, and was of quite extraordinary personal beauty, though evidently somewhat effeminate. Indeed, had it not been for the dress and the closely cropped hair, one would have said that the face, with its dreamy wistful eyes, and its delicate scarlet lips, was the face of a girl.
>
> (Ibid: 50)

The telling word here is the "though" that follows "beauty." The reason for Cyril's dedication to the theory is patent: he is just such a person himself. The uncle who raised him thought him effeminate, and at Eton Cyril turned out to be good at riding and fencing but despised football. "The two things that really gave him pleasure were poetry and acting" (p. 52). When the forgery is exposed, Cyril commits suicide. Erskine, in a letter to the narrator, frames his own death as martyrdom to the cause of Willie Hughes. The narrator's attitude to the theory, and to putting one's life on the line in the theory's defense, is presented with exquisite irony: first he dismisses it, then he embraces it, finally he holds it at an ambivalent distance. As well he might. The deaths of Cyril and Erskine imply that the fantasy of homosexual love could not be tolerated in Victorian society. "I believe there is something fatal about the idea," Erskine confesses to the narrator (p. 62).

Ambivalence is something Wilde himself was not able to maintain when he was brought to trial in 1895. Wilde's public exposure gave a voice and a body to "the male homosexual" that Freud was soon to theorize in *Three Essays on the Theory of Sexuality* (1905) and later writings. That voice and that body Wilde shared with Cyril Graham. Wilde's appearance, according to one of his friends, was anything but vigorous: "fleshly indulgence and laziness, I said to myself, were written all over him . . . He shook hands in a limp way I disliked; his hands were flabby, greasy; his skin looked bilious and dirty" (quoted in Sinfield 1994: 2). In locating sexual identity in the first 126 sonnets Wilde put the dark lady of sonnets 127–54 in a decidedly precarious position. Read in terms of Freud's binary sexual typology, the dark lady sonnets present an identity crisis. If sonnets 1–126 are homosexual poems, and sonnets 127–54 are heterosexual poems, then what about the two together? They can only constitute a pathological middle identity as "bisexual" poems. It is precisely the first seventeen sonnets' advice about marrying that makes the narrator of "The Portrait of Mr. W. H." at first doubt Cyril Graham's theory. He finally decides, however, that what Shakespeare had in mind was a "marriage" between Mr. W. H. and Shakespeare's muse. Actual women have no place in Cyril's scheme. For the both/and of the sonnets in their own day the Freudian theory of sexuality substituted either/or.

Until very recently Freudian theory and middle-class propriety have governed discussions of the sexuality implied by Shakespeare's sonnets. When W. H.

Auden dismissed the possibility of homosexuality in his preface to the 1964 Signet Classics edition, he did so in terms supplied by Sigmund Freud fifty years before. Responding to the eagerness of "the homosexual reader" "to secure our Top-Bard as the patron saint of the Homintern," Auden says of the sonnets that "men and women whose sexual tastes are perfectly normal, but who enjoy and understand poetry, have always been able to read them as expressions of what they understand by the word *love*, without finding the masculine pronoun an obstacle" (Auden 1973: 99–100). "Normal," a medical term, is the operative word here. Auden finds in the sonnets a "Vision of Eros" (capitals original) that transcends the labels "heterosexual" and "homosexual," a vision that "cannot survive an actual sexual relationship" (101). When Auden made that statement, it was still three years until the British parliament would decriminalize consensual sexual relations between adult men and two years more until the Stonewall Riot would set an agenda for gay liberation in America. Nonetheless, Auden was denying the nature of his own private life, not to mention the personal convictions about the sonnets that he shared with friends, as Joseph Pequigney reveals in *Such Is My Love: A Study of Shakespeare's Sonnets* (1985), the first systematic riposte to prevailing evasions of the sexuality question. The reluctant acceptance that Pequigney's book met with can be witnessed in Robert M. Adams's judgment in *The New York Review of Books*: "This is certainly a book that had to be written, that will make impossible any return to the old vague euphemisms, but that, after reading, one will be glad to keep distant in one's memory, if one wants to enjoy the sonnets themselves" (Adams 1986). If scholars and general readers have been more reluctant to acknowledge homoeroticism in Shakespeare's sonnets than in his plays, the reason might be found in the sonnets' insistent "I." Too many readers have too much invested in Shakespeare's speaking "I" to consider that the sexuality of that "I" may not be the same as their own. Too much is at stake, as well, for Western civilization. If Shakespeare is to remain the lynchpin in the canon, he certainly can't be gay. Or even bisexual. Or so the unspoken argument goes.

Since the middle of the twentieth century, however, the drift of academic criticism of Shakespeare's sonnets has been away from the autobiographical preoccupations of Malone and his successors. Each of the critical methodologies that have been adopted since the 1940s gives a different sort of attention to sexuality. New

criticism, with its disciplined focus on the text itself, attempts to dodge the question of sexuality entirely. "William Shakespeare was almost certainly homosexual, bisexual, or heterosexual," Stephen Booth quips. "The sonnets provide no evidence on the matter" (Shakespeare 1977: 548). Helen Vendler's extensive commentary on the sonnets is premised on the assumption that the sonnets are "lyrics" and hence bear only a tangential relationship to social and psychological concerns. "Contemporary emphasis on the participation of literature in a social matrix," she contends, "balks at acknowledging how lyric, though it may refer to the social, remains the genre that directs its *mimesis* toward the performance of the mind in *solitary* speech" (Vendler 1997: 1-2, emphasis original). The "true 'actors' in lyric" are not dramatic persons but words (3). Sonnet 144 in Vendler's reading becomes a poem about a breakdown in the distinction between the words "angel" and "fiend," reflected in the shifting places, left and right, those two words (and their synonyms) occupy in succeeding lines of the sonnet (605–6). By refusing to examine questions of sexuality, New Critics tend, by default, to assume a normative heterosexuality. Vendler will accept that the "controlling motive" of the first 126 sonnets is "sexual infatuation," but she insists that the speaker's infatuation with the young man "is so entirely an infatuation of the eye—which makes a fetish of the beloved's countenance rather than of his entire body—that gazing is this infatuation's chief (and perhaps best and only) form of intercourse" (15).

New historicism, by contrast, has made sexuality a central issue. The emphasis in new historicist studies like Margreta de Grazia's "The Scandal of Shakespeare's Sonnets" and Valerie Traub's "Sex without Issue: Sodomy, Reproduction, and Signification in Shakespeare's Sonnets" falls, not on speculation about Shakespeare's emotional life or on love as a thematic concern, but on the social work that the sonnets were doing with respect to sexuality for the poems' original readers (de Grazia 2000: 89–112; Traub 2000: 431–54). Foucault's insistence that sexuality is a cultural construct invites a reading of Shakespeare's sonnets as part of a social process whereby erotic feelings and certain bodily acts are coordinated toward politically useful ends. Thus in de Grazia's analysis it is unruly desires expressed in the dark lady sonnets, not affection for the man right fair, that threatened the social order of early modern England. Sonnet 144 epitomizes the situation by casting the man right fair as "the better angel" and the woman colored ill as "the worser spirit" (144.4). Deconstructionist readings seize on the fact that the various kinds of social work that the sonnets were performing in 1609 may not have been mutually compatible. Difference-marking is the place where such contradictions are most likely to appear. In my own essay "I, You, He, She, and We: On the Sexual Politics of Shakespeare's Sonnets" I attempt to deconstruct the seeming fixity of all these pronouns, with particular attention to the way "he" is implicated in "she," just as "she" is implicated in "he." Sonnet 144 may try to keep the two separate, but sonnets 106 ("When in the chronicle of wasted time / I see descriptions of the fairest wights") and 133 ("Beshrew that heart that makes my heart to groan / For that deep wound it gives my friend and me") demonstrate how much "he" depends on "she" for its very existence—and how much "I" depends on both (Smith 2000a: 411–29). In sonnet 144 "I" is constituted totally in terms of "he" and "she."

Sexual desire assumes existential importance in Jacques Lacan's psychoanalytical theory. For Freud, identity-formation is a function of sexual development; for Lacan, it is a function of language. Entering into the symbolic order of language, Lacan argues, entails an estrangement from the illusion of wholeness with the world that all human beings know as infants. That lost sense of wholeness becomes, for Lacan, the fundamental object of human desire, not only desire for the interiority of another person's body but desire for the escape that fictions seem to offer from one's own language-boundedness. In a sophisticated and subtle application of Lacan's theory, Joel Fineman has found in Shakespeare's sonnets a tension between the visual and the verbal that constitutes, Fineman believes, the very source of modern subjectivity. In Fineman's reading, sonnet 144 figures as a paradigm of this tension. The poet's image of "one angel in another's hell" (144.12) conflates the man right fair and the lady colored ill, so that both figures undermine the poet's ideals and the adequacy of his language. The dark lady becomes "the material conclusion of an originally immaterial imagination, the loathsome heterosexual object of an ideally homosexual desire" (Fineman 1986: 58). Correspondence is severed between the poet's vision and the words he has to express that vision.

If surviving manuscripts of Shakespeare's sonnets, successive editions, and critical interpretations have anything in common, it is the fact that sexuality is a culturally contingent concept. Hence, readings of

Shakespeare's sonnets since the 1590s inescapably reflect the concerns and the concepts of the people who have been doing the reading across those four centuries and more. As documents in the history of sexuality Shakespeare's sonnets belong to the 1690s, the 1790s, the 1890s, the 1990s, and the 2090s as much as they belong to the 1590s.

Bruce R. Smith

Notes

1. Unless otherwise noted, spelling and orthography in this and other original texts have been modernized.
2. All quotations from Shakespeare's plays are taken from *Complete Works*, ed. Stanley Wells and Gary Taylor (Oxford: Clarendon Press, 1988) and hereafter are cited in the text.
3. A census of surviving manuscripts containing sonnets by Shakespeare is provided in Beal (1980), 1, 2: 452-4.
4. Quotations from the 1609 Quarto of Shakespeare's sonnets are taken from Shakespeare's Sonnets, ed. Stephen Booth (1977) and hereafter are cited in the text.

Works Cited/For Further Study

Adams, R. M. *Review of Joseph Pequigney, Such Is My Love: A Study of Shakespeare's Sonnets. New York Review of Books*, 33, 50. 1986.

Andreadis, H. *Sappho in Early Modern England: Female Same-Sex Literary Erotics 1550–1714*. Chicago, IL: U of Chicago P., 2001.

Auden, W. H. *Forewords and Afterwards*. New York: Random House, 1973.

Baker, D. *Cavalier Shakespeare: The 1640 Poems of John Benson. Studies in Philology*, 95, 2, 152–73, 1998.

Beal, P. *Index of English Literary Manuscripts*, Vol. 1 (1450–1625), Part 2. London: Mansell. Bodleian Library, Oxford U. MS Rawlinson Poetic 152, 1980.

Bray, A. *Homosexuality in Renaissance England*. London: Gay Men's P, 1982.

_____ "Homosexuality and the Signs of Male Friendship in Elizabethan England." *Queering the Renaissance*. ed. J. Goldberg. Durham, NC: Duke UP, 1994.

Cady, J. "Masculine Love," Renaissance Writing, and the "New Invention" of Homosexuality. *Homosexuality in Renaissance and Enlightenment England: Literary Representations in Historical Context*. ed. C. J. Summers. New York: Harrington Park P, 1992.

Chalmers, A., ed. *The Works of the English Poets*, Volume 5. London: Printed for J. Johnson et al, 1810.

Crompton, L. *Byron and Greek Love: Homophobia in 19th-*

Century England. Berkeley: U of California P, 1985.

de Grazia, M. *Shakespeare Verbatim: The Reproduction of Authenticity and the 1790 Apparatus*. Oxford: Clarendon P, 1991.

_____. "The Scandal of Shakespeare's Sonnets." *Shakespeare's Sonnets: Critical Essays*. ed. J. Schiffer. London: Routledge, 2000.

Dobson, M. *The Making of the National Poet*. Oxford: Clarendon P, 1992.

Dubrow, H. "Incertainties Now Crown Themselves Assur'd": The Politics of Plotting Shakespeare's Sonnets. *Shakespeare's Sonnets: Critical Essays*. ed. J. Schiffer.London: Routledge, 2000.

Duncan-Jones, K. Was the 1609 *Shake-speares Sonnets Really Unauthorized? Review of English Studies*, 34, 151–71, 1983.

_____ *Ungentle Shakespeare: Scenes from His Life*. London: Thompson, 2001.

Fineman, J. *Shakespeare's Perjured Eye: The Invention of Poetic Subjectivity in the Sonnets*. Berkeley: U of California P. Folger Shakespeare Library, Washington. MS W.b.496, 1986.

Foucault, M. *The History of Sexuality*, Volume 1: An Introduction. trans. R. Hurley. New York: Random House, 1980.

Hutcheson, G. S. "The Sodomite Moor: Queerness in the Narrative of Reconquista." *Queering the Middle Ages*. ed. G. Burger & S. F. Kruger. Minneapolis: U of Minnesota P, 2001.

Jonson, B. *I. Donaldson*. Oxford: Oxford UP, 1985.

Keevak, M. *Sexual Shakespeare: Forgery, Authorship, Portraiture*. Detroit: Wayne State UP, 2001.

Love, H. *Scribal Publication in Seventeenth-Century England*. Oxford: Clarendon P, 1993.

Marotti, A. *Manuscript, Print, and the English Renaissance Lyric*. Ithaca, NY: Cornell UP, 1995.

Meres, F. *Palladis Tamia, Wit's Treasury* (1598), ed. D. C. Allen. New York: Scholars' Facsimiles and Reprints, 1938.

Palgrave, F. T. *The Golden Treasury of the Best Songs and Lyrical Poems in the English Language*. London: Macmillan, 1890.

Pequigney, J. *Such Is My Love: A Study of Shakespeare's Sonnets*. Chicago, IL: U of Chicago P, 1985.

Schoenbaum, S. *Shakespeare's Lives*. Oxford: Clarendon P, 1991.

Shakespeare, W. (attributed) *The Passionate Pilgrim*, ed. J. Q. Adams. New York: Scribner's, 1939.

Shakespeare, W. *Poems Written by Wil. Shake-speare*, Gent, ed. T. Benson. London: Thomas Cotes, 1640.

_____. *Works*, Volume 7. ed. C. Gildon. London: E. Curll, 1709.

_____. *Shakespeare's Sonnets*. ed. S. Booth. New Haven, CT: Yale UP, 1977.

_____. *Complete Works*. ed. S. Wells and G. Taylor. Oxford: Clarendon P, 1988.

_____. *Shakespeare in Love: The Love Poetry of William Shakespeare*. New York: Hyperion P, 1998.

_____. *Shakespeare's Sonnets*. ed. K. Duncan-Jones. The Arden Shakespeare. London: Thomas Nelson, 1998.

Sinfield, A. *The Wilde Century*. London: Cassell, 1994.

Smith, B. R. "L[o]cating the Sexual Subject." *Alternative Shakespeares*, Vol. 2. ed. T. Hawkes. London: Routledge, 1996.

_____ "I, You, He, She, and We: On the Sexual Politics of Shakespeare's Sonnets." *Shakespeare's Sonnets: Critical Essays*. ed. J. Schiffer London: Routledge, 2000.

_____ *Premodern Sexualities*. Publications of the Modern Languages Association, 115, 3, 318–29, 2000.

Spenser, E. *The Yale Edition of the Shorter Poems of Edmund Spenser*, ed. W. A. Oram et al. New Haven, CT: Yale UP, 1989.

Spevack, M. *A Complete and Systematic Concordance to the Works of Shakespeare*. Hildesheim: Olms, 1968.

Stallybrass, P. "Editing as Cultural Formation: The Sexing of Shakespeare's Sonnets." *Shakespeare's Sonnets: Critical Essays*. ed. J. Schiffer. London: Routledge, 2000.

Taylor, G. *Some Manuscripts of Shakespeare's Sonnets*. Bulletin of the John Rylands. U Library of Manchester, 68, 210–46, 1985.

Traub, V. "Sex Without Issue: Sodomy, Reproduction, and Signification in Shakespeare's Sonnets." *Shakespeare's Sonnets: Critical Essays*. ed. J. Schiffer. London: Routledge, 2000.

Trumbach, R. "The Birth of the Queen: Sodomy and the Emergence of Gender Equality in Modern Culture, 1660–1750." *Hidden from History: Reclaiming the Gay and Lesbian Past*. eds. M.B. Duberman, M. Vicinus & G. Chauncey, Jr. New York: New American Library, 1989.

_____ "Sodomy Transformed: Aristocratic Libertinage, Public Reputation and the Gender Revolution of the 18th Century." *Love Letters between a Certain Late Nobleman and the Famous Mr. Wilson*. ed. M. S. Kimmel. New York: Harrington Park P, 1990.

_____ *Heterosexuality and the Third Gender in Enlightenment London*. Chicago, IL: U of Chicago P, 1998.

Vendler, H. *The Art of Shakespeare's Sonnets*. Cambridge, MA: Harvard UP. 1997.

Vickers, B., ed. *Shakespeare: The Critical Heritage*, Volume 6: 1774–1801. London: Routledge & Kegan Paul, 1981.

Westminster Abbey. MS Dean and Chapter 41.

Wilde, O. *Complete Short Fiction.* ed. I. Small. London: Penguin Books, 1994.

Wordsworth, W. *The Poems.* 2 vols., ed. J. O. Hayden. New Haven, CT: Yale UP, 1981.

Wright, T. *The Passions of the Mind in General.* ed. W. Webster Newbold. New York: Garland, 1988.

Shylock in Love:
Economic Metaphors in Shakespeare's Sonnets

In the shadow of Freud, we have grown accustomed to talking about personality in economic terms. We take it for granted that someone can be "repressed" or "inhibited" without considering that this way of thinking tends to assume that subjective qualities are the products of quantitative relationships—a metaphorical substitution that Freud taught us how to make. But not long before Freud, and in many cultures still, selfhood was thought about principally in terms of "soul" or "spirit." Indeed, for much of the history of Western thought, especially during those eras dominated by Christianity, the self was conceived as a metaphysical essence—a pure form or identity analogous to a Platonic idea or an Aristotelian telos. Such a self could be said to lose itself in matter and find itself in the spirit. It could be adulterated or purified, It could be damned or saved. But it could not be "repressed" or "inhibited." Freud aimed deliberately to shatter such metaphysical conceptions of the self when he wrote, in a world-weary, matter-of-fact tone that belies the epochal antimetaphysical polemic behind his statement: "Happiness, in the reduced sense in which we recognize it as possible, is a problem of the economics of the individual's libido."

Thematically, Shakespeare's sonnets may be described as figurative solutions to the "problem of the economics of the individual's libido." As in Freud, economic terminology is so prevalent in these poems as to make one almost cease to notice its metaphorical status. "Debts" are everywhere "paid" and "repaid." "Accounts" are taken and given. "Losses" and "gains" are tallied. "Riches" are "stored" and "restored." The speaker celebrates his "richness" when the beloved is present and bemoans his "poverty" when the beloved is absent. He waxes full and worries about satiation, and then he wanes empty and feels the sharpness of want. He performs "audits" He takes out "leases" and forfeits them. He speaks of his beloved as "precious." a "treasure," a "gem," and refers to him most often with a pun on "dear," which means both expensive and held in great affection. By my count, no fewer than forty-six, or nearly a third, of the one-hundred-fifty-four poems in the sequence make use of economic metaphors, a rate

of 29.8 percent. In no fewer than eleven of these forty-six, economic metaphors provide the principal figurative structure of the poem as a whole, and they play a significant partial role in fifteen more.

It is relatively easy to locate the roots of Freud's economic way of talking about the psyche. From the beginning and throughout his career, Freud insisted that his approach was scientific, as indeed it was by the somatic standards of the late nineteenth century. The first map of the mind he drew was borrowed from neurological models of a "reflex arc," which attempted to chart the course of every input from its initial reception by the nerves to its eventual release as some form of translated energy. Those impulses whose entire circuit could not be accounted for were believed to be somehow bound or blocked. With this electrical paradigm as a foundation, Freud arrived logically at his conception of repression as the psychic binding of a quantum of erotic energy, and thus at his theory of human happiness as a function of libidinal "economics."

Shakespeare's sources are more difficult to find. Neither in Petrarch nor in any of the contemporary Elizabethan sonnet cycles does one find any comparable use of economic terminology. It does not appear to have been a significant part of the Elizabethan background in the history of ideas as described by Tillyard, nor even of the general Renaissance background as described by Cassirer or Kristeller. These accounts emphasize Platonic and newly revived Aristotelian ideas that seem remote from Shakespeare's frank marketplace concreteness. Another possible source is Christian scripture, where both Paul and Matthew make frequent use of monetary terms. This material does inform a sonnet such as 146— "O soul, the center of my sinful earth"—but the Christian pathos of this poem is exceptional in Shakespeare. Christian scripture does not help to account for the majority of poems where the poet seems more worldly and ironic than pious, more worried about becoming jaded than saving his soul.

How is it then that Shakespeare's imagination turned so readily to economic terms in writing these poems? The answer, like everything involving Shakespeare, has more than one level, in this case three: (1) existential/ psychological, (2) social-historical/economic, and (3) formal/aesthetic. But where Shakespeare embraced all these levels simultaneously in a given turn of phrase, we must be content to follow more slowly behind, taking up each in turn starting with the first.

✽

Two of the finest twentieth-century interpreters of Shakespeare's sonnets have agreed in seeing their economic terminology as principally expressive of a kind of existential anxiety. Northrop Frye connects the language of finance directly to a fear of ever impending oblivion:

> Time is the enemy of all things in the sonnets, the universal devourer that reduces everything to non-existence. Death is only a small part of time's power: what is really terrifying about time is its capacity for annihilation. Hence the financial metaphors of "lease," "audit," and similar bargains with time are closely associated with the more sinister images of "'expense" and "waste." The phrase "wastes of time" in sonnet 12 carries the heaviest possible weight of brooding menace.

In the most sensitive commentary on these metaphors I have found, Thomas Greene suggests that they convey an "anxiety of cosmic and existential economics" that "haunts the sonnets":

> a terrible fear of cosmic destitution overshadows the husbandry of the procreation sonnets, a fear in excess of the announced argument, not easily circumscribed. rendering the bourgeois desire for "store" more urgent, eccentric, and obsessive. In the main body of the sonnets to the young man (18-126), this fear continues to find frequent expression but is also localized much more explicitly in the poet's feelings about himself. The poetry reflects a sense of inner depletion, emptiness, poverty, which the friend is asked or stated to fill up; elsewhere it reflects a nakedness which the friend is asked to clothe. . . . The sense of depletion is . . . radical and . . . diffuse, and it is inseparable from feelings of worthlessness and deprivation.

Frye and Greene both suggest that the sonnets' obsessive adding-up acts mainly as a kind of proleptic defense against the existential certainty of eventual loss. This is a crucial insight, and it provides us with the foundation for a more complete answer. It is indeed a striking feature of Shakespeare's distinctively dark inflection of the Petrarchan tradition that his expressions or love are almost always tinged with an acute consciousness of mortality. Where Dante's love for Beatrice was the first step on an ascent toward contemplation of the eternal, Shakespeare's love for the young man in the sonnets leads to something more like what Heidegger was to call "being towards death." Although the couplets often proclaim transcendence of time, there is far more conviction in the many quiet lines in the quatrains that bespeak felt immersion in human finitude:

> *Like as the waves make towards the pibbled shore,*
> *So do our minutes hasten to their end.*
>
> (Sonnet 60)

> *Since brass, nor stone, nor earth, nor boundless sea*
> *But sad mortality o'ersways their power.*
>
> (Sonnet 65)

> *All yet doth beauty, like a dial hand*
> *teal from his figure, and no pace perceived.*
>
> (Sonnet 104)

For the author of these lines the feeling of love and the feeling of time slipping away are so closely connected as to be almost indistinguishable. There is, as Greene suggests, an element of poignant futility in the poet's use of the language of storage to attempt to arrest a process he knows to be inexorable.

But Greene goes a step too far later in his essay in extrapolating a quasi-gnostic deconstructive vision of cosmic emptiness from Shakespeare's anxieties about time passing. The characteristic strategy of the gnostic consciousness, confronting what it sees as a broken and malevolent universe of death, is escape through ecstasy. Shakespeare's sonnets, for all their genuine angst, are neither ecstatic nor nihilistic. They share with his comedies and romances (and some of the tragedies) an intuition of overarching natural order to which their response is not flight but philosophical submission. To be condemned to live in time is indeed a cruel fate. "We came crying hither," Lear says. But for Shakespeare as for Montaigne, the fact of our finitude requires us to reckon realistically with natural limits. The economic terminology in the sonnets serves as the language of this reckoning, even as it registers a quixotic resistance to loss. If you want to have a son to canyon your name, the poet argues in sonnets 1 through 17, you must pay the price in foregone freedom. If you want the high pleasure of erotic love, he argues throughout, you "buy" it at the high price of pain, jealousy, betrayal, absence, loss. This is why the beloved is "dear." Much is available to us, but, as Emerson would later put it, "nothing is got for nothing." Shakespeare in the sonnets assents to this existential economy as harsh but fair, and in any case inescapable. Like the fools in his plays, he tabulates its balances with rueful equanimity and a degree of mordant relish. Its ambivalent naturalistic fatalism seems to have appealed to him in a way that it did not to the Platonizing Sidney or the Christian and moralizing Spenser.

❧

I don't think one need be a particularly new historicist to believe that Shakespeare's imagination might also have turned to economic language in response to the pressures of his own historical moment. The poet who wrote *The Merchant of Venice* (around the same time that he wrote most of the sonnets) certainly found his era's contradictory attitudes toward money and the ethics of the marketplace a rich vein of ironies. R. H. Tawney, in *Religion and the Rise of Capitalism*, gives the classic account of how the issue of USUIY brought to a focus some of the ethical dilemmas that developed in England as Elizabethan society shifted from a static, fundamentally agrarian, late feudal form of economic organization toward a more dynamic, competitive, capitalist world market, which included colonies overseas. Trading in such a market was necessarily funded by modern forms of finance—loans on interest. But economic expediency ran afoul of traditional moral injunctions against usury—a deeply ingrained Christian teaching more appropriate to the small-scale agrarian economies of the middle ages. "It was precisely the whole conception of a social theory based ultimately on religion that was being discredited," Tawney writes:

> In 1571, the act of 1552, which had prohibited all interest as "a vyce most odyous and detestable, as in dyvers places or the hollie Scripture it is evydent to be seen," had been repealed, after a debate in the House which revealed the revolt of the plain man against the theorists who had triumphed 20 years before, and his determination that they should not

impose on business a utopian morality. Objective economic science was beginning its disillusioning career, in the form of discussions on the rise of prices, the mechanism of the money-market, and the balance of trade, by publicists concerned, not to point a moral, but to analyze forces so productive of profit to those interested in their operation.

Some studies (Fernand Braudel, E. P. Thompson, and a host of social historians) emphasize the slow, piecemeal, many-leveled, and ever incomplete nature of this transition. Still, by Shakespeare's time, a major transformation was underway. The prevailing metaphor of society was shifting from the organic—a body in which all parts cooperated under the hierarchical guidance of the head/ruler—to the mechanical—a self-regulating mechanism that could be dissected, analyzed, primed, and otherwise tinkered with. (The spreading influence of clock time epitomized this change.) And the governing attitude, if not the most common, was shifting from that expressed in Christ's expulsion of the moneylenders from the temple toward the bourgeois urbanity of John Locke or Adam Smith. In short, the value system of liberal individualism was replacing, or at least beginning subtly to undermine, the values of medieval Christian communitarianism.

Such seismic shifts in values invariably leave vivid fault lines in great works of literature, and in *The Merchant of Venice* they are easy enough to locate and trace. The whole play is built upon an opposition between what we might call "embedded" and "disembedded" capitalism. The merchant himself, the noble Antonio, represents the former. He is aggressively engaged in the pursuit of profit; when the action begins he is awaiting the return of three trading ships freighted with valuable merchandise, and we are given to understand that he is a major player in the Venetian stock market. But his ambition for personal gain is embedded within a set of countervailing social and ethical ties. When Bassanio, a wellborn friend beloved since childhood, asks Antonio to overlook his outstanding debts and finance his bid for the hand of Portia, Antonio doesn't hesitate; "if it stand, as you yourself still do,/Within the eye of honor, be assured /My purse, my person, my extremest means/Lie all unlocked to your occasions." "Honor" is the crucial term here, invoking a precapitalist social code to which Antonio gives priority. He distances himself Further from strictly capitalist values by regularly lending money without charging interest, "bringing down the rate of issuance," a frustrated Shylock reports, "here with us in Venice." He observes Christian ethical teaching in habitually coming to the aid of fellow Venetians trapped in debt. And in famously accepting Shylock's condition that he offer a pound of his own flesh as "bond" for a loan for his friend, Antonio gives the affective connotation of the word precedence over its more strictly contractual sense. His readiness to stake his life for an emotional bond lends to the pound of flesh a resonance of sacrificial solidarity that counterbalances its Shylockian significance as a stark image of capitalist commodification.

Shylock, for his part, represents "disembedded" capitalism. Shakespeare did not need Marx or Lukacs to teach him about the tendency of market mechanisms to reduce everything they touched to the status of a commodity. Disembedded from the moral, civic, and familial affiliations that constrain the Christian Antonio, Shylock pushes the logic and language of the marketplace to its reifying extreme. "My ducats and my daughter," he laments repeatedly after finding them both missing, and the two nouns' closeness of' sound is meant to suggest that Shylock does not distinguish very dearly between the value of their respective referents. "Why thou loss upon loss" has a similar effect, giving apparently equal weight to his child and his money. "Let him look to his bond" he warns Salerio repeatedly, referring to Antonio's pound of flesh, bitterly stripping the word "bond" of its (former association with human fellowship. And in insisting on tile literal payment of Antonio's pound of flesh, Shylock enacts the abstract and unfeeling legalistic processes by which unchecked capitalism reduces human subjects to the status of quantifiable and manipulable objects.

Needless to say, the plays a whole endorses Antonio's values over Shylock's. This is crudely obvious on the level of plot, where the legally outwitted moneylender is forced to give up his claim and to convert to Christianity. But it is also reinforced in subtler and more attractive ways throughout the play at the level of linguistic detail. The suitors of Portia, for example, must choose correctly among three caskets, each of which bears a riddling inscription:

> The first, of gold, which this inscription bears,
> "Who chooseth me shall gain what many men desire,"
> The second, silver, which this promise carries,
> "Who chooseth me shall get as much as he deserves,"

> This third, dull lead, with warning all as blunt,
> "Who chooseth me must give and hazard all he hath."

It is not incidental that tile inscription on the correct choice, the third, reverses the acquisitive logic of the first two in favor of a quasi-Christian economy of self-sacrifice. Bassanio gets it right, and Portia reciprocates fittingly by making a similarly unconditional offering:

> Beshrew your eyes!
> They have o'erlooked and divided me;
> One half of me is yours, the other half yours—
> Mine own, I would say, but if mine, then yours,
> And so all yours! O, these naughty times
> Put bars between the owners and their rights!

> You see me, Lord Bassanio, where I stand,
> Such as I am. Though for myself alone
> I would not be ambitious in my wish
> To wish myself much better, yet for you
> I would be trebled twenty times myself,
> A thousand times more fair, ten thousand times more rich,
> That only to stand high in your account,
> I might in virtues, beauties, livings, friends,
> Exceed account.

As in the sonnet, selfhood is represented here in starkly quantitative and legalistic terms-"divide"; "one half of me"; "the other half of me"; "owners and their rights!"; "trebled twenty times myself"'; thousand times more fair, ten thousand times more rich"; "to stand high in your account"; "exceed account." But Portia is not driving a bargain here. She effectively turns the language of commodification against itself to assert a counteraquisitive economy of passionate and total self-giving. This is an ideal kind of gift, which, as Portia later says of mercy in the play's climactic speech, "blesseth him that gives, and him that takes." Jessica and Lorenzo replicate this happier countereconomy in the fifth-act harmonies of their own "unthrift love." And the reciprocal structure of this economy is finally embodied in the concluding folk symbolism of the rings and the associated ritual testing.

In the play as a whole Shakespeare thus sets a formidable array of fundamental western-cultural structures of feeling—Christian (Portia in the "quality of mercy" speech), classical-aristocratic (the friendship of Antonio and Bassanio), folk-traditional (the caskets, the riddles, and the rings), and erotic-romantic (the love between

Portia and Bassanio, Jessica and Lorenzo, and Nerissa and Gratiano)—against a relatively new but increasingly pervasive and powerful western value structure: capitalist individualism. The sheer weight of the opposition suggests that Shakespeare, like many others since, feared that this grasping upstart had the potential to swallow up all its rivals. In response he anticipates later conservative liberals like Burke and Tocqueville in suggesting that the values and practices of the marketplace must be counterbalanced by more deeply rooted religious, civic, folk, familial, artistic, and ethical traditions. Only in this way, Shakespeare implies, might self and society be protected against capitalism's tendency to subordinate all human relations to a crass, corrosive, and alienating instrumentalism.

The Merchant of Venice also participates, of course, in a long European tradition of projecting its anxieties about the morality of the marketplace onto a Jewish scapegoat. The anti-Semitism of the play has been much debated, but I agree with Harold Bloom that it is overt and abhorrent. In this respect as in many others Shakespeare was a product of his culture. The modern tendency to play Shylock as an object of sympathy, is thus, as Bloom suggests, incoherent. Indeed, I would argue that a too-sympathetic Shylock actually obscures those few moments in the play where Shakespeare's enormous verbal momentum carries him briefly beyond his culture's entrenched bias.

In Act I, Shylock originally sets the bond of a pound of flesh as a deliberately unserious condition, a whimsical pretext for making an unprofitable loan by which he hopes only to win some relief from Antonio's habitual hostility. Bassanio greets the offer with suspicion, however, provoking Shylock to mutter as follows: "O father Abram,

what these Christians are,/Whose own hard dealing teaches them suspect / The thoughts of others." And Shylock strikes a similar note at the conclusion of his famous "Hath not a Jew eyes?" speech:

> If you prick us, do we not bleed? If you tickle us, do we not laugh? If you poison us, do we not die? And if you wrong us, shall we not revenge? If we are like you in the rest, we will resemble you in that. If a Jew wrong a Christian, what is his humility? Revenge. If a Christian wrong a Jew, what should his sufferance be by Christian example? Why, revenge. The villainy you teach me I will execute, and it shall go hard but I will better the instruction.

"You're the nigger," James Baldwin liked to tell white audiences. The point was subtle but clear: that which you fear in the demonized other is actually a repressed and alienated part of yourselves; you are yourselves the thing you hate. Shylock makes a similarly reflexive point in the lines above. Early modern Christians projected onto Jews aggressive acquisitive characteristics that they could not accept in themselves: "Your own bard dealing teaches you to suspect the thoughts of others." The repressed qualities then returned with exaggerated force in the grotesque stereotype of the carping, hard-hearted Jew: "The villainy you teach me I will execute, and it shall go hard but I will better the instruction." These great lines only achieve their effect if their speaker is indeed a fully demonic figure. The members of the audience are then forced into the uncomfortable but edifying position of recognizing themselves in an image they instinctively loathe. We are ourselves the demon we have imagined, Shakespeare suggests briefly here to his audience; we are ourselves cold, money-hungry, calculating, controlling, vindictive. And this screw is given an additional exquisite turn by Shylock's brilliant manipulation of the Christian rhetoric of universal brotherhood. Your readiness to exclude and vilify me on the basis that I am not a Christian, he says in effect, only testifies to the hypocrisy of your vaunted Christianity.

The play does not, I think, ultimately sustain this reflexively critical point of view. Perhaps this would be asking too much of an up-and-coming playwright hungry for popular success. Its conventional ending, especially the forced conversion of Shylock, caters predictably to the prejudices of its audience. But it was by no means beyond the young Shakespeare to discover in the midst of his own work a possible perspective, a budding of the moral imagination, the full unfolding of which he was not yet ready to foster.

❧

The economic idiom of the largely contemporaneous sonnets, I would like to suggest, engages on a more conflicted personal level the same anxieties about class and capitalism so vividly addressed by The Merchant of Venice.

Everyone has heard about Shakespeare retiling to the second-biggest house in Stratford. It is illuminating to review the larger acquisitive, upwardly mobile pattern of which this is a pmt. It was not, as the story implies, at the end of his playwriting days around 1613 that

Shakespeare purchased the spacious, five-gabled, three-story), home called "New Place." He bought it in 1597, only seven or eight years after Switching from itinerant acting to writing plays, and only one year after successfully acquiring the family coat of arms his father had initially sought in 1566. Such early successes as *Richard III*, *Romeo and Juliet*, *Richard II*, and *A Midsummer Night's Dream* had already substantially improved Shakespeare's financial position. And he took aggressive steps to strengthen it further. He stockpiled malt during an end-of-century recession; he loaned money on interest and twice, in 1602 and 1608, sued for repayment; he purchased the titles to £440 worth of land in and around Stratford in 1605; and in 1613 he bought a gatehouse in Blackfriars. Most of this activity was made possible by the successful outcome of a "mighty" business risk taken in 1599 by Shakespeare and his fellow actors in the Chamberlain 's Men, when they bought the Globe. Never before, Peter Thomson tells us, did an Elizabethan acting troupe have the daring or the means to buy its own theater. The move bespeaks considerable entrepreneurial energy and acumen. As one or six or seven shareholders and the designated playwright, Shakespeare himself must have contributed significantly in both nerve and capital. And his boldness paid off handsomely; Thomson speculates that the investment must have brought Shakespeare an average or £150 per year over the twelve years of his active involvement, in addition to separate payments for his plays."

It is tempting to stop here and draw a direct positive link between such aggressive involvement in the capitalist marketplace and the economic language of the sonnets. The connection is surely valid up to a point: these poems are full of "accounts" and "leases" and "costs" in part because their author's mind was preoccupied with these sorts of things. He drew on the materials available to him, and like the "dyer's hand" of sonnet 111, his verbal imagination could not help but be "subdued/To what it work[ed] in." Indeed, be often seems to revel in the sharp earthy focus of economic language, as if the rough-and-ready son of a glover were poking fun at the effete courtly decorum of the sonnet sequence convention.

But a tint, as sonnet 111 clearly implies, can also be a taint. At the same time as he was maneuvering shrewdly in the newly emerging and ever fluid world of the literary marketplace, Shakespeare was also seeking acceptance in a conservative aristocratic social sphere that regarded such middle-class grasping with suspicion and

disdain. "It was still ungentlemanly to publish," Muriel Bradbrook reminds us, "and more ungentlemanly to write for the common stages. The world of the theater was the most mixed, the most lacking in decorum of all the fields of letters." Shakespeare had obviously embraced to a considerable extent the aristocratic-hierarchical value system that structured his society: his devotion to Queen Elizabeth has been amply noted; Alvin Keman bas recently detailed his success in attracting and sustaining the patronage of King James 1; and we have seen the privileged position *The Merchant of Venice* gives to traditional aristocratic loyalties. And yet the very means by which Shakespeare had advanced within this system marked him as inferior; from the point of view of elite aristocratic society a popularly successful playwright might just as well have been a Jew. His hands were irrevocably stained, one might say, by the popular commercial milieu in which he labored— "Thence comes it," as he puts it in sonnet 111, "that my name receives a brand." From this vantage point Shakespeare's shift to the purely private and highbrow genre of the sonnet series can be seen as an attempt at sociological self-purification—"a potion of easel," to borrow again from 111, "'gainst strong infection." And to this end the language of economics becomes expressive not of emerging middle-class pride, but of deferential self-abasement. In sonnet 110 the ever protean middle-class dramatist adopts the aristocratic aversion to the marketplace and turns it upon himself: Alas, 'tis true, I have gone here and there,/And made myself a motley to the view/Gor'd my own thoughts, sold cheap what is most dear." And in sonnet 102 he pronounces aristocratic sentence upon his own knack for salesmanship: "That love is merchandiz'd whose rich esteeming/The owner's tongue doth publish everywhere.

On the social-historical level, then, we have a complex, contradictory, ambivalent situation. The author of the sonnets was at once a capitalist and a courtier, part Shylock and part Antonio, an upwardly mobile social climber who had partially internalized a worldview that disdained social mobility. Such conflictedness might well have paralyzed a lesser artist, but a crucial aspect of Shakespeare's enormous capacity as a representer of human reality is a seemingly infinite ability to turn conflict into perspective. He employs a host of different techniques, as Robert Weimann has illustrated, to achieve a kind of multidimensional sociological perspectivism in his plays, including, most prominently, the comically incongruous juxtaposition of plebian and patrician characters—the numerous clowns, rustics, mechanicals, and commoners side by side with the no-less numerous dukes, princes, and kings. The sonnet form does not normally lend itself to such broad Sociological mimesis; as a lyric it is best suited to the rendering of the intimate motions of the inner self. This holds true of Shakespeare's sonnets on the whole, but in many of these poems, nevertheless, the discourse of economics also selves as something of a rhetorical surrogate for the sociological realism of the plays. Terms of trade and finance enabled Shakespeare to smuggle resonances of middle-class social and material life into an aristocratic genre that hitherto had not been especially hospitable to them, and thus to open up a vein of class irony within it. Just as the plebian characters in the plays provide ironic perspective on the noble characters and vice versa, so the economic language of the sonnets provides ironic perspective on both the ratified young man and his déclassé admirer. As with the plays, there is no clear-cut ideological inference to be drawn from this strategy because the irony cuts in different ways in different poems, and often in more than one direction at a time. "There is no social discourse," Helen Vendler writes, "which he does not interrogate and ironize." Shakespeare uses the economic idiom in some sonnets to generate an intricate and ambiguous set of redoubling class ironies reflective of his own conflicted social status.

The distinctive structural complexity of the Shakespearean sonnet mad" it an effective agent of these many-leveled and sometimes conflicting purposes. A Shakespeare sonnet is "multiply ordered," Stephen Booth suggested persuasively thirty years ago; "[it] is organized in a multitude of different coexistent and conflicting patterns—formal, logical, ideological, syntactic, rhythmic and phonetic." The existential and social-historical resonances we have adduced could thus echo subtly, often almost imperceptibly, among what Booth characterizes as a "bewildering" quantity of frames of reference.

And economic language was at the same time particularly well-suited to the necessarily compact rhetorical organization of' the sonnet form. There isn't much time to develop a vocabulary in a sonnet. The poet can't slowly establish a field of resonance as he or she might in writing an ode. To use economic terms not only quickly evoked a response in the reader, but it also quickly set the stage for a variety of possible relationships within the dynamic of the poem. It provided Shakespeare with both a tight, self-contained rhetorical

logic and a good deal of flexibility within that containment—an ideal kind of aesthetic tension. It is revealing from this standpoint that two of the strongest sonnets in the English tradition—Milton's when I consider how my light is spent" and Wordsworth's "The world is too much with us"—are also organized in part by economic metaphors.

To summarize, we can say that Shakespeare's frequent choice of economic metaphors has, like his wit in general, many dimensions. It is a function of what James Joyce called his "myriadmindedness." Words like "dear," "account," "spend," "waste," "profit," "gain," and "loss" are nodal paints from which manifold associations ramify through many spheres of experience, from the purely psychological to the social and historical, all subsumed under a sense that existence in time is itself structured like an economy. The poems gain resonance with each passage of the reader's mind from one of these spheres to the next. And this multivalent rhetorical charge has the further rhetorical utility of concreteness, familiarity, and universal relevance. It will now be necessary to show how all of this is actually at work in some of the poems themselves.

≈

Sonnet 30 is about the economics of unconscious memory:

> When to the sessions of sweet silent thought
> I summon up remembrance or things past,
> I sigh the lack or many a thing I sought,
> And with old woes new wail my dear time's waste.
> Then can I drown an eye (unus'd to flow)
> For precious friends hid in death's dateless night,
> And weep afresh love's long since cancelled woe,
> And moan tit' expense of many a vanished sight.
> Then can I grieve at grievances foregone.
> And heavily from woe to woe tell o'er
> The sad account of fore-bemoaned moan,
> Which I new pay as if not paid before.
> > But if the while I think on thee, dear friend,
> > All losses are restored, and sorrows end.

How gracefully this beautiful poem integrates the economics of unconscious memory into the aesthetics of the sonnet! An experience of psychic repetition (grief) is so fluently worked into a repetitive form as to make the form renew the experience and the experience renew the form. Repetition is a fundamental part of the psychic structure of grief—one goes back into time and relives the pain of loss many times. Repetition is also essential to any aesthetic being, but it can soon become too safe. Both people and poems run the risk of losing intensity of feeling if the patterns of their existence are too mechanically predictable. Sonnets, because their form is so decisively preordained, are particularly susceptible. In this poem both the formal and the existential problems are resolved as repetition is experienced as surprise. A paradoxical ideal of lyric is achieved as an old feeling, "unus'd to flow," is released and hits the writer and the reader with the force of a new one—"as if not paid before." To "weep afresh" is still painful, but I think the poet is here as glad of the renewal of feeling as he is sad about the losses. That is why both the second and third quatrains begin with the phrase "Then can I"; Shakespeare wants to emphasize the enabling release achieved by grieving memory—the healthiness, Freud would say, of "working through."

"No tears in the writer, no tears in the reader. No surprise for the writer, no surprise for the reader. For me, the initial delight is in the surprise of remembering something I didn't know I knew." Robert Frost suggests that pain, memory, and surprise, the substance of sonnet 30, are at the heart of the aesthetic experience of lyric poetry. Like ritual, the poem as a "session," as a repeated form of experience, performs a kind of psychoheuristic function by providing an opportunity for the unconscious, unorganized feelings of the past to come into a controlled presence where writer and reader share their renewed life. Whether the remembered feelings are of tears or delight, or a subtle mixture of painful delight at being once again enabled to shed tears, tile poem renews access to them by finding an order at once strict enough to contain them and free enough not to block their spontaneity—"as if," to quote Wallace Stevens, "the language suddenly, ,with ease/Said things it had laboriously spoken." The very familiarity of the sonnet form lulls dangerously strong forces, "unus'd to flow," into its metrical nets. There is then a moment of surprise as the poet comes upon the buried life of his own emotions—"as if not paid before" or "something I didn't know I knew." A lyric is successful when it enables a fresh repetition rather than forcing a stale one; in this respect sonnet 30 is exemplary. Its economy, unlike that of the young man in the first seventeen sonnets, is not self-consuming, but self-renewing.

The renewal of "flow" seems all the more surprising

when one notices the intricacy of this poem's organization. An economic logic is sustained throughout: "sessions," which bas the important connotation of repeated sittings, also has a legal-economic connotation that suggests a calling to account—for the crimes, as it were, of "lack" and "waste." In the second quatrain, lost friends are said to be "precious," and their vanishing is said to be an "expense" for which woe had once been "cancelled"—like a debt. The entire economy of the poem is then stated in brief in the legal-economic pun of the first line of the third quatrain—"Then can I grieve at grievances foregone." Booth and the editors of the Riverside Shakespeare both gloss "foregone" as simply "past," but it seems to me better read as "passed up" in the sense of having avoided it by choosing another option. This would go along with the drowning of an eye unus'd to flow (line 5) to convey the sense that the poet is now grieving particularly heavily because he neglected to do so in the past. To grieve at grievances foregone is to pay double for complaints whose initial date for payment had been missed. The pain now returns with twice its original force, like the Hood of tears, as the long "o's" of lines 10 and 11 enact an extended and repeated moaning—"And heavily from woe to woe tell o'er/ The sad account fore-bemoaned moan." To "tell o'er/ The sad account" is both to repeat the story and to tally the debt, combining literary (narrative) and economic (counting) activity yet again. The debt is at last paid in the crucial line 12—which conveys both the freshness of the pang and its familiarity—"Which I new pay as if not paid before."

The economic organization of the psychological narrative is complemented by precisely balanced temporality. Oldness and newness are set next to each other wherever possible, as is appropriate to a poem about the renewed experience of an ancient feeling. The "summoning" (as if calling in a delinquent debtor) does bring the past decisively into the present as thereafter every major clause contains a present-tense verb of feeling—"sigh," "new wail," "weep afresh," "moan," "grieve," "tell," and "pay"—in connection to a noun placed in the past—"many a thing I sought," "time's waste," "friends hid," "cancelled woe," "vanished sight," "grievances foregone," and "fore-bemoaned moan." The couplet then interrupts these extended reveries (twelve lines) with an abrupt "but" to bring us back into the present. The sessions are brought to a close as grievances are redressed—"loses are restored"—and griefs are healed—"sorrows end." The couplet is made particularly effective by virtue of how aptly the phrase "losses are restored" summarizes and compensates for the pain of absence, which the poem had lamented. And with "sorrows end" as the final note, one feels a narrative resolution in a sense of relief from pain that has been once again lived through and endured.

These two organizing principles, temporal and economic, evoke a rigorously organized psyche. Once summoned, the repetitions seem to proceed on their own, as if generated by a self-governing mechanism whose laws unfold of their own accord. The poet seems to be somewhat at the mercy of these reveries, falling heavily from "woe" to "woe," as if the "sweetness" of these sessions were the pleasure of a somewhat masochistic ritual. And yet there is also a complementary motion of extreme fluidity of cadence and sound—sibilant consonants and long vowels—which is associated with the flow of tears suggested in the poem's imagery. The rigorous organization would seem to preclude such fluidity. Yet here thee poem's achieved aesthetic paradox aligns itself with its existential insight. The rules of psychological experience, like tile rules of sonnet-making, are firmly economic. You have to pay. But once you have paid, by hitting all the formal stops, the reward is freedom or fluidity within the terms of the system.

❧

Sonnet 87 also masterfully exploits the formal resources of the sonnet to register an experience of loss. But in this case the focus is intersubjective rather than strictly introspective:

> Farewell, thou art too dear for my possessing,
> And like enough thou know thy estimate;
> The charter of' thy worth gives thee releasing:
> My bonds in thee are all determinate.
> For how do I hold thee but by thy granting,
> And for that riches where is my deserving?
> The cause of this fair gift in me is wanting,
> And so my patent back again is swerving.
> Thy self thou gav'st, thy own worth then not knowing,
> Or me, to whom thou gav'st it, else mistaking;
> So thy great gift, upon misprision growing,
> Comes home again, on better judgement making.
>   Thus have I had thee as a dream doth flatter,
>   In sleep a king, but waking no such matter.

Helen Venedler has beautifully described the verbal pattern of this poem as itself a kind of "back again swerving" (line 8)—"a current coursing back and forth between two poles labeled 'speaker' and 'young man.'" She charts this current with characteristic thoroughness and precision as it moves back and forth between "I," "my," and "me" phrases on the one hand and "thou," "thy," "thee," and "thine" phrases on the other. She notes the five "melancholy repetition(s)" of forms of the word "gift," and suggests that the swerving pattern enacts the painful course of love given and withdrawn. I would only add that there is a class resonance to this polarized erotic structure. It is not incidental that the young man is the one who does all the "giving," that it is his "charter of worth," that "gives . . . releasing" in line 3, that he is the explicit subject of the verb "granting" in line 5 and the verb "gav'st" in lines 9 and 10, and that he is the giver of the "gift" in lines 7 and 11. Nor is it incidental that the speaker is by contrast principally a "possess[or]" (line 1) of "bonds" (line 4), and a "holder" (line 5) of a "patent" (line 8). Like Antonio in *The Merchant of Venice*, the young man remains embedded within an aristocratic gift economy—a network of services and hospitalities understood (mystifyingly) to be freely offered and freely reciprocated among recognized members of an elite class: from a position of secure social "worth" he "grants" (line 5), "gives" (lines 7, 9, 10, 11), and "judges" (line 12). Like Shylock, by contrast, the speaker belongs to a middle-class capitalist economy—a competitive system of exchange for profit driven, in theory at least, by individual self-interest rather than by social obligation. From a comparatively "[un]deserving" (line 6) social position, he does not give, but rather anxiously "possesses" (line 1), "hold[ing]" both "bonds" (line 4) and "patent[s]" (line 8). The abstract legalistic senses of "hold" and "bond" are played off against their more intimate physical and affective connotations. The speaker's rigid and reined clutching is thus contrasted poignantly with the young man's gracious generosity, registering at the level of the nerves a social no less than an emotional gulf.

Class difference is thus charged in this sonnet with the full emotional weight of separation and loss. The poem's touching plangency is derived in part from its successful evocation of what we might call the pathos of social distance. The first quatrain is particularly effective in this regard, but in essence all three quatrains say the same thing in different ways: "you were always too good for me; it was just a matter of time until you realized it." This is not an original or unusual sentiment for a self-doubting lover rejected by a social superior, but what is interesting about Shakespeare's version in these quatrains is its almost total absence of resentment. A democratically minded twenty-first-century reader is inclined to hear some imputation of arrogance in phrases such as "like enough thou know'st thy estimate" or "the charter of thy worth," but the poem never follows through on these intimations. Instead the string of feminine endings—"possessing," "releasing," "granting," "deserving," etc.—enacts thee speaker's acquiescence to the loss and, more remarkably, to the social appropriateness and inevitability of the loss. Shakespeare again seems to have fully, if ruefully, internalized the hierarchical value system of his society. There is palpable sadness and longing in the elongated pace of these lines, but little anger or resistance.

And whatever resistance might have remained is decisively squelched by the couplet: "Thus have I had thee as a dream doth flatter, /In sleep a king, but waking no such matter." Vendler points out that "king" here is anticipated by "mista*king*" at the end of line 10 and "ma*king*" at the end of line 12, and echoed in line 14 by "wa*king*." She notes that these endings are all phonetically close to "aching." We might synthesize these observations and read the conclusion as a playful but nonetheless decisive assertion of a sociological reality principle: to be *awake* is to not make the *mistake* of thin*king* you are a *king*. "King" stands in metonymically for the aristocracy per se, and the sobering message is clear for our speaker. To imagine kings, or even to entertain them as a playwright, does not entitle you to bond with them or their like as a lover. To be *awake* in this hierarchical world is to accept the *ache* of exclusion. The same conservative part of Shakespeare that wrote the conversion of Shylock wrote these lines. In both cases the reality principle is completely identified with extant social norms, ethno-religious in *The Merchant of Venice* and aristocratic-hierarchical here in the sonnet, and in both cases the reality principle rather starkly prevails.

و

The realism of sonnet 146 is more difficult to assess. Its unabashedly Christian economics make it an anomaly among the sonnets:

> *Poor soul, the center of my sinful earth,*
> *[. . .] these rebel powers that thee array,*

> *Why dost thou pine within and suffer dearth,*
> *Painting thy outward walls so costly gay?*
> *Why so large cost, having so short a lease,*
> *Does thou upon thy fading mansion spend?*
> *Shall worms, inheritors of this excess,*
> *Eat up thy charge? Is this thy body's end?*
> *Then, soul, live thou upon thy servant's loss,*
> *And let that pine to aggravate thy store:*
> *Buy terms divine in selling hours of dross;*
> *Within be fed, without be rich no more.*
>   *So shall thou feed on death, that feeds on men,*
>   *And death once dead, there's no more dying then.*

The gravity of this poem's tone is distinctive in a series of poems that are usually more urbane. Here the very same economic metaphors that were used somewhat wearily to calculate the expense of worldly pleasure are used to make an almost Miltonic argument in favor of spiritual inwardness. Indeed, it is the perfect blending of spirituality and economy in the poem's rhetoric that makes its argument seem so focused and intent. The crucial conceptual link at work in the first two quatrains is based, I think, on the notion of vanity. Vanity is both a sin in Christian moral terms—an excessive attention to appearances—and a mistake in economic terms—a useless expenditure. The poet accuses himself of both errors at once in the first quatrain by implying that the poverty of his poor soul is connected adversely to the "costly" array of his physical appearance. Whether "'array" means clothes ill particular or external matters generally, the plangency of "pine" suggests that the gaiety and richness of the surface is hollow because it belies an inward sense of lack—"suffering dearth." The second quatrain then develops the argument that vanity is a bad investment by pointing out that the "body" upon which such attention is now being lavished is growing old. Why spend so much on a "fading mansion"? The lease is short—which is to say that you only have possession of the building for a short while, and the inheritors, in any case, will only be the "worms." With the combined resonances of "pine," "walls," "fading mansion," and "worms," one is given a sense that the wood of this house, though brightly and freshly painted, is rotting.

"Is this thy body's end?/Then, soul, live thou upon thy servant's loss"—the poem moves into the third quatrain by summarizing the argument of the first two in a rhetorical question, and then, in conventional sonnet style, offering a proposed resolution to the problem the first two had posed. Its solution, not surprisingly, is economic; it precisely reverses the terms of the initial economic structure—benefactor becomes victim and vice versa. Indeed, the structure here is as rigorously economic as ever; nothing is got for nothing in the sense that the cost of outward gaiety was inward dearth, and now the cost of holiness, and presumably eternal life, is said to be the body's loss—"buy terms divine in selling hours of dross." Freud himself, not to mention his precursor Jonathan Swift, would have been content with a description of spirituality as "soul living upon its servant's loss." Remorse, the emotion which prompts the powerful spiritual turn of this poem, often expresses itself in economic terms in Shakespeare. One thinks of "the expense of spirit in a waste of shame" (sonnet 129) or a plaintive line from *Richard II* that cuts close to the deep feeling of this poem—"I have wasted time, and now doth time waste me."

The metaphysical word "soul" is used twice in this poem, and the couplet does suggest some kind of eternal life as a reward for the rejection of vanity. This should be hard to account for in the context of an essay that has suggested that Shakespeare's way of talking about the self is antimetaphysical in a way that anticipates Freud. But "soul" is modified the first time by the adjective "poor," which suggests a financial no less than spiritual condition, and in both cases in connection with verbs of basic economic activity—"having . . . a lease," "spending," "buying," and "selling." The almost crude simplicity of its economic activity seems to rub somewhat against the exalted mysteriousness of the word "soul." And the couplet, with its central image of "feeding on death," gives an unusually carnal, almost grotesque, feel to the reward for successful spiritual bargaining. One feels that these are the terms the converted Shylock might use if forced to defend his new faith. Is Shakespeare trying to debase the Christian myth he is using here? The intensity or the poem's tone will not permit us to draw this conclusion, but it would be consistent with Shakespeare's usual poetic practice to express at once a sincere feeling and to qualify that expression by a more or less subtly ironic inflection. The sonnets are masterful in their ability to express shaded, ambivalent attitudes.

However fleetingly the poet might have held it, I do think that sonnet 146 expresses a sincere Christian feeling, in the spirit of Matt. 6: 19-20 ("Lay not up for yourselves treasures upon earth, where moth and rust doth corrupt, and where thieves break through and steal: But lay up for yourselves treasures in heaven"). But I also think Shakespeare uses this passage of Matthew because

its language is so ironically consistent with his own naturalist economic idiom as we have seen it operating in other, less pious poems. The success of this poem, like that of many sonnets, comes from how the resonances of different discourses—in this case economic, religious, and psychological—are brought together and made to cooperate in a poetic discourse of the poet's own devising. But Shakespeare rarely forces the different terms he uses together to such an extent that the associations of one can't provide an ironic perspective on the claims of another. In the phrase "buy terms divine" he has managed at once to express sincere religious longing, real psychic pain (in the rhyme of "divine" with "pine"), and to pack in every available irony implicit in the idea that salvation—terms divine" implying the vocal blessing of God, a legal agreement, and the limitless expanse of time that could be his reward—can be so frankly bought. The poem could not have pleased either strict Protestants, who would have seen it as anti-predestinarian, or strict Catholics, who might have thought it was mocking the sale of indulgences. But it satisfies the characteristic Shakespearean demand on language, which Muriel Bradbrook captures negatively—"Shakespeare had in fact always found difficulty in saying only one thing at a time."

&

"It is wrong to call anyone a materialist," Robert Frost suggests, "simply because he attempts to say spirit in terms of matter, as if that were a sin. . . . It is the height of poetry, the height of all thinking, the height of poetic thinking, that attempt to say matter in terms of spirit and spirit in terms of matter." I have not meant to suggest that Shakespeare was a materialist, though fewer people now think that is a sin, by pointing out that he would have been sensitive to the newly materialistic terms by which people's imaginations, including his own, were being shaped in Elizabethan England. Part of the richness of Shakespeare's economic idiom in the sonnets comes from a sense that it is not taken for granted. The irony of saying "spirit" so frankly in terms of financial matters seems to have been freshly available to Shakespeare, and he made clever use of it. He also made clever use of economic matter's rare value to what Frost calls "poetic thinking"—its capacity to provide meaningful and affecting analogies to the patterns and structures of emotional experience. In doing so he contributed an important chapter to the long western-cultural story of what Marc Shell has called "thought's internalization of economic form." If this move seems somewhat disenchanting in the same way that Freud's insistence on the economic origins of happiness does, perhaps it also has the compensating Freudian virtues of a certain wry and tough-minded wisdom.

Neal Dolan

Hoarding the Treasure and Squandering the Truth: Giving and Possessing in Shakespeare's Sonnets to the Young Man

I

Not marble nor the gilded monuments
Of princes shall outlive this pow'rful rhyme,
But you shall shine more bright in these contents
Than unswept stone, besmeared with sluttish time.[1]

The speaker of the *Sonnets* promises his addressee immortality, an everlasting fame for his gifts of beauty and virtue, achieved via the speaker's gift for poetry and conferred through the gift of the poem he produces. Of course, the most immediate problem with this promise is that the *Sonnets* never actually name the "young man" to whom the majority are addressed, and therefore, the only personality to "shine more bright in these contents" of the poems is the poet himself. So it is that the *Sonnets* revert to the possession of their author, and the gift which they promise their subject and addressee is, in fact, ac-corded to Shakespeare himself. Though the poems became public property upon publication, they remain inseparable from Shakespeare; and, though they have been given as love gifts throughout time, they belong to nobody and continue to be given and received over and over again.

The relationships depicted in the *Sonnets* revolve around exchanges, or at least, attempted exchanges: of love, of favor, of praise. The break-down of relationships and the increase of antagonism and rivalry, which the *Sonnets* manifest as they progress, are often described in terms of failed, aborted, or unfair (unequal or inappropriate) exchange of gifts or love. This article will consider the nature of the poet-speaker's struggle to confer his gift upon a man of superior social status, from whom he desires reciprocation of some, perhaps many, kinds.[2] In addressing the problematic notions of valuation, ownership, and obligation in the sequence, it will also suggest that the *Sonnets* contemplate impossibilities: the impossibility of *true* representation, and the impossibility of *pure* giving.

In one of the most recent articles to apply gift

theory to Renaissance scholarship, Georgianna Ziegler remarks: "The giver of a book, who might be its 'author' or just as likely its translator, printer, or publisher, expected to be rewarded for his or her gift; in other words, the original recipient in turn became a giver, providing money, lodging, or political protection to the presenter of the book."[3] As the poem or book passes into the public realm, the "author" loses control over its circulation and interpretation, and, to a certain extent, his gift loses potency as it advances from coterie to common readers. In the marketplace, poetry (a text) is public property, and the intimate exchange between author and reader, poet and patron, is lost. The "gift books" which Ziegler examines gain value from being handmade, personally dedicated, and publicly unavailable. By striking contrast, the "increase" through copying metaphor, which Shakespeare applies to the procreation sonnets, defends the notion of the published text and implies that good material is wasted in the rejection of its reproduction.[4] Drawing attention to the paradoxical status of the *Sonnets* as both public property and private monuments, Arthur F. Marotti has examined the sequence as a commodity passing between one owner and another, yet never wholly detached from the claims of the poet or the addressee. In "Shakespeare's Sonnets as Literary Property" he highlights the importance of the patron-client relationship, with all its tensions and political implications, to the questions which modern criticism has posed about the bond between the poet-speaker and the young man of the *Sonnets*.[5] Though "the poems to the young man constantly refer to themselves as commodities," the poet re-iterates the "value of his poems as objects worthy of being presented as gifts to a patron."[6] Of course, in the context of the patronage relation-ship, gifts and commodities were difficult to separate. Depending on the balance of the two conflicting principles, the poet's gift could appear less like a gift between lovers and more like "a request for a couple of quid," as John Barrell has noted.[7]

Jacques Derrida has argued that if the gift appears

as a gift, it automatically participates in an economy of exchange, and when it is "ex-changed" then it is not "given" by nature of its expectation or receipt of a return: "From the moment the gift would appear as gift, as such, as what it is, in its phenomenon, its sense and essence, it would be engaged in a symbolic, sacrificial, or economic structure that would annul the gift in the ritual circle of debt."[8] That conundrum of giving is repeatedly addressed in the *Sonnets*; in fact, the speaker often ties him-self in knots trying to represent his poetic gift as "true" (disinterested) and the gifts of other poets as false (self-interested), "painted," or stolen (*Sonnets* 79-84). The status of the poem, which supposedly fortifies the young man's image against "this bloody tyrant Time," fluctuates throughout the sequence, along with the speaker's respect for the young man and the solidarity of their bond. From a celebration of the young man's beauty, to a persuasive device designed to induce the youth to marry and reproduce, from a lover's gift, to something which the young man discards in favor of a "fresher stamp," from a powerful weapon against time, to the impotent gift which causes a civil war within the poet, the gift is constantly in flux and repeatedly re-valued.

At times the gift of poetry evokes a sense of partnership between the donor and its recipient; more often, however, it reveals the disparity between the two-the impossibility of "friendship" or "love" other than that between a patron and his client, a relationship which itself remained under constant threat of revision. "Gifts" in the *Sonnets*, whether they relate to the young man's beauty, to the poet-speaker's praise, or to the immortality of the poetic representation, are unstable concepts; their worthiness is repeatedly revised according to their relation to each other and to the "truth." The problems raised by the *Sonnets* about giving, and, in particular, about giving praise in the hope of a re-ward, relate to the economic context of the period. In that context, the poet was stranded between total dependence upon patronage rewards and the financial independence which the marketplace of poetry might bring him in the future.[9]

II

In the first instance the poet-speaker's "gift" appears as a commissioned plea with a specific purpose—to persuade the young man to marry (give himself) and reproduce, in order to protect his beauty and virtue (gifts) against the ravages of time. The young man's refusal to give causes the poet-speaker to recapitulate his argument in numerous ways, yet the purpose of his persuasion remains constant and relates to a problem with the gift theory employed by the speaker. If the young man should give himself away for his own benefit, does the argument of the procreation sonnets rely upon the principles of self-interested profit or disinterested liberality? The question posed by Joel Fineman, "does the poet. . . identify himself with the self-centered gift or with the self-less giving?" is pivotal to the impact of the procreation sonnets, which depend upon both ideologies despite the obvious clash between their respective ideals."[10] The poet-speaker urges the young man to reproduce his image on the grounds that failure to do so would constitute the refusal to "use" his beauty correctly, thereby hoarding valuable resources only to waste them. However, while sonnet 4 extends this criticism of the youth's "Profitless" approach, it conversely promotes an ideal of liberality essentially opposed to such self-interested gain: Nature's bequest gives nothing, but doth lend, And being frank she lends to those are free: Then, beauteous niggard, why dost thou abuse The bounteous largess given thee to give?

Evoking the Senecan ideal of grace as giving, receiving, and returning, the poet-speaker castigates the young man for holding onto what was given to him only for him to give away again, in order that he might "increase" the original gift from nature.[11] Nonetheless, this sentiment of honorable and selfless giving is undercut by the sonnet's application of financial imagery and terminology, implying that the youth lacks, not necessarily honor in gift practice, but rather foresight in his investment strategy. The accusation that the young man squanders his gifts clashes with the accusation that he hoards or refuses to spend his gifts; though in both senses his "use" is wasteful. If the young man does not "treasure some place / With beauty's treasure ere it be self-killed," then he will become "death's conquest," and beauty will be lost rather than invested at credit or increased by giving. If, on the other hand, the young man should agree to "print more" of himself, then he will not merely duplicate his own image, but conquer time by living "drawn by . . . [his] own sweet skill." The correct "use" of the young man's beauty is hereby connected with the benefit of immortality, a connection which Lars Engle identifies when he sees 'Shakespeare as having taken up in the sonnets the issue of how to understand permanence in economic terms."[12]

Time is infinite, but the time given to each man is

not: one can take one's time, find the time, give some-body time off, even save time, yet time itself cannot be extended, and certainly not in Shakespeare's day. Time is not a consumable in the same way that the gift is not consumed when it is given.[13] Similarly, the ideal of giv-ing which is expressed in the assurance that "To give away yourself keeps yourself still" mimics the paradox of the promised triumph over time—"then you were / Your self again after yourself's decease." The prob-lem with this triumph lies in the copying, for when the young man gives himself, he keeps himself still because his son will be a mere "copy" in the same way that his representation in verse will be a copy of his image. If the economy of the gift is complicated by the economic discourse employed in the *Sonnets*, the idea of truthful representations is complicated by an ongoing debate dating back to Aristotle's theory of mimesis.[14] The poet-speaker repeatedly addresses the problem that art can-not render a perfect "copy" of the young man, and this observation impinges upon his promise to immortalize his beloved in verse. With this in mind, the young man is encouraged to "some other give" the "sweet semblance" of his beauty in order to achieve an "increase," a "copy" of himself to persist beyond the natural span of his life.

The proposed multiplication of the young man's physical form associates poet and patron with the mor-ally dubious industry of printing and copying, a stark contrast to conventional attempts by sonneteers to dis-tance themselves and their texts from the marketplace of print. Samuel Daniel's frequently quoted dedication to *Delia* (1592) demonstrates the perceived threat of the publication of the text for the value of the poet's "gift" to his patron:

> although I rather desired to keep in the priuate
> passions of my youth, from the multitude, as things
> vtterd to my selfe, and consecrated to silence:
> yet seeing I was betraide by the indiscretion of
> a greedie Printer, and had some of my secrets
> bewraide to the world, vncorrected . . . I am forced
> to publish that which I neuer ment . . . if my lines,
> heereafter better laboured, shall purchase grace in
> the world, they must remaine the monuments of
> your honourable fauour and recorde the zealous
> duetie of mee, who am vowed to your honour in all
> obseruancy for euer.[15]

Daniel's patron, Mary, countess of Pembroke, is the recipient of the son-nets, which remain "monuments"

of her "honourable fauour" even as they appear "rawly in publique." The clash between the poem as gift and as commodity is not easily reconciled, but Daniel does not return to this problem in the way that Shakespeare does in the *Sonnets*, perhaps because "Delia" does not occupy the position of patron in the same way that the young man does. While counsel against waste is com-mon in Petrarchan sequences, principally featured in the carpe diem-style address to the mistress, the beloved is not urged to "use" beauty as a weapon against decay. In focusing upon the use of the young man's gifts, Shake-speare draws the representation of the beloved into a con-temporary debate about the morality of the profit-able use of objects previously conceived of as "gifts." Usury—the use of money for increase—was a conten-tious issue in the late sixteenth century, and critics fo-cusing specifically upon the procreation sonnets have paid great attention to Shakespeare's employment of the images and language associated with the practice.[16] The historical context of usury has already been explored in relation to the *Sonnets*, and a number of critics have of-fered interpretations of Shakespeare's incorporation of the controversial practice of money-lending at interest within these early sonnets. What is specifically relevant to my focus, however, is the effect that references to explicitly capitalist practices—much debated and fre-quently opposed in Elizabethan society—have upon the discourse of exchange within the sequence. As Peter C. Herman has remarked, Shakespeare's association of the "means of saving the line from extinction with precisely the economic practice that many blamed for the aris-tocracy's decay" makes the poet-speaker's persuasion of the young man appear disjointed and rather ambiguous in design.[17]

The economy proposed in the procreation sonnets is significant for its failure, as Herman has observed, yet it is also significant that it concludes by instating the poem—the poet's gift—as the method of preserving the young man, preferred to the young man's own giving and receiving of a child.[18] That substitution of poetry for offspring invites the comparison of the child/gift with the poem/gift, and also of the role of the father with the role of the patron. It is significant, perhaps, that the *Son-nets* by no means demonstrate the success of either form of reproduction, nor the accomplishment of the young man in either role.[19] Herman sees Shakespeare's *Son-nets* as an "interrogation of capitalism" which demon-strates "what ensues when commodification infects the poetry of praise."[20] I would suggest that the stance of the sequence is less one-sided, and it manifests the problems of a society struggling to come to terms with a rapid and unprecedented revision of its methods of exchange and valuation. The young man's refusal to give in the opening sonnets, and the poet-speaker's difficulties with conferring a value upon his poem/gift in the face of growing competition referred to later in the sequence, characterize the prominent patronage problems of the time. Refusal to give, giving gifts of inferior worth, dishonorable motivations in giving, and competition for limited patronage gifts were all issues for patronage relations in this period.[21]

Moreover, those issues, which pervade the poet-speaker's attempt to give his patron/lover a legitimate gift deserving a reward, were de-bated in the context of the developing marketplace, and at a time when poetry was increasingly "sold" as much as it was "given." In his *Ocean to Cynthia*, Sir Walter Ralegh, for example, complains of his fall from Elizabeth's favor in terms which render his praise as a worthless commodity as much as a spurned gift:

> [s]hee cares not for thy prayse, who knowes not thers;
> Its now ann Idell labor and a tale
> tolde out of tyme that dulls the heerers eares
> a marchandize whereof ther is no sale.[22]

As Elizabeth will no longer receive his gifts with favor, his praise can at-tract no reward and is thus stripped of its value. Ralegh conveys that de-valuation by declaring that he cannot sell his outdated "merchandise," and by treating his praise in the manner of a commodity bought and sold at a price, rather than in the manner of a gift given and received as a token of affection and favor. In *The Rape of Lucrece*, Shakespeare had already depicted the delusion of those who, in the ambitious quest to possess all that they could, displayed the shortcomings of an economy that lauded the accumulation of goods above honorable bonds of loyalty and exchange:

> Those that much covet are with gain so fond
> That what they have not, that which they possess,
> They scatter and unloose it from their bond,
> And so by hoping more they have but less,
> Or, gaining more, the profit of excess
>   Is but to surfeit and such griefs sustain
>   That they prove bankrupt in this poor-rich gain.[23]

Whether Shakespeare wrote the majority of his sonnets in the late sixteenth or the early seventeenth century, they were written at a time of flux, at once for patronage and for socio-economics. The value of praise, and the value of poetry as a means to convey praise, fluctuated in response to whether praise/poetry was "given" or "sold"; and, in reality, the boundaries between the two were blurred by the poet's undeniable (if not always sizable) benefit from both. The proximity of poetry and praise to the marketplace-where flattery could be bought and lies could be fashioned for a price-placed patronage poets in defensive positions. Shakespeare's poet-speaker certainly had good reason to profess that his was the genuine article:[24]

> O let me, true in love, but truly write,
> And then believe me, my love is as fair
> As any mother's child, though not so bright
> As those gold candles fixed in heaven's air:
> Let them say more that like of hearsay well,
> I will not praise that purpose not to sell.

As the sequence progresses, however, the wasteful attitude, for which the young man is condemned in the procreation sonnets, is mirrored by the poet-speaker's apparent squander of his own love, and even of his own integrity, in the face of growing evidence that the recipient of his love is not "worth" such a gift. The remaining sonnets addressed to the young man often focus upon the relationship between the value of gifts and the value of those who receive them. When gifts are wasted or squandered, hoarded or given in excess, this affects the integrity of donor and recipient, which fundamentally alters the value of the gift itself.

III

Claiming his love to be the genuine article is a tactic employed by the poet-speaker in order to protect his poem/gift against devaluation, particularly in light of the fact that its recipient receives like gifts from many sources. Throughout the sequence the poet-speaker promotes his verse as sincere: while he does not boast of its quality, the value of his verse is raised because it is not something that can be bought or commissioned. The argument proves difficult to sustain, not least because, while the poetry is figured in terms of a gift, it is not given without the hope of a return from the young man -a return of love and of patronage. The status of the poet's gift as a currency of exchange, but a currency apparently more honorable than money itself, is similar to the status of gold in Nietzsche's *Thus Spoke Zaratlustra*:

> Tell me: how did gold attain its highest value? Because it is uncommon and use-less and gleaming and gentle in its splendour; it always gives itself. Only as the image of the highest virtue did gold attain the highest value. Goldlike gleam in the eyes of the giver. . . . Uncommon is the highest virtue and useless; it is gleaming and gentle in its splendour: a gift-giving virtue is the highest virtue.[25]

Nietzsche considers gold as a representation of the invisible virtue of the gift, and he argues that it has achieved its value only through its status as gift. Still, his thoughts on the virtues of giving and the moral rectitude of one who seeks gold in order to give it away are often am-bivalent. The image of the "goldlike gleam in the eyes of the giver," for example, leaves some doubt as to the spotlessness of the act of giving. Not only is the gleam merely like gold, that is, an imitation of gold, it is a gleam which reflects dubiously upon the eyes of the giver, al-most anticipating the satirical image of the dollar sign as a substitute for the eye. Zarathustra goes on to describe his followers as having a "thirst" for the "gift-giving virtue"—they want to "become sacrifices and gifts" themselves, to the point that they strive "[i]nsatiably . . . for treasures and gems" in order to continue giving. Metaphorically, these people become conductors of a gift-energy which is forced into them in order to "flow back . . . as the gifts of . . . [their] love." Interestingly, Zarathustra does not call this desire for self-sacrifice—this apparently devotional giving—unselfishness; rather, he implies its relation to the opposite: "Verily, such a gift-giving love must approach all values as a robber; but whole and holy I call this selfishness."[26]

The egoism of the man who exists in order to give is strikingly similar to the self-obsession of the unrequited lover. In particular, they both consider themselves robbed when they do not receive back again what they expected. The poet-lover of Elizabethan sonnet sequences often adopts the posture of love's victim; Shakespeare's speaker follows this convention, frequently describing his fruitless giving as self-corrupting (35 and 88), or as an authorized theft:[27]

> *All men make faults, and even I in this,*
> *Authórising thy trespass with compare,*
> *Myself corrupting salving thy amiss,*
> *Excusing thy sins more than their sins are;*
> *For to thy sensual fault I bring in sense —*
> *Thy adverse party is thy advocate —*
> *And 'gainst myself a lawful plea commence:*
> *Such civil war is in my love and hate*
> *That I an àccessary needs must be*
> *To that sweet thief which sourly robs from me.*

The dislocation of the perpetrator and the deed in the mind of the poet-speaker creates "civil war" within himself: he loves the young man but hates his actions, and he is led to self-corruption in his excuse of the sin out of love for the sinner. In this disrupted state the speaker is no longer giving to his lover; rather he is acting as an accessory to the lover's robbery of his love and, in effect, squandering his precious gifts. In his lack of constancy, the young man undermines the friendship with the poet-speaker, he undermines the truth of the poet's representation of his virtue, and he undermines the value of the gift for which the poet has received no return; and yet the giving continues. The poet-speaker's need to give is so insatiable that it overpowers his judgment, and he surrenders his love to the "sweet thief" regardless.

Even in possession of the young man, the poet-speaker is haunted by the fear of his leaving or being lost; when sonnet 48 takes up the metaphor of theft once again, it is applied to the poet's anticipated deprivation of his love:

> *But thou, to whom my jewels trifles are,*
> *Most worthy comfort, now my greatest grief,*
> *Thou best of dearest, and mine only care,*
> *Art left the prey of every vulgar thief.*

The poet cannot lock "up in any chest" the bond of love that is his "only care." The young man is free to "come and part" at his "pleasure," and, therefore, the poet fears he will allow himself to be "stol'n" (seduced by another love) because even honorable truth will turn "thievish" when it sees "a prize so dear." The loss or theft of the poet-speaker's treasure is inscribed as inevitable in the same way that Collatine's display of his "jewel" must result in its theft and in the destruction of Lucrece's value.[28] Sonnet 48, which maintains anxiety about the circulation of the young man even as it publishes his image, contrasts with the use of the metaphor of theft in sonnet 35 in that the young man, previously the thief, is now the object which is stolen. Though the position of the young man as subject/object fluctuates, the denial of liability is constant; the poet will admit neither his own nor the young man's responsibility for the defects of their relationship, which revolve around the inequality of the exchanges between them. In sonnet 35, the poet excuses himself from the selfishness which Nietzsche's *Zarathustra* later associates with insatiable giving by invoking the image of his lover as thief, yet in sonnet 48, he fears that his lover will be stolen from him. In each case, a force beyond the poet's control is blamed for a theft; in the first the poet's love is stolen from him so that he is passively rendered to the young man, whereas the second sees the young man inevitably taken away from the poet. All of this relates to a central problem: love cannot be stolen; it can only be given away. That essential contradiction underpins both the description of the poet as the thief's "àccessary" in sonnet 35 and the implication that the young man will be "stol'n" only at his own "pleasure" in sonnet 48. Sonnet 40 sees the poet-speaker struggle to justify his lover's betrayal and reconcile the chasm between personal control and emotional irrepressibility, between goods that can be stolen and feelings which can only be given:

> Then if for my love thou my love receivest,
> I cannot blame thee for my love thou usest;
> But yet be blamed, if thou this self deceivest
> By wilful taste of what thy self refusest.
> I do forgive thy robb'ry, gentle thief,
> Although thou steal thee all my poverty;
> And yet love knows it is a greater grief
> To bear love's wrong than hate's known injury.

Ingram and Redpath have noted the centrality of the word "love" to the ambiguities of this sonnet. "Love" refers to the poet's love for the young man, to the love that he desires from the young man, to his love in the shape of his mistress, and to the abstract quality of love itself.[29] Whatever the word applies to—and it is not always clear—the problem remains the same: true love cannot be stolen, it can only be given, and if the poet finds himself impoverished in love it must be either because his lovers have refused to give their love or else because they have transferred it elsewhere. Pointedly, sonnet 40 sees the young man "take," "receive," "use," and "steal" love, but it does not see him "give." The only gift contained here is the poet-speaker's forgiveness of

the theft of his mistress and his "love." Pronouncing that it would be easier to bear "hate's known injury" than the wrong inflicted by a loved one, the poet-speaker reveals the grief and suffering which his "love" (the young man, his mistress, or his love for one or both of these persons) has caused him.

Where "injury" has been inflicted, blame must be apportioned; and the poet's conflicting assertions about blame compound the problems associated with one-sided giving. The poet-speaker "cannot blame" his love, because he has received his love/mistress out of love for the poet, "But yet . . . [he should] be blamed" because, in truth, the poet-speaker knows that a "true love" does not behave in this manner. Booth has noted that "[o]vertones of two pertinent special contexts of receivest reflect dishonourably on the transaction"—the exchange of love carries certain connotations of receiving stolen goods and of the collection of debts or taxes.[30] In the New Cambridge edition of the *Sonnets*, Evans concurs with this interpretation of the youth as the receiver of stolen goods, while Katherine Duncan-Jones, in the Arden edition, extends the idea by suggesting that the poet will "blame" the young man for his "wilful taste" of his love because he "deceives" (that is, cheats) love by refusing to marry.[31] At the close of this sonnet, the young man has obtained everything: all the "loves" of the poet, all of the poet's love, the "use" of the poet's love, and the forgiveness which the poet appears incapable of withholding because of his love. In return, he has refused to marry the mistress he has enjoyed, yet has persisted in failing to reciprocate the poet's loyalty and affection and, as a result, the poet is left injured and impoverished; in fact, all but destroyed by his "love." By contrast, the young man is pictured once again as hoarding the gifts that he has received from others (from nature, and now, from the poet-speaker), thereby interrupting the proper flow of gift exchange and in-crease. The impetus, not only for this sonnet, but also for the expression of the poet-speaker's love throughout the sequence, is derived from the poet's inability to "alter" the nature of his feelings toward the young man. Even as he comes to realize the "alteration" of his beloved and the detrimental effect of the love upon his own integrity and wellbeing, the poet continues to love, continues to give. Steadfast in his devotion even as he is spurned, the poet-speaker declares that the young man and himself "must not be foes." Whether he is unable to sever himself from the object of his devotion because of his involuntary love, or because necessity deems that he sustain the relationship with a generous patron, is a question which draws the nature of the bond between the speaker and his addressee into contention.

IV

Aristotle identifies three types of friendship, based respectively upon goodness, utility, and pleasure. I believe that the problem with the friendship between Shakespeare's poet-speaker and his young man is related to its attempt to correlate the three. The result is Shakespeare's intricate representation of the tenuous nature of the patronage bond and the tumult of giving, expectation, and disappointment, which characterized the poet-client's position within it. If the *Sonnets* represented an actual patronage relationship and/or an actual love relationship, or even if they simply portrayed the dynamics of such relationships generally, then the "friendship" is based upon erotic pleasure and material benefit even as the poet-speaker strives to represent it as being based upon goodness. A friendship based upon pleasure might easily be dissolved when it ceased to be pleasurable: those "who are friends for the sake of utility part as soon as the advantage ceases."[32] In a friendship which has combined or appeared to combine pleasure and utility, if only the former breaks down, then what is left is a friendship which is still beneficial, but no longer pleasurable. In the case of the *Sonnets*, the advantage of the bond is reliant upon the poet's presentation of the young man as an idealized friend. The poet must represent the bond as one inspired by the "goodness" which it in fact lacks, in order to secure the reward that he needs-a reward ultimately insufficient to satisfy his erotic fervor.

Viewed in terms of the poet's erotic desires and his need of the young man, the loss of love is a continuing and colossal threat. Nonetheless, if the same situation is re-presented in terms of a friendship between the two men based upon "goodness" rather than pleasure or gain, then "All losses are restored, and sorrows end." In sonnet 42, which deals with the poet's fears about losing his mistress and his friend, the conflicting impulses of equality of exchange (a good friendship) and un-requited passion (an unfulfilled pleasure) cause the speaker to conclude with an elaborate excuse for the betrayal of his lover. The sardonic couplet then outwardly eliminates the need for the excuse fashioned in the body of the sonnet, while pointedly suggesting the self-delusion of the poet who attempts to salvage virtue from depravity:

If I lose thee, my loss is my love's gain,
And losing her, my friend hath found that loss;
Both find each other, and I lose both twain,
And both for my sake lay on me this cross.
 But here's the joy, my friend and I are one.
 Sweet flattery! then she loves but me alone.

The image of the poet bearing the "cross" obviously relates his position to the self-sacrificial acts of Jesus, suggesting his patience and constancy in the face of perpetual and unjust suffering. The excuse for the lustful behavior of the youth and the mistress—that they love each other only as an expression of their respective love for the poet-speaker—provides another opportunity for the poet-speaker to appear saintly, following his forgiveness of sin in sonnet 40. The couplets in both son-nets, however, conclude with a similar insinuation that the speaker is not so much forgiving as squandering his forgiveness upon those who should "yet be blamed" for the hoarding of their own pleasure. There is an overwhelming sense that the poet-speaker recognizes the weakness of his own argument, yet persists in deluding himself that his own gifts are given altruistically and without desire for a return.[33]

Alison V. Scott

Notes

1. All parenthetical references are to the New Cambridge Shakespeare edition of *The Sonnets*, ed. G. Blakemore Evans (Cambridge: Cambridge University Press, 1996), by son-net number and line, unless otherwise stated.
2. A. D. Cousins sees the *Sonnets* as "reflecting the contemporary adaptation of Petrarchan discourse to the pursuit of favour from socio-political superiors," thus highlighting Shakespeare's replacement of the traditional Petrarchan tension with the tensions involved in giving to, and suing for a reward from, an aristocratic patron (*Shakespeare's Sonnets and Narrative Poems* [Harlow, England: Longman, 20001, 138).
3. Ziegler, "'More Than Feminine Boldness': The Gift Books of Esther Inglis," *Women, Writing, and the Reproduction of Culture in Tudor and Stuart Britain*, ed. Mary E. Burke et al. (New York: Syracuse University Press, 2000), 33. In the same volume Jane Donawerth's "Women's Poetry and the Tudor-Stuart System of Gift Exchange," 3-18, draws attention to the odd position of women in Renaissance systems of exchange as both the objects of exchange and as the givers and recipients of gifts of poetry. On gifts at the Elizabethan court, see Lisa

M. Klein's "Your Humble Handmaid: Elizabethan Gifts of Needlework," *Renaissance Quarterly* 50 (1997): 459-93. Robert Y. Turner offers an interesting commentary upon the presentation of gifts and generosity within the patronage system in his article "Giving and Taking in Massinger's Tragicomedies," *Studies in English Literature* 35 (1995): 361-81; Mark Thorton Burnett explores the hostility and rivalry involved in exchanging gifts in his "Giving and Receiving: *Love's Labour's Lost* and the Politics of Exchange," *English Literary Renaissance* 23 (1993): 287-313. Recent work incorporating the use of gift-theory owes an incalculable debt to the work of Marcel Mauss, and mine is no exception; see *The Gift: Forms and Function of Exchange in Archaic Societies*, trans. W. D. Halls (London: Routledge, 1ggo). Natalie Zemon Davis's *The Gift in Sixteenth-Century France* (Wisconsin: University of Wisconsin Press, 2000) is an excellent introduction to what she terms "sixteenth-century gift-trouble," while Jason Scott-Warren's book *Sir John Harington and the Book as Gift* (London: Oxford University Press, 2001) provides a unique exploration of an Elizabethan poet's marketing of himself through the strategic giving of his work as a gift to various influential persons. For an accomplished examination of "Shakespeare's Gifts," see chapter two of William Flesch's book *Generosity and the Limits of Authority: Shakespeare, Herbert, Milton* (Ithaca: Cornell University Press, 1992), 85-222, though this focuses mainly upon the drama.

4. Peter C. Herman notes this unconventional linking of the text with the marketplace, arguing that the procreation sonnets enact the "delegitimizing" of reproduction rather than seeking to "legitimize the text's entry into the marketplace" through the denial of mercenary intent. See "What's the Use? Or, The Problematic of Economy in Shakespeare's Procreation Sonnets," *Shakespeare's Sonnets: Critical Essays*, ed. James Schiffer (New York: Garland, 1999), 269. Arthur F. Marotti has observed that "liln the overlapping manuscript and print cultures . . . poets contradictorily behaved as though they wished to avoid the 'stigma of print' at the same time they asserted their authorship proudly and obviously relished the measure of permanence that publication gave to their texts" ("The Transmission of Lyric Poetry and the Institutionalizing of Literature in the English Renaissance," in *Contending Kingdoms: Historical, Psychological, and Feminist Approaches to the Literature of Sixteenth-Century England and France*, ed. Marie-Rose Logan and Peter L. Rudnytsky [Detroit: Wayne State University Press, 1991], 21-41).

5. Marotti, "Shakespeare's Sonnets as Literary Property," in *Soliciting Interpretation: Literary Theory and Seventeenth-Century English Poetry*, ed. Elizabeth D. Harvey and Katharine Eisaman Maus (Chicago: University of Chicago Press, 1990), 143-73.

6. Ibid. 145-46.

7. Barrell, "Editing Out: The Discourse of Patronage and Shakespeare's Twenty-Ninth Sonnet," in *Poetry, Language and Politics* (Manchester: Manchester University Press, 1988), 42. Other commentators on the patronage discourse of the Sonnets have included Arthur F. Marotti, "'Love is not Love': Elizabethan Sonnet Sequences and the Social Order," ELH 49 (1982): 396-428, and Heather Dubrow, *Captive Victors: Shakespeare's Narrative Poems and Sonnets* (Ithaca: Cornell University Press, i987), in particular 205-30.

8. Derrida, *Given Time: 1. Counterfeit Money*, trans. Peggy Kamuf (Chicago: University of Chicago Press, 1992), 23. Even the title of Derrida's work suggests the difficulties involved in determining time, and in giving; *Given Time* goes on to explore the thwarting of the true gift by language and by structures of social exchange.

9. For an informative discussion of the tensions between patronage and publication, see Marotti's "Patronage, Poetry, and Print," Yearbook of English Studies 21 (1991): 1-21. Also, see Harold Love's *Scribal Publication in Seventeenth-Century England* (Oxford: Clarendon Press, 1993). In "The Script in the Marketplace," *Representations* 12 (1985): 101-14, Joseph Loewenstein discusses the way in which Ben Jonson "presents himself as a man ambiguously engaged with the literary marketplace" (109). In summarizing this approach Loewenstein touches upon the clash of market economics with patronage systems (see 109-10). In the first chapter of *The Imprint of Gender: Authorship and Publication in the English Renaissance* (Ithaca: Cornell University Press, 1993), Wendy Wall argues that sonnet sequences of the period occupied a curious position in relation to the development of the literary marketplace. Suggesting that sonneteers often inscribed the "exchangeability of their verse" within the verse itself, Wall examines the mirroring of erotic and social trans-actions, sexual desire and social ambition, and "textual exchange and erotic interchange" (50), raising some important questions in relation to the passage from manuscript to print culture. For more general studies of the development of a literary marketplace in the Renaissance see Elizabeth L. Eisenstein, *The Printing Press as an Agent of Change: Communications and Cultural Transformations in Early-Modern Europe* (Cambridge: Cambridge University Press, 1979), and H. S.

Bennet, *English Books and Readers*, 1558 to 1603 (Cambridge: Cambridge University Press, 1965), particularly 30-55.

10. Fineman, *Shakespeare's Perjured Eye: The Invention of Subjectivity in the Sonnets* (Los Angeles: University of California Press, 1986), 207.

11. Book 1 of Seneca's *De Beneficiis* argues that "we need to be taught to give willingly, to receive willingly to return willingly" (*Moral Essays*, trans. John W. Basore, 3 vols. [London: W. Heinemann, 19641, 1: 19). Seneca's work was widely referred to in this period, having only been recently translated by Arthur Golding. Despite the scope of Seneca's work on the theory of benefits, he never manages to overcome the contradiction inherent in his ideal of gift-giving, namely that one must give with no thought of return, but must always recognize that a return is expected of any gift received. Wall notes that the poet-speaker's urging on of the young man to copy himself in the early sonnets is contradicted later in the sequence by the argument that "sweets growne common loose their deare delight" (*Imprint of Gender*, 102); whereas the procreation sonnets see print as ensuring preservation, the later sonnets view the process as degrading to the integrity of love poetry (Ibid., 197).

12. Engle, *Shakespearean Pragmatism: Market of His Time* (Chicago: University of Chicago Press, 1993), 29.

13. The threat of time and the Sonnets' preoccupation with this theme is examined by Robert L. Montgomery, "The Present Tense Shakespeare's *Sonnets* and the Menaces of Time," *The Ben Jonson Journal* 6 (1999): 147-60.

14. See *Poetics*, trans. Malcolm Heath (London: Penguin, 1996), 3-6 (47a-48b). Heath notes in his introduction that similar ideas had already been expressed by Plato in the *Republic* (392d-98b, 595a-608b).

15. Samuel Daniel: *Poems and A Defence of Rymne*, ed. Arthur Colby Sprague (Chicago: University of Chicago Press, 1965), 9.

16. Sonnet 6 is pivotal to discussions about usury in the sonnets. See John B. Mischo's "'That use is not forbidden usury': Shakespeare's Procreation Sonnets and the Problem of Usury," in *Subjects on the Worlds Stage: Essays on British Literature of the Middle Ages and the Renaissance*, ed. David G. Allen and Robert A. White (Newark, NJ: Associated University Presses, 1995), 262-79.

17. Herman, "What's the Use," 273.

18. Ibid., 277.

19. John B. Mischo provides a useful overview of the sonneteer's use of the childbirth metaphor in the Renaissance in his article "'Great With Child to Speake': Male Childbirth and the Elizabethan Sonnet Sequence," *Explorations in Renaissance Culture* 24 (1998): 53-73. Mischo sees Shakespeare as the first sonneteer to adopt the Aristotelian theory of reproduction over the Galenic version favored by Sidney, Daniel, and Drayton in their use of the childbirth metaphor, thereby marginalizing the role of the female in procreation "by metaphorically reducing the female to a lifeless container" (67). In speaking of the prominence of corporeal metaphors in sonnets of the 1590S, Wall equates the naming of books as women with the commodification of women in Renaissance culture, but she does not comment on the gendered implications of the avoidance of the female naming convention in the publication of Shakespeare's sequence (*Imprint of Gender*, 62).

20. Herman, "What's the Use," 279.

21. For a useful overview of the decline of literary patronage in the period, see Alistair Fox, "The Complaint of Poetry for the Death of Liberality: The Decline of Literary Patronage in the 1590S," in *The Reign of Elizabeth I*, ed. John Guy (Cambridge: Cambridge University Press, 1995), 229-57. F. P. Wilson noted as early as 1948 that "After the invention of printing the old system of patronage slowly broke down under the weight of the increase in writers, books, and readers, and a new system slowly took its place. What this new system was to be reveals itself perhaps for the first time at the end of the seventeenth century when a professional writer (John Dryden) succeeded in making financial arrangements with a bookseller (Jacob Tonson) satisfactory to both parties and far more satisfactory to the author than could have been the charity of any patron" ("Some Notes on Authors and Patrons in Tudor and Stuart Times," in *Joseph Quincy Adams Memorial Studies*, ed. James G. McManaway, Giles E. Dawson, and Edwin E. Willoughby [Washington: Folger Shakespeare Library, 1948], 555).

22. *The Poems of Sir Walter Ralegh*, ed. Michael Rudick (Tempe, AZ: Arizona Center for Medieval and Renaissance Studies in conjunction with the Renaissance English Texts Society, 1999).

23. *The Oxford Shakespeare*, gen. ed. Stanley Wells and Gary Taylor (Oxford: Clarendon Press, 1998).

24. Pierre Bourdieu has reiterated the peculiar position of the gift in relation to the marketplace time and again; he stresses the distinction between lending money and giving gifts on the grounds that, while they both seek increase, the latter must appear absolutely removed from self-interest in order to appear as a gift. See *Outline of a Theory of Practice*, trans. Richard Nice (Cambridge:

Cambridge University Press, 1977).

25. Friedrich Nietzsche, "Thus Spoke Zarathustra," *The Portable Nietzschie*, ed. and trans. Walter Kaufmann, rev. ed. (New York: Penguin, 1976), 186.

26. "Thus Spoke Zarathustra," 187.

27. Heather Dubrow includes an examination of Shakespeare's use of the imagery of theft in her book *Shakespeare and Domestic Loss: Forms of Deprivation, Mourning, and Recuperation* (Cambridge: Cambridge University Press, 1999), 18-79.

28. Dubrow takes up the analogy with *The Rape of Lucrece* in *Shakespeare and Domestic Loss*, while Wall comments that "Shakespeare makes Lucrece an emblem of the dangers and pleasures of circulation itself" (*Imprint of Gender*, 215).

29. See Evans, Sonnets, 150, and Stephen Booth's commentary on the sonnet in his edition, *Shakespeare's Sonnets* (New Haven: Yale University Press, 1977), 199-200.

30. Booth, Sonnets, 199.

31. Evans, Sonnets, 150, and *Shakespeare's Sonnets*, ed. Katherine Duncan-Jones, rev. ed. (London: Arden Shakespeare, 2001), 190.

32. Aristotle, *Ethics*, trans. J. A. K. Thomson (London: Penguin, 1976), 265.

33. I would like to extend my thanks to Tony Cousins for his helpful criticism of an earlier version of this material and for his continued gifts of time and insight. I am also indebted to Clive T. Probyn for drawing my attention to Georgianna Ziegler and Jane Donawerth's work on gift-exchange in the Renaissance period while their work was still in press.

Reprinted from *Studies in Philology*, Vol. 101, No. 3 (Summer, 2004), pp. 315-331 by Allison V. Scott. Copyright © 2004 University of North Carolina Press. Reprinted with permission of the Publisher. www.uncpress.unc.edu

Without Remainder:
Ruins and Tombs in Shakespeare's Sonnets

In the sixteenth century, observes Margaret Aston, 'England acquired a whole suite of ruins.'[1] The widespread destruction of monastery buildings and church fabric—the sheer ubiquity of the destruction—is perhaps at the root of Shakespeare's oddest allusion to the dissolution: the abrupt, anachronistic appearance of a ruined monastery in the fifth act of *Titus Andronicus*. A member of the Goth forces explains to Lucius that he discovered the location of Aaron, by chance, when he 'strayed/to gaze upon a ruinous monastery,' where Aaron turned out to be hiding.[2] The anachronism here is quite startling: what is a monastery doing in ancient, pagan Rome? And a ruined monastery, at that, whose ruins cannot help but recall contemporary religious turmoils? It is as though a monastery presented itself to Shakespeare as the most obvious image of ruin in general: to depict ruin is to depict a monastery. This, though, would suggest at work a consciousness steeped in a sense of recent loss; and it is only from a particular—confessionalized—perspective that a monastery might be equated with all the symbols of loss and no talgia that come with ruin. The experience of the *Sonnets* carries some of this, but also many different, ambivalent, and mischievous responses to the dissolution and the religious upheaval of the Tudor century. This essay sets out to look at these attitudes, beginning with the *Sonnets'* relationship with the poems of Spenser. We will see, however, that the dissolution of the monasteries is only one factor in the *Sonnets'* gleeful depictions of ruins and destruction: by looking at these images of ruin alongside some of Jacques Derrida's writing on nuclear war, the archive and the biodegradable, it is possible to see that the *Sonnets* jeopardize the memories they seek to preserve and come to mime their own dissolution.

Shakespeare's *Sonnets* echo with ruin and destruction. A survey of the poems' demolitions might start with the metaphor, in Sonnet 10, that the 'lovely boy' addressed by the poems is, through his refusal to procreate, 'Seeking that beauteous roof to ruinate'—that is, be the destroyer of his own beauty, open that beauty to the ravages of time.[3] The metaphor is continued in Sonnet 13 with the line 'Who lets so fair a house fall to decay?'

and the image of the body's decay, applied now to the poet rather than the beloved, culminates in the Sonnet 73's reference to 'bare ruined choirs.' As F.W. Bateson pointed out, this can become 'a symbol not so much of the ageing poet as of a universal process of mutability.'[4] In this way, it can be read alongside the tropes of time's destructiveness, in, for example, Sonnet 64:

> *When I have seen by Time's fell hand defaced*
> *The rich proud cost of outworn buried age . . .*
> *Ruin hath taught me thus to ruminate –*
> *That Time will come and take my love away.*

The following sonnet, number 65, elaborates further: not 'brass, nor stone, nor earth, nor boundless sea' can resist 'sad mortality' and 'Time decays' both 'rocks impregnable' and 'gates of steel.' The transience of physical monuments is returned to in the opening conceit of Sonnet 125:

> *Were't aught to me that I bore the canopy,*
> *With my extern the outward honouring,*
> *Or laid great bases for eternity,*
> *Which proves more short than waste or ruining?*

We also find this in the observation that 'tyrants' crests and tombs of brass' are strictly temporary. The apotheosis of these conceits, though, is Sonnet 55, which conjures in opposition to the memorializing power of poetry a future of war and chaos:

> *When wasteful war shall statues overturn,*
> *And broils root out the work of masonry,*
> *Nor Mars his sword nor war's quick fire shall burn*
> *The living record of your memory.*

One way of situating the *Sonnets'* fascination with ruin within the religious conflict of the sixteenth century is to start with the resemblances between Sonnet 10 and the seventh sonnet of Spenser's *Ruines of Rome*.[5] A. Kent Hieatt has argued that some, at least, of the material of the *Sonnets* was generated by Shakespeare's reading of *The Ruines of Rome* and notes that Spenser's lines 'Time in time shall ruinate/Your works and names' relate to the buildings of Rome, and that of Shakespeare's line 'Seeking that beauteous roof to ruinate' employs 'a metaphor of the beloved as a building.'[6] It is not only the similarity of usage and the transmission of the coinage 'ruinate' which is interesting, though. The motif from Spenser becomes more striking when cited in full:

> And though your frames do for a time make warre
> Gainst time, yet time in time shall ruinate
> Your workes and names, and your last reliques marre.
> (Ruines 93–95)

Hieatt's analysis clips out the final phrase 'your last reliques marre.' This is fair enough; all he is trying to do is establish a verbal connection and this phrase has no bearing on it. But the word 'reliques' is one of the points at which Spenser's sonnet checks and questions itself. It is a charged, dangerous word, referring not only to the rubble and memory of a lost civilization, but also to the cult of saints outlawed by Henry VIII's Injunctions of 1538. These enjoin the people not to

> repose their trust and affiance in any other works devised by men's phantasies besides Scripture; as in wandering to pilgrimages, offering of money, candles or tapers to images or relics, or kissing or licking the same, saying over a number of beads, not understood or minded on.[7]

Under the Marian regime, relics which had been concealed were once again brought out; but this changed again with Elizabeth, as Aston outlines:

> It is . . . hardly credible what a harvest, or rather what a wilderness of superstition has sprung up in the darkness of Marian times,' wrote John Jewel to Peter Martyr early in November 1559. 'We found in all places votive relics of saints, nails with which the infatuated people dreamed that Christ had been pierced, and I know not what fragments of the sacred cross.[8]

One of the issues in all this is the falsity of relics—the official positions of the Henrician, Edwardian and Elizabethan regimes associate relics with falsehood and superstition. It is from this context that the word enters into Spenser's poem, and a sense of its uneasiness is transmitted, too, into the *Sonnets*.

If we consider Sonnets 15 and 16, in which Hieatt locates the direct influence of *Ruines* 7, we find only broad correspondences of theme. *Ruines* 7 is concerned with the transience of Rome, and by extension, the transience of the phenomenal world itself; this unsettling quality of mutability finds its way into Sonnets 15 and 16, 'Where wasteful Time debateth with decay' and the 'bloody tyrant Time' threatens the poet's 'barren rhyme.' But just as Sonnet 16 answers 15—arguing that the birth of an heir is a 'mightier way . . . to fortify yourself in your decay' than relying on immortality in verse, which is ultimately 'barren'—the argument can be seen developing further in Sonnet 17, which seems to deepen Shakespeare's dialogue with *Ruines* 7. Sonnets 15, 16, and 17 need to be taken together. Sonnet 15 evinces a belief in the commemorative power of poetry; Sonnet 16 denies it; and Sonnet 17 says why, and seems to do so by associating poetry with the falsehood of a relic, viewed from a point in the future:

> The age to come would say, 'This poet lies;
> Such heavenly touches ne'er touched earthly faces.'
> So should my papers, yellowed with their age,
> Be scorned, like old men of less truth than tongue,
> And your true rights be termed a poet's rage
> And stretche`d metre of an antique song.

Shakespeare seems here to be initiating a careful sifting of Spenser's text, at once ambivalent and ludic. We can detect, as in the other two sonnets, a profound concern with the work of mutability: what is a 'barren rhyme' in the present will be perceived, in the future, as the mere 'stretche`d metre of an antique song.' This parallels the idea that Rome's 'workes and names and . . . reliques' will be 'marred' by time. The idea of the false relic seems to be transmitted into Shakespeare's poem in two ways: first of all, in the separation of the human and the divine ('such heavenly touches ne'er touched earthly faces') and secondly, in the 'scorn' showed to the 'yellowed' poems. There is at work, here, an historical consciousness more advanced than Jewel's: not simply imagining a time of darkness giving way to a time of light, but self-consciously framing that depiction. The future will scorn the past; where the past saw the divine, the future sees superstition. Indeed, there may be a concern here other than relics: in the subtraction of the divine from 'earthly faces' there is also, perhaps, the fleeting reference to the face of the image of a saint, another of the new age's superstitious bugbears. In the new, Godly era of reformation, anything defending the cults of relics and images would be merely 'papers, yellowed with their age.' Something else persists, here, though: in Spenser's poem—and the rest of *The Ruines of Rome*—the risks of idolatry and relic-worship are introduced as self-critical, self-questioning devices.[9] In Sonnet 17, though, the possibility that the beloved's 'true rights be termed a poet's rage' is perceived as a risk opened up by committing memory to verse. According to the rhetoric of this sonnet, the divine *can* touch the earthly; but in the future, no-one may believe it. This is not to say, of course, that Shakespeare took seriously the cult of saints or relics; but if some of the terms of Spenser's Sonnet reappear in this one—or rather, in the sequence of sonnets from 15 to 17—they do so by playing with Spenser's unease at the possibility of idolatry.

Given the Catholicism that appears repeatedly in Shakespeare's background—a succession of Catholic school teachers passed through Stratford, for example, Shakespeare's mother was related to the Catholic Arden family, and his father might possibly have signed a Catholic 'spiritual testament'—we might be forgiven for expecting the *Sonnets* to betray a Catholic nostalgia similar to that of Stow's *Survey of London*. A plethora of work on Shakespeare's possible Catholicism—often focusing on the image of 'bare ruined choirs' from Sonnet 73—might lead us to expect a very different attitude to Spenser on the issue of ruins, idolatry, and iconoclasm. Eamon Duffy, for example, has argued that the phrase 'decisively aligns Shakespeare against the Reformation.'[10] But although Shakespeare's poems *do* reference the trauma of the English reformations, they do not do so, ultimately, in a way that suggests nostalgia. Moreover, other writers of the period—whose Protestant credentials are in no doubt—felt comfortable condemning the spoil of religious houses. In *The Ruines of Time*, Spenser alludes to the destruction of the abbey at Bury St Edmunds: tucked away in a lament for the transience of earthly monuments is a reference to the spoil of the abbey, 'rent for gaine':

Such one Mausolus *made, the worlds great wonder,*
But now no remnant doth thereof remaine:
Such one Marcellus, *but was torne with thunder:*
Such one Lisippus, *but is worne with raine:*
Such one King Edmond, *but was rent for gaine.*
All such vaine moniments of earthlie masse,
Deuour'd of Time, in time to nought doo passe.[11]

William Camden, similarly, has no difficulty in condemning the destruction of the same abbey and pointing a finger at Henry VIII's government:

But as great a peece of work as this was, so long in building and still encreasing, and as much as much riches as they gathered together for S. Edmunds *shrine . . . were by King Henry the Eighth utterly overthrowne. What time as at the one clappe hee suppressed all Monasteries; perswaded thereto by such as under a goodly pretense of reforming religion preferred their private and their own enriching before the honour of Prince and Country, yea and before the glory of God himselfe. And yet there remaineth still lying along the carcasse, as one would say, of that auncient monument, altogether deformed, but (for ruines, I assure you) they make a faire and goodly shew, which, who soever beholdeth, hee may both wonder there at, and withall take pity thereof.*[12]

Nostalgia, in other words, is not always Catholic nostalgia; criticism of the dissolution is not necessarily reducible to an anti-Protestant bias; and condemnation of the actions of Henry's government is not incompatible with allegiance to Elizabeth's. Shakespeare's poems, as we shall see, register the religious conflict of the Tudor century without reducing it either to nostalgia or to a single political position.

One way of bringing together these two critical positions—Shakespeare's stance in relation to Spenser, and his stance in relation to Catholicism—is through Sonnet 105, 'Let not my love be called idolatry.' The poem opens:

Let not my love be called idolatry,
Nor my belove'd as an idol show,
Since all alike my songs and praises be
To one, of one, still such, and ever so.

Joel Fineman argues that the poem 'never seems to recover from, or forget, the withdrawn ambiguity of its explanatory "since"—that is, the word 'since' in line 2 is a pivot on which the following lines can be read as both a denial of idolatry and also precisely the reason why the charge of idolatry might be levelled.[13] The poem continues:

'Fair, kind, and true' is all my argument,
'Fair, kind, and true,' varying to other words;

> *And in this change is my invention spent,*
> *Three themes in one, which wondrous scope affords.*
> *Fair, kind, and true have often lived alone,*
> *Which three till now never kept seat in one.*

Having mischievously invited the reader to entertain the possibility that the poem is flaunting idolatry, the poem proceeds to interrogate its own language of praise with a self-reflexivity which, through its very blandness of language, could be thought of as an amused, ironic comment on the anxieties of idolatry that echo through Spenser's *Ruines of Rome* and *Ruines of Time*. Jane Roessner argues that the 'till now' of the final line refers not to the beloved, but to the poem itself—that 'the real object of his worship is not the actual friend but the false (because deceptively beautiful and true) image of him that is created in the poetry.'[14] It's worth comparing the poem with *Ruines of Rome* 5:

> Rome *is no more: but if the shade of* Rome
> *May of the bodie yeeld a seeming sight,*
> *It's like a corse drawne forth out of the tombe*
> *By Magicke skill out of eternall night:*
> *The corpes of* Rome *in ashes is entombd,*
> *And her great spirite reioyned to the spirite*
> *Of this great masse, is in the same enwombed;*
> *But her braue writings, which her famous merite*
> *In spight of time, out of the dust doth reare,*
> *Doo make her Idole through the world appeare.*
>
> (Ruines 61–70)

In addition to the fraughtness of the word 'Idole,' the rhyming of 'entombed' with 'enwombed' registers a perturbation that what is dead might be mistaken for living—that the 'braue writings' of a dead civilization might inspire an idolatrous awe. Spenser's anxiety is that these texts might be better off forgotten, and that he is now trapped within the strictures of his own appalling, mistaken homage.

Unlike Spenser, however, Shakespeare seems un-ruffled by his verbal idolatry. Indeed, in its unhurried repetitions, in its laconic manipulations of both *the Homily against Idolatry* and the *Gloria Patri*, there is almost the opposite of Spenser's disquiet over the issue of idols. Moreover, fears about time and permanence that animate Spenser's poem are precisely the things caricatured in Shakespeare's. The central fear of *Ruines* 5—that what is dead might live again—responds to the proclamation in the *Homily against Idolatry* that

images are the 'destruction of Life' because 'they were not from the beginning, neither shall they continue for ever.'[15] Images are *impermanent*: to seek their disinter-ment is perverse. Sonnet 105 blithely, without concern, declares the permanence of its idol: the speaker's praise of the idol will be 'ever so,' an eternity which snigger-ingly recalls the *Gloria Patri*. He then appeals to the everlasting idol with a paean to his own constancy of affection, wherein 'my love' refers to both the idol and the speaker's feelings:

> *Kind is my love today, tomorrow kind*
> *Still constant in a wondrous excellence;*
> *Therefore my verse, to constancy confined,*
> *One thing expressing, leaves out all difference.*

There is no way to withdraw or solve the ambiguity of whether this rich constancy describes the 'lovely boy' or the poem itself; but in its willingness to set-up such an idol, the poem might be thought of as mocking both the *Homily* and the Spenser's tense enquiry. Alternatively, the neutral, repetitious surface of the poem may be the self-reflexive comment on what happens when poetry comes to close to idolatry—it becomes smooth, simplis-tic, emptied out. A third alternative is that through its deliberate creation of a verbal idol, the poem points out that no image is ever an idol *per se*—it chides the Prot-estant emphasis on the word by arguing, implicitly, that any belief system, idolatrous or not, needs a linguistic-rhetorical framework in order to exist.

This is not to say, though, that the poem is an oppo-sitional document. It toys, disdainfully, with the *Gloria Patri* just as much as with the *Homily against Idolatry*. Richard Wilson has suggested that the poem 'comple-ments Stratford's whitewashing'—the whitewashing of the frescoes and spoil of the Guild Chapel.[16] It is perhaps in its overlapping, contradictory, ambiguous diction, though—rather than any oppositional potential—that the poem most resembles the Stratford whitewash. As Patrick Collinson notes, it was not destroyed; indeed, one could argue that the whitewash was actually a kind of preservation.[17]

Elaborating on this idea, Juliet Fleming considers the whitewashed wall as an alternative to Freud's Mystic Pad as a model for consciousness. TheMystic Pad, for Freud, provided a metaphor for the apparently contradic-tory operations of a memory system that must keep trac-es, but must also remain blank in order to receive traces. Fleming makes the case for whitewash as an analogy:

Whitewash is a composition of lime and water: in the sixteenth century its cognates include 'whiting,' 'white-lime,' 'size' (lime and water to which glue has been added) and plaster or 'pargett' (a mixture of water and gypsum used to cover walls and also, when mixed thickly, for work in relief). To 'wash' a wall in the period is to clean it not by removing what was on it, but by covering it with a fresh surface—whitewash. Limewash does not restore the original writing surface, but creates a new one in the act of obliterating the old. . . . To the extent that a wall can reproduce ('from within') writing that has once been erased from it, it provides a better model for consciousness than Freud's Mystic Pad.[18]

Sonnet 105 is perhaps best imagined as a whitewashed fresco, where the lime has started to flake or peel, or has been partially scratched away—with the result that both surfaces are seen, but no distinction is made about their relative authenticity. That would be a task for an observer—someone already imbricated in a belief system. Instead, the sonnet blithely and blankly reproduces the memory traces of the past and the present, a mnemonic system whose glib, mocking neutrality borders on hypocrisy. After all, Fleming points out, 'the whitewashed or pargetted wall is an emblem for hypocrisy.'[19] Sonnet 105 is a kind of pure hypocrisy in which nothing is concealed, no truth held back, its contradictions thrust blandly into the open.

There is a point of comparison here between the mocking, ambiguous preservation of Sonnet 105, and the idea of the palimpsest. Sarah Dillon has argued for the importance of a 'palimpsestuous' reading, whereby any text or corpus of critical ideas can itself be treated as palimpsestuous, and a reading will seek 'the reappearance of the underlying script,' a repressed history or cryptic, animating figure.[20] Strikingly, for our purposes, Dillon opens with an image of the monastic past—she recalls the creation of palimpsests 'from the seventh to the ninth centuries in the scriptoriums of the great monastic institutions such as Bobbio, Luxeuil, Fleury, Corbie, and St Gall.'[21] This is a very European perspective—and as Dillon's argument tracks forward to De Quincey's 'ambivalence' about 'the Christian salvation of eternal life,' this fleeting image of the European monastic tradition is complemented by a settled sense of what Christianity might mean.[22] Effaced from the surface of Dillon's text—but palimpsestuously structuring it—is the English monastic tradition, and the violence—textual and

physical—of the Reformation, which eventually produces a nineteenth-century Anglican Christianity, about which De Quincey can be 'ambivalent.'

In mimicking and mocking the Stratford whitewash, however, Sonnet 105 does not appeal for the urgency of remembrance. Our most pressing desires for historical recovery, for readings palimpsestuous and transformational, slide frictionless from its neutral surface. Sonnet 105 wants the last word: the taking up of positions, the allying of ourselves to causes, belief itself—these are the things it sniggers at. Sonnet 105 laughs silently that it is all just text, text, text.

This image of whitewashing perhaps offers a clue to thinking about the trope of ruins in the *Sonnets*, taking in Bateson's reference to mutability along the way. The reigns of Henry, Edward, Mary, and Elizabeth seem like an extended study in mutability, with one religious reverse and recapitulation after another. Throughout these periods, physical destruction—of monasteries, church fabric, vestments, and ornaments—is paralleled by the destruction of texts. This oscillation of physical and textual destruction is one of the things played out in the *Sonnets*—almost as though these poems—apparently so detached from religious subject matter—were reviewing the preceding century. In 1560, John Bale wrote to Matthew Parker:

> And as concernynge bookes of antiquite, not printed; when I was in Ireland [i.e. February–September 1552] I had great plenty of them, whom I obtayned in tyme of the lamentable spoyle of the lybraryes of Englande, throgh much fryndeshypp, labor and expenses. Some I founde in stacyoners and bokebyndeeres store howses, some in grosers, sope sellers, taylers, and other occupyers shoppes, some in shyppes ready to be carryed over the sea into Flanders to be solde –for in those uncircumspecte and carelesse dayes, there was no quiyckar merchaundyce than lybrary bookes, and all to the destructyon of learnynge and knowledge of thynges necessary in thys fall of antichriste to be knowne . .[23]

Wiping out texts was not only a problem for the reformers: with Mary's accession, the erasure was ordered of scripture from the whitewashed church walls.[24] Textual destruction, of course, is being paralleled by the destruction of church fabric into the reign of Elizabeth. The churches were to be thoroughly refurbished, under Mary; and all these refurbishments would be ordered destroyed under Elizabeth; and by this stage, the people had every reason to expect yet another reversal. This iconoclastic ebb and flow is perhaps somewhere to be found in the *Sonnets'* continuous dialogue with mutability, culminating in Sonnet 64's lament:

> *When I have seen the hungry ocean gain*
> *Advantage on the kingdom of the shore,*
> *And the firm soil win of the wat'ry main,*
> *Increasing store with loss and loss with store;*
> *When I have seen such interchange of state,*
> *Or state itself confounded to decay,*
> *Ruin hath taught me thus to ruminate–*
> *That Time will come and take my love away.*

One of the compelling things about certain of the *Sonnets*, though, is their apparent urge to up the ante. Far from resolving classical questions of permanence—will texts outlast structures, or structures outlast texts?—the *Sonnets* seem to be consumed with the desire to annihilate *everything*. Over the Tudor century, something always survives—with the accession of Mary, out of their hiding places come saints, roods, and crosses. Scriptural phrases are obliterated; but they will be back, with Elizabeth. There is always a remainder. The *Sonnets*, though, frequently seem to be working with a logic of remainderless destruction, as though to demand, *What if nothing survives*? And this 'nothing' will encompass text, writing, speech, language, memory—in short, all the things which the Renaissance Sonnet typically promises to preserve, in the face of mutability and worldly destruction.[25]

On the surface, at least, the *Sonnets* seem to activate this classical immortality-of-poetry figure, marshalling a kind of self-confident integrity against the forces of decay, time, mutability, destruction. Ruins are outside most especially 55—come to mind. Over the course of the *Sonnets*, we envision a time when 'all the breathers of this world are dead,' we see that 'wasteful war shall statues overturn/and broils root out the work of masonry,' and, most appallingly, we see 'the earth devour her own sweet brood.' But the question of survival, for the *Sonnets*, becomes a self-questioning. The physical ruins against which the *Sonnets* hold themselves in opposition turn out to be ruin within. If the urge to depict ruin, to envisage ruin, to imagine ruin—in sum, to ruin—might be thought of as the wake of a certain *death drive*, Derrida reminds us that where there is remembrance—that is, where there is repetition, the will to repeat, the urge

to institute an archive of, for example, praise—there, *too*, is the death drive. As he puts it in *Archive Fever*:

> . . . repetition itself, the logic of repetition, indeed, the repetition compulsion, remains, according to Freud, indissociable from the death drive. Consequence: right on that which permits and conditions archivisation, we will never find anything other than that which exposes to destruction, and in truth menaces with destruction, introducing, *a priori*, forgetfulness and the archiviolithic into the heart of the monument. Into the 'by heart' itself. The archive always works, and *a priori*, against itself.[26]

In other words, when a speaker aims to create a structure of repetition—by declaring, for example, that 'Gainst death and all oblivious enmity/Shall you pace forth'—the institution of this archive may have more complicity with 'oblivious enmity' than it first appears. Ruin in these poems, then, would be only the most visible manifestation of their fascination with destruction—*son et lumie`re*, shock and awe, or the portion of an instinct directed towards the external world. Meanwhile, something far stranger, far more insidious pursues through the poems a desire for annihilation and forgetting.

What, then, does Sonnet 55—staying with this example—really want? It is worth recalling the sonnet in full:

> *Not marble nor the gilded monuments*
> *Of princes shall outlive this powerful rhyme,*
> *But you shall shine more bright in these contents*
> *Than unswept stone besmeared with sluttish time.*
> *When wasteful war shall statues overturn,*
> *And broils root out the work of masonry,*
> *Nor Mars his sword nor war's quick fire shall burn*
> *The living record of your memory.*
> *'Gainst death and all oblivious enmity*
> *Shall you pace forth; your praise shall still find room*
> *Even in the eyes of all posterity*
> *That wear this world out to the ending doom.*
> > *So, till the judgement that yourself arise,*
> > *You live in this, and dwell in lovers' eyes.*

One might begin to hazard the idea that 'this powerful rhyme' is powerful not because it will outlast ruin, decay, and the chaos of the future, but because it begins to work against its own ostensible purpose. Somewhere in the heart of this commemorative monument is the perversity of a memorial to forgetting. Is such a thing even conceivable? Who, witnessing a monument to forgetfulness, could even know, or remember, what they had witnessed? The poem seems to set up two series of ideas, opposing the animate with the inanimate: on the one hand, there is 'marble,' 'gilded monuments,' 'unswept stone,' 'statues,' death, oblivion. The poem's physical ruins, acted on by time, decay, war, and mutability represent death and oblivion by synecdoche. On the other hand, the 'powerful rhyme' which 'outlives' everything is animate—a 'living record,' 'pac[ing] forth,' 'dwell[ing] in lovers' eyes.' Helen Vendler notes the trump whereby the word 'live' is inserted into 'ob*liv*ious' in Line 9, clinching the poem's power over oblivion.[27] Ostensibly the purpose of this series of oppositions is to entrust the memory of the beloved to verse, which is untouched by the ravages of time; but the sonnet comes to evince a particular doubt: what substrate is it that carries the verse?[28]

Even as the poem completes itself with the animate figure of 'lovers's eyes,' there is the sense that this moment of finitude, the pen lifted above the manuscript, stands in for the possibility of the poem's destruction. The problem is not that beauty, 'Whose action is no stronger than a flower' cannot 'hold a plea to time'; rather, that there is no way for the poem's manuscript to survive the onslaught of time which culminates in the apocalypse ('the ending doom'). From this, one might detect in the poem a kind of dystopian science fiction: that with the land bleached white by radiation, with civilization annihilated, with language no longer even a memory, a lone figure, after decades underground, staggers into the wasteland and blurts, with no idea what the words mean, 'Not marble nor the gilded monuments/Of princes –' It is the only sound for miles. Nothing has outlasted this powerful rhyme: certainly not marble, monuments, unswept stone. But if the person—if one can say person, if ideas such as 'subjectivity' or 'identity' any longer make sense—who utters these syllables no longer knows what prompts them, no longer recognizes them as words, what exactly is it that has survived? Is it still a 'rhyme'? It declares, if there is anyone left to hear it, that 'You live in this,' but what, now, is 'this'?

What keeps Sonnet 55's fable of remainderless destruction from falling entirely into the province of science fiction is the fact that the various reformations of the sixteenth century were about, precisely, the extinction of a certain way of life. It begins with the demise of monasticism; but we see the desire for remainderless destruction at work in the actions of the Elizabethan

commissioners. As books and images had survived the Henrician and Edwardine reformations, the stakes, with the accession of Elizabeth, were higher. Roger Martin, of Long Melford, for example, expressed the intention to preserve the fabric of Catholic cultus and with it a devotion to the old religion:

> And on St James's Day, being sung Mass then by note, & the organs going in St James's chappel, which were brought into my house, with the clock and bell, that stood there, & the organs which stood upon the roodloft, that was there a little from the rood, which chappel hath been maintained by my ancestors, and therefore I will, that my heires, when times serve, shall repair, place there, & maintain, all those things again.[29]

To eradicate these intentions, the Elizabethan commissioners set out to eradicate the physical survivals of Catholicism—to annihilate its possibility by annihilating its memory. Sonnet 55, though, seems to be engaged in an attempt to outbid, to trump, even the extirpating urges of the reformers. The Reformation's aim of extincting Catholicism becomes only a synecdoche for the total destruction envisaged by the sonnet. The series of oppositions between animate and inanimate matter that structure the sonnet demand the conclusion that the sonnet's own means of transmission can be nothing like technical memory; that is, for the 'living record' to work, it cannot be entrusted to anything like a book or manuscript.

These things are too fragile—they would be easily consumed by 'war's quick fire,' or by bonfires of the sort organized by the reformers. The poem's substrate cannot be *hypomnemic*, outside the body. Which brings us back to the fabular science fiction: a lone acolyte survives the holocaust, having devoted his life to remembering words whose meaning he no longer even understands. But everything is complicated by the word 'this' in the final line of the sonnet. Nothing should be more innocuous: 'You live in this, and dwell in lovers' eyes.' We can be sure that 'this' is not technical memory—the domain of manuscript or digital information—because these are the things which are consumed when 'broils root out the work of masonry.' The 'living record' is untouched. 'Living' here could refer, it might be argued, to the posterity which will read and rehearse the poem: 'Where breath most breathes, even in the mouths of men,' as Shakespeare puts it elsewhere. But the idea that the memory is entrusted to human memory, at least insofar as one traditionally understands the term, seems to be undercut by the final line of the poem, specifically the word 'and': 'and' seems to separate 'this' from 'lovers' eyes,' that is, from the substrate of human memory. 'This' is something other than the memory appealed to by 'lovers' eyes; and as the poem has already established that 'this' cannot be technical memory, we are left with the question of what exactly 'this' might be. There is the unsettling, ghostly idea that as one reads the poem, reads it aloud, one is not reading 'this' at all. The poem is something other than it is; and in this way, forgetfulness appears at the heart of the monument. It no longer simply envisages the destruction of statues, cities, civilizations; or manuscripts, books, poetry, data. It actually works to efface itself, to annul its own presence, to destroy itself without remainder. Reducible to neither human nor technical memory, it ceases to be—one will never know what has been read under the title 'Sonnet 55.'

Curiously—and perhaps appositely, given the total destruction that the sonnet depicts, amid the demolition and iconoclasm of the sixteenth century reformations—the name that Jacques Derrida gives to the possibility of remainderless destruction is nuclear war. In his 1984 essay 'No Apocalypse, Not Now,' Derrida argues that 'the nuclear epoch is dealt with more "seriously" in texts by Mallarmé, or Kafka, or Joyce, for example, than in present-day novels that would offer direct and realistic depictions of a "real" nuclear catastrophe.'[30] What Derrida means by this is that these are texts that enter a dialog with literature's relationship to *nothingness*—we could add the *Sonnets* to this catalogue. 'There is no essence or substance of literature,' Derrida writes elsewhere. 'Literature is not. It does not exist.'[31] With no absolute properties of its own, literature is never anything more than that which is called literature. 'No Apocalypse' presses this thinking further. If literature is that which has no essence, then it is the literary archive which nuclear war threatens with absolute, remainderless annihilation:

> . . . what allows us perhaps to think the uniqueness of nuclear war, its being-for-the-first-time-and-perhaps-for-the-last-time, its absolute inventiveness, what prompts us to think it even if it remains a decoy, a belief, a phantasmatic projection, is obviously the possibility of an irreversible destruction, leaving no traces, of the juridicoliterary archive—that is, the total destruction of the basis of literature and criticism.[32]

The corollary of placing these two discussions side-by-side is that literature has no essence, no referent, because the closest thing literature has to an essence is the possibility of its absolute annihilation. One name for, or permutation of, such annihilation might be nuclear war; this, indeed, is a 'determination from something other than itself.' Without the occurrence of—for example—nuclear war, literature's referent is fabular, wholly in the future, in the absolute future of literature. The arrival of literature's referent would entail the annihilation of literature.

As the *Sonnets* gamble with this logic, the various immortalizing conceits employed by the poems become increasingly fraught. At various points in the *Sonnets*—numbers 15, 60, 63, and 107, for example—Shakespeare promises the addressee immortality. But only on one occasion does he figure this specifically as an epitaph. This occurs in Sonnet 81:

> *Or I shall live your epitaph to make,*
> *Or you survive when I in earth am rotten,*
> *From hence your memory death cannot take,*
> *Although in me each part shall be forgotten.*
> *Your name from hence immortal life shall have,*
> *Though I, once gone, to all the world must die.*
> *The earth can yield me but a common grave*
> *When you entombèd in men's eyes shall lie.*
> *Your monument shall be my gentle verse,*
> *Which eyes not yet created shall o'er-read,*
> *And tongues to be your being shall rehearse,*
> *When all the breathers of this world are dead.*
>   *You still shall live—such virtue hath my pen –*
>   *Where breath most breathes, even in the mouths of men.*

Though the sonnet purports to be an epitaph promising immortality to the bearer of 'Your name,' the name which would make an epitaph possible is precisely what is missing from the text. Again, there is a process of destruction detectable behind the sonnet's rhetoric, perhaps the same process that leads Shakespeare to remark on the impermanence of 'tombs of brass.' It might be considered particularly naive, amid the iconoclastic convulsions of sixteenth-century England, to think that entrusting the desire for memory—let alone for immortality—to a physical tomb or funeral monument was a good idea. The iconoclasm directed against tombs was sanctioned not only by texts such as the *Homily against Idolatry*, but also by the reclassification as heresy beliefs in Purgatory and in the possibility of salvation through good works. Both of these had long been targets of the reformers, and were denounced in the Forty-Two articles under Edward, and the Thirty-Nine under Elizabeth. The fact that tombs frequently listed the good deeds of the dead and requested prayers for souls in Purgatory could only provoke more iconoclastic violence. Surveying the 1590s from the early seventeenth century, John Weever—no adherant of Catholicism—deplores the iconoclasm of the period. Of the Elizabethan visitations, he writes:

> . . . they rooted vp, and battered downe, Crosses
> in Churches, and Church-yards, or also in other
> publicke places, they defaced and brake downe
> the images of Kings, Princes, and noble estates;
> erected, set vp, or pourtraied, for the onely memory
> of them to posterity, and not for any religious
> honour; they crackt a peeces the glasse-windowes
> wherein the effigies of our blessed saviour hanging
> on the Crosse, or any one of his Saints was depic-
> tured; or otherwise turned vp their heeles into the
> place where their heades vsed to be fixt; as I haue
> seene in the windowes of some of our countrey
> Churches.[33]

His stiffest condemnation, though, is reserved for iconoclasm directed against tombs:

> But the foulest and most inhumane action of those
> times was the violation of Funerall Monuments.
> Marbles which couered the dead were digged vp,
> and put to other vses (as I haue partly touched
> before). Tombes hackt and hewne apeeces; Images
> or representations of the defunct, broken, erased,
> cut or dismembered, Inscriptions or Epitaphs,
> especially if they began with an *orate pro anima*,
> or concluded with *cuius anime propitietur Deus*...
> These Commissioners . . . these Tombe-breakers,
> these graue-diggers, made such deepe and dilligent
> search into the bottome of ancient Sepulchres,
> in hope there to finde (belike) some long-hidden
> treasure . . . And hereupon the grauerakers, these
> gold-finders are called theeues, in old Inscriptions
> vpon Monuments.[34]

In this context, the fact that the only name received by the addressee is 'Your name' is significant: Shakespeare creates a tomb or monument that is already defaced, the name already struck out. Escalating its logic of

forgetfulness, the sonnet proceeds to play with how an epitaph or a poem might remember, the tension between repetition and remembrance. The poem moves from a static entombment 'in men's eyes' in the second quatrain through a 'monument' which will be 'o'er-read'; but this mausoleum of introspection is contrasted with the apparently confident, declarative speech which concludes the poem—'tongues to be' will 'rehearse' the memory of the beloved. The poem moves from silence into speech. Contemplation, the poem seems to promise, will not be enough: this epitaph will come to life.

But even this is a strategy of forgetfulness, one which returns us to the image of the broken tomb. With the name on the epitaph erased or subtracted, this poem never remembers; its work is the opposite of commemoration. It plays 'Fort/da!' with the nominal addressee of the poem, retrieving him, bringing him close, and discarding him, as the process of reading catches the reader with the word 'you,' with 'Your name.' The beloved and the reader exchange places endlessly as the poem promises immortality to each, every successive reading sounding the hollowness and glibness of the promise, turning the poem into a meditation on, precisely, hollowness and glibness. This is the secret of the poem's move from the introspective mausoleum to speech: the emphasis on 'where breath most breathes.' Breath most breathes 'in the mouths of men' because 'in the mouths of men' breath bears speech. Shakespeare uses 'breathers' at line 12 to signify 'living, alive' to set-up this equation: that to live is to remember. But this is a perverse tomb, this moving tomb, this tomb of tongues, which will not remember with the pithy, repeatable brevity of the typical epitaph; this nameless epitaph remembers without remembering, accumulating readings, repeating, 'rehearsing,' without ever repeating or rehearsing because 'Your name' will never come, and the poem will summon only the phantom of a reader, and the memory-to-come of that reader's demise.

The impossibility of remembrance is something touched on in Jonathan Dollimore's argument that Shakespeare is effectively engaged in sacrificing the young man: 'although the poet is attracted to the young man,' he argues, 'he also identifies with the destructive effects of time; there is a strange and compelling complicity between time and its chronicler such that we might go so far as to say that the author is enamored more of death than of the boy.'[35] Hence, then, the smashed tomb—the reduction of the young man to something less than even a memory. But it is not only the young man who is dissolved, according to this logic. The poet vanishes too, in a move similar to the self-immolation of Sonnet 55. If we pursue Dollimore's argument, and put together Shakespeare's identification with time and what Dollimore calls the 'indifferent power' of death and mutability, we find that in the undertow of impersonality in this, the person speaking seeks his own dissolution too. To identify with indifferent, impersonal time, death and mutability is to seek something other than a person, not a person. Identity, subjectivity, spirit—'in me each part shall be forgotten.' It will be as though they never existed.

This, though, would not be the only example of an injunction to forget attached to a tomb. Joseph Holland, addressing the Society of Antiquaries, calls their attention to

> an epitaph, wherein there is great sense comprehended in one word, and that word is written upon a large marble stone at the foot of the great staires, ascending up unto the quire in St. Paul's, to wit, OBLIVIO. Notwithstanding the brevity of this, the writer's meaning was not that the person there buried should be forgotten, because he hath sett his arms at the four corners of the stone, which was significant enough to declare who he was.[36]

If the owner of these arms intended remembrance, is there anything in the OBLIVIO other than perversity? Perhaps what this inscription marks is a prediction: that these arms will be worn down, erased, jettisoned from memory, scanned only by centuries of unregarding eyes.

This question of what may, or should, or can be remembered—whether a tomb can remember—is approached again in Sonnet 107, culminating in the image of ruination in the final line, 'When tyrants' crests and tombs of brass are spent.' The poem concludes:

> Now with the drops of this most balmy time
> My love looks fresh, and Death to me subscribes,
> Since, spite of him, I'll live in this poor rhyme,
> While he insults o'er dull and speechless tribes.
> And thou in this shall find thy monument,
> When tyrants' crests and tombs of brass are spent.

The question here is whether the poem can—or even wants to—hold 'thy monument' and 'poor rhyme' in absolute opposition to the incoherence of 'dull and speechless tribes.' Having started with the supposed

provisionality of the 'lease' of the writer's love, the poem concludes with the provisionality of 'tyrants' crests,' locating in the poem a permanence of memory. It is only 'now,' however, 'with the drops of this most balmy time,' that the love previously 'supposed as forfeit to a confined doom' seems renewed and can be excitedly hymned, breathlessly portrayed as a substance of permanent remembrance.

This remembrance is a matter of language: the poem remembers. In the poem, though, it is not only the writer who writes. Death has a language, too. In a strange, arresting anthropomorphism, Death 'insults' over the 'tribes' who have no language, writing, poetry, memory; and, it seems, Death writes, too. Death 'to me subscribes.' I am more powerful than Death, says the poem. Death to me subscribes, Death admits that I am its superior. Death cannot beat me. But Death subscribes, Death signs this declaration of my superiority. Death admits that I am superior because I write, and death admits this in writing. Death writes that I am the superior writer.

How can this be? Death is the force of forgetting. It is because the 'dull and speechless tribes' are, precisely, speechless that they are forgotten, are consigned to death, oblivion. If Death writes, if Death has a language, then there is a language of forgetting as much as there is a language of remembrance. Death forgets, but Death remarks, writes its forgetfulness. And 'I,' the inhabitant of this 'poor rhyme,' can understand Death's language. Death to me subscribes. It's a common tongue. Death, then, plays a trick on 'me' by 'subscribing' to me; the languages of remembrance and forgetting overlap and contaminate one another. 'I' can never guarantee what, precisely, will be remembered, or how, or what provisional 'now' will be preserved by this poem's recall and reading, and 'I' become quite provisional too.

The logic of the OBLIVIO infects the poem, blurring the categories of memory and forgetting. 'Spent' does not necessarily mean that 'tyrants' crests and tombs of brass' are annihilated, reduced to nothing; it suggests exhaustion—exhaustion of meaning—but not necessarily desolation. Exhausted, they signify *differently*. As a poem eventually might do. But this is only to begin to wonder about how a poem might ultimately break down. It is what Derrida calls the 'biodegradable':

> . . . for a long time I have been interested in the 'biodegradable.' In the word or the thing? Difficult to distinguish, in any case, in this case. The case: what falls, the fall [*la chute*], the falling due

[é ché ance], and the waste [dé chet].[37]

This is an unsettling triptych, mapping together literature and waste and ruin through the figure of falling, of falling due. In the classical immortality topos, literature is what resists falling, *ruere, cadere, degradere*. But literature may still fall, fall due, fall into waste. Derrida goes on:

> Is not what we call rhetoric a large discourse, itself in a constant state of recycling, of that which in a discourse submits to composition, decomposition, recomposition? These processes could affect the very essence of language and proper meaning of words. Can one speak nonfiguratively of biodegradability with regard to the identity attributed to a supposedly proper meaning? As a result of the action of certain bacteria . . . the aforementioned proper meaning would decompose in order to pass, having become unrecognisable, into other forms, other figures. It would let itself be assimilated, circulating anonymously within the great organic body of culture, as would one of those metaphors we call 'dead.'[38]

This, perhaps, envisages another end for the *Sonnets*, and for the entire Shakespearean archive: 'To be biodegradable means at least two things: on the one hand, the annihilation of identity; on the other hand, the chance to pass into the general milieu of culture, into the 'life' of 'culture' while enriching it with anonymous but nourishing substances.'[39] This entails survival, but at the loss of identity—so that one no longer even knows what has survived. It would mean that some fragment of the *Sonnets* may, indeed, be 'powerful,' may outlive marble, guildedmonuments, tombs of brass—but at the cost of ever being recognizable as a part of a sonnet, having jettisoned even the name of Shakespeare. The name of Shakespeare, the Shakespearean canon: these are the things that would degrade, dissolve, become less than memories. Some waste product, some chemical by-product, may survive in the form of catch-phrase, cliché, or even concept: but not a concept that is remembered through its association with Shakespeare. As Derrida puts it elsewhere, 'every conceptual breakthrough amounts to transforming, that is, to deforming, an accredited, authorized relationship between a word and a concept, between a trope and what one had every interest to consider to be an unshiftable primary sense,

a proper, literal, or current usage.'[40] In this way, some fraction of the 'powerful rhyme' would outlive even itself, 'float[ing] on the surface of culture like the wastes whose survival rivals that of the masterpieces of our culture and the monuments that we promise eternity.'[41] Like this, perhaps, Shakespeare comes to the identification with time and death that Dollimore discusses; and the nameless monument of the young man foreshadows the erasure of Shakespeare's own name.

I would like to conclude, however, with another way of thinking about these poems and ruins, via the status of the *Sonnets* as gifts. Whether or not they seek patronage in return, the dedication of these poems to the 'onlie begetter,' and their repeated, ardent address to a singular 'lovely boy' codifies this status. Moreover, they seek to give—they seek to give *time*. Time, the future, remembrance, repetition—these are the things promised by the *Sonnets*. But these are gifts contorted by images of chaos, war, and demolition, by promises of forgetfulness as much as remembrance, by the infection of the OBLIVIO. In this way, they remind me of Blanchot's strange, unsettling motto: 'The disaster is a gift; it gives disaster.'[42]

What could this mean, in relation to the *Sonnets*? One way of thinking about it is through Derrida's notion of the gift. In this way, we begin to approach the idea of the present as a ruin. Derrida writes:

> For there to be gift, *it is necessary* [il faut] that the donee not give back, amortise, reimburse, acquit himself, enter into a contract, and that he never have contracted a debt. . . . The donee owes it *to himself* even not to give back, he *ought* not to owe . . . It is thus necessary, at the limit, that he *ought* not to *recognise* the gift as gift. If he recognises it *as* gift, if the gift *appears to him as such*, if the present is present to him *as present*, this simple recognition suffices to annul the gift.[43]

This insistent punning on the word 'present' signals the definition of the problem: the problem of the gift will also be a problem of time. '[E]ven before *recognition* becomes *gratitude*' the gift is being annulled: pulled back into the mechanisms of exchange.[44] There is at least the possibility of debt, and countergift. Countergift, even in the future, would annul the gift: an exchange would have taken place. However, Derrida continues, it would not even be enough for the donor to give in secret, to never reveal the origin of the gift or the identity of the giver:

At the limit, the gift as gift ought not to appear as gift: either to the donee or to the donor. It cannot be gift as gift except by not being present as gift. Neither to the 'one' nor to the 'other.' If the other perceives or receives it, if he or she keeps it as gift, the gift is annulled. But the one who gives it must also not know it either: otherwise, he begins, at the threshold, as soon as he intends to give, to pay himself, to gratify himself with a symbolic recognition, to praise himself, to approve of himself, to gratify himself, to congratulate himself, to give back to himself symbolically the value of what he thinks he has given or what he is preparing to give. The temporalisation of time (memory, present, anticipation; retention, protention, imminence of the future; 'ecstases,' and so forth) always sets in motion the process of a destruction of the gift: through keeping, restitution, reproduction, the anticipatory expectation or apprehension that grasps or comprehends in advance.[45]

What this means is that no gift is ever entirely possible; no gift is ever an experience of the present. Even if the issue of patronage had never occurred to Shakespeare, the presentation of these poems would have begged something both of him and of their dedicatee. In order to be gifts, in this formulation, the poems would have to detach themselves from the present, from all tenses.

This, perhaps, is the reason for the *Sonnets'* repeated invocations of destruction, demolition, ruins, chaos, forgetting. The gift, in its impossibility, is no experience of time. Its timelessness unravels the timelessness which the *Sonnets* only pretend to give. Unravels, too, an essay such as the present one, which wants, it seems, to preserve the name 'Shakespeare,' the corpus 'Sonnets,' and perhaps even some sense of 'the history of the English reformations.' The disaster 'gives disaster': the gifts of the *Sonnets* could arrive only at the expense of time, which is to say, at the expense of everything—literature, history, modernity, the name of Shakespeare, subjectivity. It is the gift, if anything, of nuclear war.

Tom Muir

Notes

1. Margaret Aston, 'English Ruins and English History: The Dissolution and the Sense of the Past' in *Lollards and Reformers: Images and Literacy in Late Medieval Religion* (London: Hambledon Press, 1984), p. 313.
2. William Shakespeare, *Titus Andronicus*, ed. Jonathan Bate (London: Arden, 2006), v.i.21.
3. William Shakespeare, *The Sonnets and A Lover's Complaint*, ed. John Kerrigan (Harmondsworth: Penguin, 1995), 126 : 1, 10 : 7. All further references by sonnet and line number are to this edition.
4. F.W. Bateson, 'The function of criticism,' *Essays in Criticism*, 3 (1953), p. 9.
5. Very little work treats the possible connections between the *Sonnets* and Spenser. R. L. Kesler suggests that Sonnet 18 carries within itself a 'virtual' version of *Amoretti* 15, from which it seeks to distance itself and surpass: see Kesler, 'Formalism and the Problem of History: Sonnets, Sequence and Linear Time' in Stephen Cohen (ed.), *Shakespeare and Historical Formalism* (Aldershot: Ashgate, 2007), pp. 183–184. In 'Confounded by Winter: Speeding Time in Shakespeare's Sonnets,' Dympna Callaghan contrasts the Sonnets' depiction of time as destructive with the 'unmotivated cyclical progression of the natural order, as presented, for example, in the Garden of Adonis in Spenser's *Faerie Queene'* (Michael Schoenfeldt (ed.), *A Companion to Shakespeare's Sonnets* (Oxford: Blackwell, 2007), p. 108). More apposite to the present discussion is Andrew Hadfield's argument that Shakespeare enjoys a satirical relationship to the poems of Spenser: comparing Sonnet 130 with *Amoretti* 64, for example, he speculates that Shakespeare's poem 'can be read as a cheeky response to the intricately wrought religious language of the great Protestant poet, as well as a satire of the general conventions of Elizabethan love poetry' (Hadfield, 'Poetry, Politics and Religion' in Patrick Cheney (ed.), *The Cambridge Companion to Shakespeare's Poetry* (Cambridge: Cambridge UP, 2007), p. 174).
6. Edmund Spenser, *The Ruines of Rome: by Bellay* in *The Shorter Poems*, ed. Robert McCabe (Harmondsworth: Penguin, 1999), ll, pp. 94–95; A. Kent Hieatt, 'The Genesis of Shakespeare's Sonnets: Spenser's *Ruines of Rome: by Bellay,'* PMLA, 98 (1983), p. 805. Hieatt continues:

    'Ruinate' does not appear in the corpus [i.e. the corpus of contemporary sonnet sequences] except in *Amoretti* 56, 'Finding a tree alone all comfortlesse/ Beats on it strongly it to ruinate.' In Shakespeare's other works the only other occurrences are *Lucrece* 944, 'To ruinate proud buildings with thy hours'; in *Henry VI* part 3 5.1.83 (first quarto, 1595), 'I will not ruinate my father's house'; in *Titus Andronicus* 5.3.203-04 (last lines of play, second quarto, 1600; not in first quarto, 1594), 'Then afterwards, to order well the state/That like events may ne'er it ruinate'; *Comedy of Errors* 3.2.4 (folio of 1623), 'Shall love in building grow so ruinate?'

In addition, Hieatt notes a second effect transmitted from *Ruines* 7 to the *Sonnets*. This is the use of '"war" and "time" in a combination signifying war against time' (p. 803). In Spenser, we find this as 'though your frames do for a time make warre/ Gainst time' (*Ruines* 93–94); the trope makes its way into Sonnets 15 and 16 as:

> And all in war with time for love of you,
> As he takes from you I engraft you new.

and:

> But wherefore do not you a mightier way
> Make war upon this bloody tyrant Time . . .

7. See Eamon Duffy, *The Stripping of the Altars: Traditional Religion in England c.1400–c.1580*, 2nd ed. (New Haven: Yale UP, 2005), p. 407.
8. Margaret Aston, England's Iconoclasts Vol 1: *Laws Against Images* (Oxford: Clarendon Press, 1988), Vol. 1, p. 278.
9. See, for example, *Ruines of Rome* 65–70:

> The corpes of Rome in ashes is entombed,
> And her great spirite reioyned to the spirite
> Of this great masse, is in the same enwombed;
> But her braue writings, which her famouse merite
> In spight of time, out of the dust doth reare,
> Doo make her Idole through the world appeare.

In this poem, the terms of admiration—'braue writings' and 'famouse merite'—are immediately undercut by the possibility that such admiration may seduce both writer and reader into idolatry. The poem anxiously evokes the *Homily against Idolatry*—which seeks to establish the equivalence of images and idols—at its most fervid:

The seeking out of Images is the beginning of Whoredom . . . and the bringing up of them, is the destruction of Life: For they were not from the beginning, neither shall they continue for ever. . . . the honouring of abominable images is the Cause, the beginning, and end, of all evil, and . . . the Worshippers of them be either mad, or most wicked. . . .Nevertheless, they that love such evil things, they that trust in them, they that make them, they

that favour them, and they that honour them, are all worthy of death, and so forth (*Certain sermons or homilies appointed to be read in churches in the time of Queen Elizabeth of famous memory and now reprinted for the use of private families, in two parts.*)

(London: 1687), pp. 182–3).

On Spenser, Rome, and idolatry, see Margaret W. Ferguson, '"The Afflatus of Ruin": Meditations on Rome by Du Bellay, Spenser and Stevens' in Annabel Patterson (ed.), *Roman Images: Selected Papers from the English Institute*, 1982 (Baltimore: Johns Hopkins UP, 1984), pp. 23–50.

10. Eamon Duffy, 'Bare Ruined Choirs: Remembering Catholicism in Shakespeare's England' in Richard Dutton, Alison Findlay and Richard Wilson (eds), *Theatre and Religion: Lancastrian Shakespeare* (Manchester: Manchester UP, 2003), p. 53. He continues:

The word 'late' there has in fact been taken by some commentators to rule out the application of the image to the monasteries at all, for in the 1590s the dissolution of the monasteries was two generations back, and so could hardly be described as 'late.' On the contrary, however, I believe the telltale word 'late' once again aligns Shakespeare with a dangerously positive reading of the religious past. . . . open assertions of the last stages of monasticism were 'rare'

(pp. 53–54).

Margaret Aston, similarly, has taken this to be a reference to the ruined choirs of the monastic houses, arguing that it 'bears witness to an awareness of the departed monastic period' (Aston, '*English Ruins*,' p. 314). The most elaborate reading of the whole line—'bare ruined choirs, where late the sweet birds sang'—is still William Empson's, tracing the comparison to 'choirs' from the previous line, 'those boughs which shake against the cold':

. . . the comparison holds for many reasons; because ruined monastery choirs are places in which to sing, because they involve sitting in a row, because they are made of wood, are carved into knots and so forth, because they used to be surrounded by a sheltering building crystallised out of the likeness of a forest, and coloured with stained glass and painting like flowers and leaves, because they are

now abandoned by all but the grey walls coloured
like the skies of winter . . .
> (William Empson, *Seven Types of Ambiguity* (Har-
> mondsworth: Penguin, 1995), p. 21).

Just as fascinating, though, is Bateson's rejoinder to this: quite feverishly, he writes that

> the suggested allusion to monastic choirs is not
> only historically improbable, it is also poetically
> disastrous. In 1593 an allusion to the suppressed
> monasteries would have been topical and con-
> troversial. The contemporary equivalent would
> perhaps be an anti-English simile from the Boer
> War (e.g., 'like grand old Kruger'). And this sort of
> allusion isn't wanted in Sonnet LXXXIII. It would
> immediately vulgarise the pathetic portrait Shake-
> speare is painting of himself. In so far as such a
> meaning suggests itself to the reader it must surely
> be suppressed or attenuated rather than encouraged
> (F.W. Bateson and William Empson, 'Bare Ruined
> Choirs' in *Essays in Criticism* 3 (1953), p. 361).

This final sentence seems extraordinary, not least in its use of the word 'suppressed,' which we might also call, in the context of a discussion of the dissolution of the monasteries, 'topical and controversial.' And in the stridency of this call for the attenuation or suppression of meaning—the ruination of a meaning, perhaps?—there seems to be the hint of a higher stake. After all, for whom would this allusion to monastic choirs be 'poetically disastrous' in 1593, or thenabouts? For whom is it poetically disastrous in 1953—the time of Bate-son's enquiry—or now? The assumption here seems to be that the population of England switched, en masse and wholeheart-edly, from Catholicism to Protestantism at a particular point in the mid-sixteenth century; and behind this—hence the striden-cy—we can perhaps also hear what Arthur Marotti calls "the Protestant–Whig narrative into which Shakespeare and other early modern writers have been inserted" (Arthur F. Marotti, 'Shakespeare and Catholicism' in Dutton et al. (eds), Theatre and Religion, p. 218).

11. Edmund Spenser, *The Ruines of Time* in *The Shorter Po-ems*, ed. McCabe, pp. 414–420.
12. William Camden, *Britain, or A chorographicall descrip-tion of the most flourishing kingdomes, England, Scot-land, and Ireland, and the ilands adioyning, out of the depth of antiquitie beautified vvith mappes of the severall shires of England: written first in Latine by William Cam-*

den Clarenceux K. of A. Translated newly into English by Phile'mon Holland Doctour in Physick: finally, revised, amended, and enlarged with sundry additions by the said author (London, 1610), p. 461. Camden is critical of the dissolution throughout the Britannia: early on, he delivers a salvo to those who would want to extirpate even the memory of the religious past:

> There are certaine, as I heare who take it impatient-
> ly that I have mentioned some of the most famous
> Monasteries and their founders. I am sory to heare
> it, and with their good favour will say thus much,
> They may take it as impatiently, and peradventure
> would haue vs forget that our ancestoures were,
> and we are of the Christian profession when as
> there are not extant any other more conspicuous,
> and certaine Monuments, of their piety and zealous
> devotion toward God. Neither were there any other
> seed-gardens from whence Christian Religion,
> and good learning were propagated over this isle,
> howbeit in corrupt ages some weeds grew out over-
> ranckly (p. 6).

13. Joel Fineman, *Shakespeare's Perjured Eye: The Inven-tion of Poetic Subjectivity in the Sonnets* (Berkeley: Cali-fornia UP, 1986), p. 141.
14. Jane Roessner, 'Double exposure: Shakespeare's Sonnets 100–114' *English Literary History*, 46(3) (1979), p. 360.
15. *Homily against Idolatry*, p. 182.
16. Richard Wilson, *Secret Shakespeare: Studies in Theatre, Religion and Resistance* (Manchester: Manchester UP, 2004), p. 152. He suggests that the poem is 'a secret prayer to the Holy Trinity, whispered as lip-service to the "Homily against Idolatry".' Just as the paintings might still be seen beneath the whitewash, the prayer can be heard beneath the 'lip-service.'
17. Patrick Collinson, 'William Shakespeare's Religious In-heritance' in *Elizabethan Essays* (London: Hambledon, 1994), p. 250. 'The fact,' says Collinson, 'that the great doom painting was whitewashed over rather than de-stroyed suggests the kind of crypto-Catholic conduct of which Puritans often complained.' 'The reversibility of whitewashing,' notes Duffy, 'was an established fact: at Chichester a painting of the Passion of Christ in the Ca-thedral was whitewashed over in the early 1580s, but "some well wishers of that waie" rubbed at the white-wash so that "it is almost as bright as ever it was"' (*Strip-ping of the Altars*, p. 583).
18. Juliet Fleming, Graffiti *and the Writing Arts of Early*

Modern England (London: Reaktion, 2001), pp. 76, 78.

19. Ibid., p. 76.
20. Sarah Dillon, *The Palimpsest: Literature, Criticism, Theory* (London: Continuum, 2007), p. 4.
21. Ibid., p. 13.
22. Ibid., p. 33.
23. Quoted in C. E. Wright, 'The Dispersal of the Libraries in the Sixteenth Century' in Francis Wormald and C. E. Wright (eds), *The English Library Before 1700* (London: Athlone, 1958), pp. 153–154.
24. 'It is interesting to see,' Aston remarks, 'how words went down as images went up':

> The scriptures written on roodlofts and about the churches in London, with the arms of England, was washed out against the feast of Easter [1554] in most part of all the parish churches of the diocese of London, wrote Wriothesley. Archdeacon Harpsfield saw to it that the scripture was 'put out' of the church window at Headcorn in Kent, from its place over the rood at St James, Dover, and from the rood loft at Harrietsham. In 1555 the churchwardens of St Mary's, Devizes, paid 'for defacing the scriptures on the walls . . . and for defacing the ten commandments'
> (Aston, *England's Iconoclasts*, pp. 292–293).

25. In *The Ruines of Rome*, for example, we find what is at least on the surface a lament for the city's smashed grandeur combined with the desire to remember in writing its greatness:

> *If vnder heauen anie endurance were,*
> *These monuments, which not in paper writ,*
> *But in Porphyre and Marble doo appeare,*
> *Might well haue hop'd to haue obtained it.*
> *Nath'les my Lute, whom* Phoebus *deignd to give*
> *Cease not to sound these old antiquities . . .*
> (*Ruines of Rome* 439–444).

Similarly, Samuel Daniel contrasts the demolition of 'walls which ambition reared' with 'Th'eternal annals of a happy pen' (Samuel Daniel, Sonnet 37 in *Poems and A Defence of Ryme*, ed. Arthur Colby Sprague (Chicago: Chicago UP, 1950), ll. 2,8. These and similar tropes reactivate what Anne Janowitz refers to as the classical 'immortality-of-poetry' topos: she traces it back to Ovid, citing Frank Justus Miller's translations of the *Metamorphoses*:

> Still in my better part I shall be borne immortal far beyond the lofty stars and I shall have an undying name. Wherever Rome's power extends over the conquered world, I shall have mention on men's lips and, if the prophecies of the bards have any truth, through all the ages shall I live in fame.

See Janowitz, *England's Ruins: Poetic Purpose and the National Landscape* (Oxford: Blackwell, 1990), pp. 183–184.

26. Jacques Derrida, *Archive Fever: A Freudian Impression*, trans. Eric Prenowitz (Chicago: Chicago UP, 1996), pp. 11–12. Of the silence of the death drive, Freud writes:

> It was not easy . . . to demonstrate the activities of this supposed death instinct. The manifestations of Eros were conspicuous and noisy enough. It might be assumed that the death instinct operated silently within the organism towards its dissolution, but that, of course, was no proof. A more fruitful idea was that a portion of the instinct is diverted towards the external world and comes to light as an instinct of aggressiveness and destructiveness. In this way the instinct itself could be pressed into the service of Eros, in that the organism was destroying some other thing, whether animate or inanimate, instead of destroying itself.

See Freud, *Civilisation and its Discontents*, trans. James Strachey in *Penguin Freud Library*, Vol. 12: *Civilisation, Society and Religion* (Harmondsworth: Penguin, 1991), p. 310. An instinct of destruction placed in the service of Eros sounds like an uncannily accurate characterization of the *Sonnets*. But we should note that it is only a *portion* of the instinct which is being directed outwards: in other words, the outward destruction could be thought of as a feint, a kind of bluff. It should call attention to whatever it is in the *Sonnets* that seeks something other than remembrance, commemoration, immortalization.

27. Helen Vendler, *The Art of Shakespeare's Sonnets* (Cambridge, MA: Harvard UP, 1997), p. 268.
28. 'Substrate' is a term from printing, meaning the material onto which text or images might be printed, pressed, imprinted—the material on which an *impression* is made. For Derrida, however, the term comes to signify any mnemonic system, and the possibility of memory generally. Recalling in *Archive Fever* his earlier discussion of the 'Mystic Writing Pad,' he makes it clear that a descrip-

tion of memory systems—such as Freud's—that mobilizes metaphors of partitioning and prosthesis necessarily begins to collapse distinctions between 'interior' and 'exterior,' between 'human' and 'technical' memory. The term 'substrate,' then, ceases to signify the merely external—if functions as a supplement, signifying any form of memory, becoming the condition of thinking about memory itself. See, in particular, *Archive Fever*, pp. 14–20.

29. Roger Martin, *The State of Melford Church and Our Ladie's Chappell at the East End, as I did know it* in David Dymond and Clive Paine, *The Spoil of Melford Church: the Reformation in a Suffolk Parish*, 2nd ed. (Ipswich: Salient Press, 1992), p. 8.

30. Jacques Derrida, 'No apocalypse, not now: full speed ahead, seven missiles, seven missives' trans. Catherine Porter and Philip Lewis in Diacritics, 14(2) (1984), pp. 27–28.

31. Jacques Derrida, *Demeure: Fiction and Testimony* published with Maurice Blanchot, *The Instant of My Death*, both trans. Elizabeth Rottenberg (Stanford: Stanford UP, 2000), pp. 28. He continues:

> *No exposition, no discursive form is intrinsically or essentially* literary *before and outside of the function it is assigned by a right, that is, a specific intentionality inscribed directly on the social body. The same exposition may be taken to be literary here, in one situation according to given conventions, and non-literary there. This is the sign that literarity is not an intrinsic property of this or that discursive event. Even where it seems to* reside *[demeurer], literature remains an unstable function, and it depends on a precarious judicial status. Its passion consists in this—that it receives its determination from something other than itself. Even when it harbours the unconditional right to say anything, including the most savage antinomies, disobedience itself, its status is never assured or guaranteed permanently [*à demeure*], at home, in the inside of an 'at home.' This contradiction is its very existence, its ecstatic process.*

32. Derrida, 'No Apocalypse,' p. 26.
33. John Weever, *Ancient Funeral Monuments* (London, 1631), p. 50. See, too, Nigel Llewellyn, *Funeral Monuments in Post-Reformation England* (Cambridge: Cambridge UP, 2000), p. 259: 'In some quarters, passions were aroused to such [an iconoclastic] pitch that funeral monuments were physically attacked. In response, the state issued proclamations and using heralds and antiquaries as apologists, sought to protect monuments by presenting them as examples of order and virtue. Some tomb-breaking was part of a wider attack on religious institutions but other damage was the result of social circumstance. The effigy of an unpopular landowner might earn the attention of a mob, otherwise untutored in image theory.'

34. Weever, *Funerall Monuments*, p. 51. John Stow is equally appalled at the destruction of tombs. At St Dunstan in the East, he observes that buried there are 'many other worshipfull persons besides, whose monuments are altogether defaced': see Stow, *A Survey of London*, ed. C.L. Kingsford (Oxford: Clarendon Press, 1908), Vol. I, p. 135. Similarly, at St Mary Somerset, he writes, 'it is a proper church, but the monuments are all defaced' (Vol. II, p. 6). Given that 'defacement' is Stow's choice of verb for the work of iconoclasts suggesting some remainder, at least—it is striking that at St Peter's church in Queen Hithe ward, the demolition seems total: 'In this Church no Monuments doe remain' (Vol. II, p. 6).

35. Jonathan Dollimore, *Death, Desire and Loss in Western Culture* (Harmondsworth: Penguin, 1999), p. 105.
36. Thomas Hearne, *A Collection of Curious Discourses written by Eminent Antiquaries upon Several Heads in our English Antiquities* (London, 1771), Vol. I, pp. 259–260.
37. Jacques Derrida, 'Biodegradables: seven diary fragments' trans. Peggy Kamuf in *Critical Inquiry*, 15 (1989), p. 815.
38. Ibid., pp. 815–816.
39. Ibid., p. 837.
40. Jacques Derrida, 'The Time of a Thesis: Punctuations' in Alan Montefiore (ed.), *Philosophy in France Today* (Cambridge: Cambridge UP, 1983), pp. 40–41.
41. Derrida, 'Biodegradables,' p. 815.
42. Maurice Blanchot, *The Writing of the Disaster* trans. Ann Smock (Lincoln: Nebraska UP, 1995), p. 5.
43. Jacques Derrida, *Given Time: 1. Counterfeit Money* trans. Peggy Kamuf (Chicago: Chicago UP, 1992), p. 13.
44. Ibid.
45. Ibid., p. 14.

Reprinted from *Textual Practice* 24 (1), pp. 21-49 by Tom Muir. Copyright © 2010 Routledge, Francis Group. Reprinted with permission of the Publisher.

Ecosystemic Shakespeare:
Vegetable Memorabilia in the Sonnets

The paperback cover of one of my copies of *Shakespeare's Sonnets* has been defaced. The cover image is an enlarged detail from Rembrandt's *Man Sharpening a Quill* (1632), but the man's face is missing.[1] Only his hands are there, husbanding a few of the natural elements in what we might call a textual economy. The left hand holds a bird's feather, its tip, the nib, turned toward the man. The right hand grips the bone handle of a knife, its mineral blade preparing animal matter to put "mind . . . in character." Plants are also here among the animals and minerals: the man's paper, not shown in this detail, awaits the freshly sharpened quill, and the edge of a linen ruff spreads above the quill's nib, invoking the relationship between rag-based paper and the collar's flax fibers. (Recycled cloth was the stuff of paper for most of the history of Western printing.) My cover, tattered at the corners, stained from use as a coaster, and splitting at the spine is past prime, and yet the copyright page demands that it remain this volume's sole cover in perpetuity: "You must not circulate this book in any other binding or cover and you must impose this same condition on any acquirer." Surely this is an in-joke for readers already familiar with the volume's contents, for it defies nature and limits conferral. Can one really be expected to guard this flimsy cover, mere paper plus a plastic film, 'gainst Time's scythe (and coffee spills)? The legal injunction is an economical safeguard, but in emphasizing one economy, the book trade, it de-emphasizes another economy, nature. Cover and copyright renew and contribute to the *Sonnets'* central preoccupation with preservation and decay. Like the things it depicts, the cover must disintegrate.

In the opening sonnets, the poet seeks a preservatory that might evade decay and death, reaching a cobbled solution at the end of sonnet 17, where the poet's papers and the beloved's child dually preserve the beloved's beauty. In sonnet 18, the poet is commonly thought to switch preservation strategies and "flatly contradict the overriding procreation theme of 1–17."[2] One is tempted to read this sonnet as a throwing up of hands, a decision to put a brave face on a flawed preservation effort (an effort mocked later in the first quarto, hereafter *Q*, by

"a fickle maid full pale, / Tearing of papers" [*A Lover's Complaint*, ll. 5–6]).[3] However, given the *Sonnets'* repeated emphasis on husbandry, a preservation strategy that simply denies or ignores natural decay would seem willfully negligent. Outright defiance is uncharacteristic of the *Sonnets*, too. Their rhetorical tendency is toward "systems" and "economies" that comprehend divergent ideas through arrangement and re-arrangement.[4] Thomas M. Greene, for instance, considers the "rhetorical economics" of the *Sonnets* and suggests that the poetry's "rhetorical density" may be meant to "refute its own self-accusations of dearth."[5] In Greene's analysis, poetry is never able to produce its desired result: "The increase we desire from fairest creatures never materializes." And yet, here it is. The non-referential "this" of sonnet 18—"So long lives this, and this gives life to thee"—simultaneously implies a nearness to the original poet and a nearness to the eventual reader.[6] Reading "this," holding "this" in our hands, we are implicated into the textual economy of the *Sonnets* because we hold the material offspring of Shakespeare's papers. His flax-fiber pages and our tree-pulp pages are systemically linked.

While sonnets 15 through 17 introduce and consider the idea of replacing progeny with poems, sonnet 18 does something different, something subtle and more systemically complex. The poet finds a biological solution to textual decay by envisioning his perishable writing materials as part of a larger system of natural matter—an ecosystem in which decay and renewal are symbiotic.[7] The poet's decaying "papers (yellowed with their age)" give way to "this," a free-floating demonstrative pronoun without a clear referent, a timeless pronoun capable of attaching itself to the varied papers on which it will appear in the future. This essay is an attempt to narrate possibilities, to consider what an ecosystemic reading of the *Sonnets* might reveal about the poetic complexities of recording–and preserving–human ideas with vegetable matter.[8] I want to further suggest that an ecosystemic reading might provide speare's habitat and in ours. More specifically, though, I focus on the systemic link between plants and poetic preservation in sonnets 15 to 18. I argue here that the poet deliberately "engraft[s]" his beloved into a textual lineage, a dynamic biological system in which poetic reproduction relies upon decayed textiles.

Sonnet 15 likens men and plants in an extended simile that seems imprecise. In the first two lines of the sonnet, the speaker "consider[s]" a general claim: "every thing that grows / Holds in perfection but a little moment." Lines 3–8, where he particularizes and exemplifies the opening claim, are less clear:

> When I perceive that men as plants increase,
> Cheere'd and checked even by the selfsame sky,
> Vaunt in their youthful sap, at height decrease,
> And wear their brave state out of memory;

Stephen Booth writes, "The reader's experience of this line is a type of his experience of this sonnet and the sonnets in general. The line is easy to understand, but it would be hard to say just what it says or how it says it." Metaphors interweave and change forms. Line 6 seems to comment on the stars and stage, creating "A somewhat confused theatrical metaphor" in lines 3–8. Also confusing is the fact that, in the second quatrain, both men and plants "increase," "Vaunt," and "decrease," but in line 8, the plants seem to disappear from the equation as men "wear their brave state out of memory." This essay is particularly interested in the poetic role of these plants. Syntactically, the plants might also "wear their brave state out of memory," but I have not found a gloss or critical reading that considers just how a plant might wear itself out.

The "men as plants" analogy grows more systemically complex, rather than collapsing in line 8, if we consider that this is the first of a series of sonnets that are actively concerned with the ecology of writing as a means of preservation. Plants, textiles, and texts were biologically connected, and the verb "wear" in this context can summon all three, though "wear" is most frequently glossed only as a reference to clothing. For instance, Burrow writes of line 8: "young men wear out their proud clothes, their elevated status, and their exhilarated condition all at once." (Burrow 410).[9] But plants participate, too: when men wear their "brave state out of memory," they also wear out the memory of plants because clothing fibers are plant fibers. Line 8 of sonnet 15 recalls and reconsiders the simultaneous decay of finery and flora signaled by "tattered weed" in sonnet 2: "Thy youth's proud livery so gazed on now / Will

be a tattered weed of small worth held." Sonnet 2 fails to convince the beloved to procreate, "to be new made when thou art old," but sonnet 15 salvages the "tattered weed" and recontextualizes it. In sonnet 2, old clothes are merely frayed reminders of the beloved's prime; in sonnet 15, worn-out clothing takes on new worth as part of a textual economy.

Paper, an object essential to the poetic preservation first suggested in these lines, was the product of exactly the kinds of disintegration described in sonnet 15: wearing out (paper fibers needed to be broken in through wearing before they could be used for papermaking) and decay (piling rags and letting them rot helped to further break down the fibers). Sonnet 15, then, introduces a material twist that subtly glosses sonnet 2 and redirects the preservation project: the beloved's worn-out, time-decayed clothing might become the stuff of a more lasting memorial (cf. sonnet 55). Space does not permit a full consideration of known variants between *Q* and the numerous surviving manuscript versions of sonnet 2, but it is worth noticing that the wording of lines 3–4 in most versions of "Spes Altera" offers less hope of preservation than *Q*. In "Spes Altera," the beloved's clothing "so accounted now" becomes "like rotten weeds of no worth held."[10] Rotten weeds are worthless in this context because they are just weeds, decayed plants that are physically distinct from the beloved's clothing. Where "Spes Altera" likens plants and clothing via simile, *Q* links them in an ecosystem: the livery "*Will be* a tattered weed" (emphasis mine). In *Q,* lines 3–4 work better biologically and, I would argue, they make better poetry in the sense that they are more consistent with the *Sonnets'* counterpointed aesthetic. The "tattered weed" with its tiny value offers another way to re-member a beloved through the reuse of the sort of memory-rich clothing Peter Stallybrass has written about.[11] Tears, stains, and stitches signal narratives. Wearing clothes, one impresses his or her body and life onto plant matter. In Renaissance society, this inhabiting process also served the purpose of breaking down stiff fibers and preparing clothing for paper. Texts required worn-out plants and people; decay was a precondition of poetic preservation.

The war that the poet makes with Time, then, is more subtle than defiant, for he discovers one way to convert biological decay into textual reproduction, reusing and renewing that which Time takes. In line 12, "To change your day of youth to sullied night," decay is like the onset of night. But how can the night, something that is already dark, be sullied? Elsewhere in Shakespeare, to sully is to stain or soil white cloth.[12] Here, "sullied" works not only with "night" but also with "most rich" to effect a layered metaphor: Time decays or sullies the fine clothes of youth, changing bright to dark. In the final line of sonnet 15,"As he [Time] takes from you, I engraft you new," the poet promises to graft the beloved into another, more reproductive lineage. The first quatrain of sonnet 16 anxiously reveals the textual nature of this engrafting project, and sonnet 18 ultimately proclaims its superiority as a preservation strategy. The beloved will live in "this," whatever paper form it has taken, "[w]hen in eternal lines to time thou grow'st." Would it be going too far to imagine rhetorical connections among eternal lines, poetic lineage, and linen? Ben Jonson makes just these associations in his poetic tribute to Shakespeare. Three lines after the infamous claim that Shakespeare "*was not of an age, but for all time!*" Jonson writes, "*Nature her selfe was proud of his designes, / And ioy'd to weare the dressing of his lines! / Which were so richly spun, and wouen so fit*" (A4v).[13] Playing on the material and orthographical similarities of poetic lines and linen, Jonson likens the making of "*well torned . . . lines*" to the spinning of plant matter on a flax wheel (A4v).[14]

As Jonson's lines suggest, Renaissance writers and readers understood the systemic links among plants, clothing, and paper. John Taylor, the "Water Poet," offers something like a natural history of the book in *The Praise of Hemp-seed*, explaining how a plant like hemp (or flax) "to paper doth conuert" via cloth economies and how this conversion imbues texts with alternate narratives.[15] Considering the origins of paper, and especially how its raw materials cycle through society, Taylor calls attention to the fiber contents of pages—perhaps, for the reader, to the very page on which the lines are printed:

> *For when I thinke but how is paper made*
> *Into Philosophy I straight waies wade:*
> *How here, and there, and euery where lies scatter'd*
> *Old ruind rotten rags, and ropes, all tatter'd.*

Having invoked a peculiar kind of *rime sparse*, Taylor attempts to gather that which is scattered into "tatters Allegoricall / Tropes, tipes, and figures, of mans rise or fall." Here he imagines several specific origin stories in which paper becomes a rhetorical under-text that inflects and in some cases subverts the over-text. A Brownist's "zealous ruffe," for instance, might "Be turnd to paper, and a Play writ in't."

In Taylor's account, Hempseed, and the cloth it becomes, has something to say. But rather than speak in the first person (like the traveling Shilling of another of Taylor's works), Hempseed is spoken about and spoken on when print meets paper. In one sense, in the moment we might have had prosopopoeia, paper or its raw resources speaking, we find antiprosopopoeia, poets as paper: "In paper, many a Poet now suruiues / Or else their lines had perish'd with their liues." Shakespeare is named among the English poets who, thanks to Hempseed "immortally / Do liue in spight of death, and cannot die." In light of Taylor's botanical insights, we might rephrase line 6 of Sonnet 15: men increase—as plants. For some, this "reduction of human subjects to the status of things or commodities" leads to economic crisis: "The Sonnets . . . demonstrat[e] what ensues when commodification infects the poetry of praise."[16] An ecosystemic approach acknowledges this interchangeableness of "human subjects," "things," and "poetry," but without the pessimism.[17] Infection is part of the ecosystem; decay both obliterates and funds textual subjects and objects.

Plants still provide us with paper and, by extension, with Shakespeare. And though we no longer socially interact with them in cloth form, we still materially and metaphorically link paper and plants, describing reuse and electronic document delivery in terms of arboreal salvation narratives. Our books about the *Sonnets* still ask us to think about plants, preservation, and the recycling of organic matter: one secondary source cited above is printed on "*permanent* paper from mills that operate a sustainable forestry policy."[18] Because our link with Shakespeare is botanical, an ecosystemic reading is another way of asking questions about the very poetics with which the sonnets are involved. It is a close reading that attends not only to what is on the page, but also to what is in the page—not only to the text as it has changed editorially, but also to the text as it has changed ecologically. Ecosystemic reading, like close reading, is drawn to complexity, play, and possibility. The sonnets, so concerned with the way poetry survives "the interchange of state," invite us to notice the recycling of animal, vegetable, and mineral matter both in their poetic language and in their physical incarnations. Elemental questions raised in earlier poems are restated and reworked in poems appearing later in the sequence, and a longer essay might more fully consider the shifts, revisions, and inconsistencies in the poet's attitude toward preservation through poetry.

In closing, I return to the non-referential

demonstrative pronoun "this" as a physical word on the page that is employed repeatedly and conspicuously in the *Sonnets* to identify the text without identifying a specific incarnation of it. After the couplet of sonnet 18, where it appears twice, the next non-referential "this" appears in the couplet of sonnet 55: "So, till the judgement that yourself arise, / You live in this, and dwell in lovers' eyes." The simple point I wish to make is that, while it is natural to assume that "this," in the context of the poems, is the poet's papers or a copy intended for the beloved, we are drawn in as voyeur-readers by a poet who needs our eyes. The trick of making a non-referential "this" do double duty across time is used again in the couplets of sonnets 74 ("And that is this, and this with thee remains") and 107 ("And thou in this shalt find thy monument, / When tyrants' crests and tombs of brass are spent").[19] A common feature of all three sonnets that repeat the non-referential "this" of sonnet 18 in their couplets (55, 74, and 107) is an emphasis on poetry as "monument" or "memorial." In sonnet 55, the poet praises the superiority of his "pow'rful rhyme" over stone monuments because it is a "living record": "Nor Mars his sword, nor war's quick fire shall burn / The living record of your memory."[20] Booth notes the irony that these lines "assert the immortality of the poem" just as they "remind a reader of the flimsiness and vulnerability of anything written on paper" (Booth, *Sonnets* 229). The poet is not blind to this seeming irony. In fact, as I have been arguing, his preservation strategy relies upon it. The beloved's praise—and the poet's glory—will be a "living record" that survives in the eyes of readers who are also wearers: "Even in the eyes of all posterity / That wear this world out to the ending doom." It is the very flimsiness of paper that makes it a better monument, for the "living record" lives by wear and tear.

Close reading the lines of the *Sonnets*, we are drawn into even closer readings between their lines, for Shakespeare's poetry is concerned with making in every sense of the word. In the context of this forum on Shakespeare and Ecology, I would also add that I think ecosystemic readings can offer insights that might be particularly timely and meaningful to us and to our students. In a previous *Shakespeare Studies* forum, Jean Howard asks "an obvious question, but one we too seldom ask of our scholarship: why should one care about early modern cosmopolitanism?"[21] The answer, she claims, is that the issue matters to us now, and that "the mirror of the past" might nuance our own present-day conversations about the

topic. Exchanging "ecology" for "cosmopolitanism," I recycle the sentiment.

Joshua Calhoun

Notes

1. The cover cited appears on the reissued edition of *The Complete Sonnets and Poems*, ed. Colin Burrow (Oxford: Oxford University Press, 2008); interestingly, the previous cover (2002) emphasized a face—Giovanni Bellini's *Portrait of a Boy*. All citations of Shakespeare's poetry are from this edition.

2. G. Blakemore Evans, ed., William Shakespeare, *The Sonnets* (Cambridge: Cambridge University Press, 2006), 123.

3. Cf. Sasha Roberts, *Reading Shakespeare's Poems in Early Modern England* (New York: Palgrave, 2003). Roberts convincingly argues, "Thorpe's quarto pairs Shakespeare's sonnet sequence with *A Lover's Complaint* to produce a *composite* volume that invites intertextual readings" (143). Following Roberts, I would argue that the "narrative of the 1609 sequence" (174) allows us to emphasize thematic groupings like the "procreation sonnets" without overemphasizing authorial intent.

4. The Shakespearean sonnet is "a system in motion . . . with several subsystems," writes Helen Vendler (*The Art of Shakespeare's Sonnets* [Cambridge: Belknap Press of Harvard University Press, 1997], 22); Stephen Booth claims, "Shakespeare copes with the problem of the conflicting obligations of a work of art by multiplying the number of ordering principles, systems of organization, and frames of reference" ("The Value of the Sonnets," *A Companion to Shakespeare's Sonnets*, ed. Michael Schoenfeldt [Malden: Blackwell Publishing, 2007], 15–26, esp. 16).

5. Thomas M. Greene, "Pitiful Thrivers: Failed Husbandry in the Sonnets," in *Shakespeare's Poems: The Scholarly Literature*, eds. Stephen Orgel and Sean Keilen (New York: Routledge, 1999), 50–64, esp. 55.

6. Cf. "this, *dem. pron.* and *a.*": "B. I. 1. Indicating a thing or person present or near (actually in space or time . . . spec. as being nearer than some other (hence opposed to that . . ." (*OED Online*).

7. Cf. "ecosystem *n.*": "A biological system composed of all the organisms found in a particular physical environment, interacting with it and with each other. Also in extended use: a complex system resembling this" (*OED Online*).

8. Sonnet 59 in some ways narrates the imagined experience of the poet doing what I am describing: considering cycles of thought by looking at "some antique book," a half-

century-old "record" of the "mind . . . in character."

9. Cf. Stephen Booth, ed., *Shakespeare's Sonnets* (New Haven: Yale University Press, 1977), 157; the line may also extend the theatrical metaphor of the first quatrain, alluding to the recycled clothing used by actors. Cf. "The currency of clothing" in Ann Rosalind Jones and Peter Stallybrass, *Renaissance Clothing and the Materials of Memory* (Cambridge: Cambridge University Press, 2000), 17–33.

10. Here I quote Burrow's collated version of "Spes Altera." Cf. Evans, "Appendix: Manuscript Copies of the Sonnets," *The Sonnets*, 268–70.

11. Cf. Peter Stallybrass, "Marx's Coat," *Border Fetishisms: Material Objects in Unstable Spaces*, ed. Patricia Spyer (New York: Routledge, 1998),183–207; and "Worn Worlds: Clothes and Identity on the Renaissance Stage," *Subject and Object in Renaissance Culture*, eds. Margreta de Grazia, Maureen Quilligan, and Peter Stallybrass (Cambridge: Cambridge University Press, 1996), 289–320. Stallybrass's discussion of Renaissance England as "a livery society" ("Worn Worlds" 289) is especially pertinent to my discussion of sonnets 2 and 15. I am grateful to him for generously sharing research notes and conversation about rag-based paper.

12. Cf. *The Winter's Tale*, 1.2.329: "Sully the purity and whiteness of my sheets"; and *1 Henry IV*, 2.5.73–74: "For look you, Francis, your white canvas doublet will sully." Both cited from *The Complete Works*, 2nd ed., eds. Stanley Wells, Gary Taylor, John Jowett, and William Montgomery (Oxford: Clarendon Press, 2005).

13. I cite a version of the First Folio accessed via the publicly available Schoenberg Center for Electronic Text & Image (SCETI) database because, paradoxically, electronic databases like SCETI have made the plant and cloth nature of Renaissance books more visible to those who may not have access to them in rare books collections. At 8x magnification, these high-quality images reveal flecks of plant and cloth matter in many of the Folio's pages.

14. The spelling ("torned" for "turned"), whether accidental or not, further suggests the shared nature of lines and linen.

15. John Taylor, *The Praise of Hemp-seed* (London, 1620), D4r. Taylor asserts that flax and hemp "Are male and female, both one, and the same" (B2r).

16. Peter C. Herman, "What's the Use? Or, The Problematic of Economy in Shakespeare's Procreation Sonnets," *Shakespeare's Sonnets: Critical Essays*, ed. James Schiffer (New York: Garland Publishing, Inc., 1999), 263–83, esp. 264, 279.

17. Laurie Shannon finds a useful critique of human exceptionalism in Renaissance cosmology: "early modern humanity is relatively ecosystemic: it always has animality (and divinity and plants and elements) in or with it" ("The Eight Animals in Shakespeare: or, Before the Human," *PMLA* 124.2 [2009]: 472–79, esp. 477).

18. Schoenfeldt, ed., *Companion*, title page, emphasis mine. The oxymoronic term "permanent paper" indicates, among other things, paper that does not yellow within a few years; cf. <http://www.permanencematters.com/the-issue/>.

19. The relativity of "this"—its ability to indicate a material thing held in some future reader's hands—is also suggested in the couplets of sonnets 116, 123, and 124.

20. "The living record of your memory" recalls the growth of eternal lines in 18.12 and anticipates the poet's claim that "My life hath in this line some interest, / Which for memorial still with thee shall stay" (74.3–4). The boast that "war's quick fire" cannot burn a written record is not original here; as Burrow notes, Ovid makes the same claim, although he ties the preservation of his verse to the fate of the Roman Empire (490). Katherine Duncan Jones regards the boast as "support for Shakespeare's intention to publish [the *Sonnets*], to ensure the proliferation of copies" (*Shakespeare's Sonnets* [London: Thomson Learning, 2007], 220).

21. Jean E. Howard, "Introduction: English Cosmopolitanism and the Early Modern Moment," *Shakespeare Studies* 35 (2007): 19–23, esp. 23

The Social Masochism of Shakespeare's Sonnets

Figuring linguistic ambiguity as Shakespeare's "fatal *Cleopatra*," the temptation "for which he lost the world, and was content to lose it," Samuel Johnson conjures up a mixture of "dark" womanhood, implications of gratified lust, and the exoticism of cross-rank erotics—opposing a standard of verbal economy to a sense of pleasant, feminized, and useless diversion.[1] The image deals in durable categories. The modern term "wordplay," for instance, retains this distinction between the productivity of work and the waste of fun, a dividing line that, as Margreta de Grazia has argued, was not widely incorporated into English usage until Johnson's own eighteenth-century efforts at "lexical standardization."[2] Work and play, de Grazia claims, do not map so cleanly onto the language of Shakespearean texts. As an example, she follows the variations on one word ("bear") in *The Winter's Tale*, and shows how the capacity of a single sound to gather together multiple meanings could be a definitive source of both structure and action.[3] To disregard the "wordplay" in the play, then, may be to miss the very ways it makes sense, to lose what makes it work.

Although Johnson's distinction between productivity and waste seems worth complicating, his Cleopatra aptly suggests the vague air of eroticism that so often marks Shakespeare's use of homonyms. The puns, as everybody knows, are bawdy, particularly in the sonnets, where a dangerously alluring "dark lady" and a reluctant young man are surrounded by what has been called an "imprecise[ly] create[d] . . . aura of sexuality," a suggestiveness that "abides in the half-light of wordplay, implication, and insinuation."[4] I want to question the value of reading this text as a coherent whole, but first would like to note how central the collective "aura" created by ambiguous language has been to the long and contested tradition of making sense of the sonnets. Peter Stallybrass and de Grazia have both traced the cultural anxiety that has marked these poems' reception, exemplified by the fervent denials of Shakespeare's homosexuality by critics such as Samuel Coleridge and George Chalmers.[5] More recently, Joseph Pequigney has reversed these claims, arguing in *Such Is My Love: A Study of Shakespeare's Sonnets* that, if read correctly, the sonnets tell the clear story of an "amorous transaction" between Shakespeare and his male addressee.[6] In these readings, Shakespeare's bawdy ambiguities are signposts to a specific kind of biographical subtext—whether homosexual or heterosexual, they seem to confess the truths of an "interiorized" sexuality.[7]

Stephen Booth, perhaps the editor most attuned to the verbal play of the sonnets, voices a strong impatience with these biographical interpretations. "Hermaphroditic wordplay," he writes, "is not likely to confuse any readers but those who treat the poems as biographical spoor: sexual wordplay has always been anatomically eclectic—as any reader of walls knows."[8] Sexually overcharged language, Booth argues, is only natural. But here, defending the sonnets from being read as authorial confession comes at the price of universalizing a very different kind of text: the obscene graffiti "any reader" might find in a modern (men's) bathroom. Booth's argument resonates here with de Grazia's critique of his extraordinarily thorough readings of Shakespeare's language: "while he may have done more than anyone to animate Shakespearean homonyms, Booth also has done more to render them *unimportant*, that is, incapable of importing or delivering meaning."[9] In terms of the sonnets, Booth attends to the multiple nuances of each word but ascribes to one of the poems' most defining characteristics—their erotic aura—the unimportance of an everyday thing.

Although little can be said with certainty about the specific social context(s) for which Shakespeare originally wrote the sonnets, the scant surviving evidence of at least some of the poems' early circulation suggests a different way to read their verbal ambiguities. In 1598, in what has become a much-cited line in Shakespeare studies, author Francis Meres noted in his *Palladis Tamia* that Shakespeare's "sugred *Sonnets*" were passing among his "priuate friends."[10] The following year, a full decade before the sequence we know as the *Sonnets* appeared in print, a published collection of miscellaneous verse called *The Passionate Pilgrim* included versions of what would become Sonnets 138 and 144, the two poems likely reaching the printer after circulating on their own in manuscript. As Gary Taylor and Arthur F. Marotti have shown, since the few examples of Shakespeare's sonnets that have been found in private copybooks all date from 1620 or later, *The Passionate Pilgrim* poems offer the only textual evidence of the circulation Meres mentioned in 1598.[11] Approaching the

Sonnets by way of the two poems that were published in *The Passionate Pilgrim*, I would like to argue that reading Shakespeare's wordplay apart from the familiar contiguity of the 1609 text can offer fresh ways to historicize his fondness for the bawdy pun. In the grain of de Grazia's analysis of *The Winter's Tale*, I hope to show that conceptualizing the specific ways wordplay may have been at work within the scene of manuscript production and circulation allows for readings of the poems apart from both Shakespeare's sexual biography and Booth's transhistoricism—both the interiorized self and the universal men's room.

Significantly, *The Passionate Pilgrim* poems belong to the "dark lady" group, not the "young man" sonnets that, praising an apparently aristocratic addressee, seem to have recognizable roots in manuscript circulation between writer and patron. And if these "dark lady" verses were indeed products of some kind of manuscript culture, they fit uneasily within the figures of homosociality through which the Renaissance craze for sonnets has most often been understood. The central role played by Petrarchan verse within elite male social networks of the late sixteenth century has been well documented, beginning with the terms set out by J. W. Saunders in *The Profession of English Letters*. Renaissance sonneteers, Saunders shows, circulated verse within a "group system" of similarly positioned, similarly ambitious men he describes (recalling Meres's comment) as a "circle of friends."[12] Providing a kind of decorum practice, a manner of solidifying ties, and the possibility of upward mobility through display, this manuscript culture developed male bonds and aspirations through the idiom of courtly love. Shakespeare's "young man" sonnets, read as making a bid for favor from an upper-class patron, make sense within this model of sonnets as vehicles of ambition and homosocial bonds. If the "dark lady" sonnets performed a similar role, they did so in a more complicated way.

More recent work on sonnet circulation by Marotti and Wendy Wall has stressed ways in which the dynamics of this gentlemanly social world informed the poetry's themes and content. "In the Tudor and early Stuart periods," Marotti claims, "lyric poetry was basically a genre for gentleman-amateurs who regarded their literary 'toys' as ephemeral works that were part of a social life that also included dancing, singing, gaming, and civilized conversation."[13] Within this social life, he argues, in which writer and reader knew one another well and participated in the same system of worldly aspirations,

the conventions of love poetry could "express figuratively the realities of suit, service, and recompense with which ambitious men were insistently concerned."[14] Philip Sidney serves as Marotti's prime example of this type of "gentleman-amateur," allegorizing his own frustrated social situation in the language of love for an audience of peers readily able to decode and to sympathize with his hopes.[15]

Drawing on Eve Kosofsky Sedgwick's conception of homosociality in English literature, Wall details ways in which coterie verse written to and about women inscribed the relations "between men" at the heart of this manuscript culture. The acts of judging, responding, and rewriting through which male readers forged relationships with male writers, Wall claims, were often figured in the poems' urgent pleas for a lover's response. In various ways, the unrequiting women addressed in the verse play the role of third term in the triangulated desire of men for the society of men.[16] For Saunders, Marotti, and Wall, the male relationships negotiated through sonnet circulation turn on the gendered social similarities of writer and reader, expressed and solidified by the foil of the female "other."

These studies present convincing formulations of how the thematics of Renaissance sonnets worked within the particularly coded setting of gentlemanly amateurism, but I would argue that Shakespeare's sonnets, written from a very different social position, inscribe another series of relationships among writer, theme, and reader. And it is the highly sexualized linguistic slippage of the "dark lady" sonnets, not the deferential (though still, of course, bawdy) "young man" verses that may best exemplify this difference. Although Meres has memorialized Shakespeare's audience as "friends," as Marotti notes, it is worth keeping in mind the early modern connotation of patronage, not equality, in the term; written by an actor, playwright, and theater shareholder, Shakespeare's verse would have crossed a major class divide to reach any audience of gentlemanly readers.[17] And if, in the two "dark lady" *Passionate Pilgrim* poems, we have a glimpse of some of the works Shakespeare produced for the kind of readership that Saunders, Marotti, and Wall describe in their discussions of manuscript circulation—male readers of higher social status than Shakespeare, and for whom sonnet consumption foregrounded concerns of class—how might these works have played in this original setting?

Loaded with sexual wordplay, both poems depict a male speaker in a losing struggle with chastity and integrity. In the 1599 version of Sonnet 138, "When My Love Swears that She is Made of Truth," Shakespeare dramatizes the speaker's choice to "lie" with his love in different terms than would appear in 1609. In line 8, he describes their lying as "Outfacing faults in love, with love's ill rest." And the poem ends,

> *O loves best habit's in a soothing toung*
> . . . .
> *Therefore I'll lye with Love, and love with me,*
> *Since that our faultes in love thus smother'd be.*
> (lines 11–4)

Lying without resting, smothered by soothing tongues, the speaker here knits together a clever argument about vanity with a highly suggestive erotic vocabulary. The echo of "mother" in the "smother'd" of the last line puts a feminine spin on this intrusion of desire. The two participants are shown to be "mother'd" just as Lear is as he loses his wits—"O, how this mother swells up toward my heart!"—the *s* from "this" making a similar pun on "smother."[18] Here linguistic ambiguities replicate the theme: as the speaker loses integrity to feminine encroachment, so the "mother'd" word equivocates into a mess of meaning.

This sense of an overwhelming, gendered disorder underlies the tension in the second sonnet published in *The Passionate Pilgrim* as well. Like 138, 144 turns on ambiguities in the word "ill." "Two loves I have of comfort and despaire," the speaker explains, "My better Angell, is a Man (right faire) / My worser spirite a Woman (colour'd ill)" (lines 1, 3–4). These lines are often interpreted within the framework of the traditional plot of the *Sonnets*, a triangular love affair with the speaker at the center. Booth, for instance, translates the opening line as, "I have two beloveds; one gives me comfort, and the other drives me to despair."[19] The sentiment, however, could just as easily be read as a conflict within the self: along the lines of Sonnet 138, the speaker torn between a fair, masculine orderliness and an ill, feminine, and sexual energy—a gendered early modern version of the tiny angel and devil perched at either ear. Booth glosses venereal disease as one sense of the concluding line: "Till my bad Angell fire my good one out" (line 14). But, if the poem is read as dramatizing a conflict within the speaker, this sexual meaning also entails the same moral victory of illness, femininity, and lust as does the concluding play on smother'd/mother'd in 138. In other words, the very same terms that describe sexual

intercourse describe the deterioration, or contamination, of manhood. As the words themselves demonstrate a kind of loss of integrity—ambiguity after ambiguity sliding Petrarchan conventions into admissions of bodily disorder—so the speaker dramatizes his own slide from a masculinized self-control to a feminized indulgence. Homonyms break sense in two, repeating at the level of the word the division of the "mother'd" man.

The poems recall the terms of Johnson's Cleopatra: the "dark lady," the controlling voice given over to wasteful indulgence, and the aura of innuendo. But reading their gendered presentation with the class dynamics of gentlemanly readership in mind offers a way of seeing how the ambiguities of quibbles may have been a crucial part of their sense rather than a Johnsonian diversion. If these poems were written to circulate within the homosocial networks described by historians of early modern manuscript culture, for a readership accustomed to finding specific social relationships embedded in conventions of verse, they met their audience not as communications among equals coded in terms of desire for an other gender but as markers of same-sex inequality, caricatures of another other: the socially abject author. Put differently, the two *Passionate Pilgrim* sonnets can be read as introducing a fourth term to the triangle of desire that critics have found to be at work in Renaissance sonnet circulation. Rather than providing an avenue for males to bond over depictions of women, they might have enabled a kind of rank-reinforcing sense of the *difference* between writer and reader.

Within this social context, the indistinct aura of eroticism created by the double valence of words such as "lie," "faultes," "angell," and "smoth'r" would (literally) have made all the difference. Any reader of Sidney and his imitators could have encountered expressions of absolute enthrallment to his beloved, a few muted gestures toward images of bodily satisfactions, and clever turns on linguistic ambiguities. Readers of Richard Barnfield's poems (which perhaps played a role in his disinheritance)[20] would have found extended sexual similes involving birds, bees, and flowers. But Shakespeare's far more polyvocal and indeterminate bawdiness raises the Petrarchan trope of disempowerment to a new pitch. In dramatizing a speaker's loss of control in love and language—the permeability of a masculine self subject to feminine encroachment—his sonnets present both voice and diction equally subject to a loss of integrity, to carnal intrusions. Enthrallment appears in patently erotic terms, reproduced or mirrored at the level of the word. And the audience is invited to observe the "mothered" author feminized in both the narrated action and the act of writing; as he gives in to his very corporal beloved, his language performs a similar kind of lapse.

Displacing class anxieties onto distinctions of gender, this deferential self-presentation prefigures the terms that, as Wall shows, governed the shift from manuscript circulation to book publication that would occur around the turn of the seventeenth century. As more and more circulated manuscripts were collected in print and made available to a wide audience, Wall observes, "writers and publishers ushered printed texts into the public eye by naming that entrance as a titillating and transgressive act . . . They did so, I argue, as a means of addressing the vexed class concerns that were bound up with the act of publication. In this way, readers and writers could safeguard the social boundaries that relied on the coterie network by translating that boundary into sexualized terms. The view of the author that emerges from this metaphoric inscription is one defined against a wanton and feminized textual commodity."[21] Crossing the same class boundary in the opposite direction, the two *Passionate Pilgrim* sonnets can be read as inversions of this gendered imagery of authorship and reading that Wall finds pervading early modern prefaces. In print, the maintenance of class status called for a distancing between masculine author and feminine text, and reading was figured as a kind of voyeurism from below, whereas in both the narratives and the diction of Shakespeare's circulating manuscripts the speaking voice persistently collapses into feminized disorder. The author appears as irretrievably enmeshed in a "wanton" text, in language that refuses to behave properly. And reading presents the effect of observation from above.

The sexualized, abject persona that appears elsewhere in the *Sonnets*, then, might record Shakespeare's attempts to charm an audience that outclassed him, not the events of what we would call his personal life. This helps make sense of the persistent combination of verbal ambiguity, language of bodily disorder, and terms of social movement that informs many of the "dark lady" sonnets. The opening lines of Sonnet 147, for instance, return to the trope of love as physical illness that underlies both *Passionate Pilgrim* sonnets:

> My love is a feaver longing still
> For that which longer nurseth the disease,
> Feeding on that which doth preserve the ill,
> Th' uncertain sicklie appetite to please.

(lines 1–4)

And the syntactic ambiguity of the fourth line supports two different readings: either the speaker's love feeds on "that which doth preserve the ill" *in order to* please the "sicklie appetite," or the "uncertain sicklie appetite to please" *is* "that which doth preserve the ill." The slipperiness of the language, then, couples the speaker's disordered erotic desire with the suggestion that at the root of his "disease" is the "appetite to please"—a suggestion that, embedded in a class-conscious sonnet, aligns the hopes of entertaining an audience with the fall into an unruly sexuality.

Sonnet 128, packed with bawdy puns, makes more insistent connections between social aspirations, aesthetic performance, and unruly language. The main conceit of the poem, the beloved as musician, Booth notes, turns on "the sexual potential in the name of the instrument in question: a 'virginal.'"[22] And in the imagery of frustrated desire—"Do I envy those jacks that nimble leape / To kisse the tender inward of thy hand"—the word "jacks" suggests several meanings, glossed by Booth as part of the virginal, a term for lower-class social upstarts, and slang for male organs (lines 5–6).[23] To a readership accustomed to poems in which, as Marotti and Wall show, a language of erotic desire thematized social aspirations, the associations drawn among the speaker's envy, the involuntary sexual physicality of the rising "jack," and the sense of low class position would likely have carried a weight that the poem loses out of context. Once again, the effect hinges on a bawdy pun.

The speaker who "rises and falls" for love in Sonnet 151 similarly conflates bawdiness with aspirations, and a lack of autonomy with the feminized, unruly body. The beloved woman's unfaithfulness not only highlights the fact that the speaker will accept mistreatment; it also causes a kind of chain reaction that ends in the "treason" of the lover's body over his composure in lines 5 and 6: "For thou betraying me, I doe betray / My nobler part to my grose bodies treason." The overpowering, sexualized body serves as a guarantee of the sonneteer as social masoch ist, a sign of subordination. "No want of conscience," he claims, leads him to declare this position (line 13), the term "conscience" ringing three times in the sonnet (lines 1, 2, and 13) and carrying, Booth suggests, what would have been a highly recognizable sexual meaning: "any word with *con* in it appears to have invited Shakespeare and his contemporaries . . . to play on the commonest name for the female sex organ."[24] In the ambiguity, this sexual physiology inflects the language of the sonnet's argument just as the speaker's "grose" body overwhelms his better judgment. Again the female body helps signify the speaker's lack of control. These moments from the "dark lady" poems present shades of the more conventionally deferential persona found in some of the "young man" group (Sonnet 26, for instance: "Lord of my love, to whom in vassalage / Thy merrit hath my dutie strongly knit" [lines 1–2]). But in their persistent mixture of feminization, grotesque embodiment, and unruly language, they move beyond acts of deference toward performances of self-abjection.

In historicizing the pleasure these verses may have offered to a homosocial coterie of readers, then, it is useful to keep in mind David M. Halperin's note on the place of rank in premodern homosexuality: "Within the horizons of the male world," Halperin writes, "hierarchy itself is *hot*: it is indissociably bound up with at least the potential for erotic signification."[25] Combining a sense of voyeurism from above with a titillating vocabulary, the figure of the abject author could have played a gendered and hierarchized world-reinforcing role with a potently overdetermined blend of effects. Here the insistent aura created by multiple meanings enables the pleasures of the text, producing a language of desire that can accommodate both the author's self-presentation as feminized other *and* the formal demands of a sonnet. The sensemaking capabilities of homonyms allow the poems to flicker between demonstrating the overwhelming power of lust and the restraint of witty argument—in which neither sense is primary, neither parasitical, but both belong to the same dramatization of classed concerns.

Although historians disagree over the exact causes and progression of the changes that took place for the English gentry in the late sixteenth century, the general consensus over the era's class crisis or decline begins to illustrate why an abject-able sonneteer might have been particularly in order in the 1590s. Within his painstaking statistical history of economic debility and eroding class barriers, Lawrence Stone sees a fundamental shift in cultural attitudes occurring around the century's end. In what he terms a "decay of respect," the English elite lost not only material ground but also the intangible cultural capital of esteem, with insubordination and public insult becoming both more prevalent and more tolerated.[26] In a similar vein, Frank Whigham reads the gentry's late-sixteenth-century rage for courtesy and behavior manuals as a reactionary effort at reviving a respect for class boundaries that was rapidly slipping away. In the

period's literature of courtly decorum, Whigham shows work increasingly came to be used as a border-policing criteria: "there arose a basic governing principle of the display of effortlessness (called *sprezzatura* by [Baldassare] Castiglione), designed to imply the natural or given character of one's social identity, and to deny any earnedness, any labor or arrival from a social elsewhere."[27]

Depicting just such a "social elsewhere," Shakespeare's two earliest published sonnets and others like them from the 1609 text can be read as reversing this imperative of courtly *effortlessness*. They present a language of desire unable to cover chaos and disorder smoothly—a vision of *sprezzatura* gone wrong. Along with trafficking in the gentlemanly anxiety of origins, they also play with the aristocratic nightmare of impure issue. In what has been called the "horror of gynerasty" portrayed in the "dark lady" sonnets, Shakespeare inscribes the fears of mixed blood and illegitimacy that made unbounded heterosexual lust seem to many to be the most socially destructive type of early modern inclination.[28] Locating these anxieties in the voice of a social other, Shakespeare might have provided a uniquely effective combination of excitement and disavowal, a textual object that ultimately, through the figure of the abject author, allowed for a much-needed reminder of the class boundary across which it moved. Where many of the "young man" sonnets take on an advising and even admonishing role, playing with and possibly throwing into question the social relationship between writer and reader, these others might have placed the reader on top in a much less equivocal way. We can only speculate whether the young man was among the "friends" for whom the *Passionate Pilgrim* sonnets were written, or whether they were meant to support any other relationship of patronage. If they were, they present a very unique mode of deference.

This is—hopefully—not to join the tradition of tortured logic and bowdlerization in the name of reading the sex out of Shakespeare. If erotic language functioned in a social setting, in ways that call for a broad conception of sexuality, this hardly cancels out either its possible entanglements in the localities of Shakespeare's personal life or its ability to signify beyond its scene of production. Focusing on how the sonnets' rhetoric might have functioned within the culture of manuscript circulation, however, does provide alternatives to readings of the poems that are perhaps overly reliant on two back-formations of the book: the ordering of the 1609 text (with which we have no record of Shakespeare's involvement) and the figure of Shakespeare as a widely respected author. The title page of the 1609 quarto announced that it presented Shakespeare's sonnets, "Neuer before Imprinted."[29] But before he could have been portrayed in the book market as part of an exclusive circle of sonneteers, and the text as a site of trespass into his individual privacy, Shakespeare had to pass his pages in from the outside, catering to a different kind of voyeurism.

"The major portion of Shakespeare's sonnet collection," Marotti writes, "consists of poems written to a younger man who is clearly treated as a patron. The context in which these sonnets should first be read is that of manuscript-circulated patronage poetry, a set of circumstances in which literary property was conceived of in different ways than it was in the culture of the book."[30] But in privileging the narrative behind the "procreation" sonnets, Marotti's approach to the poems as manuscripts reintroduces the priorities of the 1609 text, in which the "young man" poems come first and are more numerous than any other grouping. Compared to the "procreation" sonnets, which in apparently addressing a specific patron turn on a relationship between writer and gentleman that has in some ways already been established, these early "dark lady" poems might more accurately record the conditions of Shakespeare's emergence as a coterie writer.

De-emphasizing the authority of the 1609 book also lends support to readings of the *Sonnets'* bawdiness that depart from any narrative of sexuality issuing from a discrete, interiorized subject. Not only did at least two of the poems apparently circulate well before 1609, but they would also, as manuscripts traveling singly or in small groups, very likely have functioned only loosely within the kinds of plotlines critics have located in the 1609 arrangement. If the verse is approached in this way, seen as lexical and symbolic performances rather than episodes in one or more allegorical narratives, the pursuit of direct correspondences between Shakespeare's private sexual life and the voice of the poems increasingly begins to seem beside the point. As Stallybrass argues, following Michel Foucault's suggestions in *The History of Sexuality*, eighteenth- and nineteenth-century responses to the transgressive aura of the sonnets can be seen to reveal more about the cultural need to align speech, "interiorized" sexuality, and knowledge than about the writing of the poems themselves.[31] Readings of the *Sonnets* as confessional biography, in other words, seem to reveal more about the reader than anything else.

Perhaps an editorial practice attuned to reading around the textual back-formation of the book can best avoid this sexual back-formation of the confessional speaker, without taking for granted the questions of property— the unified work as the domain of an author, desire as produced and owned by an originating self—that, as Foucault's work suggests, only come to seem natural through the disappearance of their history.[32]

These kinds of critical chronologies take on a particular selfreflexivity and breadth with regard to Shakespeare, *the* figure of a canonical author, whose reception has been such a defining force in the construction of the aesthetic, textual, and psychological discourses—not to mention the institutional arrangements—through which the discipline of literary studies takes place. The hyperbolic claims made in his name—that he invented the human (Harold Bloom), that his work represents the construction of the modern subject (Francis Barker), or that he founded the modern "subjectivity effect" (Joel Fineman)—attest to the lure of the concept of *origination* in Shakespearean scholarship.[33] And although the facts of his life remain mostly hidden, reading closely for the imprint of the social allows for fresh inquiry not only into the discourses that informed the verse but also into those the verse made possible in turn. For Shakespeare, who has made so much linguistic proliferation happen, the stakes of this attention can be expansive.

In reading connections between Shakespearean performances and constructions of psychoanalysis, chronology becomes especially entangled, and here it is perhaps significant that the ordering of the 1609 *Sonnets* often figures heavily. In Fineman's reading of the *Sonnets*, the shift from the "procreation" sonnets' praise of the idealized young man to the "dark lady" poems' exploration of misogynistic desire presents a subjective break from the past that is still being worked out in the registers of Freudian and Lacanian theory. In this analysis, the 1609 ordering literally maps onto a chronology of human thought. The identification that Fineman sees as the sonnets' innovation is feminizing selfabjection: "identifying himself with the heterogeneous look of the lady, or with the duplicity of her speech, the poet identifies himself with difference, with that which resists or breaks identification."[34] Relying on the order of 1609, Fineman places this identification within the very literary time of tradition, reading the motivation of this groundbreaking move in terms of his experience of belatedness as a Petrarchan poet.[35] In this conception, the sonnets' innovation takes place less in a particular social scene than in a relatively exclusive and autonomous aesthetic and humanistic chronology.

In Richard Halpern's more recent *Shakespeare's Perfume*, a remarkably wide-ranging study of the ideals of sodomy and the sublime in Saint Paul, Shakespeare, Oscar Wilde, Sigmund Freud, and Jacques Lacan, the ordering of the 1609 *Sonnets* takes on the apparent solidity of a chemical process. Here the poems' wordplay serves as a symptom of a separation that has already taken place. Drawing their thematics from the discourse of alchemy, Halpern argues, the *Sonnets* perform a division of a purely aesthetic homoeroticism expressed in the "rhetoric of sublimation" from an abjected sexual "anti-idealizing" stance, first abiding in its "exuberantly bawdy taste for sexual wordplay" and later "displaced from the young man onto the Dark Lady."[36] Like Fineman's "dark lady," Halpern's comes second: born from the symbolic tensions of the "procreation" sonnets. And the chronology, here figured as a chemistry experiment, allows for a very specific formulation of the place of Shakespeare's poetry within a Western discourse of sexuality and self.

As Jeffrey Masten claims in a response to *Shakespeare's Perfume*, the thematic and linguistic continuities that connect the rhetoric of alchemical sublimation to that of modern psychoanalysis are worth complicating: "I want at least to pose as a possibility that—in a context where the lines between words . . . are much less strenuously drawn than they are post-standardization—familiar psychological structures like 'repression,' 'negation,' or 'sublimation' may exist only in very different forms."[37] I would argue that the linguistic ambiguities of the abject author are examples of this kind: seemingly familiar things—sexualized puns—in a historically unfamiliar form. If this persona did inscribe hierarchy through the use of linguistic ambiguity, it represents an instance in which discourse is moving toward modern configurations but has not yet arrived. Expressing social positions in the doubleness of bawdy terms, the poems set the stage for a Johnsonian separation of primary (masculinized) sense and secondary (feminized) waste. Presenting a persona who can be located in the slippage of his language toward an unruly sexuality, they also depict something like a Freudian subject, who reveals the hidden erotic desires of an unconscious through double meanings in jokes, puns, or slips of the tongue. But the pleasures of these texts, in their social and hierarchical character, operated along lines that differ from the drives of Freudian theory; and they rely on a kind of

linguistic ambiguity in which the Johnsonian criteria of primary, working meaning and unnecessary or distracting waste do not apply.

To understand these sonnets, then, may be to come to terms with the ways they elude (rather than originate or create) some of our own culturally commonplace ideas about wordplay—that it is unproductive, peripheral—and about the location of desire—that its source is somehow rooted and hidden in every discrete individual. The abject author texts, though involved with an erotic language of voyeurism and bodily stimulation, likely addressed desires better described as "social" than "private." And some of the sonnets that have often been taken as windows (however obscure) into the private life of Shakespeare, might instead turn on a language meant to frustrate any sense of the stability of origins. In other words, although this self-presentation might have worked within very local hierarchical social conditions and relied on specific Renaissance definitions of sex, gender, and class, the same markers that portray the speaker as outside the game of *sprezzatura* and the coterie of gentleman-amateurs depict him as coming from no determinable place. Ungentlemanly, torn by femininity, entangled with an unnamed and lowly mistress, Shakespeare shows himself writing a language that cannot readily be traced back to any accountable source. Reading this as a deliberate effect offers, among other things, a way to think historically about the concept of negative capability that, since the nineteenth century, has been invoked to account for his charm.[38] It is often supposed that the authorial personality so difficult to locate within the plays can be found with his heart on his sleeve in the sonnets. Perhaps, instead, in at least some of the poems Shakespeare practiced the art of *not* appearing.

This identification with slippery origins reappears elsewhere in the sequence, most conspicuously in the poems that play with the name "Will." In 111, for instance, a disoriented and disordered speaker asks his reader to "chide" (line 1) the "guiltie goddesse" (line 2) of his "harmfull deeds" (line 2), and confesses a loss of self-control by offering himself as a "willing pacient" (line 9) for correction. As inclination, as proper name, and, here, as a mark of submission, "Will" powerfully encapsulates the connections among authorial identity, desire, and abjection. Bawdiness and social aspiration come together even more insistently in 135, in which, through thirteen repetitions, "Will" slides from desire for social gain, to estate, to both male and female sex organs (lines 1, 2, 4, 5, 6, 7, 8, 11, 12, and 14). Unsettling the proper name, these ambiguities put a personal spin on the linguistic mode of dislocating self-designation—of throwing origins into question—found in the abject authorial voice of many of the "dark lady" sonnets.

Seeing masochism as social action raises basic questions about who, or what, benefits—and why. In Cynthia Marshall's compelling analysis, *The Shattering of the Self*, moments of self-dissolution inscribed in Renaissance writing represent "allowable reversion" to earlier "unstable and poorly defined idea[s] of selfhood."[39] In this narrative of subject formation, masochistic moments resist powers of social discipline. The self-shattering authorial voice in the sonnets, however, might be best understood as a bid for visibility within existing class structures, not a temporary return to some previously enjoyed freedom. If so, the sonnets are an important episode in the cultural history of interiority-in-performance (and the ascendancy of the middle class) that Stephen Greenblatt discusses in *Renaissance Self-Fashioning*. The figures that Greenblatt investigates, Shakespeare among them, all participated in the unprecedented social mobility of sixteenth-century England, and all found ways of entering society from its margins by imagining selfhood as a malleable performance. Othello, plagued by a sense of his own illegitimacy as an outsider and his reliance on a self-presentation as exotic other, provides Greenblatt with an emblem of these kinds of self-dramatizations.[40] But the characteristics he finds in Othello's self-fashioning—that it occurs in language, in deference to an "authority situated at least partly outside the self" and "in relation to something perceived as alien"—could just as easily describe the way the *Passionate Pilgrim* sonnets play with self-alienation as an authorial image.[41] Reading the abject author not only as a major persona of the *Sonnets* but also as one situated in a practice of manuscript circulation allows us to imagine one way in which this self-fashioning was itself fashioned by a very particularized use of texts and by an especially slippery moment in the standardization of English.

But most of all, these sonnets show the looseness of speech at work. The homonyms' power of making sense cannot be separated from the social significance of these poems any more than Shakespeare's ability to appeal to gentlemanly audiences can be divided from his especially successful emergence into English society. The categories of primary and secondary meaning would come later, along with the increasing differentiation between masculine author and feminine text, as voices of the rising middle class—like Johnson's, a bookseller's

son—struggled to adapt Shakespeare's charm to a drastically new social scene.

Hugh Mcintosh

Notes

1. Samuel Johnson, *Mr. Johnson's Preface to His Edition of Shakespeare's Plays* (London: Printed for J. and R. Tonson, H. Woodfall, J. Rivington, R. Baldwin, C. Hawes, Clark and Collins, T. Longman, W. Johnston, T. Caslon, C. Corbet, T. Lownds, and the executors of B. Dodd, 1765), p. xxiv.
2. Margreta de Grazia, "Homonyms Before and After Lexical Standardization," *Deutsche Shakespeare-Gesellschaft West Jahrbuch* (1990): 143–56.
3. De Grazia, esp. pp. 143–6.
4. Wendy Wall, *The Imprint of Gender: Authorship and Publication in the English Renaissance* (Ithaca: Cornell Univ. Press, 1993), p. 198; Richard Halpern, *Shakespeare's Perfume: Sodomy and Sublimity in the Sonnets, Wilde, Freud, and Lacan* (Philadelphia: Univ. of Pennsylvania Press, 2002), p. 21.
5. Peter Stallybrass, "Editing as Cultural Formation: The Sexing of Shakespeare's Sonnets," *MLQ* 54, 1 (March 1993): 91–103, 95. See also de Grazia, *Shakespeare Verbatim: The Reproduction of Authenticity and the 1790 Apparatus* (Oxford: Clarendon Press, 1991), pp. 152–4.
6. Joseph Pequigney, *Such is My Love: A Study of Shakespeare's Sonnets* (Chicago: Univ. of Chicago Press, 1985), p. 40.
7. Stallybrass, p. 97.
8. Stephen Booth, "Facts and Theories About Shakespeare's Sonnets," in *Shakespeare's Sonnets*, ed. Booth (New Haven: Yale Nota Bene, 2000), pp. 543–9, 548. All subsequent references to the sonnets—excepting the versions of Sonnets 138 and 144 that appeared in 1599's *The Passionate Pilgrim*—are cited from this reprint of the 1609 quarto and will appear parenthetically in the text by line number. The two *Passionate Pilgrim* sonnets are cited from the electronic version of a copy of the second edition (London: T. Judson? For W. Jaggard?, 1599?), held by the Folger Shakespeare Library, STC (2d edn.) 22341.5. References to this electronic version of the second edition will also appear parenthetically in the text by line number.
9. De Grazia, "Homonyms," p. 147.
10. Francis Meres, *Palladis Tamia: Wits Treasury, Being the Second Part of Wits Common Wealth* (London: P. Short, 1598), EEBO STC (2d edn.) 17834. Arthur F. Marotti,

"'Love is Not Love': Elizabethan Sonnet Sequences and the Social Order," *ELH* 49, 2 (Summer 1982): 396–428, 410.

11. Gary Taylor, "Some Manuscripts of Shakespeare's Sonnets," *BJRL* 68, 1 (Fall 1985): 210–46; and Marotti, "Shakespeare's Sonnets and the Manuscript Circulation of Texts in Early Modern England," in *A Companion to Shakespeare's Sonnets*, ed. Michael Shoenfeldt (Oxford: Blackwell, 2007), pp. 185–203, 185–6.

12. J. W. Saunders, *The Profession of English Letters* (London: Routledge and Kegan Paul, 1964), pp. 44, 45. See also Saunders, "The Stigma of Print: A Note on the Social Bases of Tudor Poetry," *EIC* 1, 2 (April, 1951): 139–64, 153.

13. Marotti, *John Donne, Coterie Poet* (Madison: Univ. of Wisconsin Press, 1986), p. 3.

14. Marotti, "Love," p. 398.

15. Marotti, "Love," pp. 396–406.

16. Wall, pp. 38–9.

17. Marotti, "Love," p. 411.

18. Shakespeare, *King Lear*, ed. R. A. Foakes (London: Arden, 1997), II.ii.246.

19. Booth, p. 497.

20. Claude J. Summers, foreword to *The Affectionate Shepherd: Celebrating Richard Barnfield*, ed. Kenneth Borris and George Klawitter (Selinsgrove PA: Susquehanna Univ. Press, 2001), pp. 9–12, 10.

21. Wall, pp. 172–3.

22. Booth, pp. 438–9.

23. Ibid.

24. Booth, p. 526.

25. David M. Halperin, *How to Do the History of Homosexuality* (Chicago: Univ. of Chicago Press, 2002), p. 118.

26. Lawrence Stone, *The Crisis of Aristocracy, 1558–1641* (Oxford: Clarendon, 1965), p. 10.

27. Frank Whigham, "Interpretation at Court: Courtesy and the Performer-Audience Dialectic," *NLH* 14, 3 (Spring 1983): 623–39, 626.

28. De Grazia, "The Scandal of Shakespeare's Sonnets," in *Shakespeare's Sonnets: Critical Essays*, ed. James Schiffer (New York: Garland, 1999), pp. 89–112, 105.

29. *Shakespeare's Sonnets: Neuer before Imprinted* (London: G. Eld, 1609), reproduced in Booth, p. xxi.

30. Marotti, "Shakespeare's Sonnets as Literary Property," in *Soliciting Interpretation: Literary Theory and Seventeenth-Century English Poetry*, ed. Elizabeth D. Harvey and Katherine Eisaman Maus (Chicago: Univ. of Chicago, 1990), pp. 143–73, 145.

31. Stallybrass, p. 97.

32. See Michel Foucault, *The History of Sexuality: Volume One, An Introduction*, trans. Robert Hurley (New York: Vintage, 1990).

33. These respective claims appear in Harold Bloom, *Shakespeare: The Invention of the Human* (New York: Riverhead Books, 1998), pp. 16–7; Francis Barker, *The Tremulous Private Body: Essays on Subjection* (Ann Arbor: Univ. of Michigan Press, 1995), pp. 52–9; and Joel Fineman, *The Subjectivity Effect in Western Literary Tradition: Essays toward the Release of Shakespeare's Will* (Cambridge MA: MIT Press, 1991), pp. 1–23.

34. Fineman, p. 111.

35. Fineman, p. 113.

36. Halpern, pp. 12, 28.

37. Jeffrey Masten, "Gee, Your Heir Smells Terrific: Response to 'Shakespeare's Perfume,'" *http://emc.eserver.org/1-2/masten.html*, paragraph 8 (accessed 10 June 2009).

38. I am grateful to Jeffrey Masten for suggesting the relevance of negative capability to this discussion.

39. Cynthia Marshall, *The Shattering of the Self: Violence, Subjectivity, and Early Modern Texts* (Baltimore MD: Johns Hopkins Univ. Press, 2002), p. 4. See especially pp. 7–9 for a discussion of theoretical approaches to masochism.

40. Stephen Greenblatt, *Renaissance Self-Fashioning: From More to Shakespeare* (Chicago: Univ. of Chicago Press, 1980), pp. 237–9.

41. Greenblatt, p. 9.

Reprinted from *SEL Studies in English Literature 1500-1900*, Vol. 50, No. 1, (Winter, 2010), pp. 109-125 by Hugh McIntosh. Copyright © 2010 Rice University Press.

Love's Usury, Poet's Debt:
Borrowing and Mimesis in Shakespeare's Sonnets

I

The development of mercantile capitalism in early modern Europe was a defining feature of the society in which Shakespeare lived and wrote. New Historicist scholarship has achieved much in its attempts to elucidate these socio-economic conditions and to understand the ways in which Shakespeare would have encountered the world of finance, capital, debt and interest. Buying and selling, borrowing and lending are dominant, even on the superficial level of plot, in many of the plays; more subtle, and perhaps more interesting, is the infusion of this imagery into Shakespearc's language, developing a powerful symbolic value. For instance, we are able to read and hear in Shylock's desperation over his 'bond' not just the comic machinations of a stock character (the money-lending Jew) but the cry of a victim of bigotry and discrimination—a demand for recognition. This is a 'repayment' that has both literal and metaphorical significance; 'paying the debt' is bound up in the notions of justice, mercy or revenge and love or hate that are central not just in *The Merchant of Venice* but in plays ranging from *The Comedy of Errors* to *Measure for Measure*. The focus of the present paper, however, will be on the 'use' of usury in Shakespeare's sonnets.

In an article on "Sodomy, Usury and the Narrative of Shakespeare's Sonnets" (2001), David Hawkes provides a reading of the sonnets that depends in part on the above-mentioned concurrence of (or conflict between) capital and social mores in *The Merchant of Venice*. Following Michel Foucault, he emphasizes the role of a nascent capitalist ideology in the 'definitive emergence of deviant sexualities into public discourse':

> The official Aristotelian-Thomistic morality of precapitalist Europe condemned as unnatural those sexual acts that do not result in reproduction, on the grounds that reproduction is the natural telos of sex. Similarly, teleological objections to usury—the [unnatural] reproduction, or 'breeding,' of money—formed the major ideological obstacle to the accumulation of capital. (96)

Hawkes sees this twinning of usury and sodomy as the key to understanding the seventeen sonnets that traditionally open the collection (following Thomas Thorpe's arrangement in the 1609 Quarto), encouraging a young man to marry and have children. Identifying the young man being addressed with the 'fair youth,' the subject and object of the poet's apparent homosexual love, Hawkes argues that by using the language of 'unnatural' usury to expound the merits of 'natural' marriage and procreation, Shakespeare is ironically undermining the assumption that, because homosexual sex is non-reproductive, homoerotic desire is 'unnatural.'

This is only one point of access to the sonnets' images of borrowing and lending, which recur in very different contexts—as Hawkes himself insists, the complete work is full of ambiguities, inconsistencies and even contradictions. Such contradictory thoughts and emotions are characteristic of what Stanley Wells has called 'an internal drama of great psychological complexity' and do not necessarily detract from the overall patterning and internal logic of the sequence, the unity of which seems to depend on overlapping strands of imagery rather than on a 'sequential' argument (369). Indeed, any attempt to trace such an argument is partly confounded by the continuing debate over the sonnets' dates of composition and, more significantly, over the extent of Shakespeare's involvement in their ordering and publication.[1] Nevertheless, for the sake of consistency, in this article I will accept the sonnets' status as a 'sequence.'

Insofar as the first group of seventeen can be seen to introduce the strain of imagery conflating sex and usury, it also acquaints the reader with the meta-poetic anxiety that pervades the rest of the sequence. In the opening sonnets, the speaker uses the heavy weight of mortality to exhort his young friend to marry and have children ('Make thee another self,' sonnet 10) and, in so doing, defy death ('Then what could death do if thou shouldst depart,/Leaving thee living in posterity?,' sonnet 6). The sonnets remind the reader again and again of the ephemerality and fragility of life—a theme echoing in and echoed by many of the plays. Prospero reminds us that 'our little life is rounded with a sleep' (*The Tempest*

IV.i.157–8). It is a life temporarily borrowed from death, the life Lear 'usurp'd' (*King Lear* V.iii.317), a life that is less 'owned' than 'owed.' In the famous sonnet 18, it is not just human existence that is subject to death; nature, too, is subject to decay and its 'summer' has a 'lease' that will expire. Images of financial exchange are appropriate because they foreground contingency and impermanence, reminding us of the Biblical disdain for 'treasures of this world' (Matthew 6.19).

One of the most common assumptions regarding the sonnets is that, in contrast to this mortality, they assert the power of language and literature to immortalize. Sonnet 55 is distinctly and distinctively celebratory: 'Not marble nor the guilded monuments / Of princes' (whose apparent longevity, greater than that of man or nature, is nevertheless subject to destruction) 'shall outlive this powerful rhyme.' This assumption is flawed, however, and is brought into question in the very sonnets in which the meta-poetic idiom is inaugurated. Referring to sonnet 16, Hawkes claims that 'the prospect of poetic immortality is unfavorably compared with genetic reproduction' (109):

> *But wherefore do not you a mightier way*
> *Make war upon this bloody tyrant, time,*
> *And fortify yourself in your decay*
> *With means more blessed than my barren rhyme?*

The poet's self-abasement in order to flatter his love is a convention of the genre: consider sonnet 103, where his muse is associated with 'poverty,' because 'more, much more, than in my verse can sit / Your own glass shows you when you look in it'; or sonnet 106, in which we read that past poets have 'prefigured' his love's beauty, but that he and his contemporaries 'lack tongues to praise.' There are aspects to this impugnment of language and its ability to represent reality, however, which are more complex than the convention suggests; as we shall see, they are intricately linked to Shakespeare's conceptualization of 'Love's Usury.'[2]

II

In the sonnets, the abundant images of borrowing and lending, leasing and payment present love as 'merchandised' (sonnet 102): love is exchanged as a commodity between such traders as the rival poets, the fair youth and the dark lady. The latter two figures invert another convention of the sonnet form—the 'fair lady' to whom

love poems in the style of Petrarch would be addressed. In the improbably complicated love-triangle depicted in sonnet 134, the protagonists seem trapped within the idiom of *The Merchant of Venice*. The poet is 'mortgaged' and will have to 'forfeit' himself; his 'friend' (presumably, the fair youth) had 'learned but surety-like to write for me, / Under that bond that him as fast doth bind'; the third party (the dark lady, or perhaps an additional rival) is a 'usurer,' who 'sue[s] a friend came debtor.' Such densely packed images undermine any sense of 'owning' love—that is to say, being certain of one's faith in love or in the loved one. James Dawes describes the beloved of sonnet 53 as 'a merchant in shadows' (45):

> *What is your substance, whereof are you made,*
> *That millions of strange shadows on you tend?*
> *Since every one hath, every one, one shade,*
> *And you, but one, can every shadow lend.*
> *Describe Adonis, and the counterfeit*
> *Is poorly imitated after you.*
> . . .
> *Speak of the spring and foison of the year:*
> *The one doth shadow of your beauty show,*
> *The other as your bounty doth appear;*
> *And you in every blessed shape we know.*
> *In all external grace you have some part,*
> *But you like none, none you, for constant heart.*

We are reminded of the uncertainty regarding social relations that grew with the development of capitalist economics: accompanying 'lending,' 'bounty' and 'foison' is an increasingly unstable and tentative sense of identity. The psyche and 'substance' of the other cannot be known or understood objectively, which has the effect of further undermining any attempt at creating a 'counterfeit' of that other—the problem of mimesis. Moreover, the ambiguous phrasing of the closing couplet implicates the beloved as a primary cause of this unreliability (as Stephen Booth points out, Elizabethan pronunciation of 'constant heart' may well have punned on 'constant art' [226]).

Writing about 'Truth and Decay in Shakespeare's Sonnets' (1995), Dawes brings the reader's attention to the notion of 'constancy' as it is expressed in the sequence. The poet fears the infidelity of both the fair youth and the dark lady, but is himself complicit in breaking the 'bonds' of love: 'I have been frequent with unknown minds, / and given to time your own dear-purchased right' (sonnet 117). Dawes joins those critics who read in the subtext of the sonnets that 'monumentalize' love and the beloved—most notably, sonnet 55—a desperate attempt by the poet to idealize that which, he recognizes intuitively, can be corrupted. If these ideals are corruptible then, by association, so too is the poetry that extols them. Notwithstanding his contention that the poet's creations are tainted by their subject matter, Dawes does not fully explore the relationship between beloved and love-poem; he neglects one of the fair youth sonnets, 101, which speaks compellingly to the poet's obsessive and idealized notions of 'truth' and 'beauty':

> *O truant muse, what shall be thy amends*
> *For thy neglect of truth in beauty dyed?*
> *Both truth and beauty on my love depends;*
> *So dost thou too, and therein dignified.*
> *Make, answer, muse.*
> . . .
> *Because he needs no praise wilt thou be dumb?*
> *Excuse not silence so, for 't lies in thee*
> *To make him much outlive a gilded tomb,*
> *And to be praised of ages yet to be.*
> *Then do thy office, muse; I teach thee how*
> *To make him seem long hence as he shows now.*

In the discussion that follows, I will assess the poet's attempt to come to terms with the impermanence and imperfection of his 'borrowed' love and its place in the ostensibly eternalising, idealising medium of poetry.

If 'truth' and 'beauty'—those supposed prerequisites of art—depend on the poet's love (both abstract and particular), and that love is in turn inconstant, then it is not surprising that the poet's muse is 'truant.' When the inspiration for poetry (truth, beauty, love's constancy) is lacking, the poet must either invoke his muse through incantation, as in sonnet 100 ('Rise, resty muse'), or excuse its absence, as in sonnet 102 ('I sometime hold my tongue, / Because I would not dull you with my song'). In sonnet 83, one of a group in which the poet expresses a lack of confidence in his poetic prowess as he confronts the challenge of a rival, he excuses his 'silence' by emphasizing how his words would be inadequate as description: 'There lives more life in one of your fair eyes / Than both your poets can in praise devise.' Once more, Shakespeare returns to the failings of artistic mimesis: it is unable to reflect reality accurately. The language of usury is evident again as we read, 'I found—or thought I found—you did exceed / The barren tender of a poet's debt.' The proposition here would be that, although

beauty obliges the poet to pay tribute—as poet and lover he 'owes' such praise—his language is too poor to pay it. This is not the case, however; the modification, 'or thought I found' implies that the poet has since discovered that the value or significance of his poetry at least matches (if not outweighs) that of his beloved.

This resonates with one of the poet's questions in sonnet 101. He asks his 'truant muse,' 'Because he [the beloved] needs no praise wilt thou be dumb?,' and chastises his own lack of inspiration: 'Excuse not silence so.' The poet exhorts himself to continue ('do thy office, muse') precisely because the beloved does need praise. He does not 'need' it in the sense that he deserves it; on the contrary, because he has earned an 'ill report' (sonnet 95), he 'needs' to be praised for the poet's sake. The conventions of love poetry demand that the poet's beloved is perfect—a perfection that, if captured by the poet, will immortalize both the beloved and the poet. In Shakespeare's sonnets, the subject (in this case the fair youth) is far from perfect, exposed to 'the canker in the fragrant rose' (95); the poet must therefore create an aggrandized image of his love through his 'praise.' Sonnet 101 expresses a determination to make the beloved 'seem long hence as he shows now.' This presents a paradox. We have seen that Shakespeare's investigation into the possibility of accurate portrayal or representation in fact derides his poetry's mimetic power and asserts the unreliability of language. How do we reconcile the attempt to create an idealized image of the 'constant' beloved (an attempt that would seem to follow convention) with the subtextual suggestion that not even poetry is 'constant'? The answer lies in the importance of appearance—the vital words are 'seem' and 'shows.' The poet knows that his love is a cankerous rose, one that will decay or simply abandon him, but, like 'beauty's veil,' he will 'cover every blot / and all things [turn] to fair that eyes can see' (sonnet 95). In sonnet 146, however, the monetary images resurface in a strong indictment of the process of improving external appearances through 'art' (see also sonnet 53):

> *What so large cost, having so short a lease,*
> *Dost thou upon thy fading mansion spend?*
> . . .
> *Buy terms divine in selling hours of dross;*
> *Within be fed, without be rich no more.*

Sonnet 101 thus draws our attention to the detractions of mimesis and to the means by which the poetic subject is created. It is precisely because the beloved falls short of 'ideal' that he or she is 'idealized' by Shakespeare the lover-poet; and it is precisely because he realizes that this illusory process of representation and re-creation necessarily fails that Shakespeare the poet-lover foregrounds the mimetic function. The dynamics of usury—in the sequence, 'love's usury'—are analogous to those of poetic practice—the 'poet's debt.' The 'false compare' of sonnet 130 is that of metaphor, upon which poetry (particularly conventional love poetry) depends. To utilize metaphor is to borrow meaning; the scheme of reference of the vehicle is borrowed so that it can temporarily be imposed on the tenor. If the poet is called upon to give an account of this linguistic loan, however, he cannot repay the debt. He is bankrupt, having spent all of his verbal resources in the descriptive effort, and is consequently 'forfeit' to the admission that 'this poet lies' (sonnet 17). 'Lean penury within that pen doth dwell / That to his subject lends not some small glory,' proclaims sonnet 84. Yet it is the very attempt to 'borrow' 'glory' that results in 'penury' for the poet: epideixis, or giving praise, leads to poverty.

In *Shakespeare's Perjured Eye: The Invention of Poetic Subjectivity in the Sonnets* (1986), Joel Fineman elaborates on the limitations of 'praise, poetical or rhetorical,' which 'is what happens when mimesis and metaphor meet' (3). Recently, however, David Schalkwyk has challenged Fineman's claim 'that Shakespeare's sonnets make the revolutionary discovery that words can *never* match the world' (10).[3] In *Speech and Performance in Shakespeare's Sonnets and Plays* (2002), Schalkwyk maintains that the sonnets are not merely descriptive but also 'performative': 'the pre-eminence of rhetoric in the early modern period shows that language was principally appreciated as a *force* working in the world rather than as a (always-already-failed) reflection of it.' Nevertheless, although the prospect of perlocutionary action—forming, changing or even constituting reality through speech—might encourage the poet's attempts to make his beloved 'seem' praiseworthy to those who read or hear his poems 'long hence,' he cannot ultimately ignore the falseness or 'show' of the loved one.

III

Thomas Greene provides an alternative account of the poet's bankruptcy in "Pitiful Thrivers: Failed Husbandry in the Sonnets" (1985). Like Hawkes, he points out

'Shakespeare's ability to manipulate words which in his language belonged both to the economic and the sexual/biological semantic fields' (231). There are a number of areas of convergence between Greene's essay and the present one. He sees in the husbandry motif of the procreation sonnets a 'bourgeois desire for "store"' that is aimed at resisting change and decay; the poet's later despondency and lack of self-esteem or confidence in his beloved have an 'economic character' (233). Furthermore, Greene suggests that 'the worth of the friend may reside after all in the poet's fancy' and although, following on from this, 'an alternative economic system situates the source of value in the poetry of the sonnets,' this value is often affirmed without confidence or in an unconvincing concluding couplet (234).

Greene also identifies a strong desire on the part of the poet for a relationship with his subject based on mutuality and equality. Against the power struggles and the 'unkind abuse' of sonnet 134, he quotes the reciprocity offered in sonnet 120—a recognition that neither poet nor beloved is able to adopt a position of moral superiority: 'your trespass now becomes a fee; / Mine ransoms yours, and yours must ransom me.' This sentiment is echoed in the 'mutual render' of sonnet 125. Such an egalitarian desire might seem at odds with the framework of usury, in which the exchanges that take place typically give the usurer power over the debtor. If so, it is an incongruity that, in Terry Eagleton's terms, is entirely Shakespearean: extrapolating Eagleton's approach to 'Language' in the opening chapter of his *William Shakespeare* (1985), we can see how the ambiguity of financial signifiers such as 'use' or 'debt,' which is what allows usury to be employed as such an effective metaphor, also acts in opposition to the stability of power relationships in an established social order. In other words, the uncertainty created by the vagaries of language is akin to the uncertainty and social instability created by the development of mercantile capitalism.[4]

John Mischo, in his assessment of the 'procreation sonnets,' returns the usury trope to this historical context; he focuses on the broader political and socio-economic implications of Shakespeare's manipulation of an issue that was 'a touchstone for theories of political economy' (262). Mischo describes the inconsistencies in the attitudes of both church and state towards usury during the years leading up to and following the 'Compromise' of 1571—which, as its name suggests, served only to make such inconsistencies legal. The guiding principle was that of 'par' or parity: no economic transaction should occur to the detriment of any party. Apologists for usury increasingly argued that the practice should not be condemned in moral or 'Christian' terms if it served the greater societal good, and propounded the 'ameliorative effects of usury' (264). For the middle classes, the greatest of these would be the generation of capital, allowing for social mobility. It was for this reason that the aristocracy joined the moral opposition to 'money breeding money' (even though many families in the landed classes were themselves dependent on the loans offered by merchant bankers): they felt threatened by the opportunities that usury created for the lower classes. Mischo suggests that the sonnets figure usury as a means of attaining equality. On a wider egalitarian level, it narrows the gap between the classes of a divided society; in specific relationships between individuals, it can still subscribe to the principle of parity because 'that use is not forbidden usury / Which happies those that pay the willing loan' (sonnet 6). Therefore, he argues, in the sonnets Shakespeare 'not only acknowledges the necessity of usury . . . [he] comes to celebrate usury as consonant with the Christian concept of caritas' or brotherly love (262).

This may be true of the first seventeen sonnets, but in other groupings within the sonnets the skeptical reading of 'mutual render' offered by Greene is more convincing: although the poet wishes for equality, his assertions of reciprocity in the later fair youth sonnets may be seen as 'repressing artificially the pain and guilt which have already surfaced, and which will surface even more harshly in the dark lady group to follow' (239). The poet is always borrowing: borrowing his experience of love, which will become forfeit to infidelity, decay or death, and borrowing meaning to create metaphors in the very process of mimesis, which will leave him spent. Because he is always in debt, and never able to play the usurer, he sees himself in a position of inferiority to a fair youth, a rival poet and a dark lady who exercise their power and manipulate him. Sonnet 42 may end with a couplet that denounces sexual jealousy, celebrating with 'joy' that 'my friend and I are one; / Sweet flattery! then she loves but me alone,' but the argument of the sonnet is more convincingly concluded with the resignation of the preceding lines: 'I lose both twain, / and both for my sake lay on me this cross.' Again, one of the conventions of the sonnet form is subverted. Shakespeare's sonnets cannot take on a traditional role as weapons in battles of 'courtly rivalry,' or 'rivalry in courtship,' and the poet depicts himself as the losing suitor.

IV

The order in which Shakespeare composed the sonnets and the order in which he first intended them to be read are, as I have mentioned, largely matters of conjecture; it seems unlikely that the order in the 1609 Quarto edition corresponds directly to either. Correlation between the chronology of events depicted in the sequencing we have inherited and Shakespeare's sketchy biography is, at best, partial. Indeed, the connection of the characters as well be the dramatis personae of another of Shakespeare's 'fictional' dramas.[5] Our separation from the circumstances of composition lends a particular resonance to Barthes' 'death of the author' when we read the sonnets. This, along with the sequence's preoccupation with the nature of writing, language and signification, has attracted the attention of poststructuralist critics. Even in post-structural analyses, however, there is a temptation to identify some form of coherent internal structure and to follow a narrative progression. Howard Felperin, for example, seems to make this error in his reading of the sonnets in *Beyond Deconstruction: The Uses and Abuses of Literary Theory* (1985).

After the opening seventeen sonnets, Felperin suggests, the poet concedes the inadequacy of mimesis to the natural object and moves his focus to 'supermimesis'—replacing the object with the version that he has created (163). Felperin assesses the performative function of sonnet 55 in this light: the power to endure comes from the force of the claim to such power (a process of the same kind as that described earlier with regard to sonnet 101, in which the poet's articulated assurance depends on the very expression of praise for the beloved). Yet this claim is called into question by sonnets 60 to 64, a sub-group that continues the 'monumentalizing' theme of sonnet 55 but undermines its effect by amplifying the imagery of ruin and deterioration, encouraging an acceptance of the transience of poetry and a mistrust of language. A meta-mimetic awareness thus predominates. Felperin argues that the poet is prompted to 'create' an object appropriate to the problematic nature of representation in poetry, the duplicitous dark lady: 'The relationship now represented—or is it generated—is as unstable, polymorphous, and perverse as the language which represents, or generates it' (195).

Although many aspects of Felperin's reading are consonant with the ideas presented in this article, it nevertheless depends on a linear development throughout the sonnets, which we have seen cannot be assumed.

Neither Shakespeare nor his poetic persona 'realizes' belatedly that language, like human relationships, is 'unstable, polymorphous, and perverse'—he has been grappling with this problem all along. Perhaps it would be more accurate to say that the problem is addressed throughout the sonnets, irrespective of their order. In sonnet 15, when Shakespeare 'engraft[s]' his beloved '[a]new,' he knows that 'this poet lies' (sonnet 17) in the same way that in sonnet 138 he equivocally declares, 'I lie with her, and she with me, / and in our faults by lies we flattered be.' A similar ambivalence is found in sonnet 20, another 'early' sonnet that anticipates much of the above discussion:

> *A woman's face with nature's own hand painted*
> *Hast thou, the master-mistress of my passion;*
> *A woman's gentle heart, but not acquainted*
> *With shifting change as is false woman's fashion;*
> . . .
> *A man in hue, all hues in his controlling,*
> *Which steals men's eyes and women's souls amazeth.*
> . . .
> *Mine be thy love and thy love's use their treasure.*

I have already demonstrated the dilemma created by improvement through 'art' (sonnets 53 and 146), embellishing the dichotomy between nature and artifice: not only is art unable to match nature, but artifice implies inconstancy, which further detracts from that nature. In sonnet 20, the interrelation between this problem of 'hues' and that of poetic 'use' (usury) is acutely evident. 'Master-mistress' evokes both the confusion of 'natural' gender roles and the lovers' tussle for superiority; there are undertones of possession and ownership in 'controlling' and 'steals.' This returns us, finally, to the explication offered by Hawkes and Greene. The poet's aim to 'loan' out his beloved to others for sexual 'use'—whilst preserving his own version of idealized love—is a project of husbandry in which he fails, leaving him bankrupt. 'Mine be thy love and thy love's use their treasure' expresses a generous hope, but one that is flouted by the poet's debt: there is inevitably a shortfall in transactions between love's usury and poetic mimesis.

Christopher Thurman

Notes

1. See Jackson, 'Vocabulary and Chronology' and 'Shakespeare's Sonnets.'
2. I borrow the term from the title of Donne's poem, al-

though I use it here in an entirely different context.
3. Schalkwyk does concede some ground to Fineman in 'the abstract context of print,' where 'the inadequacy of words to their object is entirely grammatical,' but suggests that 'the now well-known problem of difference between that which is spoken and that which is spoken about' has altogether different implications in the theatre, where 'the grammatical is brought into contact with the referential' onstage (80–1).
4. Eagleton also quotes Marx and Engels's acclaimed observation that 'uninterrupted disturbance of all social conditions, everlasting uncertainty and agitation distinguish the bourgeois epoch from all earlier ones. All fixed, fast-frozen relations, with their train of ancient and venerable prejudices and opinions, are swept away . . . All that is solid melts into air' (Marx 1942).
5. As Schalkwyk notes, the sonnets are simultaneously rooted in 'real experiences and relationships' and 'abstracted . . . open to subsequent appropriation and projection'; there is a 'referential emptiness' to the ambiguous pronouns in the sequence (26–7).

Works Cited

Dawes, James. "Truth and Decay in Shakespeare's Sonnets." *Cahiers Elisabethains* 47 (1995): 43-53.

Eagleton, Terry. *William Shakespeare*. Oxford: Blackwell, 1985.

Felperin, Howard. *Beyond Deconstruction: The Uses and Abuses of Literary Theory*. New York: Oxford UP, 1985.

Fineman, Joel. *Shakespeare's Perjured Eye: The Invention of Poetic Subjectivity in the Sonnets*. Berkeley: U of California P, 1986.

Greene, Thomas. "Pitiful Thrivers: Failed Husbandry in the Sonnets." *Shakespeare and the Question of Theory*. eds. Patricia Parker & Geoffrey Hartman. New York & London: Methuen, 1985. 230–44.

Hammond, Gerald. *The Reader and Shakespeare's Young Man Sonnets*. London: Macmillan, 1981.

Hawkes, David. "Sodomy, Usury and the Narrative of Shakespeare's Sonnets." *Idols of the Marketplace: Idolatry and Commodity Fetishism in English Literature, 1580–1680*. Basingstoke: Palgrave, 2001. 93–114.

Jackson, MacDonald. "Shakespeare's Sonnets: Rhyme and Reason in the Dark Lady Series." *Notes and Queries* 46.2 (1999): 219–21.

_____. "Vocabulary and Chronology: The Case of Shakespeare's Sonnets." *Review of English Studies* 52 (2001): 59–75.

Marx, Karl. *Selected Works Volume 1*. ed. V. Adoratsky. London: Lawrence & Wishart, 1942.

Mischo, John. "That Use Is Not Forbidden Usury: Shakespeare's Procreation Sonnets and the Problem of Usury." *Subjects on the World's Stage: Essays on British Literature of the Middle Ages and the Renaissance.* eds. David Allen & Robert White. Newark & London: Associated UP, 1995. 262–79.

Schalkwyk, David. *Speech and Performance in Shakespeare's Sonnets and Plays.* Cambridge: Cambridge UP, 2002.

Shakespeare, William. *The Oxford Shakespeare: Histories with the Poems and Sonnets.* Ed. Stanley Wells. New York: Oxford UP, 1994.

_____. *Shakespeare's Sonnets.* ed. Stephen Booth. New Haven & London: Yale UP, 2000.

Vendler, Helen. *The Art of Shakespeare's Sonnets.* Cambridge, MA: Harvard UP, 1997.

Reprinted from *Literature Compass* 4/3 (2007): pp. 809-819, 10.1111/j.1741-4113.2007.00433.x by Christopher Thurman. Copyright © 2007 Wiley-Blackwell Publishing. Reprinted with permission of the Publisher.

Who Bore the Canopy in Sonnet 125?

The first four lines of sonnet 125 have puzzled many commentators.

Wer't ought to me I bore the canopy,
With my extern the outward honoring,
Or layd great bases for eternity,
Which proues more short then wast or ruining?

A possible reading of the first line is 'Did it mean anything to me that I *did* bear the canopy?' If so, line 3 would read: 'Did it mean anything to me that I *had* laid great bases?,' which perhaps refers to the foundations of a stately home, or to a flourishing family, or to a costly tomb, or to some provision for the afterlife.

However, there seems to be general agreement that the subjunctive mood offers the more probable meaning of the words: 'Would it have meant anything to me if I *had* borne the canopy?' (which I didn't), 'or *had* laid . . . bases . . . ?' (which I also didn't). Another reading might be 'Would it mean anything to me if I *were to* bear the canopy.' Whichever sense the poet had in mind, the underlying thought (expressed later in the sonnet) is, 'No—these are matters of general concern that mean little to me—it is my private devotion to you (his young friend) which is all consuming.' Nevertheless, by saying 'Were't ought to me I *bore* etc.,' the poet seems to be indicating that he might have been one of those selected to do so on some particular occasion; otherwise he could have written 'Were't ought to me *to bear* etc.' (with 'lay' replacing 'layd'), which would have had the effect of distancing himself from any such ceremony.

A number of commentators allow for the possibility that Shakespeare did once bear the canopy, or might have done so.[1] It therefore seems worthwhile to find out more about canopies, who bore them, who might aspire to bear them, and when. Our starting point is Leslie Hotson's finding that by law they could only be carried over the sovereign (and by extension his consort, or child, or his or their coffins), and over nobody else.[2]

A ceremonial canopy consists of a square or rectangle of richly embroidered fabric carried on four staves (occasionally six or more) some six to eight feet long, which would often be ornamented with silver finials and bells. Research using the ODNB (Oxford Dictionary of National Biography) and other resources has shown who were reported as carrying canopies over the monarch in processions on public occasions of state at this period.[3] Broadly speaking, they were knights or gentlemen, 'barons of the Cinque Ports' (commoners) at coronations, and senior academics at Cambridge and Oxford.[4] The three public processions in the early 1600s which involved canopies took place at the funeral of Queen Elizabeth on 28 April 1603, the coronation of James I on 25 July 1603, and the triumphal entry of King James into the City of London on 15 March 1604 (ns), postponed from the coronation celebrations because of plague.

The names of the knights and others who were summoned to act as canopy bearers in the Queen's funeral procession are recorded in a document in the College of Arms, together with the names of the 'assistant earls.'[5] The bearers of the canopy carried over James on his coronation procession from Parliament Stairs to Westminster Abbey were barons of the Cinque Ports,[6] and on his triumphal entry the following year were Scotsmen from his privy chamber.[7] Any of these three occasions might have suggested the opening line of sonnet 125, but at none of them would there have been any possibility that Shakespeare might have been one of the bearers.

There are other events of the period, less public, when a canopy was employed, principally at the opening of a parliament, as part of the Garter festivities, at the christening of a royal infant, and during the anointing ceremony at a coronation. In addition, a canopy was borne over Queen Elizabeth at a special service of thanksgiving for the victory over the Armada, which was held in St Paul's Church on 24 November 1588. A canopy is also depicted in the painting known as 'Eliza Triumphans.'[8]

At the opening of Parliament on 12 January, 1563 (ns), a canopy was borne over Queen Elizabeth inside Westminster Abbey by an esquire and five knights.[9] The canopy for the procession which was part of the Garter ceremony at Windsor in April 1596 was carried by 'four men' otherwise unidentified, on the only occasion of which a record has surfaced.[10] At a royal christening, the bearers were usually related to the monarch, and were often members of the higher nobility. For example, a canopy was held over the infant Princess Elizabeth at her christening at Greenwich Palace by four bearers chosen by King Henry VIII, including a duke and a viscount.[11] At a coronation, a canopy is held over the sovereign at the most sacred moment of the ceremony when he or she is anointed with holy oil. These canopy bearers are traditionally Knights of the Garter who are also members of the higher nobility. At the coronation of James I one duke and several earls were available to officiate;[12] it is not known who did so. At that of Charles II two dukes and two earls officiated,[13] and at that of James II three dukes and one earl.[14]

If the first line of the sonnet was suggested to the poet by some particular occasion when a canopy was employed, one might enquire whether the sonnet contains any clues as to the nature of the occasion. It has been observed in the past that some of the words used appear to refer to the coronation of James I, for example, canopy, obsequious, oblation. The coronation service (which was essentially an interrupted Holy Communion service[15]) included oblations of a pall of cloth-of-gold and a pound ingot of gold offered by the King, and also oblations of the communion wine and bread, which latter according to the order of the communion service should be '*the purest wheat bread that conveniently may be gotten,*' that is, 'not mixt with seconds' (line 11).[16] Furthermore 'layd great bases for eternity' (line 3) resonates with the communion service prayer: '*laying up in store for them selves a good foundacion, against the time to come, that they may attayne eternal lyfe.*'[17] But it is unlikely that Shakespeare would have witnessed King James's coronation, as attendance was strictly limited because of plague.[18]

Thus the records indicate that Shakespeare would never have been chosen to carry the pole of a canopy either in a procession or at any of the more private ceremonies, and was probably absent from James's coronation. It is possible that he might have pictured himself so doing in his imagination, or maybe he is simply finding a way of saying that such ceremonies mean little to him compared with his love for his friend.

John M. Rollett

Notes

1. In their editions of (or commentaries on) the Sonnets the following make this allowance, or hint at it: A. L. Rowse (1964), John Dover Wilson (1967), Stephen Booth (1977), Kenneth Muir (1979), Robert Giroux (1982), John Kerrigan (1986), Colin Burrow (2002). While a number of editors consider the canopy to be metaphorical or figurative, others leave the matter open.

2. Leslie Hotson, *Mr W. H.* (London, 1964), 38–9.

3. A search on the word 'canopy' in the *Oxford Dictionary of National Biography (ODNB)* and via the internet (including variant spellings) yielded details of some 30 occasions when canopies were carried, always over royalty. Canopies in public processions were carried by commoners with one exception. At Queen Jane Seymour's funeral on 12 November, 1537, Thomas Fiennes, ninth Baron Dacre *(ODNB)*, and Thomas West, eighth Baron West and ninth Baron de la Warr *(ODNB)*, were two of those who bore the canopy over her hearse.

4. When Queen Elizabeth visited Cambridge on 5 August 1564, Robert Beaumont, Master of Trinity College *(ODNB)*, Edward Hawford, Master of Christ's College *(ODNB)*, and John Pory, Master of Corpus Christi College *(ODNB)* were recorded as carrying a canopy over the Queen as she entered King's College Chapel (the name of the fourth bearer has not come to light). The richly embroidered cloth, 'a Florentine fabric of the highest quality,' held in the Armour Room of the Fitzwilliam Museum, Cambridge, known as Henry VII's hearse-cloth, is believed to have been used on this occasion. Hugh Tait, 'The Hearse-Cloth of Henry VII Belonging to the University of Cambridge,' *Journal of the Warburg and Courtauld Institutes*, xix, 3–4 (Jul.–Dec. 1956), 294–8. On the Queen's visit to Oxford University in 1592 a canopy was 'supported by four Doctors.' John Nichols, *The Progresses and Public Processions of Queen Elizabeth* (London, John Nichols and son, 1823), 145.

5. These are the names of the twelve people chosen as the bearers of the six poles of the canopy borne over Queen Elizabeth's hearse at her funeral procession on 28 April 1603, taken from a document in the College of Arms: MS. R.20 Funeral Ceremony (Anstis), f. 296. 'Knightes for the Canopie: Sir ffrancis Knolls, Lieftenant of the Tower, Sir Jerome BowesX, Sir Jo: Peeter, Sir Edw. Hobby, Sir Richard BarkleyX, Sir Henry Gle[nm]aid, Sir Edw. Wynter, Sir Henry Guilford, Sir Robert Croft, Sir George Moore, Sir Richard Ward, Sir Richard [Lea]'; they perhaps formed two teams, turn and turn about. This is followed by a list of fifteen knights and gentlemen as reserves (those marked 'x' on the first list may have turned out to be unavailable). 'Sir Charles Perry, Mr Tho. Somerset, Mr ffrauncis Manners, Sir George Boucher, Mr Philip Herbert, Mr Oliver Manners, Sir Moyles [ffinche], Sir Tho. Monson, Sir Robert Wroth, Mr ffra. Clifford, Sir Robert Sidney, Sir Edw. Stafford, Sir George [Carew], Sir Wm. Cornwallis, Sir Robert [Wrothe]; square brackets indicate uncertainties. The names of the earls chosen as 'Assistants to the Corps Royall' (f. 337),

processing two on either side of the hearse adjacent to the canopy bearers (as shown in a marginal sketch) are as follows: 'E. of Northumberland, E. of Salop, E. of Derby, E. of Cumberland, E. of Hartford, E. of Lincoln'; either all six took part or two stood by as reserves. I thank Matthew Jones, Archivist of the College of Arms, for checking the names of the canopy bearers.

6. 'The King under a Canopy born by the Barons of the Cinque Ports.' Anon., *The Ceremonies, Form of Prayer, and Services used in Westminster-Abby at the Coronation of King James the First and Queen Ann his consort* (London, Randal Taylor, 1685). A canopy was also borne over his Queen. The bearers were required to wear clothes specified in considerable detail and pay for them, including scarlet gowns. As 'scarlet is valued at £3 10s. the yard at least,' it was an expensive honour to be a canopy bearer. Historical Manuscripts Commission, Mss. Rye and Herefordshire Corporations (London, 1892), 15 July 1603; <http:// www.british-history.ac.uk/report. aspx?compid¼67148>.

7. 'The King, richly mounted on a white gennet, under a rich canopie susteind by eyght gentlemen of the Privie Chamber, for [ie in place of] the Barons of the Cinque Ports, entered the Royal Cittie of London, etc.,' 15 March 1603/4. John Nichols, *The Progresses, Processions and Magnificent Festivities of King James the First* (London, J. B. Nichols, 1828), 324. According to Nicolo Molin, the Venetian Ambassador, twenty-four gentlemen participated, 'splendidly dressed, eight of whom took it turn and turn about.' Calendar of State Papers (Venetian), 26 March 1604 (London, 1900); <http://www.british-history.ac.uk/ report.aspx?compid¼95611>.

8. Roy Strong, *The Cult of Elizabeth* (Pimlico, 1999), 17–55. Three of the canopy-bearers are visible, and have been identified as Sir Robert Cecil and two sons of the Earl of Worcester (all commoners).

9. 'In which Order Her Majesty proceeded to the North Door of the church of *Westminster*, where the dean there and the Dean of the Chappel met her, and the whole Chappel in Copes; and St *Edward's* staff with the Inlet in the top was delivered unto her, her Arm, for the bearing thereof, assisted by the Baron of Hunsdon; the Canopy born over her by *Charles Howard* Esq; Sir *George Howard*, *Sir Richard Blunt*, Sir *Ed. Warner*, Sir *John Perrott*, and Sir *William Fitz-Williams*, Knights; her Grace's Train borne up and assisted, for the weight thereof from her arms, by the Lord *Robert Dudley*, Master of the Horse, and Sir *Francis Knollys*, Vice Chamberlain; and so orderly proceeded to the Travers beside the Table of Ad-

ministration . . .' Simonds D'Ewes, *The Journals of all the Parliaments during the reign of Queen Elizabeth* (London, 1682), 58.

10. Ralph M. Sargent, *The Life and Lyrics of Sir Edward Dyer* (Oxford, 1968), 130.

11. The bearers at the christening of the infant Elizabeth, which took place on 10 September 1533, in Greyfriars Church, Greenwich, were: Thomas Boleyn, Earl of Wiltshire (grandfather), John Hussey, first Baron Hussey, Thomas Howard, third Duke of Norfolk (brother of Thomas Boleyn's wife, ne'e Elizabeth Howard), and William Howard, first Baron Effingham (half-brother to Elizabeth Howard). James Gairsner (ed.), *Letters and Papers Foreign and Domestic, Henry VIII*, vol. 6 (London, Longmans Green, 1882), 1111.

12. No contemporary account has so far come to light naming those who officiated at King James's coronation. However, on 25 July 1603 there were twelve Knights of the Garter available who were also members of the higher nobility, one duke and eleven earls; of these, the Duke of Lennox and the earls of Mar, Pembroke, and Southampton had been newly installed earlier that month. The honour of performing the hugely prestigious duty of acting as canopy bearer would have fallen to the Duke of Lennox (James's cousin) and three of the eight more senior earls (or four, if the Duke did not officiate). Among these the earl of Nottingham was Lord High Steward, in overall charge of everything relating to the coronation, the earl of Worcester was Earl Marshal, responsible for ceremonial details, and the earl of Ormond was too ill to attend. The remaining five were the earls of Shrewsbury, Cumberland, Northumberland, Sussex, and Derby, listed in order of appointment. If the proceedings went according to tradition, the Duke and three of these (or four without the Duke) would have borne the canopy, with those remaining perhaps standing by in reserve. To see the anointing of Queen Elizabeth II at her coronation in 1953 go to <http://pirate. shu.edu/_wisterro/coronation.htm>, scroll down to the end of the paragraph headed 'The Anointing,' and click on the word Anointing.

13. 'During the time of unction, a rich pall of cloth of gold (brought from the great wardrobe by Mr. Rumbal) was held over the king's head by the dukes of Buckingham and Albemarle, the earls of Berks and Sandwich, as knights of the most noble Order of the Garter.' T. C. Banks, *An Historical and Critical Enquiry into the Nature of the Kingly Office, etc.* (London, Sherwood, Neely and Jones, 1814), 49–50.

14. 'Then four Knights of the Garter, appointed by His Maj-

esty, viz. the Duke of Ormond, the Duke of Albemarle, the Duke of Beaufort, and the Earl of Mulgrave held a Pall or Pallet of Cloth of Gold over the KING during the whole Ceremony of the Anointing.' Francis Sandford, *The History of the Coronation of James II* (London, 1687), 91.

15. Anon., *The ceremonies, form of prayer, and services used in Westminster-Abby at the coronation of King James the First and Queen Ann his consort* (London, Randal Taylor, 1685).

16. Stephen Booth, who also finds other 'incidental likenesses between the diction of the service and that of the sonnet.' *Shakespeare's Sonnets* (New Haven, CT, 1977), 429–30.

17. Peter Farey, 'Sonnet 125,' *The Shakespeare Conference*, 17 October 2006, <http://shaksper.net/archive/2006/242-october/25020-sonnet-125>, quoting the 1559 Prayer Book, Holy Communion <http://justus.anglican.org/resources/bcp/1559/BCP_1559.htm>.

18. Attendance at the Abbey was strictly controlled because of plague. Apart from the Mayor and Aldermen, only twelve 'distingished citizens' of London were allowed to attend. Nichols, v.s., 228.

Resources

Chronology of Shakespeare's Life

1533: King Henry VIII divorces Catherine of Aragon and marries Anne Boleyn, who gives birth to Elizabeth. Henry breaks with the Church of Rome; the English Reformation begins.

1534: The Act of Supremacy is passed by the Reformation Parliament; Henry VIII is now head of the Church of England.

1547: Henry VIII dies; Edward VI, his son with Jane Seymour, becomes king of England and continues the Reformation in England.

1549: The Act of Uniformity is passed. The first Book of Common Prayer is issued; it is revised in 1552.

1553: Edward VI dies; his sister Mary, daughter of Catherine of Aragon and wife of Philip II of Spain, becomes queen of England. She restores Roman Catholicism to England, and Protestants are persecuted.

1557: John Shakespeare, a glover, marries Mary Arden of Wilmcote; they live in a house on Henley Street in Stratford-upon-Avon.

1558: Queen Mary dies childless; her sister, Elizabeth, becomes queen.

1560: The Geneva Bible is published.

1563: John Foxe's *Book of Martyrs* is published in English.

1564: William Shakespeare is born on April 23 and is baptized on April 26.

1565: John Shakespeare is elected one of fourteen alderman of Stratford on July 4; he will become bailiff for one year in 1568 and chief alderman in 1571.

1570: Pope Pius V excommunicates Elizabeth I. Shakespeare presumably enters Stratford's grammar school.

1576: James Burbage builds the Theatre in Shoreditch, London.

1577: A rival theater, the Curtain, opens in Bishopsgate.

1580: Pope Gregory XIII proclaims Elizabeth an enemy of the Church and asks loyal Catholics to assassinate her.

1582: Shakespeare courts Anne Hathaway, who becomes pregnant; the two marry on November 28. They live with William's parents in the Henley Street house.

1583: Shakespeare's daughter Susanna is christened on May 26.

1585: Shakespeare's twins, Judith and Hamnet, are born on February 2.

1585–1592: The "lost years": nothing definite is known of Shakespeare during this period.

1587: Mary Queen of Scots is executed. The second edition of Raphael Holinshed's *Chronicles of England, Scotland, and Wales*, a primary source of Shakespeare's English history plays, is published. The Rose Theatre is built on the south bank of the Thames. Thomas Kyd's *The Spanish Tragedy* and Christopher Marlowe's *Tamburlaine* are produced.

1588: The Spanish Armada, sent to invade England and restore Catholicism, is defeated.

1589: Possible date of Shakespeare's arrival in London as actor and playwright. An early version of *Hamlet* (often attributed to Thomas Kyd and known as *Ur-Hamlet*) is produced. Marlowe's *The Jew of Malta* is produced.

1589–1592: Shakespeare's early comedies are produced, as are *Titus Andronicus, Henry VI, Parts I-III*, and *Richard III*.

1592: First mention of Shakespeare in London (by rival dramatist Robert Greene, who calls Shakespeare an "upstart Crow").

1592–1593: The Plague sweeps through London, and theaters are closed. Shakespeare writes *Venus and Adonis* (published 1593) and *The Rape of Lucrece* (published 1594) and dedicates both to Henry Wriothesley, third earl of Southampton.

1593–1594: Shakespeare's early sonnets to the "Fair Youth" are written. *The Comedy of Errors* is produced.

1594: The Lord Chamberlain's Men theater troupe forms, with Richard Burbage as leading actor and Shakespeare as part of the troupe.

1595–1596: *Love's Labour's Lost, Richard II, Romeo and Juliet*, and *A Midsummer Night's Dream* are produced.

1596: Shakespeare's son Hamnet dies. Shakespeare's coat of arms is approved by the Heralds' College.

1596–1598: The Swan theater opens. *Henry IV, Part I, King John, The Merchant of Venice, The Merry Wives of Windsor*, and *Henry IV, Part II* are produced.

1597: Shakespeare purchases New Place, the second-largest house in Stratford-upon-Avon. James Burbage dies.

1598: Francis Meres, in *Palladis Tamia*, catalogs Shakespeare's plays and poems.

1599: *Henry V* is produced. The Globe Theatre is built on the south bank of the Thames from the timbers of the Theatre.

1599–1600: *Much Ado About Nothing, As You Like It, Julius Caesar*, and *Twelfth Night* are produced.

1600–1601: *Hamlet* and *Troilus and Cressida* are produced.

1601: John Shakespeare dies. Ben Jonson's *Every Man in His Humour* is published.

1603: Elizabeth I dies, and James VI of Scotland succeeds her as James I of England. The Lord Chamberlain's Men become the King's Men. Shakespeare's *Hamlet* (Quarto 1) is published for the first time.

1603–1604: Plague closes theaters, March 19, 1603-April 9, 1604. *Othello* is produced.

1604–1605: *Measure for Measure* and *All's Well That Ends Well* are produced.

1605: The Gunpowder Plot is uncovered on November 5.

1605–1606: *King Lear*, *Macbeth*, and *Timon of Athens* are produced.

1607: Susanna Shakespeare marries Dr. John Hall. They live in Hall's Croft, Stratford-upon-Avon. Ben Jonson's *Volpone* is published.

1607–1608: *Antony and Cleopatra*, *Pericles*, and *Coriolanus* are produced.

1608: The first edition of *King Lear* (Quarto 1) is published. Mary Shakespeare dies.

1609: An unauthorized first edition of Shakespeare's *Sonnets* is published. The King's Men start performing at Blackfriars (private) indoor theater as well as at the Globe.

1609–1610: *The Winter's Tale* and *Cymbeline* are produced.

1611: *The Tempest* is produced. The Authorized Version (King James) Bible is published.

1613: *Henry VIII*, written by Shakespeare with John Fletcher, is produced; the Globe burns down during a performance of the play. Shakespeare and Fletcher's lost play *Cardenio* is produced.

1613–1614: *The Two Noble Kinsmen*, written by Shakespeare and Fletcher, is produced.

1616: Shakespeare dies on April 23. He is buried in the chancel of Holy Trinity Church, Stratford-upon-Avon. *The Works of Benjamin Jonson* is published in folio.

1623: Shakespeare's effigy is installed in Holy Trinity Church. John Heminges and Henry Condell edit the first collection of Shakespeare's plays (First Folio): *Mr. William Shakespeare's Comedies, Histories, and Tragedies*

Works by William Shakespeare

The following list provides dates of the writing (wr.), production (pr.), and publication (pb.) of Shakespeare's works. The writing and production dates that appear here are based on consensus culled from current scholarship; they may differ in some particulars from what individual scholars have determined for themselves to be most accurate.

Drama

Henry VI, Part I, wr. 1589-1590, pr. 1592, pb. 1623

Edward III, wr., pr. c. 1589-1595, pb. 1596 (attributed to Shakespeare)

Henry VI, Part II, pr. c. 1590-1591, pb. 1594

Henry VI, Part III, pr. c. 1590-1591, pb. 1595

Richard III, pr. c. 1592-1593, pb. 1597 (revised 1623)

The Comedy of Errors, pr. c. 1592-1594, pb. 1623

The Taming of the Shrew, pr. c. 1593-1594, pb. 1623

Titus Andronicus, pr., pb. 1594

Love's Labour's Lost, pr. c. 1594-1595, pb. 1598 (revised 1597 for court performance)

The Two Gentlemen of Verona, pr. c. 1594-1595, pb. 1623

Romeo and Juliet, pr. c. 1595-1596, pb. 1597

Richard II, pr. c. 1595-1596, pb. 1600

A Midsummer Night's Dream, pr. c. 1595-1596, pb. 1600

The Merchant of Venice, pr. c. 1596-1597, pb. 1600

King John, pr. c. 1596-1597, pb. 1623

The Merry Wives of Windsor, pr. 1597, pb. 1602 (revised c. 1600-1601)

Henry IV, Part I, pr. c. 1597-1598, pb. 1598

Henry IV, Part II, pr. 1598, pb. 1600

Much Ado About Nothing, pr. c. 1598-1599, pb. 1600

Henry V, pr. c. 1598-1599, pb. 1600

Julius Caesar, pr. c. 1599-1600, pb. 1623

As You Like It, pr. c. 1599-1600, pb. 1623

Hamlet, Prince of Denmark, pr. c. 1600-1601, pb. 1603

Twelfth Night: Or, What You Will, pr. c. 1600-1602, pb. 1623

Troilus and Cressida, pr. c. 1601-1602, pb. 1609

All's Well That Ends Well, pr. c. 1602-1603, pb. 1623

Othello, the Moor of Venice, pr. 1604, pb. 1622 (revised 1623)

Measure for Measure, pr. 1604, pb. 1623

King Lear, pr. c. 1605-1606, pb. 1608

Macbeth, pr. 1606, pb. 1623

Antony and Cleopatra, pr. c. 1606-1607, pb. 1623

Pericles, Prince of Tyre, pr. c. 1607-1608, pb. 1609

Timon of Athens, pr. c. 1607-1608, pb. 1623

Coriolanus, pr. c. 1607-1608, pb. 1623

Cymbeline, pr. c. 1609-1610, pb. 1623

The Winter's Tale, pr. c. 1610-1611, pb. 1623

The Tempest, pr. 1611, pb. 1623

The Two Noble Kinsmen, pr. c. 1612-1613, pb. 1634 (with John Fletcher)

Henry VIII, pr. 1613, pb. 1623 (with John Fletcher)

Poetry

Venus and Adonis, 1593

The Rape of Lucrece, 1594

The Passionate Pilgrim, 1599 (miscellany with poems by Shakespeare and others)

The Phoenix and the Turtle, 1601

A Lover's Complaint, 1609

Sonnets, 1609

Editions of the Sonnets

Shakespeare's sonnets, like his other work, have been reprinted countless times over the years. This chronological listing includes the various editions published in the second half of the twentieth and first half of the twenty-first century. They range from standard paperback reprints of the original 1609 edition, to reprints with commentary, illustrated and gift editions of the original, as well as unabridged recordings.

1963: *Shakespeare's Sonnets*, ed. Martin Seymour-Smith (Oxford, Heinemann Educational)

1964: *The Sonnets, Songs and Poems of Shakespeare*, ed. Oscar James Campbell (Bantam Books)

1967: *Shakespeare's Sonnets*, ed. W. G. Ingram and Theodore Redpath (University of London Press)

1973: *Shakespeare's Sonnets—The Problems Solved: A Modern Edition with Prose Versions, Introduction and Notes*, ed. A.L. Rowse (Macmillan)

1977: *Shakespeare's Sonnets,* ed. Stephen Booth (Yale University Press)

1980: *The Sonnets: Poems of Love*, ed. William Burto (St. Martin's Press)

1986: *The Sonnets and a Lover's Complaint*, ed. John Kerrigan (Penguin Classics)

1990: Love Sonnets of Shakespeare: Miniature Edition (Running Press)

1992: *Illustrated Shakespeare: The Shakespeare Sonnets*, unabridged recording of the sonnets by Alex Jennings (Gramercy)

1996: *The Sonnets*, ed. G. Blakemore Evans (Cambridge University Press)

1997: *Shakespeare's Sonnets,* ed. Katherine Duncan-Jones (Arden Shakespeare: Third Series)

1993: The Sonnets, illus. Ian Penney (Tiger Books)

1999: *The Art of Shakespeare's Sonnets,* ed. Helen Vendler (Belknap Press)

2001: *The Sonnets*, ed. Stephen Orgel, with an introduction by John Hollander (Pelican Shakespeare, Penguin Classics)

2002: *The Complete Sonnets and Poems,* ed. Colin Burrow (Oxford University Press)

2004: *Shakespeare's Sonnets*, ed. Barbara A. Mowat and Paul Werstine (Folger Shakespeare Library, Simon & Schuster)

2007: *Shakespeare's Sonnets*, collectors format, with commentary by David West (Overlook)

2010: *Shakespeare's Sonnets: Gift Edition*, ed. Katherine Duncan-Jones (Bloomsbury Arden Shakespeare)

Guide to Free Online Resources on the Sonnets

While William Shakespeare, in the words of fellow writer Ben Johnson, "was not of an age, but for all time," the World Wide Web of course changes day by day, hour by hour, minute by minute—new pages are built, old ones go dead, links break, and information grows at a rate difficult to comprehend, with classic texts, groundbreaking literary and historical research, and wild speculation alike all infinitely searchable. It is this searchability that is so important, for now any scholar or student with an internet connection can access wisdom once unreachable except by a lifetime of travel from one major university library to another, from one archive to another, from one continent to another. Yet after these resources are found, they also must be evaluated, weighed, understood in context—this list is to help with that.

The following is not exhaustive, and of course it is a snapshot of one instant in a world of constantly changing information. Below are more than three-dozen websites containing a great wealth of useful free resources for students and educators alike on the works, life, and era of Shakespeare. These sites, evaluated and with their main features noted, are grouped into six broad categories:

The Sonnets Themselves: Text, Audio, and Video—Here the sonnets themselves are presented, sometimes in familiar text-only but sometimes in other media as well, for reference and appreciation, without commentary or other apparatus.

For New Students—Students new to Shakespeare can find introductory information on the author's works, biography, and times. Generally, however, neither citations nor other references to scholarly work are given, so students working on class assignments usually will want to follow up in the Sites That Include Biography, History, and Analysis area.

For Educators—Pages here give many useful resources for K-12 teachers, including lesson plans.

Concordances—These sites make the works of Shakespeare searchable by specific words or phrases for easy reference.

Sites That Include Biography, History, and Analysis—Such "full-service" web pages cover almost every topic that students, either in high school or in college, may need. Often information is attributed and cited, and links to other scholarly resources usually are given as well.

Links of Links—Rather than hosting a great deal of Shakespeare information themselves, these sites instead have compiled lists of many other web sites for further research.

The Sonnets Themselves: Text, Audio, and Video

http://www.bartleby.com/people/Shakespe.html
The site gives the full text of thirty-seven plays, all one-hundred-fifty-four sonnets, "Venus and Adonis," "The Rape of Lucrece," "Sonnets to Sundry Notes of Music," and "The Phoenix and the Turtle" from the 1914 Oxford edition of The Complete Works of William Shakespeare edited by W.J. Craig. Each play links to its own base page, where it then is linked scene by scene; the poetry base page similarly links each poem to its own page, and an index of first lines is given as well.

http://www.gutenberg.org/ebooks/1041
The site gives the full text of the sonnets as an electronic book. Aside from html, UTF-8, and txt online, downloadable options include EPUB and Kindle.

https://librivox.org/sonnets-by-william-shakespeare/
Run by a non-profit organization whose aim is to make public-domain books available for as free audio files, the site gives no history or criticism but presents the sonnets as recorded by a dozen-odd readers. The entirety, with a running time of 2:44:21, can be downloaded as an mp3 zip file of around 77 MB; the poems also can be accessed as ten-sonnet blocks, either downloaded or played on the site itself. The readings vary in pacing and skill, but all are at least decent.

http://www.numberphile.com/videos/14_shakespeare.html
Supported by the Mathematical Sciences Research Institute of Berkeley, California, the site presents entertaining short videos by video-journalist and filmmaker Brady Haran on various mathematical topics. At 4:37 minutes long, Number 14 shows Roger Bowley, Professor Emeritus of the University of Nottingham, discussing Sonnet 18, "Shall I compare thee to a summer's day?" Bowley reads the poem, explains the structure of the Shakespearean sonnet, and discusses the general meaning of the

sonnets as a whole, while meter and rhyme are reinforced visually.

http://poetry.eserver.org/sonnets/
Hosted by Iowa State University, the site presents all of Shakespeare's sonnets, each one linked from its number to a single page.

http://www.sonnets.org/shakespeare.htm
This subpage of www.sonnets.org provides 14 of Shakespeare's sonnets as full text, scrollable, without commentary. The homepage, however, covers the sonnet form in general, both in Great Britain and elsewhere, with a small amount of history and explanation, plus the full text of sonnets from a great number of poets; "The Sonnet in Great Britain," for example, is divided into seven periods, each of which features up to a dozen poets who then have at least several sonnets given.

http://www.touchpress.com/titles/shakespeares-sonnets/
Run by a company that produces multimedia books, the site provides the sonnets in an iTunes file of around 1.5 GB. Each sonnet is performed on video by noted actors such as Patrick Stewart, David Tennant, and Kim Cattrall. The text is shown during readings, and highlighted line by line.

http://www.web-l.com/shakespeare/poetry/sonnets/
The site gives the full text of the sonnets, listed by number and first line, then linked one per page.

http://www.youtube.com/playlist?list=PLB95F4388 26F3CE36
This playlist presents mellifluous readings of the sonnets by Bertram Selwyn, one per link. As each line is read, it is displayed in large, quaint-seeming type over across the Chandos portrait.

For New Students
http://www.cliffsnotes.com/literature/s/ shakespeares-sonnets/about-shakespeares-sonnets
The site begins with a brief one-paragraph definition of the Shakespearean sonnet form, then discusses the original publishing of the sonnets, and gives an overview of the "Young Man" and "Dark Lady" sections of Shakespeare's sonnet sequence. Under "Summary and Analysis" in the column at the left, each sonnet is linked to a page giving an explanatory summary at one tab and at the full text of the poem at the other tab; a brief biography is given, as well as is a glossy of now-unusual terms from the sonnets. No citations or references to scholarship are given, however.

http://www.nosweatshakespeare.com/
Run by a father-and-son team of Shakespeare enthusiasts named John and Warren King, the site sells e-books of around a dozen of the plays that have been modernized for easier reading, including some specifically adapted for children, and an e-book of the sonnets that also includes a modern "translation" for each. Free resources include an overview, list of characters, plot summary, and interactive setting map of each play; quotations about and by Shakespeare, the latter with modernized "translations"; brief introductory essays on the life, historical context, and language of Shakespeare; and all sonnets individually linked as full text plus "translation." Really, it is difficult to determine whether these sometimes-flat rewritings ultimately help elevate us or dumb us down—many times, after all, simple footnotes to explain unfamiliar vocabulary or syntax might be better—but perhaps they may serve as a jumping-off point for appreciation that leads to further reading and research.

http://www.shmoop.com/shakespeare/
Run by an online publishing company that provides web-based study courses for purchase by high school students and teachers, the site also provides some free resources. Brief information is given on twenty of the plays: an "In a Nutshell" and "Why Should I Care?" plus "Themes," "Characters," "Analysis," and others. The texts themselves are not given, however. Currently four sonnets are discussed as well: Numbers 2, 18, 116, and 130. Full text without annotations are given, although each "Summary" tab gives a brief overview of a particular poem, and "Analysis" and "Themes" are subdivided to give several little paragraph-sized chunks. The site is decent for the first-time Shakespeare reader, but its "Best of the Web" tabs unfortunately link very, very few actual critical resources.

http://shakespeare.about.com/
This commercial site gives a fair deal of introductory information, filed under the broad headers of "Shakespeare," "Shakespeare's Life," "Plays," and "Sonnets." Aside from biography and historical context, also given are study guides are given for a handful of the plays. The section on the sonnets defines the sonnet form and

explains the iambic pentameter. The "Fair Youth" and "Dark Lady" sections each receive small introductions, and Sonnets 18, 19, 20, and 21 are given as full text, with Sonnet 18 also having a very brief study guide. No bibliographic or critical resources are given, and navigation, which could be clearer, is impeded somewhat by a great many advertisements.

http://www.sparknotes.com/shakespeare/shakesonnets/

The site gives basic resources for students to approach and understand the sonnets. After links to fairly brief pages on "Context," "The Sonnet Form," and "Themes, Motifs & Symbols," ten sonnets are given, one to a page, as full text followed by one paragraph of summary and two or three paragraphs of commentary; no critical sources are cited or listed at the commentaries. Under the heading "Study Tools" are given half a dozen study questions and a bibliography of only one critical text—Stephen Booth's 1977 Shakespeare's Sonnets—along with examples of how to cite the "SparkNote" in MLA, Chicago, and APA style.

For Educators
http://www.pbs.org/shakespeare/educators/

Hosted by the Public Broadcasting System, the site gives a wealth of resources for using Shakespeare in classroom, from elementary school through high school. Subpages give information filed under "Professional Development," "Lesson Plans," and "Resources," while the pages linked at "Multimedia Digital Library" and "In Your State" are searchable. The "Lesson Plans" area is very helpful for faculty, and filed under the heading "Shakespeare's Language" is a step-by-step lesson plan by high school teacher Joan Snyder for introducing and discussing Sonnets 18, 29, and 130 in two 45-minute periods.

http://www.uen.org/core/languagearts/shakespeare/

Hosted by the Utah Education Network, which includes the state's Board of Education and its System of Higher Education, the site provides links out to over a dozen other useful Shakespeare websites, plus links to several lesson plans for different grade levels from the Folger Library, the John F. Kennedy Center for the Performing Arts, the National Endowment for the Humanities, and ReadWriteThink.org. Also linked are study guides to each play from the Utah Shakespeare Festival; all guides include the same eleven brief essays of useful

context, but the synopsis, list and description of characters, and scholarly articles of course are specific to the particular play.

Concordances
http://www.doc.ic.ac.uk/~rac101/concord/texts/sonnets/

The site gives a concordance to the sonnets. The base page shows the full text of Sonnet 1, and remaining sonnets are linked, one per page, from their Roman numerals at the top of the page. Any word's occurrence across the entirety of the sonnets can be checked either by typing into the search field or by clicking on any word within the displayed sonnet. The results are shown in two columns, the left giving the Roman numerals and first lines of poems, the right listing the line numbers of any matches; the left column links out again to each sonnet, and the right column again is searchable by clicking on any word.

http://www.opensourceshakespeare.org/

Hosted by George Mason University, the site gives full text of all plays and poems, including the sonnets, with all works fully searchable by word, by character, and by phrase keyed into the search box. An extensive concordance also is searchable by letter; the frequency of each word is given, and all occurrences are listed by location in works, while links give the text of each use, including wide surrounding context—the entirety of a sonnet, for example. A function also exists for the searcher to compare two sonnets side-by-side if desired.

http://www.shakespeare-monologues.org/home

The site provides all monologues in Shakespeare's plays, organized by "The Men" and "The Women," and then within each by play, categorized under the headers of "Comedies," "Histories," and "Tragedies"; a search box also is provided. Each monologue, listed by first line, then is linked out, either to a page on Bartleby.com or to a pdf version.

http://sydney.edu.au/engineering/it/~matty/Shakespeare/

Run by James Matthew Farrow of the University of Sydney, the site gives full text for all of Shakespeare's plays and poems. The plays, grouped under the headers of "Histories," "Tragedies," and "Comedies," are linked to their own base pages, then given scene by scene, while the sonnets are presented in one scrollable page, and a glossary of unfamiliar Shakespearean terms is provided at its own link. The "Shakespeare search engine" near the top of the homepage can search any word or group of words in Shakespeare's work; it allows for use of operators such as and, or, not, before, after, and near, along narrowing by play, character, or scene, and weighting, and results are given with wide surrounding context.

Sites That Include Biography, History, and Analysis

http://absoluteshakespeare.com/

The easily navigable site give a broad range of information about Shakespeare's life and works, including a very large glossary of less familiar Shakespearean words, over 130 quotes indexed by work, trivia, and a useful timeline. Summaries and commentaries on ten major plays are given, and full text for all plays is provided by scenes. Full text is given for all the sonnets, usually presented in groups of 25 to a scrollable page, along with full text of "A Lover's Complaint," "The Passionate Pilgrim," "The Phoenix and the Turtle," "The Rape of Lucrece," and "Venus and Adonis," though none have commentary or editorial notes. No scholarly or other resources are given, and the "Bibliography" link gives a list of Shakespeare's works, not links to other sources.

http://www.bardweb.net/index.html

Run by writer J.M. Pressley, the site gives a variety of information about a number Shakespeare's works, plus the author's biography, Elizabethan history, and Shakespeare's language. While each pages themselves are short, each gives a number of useful links—fully three-dozen on the "works" page, for example, including criticism and journals. The sonnets are treated very broadly in only a few paragraphs, without full text, but links out lead to other sites giving in-depth treatment.

http://www.english.emory.edu/classes/Shakespeare_ Illustrated/Shakespeare.html

Run by Harry Rusche, a professor of English at Emory University, the site provides a brief introduction on the relationship between painted art and Shakespeare's plays, then presents a great number of eighteenth- and nineteenth-century paintings and engravings depicting scenes from the plays. One page organizes the works according to the plays they represent, giving each picture a link for its own page, while another page gives the alphabetized names of the roughly 100 artists on the site

and links the works out from their subpages. Other brief essays and explanation are linked from the introduction as well.

http://www.folger.edu/Content/Teach-and-Learn/ Teaching-Resources/Teaching-Sonnets/

Hosted by the Folger Shakespeare Library of Washington, D.C., the site provides teachers with a lesson plan for exploring sonnets across ten class periods of 40 to 45 minutes. After a brief rationale on the value of teaching sonnets, along with a concise history of the sonnet and details on sonnet structure, lessons begin by introducing students to an approachable work by Edna St. Vincent Millay, then continue to discuss Petrarch in translation, examine Shakespeare sonnets from the collection and from Romeo and Juliet, perform close readings, dramatize a sonnet by reading aloud, and other activities. The folger.edu base page of course provides a wealth of information and resources on Shakespeare's works and life.

http://internetshakespeare.uvic.ca/

Run by the University of Victoria in British Columbia, Canada, the site provides a tremendous wealth of well-organized information organized under the tabs labeled "Plays & Poems," "Life & Times," "Performance," "Reviews," and "Resources." Full text is given of the entire works of Shakespeare, the plays scene by scene and the sonnets play by play. In addition to modern printings, facsimiles of folios often are given as well, with the capacity for magnification; each play also has a "Text analysis tools" link that gives a variety of statistics on character appearance, lines spoken, and other factors, including location with the work. Topics in the "Life & Times" tab are divided into "Life," "Stage," "Society," "History," "Ideas," "Drama," "Literature," and "Plays," with several concise informative essays linked under each. The "Resources" tab gives a very great number of useful links out, all thoroughly categorized.

http://www.ipl.org/div/litcrit/bin/litcrit.out. pl?au=sha-9

Hosted by the Internet Public Library consortium, which is comprised of a number of universities in the United States and abroad, the site provides carefully annotated bibliographies linking out to sources on the web, each of which is identified as academically "Critical," "Biographical," or "Other (non-critical)" in emphasis. All source listings, whether for broader webpages or for articles or books posted online, are headed with a linked title; the URL for each also is visible, and in addition to listing author and title and, where applicable, full information on journal, volume, year, and inclusive pagination, the annotations give at least a sentence or two, and sometimes more, of description. Aside from its broader Shakespeare homepage, the site also has similarly categorized annotated bibliographies on its pages focusing on specific plays and on the sonnets and other poems.

http://www.poets.org/poet.php/prmPID/122
Run by the Academy of American Poets, the site provides a brief biography of Shakespeare and broadly discusses the plays and sonnets, in addition to giving a paragraph on his invention of new words. In the column labelled "Poems by William Shakespeare" on the page's right are linked, one to a page, full text of speeches from around 20 of the plays, plus around 16 sonnets, including one that has an audio option. The "Further Reading" column is linked a concise introduction to the history and forms of the sonnet, and a few links out are given, including an interesting one from the December 1999 issue of the London Review of Books by critic Frank Kermode .

http://www.shakespeareforalltime.com/resources/
Run by a self-taught Shakespeare enthusiast who goes only by the first name of Peter but shows wide reading and study, the site is both a blog—updated very regularly through 2012 though more sporadically through 2013 and beyond—and a source of factual and critical information. The plays link out to the annotated scene-by-scene presentation at www.shakespeare-online.com, while the sonnets are given without notes or explanation. In addition to giving a list of nearly a dozen other live-linked websites on Shakespeare, the site also gives a suggested reading list of over a dozen scholarly texts, from William Hazlitt and Samuel T. Coleridge to Harold Bloom; the listing for each book on the suggested reading page links to Amazon.com for purchase if desired.

http://shakespeare.mit.edu
Hosted by the Massachusetts Institute of Technology, the site gives the full texts of the complete work of Shakespeare: all plays, listed alphabetically in categories of "Comedy," "History," and Tragedy, along with poetry, including the sonnets. Plays are given both in their entirety and broken into scenes, one scene to a link; from the sonnet base page, each sonnet links out to its own page. No literary criticism, history, or even textual annotations are given, but for basic full-text the site is complete and easy to use. The base page of each work links out Amazon.com for purchase, if desired, of the appropriate Arden Shakespeare paperback.

http://www.shakespeare-online.com
Run by Amanda Mabillard, a university-trained independent scholar and writer, the site offers a great wealth of information—biographical and historical, explanation and analysis of Shakespeare's works, and the effect of Shakespeare upon literature, language and culture. Some work is that of Mabillard, some that of other scholars, all clearly attributed. The site directory organizes topics under headings such as "plays" and "sonnets"—both given in full text, with explanatory notes—"analysis," "sources," "biography," "plots," "faq," "glossary," and whatnot. Although the layout may be just a little bit "busy," as if intended for early high school students rather than those in college, the amount of fact, context, and interpretation given is tremendous, useful, and painstaking. Following interesting side-trails and delving through link upon link may remind the searcher of the nursery rhyme about the journey to St. Ives, during which is met the man seven wives, each of whom has seven sacks containing seven cats each, who then each have seven kittens. It is probable that only a finite number of articles is kept on this website; it is unlikely, however, that the average researcher ever could determine the figure.

http://www.shakespeares-sonnets.com/sonnet/index.php
Hosted by UK publisher Oxquarry Books, the site focuses mainly on Shakespeare's sonnets but also includes "A Lover's Complaint" and "Venus and Adonis," along with poetry by Sir Thomas Wyatt, Sir Philip Sydney's "A Defence of Poesie," and a few other miscellaneous works. Each sonnet, individually linked, is given in current typeface and in a reproduction closer to that of the 1609 quarto, and receives a summary introduction and then a line-by-line explanation that includes glosses on less familiar vocabulary. Sources often are cited, though the commentary is explicatory rather than examining delving into literary criticism per se. The sonnets also are presented in a scrollable full list, though without commentary.

http://web.cn.edu/kwheeler/resource_lit.shakespeare.html
Run by L. Kip Wheeler, a professor of English at

Carson-Newman University in Tennessee, the site gives, both on separate pages and in pdf form, much useful historical information: overviews of the Hundred Years' War and the War of the Roses, definitions of classical tragedy and comedy, a discussion of the Great Chain of Being, a delineation of Renaissance views of ghosts, and a handout on the wives of Henry VIII, for example. One pdf defines the Petrarchan and Shakespearean sonnets, shows structure and rhyme in Sonnet 1 and Sonnet 29, and presents with Yeats' "Leda and the Swan" for discussion as well. A chronological list of Shakespeare's works is provided, as are links to other useful Shakespeare pages. In addition, buttons on the left of the page include, aside from class-related matters, other literature and poetry resources and a solid history of the English language.

http://en.wikipedia.org/wiki/Shakespeare's_sonnets
Despite the introductory disclaimer that "Wikipedia is allowed to be imperfect," the site of course is a fine place to begin, as the oversight of a multitude of interested contributor/editors generally provides good information and should correct any errors or mischief fairly quickly. Main topics covered include "Dedication," "Structure," "Characters," "Themes," and "Legacy," and almost any pertinent or tangential items of potential interest—all historical figures and modern critics, for example, along with other literary and historical topics such as poetic meter and Shakespeare's sexuality, to name only two—are linked out to their own articles on Wikipedia. The article is cited throughout with footnotes that primarily refer to scholarly works. In addition to these sources, links to other useful websites are given as well.

http://www.williamshakespearefacts.net/
The site gives a great number of quick facts and statistics on Shakespeare's life and works, plus various quotes on life, quotes on love, and humorous quotes from the plays. All plays are listed with pertinent dates and interesting stats, while the sonnets are given in full text, linked one to a page.

http://www.william-shakespeare.info/site-map.htm
The site, designed with light text upon a black background, provides a great deal of information on Shakespeare, subdivided in columns under the broad headings of "The LIFE of Shakespeare," "The WORLD of Shakespeare," and "The WORKS of Shakespeare."

Each column then has from around 10 to 20 subpages, each of whose essays are laid out in short paragraphs with clear labels. From the base page of plays, all works have their own base page with brief introduction, and then full text is given by act. From the base page of sonnets, each sonnet links out to full text on its own page, though no notes or interpretations are given. Surprisingly for a site on Shakespeare, language is sometimes a little bit spotty, and unfortunately, none of the information on history, biography, and whatnot is cited, nor are links to any sources or criticism given.

Links of Links
http://libguides.libraries.claremont.edu/content.php?pid=45958&sid=339510
Hosted by the Claremont Colleges of California, the library website of the consortium provides some two-dozen links to sites useful in studying Shakespeare and his works. Some sites themselves hold a wealth of information, while others are compendia of lists of still further links.

http://www.michellehenry.fr/shak.htm
The site provides, in one illustrated scrollable list, links to a wide variety of sites. The external sites are categorized under headers such as "Resources," "PowerPoint Presentations," "The Globe Theater," "Glossary," "Listening," "Activities," "Lesson Plans," "Interactive Games," and others, including, of course, several plays and the sonnets in general.

http://www.onlinecollege.org/2009/12/16/100-incredibly-useful-links-for-teaching-and-studying-shakespeare/
The site provides around 100 links out for teaching and studying Shakespeare, grouped in the following categories: "Comprehensive Resources," "Reading Shakespeare," "Articles," "Quizzes," "Aids to Teaching and Studying Shakespeare," "Teacher's Guides," "Audio and Video," "Glossaries, Dictionaries, and More," "Other Fun Stuff," and "Shakespeare for Homeschoolers."

http://www.webenglishteacher.com/shakespeare.html
Run by longtime English teacher Carla Beard, the site in its "Shakespeare" section has pages devoted to "Shakespeare and the Elizabethan Age," to "The Globe Theater," to "Shakespeare's Sonnets," and to many of the plays, with the pages each providing links out to

other useful resources. Some of the linked external sites give context or study guides for students, while many—especially that devoted to the sonnets—also give lesson plans for teachers.

Rafeeq McGiveron

Guide to Literary Criticism on the Sonnets

The following list highlights works concerning William Shakesepeare's sonnets and the art form of the sonnet itself. The books include histories of the sonnets as well as literary dissection of the works in terms of their creation, authenticity, interpretations, and publication.

Baldwin, T. W. *On the Literary Genetics of Shakespeare's Poems and Sonnets*. University of Illinois Press. 1951.
"The Literary Genetics of Shakespeare's Sugred Sonnets" is but one of the chapters in this volume analyzing Shakespeare's poetry. The book also contains detailed dissections of the non-sonnet writings including chapters on "The Construction of Venus and Adonis," "Shaping Ideas in Venus and Adonis: Chaos to Cosmos Through Love," "Shaping Ideas in Venus and Adonis: Platonic Love," "Basic Sources of Lucrece," and "William Shakespeare, Renaissance Poet," plus an index.

Bate, Jonathan. *Shakespeare and the English Romantic Imagination*. Oxford: Clarendon Press. 1989.
Bate, professor of Shakespeare and Renaissance Literature at the University of Warwick, chronicles the strong influence of Shakespeare's writing on the most noteworthy Romantic-era poets both in terms of their perspectives on love, nature, and numerous other themes paramount to their poems and plays. The book takes a deep look at Shakespeare and William Wordsworth, William Blake, Samuel Taylor Coleridge, John Keats, Lord, Byron, and Percy Shelley. Bates also presents his argument for debunking critic Harold Bloom's notion that John Milton was the Romantics' leading influence.

Boaden, James & Abraham Wivell. *Portraits of Shakespeare, and On the Sonnets of Shakespeare*. Cambridge University Press. 2013.
Numerous portraits of Shakespeare date back to the years when he was still alive, but if the works credited to William Shakespeare were written by others then who is the man whose image appears in the illustrations? Boaden investigates the authenticity of these early images, which segues into an examination of the sonnets and names William Herbert, the Earl of Pembroke, as the mysterious "W.H." to whom the first publication of the poems is dedicated.

Boyd, Brian. *Why Lyrics Last: Evolution, Cognition and Shakespeare's Sonnets*. Harvard University Press. 2012.
Boyd proposes that song lyrics, rap rhythms, and puns encountered daily in print and TV jingles in ads have replaced poetry and verse in the modern world. The psychology behind why the lyrics of the new world and the poetics of the old world grab our attention, however, are the same. Chapters analyze "Poetry, Pattern, and Attention," "Lyric and Sonnet," "A First Shakespeare Sonnet," "Love: The Mistress," "Love and Time: The Youth," and "Lyric and Narrative." The book also includes scholarly notes, a bibliography, and an index.

Briggs, E.D.P., ed. *English Sonnets*. Orion. 1999.
This book is an amalgam of sonnets from throughout English-language literature, and both British and American authors are present. Besides Shakespeare, the volume includes sonnets from numerous authors including Matthew Arnold, Coleridge, Robert Burns, Elizabeth Barrett Browning, George Eliot, Thomas Gray, Thomas Hardy, George Herbert, Thomas Hood, Ben Johnson, John Keats, John Milton, Herman Melville, Edgar Allen Poe, Christina Rossetti, Percy Shelley, and Edmund Spencer. Along with the more than one hundred sonnets, the book also sports scholarly notes, an index of authors, and a list of titles and first lines.

Brown, Henry. *The Sonnets of Shakespeare Solved, and the Mystery of His Friendship, Love, and Rivalry Revealed*. Nabu Press. 2014.
Originally published in the 1870s, Brown theorizes that Shakespeare's sonnets are purely autobiographical and studying them provides a map of his innermost thoughts and feelings, which are not present in any of his plays. The sonnets, claims Brown, reveal what Shakespeare was like as a man. Chapters present Brown's argument for his findings, a table of the sonnets, an explanation of the sonnets, and numerous scholarly notes concerning the sonnets, which he divides into four groups.

Callaghan, Dympna. *Shakespeare's Sonnets*. **Wiley-Blackwell. 2006.**
Callaghan focuses on the composition of the sonnets to provide general readers with an introduction to the works rather than discuss the endless theories regarding their authorship, sexual references, and other theoretical aspects. He asserts that scholarship has ignored the parameters of their form and what thoughts can be expressed within the limits of their 14-line frame. He applies more modern critical thinking regarding the many intricacies of Shakespeare's composition of the sonnets as individual poems.

De Grazia, Marreta. *The Scandal of Shakespeare's Sonnet Sonnets: Volume 46 Shakespeare and Sexuality*. **Cambridge University Press. 2007.**
Grazia addresses the long-held belief that John Benson altered Shakespeare's sonnets for an edition published in 1640 in order to hide that the first one-hundred-twenty-six poems were written to a man and therefore were of a homosexual nature. Grazia argues that Benson in fact changed very little of the poems and that they appear primarily as Shakespeare wrote them. Grazia further chronicles alterations made in subsequent publications of Shakespeare's sonnets and the criticism thereof.

Dubrow, Heather. *Captive Victors: Shakespeare's Narrative Poems and Sonnets*. **Cornell University Press. 1987. 288p.**
Dubrow, the John Bascom Professor and Tighe-Evans Professor of English at the University of Wisconsin—Madison, provides a detailed analysis of Shakespeare's longer narrative poems Venus and Adonis and The Rape of Lucrece and how those two works compare with his sonnets. There also are scholarly analysis of the language Shakespeare incorporates in the works especially in terms of the presentation of the description of the rape scenes in the works.

Duncan Jones, Katherine. *Shakespeare's Sonnets*. **Bloomsbury. 2014.**
This revised edition of Duncan Jones's 1997 original has been dubbed by scholars and reviewers as "the edition of first resort." For this updated paperback, Jones, a professor of Early Modern English at Somerville College, Oxford, specializing in Elizabethan literature, history, and biography, has updated and corrected the text to include new scholarship and Shakespearean criticism that has surfaced since the original volume was released.

The author provides full background on Shakespeare's sonnets and the scholarly debates concerning their origins as well as their franks sexual references.

Edmonson, Paul & Stanley Wells. *Shakespeare's Sonnets*. **Oxford University Press. 2004.**
Edmonson and Wells analyze Shakespeare's sonnets in terms of their publishing history and context to his plays and longer poems. Subjects covered include the early publications of the sonnets, the history and emergence of the sonnet as a literary form, the sonnets in relations to Shakespeare's life, the sonnets as theater, concerns of the sonnets, the place of *A Lover's Complaint,* the sonnets later publication, and the sonnets critical reputation and influence on later writers.

Empson, William. *Seven Types of Ambiguity*. **New Directions. 1966.**
First published in 1930, British literary critic and writer Empson has revised the volume's text twice to reflect the latest scholarship. As the title indicates, the book focuses on seven types of ambiguity that could be present in a literary text, which would make it open to numerous angles of interpretation based on individual perspective. Works discussed include Shakespeare's sonnets and plays, and the poetry of Geoffrey Chaucer, John Donne, Alexander Pope, William Wordsworth, T.S. Eliot, and others.

Evans, Maurice. *Elizabethan Sonnets*. **Phoenix Press. 2003.**
This collection was assembled to honor the 400th anniversary of Queen Elizabeth I's death. Evans gathers works from a number of Shakespeare's contemporaries but not the bard himself. Works include Philip Sidney's "Astrophel and Stella," Edmund Spencer's "Amoretti," and numerous other signature authors of the day. To provide readers with historical context in which to place the works, the volume also sports a scholarly introduction, notes, and a chronology of the sonnets and their authors lives and times.

Fairhead, Jane. Shakespeare's *Sonnets Re-Visited*. **CreateSpace Publishing. 2013.**
Fairhead theorizes that the sonnets assigned to Shakespeare in fact were written by Sir Thomas More during his incarceration in the Tower of London from 1534 until he was executed for treason by King Henry VIII in 1535. Furthermore, she asserts that the poems were a

correspondence between More and his oldest daughter, Meg.

Fenton, James. *The Strength of Poetry*. Oxford University Press. 2003.
Fenton, a Whitbread Prize–winning poet, professor, and critic offers a sampling of the lectures he delivered on poetry while teaching at Oxford from 1994 to 1999. His critical writings proved Fenton equally adept at prose. This volume offers his thoughts on poetry across the ages as seen through a very wide angle lens. Not only does he discuss poets and their works, but also poets thoughts on other poets output, including W. H. Auden's thoughts on the perceived homoerotic qualities of Shakespeare's sonnets.

Fuller, John, ed. *The Oxford Book of Sonnets*. Oxford University Press. 2000.
Fuller offers a survey of the sonnet throughout literary history in this collection of 328 individual works. The volume reaches as far back as Shakespeare through the form's revival in the eighteenth century through modern poets like Seamus Heaney and Carol Ann Duffy. Fuller also includes a scholarly introduction that places the sonnet in its artistic and historic context.

Gordon, Helen Heightsman. *The Secret Love Story in Shakespeare's Sonnets*. Xlibris Corporation. 2008.
This volume presents Gordon's theory that Shakespeare's sonnets were love poems written by nobleman Edward De Vere, the 17th Earl of Oxford, to Queen Elizabeth the First with whom he allegedly had a torrid affair. Gordon further contends that the hyphenation of "Shake-speare" in the first publication of the sonnets indicates that it actually was a pen name for Oxford, who was known to be a talented writer. She further claims that since the sonnets were never meant for public consumption that they represent the author's purest writing, unlike the plays which underwent alterations over time.

Halpern, Richard. *Shakespeare's Perfume. Sodomy and Sublimity in the Sonnets, Wilde, Freud and Lacan*. University of Pennsylvania Press. 2002.
Halpern examines the asserted homosexuality present in Shakespeare's sonnets, Oscar Wilde's works, Sigmund Freud's writings on Leonardo da Vinci, and Jacques Lacan's seminar on the ethics in regard to psychoanalysis. The four chapters cover Shakespeare, Wilde's The Portrait of Mr. W.H., "Leonardo da Vinci and the Memory of

his Childhood," and "Lacan's Anal Thing, The Ethics of Psychoanalysis. The book also is capped with scholarly notes on the texts, a bibliography, and an index.

Hammond, Paul. *Figuring Sex Between Men from Shakespeare to Rochester*. Oxford University Press. 2002.
Hammond, professor of Seventeenth-Century English Literature, University of Leeds, in this volume surveys the homoeroticism and homophobia present in literature dating to the period. The material graciously is presented in laymen's terms so that both scholars and casual readers can understand it. He has compiled significant examples of writings from Shakespeare's sonnets, which many have theorized were the bard's love poems to another man, and plays through works by lesser-known poets, playwrights, and others gleaned from published and unpublished sources.

Hammond, Paul. *Shakespeare's Sonnets: An Original Spelling Text*. Oxford University Press. 2012.
Hammond presents the sonnets in the exact spelling in which they were first printed in 1609 sans the editorial alterations that were incorporated into the numerous editions by various publishers over the years. The text includes explanations of the different spellings and punctuations to help readers understand the original word in context with today's spelling.

Healy, Margaret. *Shakespeare, Alchemy and Creative Imagination: The Sonnets and A Lover's Complaint*. Cambridge University Press. 2011.
Healy proposes that the true meaning of Shakespeare's references to alchemy, metal, and assorted imagery of nature's mystical powers are lost to readers in modern times who view them as fanciful, false, and archaic notions. Reader's of the time, however, believed them. This volume explains how these references were used and what their meanings are so that modern readers can better understand the sonnets and Shakespeare's other poetry. The volume also includes scholarly notes.

Heylin, Clinton. *So Long as Men Can Breathe: The Untold Story of Shakespeare's Sonnets*. Da Capo. 2009.
This volume follows the sordid history of the publications of numerous editions of Shakespeare's sonnets beginning with the first edition in 1609, which was assembled and released through the collective efforts of

a shady publisher, a printer, and a bookseller. The text addresses the question of whether Shakespeare was involved in—or was even aware of—the book's publication. The text also chronicles subsequent publications and the alterations made to the works over time.

Jakobson, Roman & Lawrence G. Jones. *Shakespeare's Verbal Art in Th'Experience of Spirit.* **Mouton De Gruyter. 1970.**
Volume 35 of De Proprietatibus literarum: Series practica, this is a minutely detailed examination of Shakespeare's sonnet 129. It presents the poem with sections analyzing "spelling and punctuation," "interpretation," "pervasive features," "odd against even," "outer against inner," "anterior against posterior," "couplet against quatrains," "center against marginals," "Anagrams?," "concluding questions," and "references."

Jensen, Peter. *Secrets of the Sonnets: Shakespeare's Code.* **Lulu.com. 2007.**
Jensen proposes that Shakespeare incorporated a code in the sonnets, which when cracked, offers a new world of insight into who the characters of the Dark Lady and other players were in real life. The analysis also places a strong emphasis on the often bawdy and even juvenile humor incorporated into the otherwise serious sounding works. Jensen explains how he discovered the "code" and how readers can use it to see behind the facade of romance presented in the poems and appreciate their humor.

Jong, Erica. *Serenissima: A Novel of Venice.* **Houghton Mifflin. 1987.**
This novel's protagonist is Hollywood actress Jessica Pruitt who travels to Venice to judge a film festival while also trying to wrangle the part of Shylock's daughter in a top film adaptation of Shakespeare's The Merchant of Venice. Pruitt mysteriously is transported back in time to the Venice of Shakespeare and where his sonnets light the path to her romantic adventure with the bard and numerous other amorous contenders.

Kinney, Arthur F., ed. *The Cambridge Companion to English Literature, 1500–1600.* **Cambridge University Press. 1999.**
A highly detailed comprehensive study of all facets of English literature and the authors producing it during a single century. Along with editor Kinney's introduction, the volume offers fourteen essays. Chapters cover

Tudor aesthetics, authorship and the material conditions of writing, religious writing, poetry and patronage, dramatic achievements, the evolution of satire, lyric forms, chronicling private life, and popular culture of the time. The book also includes a chronology and index.

Koch, Mathias. *Shakespeare's Sonnet 60: A Detailed Interpretation and Analysis.* **GRIN Verlag. 2013.**
The text concentrates solely on Shakespeare's sonnet number 60, which focuses on time. The volume includes an introduction stating the author's theses followed by a history of the sonnet, a discussion of Shakespeare's sonnet writing and how his output generally is divided into two essential groupings with the first being written to a "lover" and the second addressed to a "Dark Mistress," and analysis and interpretation of Sonnet 60, and a bibliography.

Knight, G. Wilson. *The Mutual Flame: On Shakespeare's Sonnets and The Phoenix and the Turtle.* **Routledge. 2014.**
A reprint of the 1955 original, the volume is divided into matching sections covering the two disparate bodies of work described in the title. The section on Shakespeare's sonnets includes "Facts and Problems," "The Integration pattern," "Symbolism," "Time and Eternity," "The Expansion," and "Conclusion." The Phoenix and Turtle section covers "Preliminary Remarks," "Love's Martyr," "The Poetical Essays," "Shakespeare's Poems," "Other Poets." There volume also includes two indexes.

Legault, Paul & Sharmila Cohen, eds. *The Sonnets: Translating and Rewriting Shakespeare.* **Nightboat/Telephone Books. 2012.**
Editors and publishers Paul Legault and Sharmila Cohen, the author of three collections of poems, and a poet and translator, respectively, rewrite Shakespeare's sonnets by presenting the one-hundred-fifty-four poems as they were "translated" by an equal number of individual modern poets including Rae Armantrout, Mary Jo Bang, Jen Bervin, Paul Celan, Tan Lin, Harryette Mullen, Ron Padgett, Donald Revell, Jerome Rothenberg, Juliana Spahr, and others, who present the identical themes employed in the originals in different words.

Leishman, James. *Themes and Variations in Shakespeare's Sonnets.* **Routledge. 2013.**
The book is divided into three sections: Poetry as Immortalization from Pindar to Shakespeare; Devouring

Time and Fading Beauty from the Greek Anthology to Shakespeare; and 'Hyperbole' and 'Religiousness' in Shakespeare's Expressions of His Love, which examine Shakespeare's use of beauty, love, and other universal literary themes as well as comparing his work to those of other English and international sonneteers. The volume also includes an index of first lines for all the sonnets discussed and a general index.

Levin, Phyllis. ed. *The Penguin Book of the Sonnet: 500 Years of a Classic Tradition in English*. Penguin Books. 2001.
The volume incorporates sonnets beginning in 1304 through works of the twentieth century—more than six hundred poems in all. Authors represented range from Geoffrey Chaucer, Sir Philip Sidney, Shakespeare, John Donne, Robert Burns, Charles Lamb, and John Keats to Robert Frost, Ezra Pound, and John Updike. The volume also includes an introduction, an appendix titled "The Architecture of a Sonnet," explanatory notes, suggestions for further reading, biographical notes, index of poets, index of titles and first lines, and credits.

Martin, Philip. *Shakespeare's Sonnets: Self, Love and Art*. Cambridge University Press. 2010.
Shakespeare's sonnets are heavy with references to two kinds of self love; one harmful, the other not. Martin emphasizes the positive aspects of self-love contained in the poems and how despite the heartbreak and despair often expressed in the works the narrator manages to retain a notion of self worth and self awareness. Martin also addresses Shakespeare sense of mortality, both in the artistic sense and as a mortal man.

Muir, Kenneth. *Shakespeare's Sonnets*. Routledge. 2013.
Muir puts Shakespeare's sonnets into context by comparing them to the compositions of fellow English poets as well as those of Italian and French writers. The text also discusses the influence of Ovid and other classical authors on Shakespeare in addition to the influence they had on his theater writings. The volume also sports scholarly notes; a bibliography; appendixes on "The Dark Lady," The Rival Poets, "A Lovers Complaint," "The Passionate Pilgrim"; and an index.

Mussari, Mark. *The Sonnets (Shakespeare Explained)*. Marshall Cavendish. 2010.
Mussari presents Shakespeare's sonnets for the lay reader. Each sonnet is offered individually with Mussari explaining the action that is occurring in each fourteen-line poem—what the themes, symbols, etc., are—who is speaking and being spoken to; and what the meaning of each piece is. The text also supplies background on each works' historical and social context to provide deeper meaning to the poems and how they fit into Shakespeare's canon and his world.

Noonan, John. *Shakespeare's Spiritual Sonnets*. CreateSpace Publishing. 2011.
Noonan's theory is that while some of the sonnets surely were love poems written by Shakespeare as works for hire, many were composed simply to convey his own thoughts. He selects twenty-two sonnets and makes a case that they were the author's musings on the reigning theology of Elizabethan Britain and his personal relationship with God.

Paterson, Don. *101 Sonnets*. Faber & Faber. 2012.
As the title denotes, Paterson collects one-hundred-one sonnets from throughout literature for this brief collection. Along with the works , Paterson offers his own insights as well as a general introduction to the sonnet as a form. Paterson won the Forward Prize for Best Collection as well as Queen's Gold Medal for Poetry in 2009, so he's well qualified to discuss the subject with genuine insight. The book is serious enough for literature scholars while also being quite approachable to students and lay readers.

Paterson, Don. *Reading Shakespeare's Sonnets: A New Commentary*. Faber & Faber. 2012.
Paterson's analysis of Shakespeare's sonnets is based on his theories that earlier interpretations are not as accurate as believed and that the works convey vastly different meanings today than those presented by outdated scholarship. To provide current value he presents each of the 154 works accompanied by his own interpretation of what these poems say to modern readers and if the messages remain relevant. The volume also includes two appendixes, "A Note on Sonnet Form," and "A Note on Metre."

Pujante, A. Luis & Ton Hoenselaars, eds. *Four-Hundred Years of Shakespeare in Europe*. University of Delaware Press. 2003.
Although English born, Shakespeare was a citizen of the world and this volume provides an overview of the

influence his works have wielded in European history. Or particular interest is Manfred Pfister's essay, Route 66: the political performance of Shakespeare's Sonnet 66 in Germany and Elsewhere. Pfister contends that while English and American readers long have dismissed this sonnet as a minor outing, Europeans—particularly Germans—hold it in great esteem. He argues that the poem especially was a source of strength to those suffering under the Nazis during the second world war.

Rodenburg, Patsy. *Speaking Shakespeare*. Palgrave Macmillan. 2004.
The text demonstrates the proper way to speak and pronounce the words in Shakespeare's writing so that they are understood in the way that the author intended. Rodenburg covers both Shakespeare's plays and poetry so that readers or actors will correctly comprehend the writer's intent and what the words actually mean in context with the plot of the individual work for the purpose of making the words seem natural to speak.

Schalkwyk, David. *Speech and Performance in Shakespeare's Sonnets and Plays*. Cambridge University Press. 2007.
South African Shakespeare scholar Schalkwyk takes an alternate approach to the study of the bard's sonnets by juxtaposing them against his plays. He maintains that as the author earned his bread and butter in the theater and that regardless if the piece was drama, comedy, tragedy, or history the plays were composed in poetic and lyrical language and contents that readers can apply that mindset to the straight poetry being theatrical snippets that are equally ripe for performing.

Schiffer, James, ed. *Shakespeare's Sonnets: Critical Essays*. Routledge. 2000.
With Shakespeare studies it often seems like everything already has been said, but Schiffer assembles a massive collection of essays on the sonnets by leading modern scholars who provide new perspectives on the works while also challenging some of the older and established criticism as outdated. Current scholars have a freer hand to examine the sexual facets of the poems including the perceived homosexual aspects of the works that were ignored by earlier critics.

Schoenfeldt, Michael, ed. *A Companion to Shakespeare's Sonnets*. Wiley-Blackwell. 2007.
Schoenfeldt presents a study of Shakespeare's sonnets

divided into nine sections sporting essays by numerous scholars. Sections cover: Sonnet Form and Sonnet Sequence, Shakespeare and His Predecessors, Editorial Theory and Biographical Theory, The Sonnets in Manuscript and Print, Models of Desire in the Sonnets, Ideas of Darkness in the Sonnets, Memory and Repetition in the Sonnets, and The Sonnets and A Lover's Complaint. The volume also includes an appendix: "The 1609 Text of Shakespeare's Sonnets and A Lover's Complaint."

Spiller, Michael R.G. *The Development of the Sonnet: An Introduction*. Routledge. 2003.
Spiller was the senior lecturer in English and cultural history at the University of Aberdeen, Scotland, when compiling this title, which traces the sonnet as a poetic form from its roots in thirteenth century Italy through John Milton and others to illustrate the changes the sonnet experienced. Along with Milton, the volume analyzes the works of poets Petrarch, Dante, and Shakespeare. Chapters cover, The Sonnet and its Place, Sicilians and Citizens: The Early Sonnet, and The Fortunate Isles: The Sonnet Moves Abroad. The book also features an appendix, scholarly notes, a bibliography, and an index.

Vendler, Helen. *The Art of Shakespeare's Sonnets*. Harvard University Press. 1999.
Vendler, a noted poetry scholar, dissects each of Shakespeare's sonnets by breaking them down into their four sections and analyzing each one individually to illustrate how the parts fit together to illicit the emotion and response desired by the poet. Vendler's analysis is printed on the page next to the original verses so readers can view them in tandem.

Vickers, Brian. *Shakespeare, "A Lover's Complaint," and John Davies of Hereford*. Cambridge University Press. 2007.
Shakespeare studies have been fraught with mystery for hundreds of years as scholars have exhaustedly debated the authorship of his plays as well as numerous poems that it is believed he may have written under an assumed name or no name as a pen for hire by a wealthy patron. Some scholars have assigned him authorship of the poem A Lover's Complaint, while others contend that it is so ghastly bad that Shakespeare couldn't possibly have written it. Vickers comes out swinging in this exhaustive study, which debunks the old arguments and grants authorship to Jacobean poet John Davies.

Vickers, Brian. *Counterfeiting Shakespeare: Evidence, Authorship and John Ford's "Funeral Elegye."* **Cambridge University Press. 2009.**
Vickers once again steps up to debunk additional compositions allegedly written by Shakespeare. Rather than just heap his own arguments on the pile, Vickers dissects how authorship of anonymous works is granted to a particular writers by examining the various pieces of evidence. Scholars have attributed authorship of the two poems, Shall I Die? and A Funeral Elegye to Shakespeare, but Vickers makes a case for why he believes these works belong to other poets and assigns authorship of the Elegye to John Ford.

Wells, Stanley. *Looking for Sex in Shakespeare.* **Cambridge University Press. 2004.**
You don't have to look far according to Wells who offers perspectives from a cadre of leading modern scholars. The subject of sex on Shakespeare's works has long been a hotly debated subject as numerous scholars have suggested a plethora of sexually oriented interpretations of the plays and sonnets. The author contends that much of the supposed sexual innuendo present in the works is a byproduct of the actor's or reader's interpretation of the material.

Whittenmore, Hank. *Shakespeare's Son and His Sonnets.* **Martin and Lawrence. 2011.**
Whittenmore uses Shakespeare's sonnets as a historical chronicle of the demise of the Tudor dynasty and a litany of the political intrigue, passion, and betrayal that were the hallmarks of the Elizabethan era. He divides the sonnets into groupings of 1-126 marking the poems regarding the Fair Youth, who he claims is Henry Wriothesley; twenty follow-up sonnets cover Wriothesley's incarceration in the Tower of London; and the remaining sonnets concerning his release after Elizabeth the First's death.

Zak, William F. *A Mirror for Lovers: Shake-speare's Sonnets as Curious Perspective.* **Lexington Books. 2013.**
Zak examines each of the sonnets "under a labor intensive, microscopic lens while grouping them into thematic clusters, clarifying along the way the connection between the sequence and both the runic dedication introducing the sonnets and the female complaint, a seemingly unrelated appendage, that concludes the original Q manuscript of these poems." The seven chapters capped with a bibliography cover such themes as the struggle between Shakespeare's use of love and hate, the poems that include the Dark Lady, the procreation group of poems, and more.

Zinman, Ira B. *Shakespeare's Sonnets and the Bible: A Spiritual Interpretation with Christian Sources.* **World Wisdom. 2009.**
Although the Bible figured prominently into the lives of the Elizabethans, direct references to religion in drama and verse were forbidden in Shakespeare's time, so all such allusions are hidden in the subtext of the works. The religious aspects of Shakespeare's plays have been well explored, but that facet of the sonnets largely has been ignored. Zinman looks at the poems through the lens of religious interpretation and how it fits in with other areas of Shakespearean criticism.

Michael Rogers

General Bibliography

Ackroyd, Peter. *Shakespeare: The Biography*. New York: Nan A. Talese, 2005.

Akrigg, G.P.V. *Shakespeare and the Earl of Southampton*. Cambridge, MA: Harvard UP. 1968.

Archer, John Michael. *Technically Alive: Shakespeare's Sonnets*. New York: Palgrave, 2012.

Atkins, Carl D., ed. *Shakespeare's Sonnets: With Three Hundred Years of Commentary*. Cranbury: Associated UPs, 2007.

Auden, W.H. *Shakespeare's Sonnets*. ed. William Burto. 1965. New York: Signet, n.d.

Baldwin, T.W. *Shakespeare's Small Latine and Lesser Greeke*. Urbana: U of IL P, 1944.

Bate, Jonathan. *Soul of the Age: A Biography of the Mind of William Shakespeare*. New York: Random House, 2009.

_____. *The Genius of Shakespeare*. New York: Oxford UP, 1998.

Baugh, Albert C. & Thomas Cable. *A History of the English Language*. 3rd ed. Englewood Cliffs, NJ: Prentice, 1978.

Bearman, Robert. *Shakespeare in the Stratford Records*. Phoenix Mill, UK: Sutton, 1994.

Bell, Ilona. "Rethinking Shakespeare's Dark Lady." *A Companion to Shakespeare's Sonnets*. ed. Michael Schoenfeldt. Malden, MA: Blackwell, 2007.

_____. *Elizabethan Women and the Poetry of Courtship*. Illustrated ed. New York: Cambridge UP, 1999.

Bender, Robert M. & Squier, Charles L. eds. *The Sonnet: An Anthology: A Comprehensive Selection of British and American Sonnets from the Renaissance to the Present*, Washington Square Press, New York. 1987.

Blades, John. Shakespeare: *The Sonnets*. Analyzing Texts Series. Houndmills, UK: Palgrave, 2007.

Blevins, Jacob. *Catullan Consciousness and the Early Modern Lyric in England: From Wyatt to Donne*. Farnham, Surrey, England: Ashgate, 2004.

Bloom, Harold, ed. *The Sonnets*. New York: Bloom's Literary Criticism, 2008.

_____. *William Shakespeare's Sonnets*. New York: Chelsea, 1987.

Booth, Stephen, ed. *Shakespeare's Sonnets*. New Haven: Yale UP, 1977.

_____. *An Essay on Shakespeare's Sonnets*. New Haven: Yale UP, 1969.

Braden, Gordon. *Sixteenth-Century Poetry: An Annotated Anthology*. Hoboken, NJ: Wiley Blackwell, 2005.

Bromley, James M. *Intimacy and Sexuality in the Age of Shakespeare*. Cambridge: Cambridge UP, 2011.

Burrow, Colin, ed. *The Complete Sonnets and Poems, William Shakespeare*. New York: Oxford UP, 2002.

Butler, Samuel. *Shakespeare's Sonnets Reconsidered*. London: Jonathon Cape, 1927.

Callaghan, Dympna. *Shakespeare's Sonnets*. Malden: Blackwell, 2007.

Chambers, E. K. *William Shakespeare: A Study of Facts and Problems*. 2 vols. Oxford: Clarendon Press, 1930.

Cheney, Patrick, Andrew Hadfield, & Garrett A. Sullivan, Jr., eds. *Early Modern English Poetry: A Critical Companion*. New York: Oxford UP, 2006.

Cheney, Patrick. *The Cambridge Companion to Shakespeare's Poetry*. New York: Cambridge UP, 2007.

Cousins, A. D. & Peter Howarth. *The Cambridge Companion to the Sonnet*. Cambridge: Cambridge UP, 2011.

De Grazia, Margreta & Stanley Wells, eds. *The Cambridge Companion to Shakespeare*. New York: Cambridge UP, 2001.

Dobson, Michael & Stanley Wells, eds. *The Oxford Companion to Shakespeare*. New York: Oxford UP, 2001.

Dubrow, Heather. *Captive Visitors: Shakespeare's Narrative Poems and Sonnets*. Ithaca: Cornell UP, 1987.

Duncan-Jones, Katherine, ed. *Shakespeare's Sonnets*. London: Nelson, 1997.

Edmondson, Paul & Stanley Wells. *Shakespeare's Sonnets*. Oxford, UK: Oxford UP, 2004.

Evans, G. Blakemore, ed. *The Riverside Shakespeare*. Boston: Houghton, 1974.

_____, ed. *The Sonnets*. New Cambridge Shakespeare Series. Cambridge; Cambridge UP, 1996.

Ferry, Anne Davidson. *The "Inward" Language: Sonnets of Wyatt, Sidney, Shakespeare, Donne*. Chicago: Univ. of Chicago Press, 1983.

Fiedler, Leslie. "Some Contexts of *Shakespeare's Sonnets*." *The Riddle of Shakespeare's Sonnets*. London: Routledge & Kegan Paul. 1962.

Finneman, Joel. *Shakespeare's Perjured Eye: The Invention of Poetic Subjectivity in the Sonnets*. Berkeley, CA: U of California P, 1986.

Fontana, Ernest. "Shakespeare's Sonnet 55." *Explicator* 45.3 (Spring 1987): 6-8.

Gajowski, Evelyn. *Presentism, Gender, and Sexuality in Shakespeare*. New York: Palgrave, 2009.

Green, Martin. *The Labyrinth of Shakespeare's Sonnets: An Examination of Sexual Elements in Shakespeare's Language*. London: Skilton, 1974.

Greenblatt, Stephen. *Will in the World: How Shakespeare Became Shakespeare*. New York: W. W. Norton, 2004.

Hale, J.R. *Renaissance Exploration*. New York: Norton, 1968.

Hammond, Gerald. *The Reader and Shakespeare's Young Man Sonnets*. London: Macmillan, 1981.

Harrison, James. "Shakespeare's Sonnet 129." *Explicator* 47.4 (Summer 1989): 6-7.

Hart, Jonathan. *Shakespeare: Poetry, Culture, and History*. New York: Palgrave Macmillan, 2009.

_____. *Shakespeare: Poetry, History, and Culture*. New York: Palgrave, 2009.

Hayashi, Tetsumaro. *Shakespeare's Sonnets: A Record of 20th-Century Criticism*. Metuchen, NJ: Scarecrow Press. 1972.

Herrnstein, Barbara, ed. *Discussions of Shakespeare's Sonnets*. Discussions of Literature Series. Boston: Heath, 1964.

Heylin, Clinton. *So Long as Men Can Breathe: The Untold Story of Shakespeare's Sonnets*. Philadelphia: Da Capo Press, 2009.

Hope, Warren & Kim Holston. *The Shakespeare Controversy: An Analysis of the Authorship Theories*. 2d ed. Jefferson, N.C.: McFarland, 2009.

Hotson, Leslie. *Shakespeare's Sonnets Dated*. London: Rupert Hart-Davis. 1947.

Howell, Mark. "Shakespeare's Sonnet 18." *Explicator* 40.3 (Spring 1982): 12.

Hubler, Edward, et al. *The Riddle of Shakespeare's Sonnets*. New York: Basic Books, 1962.

_____. *The Sense of Shakespeare's Sonnets*. Princeton, NJ: Princeton UP, 1952.

Huntington, John. *Ambition, Rank, and Poetry in 1590s England*. Urbana: U of Illinois P, 2001.

Ingram, W. G. & Theodore Redpath, eds. *Shakespeare's Sonnets*. 3rd impression. London: Hodder and Stoughton, 1978.

Kinney, Arthur F., ed. *The Cambridge Companion to English Literature, 1500–1600*. New York: Cambridge UP, 2000.

Krieger, Murray. A Window to Criticism: Shakespeare's Sonnets and Modern Poetics. Princeton, NJ: Princeton UP, 1964.

Landry, Hilton. Interpretations of Shakespeare's Sonnets. Princeton, NJ: Princeton UP, 1964.

Leishman, J.B. *Themes and Variations in Shakespeare's Sonnets*. 2nd ed. London: Hutchinson, 1963.

Lewis, C. S. *Poetry and Prose in the Sixteenth Century*. Oxford, UK: Clarendon Press, 1990.

Mapstone, Sally, ed. *Older Scots Literature*. Edinburgh: John

Donald, 2005.

Matz, Robert. *An Introduction to the World of Shakespeare's Sonnets*. Jefferson, NC: McFarland, 2008.

_____. *The World of Shakespeare's Sonnets: An Introduction*. Jefferson, NC: McFarland, 2008.

McRae, William. "Shakespeare's Sonnet 29." *Explicator* 46.1 (Fall 1987): 6-8.

Morotti, Arthur F. *Manuscript, Print, and the English Renaissance Lyric*. Ithaca, NY: Cornell UP, 1995.

Muir, Kenneth. *Shakespeare's Sonnets*. 1979. London: Allen, 2005.

_____. *Shakespeare's Sonnets*. London: George Allen and Unwin, 1979.

Nicoll, Allardyce, ed. *Shakespeare Survey 15*. Cambridge: Cambridge UP, 1962.

Park, Honan. *Shakespeare: A Life*. Oxford: Oxford UP, 2000.

Pequigney, Joseph. *Such Is My Love: A Study of Shakespeare's Sonnets*. Chicago: U of Chicago P, 1985.

Price, George R. *Reading Shakespeare's Plays*. Woodbury, NY: Barron's, 1962.

Ramsey, Paul. *The Fickle Glass: A Study of Shakespeare's Sonnets*. New York: AMS, 1979.

Rivers, Isabel. *Classical and Christian Ideas in English Renaissance Poetry: A Student's Guide*. 2d ed. New York: Routledge, 1994.

Rivers, Isabel. *Classical and Christian Ideas in English Renaissance Poetry: A Student's Guide*. 2d ed. New York: Routledge, 1994.

Robertson, J. M. *The Problems of Shakespeare's Sonnets*. London: 1926.

Rollins, Hyder, E., ed. *A New Variorum Edition of Shakespeare: The Sonnets*. 2 vols. London, 1944.

Rowse, A.L, ed. *Shakespeare's Sonnets*. New York: Harper, 1964.

_____. *Shakespeare the Man*. Rev. ed. Houndmills, UK: Macmillan, 1988.

_____. *The Poems of Shakespeare's Dark Lady*. New York: Potter. 1979.

Schaar, Claes. *Elizabethan Sonnet Themes and the Dating of Shakespeare's Sonnets*. Copenhagen: Lund. 1962.

Schiffer, James, ed. *Shakespeare's Sonnets: Critical Essays*. New York: Garland, 2000.

Schoenbaum, S. *Shakespeare's Lives*. 2d ed. Oxford: Clarendon Press, 1991.

_____. *William Shakespeare: A Compact Documentary Life*. New York: Oxford UP, 1977.

_____. *William Shakespeare: A Documentary Life*. Oxford: Clarendon Press, 1975.

_____. *William Shakespeare: Records and Images*. New

York: Oxford UP, 1981.

Schoenfeldt, Michael, ed. *A Companion to Shakespeare's Sonnets*. Malden, MA: Blackwell, 2007.

Seymour-Smith, Martin, ed. *Shakespeare's Sonnets*. London: William Heinemann.

Shakespeare, William. *The Complete Works of Shakespeare*. Ed. David Bevington. 4th ed. New York: Longman, 1997.

_____. *The Complete Works of Shakespeare*. Ed. David Bevington. 4th ed. New York: Longman, 1997.

Shapiro, James. *1599: A Year in the Life of William Shakespeare*. London: Faber & Faber, 2005.

_____. *Contested Will: Who Wrote Shakespeare?* New York: Simon & Schuster, 2010.

Swisher, Clarice, ed. *Readings on the Sonnets*. Greenhaven Literary Companions to British Literature Series. San Diego: Greenhaven, 1997.

Tillyard, E.M.W. *The Elizabethan World Picture*. New York: Vintage, n.d.

Vendler, Helen. *The Art of Shakespeare's Sonnets*. Cambridge: Belknap, 1997.

Vickers, Brian, ed. *English Renaissance Literary Criticism*. 1999. Reprint. Oxford, UK: Clarendon Press, 2003.

Wait, R.J.C. *The Background to Shakespeare's Sonnets*. New York: Schocken, 1972.

Watson, Thomas Ramey. "Shakespeare's Sonnet 29." *Explicator* 45.1 (Fall 1986): 12-13.

Wells, Stanley. *Shakespeare, Sex, & Love*. Oxford: Oxford UP, 2010.

Willen, Gerald & Victor B. Reed, eds. *A Casebook on Shakespeare's Sonnets*. New York: Crowell, 1964.

Wilson, J. Dover. *An Introduction to the Sonnets of Shakespeare*. New York: 1964.

All Sonnets

1

From fairest creatures we desire increase,
That thereby beauty's rose might never die,
But as the riper should by time decease,
His tender heir might bear his memory:
But thou contracted to thine own bright eyes,
Feed'st thy light's flame with self-substantial fuel,
Making a famine where abundance lies,
Thy self thy foe, to thy sweet self too cruel:
Thou that art now the world's fresh ornament,
And only herald to the gaudy spring,
Within thine own bud buriest thy content,
And, tender churl, mak'st waste in niggarding:
    Pity the world, or else this glutton be,
    To eat the world's due, by the grave and thee.

2

When forty winters shall besiege thy brow,
And dig deep trenches in thy beauty's field,
Thy youth's proud livery so gazed on now,
Will be a totter'd weed of small worth held:
Then being asked, where all thy beauty lies,
Where all the treasure of thy lusty days;
To say, within thine own deep sunken eyes,
Were an all-eating shame, and thriftless praise.
How much more praise deserv'd thy beauty's use,
If thou couldst answer 'This fair child of mine
Shall sum my count, and make my old excuse,'
Proving his beauty by succession thine!
    This were to be new made when thou art old,
    And see thy blood warm when thou feel'st it cold.

3

Look in thy glass and tell the face thou viewest
Now is the time that face should form another;
Whose fresh repair if now thou not renewest,
Thou dost beguile the world, unbless some mother.

For where is she so fair whose uneared womb
Disdains the tillage of thy husbandry?
Or who is he so fond will be the tomb
Of his self-love, to stop posterity?
Thou art thy mother's glass and she in thee

Calls back the lovely April of her prime;
So thou through windows of thine age shalt see,
Despite of wrinkles, this thy golden time.
    But if thou live, remembered not to be,
    Die single and thine image dies with thee.

4

Unthrifty loveliness, why dost thou spend
Upon thy self thy beauty's legacy?
Nature's bequest gives nothing, but doth lend,
And being frank she lends to those are free:
Then, beauteous niggard, why dost thou abuse
The bounteous largess given thee to give?
Profitless usurer, why dost thou use
So great a sum of sums, yet canst not live?
For having traffic with thy self alone,
Thou of thy self thy sweet self dost deceive:
Then how when nature calls thee to be gone,
What acceptable audit canst thou leave?
    Thy unused beauty must be tombed with thee,
    Which, used, lives th' executor to be.

5

Those hours, that with gentle work did frame
The lovely gaze where every eye doth dwell,
Will play the tyrants to the very same
And that unfair which fairly doth excel;
For never-resting time leads summer on
To hideous winter, and confounds him there;
Sap checked with frost, and lusty leaves quite gone,
Beauty o'er-snowed and bareness every where:
Then were not summer's distillation left,

A liquid prisoner pent in walls of glass,
Beauty's effect with beauty were bereft,
Nor it, nor no remembrance what it was:
　　But flowers distilled, though they with winter meet,
　　Leese but their show; their substance still lives sweet.

6

Then let not winter's ragged hand deface,
In thee thy summer, ere thou be distilled:
Make sweet some vial; treasure thou some place
With beauty's treasure ere it be self-killed.
That use is not forbidden usury,
Which happies those that pay the willing loan;
That's for thy self to breed another thee,
Or ten times happier, be it ten for one;
Ten times thy self were happier than thou art,
If ten of thine ten times refigured thee:
Then what could death do if thou shouldst depart,
Leaving thee living in posterity?
　　Be not self-willed, for thou art much too fair
　　To be death's conquest and make worms thine heir.

7

Lo! in the orient when the gracious light
Lifts up his burning head, each under eye
Doth homage to his new-appearing sight,
Serving with looks his sacred majesty;
And having climbed the steep-up heavenly hill,
Resembling strong youth in his middle age,
Yet mortal looks adore his beauty still,
Attending on his golden pilgrimage:
But when from highmost pitch, with weary car,
Like feeble age, he reeleth from the day,
The eyes, 'fore duteous, now converted are
From his low tract, and look another way:
　　So thou, thyself outgoing in thy noon
　　Unlooked on diest unless thou get a son.

8

Music to hear, why hear'st thou music sadly?
Sweets with sweets war not, joy delights in joy:
Why lov'st thou that which thou receiv'st not gladly,

Or else receiv'st with pleasure thine annoy?
If the true concord of well-tuned sounds,
By unions married, do offend thine ear,
They do but sweetly chide thee, who confounds
In singleness the parts that thou shouldst bear.
Mark how one string, sweet husband to another,
Strikes each in each by mutual ordering;
Resembling sire and child and happy mother,
Who, all in one, one pleasing note do sing:
　　Whose speechless song being many, seeming one,
　　Sings this to thee: 'Thou single wilt prove none.'

9

Is it for fear to wet a widow's eye,
That thou consum'st thy self in single life?
Ah! if thou issueless shalt hap to die,
The world will wail thee like a makeless wife;
The world will be thy widow and still weep
That thou no form of thee hast left behind,
When every private widow well may keep
By children's eyes, her husband's shape in mind:
Look what an unthrift in the world doth spend
Shifts but his place, for still the world enjoys it;
But beauty's waste hath in the world an end,
And kept unused the user so destroys it.
　　No love toward others in that bosom sits
　　That on himself such murd'rous shame commits.

10

For shame deny that thou bear'st love to any,
Who for thy self art so unprovident.
Grant, if thou wilt, thou art beloved of many,
But that thou none lov'st is most evident:
For thou art so possessed with murderous hate,
That 'gainst thy self thou stick'st not to conspire,
Seeking that beauteous roof to ruinate
Which to repair should be thy chief desire.
O! change thy thought, that I may change my mind:
Shall hate be fairer lodged than gentle love?
Be, as thy presence is, gracious and kind,
Or to thyself at least kind-hearted prove:
　　Make thee another self for love of me,
　　That beauty still may live in thine or thee.

11

As fast as thou shalt wane, so fast thou grow'st
In one of thine, from that which thou departest;
And that fresh blood which youngly thou bestow'st,
Thou mayst call thine when thou from youth convertest.
Herein lives wisdom, beauty, and increase;
Without this folly, age, and cold decay:
If all were minded so, the times should cease
And threescore year would make the world away.
Let those whom nature hath not made for store,
Harsh, featureless, and rude, barrenly perish:
Look whom she best endowed, she gave the more;
Which bounteous gift thou shouldst in bounty cherish:
     She carved thee for her seal, and meant thereby,
     Thou shouldst print more, not let that copy die.

12

When I do count the clock that tells the time,
And see the brave day sunk in hideous night;
When I behold the violet past prime,
And sable curls, all silvered o'er with white;
When lofty trees I see barren of leaves,
Which erst from heat did canopy the herd,
And summer's green all girded up in sheaves,
Borne on the bier with white and bristly beard,
Then of thy beauty do I question make,
That thou among the wastes of time must go,
Since sweets and beauties do themselves forsake
And die as fast as they see others grow;
     And nothing 'gainst Time's scythe can make defence
     Save breed, to brave him when he takes thee hence.

13

O! that you were your self; but, love, you are
No longer yours, than you your self here live:
Against this coming end you should prepare,
And your sweet semblance to some other give:
So should that beauty which you hold in lease
Find no determination; then you were
Yourself again, after yourself's decease,
When your sweet issue your sweet form should bear.
Who lets so fair a house fall to decay,

Which husbandry in honour might uphold,
Against the stormy gusts of winter's day
And barren rage of death's eternal cold?
     O! none but unthrifts. Dear my love, you know,
     You had a father: let your son say so.

14

Not from the stars do I my judgement pluck;
And yet methinks I have Astronomy,
But not to tell of good or evil luck,
Of plagues, of dearths, or seasons' quality;
Nor can I fortune to brief minutes tell,
Pointing to each his thunder, rain and wind,
Or say with princes if it shall go well
By oft predict that I in heaven find:
But from thine eyes my knowledge I derive,
And, constant stars, in them I read such art
As truth and beauty shall together thrive,
If from thyself, to store thou wouldst convert;
     Or else of thee this I prognosticate:
     Thy end is truth's and beauty's doom and date.

15

When I consider every thing that grows
Holds in perfection but a little moment,
That this huge stage presenteth nought but shows
Whereon the stars in secret influence comment;
When I perceive that men as plants increase,
Cheered and checked even by the self-same sky,
Vaunt in their youthful sap, at height decrease,
And wear their brave state out of memory;
Then the conceit of this inconstant stay
Sets you most rich in youth before my sight,
Where wasteful Time debateth with decay
To change your day of youth to sullied night,
     And all in war with Time for love of you,
     As he takes from you, I engraft you new.

16

But wherefore do not you a mightier way
Make war upon this bloody tyrant, Time?
And fortify your self in your decay

With means more blessed than my barren rhyme?
Now stand you on the top of happy hours,
And many maiden gardens, yet unset,
With virtuous wish would bear you living flowers,
Much liker than your painted counterfeit:
So should the lines of life that life repair,
Which this, Time's pencil, or my pupil pen,
Neither in inward worth nor outward fair,
Can make you live your self in eyes of men.
> *To give away yourself, keeps yourself still,*
> *And you must live, drawn by your own sweet skill.*

17

Who will believe my verse in time to come,
If it were filled with your most high deserts?
Though yet heaven knows it is but as a tomb
Which hides your life, and shows not half your parts.
If I could write the beauty of your eyes,
And in fresh numbers number all your graces,
The age to come would say 'This poet lies;
Such heavenly touches ne'er touched earthly faces.'
So should my papers, yellowed with their age,
Be scorned, like old men of less truth than tongue,
And your true rights be termed a poet's rage
And stretched metre of an antique song:
> *But were some child of yours alive that time,*
> *You should live twice, in it, and in my rhyme.*

18

Shall I compare thee to a summer's day?
Thou art more lovely and more temperate:
Rough winds do shake the darling buds of May,
And summer's lease hath all too short a date:
Sometime too hot the eye of heaven shines,
And often is his gold complexion dimmed,
And every fair from fair sometime declines,
By chance, or nature's changing course untrimmed:
But thy eternal summer shall not fade,
Nor lose possession of that fair thou ow'st,
Nor shall death brag thou wander'st in his shade,
When in eternal lines to time thou grow'st,
> *So long as men can breathe, or eyes can see,*
> *So long lives this, and this gives life to thee.*

19

Devouring Time, blunt thou the lion's paws,
And make the earth devour her own sweet brood;
Pluck the keen teeth from the fierce tiger's jaws,
And burn the long-lived phoenix in her blood;
Make glad and sorry seasons as thou fleet'st,
And do whate'er thou wilt, swift-footed Time,
To the wide world and all her fading sweets;
But I forbid thee one most heinous crime:
O! carve not with thy hours my love's fair brow,
Nor draw no lines there with thine antique pen;
Him in thy course untainted do allow
For beauty's pattern to succeeding men.
> *Yet, do thy worst old Time: despite thy wrong,*
> *My love shall in my verse ever live young.*

20

A woman's face with nature's own hand painted,
Hast thou, the master mistress of my passion;
A woman's gentle heart, but not acquainted
With shifting change, as is false women's fashion:
An eye more bright than theirs, less false in rolling,
Gilding the object whereupon it gazeth;
A man in hue all hues in his controlling,
Which steals men's eyes and women's souls amazeth.
And for a woman wert thou first created;
Till Nature, as she wrought thee, fell a-doting,
And by addition me of thee defeated,
By adding one thing to my purpose nothing.
> *But since she prick'd thee out for women's pleasure,*
> *Mine be thy love and thy love's use their treasure.*

21

So is it not with me as with that Muse,
Stirred by a painted beauty to his verse,
Who heaven itself for ornament doth use
And every fair with his fair doth rehearse,
Making a couplement of proud compare
With sun and moon, with earth and sea's rich gems,
With April's first-born flowers, and all things rare,
That heaven's air in this huge rondure hems.
O! let me, true in love, but truly write,

And then believe me, my love is as fair
As any mother's child, though not so bright
As those gold candles fixed in heaven's air:
　Let them say more that like of hearsay well;
　I will not praise that purpose not to sell.

22

My glass shall not persuade me I am old,
So long as youth and thou are of one date;
But when in thee time's furrows I behold,
Then look I death my days should expiate.
For all that beauty that doth cover thee,
Is but the seemly raiment of my heart,
Which in thy breast doth live, as thine in me:
How can I then be elder than thou art?
O! therefore, love, be of thyself so wary
As I, not for myself, but for thee will;
Bearing thy heart, which I will keep so chary
As tender nurse her babe from faring ill.
　Presume not on thy heart when mine is slain,
　Thou gav'st me thine not to give back again.

23

As an unperfect actor on the stage,
Who with his fear is put beside his part,
Or some fierce thing replete with too much rage,
Whose strength's abundance weakens his own heart;
So I, for fear of trust, forget to say
The perfect ceremony of love's rite,
And in mine own love's strength seem to decay,
O'ercharged with burthen of mine own love's might.
O! let my looks be then the eloquence
And dumb presagers of my speaking breast,
Who plead for love, and look for recompense,
More than that tongue that more hath more express'd.
　O! learn to read what silent love hath writ:
　To hear with eyes belongs to love's fine wit.

24

Mine eye hath played the painter and hath steeled,
Thy beauty's form in table of my heart;

My body is the frame wherein 'tis held,
And perspective that is best painter's art.
For through the painter must you see his skill,
To find where your true image pictured lies,
Which in my bosom's shop is hanging still,
That hath his windows glazed with thine eyes.
Now see what good turns eyes for eyes have done:
Mine eyes have drawn thy shape, and thine for me
Are windows to my breast, where-through the sun
Delights to peep, to gaze therein on thee;
　Yet eyes this cunning want to grace their art,
　They draw but what they see, know not the heart.

25

Let those who are in favour with their stars
Of public honour and proud titles boast,
Whilst I, whom fortune of such triumph bars
Unlook'd for joy in that I honour most.
Great princes' favourites their fair leaves spread
But as the marigold at the sun's eye,
And in themselves their pride lies buried,
For at a frown they in their glory die.
The painful warrior famoused for fight,
After a thousand victories once foiled,
Is from the book of honour razed quite,
And all the rest forgot for which he toiled:
　Then happy I, that love and am beloved,
　Where I may not remove nor be removed.

26

Lord of my love, to whom in vassalage
Thy merit hath my duty strongly knit,
To thee I send this written embassage,
To witness duty, not to show my wit:
Duty so great, which wit so poor as mine
May make seem bare, in wanting words to show it,
But that I hope some good conceit of thine
In thy soul's thought, all naked, will bestow it:
Till whatsoever star that guides my moving,
Points on me graciously with fair aspect,
And puts apparel on my tottered loving,
To show me worthy of thy sweet respect:

Then may I dare to boast how I do love thee;
Till then, not show my head where thou mayst prove me.

27

Weary with toil, I haste me to my bed,
The dear repose for limbs with travel tired;
But then begins a journey in my head
To work my mind, when body's work's expired:
For then my thoughts--from far where I abide--
Intend a zealous pilgrimage to thee,
And keep my drooping eyelids open wide,
Looking on darkness which the blind do see:
Save that my soul's imaginary sight
Presents thy shadow to my sightless view,
Which, like a jewel hung in ghastly night,
Makes black night beauteous, and her old face new.
   Lo! thus, by day my limbs, by night my mind,
   For thee, and for myself, no quiet find.

28

How can I then return in happy plight,
That am debarred the benefit of rest?
When day's oppression is not eas'd by night,
But day by night and night by day oppressed,
And each, though enemies to either's reign,
Do in consent shake hands to torture me,
The one by toil, the other to complain
How far I toil, still farther off from thee.
I tell the day, to please him thou art bright,
And dost him grace when clouds do blot the heaven:
So flatter I the swart-complexion'd night,
When sparkling stars twire not thou gild'st the even.
   But day doth daily draw my sorrows longer,
   And night doth nightly make grief's length seem stronger.

29

When in disgrace with fortune and men's eyes
I all alone beweep my outcast state,
And trouble deaf heaven with my bootless cries,
And look upon myself, and curse my fate,
Wishing me like to one more rich in hope,

Featured like him, like him with friends possessed,
Desiring this man's art, and that man's scope,
With what I most enjoy contented least;
Yet in these thoughts my self almost despising,
Haply I think on thee, and then my state,
Like to the lark at break of day arising
From sullen earth, sings hymns at heaven's gate;
   For thy sweet love remembered such wealth brings
   That then I scorn to change my state with kings.

30

When to the sessions of sweet silent thought
I summon up remembrance of things past,
I sigh the lack of many a thing I sought,
And with old woes new wail my dear time's waste:
Then can I drown an eye, unused to flow,
For precious friends hid in death's dateless night,
And weep afresh love's long since cancelled woe,
And moan the expense of many a vanished sight:
Then can I grieve at grievances foregone,
And heavily from woe to woe tell o'er
The sad account of fore-bemoaned moan,
Which I new pay as if not paid before.
   But if the while I think on thee, dear friend,
   All losses are restor'd and sorrows end.

31

Thy bosom is endeared with all hearts,
Which I by lacking have supposed dead;
And there reigns Love, and all Love's loving parts,
And all those friends which I thought buried.
How many a holy and obsequious tear
Hath dear religious love stol'n from mine eye,
As interest of the dead, which now appear
But things removed that hidden in thee lie!
Thou art the grave where buried love doth live,
Hung with the trophies of my lovers gone,
Who all their parts of me to thee did give,
That due of many now is thine alone:
   Their images I loved, I view in thee,
   And thou (all they) hast all the all of me.

32

If thou survive my well-contented day,
When that churl Death my bones with dust shall cover
And shalt by fortune once more re-survey
These poor rude lines of thy deceased lover,
Compare them with the bett'ring of the time,
And though they be outstripped by every pen,
Reserve them for my love, not for their rhyme,
Exceeded by the height of happier men.
O! then vouchsafe me but this loving thought:
'Had my friend's Muse grown with this growing age,
A dearer birth than this his love had brought,
To march in ranks of better equipage:
    But since he died and poets better prove,
    Theirs for their style I'll read, his for his love'.

33

Full many a glorious morning have I seen
Flatter the mountain tops with sovereign eye,
Kissing with golden face the meadows green,
Gilding pale streams with heavenly alchemy;
Anon permit the basest clouds to ride
With ugly rack on his celestial face,
And from the forlorn world his visage hide,
Stealing unseen to west with this disgrace:
Even so my sun one early morn did shine,
With all triumphant splendour on my brow;
But out, alack, he was but one hour mine,
The region cloud hath mask'd him from me now.
    Yet him for this my love no whit disdaineth;
    Suns of the world may stain when heaven's sun staineth.

34

Why didst thou promise such a beauteous day,
And make me travel forth without my cloak,
To let base clouds o'ertake me in my way,
Hiding thy bravery in their rotten smoke?
'Tis not enough that through the cloud thou break,
To dry the rain on my storm-beaten face,
For no man well of such a salve can speak,
That heals the wound, and cures not the disgrace:
Nor can thy shame give physic to my grief;

Though thou repent, yet I have still the loss:
The offender's sorrow lends but weak relief
To him that bears the strong offence's cross.
    Ah! but those tears are pearl which thy love sheds,
    And they are rich and ransom all ill deeds.

35

No more be grieved atthat which thou hast done:
Roses have thorns, and silver fountains mud:
Clouds and eclipses stain both moon and sun,
And loathsome canker lives in sweetest bud.
All men make faults, and even I in this,
Authorizing thy trespass with compare,
Myself corrupting, salving thy amiss,
Excusing thy sins more than thy sins are;
For to thy sensual fault I bring in sense,
Thy adverse party is thy advocate,
And 'gainst myself a lawful plea commence:
Such civil war is in my love and hate,
    That I an accessary needs must be,
    To that sweet thief which sourly robs from me.

36

Let me confess that we two must be twain,
Although our undivided loves are one:
So shall those blots that do with me remain,
Without thy help, by me be borne alone.
In our two loves there is but one respect,
Though in our lives a separable spite,
Which though it alter not love's sole effect,
Yet doth it steal sweet hours from love's delight.
I may not evermore acknowledge thee,
Lest my bewailed guilt should do thee shame,
Nor thou with public kindness honour me,
Unless thou take that honour from thy name:
    But do not so, I love thee in such sort,
    As thou being mine, mine is thy good report.

37

As a decrepit father takes delight
To see his active child do deeds of youth,
So I, made lame by Fortune's dearest spite,

Take all my comfort of thy worth and truth;
For whether beauty, birth, or wealth, or wit,
Or any of these all, or all, or more,
Entitled in thy parts, do crowned sit,
I make my love engrafted to this store:
So then I am not lame, poor, nor despised,
Whilst that this shadow doth such substance give
That I in thy abundance am sufficed,
And by a part of all thy glory live.
 Look what is best, that best I wish in thee:
 This wish I have; then ten times happy me!

38

How can my muse want subject to invent,
While thou dost breathe, that pour'st into my verse
Thine own sweet argument, too excellent
For every vulgar paper to rehearse?
O! give thy self the thanks, if aught in me
Worthy perusal stand against thy sight;
For who's so dumb that cannot write to thee,
When thou thy self dost give invention light?
Be thou the tenth Muse, ten times more in worth
Than those old nine which rhymers invocate;
And he that calls on thee, let him bring forth
Eternal numbers to outlive long date.
 If my slight muse do please these curious days,
 The pain be mine, but thine shall be the praise.

39

O! how thy worth with manners may I sing,
When thou art all the better part of me?
What can mine own praise to mine own self bring?
And what is't but mine own when I praise thee?
Even for this, let us divided live,
And our dear love lose name of single one,
That by this separation I may give
That due to thee which thou deserv'st alone.
O absence! what a torment wouldst thou prove,
Were it not thy sour leisure gave sweet leave,
To entertain the time with thoughts of love,
Which time and thoughts so sweetly doth deceive,
 And that thou teachest how to make one twain,
 By praising him here who doth hence remain.

40

Take all my loves, my love, yea take them all;
What hast thou then more than thou hadst before?
No love, my love, that thou mayst true love call;
All mine was thine, before thou hadst this more.
Then, if for my love, thou my love receivest,
I cannot blame thee, for my love thou usest;
But yet be blam'd, if thou thy self deceivest
By wilful taste of what thyself refusest.
I do forgive thy robbery, gentle thief,
Although thou steal thee all my poverty:
And yet, love knows it is a greater grief
To bear love's wrong, than hate's known injury.
 Lascivious grace, in whom all ill well shows,
 Kill me with spites yet we must not be foes.

41

Those pretty wrongs that liberty commits,
When I am sometime absent from thy heart,
Thy beauty, and thy years full well befits,
For still temptation follows where thou art.
Gentle thou art, and therefore to be won,
Beauteous thou art, therefore to be assailed;
And when a woman woos, what woman's son
Will sourly leave her till he have prevailed?
Ay me! but yet thou mightst my seat forbear,
And chide thy beauty and thy straying youth,
Who lead thee in their riot even there
Where thou art forced to break a twofold truth:
 Hers by thy beauty tempting her to thee,
 Thine by thy beauty being false to me.

42

That thou hast her it is not all my grief,
And yet it may be said I loved her dearly;
That she hath thee is of my wailing chief,
A loss in love that touches me more nearly.
Loving offenders thus I will excuse ye:
Thou dost love her, because thou know'st I love her;
And for my sake even so doth she abuse me,
Suffering my friend for my sake to approve her.
If I lose thee, my loss is my love's gain,

And losing her, my friend hath found that loss;
Both find each other, and I lose both twain,
And both for my sake lay on me this cross:
 But here's the joy; my friend and I are one;
 Sweet flattery! then she loves but me alone.

43

When most I wink, then do mine eyes best see,
For all the day they view things unrespected;
But when I sleep, in dreams they look on thee,
And darkly bright, are bright in dark directed.
Then thou, whose shadow shadows doth make bright,
How would thy shadow's form form happy show
To the clear day with thy much clearer light,
When to unseeing eyes thy shade shines so!
How would, I say, mine eyes be blessed made
By looking on thee in the living day,
When in dead night thy fair imperfect shade
Through heavy sleep on sightless eyes doth stay!
 All days are nights to see till I see thee,
 And nights bright days when dreams do show thee me.

44

If the dull substance of my flesh were thought,
Injurious distance should not stop my way;
For then despite of space I would be brought,
From limits far remote, where thou dost stay.
No matter then although my foot did stand
Upon the farthest earth removed from thee;
For nimble thought can jump both sea and land
As soon as think the place where he would be.
But ah! thought kills me that I am not thought,
To leap large lengths of miles when thou art gone,
But that, so much of earth and water wrought,
I must attend time's leisure with my moan,
 Receiving nought by elements so slow
 But heavy tears, badges of either's woe.

45

The other two, slight air and purging fire,
Are both with thee, wherever I abide;
The first my thought, the other my desire,
These present-absent with swift motion slide.
For when these quicker elements are gone
In tender embassy of love to thee,
My life, being made of four, with two alone
Sinks down to death, oppressed with melancholy;
Until life's composition be recured
By those swift messengers return'd from thee,
Who even but now come back again, assured
Of thy fair health, recounting it to me:
 This told, I joy; but then no longer glad,
 I send them back again and straight grow sad.

46

Mine eye and heart are at a mortal war,
How to divide the conquest of thy sight;
Mine eye my heart thy picture's sight would bar,
My heart mine eye the freedom of that right.
My heart doth plead that thou in him dost lie,
A closet never pierced with crystal eyes,
But the defendant doth that plea deny,
And says in him thy fair appearance lies.
To 'cide this title is impannelled
A quest of thoughts, all tenants to the heart;
And by their verdict is determined
The clear eye's moiety, and the dear heart's part:
 As thus: mine eye's due is thine outward part,
 And my heart's right, thine inward love of heart.

47

Betwixt mine eye and heart a league is took,
And each doth good turns now unto the other:
When that mine eye is famish'd for a look,
Or heart in love with sighs himself doth smother,
With my love's picture then my eye doth feast,
And to the painted banquet bids my heart;
Another time mine eye is my heart's guest,
And in his thoughts of love doth share a part:
So, either by thy picture or my love,
Thy self away, art present still with me;
For thou not farther than my thoughts canst move,
And I am still with them, and they with thee;

Or, if they sleep, thy picture in my sight
  Awakes my heart, to heart's and eyes' delight.

48

How careful was I when I took my way,
Each trifle under truest bars to thrust,
That to my use it might unused stay
From hands of falsehood, in sure wards of trust!
But thou, to whom my jewels trifles are,
Most worthy comfort, now my greatest grief,
Thou best of dearest, and mine only care,
Art left the prey of every vulgar thief.
Thee have I not locked up in any chest,
Save where thou art not, though I feel thou art,
Within the gentle closure of my breast,
From whence at pleasure thou mayst come and part;
  And even thence thou wilt be stol'n I fear,
  For truth proves thievish for a prize so dear.

49

Against that time, if ever that time come,
When I shall see thee frown on my defects,
When as thy love hath cast his utmost sum,
Called to that audit by advis'd respects;
Against that time when thou shalt strangely pass,
And scarcely greet me with that sun, thine eye,
When love, converted from the thing it was,
Shall reasons find of settled gravity;
Against that time do I ensconce me here,
Within the knowledge of mine own desert,
And this my hand, against my self uprear,
To guard the lawful reasons on thy part:
  To leave poor me thou hast the strength of laws,
  Since why to love I can allege no cause.

50

How heavy do I journey on the way,
When what I seek, my weary travel's end,
Doth teach that ease and that repose to say,
'Thus far the miles are measured from thy friend!'
The beast that bears me, tired with my woe,
Plods dully on, to bear that weight in me,
As if by some instinct the wretch did know
His rider lov'd not speed being made from thee.

The bloody spur cannot provoke him on,
That sometimes anger thrusts into his hide,
Which heavily he answers with a groan,
More sharp to me than spurring to his side;
  For that same groan doth put this in my mind,
  My grief lies onward, and my joy behind.

51

Thus can my love excuse the slow offence
Of my dull bearer when from thee I speed:
From where thou art why should I haste me thence?
Till I return, of posting is no need.
O! what excuse will my poor beast then find,
When swift extremity can seem but slow?
Then should I spur, though mounted on the wind,
In winged speed no motion shall I know,
Then can no horse with my desire keep pace.
Therefore desire, (of perfect'st love being made)
Shall neigh, no dull flesh, in his fiery race;
But love, for love, thus shall excuse my jade-
  Since from thee going, he went wilful-slow,
  Towards thee I'll run, and give him leave to go.

52

So am I as the rich, whose blessed key,
Can bring him to his sweet up-locked treasure,
The which he will not every hour survey,
For blunting the fine point of seldom pleasure.
Therefore are feasts so solemn and so rare,
Since, seldom coming in the long year set,
Like stones of worth they thinly placed are,
Or captain jewels in the carcanet.
So is the time that keeps you as my chest,
Or as the wardrobe which the robe doth hide,
To make some special instant special-blest,
By new unfolding his imprisoned pride.
  Blessed are you whose worthiness gives scope,
  Being had, to triumph, being lacked, to hope.

53

What is your substance, whereof are you made,
That millions of strange shadows on you tend?
Since every one hath, every one, one shade,
And you but one, can every shadow lend.

Describe Adonis, and the counterfeit
Is poorly imitated after you;
On Helen's cheek all art of beauty set,
And you in Grecian tires are painted new:
Speak of the spring, and foison of the year,
The one doth shadow of your beauty show,
The other as your bounty doth appear;
And you in every blessed shape we know.
    In all external grace you have some part,
    But you like none, none you, for constant heart.

54

O! how much more doth beauty beauteous seem
By that sweet ornament which truth doth give.
The rose looks fair, but fairer we it deem
For that sweet odour, which doth in it live.
The canker blooms have full as deep a dye
As the perfumed tincture of the roses,
Hang on such thorns, and play as wantonly
When summer's breath their masked buds discloses:
But, for their virtue only is their show,
They live unwoo'd, and unrespected fade;
Die to themselves. Sweet roses do not so;
Of their sweet deaths are sweetest odours made:
    And so of you, beauteous and lovely youth,
    When that shall vade, my verse distills your truth.

55

Not marble, nor the gilded monuments
Of princes, shall outlive this powerful rhyme;
But you shall shine more bright in these contents
Than unswept stone, besmear'd with sluttish time.
When wasteful war shall statues overturn,
And broils root out the work of masonry,
Nor Mars his sword, nor war's quick fire shall burn
The living record of your memory.
'Gainst death, and all oblivious enmity
Shall you pace forth; your praise shall still find room
Even in the eyes of all posterity
That wear this world out to the ending doom.
    So, till the judgment that yourself arise,
    You live in this, and dwell in lovers' eyes.

56

Sweet love, renew thy force; be it not said
Thy edge should blunter be than appetite,
Which but to-day by feeding is allayed,
To-morrow sharpened in his former might:
So, love, be thou, although to-day thou fill
Thy hungry eyes, even till they wink with fulness,
To-morrow see again, and do not kill
The spirit of love, with a perpetual dulness.
Let this sad interim like the ocean be
Which parts the shore, where two contracted new
Come daily to the banks, that when they see
Return of love, more blest may be the view;
    As call it winter, which being full of care,
    Makes summer's welcome, thrice more wished, more rare.

57

Being your slave what should I do but tend
Upon the hours, and times of your desire?
I have no precious time at all to spend;
Nor services to do, till you require.
Nor dare I chide the world without end hour,
Whilst I, my sovereign, watch the clock for you,
Nor think the bitterness of absence sour,
When you have bid your servant once adieu;
Nor dare I question with my jealous thought
Where you may be, or your affairs suppose,
But, like a sad slave, stay and think of nought
Save, where you are, how happy you make those.
    So true a fool is love, that in your will,
    Though you do anything, he thinks no ill.

58

That god forbid, that made me first your slave,
I should in thought control your times of pleasure,
Or at your hand the account of hours to crave,
Being your vassal, bound to stay your leisure!
O! let me suffer, being at your beck,
The imprison'd absence of your liberty;
And patience, tame to sufferance, bide each check,
Without accusing you of injury.
Be where you list, your charter is so strong

That you yourself may privilege your time
To what you will; to you it doth belong
Yourself to pardon of self-doing crime.
  I am to wait, though waiting so be hell,
  Not blame your pleasure be it ill or well.

59

If there be nothing new, but that which is
Hath been before, how are our brains beguil'd,
Which labouring for invention bear amiss
The second burthen of a former child.
Oh that record could with a backward look,
Even of five hundred courses of the sun,
Show me your image in some antique book,
Since mind at first in character was done,
That I might see what the old world could say
To this composed wonder of your frame;
Whether we are mended, or where better they,
Or whether revolution be the same.
  Oh sure I am the wits of former days,
  To subjects worse have given admiring praise.

60

Like as the waves make towards the pebbled shore,
So do our minutes hasten to their end;
Each changing place with that which goes before,
In sequent toil all forwards do contend.
Nativity, once in the main of light,
Crawls to maturity, wherewith being crown'd,
Crooked eclipses 'gainst his glory fight,
And Time that gave doth now his gift confound.
Time doth transfix the flourish set on youth
And delves the parallels in beauty's brow,
Feeds on the rarities of nature's truth,
And nothing stands but for his scythe to mow:
  And yet to times in hope, my verse shall stand
  Praising thy worth, despite his cruel hand.

61

Is it thy will, thy image should keep open
My heavy eyelids to the weary night?
Dost thou desire my slumbers should be broken,
While shadows like to thee do mock my sight?

Is it thy spirit that thou send'st from thee
So far from home into my deeds to pry,
To find out shames and idle hours in me,
The scope and tenor of thy jealousy?
O, no! thy love, though much, is not so great:
It is my love that keeps mine eye awake:
Mine own true love that doth my rest defeat,
To play the watchman ever for thy sake:
  For thee watch I, whilst thou dost wake elsewhere,
  From me far off, with others all too near.

62

Sin of self-love possesseth all mine eye
And all my soul, and all my every part;
And for this sin there is no remedy,
It is so grounded inward in my heart.
Methinks no face so gracious is as mine,
No shape so true, no truth of such account;
And for myself mine own worth do define,
As I all other in all worths surmount.
But when my glass shows me myself indeed
Beated and chopp'd with tanned antiquity,
Mine own self-love quite contrary I read;
Self so self-loving were iniquity.
  Tis thee, myself, that for myself I praise,
  Painting my age with beauty of thy days.

63

Against my love shall be as I am now,
With Time's injurious hand crushed and o'erworn;
When hours have drained his blood and filled his brow
With lines and wrinkles; when his youthful morn
Hath travelled on to age's steepy night;
And all those beauties whereof now he's king
Are vanishing, or vanished out of sight,
Stealing away the treasure of his spring;
For such a time do I now fortify
Against confounding age's cruel knife,
That he shall never cut from memory
My sweet love's beauty, though my lover's life:
  His beauty shall in these black lines be seen,
  And they shall live, and he in them still green.

64

When I have seen by Time's fell hand defaced
The rich proud cost of outworn buried age;
When sometime lofty towers I see down-razed,
And brass eternal slave to mortal rage;
When I have seen the hungry ocean gain
Advantage on the kingdom of the shore,
And the firm soil win of the watery main,
Increasing store with loss, and loss with store;
When I have seen such interchange of state,
Or state itself confounded to decay;
Ruin hath taught me thus to ruminate
That Time will come and take my love away.
　　This thought is as a death which cannot choose
　　But weep to have that which it fears to lose.

65

Since brass, nor stone, nor earth, nor boundless sea,
But sad mortality o'ersways their power,
How with this rage shall beauty hold a plea,
Whose action is no stronger than a flower?
O! how shall summer's honey breath hold out,
Against the wrackful siege of battering days,
When rocks impregnable are not so stout,
Nor gates of steel so strong but Time decays?
O fearful meditation! where, alack,
Shall Time's best jewel from Time's chest lie hid?
Or what strong hand can hold his swift foot back?
Or who his spoil of beauty can forbid?
　　O! none, unless this miracle have might,
　　That in black ink my love may still shine bright.

66

Tired with all these, for restful death I cry,
As to behold desert a beggar born,
And needy nothing trimm'd in jollity,
And purest faith unhappily forsworn,
And gilded honour shamefully misplaced,
And maiden virtue rudely strumpeted,
And right perfection wrongfully disgraced,
And strength by limping sway disabled
And art made tongue-tied by authority,

And folly, doctor-like, controlling skill,
And simple truth miscalled simplicity,
And captive good attending captain ill:
　　Tired with all these, from these would I be gone,
　　Save that, to die, I leave my love alone.

67

Ah! wherefore with infection should he live,
And with his presence grace impiety,
That sin by him advantage should achieve,
And lace itself with his society?
Why should false painting imitate his cheek,
And steal dead seeming of his living hue?
Why should poor beauty indirectly seek
Roses of shadow, since his rose is true?
Why should he live, now Nature bankrupt is,
Beggared of blood to blush through lively veins?
For she hath no exchequer now but his,
And proud of many, lives upon his gains.
　　O! him she stores, to show what wealth she had
　　In days long since, before these last so bad.

68

Thus is his cheek the map of days outworn,
When beauty lived and died as flowers do now,
Before these bastard signs of fair were born,
Or durst inhabit on a living brow;
Before the golden tresses of the dead,
The right of sepulchres, were shorn away,
To live a second life on second head;
Ere beauty's dead fleece made another gay:
In him those holy antique hours are seen,
Without all ornament, itself and true,
Making no summer of another's green,
Robbing no old to dress his beauty new;
　　And him as for a map doth Nature store,
　　To show false Art what beauty was of yore.

69

Those parts of thee that the world's eye doth view
Want nothing that the thought of hearts can mend;
All tongues, the voice of souls, give thee that due,

Uttering bare truth, even so as foes commend.
Thy outward thus with outward praise is crown'd;
But those same tongues, that give thee so thine own,
In other accents do this praise confound
By seeing farther than the eye hath shown.
They look into the beauty of thy mind,
And that in guess they measure by thy deeds;
Then, churls, their thoughts, although their eyes were kind,
To thy fair flower add the rank smell of weeds:
*   But why thy odour matcheth not thy show,*
*   The soil is this, that thou dost common grow.*

70

That thou art blamed shall not be thy defect,
For slander's mark was ever yet the fair;
The ornament of beauty is suspect,
A crow that flies in heaven's sweetest air.
So thou be good, slander doth but approve
Thy worth the greater, being wooed of time;
For canker vice the sweetest buds doth love,
And thou present'st a pure unstained prime.
Thou hast passed by the ambush of young days
Either not assailed, or victor being charged;
Yet this thy praise cannot be so thy praise,
To tie up envy, evermore enlarged,
*   If some suspect of ill masked not thy show,*
*   Then thou alone kingdoms of hearts shouldst owe.*

71

No longer mourn for me when I am dead
Than you shall hear the surly sullen bell
Give warning to the world that I am fled
From this vile world with vilest worms to dwell:
Nay, if you read this line, remember not
The hand that writ it, for I love you so,
That I in your sweet thoughts would be forgot,
If thinking on me then should make you woe.
O! if, I say, you look upon this verse,
When I perhaps compounded am with clay,
Do not so much as my poor name rehearse;
But let your love even with my life decay;
*   Lest the wise world should look into your moan,*
*   And mock you with me after I am gone.*

72

O! lest the world should task you to recite
What merit lived in me, that you should love
After my death,--dear love, forget me quite,
For you in me can nothing worthy prove.
Unless you would devise some virtuous lie,
To do more for me than mine own desert,
And hang more praise upon deceased I
Than niggard truth would willingly impart:
O! lest your true love may seem false in this
That you for love speak well of me untrue,
My name be buried where my body is,
And live no more to shame nor me nor you.
*   For I am shamed by that which I bring forth,*
*   And so should you, to love things nothing worth.*

73

That time of year thou mayst in me behold
When yellow leaves, or none, or few, do hang
Upon those boughs which shake against the cold,
Bare ruined choirs, where late the sweet birds sang.
In me thou see'st the twilight of such day
As after sunset fadeth in the west;
Which by and by black night doth take away,
Death's second self, that seals up all in rest.
In me thou see'st the glowing of such fire,
That on the ashes of his youth doth lie,
As the death-bed, whereon it must expire,
Consumed with that which it was nourish'd by.
*   This thou perceiv'st, which makes thy love more strong,*
*   To love that well, which thou must leave ere long.*

74

But be contented when that fell arrest
Without all bail shall carry me away,
My life hath in this line some interest,
Which for memorial still with thee shall stay.
When thou reviewest this, thou dost review
The very part was consecrate to thee:
The earth can have but earth, which is his due;
My spirit is thine, the better part of me:
So then thou hast but lost the dregs of life,

The prey of worms, my body being dead;
The coward conquest of a wretch's knife,
Too base of thee to be remembered.
    The worth of that is that which it contains,
    And that is this, and this with thee remains.

75

So are you to my thoughts as food to life,
Or as sweet-season'd showers are to the ground;
And for the peace of you I hold such strife
As 'twixt a miser and his wealth is found.
Now proud as an enjoyer, and anon
Doubting the filching age will steal his treasure;
Now counting best to be with you alone,
Then better'd that the world may see my pleasure:
Sometime all full with feasting on your sight,
And by and by clean starved for a look;
Possessing or pursuing no delight
Save what is had, or must from you be took.
    Thus do I pine and surfeit day by day,
    Or gluttoning on all, or all away.

76

Why is my verse so barren of new pride,
So far from variation or quick change?
Why with the time do I not glance aside
To new-found methods, and to compounds strange?
Why write I still all one, ever the same,
And keep invention in a noted weed,
That every word doth almost tell my name,
Showing their birth, and where they did proceed?
O! know sweet love I always write of you,
And you and love are still my argument;
So all my best is dressing old words new,
Spending again what is already spent:
    For as the sun is daily new and old,
    So is my love still telling what is told.

77

Thy glass will show thee how thy beauties wear,
Thy dial how thy precious minutes waste;
The vacant leaves thy mind's imprint will bear,
And of this book, this learning mayst thou taste.

The wrinkles which thy glass will truly show
Of mouthed graves will give thee memory;
Thou by thy dial's shady stealth mayst know
Time's thievish progress to eternity.
Look what thy memory cannot contain,
Commit to these waste blanks, and thou shalt find
Those children nursed, delivered from thy brain,
To take a new acquaintance of thy mind.
    These offices, so oft as thou wilt look,
    Shall profit thee and much enrich thy book.

78

So oft have I invoked thee for my Muse,
And found such fair assistance in my verse
As every alien pen hath got my use
And under thee their poesy disperse.
Thine eyes, that taught the dumb on high to sing
And heavy ignorance aloft to fly,
Have added feathers to the learned's wing
And given grace a double majesty.
Yet be most proud of that which I compile,
Whose influence is thine, and born of thee:
In others' works thou dost but mend the style,
And arts with thy sweet graces graced be;
    But thou art all my art, and dost advance
    As high as learning, my rude ignorance.

79

Whilst I alone did call upon thy aid,
My verse alone had all thy gentle grace;
But now my gracious numbers are decayed,
And my sick Muse doth give an other place.
I grant, sweet love, thy lovely argument
Deserves the travail of a worthier pen;
Yet what of thee thy poet doth invent
He robs thee of, and pays it thee again.
He lends thee virtue, and he stole that word
From thy behaviour; beauty doth he give,
And found it in thy cheek: he can afford
No praise to thee, but what in thee doth live.
    Then thank him not for that which he doth say,
    Since what he owes thee, thou thyself dost pay.

80

O! how I faint when I of you do write,
Knowing a better spirit doth use your name,
And in the praise thereof spends all his might,
To make me tongue-tied speaking of your fame.
But since your worth, wide as the ocean is,
The humble as the proudest sail doth bear,
My saucy bark, inferior far to his,
On your broad main doth wilfully appear.
Your shallowest help will hold me up afloat,
Whilst he upon your soundless deep doth ride;
Or, being wracked, I am a worthless boat,
He of tall building, and of goodly pride:
    Then if he thrive and I be cast away,
    The worst was this, my love was my decay.

81

Or I shall live your epitaph to make,
Or you survive when I in earth am rotten,
From hence your memory death cannot take,
Although in me each part will be forgotten.
Your name from hence immortal life shall have,
Though I, once gone, to all the world must die:
The earth can yield me but a common grave,
When you entombed in men's eyes shall lie.
Your monument shall be my gentle verse,
Which eyes not yet created shall o'er-read;
And tongues to be your being shall rehearse,
When all the breathers of this world are dead;
    You still shall live, such virtue hath my pen,
    Where breath most breathes, even in the mouths of men.

82

I grant thou wert not married to my Muse,
And therefore mayst without attaint o'erlook
The dedicated words which writers use
Of their fair subject, blessing every book.
Thou art as fair in knowledge as in hue,
Finding thy worth a limit past my praise;
And therefore art enforced to seek anew
Some fresher stamp of the time-bettering days.
And do so, love; yet when they have devised,
What strained touches rhetoric can lend,
Thou truly fair, wert truly sympathized
In true plain words, by thy true-telling friend;

And their gross painting might be better used
Where cheeks need blood; in thee it is abused.

83

I never saw that you did painting need,
And therefore to your fair no painting set;
I found, or thought I found, you did exceed
The barren tender of a poet's debt:
And therefore have I slept in your report,
That you yourself, being extant, well might show
How far a modern quill doth come too short,
Speaking of worth, what worth in you doth grow.
This silence for my sin you did impute,
Which shall be most my glory being dumb;
For I impair not beauty being mute,
When others would give life, and bring a tomb.
    There lives more life in one of your fair eyes
    Than both your poets can in praise devise.

84

Who is it that says most, which can say more,
Than this rich praise, that you alone, are you,
In whose confine immured is the store
Which should example where your equal grew?
Lean penury within that pen doth dwell
That to his subject lends not some small glory;
But he that writes of you, if he can tell
That you are you, so dignifies his story.
Let him but copy what in you is writ,
Not making worse what nature made so clear,
And such a counterpart shall fame his wit,
Making his style admired every where.
    You to your beauteous blessings add a curse,
    Being fond on praise, which makes your praises worse.

85

My tongue-tied Muse in manners holds her still,
While comments of your praise richly compiled,
Reserve thy character with golden quill,
And precious phrase by all the Muses filed.
I think good thoughts, whilst others write good words,
And like unlettered clerk still cry 'Amen'
To every hymn that able spirit affords,
In polished form of well-refined pen.
Hearing you praised, I say "tis so, 'tis true,'

And to the most of praise add something more;
But that is in my thought, whose love to you,
Though words come hindmost, holds his rank before.
    Then others, for the breath of words respect,
    Me for my dumb thoughts, speaking in effect.

86

Was it the proud full sail of his great verse,
Bound for the prize of all too precious you,
That did my ripe thoughts in my brain inhearse,
Making their tomb the womb wherein they grew?
Was it his spirit, by spirits taught to write
Above a mortal pitch, that struck me dead?
No, neither he, nor his compeers by night
Giving him aid, my verse astonished.
He, nor that affable familiar ghost
Which nightly gulls him with intelligence,
As victors of my silence cannot boast;
I was not sick of any fear from thence:
    But when your countenance filled up his line,
    Then lacked I matter; that enfeebled mine.

87

Farewell! thou art too dear for my possessing,
And like enough thou know'st thy estimate,
The charter of thy worth gives thee releasing;
My bonds in thee are all determinate.
For how do I hold thee but by thy granting?
And for that riches where is my deserving?
The cause of this fair gift in me is wanting,
And so my patent back again is swerving.
Thy self thou gavest, thy own worth then not knowing,
Or me to whom thou gav'st it else mistaking;
So thy great gift, upon misprision growing,
Comes home again, on better judgement making.
    Thus have I had thee, as a dream doth flatter,
    In sleep a king, but waking no such matter.

88

When thou shalt be disposed to set me light,
And place my merit in the eye of scorn,
Upon thy side, against myself I'll fight,
And prove thee virtuous, though thou art forsworn.
With mine own weakness being best acquainted,
Upon thy part I can set down a story

Of faults concealed, wherein I am attainted;
That thou in losing me shalt win much glory:
And I by this will be a gainer too;
For bending all my loving thoughts on thee,
The injuries that to myself I do,
Doing thee vantage, double-vantage me.
    Such is my love, to thee I so belong,
    That for thy right, myself will bear all wrong.

89

Say that thou didst forsake me for some fault,
And I will comment upon that offence:
Speak of my lameness, and I straight will halt,
Against thy reasons making no defence.
Thou canst not, love, disgrace me half so ill,
To set a form upon desired change,
As I'll myself disgrace; knowing thy will,
I will acquaintance strangle, and look strange;
Be absent from thy walks; and in my tongue
Thy sweet beloved name no more shall dwell,
Lest I, too much profane, should do it wrong,
And haply of our old acquaintance tell.
    For thee, against my self I'll vow debate,
    For I must ne'er love him whom thou dost hate.

90

Then hate me when thou wilt; if ever, now;
Now, while the world is bent my deeds to cross,
Join with the spite of fortune, make me bow,
And do not drop in for an after-loss:
Ah! do not, when my heart hath 'scaped this sorrow,
Come in the rearward of a conquered woe;
Give not a windy night a rainy morrow,
To linger out a purposed overthrow.
If thou wilt leave me, do not leave me last,
When other petty griefs have done their spite,
But in the onset come: so shall I taste
At first the very worst of fortune's might;
    And other strains of woe, which now seem woe,
    Compared with loss of thee, will not seem so.

91

Some glory in their birth, some in their skill,
Some in their wealth, some in their body's force,
Some in their garments though new-fangled ill;

Some in their hawks and hounds, some in their horse;
And every humour hath his adjunct pleasure,
Wherein it finds a joy above the rest:
But these particulars are not my measure,
All these I better in one general best.
Thy love is better than high birth to me,
Richer than wealth, prouder than garments' cost,
Of more delight than hawks and horses be;
And having thee, of all men's pride I boast:
> *Wretched in this alone, that thou mayst take*
> *All this away, and me most wretched make.*

92

But do thy worst to steal thyself away,
For term of life thou art assured mine;
And life no longer than thy love will stay,
For it depends upon that love of thine.
Then need I not to fear the worst of wrongs,
When in the least of them my life hath end.
I see a better state to me belongs
Than that which on thy humour doth depend:
Thou canst not vex me with inconstant mind,
Since that my life on thy revolt doth lie.
O what a happy title do I find,
Happy to have thy love, happy to die!
> *But what's so blessed-fair that fears no blot?*
> *Thou mayst be false, and yet I know it not.*

93

So shall I live, supposing thou art true,
Like a deceived husband; so love's face
May still seem love to me, though altered new;
Thy looks with me, thy heart in other place:
For there can live no hatred in thine eye,
Therefore in that I cannot know thy change.
In many's looks, the false heart's history
Is writ in moods, and frowns, and wrinkles strange.
But heaven in thy creation did decree
That in thy face sweet love should ever dwell;
Whate'er thy thoughts, or thy heart's workings be,
Thy looks should nothing thence, but sweetness tell.
> *How like Eve's apple doth thy beauty grow,*
> *If thy sweet virtue answer not thy show!*

94

They that have power to hurt, and will do none,
That do not do the thing they most do show,
Who, moving others, are themselves as stone,
Unmoved, cold, and to temptation slow;
They rightly do inherit heaven's graces,
And husband nature's riches from expense;
They are the lords and owners of their faces,
Others, but stewards of their excellence.
The summer's flower is to the summer sweet,
Though to itself, it only live and die,
But if that flower with base infection meet,
The basest weed outbraves his dignity:
> *For sweetest things turn sourest by their deeds;*
> *Lilies that fester, smell far worse than weeds.*

95

How sweet and lovely dost thou make the shame
Which, like a canker in the fragrant rose,
Doth spot the beauty of thy budding name!
O! in what sweets dost thou thy sins enclose.
That tongue that tells the story of thy days,
Making lascivious comments on thy sport,
Cannot dispraise, but in a kind of praise;
Naming thy name blesses an ill report.
O! what a mansion have those vices got
Which for their habitation chose out thee,
Where beauty's veil doth cover every blot
And all things turns to fair that eyes can see!
> *Take heed, dear heart, of this large privilege;*
> *The hardest knife ill-used doth lose his edge.*

96

Some say thy fault is youth, some wantonness;
Some say thy grace is youth and gentle sport;
Both grace and faults are lov'd of more and less:
Thou mak'st faults graces that to thee resort.
As on the finger of a throned queen
The basest jewel will be well esteem'd,
So are those errors that in thee are seen
To truths translated, and for true things deem'd.
How many lambs might the stern wolf betray,
If like a lamb he could his looks translate!
How many gazers mightst thou lead away,

If thou wouldst use the strength of all thy state!
  But do not so, I love thee in such sort,
  As thou being mine, mine is thy good report.

97

How like a winter hath my absence been
From thee, the pleasure of the fleeting year!
What freezings have I felt, what dark days seen!
What old December's bareness everywhere!
And yet this time removed was summer's time;
The teeming autumn, big with rich increase,
Bearing the wanton burden of the prime,
Like widow'd wombs after their lords' decease:
Yet this abundant issue seemed to me
But hope of orphans, and unfathered fruit;
For summer and his pleasures wait on thee,
And, thou away, the very birds are mute:
  Or, if they sing, 'tis with so dull a cheer,
  That leaves look pale, dreading the winter's near.

98

From you have I been absent in the spring,
When proud pied April, dressed in all his trim,
Hath put a spirit of youth in every thing,
That heavy Saturn laughed and leapt with him.
Yet nor the lays of birds, nor the sweet smell
Of different flowers in odour and in hue,
Could make me any summer's story tell,
Or from their proud lap pluck them where they grew:
Nor did I wonder at the lily's white,
Nor praise the deep vermilion in the rose;
They were but sweet, but figures of delight,
Drawn after you, you pattern of all those.
  Yet seemed it winter still, and you away,
  As with your shadow I with these did play.

99

The forward violet thus did I chide:
Sweet thief, whence didst thou steal thy sweet that smells,
If not from my love's breath? The purple pride
Which on thy soft cheek for complexion dwells
In my love's veins thou hast too grossly dy'd.
The lily I condemned for thy hand,
And buds of marjoram had stol'n thy hair;

The roses fearfully on thorns did stand,
One blushing shame, another white despair;
A third, nor red nor white, had stol'n of both,
And to his robbery had annexed thy breath;
But, for his theft, in pride of all his growth
A vengeful canker eat him up to death.
  More flowers I noted, yet I none could see,
  But sweet, or colour it had stol'n from thee.

100

Where art thou Muse that thou forget'st so long,
To speak of that which gives thee all thy might?
Spend'st thou thy fury on some worthless song,
Darkening thy power to lend base subjects light?
Return forgetful Muse, and straight redeem,
In gentle numbers time so idly spent;
Sing to the ear that doth thy lays esteem
And gives thy pen both skill and argument.
Rise, resty Muse, my love's sweet face survey,
If Time have any wrinkle graven there;
If any, be a satire to decay,
And make Time's spoils despised every where.
  Give my love fame faster than Time wastes life,
  So thou prevent'st his scythe and crooked knife.

101

O truant Muse what shall be thy amends
For thy neglect of truth in beauty dyed?
Both truth and beauty on my love depends;
So dost thou too, and therein dignified.
Make answer Muse: wilt thou not haply say,
'Truth needs no colour, with his colour fixed;
Beauty no pencil, beauty's truth to lay;
But best is best, if never intermixed'?
Because he needs no praise, wilt thou be dumb?
Excuse not silence so, for 't lies in thee
To make him much outlive a gilded tomb
And to be praised of ages yet to be.
  Then do thy office, Muse; I teach thee how
  To make him seem, long hence, as he shows now.

102

My love is strengthened, though more weak in seeming;
I love not less, though less the show appear;
That love is merchandized, whose rich esteeming,

The owner's tongue doth publish every where.
Our love was new, and then but in the spring,
When I was wont to greet it with my lays;
As Philomel in summer's front doth sing,
And stops his pipe in growth of riper days:
Not that the summer is less pleasant now
Than when her mournful hymns did hush the night,
But that wild music burthens every bough,
And sweets grown common lose their dear delight.
     Therefore like her, I sometime hold my tongue:
     Because I would not dull you with my song.

103

Alack! what poverty my Muse brings forth,
That having such a scope to show her pride,
The argument all bare is of more worth
Than when it hath my added praise beside!
O! blame me not, if I no more can write!
Look in your glass, and there appears a face
That over-goes my blunt invention quite,
Dulling my lines, and doing me disgrace.
Were it not sinful then, striving to mend,
To mar the subject that before was well?
For to no other pass my verses tend
Than of your graces and your gifts to tell;
     And more, much more, than in my verse can sit,
     Your own glass shows you when you look in it.

104

To me, fair friend, you never can be old,
For as you were when first your eye I ey'd,
Such seems your beauty still. Three winters cold,
Have from the forests shook three summers' pride,
Three beauteous springs to yellow autumn turned,
In process of the seasons have I seen,
Three April perfumes in three hot Junes burned,
Since first I saw you fresh, which yet are green.
Ah! yet doth beauty like a dial-hand,
Steal from his figure, and no pace perceived;
So your sweet hue, which methinks still doth stand,
Hath motion, and mine eye may be deceived:
     For fear of which, hear this thou age unbred:
     Ere you were born was beauty's summer dead.

105

Let not my love be called idolatry,
Nor my beloved as an idol show,
Since all alike my songs and praises be
To one, of one, still such, and ever so.
Kind is my love to-day, to-morrow kind,
Still constant in a wondrous excellence;
Therefore my verse to constancy confined,
One thing expressing, leaves out difference.
Fair, kind, and true, is all my argument,
Fair, kind, and true, varying to other words;
And in this change is my invention spent,
Three themes in one, which wondrous scope affords.
     Fair, kind, and true, have often lived alone,
     Which three till now, never kept seat in one.

106

When in the chronicle of wasted time
I see descriptions of the fairest wights,
And beauty making beautiful old rhyme,
In praise of ladies dead and lovely knights,
Then, in the blazon of sweet beauty's best,
Of hand, of foot, of lip, of eye, of brow,
I see their antique pen would have expressed
Even such a beauty as you master now.
So all their praises are but prophecies
Of this our time, all you prefiguring;
And for they looked but with divining eyes,
They had not skill enough your worth to sing:
     For we, which now behold these present days,
     Have eyes to wonder, but lack tongues to praise.

107

Not mine own fears, nor the prophetic soul
Of the wide world dreaming on things to come,
Can yet the lease of my true love control,
Supposed as forfeit to a confined doom.
The mortal moon hath her eclipse endured,
And the sad augurs mock their own presage;
Incertainties now crown themselves assured,
And peace proclaims olives of endless age.
Now with the drops of this most balmy time,
My love looks fresh, and Death to me subscribes,
Since, spite of him, I'll live in this poor rhyme,
While he insults o'er dull and speechless tribes:

And thou in this shalt find thy monument,
When tyrants' crests and tombs of brass are spent.

108

What's in the brain that ink may character
Which hath not figured to thee my true spirit?
What's new to speak, what now to register,
That may express my love, or thy dear merit?
Nothing, sweet boy; but yet, like prayers divine,
I must each day say o'er the very same;
Counting no old thing old, thou mine, I thine,
Even as when first I hallowed thy fair name.
So that eternal love in love's fresh case,
Weighs not the dust and injury of age,
Nor gives to necessary wrinkles place,
But makes antiquity for aye his page;
    Finding the first conceit of love there bred,
    Where time and outward form would show it dead.

109

O! never say that I was false of heart,
Though absence seemed my flame to qualify,
As easy might I from my self depart
As from my soul which in thy breast doth lie:
That is my home of love: if I have ranged,
Like him that travels, I return again;
Just to the time, not with the time exchanged,
So that myself bring water for my stain.
Never believe though in my nature reigned,
All frailties that besiege all kinds of blood,
That it could so preposterously be stained,
To leave for nothing all thy sum of good;
    For nothing this wide universe I call,
    Save thou, my rose, in it thou art my all.

110

Alas! 'tis true, I have gone here and there,
And made my self a motley to the view,
Gored mine own thoughts, sold cheap what is most dear,
Made old offences of affections new;
Most true it is, that I have looked on truth
Askance and strangely; but, by all above,
These blenches gave my heart another youth,

And worse essays proved thee my best of love.
Now all is done, have what shall have no end:
Mine appetite I never more will grind
On newer proof, to try an older friend,
A god in love, to whom I am confined.
    Then give me welcome, next my heaven the best,
    Even to thy pure and most most loving breast.

111

O! for my sake do you with Fortune chide,
The guilty goddess of my harmful deeds,
That did not better for my life provide
Than public means which public manners breeds.
Thence comes it that my name receives a brand,
And almost thence my nature is subdued
To what it works in, like the dyer's hand:
Pity me, then, and wish I were renewed;
Whilst, like a willing patient, I will drink
Potions of eisel 'gainst my strong infection;
No bitterness that I will bitter think,
Nor double penance, to correct correction.
    Pity me then, dear friend, and I assure ye,
    Even that your pity is enough to cure me.

112

Your love and pity doth the impression fill,
Which vulgar scandal stamped upon my brow;
For what care I who calls me well or ill,
So you o'er-green my bad, my good allow?
You are my all-the-world, and I must strive
To know my shames and praises from your tongue;
None else to me, nor I to none alive,
That my steeled sense or changes right or wrong.
In so profound abysm I throw all care
Of others' voices, that my adder's sense
To critic and to flatterer stopped are.
Mark how with my neglect I do dispense:
    You are so strongly in my purpose bred,
    That all the world besides methinks y'are dead.

113

Since I left you, mine eye is in my mind;
And that which governs me to go about

Doth part his function and is partly blind,
Seems seeing, but effectually is out;
For it no form delivers to the heart
Of bird, of flower, or shape which it doth latch:
Of his quick objects hath the mind no part,
Nor his own vision holds what it doth catch;
For if it see the rud'st or gentlest sight,
The most sweet favour or deformed'st creature,
The mountain or the sea, the day or night,
The crow, or dove, it shapes them to your feature.
    Incapable of more, replete with you,
    My most true mind thus maketh mine eye untrue.

114

Or whether doth my mind, being crowned with you,
Drink up the monarch's plague, this flattery?
Or whether shall I say, mine eye saith true,
And that your love taught it this alchemy,
To make of monsters and things indigest
Such cherubins as your sweet self resemble,
Creating every bad a perfect best,
As fast as objects to his beams assemble?
O! 'tis the first, 'tis flattery in my seeing,
And my great mind most kingly drinks it up:
Mine eye well knows what with his gust is 'greeing,
And to his palate doth prepare the cup:
    If it be poisoned, 'tis the lesser sin
    That mine eye loves it and doth first begin.

115

Those lines that I before have writ do lie,
Even those that said I could not love you dearer:
Yet then my judgment knew no reason why
My most full flame should afterwards burn clearer.
But reckoning Time, whose million'd accidents
Creep in 'twixt vows, and change decrees of kings,
Tan sacred beauty, blunt the sharp'st intents,
Divert strong minds to the course of altering things;
Alas! why, fearing of Time's tyranny,
Might I not then say, 'Now I love you best,'
When I was certain o'er incertainty,
Crowning the present, doubting of the rest?
    Love is a babe, then might I not say so,
    To give full growth to that which still doth grow?

116

Let me not to the marriage of true minds
Admit impediments. Love is not love
Which alters when it alteration finds,
Or bends with the remover to remove:
O, no! it is an ever-fixed mark,
That looks on tempests and is never shaken;
It is the star to every wandering bark,
Whose worth's unknown, although his height be taken.
Love's not Time's fool, though rosy lips and cheeks
Within his bending sickle's compass come;
Love alters not with his brief hours and weeks,
But bears it out even to the edge of doom.
    If this be error and upon me proved,
    I never writ, nor no man ever loved.

117

Accuse me thus: that I have scanted all,
Wherein I should your great deserts repay,
Forgot upon your dearest love to call,
Whereto all bonds do tie me day by day;
That I have frequent been with unknown minds,
And given to time your own dear-purchased right;
That I have hoisted sail to all the winds
Which should transport me farthest from your sight.
Book both my wilfulness and errors down,
And on just proof surmise accumulate;
Bring me within the level of your frown,
But shoot not at me in your wakened hate;
    Since my appeal says I did strive to prove
    The constancy and virtue of your love.

118

Like as, to make our appetites more keen,
With eager compounds we our palate urge;
As, to prevent our maladies unseen,
We sicken to shun sickness when we purge;
Even so, being full of your ne'er-cloying sweetness,
To bitter sauces did I frame my feeding;
And, sick of welfare, found a kind of meetness
To be diseased, ere that there was true needing.
Thus policy in love, to anticipate
The ills that were not, grew to faults assured,
And brought to medicine a healthful state

Which, rank of goodness, would by ill be cured;
  But thence I learn and find the lesson true,
  Drugs poison him that so fell sick of you.

119

What potions have I drunk of Siren tears,
Distilled from limbecks foul as hell within,
Applying fears to hopes, and hopes to fears,
Still losing when I saw myself to win!
What wretched errors hath my heart committed,
Whilst it hath thought itself so blessed never!
How have mine eyes out of their spheres been fitted,
In the distraction of this madding fever!
O benefit of ill! now I find true
That better is by evil still made better;
And ruined love, when it is built anew,
Grows fairer than at first, more strong, far greater.
  So I return rebuked to my content,
  And gain by ill thrice more than I have spent.

120

That you were once unkind befriends me now,
And for that sorrow, which I then did feel,
Needs must I under my transgression bow,
Unless my nerves were brass or hammered steel.
For if you were by my unkindness shaken,
As I by yours, you've passed a hell of time;
And I, a tyrant, have no leisure taken
To weigh how once I suffered in your crime.
O! that our night of woe might have remembered
My deepest sense, how hard true sorrow hits,
And soon to you, as you to me, then tendered
The humble salve, which wounded bosoms fits!
  But that your trespass now becomes a fee;
  Mine ransoms yours, and yours must ransom me.

121

'Tis better to be vile than vile esteemed,
When not to be receives reproach of being;
And the just pleasure lost, which is so deemed
Not by our feeling, but by others' seeing:
For why should others' false adulterate eyes
Give salutation to my sportive blood?
Or on my frailties why are frailer spies,

Which in their wills count bad what I think good?
No, I am that I am, and they that level
At my abuses reckon up their own:
I may be straight though they themselves be bevel;
By their rank thoughts, my deeds must not be shown;
  Unless this general evil they maintain,
  All men are bad and in their badness reign.

122

Thy gift, thy tables, are within my brain
Full charactered with lasting memory,
Which shall above that idle rank remain,
Beyond all date, even to eternity:
Or, at the least, so long as brain and heart
Have faculty by nature to subsist;
Till each to razed oblivion yield his part
Of thee, thy record never can be missed.
That poor retention could not so much hold,
Nor need I tallies thy dear love to score;
Therefore to give them from me was I bold,
To trust those tables that receive thee more:
  To keep an adjunct to remember thee
  Were to import forgetfulness in me.

123

No, Time, thou shalt not boast that I do change:
Thy pyramids built up with newer might
To me are nothing novel, nothing strange;
They are but dressings of a former sight.
Our dates are brief, and therefore we admire
What thou dost foist upon us that is old;
And rather make them born to our desire
Than think that we before have heard them told.
Thy registers and thee I both defy,
Not wondering at the present nor the past,
For thy records and what we see doth lie,
Made more or less by thy continual haste.
  This I do vow and this shall ever be;
  I will be true despite thy scythe and thee.

124

If my dear love were but the child of state,
It might for Fortune's bastard be unfathered,
As subject to Time's love or to Time's hate,

Weeds among weeds, or flowers with flowers gathered.
No, it was builded far from accident;
It suffers not in smiling pomp, nor falls
Under the blow of thralled discontent,
Whereto th' inviting time our fashion calls:
It fears not policy, that heretic,
Which works on leases of short-number'd hours,
But all alone stands hugely politic,
That it nor grows with heat, nor drowns with showers.
    To this I witness call the fools of time,
    Which die for goodness, who have lived for crime.

125

Were't aught to me I bore the canopy,
With my extern the outward honouring,
Or laid great bases for eternity,
Which proves more short than waste or ruining?
Have I not seen dwellers on form and favour
Lose all and more by paying too much rent
For compound sweet, forgoing simple savour,
Pitiful thrivers, in their gazing spent?
No; let me be obsequious in thy heart,
And take thou my oblation, poor but free,
Which is not mixed with seconds, knows no art,
But mutual render, only me for thee.
    Hence, thou suborned informer! a true soul
    When most impeached stands least in thy control.

126

O thou, my lovely boy, who in thy power
Dost hold Time's fickle glass, his sickle, hour;
Who hast by waning grown, and therein showest
Thy lovers withering, as thy sweet self growest.
If Nature, sovereign mistress over wrack,
As thou goest onwards still will pluck thee back,
She keeps thee to this purpose, that her skill
May time disgrace and wretched minutes kill.
Yet fear her, O thou minion of her pleasure!
She may detain, but not still keep, her treasure:
Her audit (though delayed) answered must be,
And her quietus is to render thee.
    Her audit, though delay'd, answer'd must be
    And her quietus is to render thee.

127

In the old age black was not counted fair,
Or if it were, it bore not beauty's name;
But now is black beauty's successive heir,
And beauty slandered with a bastard shame:
For since each hand hath put on Nature's power,
Fairing the foul with Art's false borrowed face,
Sweet beauty hath no name, no holy bower,
But is profaned, if not lives in disgrace.
Therefore my mistress' eyes are raven black,
Her eyes so suited, and they mourners seem
At such who, not born fair, no beauty lack,
Sland'ring creation with a false esteem:
    Yet so they mourn becoming of their woe,
    That every tongue says beauty should look so.

128

How oft when thou, my music, music play'st,
Upon that blessed wood whose motion sounds
With thy sweet fingers when thou gently sway'st
The wiry concord that mine ear confounds,
Do I envy those jacks that nimble leap,
To kiss the tender inward of thy hand,
Whilst my poor lips which should that harvest reap,
At the wood's boldness by thee blushing stand!
To be so tickled, they would change their state
And situation with those dancing chips,
O'er whom thy fingers walk with gentle gait,
Making dead wood more bless'd than living lips.
    Since saucy jacks so happy are in this,
    Give them thy fingers, me thy lips to kiss.

129

The expense of spirit in a waste of shame
Is lust in action: and till action, lust
Is perjured, murderous, bloody, full of blame,
Savage, extreme, rude, cruel, not to trust;
Enjoyed no sooner but despised straight;
Past reason hunted; and no sooner had,
Past reason hated, as a swallowed bait,
On purpose laid to make the taker mad.
Mad in pursuit and in possession so;
Had, having, and in quest to have extreme;

A bliss in proof, and proved, a very woe;
Before, a joy proposed; behind a dream.
All this the world well knows; yet none knows well
To shun the heaven that leads men to this hell.

130

My mistress' eyes are nothing like the sun;
Coral is far more red, than her lips red:
If snow be white, why then her breasts are dun;
If hairs be wires, black wires grow on her head.
I have seen roses damasked, red and white,
But no such roses see I in her cheeks;
And in some perfumes is there more delight
Than in the breath that from my mistress reeks.
I love to hear her speak, yet well I know
That music hath a far more pleasing sound:
I grant I never saw a goddess go,
My mistress, when she walks, treads on the ground:
And yet by heaven, I think my love as rare,
As any she belied with false compare.

131

Thou art as tyrannous, so as thou art,
As those whose beauties proudly make them cruel;
For well thou know'st to my dear doting heart
Thou art the fairest and most precious jewel.
Yet, in good faith, some say that thee behold,
Thy face hath not the power to make love groan;
To say they err I dare not be so bold,
Although I swear it to myself alone.
And to be sure that is not false I swear,
A thousand groans, but thinking on thy face,
One on another's neck, do witness bear
Thy black is fairest in my judgment's place.
In nothing art thou black save in thy deeds,
And thence this slander, as I think, proceeds.

132

Thine eyes I love, and they, as pitying me,
Knowing thy heart torments me with disdain,
Have put on black and loving mourners be,
Looking with pretty ruth upon my pain.
And truly not the morning sun of heaven
Better becomes the grey cheeks of the east,
Nor that full star that ushers in the even,

Doth half that glory to the sober west,
As those two mourning eyes become thy face:
O! let it then as well beseem thy heart
To mourn for me since mourning doth thee grace,
And suit thy pity like in every part.
Then will I swear beauty herself is black,
And all they foul that thy complexion lack.

133

Beshrew that heart that makes my heart to groan
For that deep wound it gives my friend and me!
Is't not enough to torture me alone,
But slave to slavery my sweet'st friend must be?
Me from myself thy cruel eye hath taken,
And my next self thou harder hast engrossed:
Of him, myself, and thee I am forsaken;
A torment thrice three-fold thus to be crossed.
Prison my heart in thy steel bosom's ward,
But then my friend's heart let my poor heart bail;
Whoe'er keeps me, let my heart be his guard;
Thou canst not then use rigour in my jail:
And yet thou wilt; for I, being pent in thee,
Perforce am thine, and all that is in me.

134

So now I have confessed that he is thine,
And I my self am mortgaged to thy will,
Myself I'll forfeit, so that other mine
Thou wilt restore to be my comfort still:
But thou wilt not, nor he will not be free,
For thou art covetous, and he is kind;
He learned but surety-like to write for me,
Under that bond that him as fast doth bind.
The statute of thy beauty thou wilt take,
Thou usurer, that put'st forth all to use,
And sue a friend came debtor for my sake;
So him I lose through my unkind abuse.
Him have I lost; thou hast both him and me:
He pays the whole, and yet am I not free.

135

Whoever hath her wish, thou hast thy Will,
And Will to boot, and Will in over-plus;
More than enough am I that vexed thee still,
To thy sweet will making addition thus.

Wilt thou, whose will is large and spacious,
Not once vouchsafe to hide my will in thine?
Shall will in others seem right gracious,
And in my will no fair acceptance shine?
The sea, all water, yet receives rain still,
And in abundance addeth to his store;
So thou, being rich in Will, add to thy Will
One will of mine, to make thy large will more.
    Let no unkind, no fair beseechers kill;
    Think all but one, and me in that one Will.

136

If thy soul check thee that I come so near,
Swear to thy blind soul that I was thy Will,
And will, thy soul knows, is admitted there;
Thus far for love, my love-suit, sweet, fulfil.
Will, will fulfil the treasure of thy love,
Ay, fill it full with wills, and my will one.
In things of great receipt with ease we prove
Among a number one is reckoned none:
Then in the number let me pass untold,
Though in thy store's account I one must be;
For nothing hold me, so it please thee hold
That nothing me, a something sweet to thee:
    Make but my name thy love, and love that still,
    And then thou lovest me for my name is 'Will.'

137

Thou blind fool, Love, what dost thou to mine eyes,
That they behold, and see not what they see?
They know what beauty is, see where it lies,
Yet what the best is take the worst to be.
If eyes, corrupt by over-partial looks,
Be anchored in the bay where all men ride,
Why of eyes' falsehood hast thou forged hooks,
Whereto the judgment of my heart is tied?
Why should my heart think that a several plot,
Which my heart knows the wide world's common place?
Or mine eyes, seeing this, say this is not,
To put fair truth upon so foul a face?
    In things right true my heart and eyes have erred,
    And to this false plague are they now transferred.

138

When my love swears that she is made of truth,
I do believe her though I know she lies,
That she might think me some untutored youth,
Unlearned in the world's false subtleties.
Thus vainly thinking that she thinks me young,
Although she knows my days are past the best,
Simply I credit her false-speaking tongue:
On both sides thus is simple truth suppressed:
But wherefore says she not she is unjust?
And wherefore say not I that I am old?
O! love's best habit is in seeming trust,
And age in love, loves not to have years told:
    Therefore I lie with her, and she with me,
    And in our faults by lies we flattered be.

139

O! call not me to justify the wrong
That thy unkindness lays upon my heart;
Wound me not with thine eye, but with thy tongue:
Use power with power, and slay me not by art,
Tell me thou lov'st elsewhere; but in my sight,
Dear heart, forbear to glance thine eye aside:
What need'st thou wound with cunning, when thy might
Is more than my o'erpressed defence can bide?
Let me excuse thee: ah! my love well knows
Her pretty looks have been mine enemies;
And therefore from my face she turns my foes,
That they elsewhere might dart their injuries:
    Yet do not so; but since I am near slain,
    Kill me outright with looks, and rid my pain.

140

Be wise as thou art cruel; do not press
My tongue-tied patience with too much disdain;
Lest sorrow lend me words, and words express
The manner of my pity-wanting pain.
If I might teach thee wit, better it were,
Though not to love, yet, love to tell me so;
As testy sick men, when their deaths be near,
No news but health from their physicians know;
For, if I should despair, I should grow mad,
And in my madness might speak ill of thee;
Now this ill-wresting world is grown so bad,

Mad slanderers by mad ears believed be.
  That I may not be so, nor thou belied,
  Bear thine eyes straight, though thy proud heart go wide.

141

In faith I do not love thee with mine eyes,
For they in thee a thousand errors note;
But 'tis my heart that loves what they despise,
Who, in despite of view, is pleased to dote.
Nor are mine ears with thy tongue's tune delighted;
Nor tender feeling, to base touches prone,
Nor taste, nor smell, desire to be invited
To any sensual feast with thee alone:
But my five wits nor my five senses can
Dissuade one foolish heart from serving thee,
Who leaves unswayed the likeness of a man,
Thy proud heart's slave and vassal wretch to be:
  Only my plague thus far I count my gain,
  That she that makes me sin awards me pain.

142

Love is my sin, and thy dear virtue hate,
Hate of my sin, grounded on sinful loving:
O! but with mine compare thou thine own state,
And thou shalt find it merits not reproving;
Or, if it do, not from those lips of thine,
That have profaned their scarlet ornaments
And sealed false bonds of love as oft as mine,
Robbed others' beds' revenues of their rents.
Be it lawful I love thee, as thou lov'st those
Whom thine eyes woo as mine importune thee:
Root pity in thy heart, that, when it grows,
Thy pity may deserve to pitied be.
  If thou dost seek to have what thou dost hide,
  By self-example mayst thou be denied!

143

Lo, as a careful housewife runs to catch
One of her feathered creatures broke away,
Sets down her babe, and makes all swift dispatch
In pursuit of the thing she would have stay;
Whilst her neglected child holds her in chase,
Cries to catch her whose busy care is bent
To follow that which flies before her face,

Not prizing her poor infant's discontent;
So runn'st thou after that which flies from thee,
Whilst I thy babe chase thee afar behind;
But if thou catch thy hope, turn back to me,
And play the mother's part, kiss me, be kind;
  So will I pray that thou mayst have thy 'Will,'
  If thou turn back and my loud crying still.

144

Two loves I have of comfort and despair,
Which like two spirits do suggest me still:
The better angel is a man right fair,
The worser spirit a woman coloured ill.
To win me soon to hell, my female evil,
Tempteth my better angel from my side,
And would corrupt my saint to be a devil,
Wooing his purity with her foul pride.
And whether that my angel be turned fiend,
Suspect I may, yet not directly tell;
But being both from me, both to each friend,
I guess one angel in another's hell:
  Yet this shall I ne'er know, but live in doubt,
  Till my bad angel fire my good one out.

145

Those lips that Love's own hand did make,
Breathed forth the sound that said 'I hate',
To me that languished for her sake:
But when she saw my woeful state,
Straight in her heart did mercy come,
Chiding that tongue that ever sweet
Was used in giving gentle doom;
And taught it thus anew to greet;
'I hate' she altered with an end,
That followed it as gentle day,
Doth follow night, who like a fiend
From heaven to hell is flown away.
  'I hate', from hate away she threw,
  And saved my life, saying 'not you'.

146

Poor soul, the centre of my sinful earth,
... ... these rebel powers that thee array
Why dost thou pine within and suffer dearth,

Painting thy outward walls so costly gay?
Why so large cost, having so short a lease,
Dost thou upon thy fading mansion spend?
Shall worms, inheritors of this excess,
Eat up thy charge? Is this thy body's end?
Then soul, live thou upon thy servant's loss,
And let that pine to aggravate thy store;
Buy terms divine in selling hours of dross;
Within be fed, without be rich no more:
    So shall thou feed on Death, that feeds on men,
    And Death once dead, there's no more dying then.

147

My love is as a fever longing still,
For that which longer nurseth the disease;
Feeding on that which doth preserve the ill,
The uncertain sickly appetite to please.
My reason, the physician to my love,
Angry that his prescriptions are not kept,
Hath left me, and I desperate now approve
Desire is death, which physic did except.
Past cure I am, now Reason is past care,
And frantic-mad with evermore unrest;
My thoughts and my discourse as madmen's are,
At random from the truth vainly expressed;
    For I have sworn thee fair, and thought thee bright,
    Who art as black as hell, as dark as night.

148

O me! what eyes hath Love put in my head,
Which have no correspondence with true sight;
Or, if they have, where is my judgment fled,
That censures falsely what they see aright?
If that be fair whereon my false eyes dote,
What means the world to say it is not so?
If it be not, then love doth well denote
Love's eye is not so true as all men's: no,
How can it? O! how can Love's eye be true,
That is so vexed with watching and with tears?
No marvel then, though I mistake my view;
The sun itself sees not, till heaven clears.
    O cunning Love! with tears thou keep'st me blind,
    Lest eyes well-seeing thy foul faults should find.

149

Canst thou, O cruel! say I love thee not,
When I against myself with thee partake?
Do I not think on thee, when I forgot
Am of my self, all tyrant, for thy sake?
Who hateth thee that I do call my friend,
On whom frown'st thou that I do fawn upon,
Nay, if thou lour'st on me, do I not spend
Revenge upon myself with present moan?
What merit do I in my self respect,
That is so proud thy service to despise,
When all my best doth worship thy defect,
Commanded by the motion of thine eyes?
    But, love, hate on, for now I know thy mind,
    Those that can see thou lov'st, and I am blind.

150

O! from what power hast thou this powerful might,
With insufficiency my heart to sway?
To make me give the lie to my true sight,
And swear that brightness doth not grace the day?
Whence hast thou this becoming of things ill,
That in the very refuse of thy deeds
There is such strength and warrantise of skill,
That, in my mind, thy worst all best exceeds?
Who taught thee how to make me love thee more,
The more I hear and see just cause of hate?
O! though I love what others do abhor,
With others thou shouldst not abhor my state:
    If thy unworthiness raised love in me,
    More worthy I to be beloved of thee.

151

Love is too young to know what conscience is,
Yet who knows not conscience is born of love?
Then, gentle cheater, urge not my amiss,
Lest guilty of my faults thy sweet self prove:
For, thou betraying me, I do betray
My nobler part to my gross body's treason;
My soul doth tell my body that he may
Triumph in love; flesh stays no farther reason,
But rising at thy name doth point out thee,
As his triumphant prize. Proud of this pride,
He is contented thy poor drudge to be,

To stand in thy affairs, fall by thy side.
　　No want of conscience hold it that I call
　　Her love, for whose dear love I rise and fall.

152

In loving thee thou know'st I am forsworn,
But thou art twice forsworn, to me love swearing;
In act thy bed-vow broke, and new faith torn,
In vowing new hate after new love bearing:
But why of two oaths' breach do I accuse thee,
When I break twenty? I am perjured most;
For all my vows are oaths but to misuse thee,
And all my honest faith in thee is lost:
For I have sworn deep oaths of thy deep kindness,
Oaths of thy love, thy truth, thy constancy;
And, to enlighten thee, gave eyes to blindness,
Or made them swear against the thing they see;
　　For I have sworn thee fair; more perjured eye,
　　To swear against the truth so foul a lie!

153

Cupid laid by his brand and fell asleep:
A maid of Dian's this advantage found,
And his love-kindling fire did quickly steep
In a cold valley-fountain of that ground;

Which borrowed from this holy fire of Love,
A dateless lively heat, still to endure,
And grew a seething bath, which yet men prove
Against strange maladies a sovereign cure.
But at my mistress' eye Love's brand new-fired,
The boy for trial needs would touch my breast;
I, sick withal, the help of bath desired,
And thither hied, a sad distempered guest,
　　But found no cure, the bath for my help lies
　　Where Cupid got new fire; my mistress' eyes.

154

The little Love-god lying once asleep,
Laid by his side his heart-inflaming brand,
Whilst many nymphs that vowed chaste life to keep
Came tripping by; but in her maiden hand
The fairest votary took up that fire
Which many legions of true hearts had warmed;
And so the General of hot desire
Was, sleeping, by a virgin hand disarmed.
This brand she quenched in a cool well by,
Which from Love's fire took heat perpetual,
Growing a bath and healthful remedy,
For men diseased; but I, my mistress' thrall,
　　Came there for cure and this by that I prove,
　　Love's fire heats water, water cools not love.

Contributors

Elizabeth Jane Bellamy is Professor and John C. Hodges Chair of Excellence in the Department of English. Her teaching and research interest is sixteenth-century British poetry, with particular emphasis on Spenser and the Renaissance comparative epic tradition. Her secondary interest is in the field of psychoanalytic literary criticism. Bellamy has also published in such journals as *English Literary History, Spenser Studies, The Shakespeare Yearbook, Comparative Literature Studies, Montaigne Studies, Annali d'Italianistica, Diacritics, Textual Practice, Parallax, The Yale Journal of Criticism, Clio, The South Atlantic Quarterly, Thesis Eleven, LIT: Literature / Interpretation / Theory,* and *Literature and Psychology.* She has also contributed essays on Renaissance literature and/or psychoanalytic literary criticism in edited collections published by Routledge and several university presses.

Robert C. Evans is I. B. Young Professor of English at Auburn University at Montgomery. He earned his Ph.D. from Princeton University in 1984. In 1982 he began teaching at AUM, where he has been named Distinguished Research Professor, Distinguished Teaching Professor, and University Alumni Professor. External awards include fellowships from the American Council of Learned Societies, the American Philosophical Society, the National Endowment for the Humanities, the UCLA Center for Medieval and Renaissance Studies, and the Folger, Huntington, and Newberry Libraries. He is the author or editor of more than thirty books and of numerous essays, including four books on Shakespeare (in print or forthcoming) as well as a variety of essays on Shakespeare's plays and poetry.

T. Fleischmann, is an essayist with a Masters of Fine Arts in Nonfiction Writing from the University of Iowa.

Andrew Hadfield is Professor of English at the University of Sussex and visiting professor at the University of Granada. He is the author of a number of works on the early modern period, including *Shakespeare and Republicanism* (Cambridge University Press, 2005) and Edmund *Spenser: A Life* (Oxford University Press, 2012). He is currently working on a study of lying in early modern England and will be editing the works of Thomas Nashe. He writes reviews for the *The Times Literary Supplement* and *The Irish Times* and is currently vice chair of the Society of Renaissance Studies.

Ashleigh Imus holds a Ph.D. in Medieval studies (English, Latin, and Italian literature) from Cornell University. She has taught English and world literature as well as Italian language at several colleges in New York. She has published articles and book reviews on culture, history, and literature from the ancient world to the present. Her translations of Latin literature appear at *Epistolae,* a free online database of medieval women's letters.

Rafeeq O. McGiveron holds a B.A. with Honor in English and History from Michigan State University, an M.A. in English and History from MSU, and an M.A. in English from Western Michigan University. Having taught literature and composition for many years at a number of schools, including MSU, WMU, and Lansing Community College, in positions that have allowed his scholarship to be driven by personal interest and the serendipity of the classroom rather than by necessity, he has published some two-dozen articles of literary criticism, most recently editing *Critical Insights:* Fahrenheit 451 for Salem Press in 2013. Currently he works as an academic advisor and interdepartmental liaison at Lansing Community College, where he has served since 1992. He also dabbles in fiction, occasionally poetry, and mobile art. His website is www.rafeeqmcgiveron. com, and his novel *Student Body* was released in 2014.

Michael Rogers is a freelance writer and editor from Long Island, NY, who has had a life-long affair with literature. For more than twenty years he was a Senior Editor at *Library Journal* magazine. During his tenure at *Library Journal,* he wrote Classic Returns, the only regularly featured column in a book-review publication to highlight out-of-print titles brought back into print in new editions. He also served as a Book Review Editor and Media Editor. He has written hundreds of book, audio book, and DVD reviews, and is the most quoted reviewer in *Library Journal*'s more than one-hundred-twenty-five-year history. Along with writing and editing reviews, Rogers also held posts as *Library Journal*'s News and Technology Editor for which he was awarded the Jesse H. Neal Gold Award. He has written numerous book-related news stories and author Q&As as well as contributed to the *Dictionary of Literary Biography*, *Publishers Weekly*, and a variety of literary reference works.

Mirela Roncevic is an editor, literary journalist, and book reviewer, with eighteen years of experience in book publishing as well as librarianship. She was Senior Editor at *Library Journal* for twelve years, where she assigned for review and reviewed books in a wide range of categories, including literary fiction, literary criticism, poetry, creative nonfiction, and arts and humanities. She has published countless book reviews, author interviews, and articles in various literary journals, including *Publishers Weekly*. She is Managing Editor of Salem Press' Critical Insights series, editor of American Library Association's *eContent Quarterly* journal, and regular contributor to No Shelf Required, a blog about ebooks in libraries. She holds a Master of Arts in the Humanities, with specialization in Comparative Literature, from New York University.

Index